CONFLUENCES OF LAW AND HISTORY

Confluences of Law and History

Irish Legal History Society Discourses and Other Papers, 2011–21

NIAMH HOWLIN

AND

FELIX M. LARKIN

EDITORS

FOUR COURTS PRESS

in association with

THE IRISH LEGAL HISTORY SOCIETY

Typeset in 10.5pt on 12.5pt EhrhardtMtPro by
Carrigboy Typesetting Services for
FOUR COURTS PRESS LTD
7 Malpas Street, Dublin 8, Ireland
www.fourcourtspress.ie
and in North America for
FOUR COURTS PRESS
c/o IPG, 814 N Franklin Street, Chicago, IL 60610.

References to this publication should cite the publisher as Four Courts Press in association with the Irish Legal History Society.

A catalogue record for this title is available
from the British Library.

ISBN 978–1–80151–085–1

Printed in England,
by Antony Rowe Ltd, Chippenham, Wilts.

Contents

Contributors

PAUL BEW is emeritus professor of Irish politics, Queen's University Belfast. He is the author of numerous books and articles on Irish political history, including *Ireland: the politics of enmity, 1789–2006* (Oxford, 2007) and *Enigma: a new life of Charles Stewart Parnell* (Dublin, 2011). His latest book is *Ancestral voices in Irish politics: judging Dillon and Parnell* (Oxford, 2023). Created Baron Bew of Donegore in the county of Antrim in 2007, he sits in the House of Lords as a crossbencher.

KEVIN COSTELLO teaches legal history at University College Dublin. He has research interests in aspects of British and Irish legal history, and, in particular, the history of administrative law 1600 to 1900. His monograph *The court of admiralty of Ireland, 1575–1893* was published by the Irish Legal History Society in 2011.

L. PERRY CURTIS JR was an American scholar who made a significant contribution to the study of Irish history. He held academic appointments successively at Princeton, the University of California at Berkeley and Brown University (where he was professor in history and in modern culture and media). His publications include *Coercion and conciliation in Ireland* (Princeton, 1963), *Apes and angels* (London, 1971, 1997), *Images of Erin in the age of Parnell* (Dublin, 2000) and *The depiction of eviction in Ireland* (Dublin, 2011). He died on 9 April 2019.

DONNELL DEENY was appointed to the supreme court of judicature in Northern Ireland in 2004, was knighted and served on the high court and the court of appeal. He is now principally a mediator and also chairman of the UK Spoliation Advisory Panel and chairman of the Advisory Committee on Cultural Restitution for the Irish government. He was educated at Dublin University, of which he is pro-chancellor, and Queen's University Belfast, of which he is an LLD (h.c.)

PATRICK M. GEOGHEGAN was president of the Irish Legal History Society 2018–21. A professor in history at Trinity College Dublin, he is the author of an acclaimed two-volume study of Daniel O'Connell as well as other works on eighteenth- and nineteenth-century political history. He presents the award-winning *Talking history* on Newstalk radio.

ANTHONY HART was a pillar of the Irish Legal History Society from its inception in 1988 until his sudden death on 9 July 2019. He was president of the Society 1991–4, and was awarded the Society's Gold Medal in 2012. He had a distinguished legal career: called to the bar of Northern Ireland in 1969; became a QC in 1983; appointed a county court judge in 1985, recorder of Belfast in 1997 and a judge of the high court of Northern Ireland in 2005. After his retirement from the bench in 2012, he chaired Northern Ireland's historical institutional abuse inquiry. His publications include *A history of the king's serjeants at law in Ireland: honour rather than advantage?* (Dublin, 2000) and *A history of the bar and inn of court of Northern Ireland* (Belfast, 2013).

DAIRE HOGAN was president of the Irish Legal History Society 1994–7. He is the author of *The legal profession in Ireland, 1789–1922* (Dublin, 1986), and, with Patrick Maume, edited *The reminiscences of Ignatius O'Brien, lord chancellor of Ireland 1913–18* (Dublin, 2021). He is currently researching aspects of the history of the judiciary in Ireland in the nineteenth and early twentieth centuries.

NIAMH HOWLIN teaches at the Sutherland School of Law, University College Dublin. She has published several books on Irish legal history, including *A century of courts: the Courts of Justice Act 1924* (Dublin, 2024); *Barristers in Ireland: an evolving profession since 1921* (Dublin, 2023) and *Juries in Ireland: laypersons and law in the long nineteenth century* (Dublin, 2017). She has advised the Irish government on historical miscarriages of justice, is a fellow of the Royal Historical Society, and sits on the Irish Manuscripts Commission.

PATRICK HYDE KELLY is an Emeritus Fellow of Trinity College Dublin. His publications include critical editions of *Locke on money* (Oxford, 1991), and William Molyneux, *The case of Ireland's being bound by acts of parliament in England, stated* (Dublin, 2018), as well as articles on Locke and Irish political and intellectual history of the seventeenth and eighteenth centuries.

FELIX M. LARKIN is a historian and retired public servant. He has written extensively about the history of the press in Ireland, and was co-founder of the Newspaper and Periodical History Forum of Ireland. His publications include *Terror and discord: the Shemus cartoons in the* Freeman's Journal, *1920–1924* (Dublin, 2009) and *Living with history: occasional writings* (Dublin, 2021). He is a Fellow of the Royal Historical Society.

JOHN F. LARKIN is one of the founders of the Irish Legal History Society. He is a Vice President of the Society. Since 2001 he has practised as Queen's (now King's) Counsel at the Bar of Northern Ireland principally in public law. Between 2010 and 2020 he served as Attorney General for Northern Ireland. He is also a member of the Bar of Ireland and was Reid Professor in Trinity College Dublin, 1989–91.

ROBERT D. MARSHALL is a solicitor in holy orders of the Anglican tradition, serving as an auxiliary curate in Dublin. He was appointed registrar of the United Dioceses of Dublin and Glendalough and of the province of Dublin in 2022, having been deputy registrar 2007–22. For 30 years until retirement in 2009, he practised as a property lawyer with A&L Goodbody where he became familiar with the property law and procedures then largely unchanged from those described in his chapter of this volume. An officer of the Society since 1994, he served as president 2012–15. He is a member of the Historical Studies Committee of the Royal Irish Academy and writes in an independent capacity.

THOMAS MOHR is an associate professor at the Sutherland School of Law, University College Dublin. He is president of the Irish Legal History Society and book review editor of the *Irish Jurist*, Ireland's oldest law journal. His publications on Irish legal history range from medieval Gaelic law to the law of the independent Irish state in the twentieth century. His latest books are *Guardian of the Treaty: the privy council appeal and Irish sovereignty* (Dublin, 2016) and, with Peter Crooks, he edited *Law and the idea of liberty in Ireland: from Magna Carta to the present* (Dublin, 2023).

JANE OHLMEYER is Erasmus Smith's professor of modern history (1762) at Trinity College Dublin. She is a Fellow of Trinity College Dublin, a Fellow of the Royal Historical Society, and a Member of the Royal Irish Academy. She received the Academy's Gold Medal in 2023. She is the author or editor of numerous articles and eleven books. Her most recent book is *Making empire: Ireland, imperialism and the early modern world* (Oxford, 2023), based on the Ford Lectures delivered in Oxford in 2021.

MARION RÖWEKAMP is a historian and a full-time lawyer. She was the holder of the Wilhelm and Alexander von Humboldt chair of the DAAD at the Colegio de México in Mexico City. Previously, she worked in the US at Columbia University, the Five Women College Studies and Research Center, and at the Center for European Studies at Harvard University. She has also worked in Mexico City at the Colegio de México and at the Instituto de Investigaciones Históricas of the UNAM and the Latin American Institute of the Free University of Berlin. She has published six books and various articles in the area of women's legal studies.

BLÁTHNA RUANE is a senior counsel, who has written widely on the constitution, law and legal history. She is an adjunct professor of law at the Sutherland School of Law at University College Dublin.

Abbreviations

ADF	Allgemeiner Deutscher Frauenbund
Att Gen	Attorney General
BL	Barrister at law / British Library
Bodleian	Bodleian Library, Oxford
CAB	Cabinet Papers
CB	Chief Baron
CID	Criminal investigation department
CJ	Chief Justice
Cl & Fin	Clark and Finelly's House of Lords Cases
Cmnd.	Command paper
CO	Colonial Office
CSPI	Calendar of State Papers Ireland
DCA	Dublin City Archives
DE	Dáil Éireann
Deb.	Debates
DFA	Department of Foreign Affairs
DIB	*Dictionary of Irish biography*
DMP	Dublin Metropolitan Police
DO	Dominion Office
ER	English Reports
Exch R	Exchequer Reports
HC	House of Commons / high court
HMC	Historical Manuscripts Commission
How St Tr	Howell's State Trials
ICW	International Council of Women
IHS	*Irish Historical Studies*
ILTR	Irish Law Times Reports
ILTSJ	*Irish Law Times and Solicitors' Journal*
IR	Irish Reports
J	Judge / Justice / Journal
JP	Justice of the Peace
KB	King's Bench
KC	King's Counsel
LCJ	Lord Chief Justice
LR Ir	Law Reports Ireland
MP	Member of Parliament
NAI	National Archives of Ireland
NGI	National Gallery of Ireland

NILQ	*Northern Ireland Legal Quarterly*
NLI	National Library of Ireland
NPG	National Portrait Gallery, London
Oxford DNB	*Oxford dictionary of national biography*
PA	Parliamentary Archives
PC	Privy Council
PRONI	Public Record Office of Northern Ireland
QC	Queen's Counsel
QUB	Queen's University Belfast
RIA	Royal Irish Academy
RIC	Royal Irish Constabulary
RM	Resident Magistrate
SC	Senior Counsel / Supreme Court
TCD	Trinity College Dublin
TD	Teachta Dála
TNA	The National Archives, Kew
TSCH	Department of the Taoiseach
UCDA	University College Dublin Archives
WO	War Office

Illustrations

PLATES

Between pages 176 and 177

Between pages 304 and 305

FIGURES

Acknowledgments

A book like this is always the result of teamwork. Having two joint editors certainly lightens the load, but there are also a host of other people whose combined efforts have made the book a reality.

We most sincerely thank each of the contributors to this volume. Not only have they produced written work of a very high standard, but many of them also delivered engaging and entertaining discourses to members of the Irish Legal History Society over the past ten years or so.

We thank our colleagues on the ILHS publications committee for their support, particularly, Robert Marshall, president 2012–15 and chair of the publications committee, who not only stewarded this book, but also contributed one of its chapters based on his presidential address to the Society. We also acknowledge the support and leadership of the most recent past president of the Society, John Gordon, and past presidents Patrick Geoghegan (2018–21) and Donnell Deeny (2015–18), both of whose presidential addresses are included in this volume.

The years since the publication of the last collection of Irish Legal History Society discourses have also been tempered with sadness for members of the Society. We lost two former presidents, Nial Osborough and Tony Hart, and four former patrons: Lords Hutton, Carswell and Kerr and Chief Justice Murray. Also in this period our former treasurer, John Leckey, passed away, as well as former Council member Hugh Geoghegan. Two of the contributing authors in this volume have died since writing their papers – Tony Hart and Perry Curtis – while the late Gregory O'Connor is singled out for thanks by Donnell Deeny and Robert Marshall in their respective chapters. We acknowledge these losses and remember our friends and colleagues while celebrating the contribution they have made to the discipline of legal history.

We thank Mary Hart for allowing us to proceed with the publication of Tony Hart's paper. Michael Curtis also agreed to let us publish Perry Curtis' paper (as had been his father's wish), and we are grateful to Bruce Perkins, Dave Kay and Stephanie Dearmont for their assistance in preparing it for publication.

This book is greatly enhanced by the illustrations which we have been fortunate to include. Thanks to the National Library of Ireland, the National Gallery of Ireland, the National Portrait Gallery (London), the Calton Gallery (Edinburgh) and some private individuals for permission to use their images. We are particularly grateful to James Harte in the National Library of Ireland for his assistance.

We are, as ever, grateful to Four Courts Press for their expertise; in particular we wish to acknowledge the hard work and patience of Martin Fanning, Anthony Tierney and Martin Healy. Thanks also to Julitta Clancy for indexing.

A decade of legal history scholarship

NIAMH HOWLIN & FELIX M. LARKIN

Ireland's Decade of Centenaries commemorations programme,[1] initiated in 2012, focused a spotlight on the events, personalities and social movements that have shaped the last hundred years. It encouraged public interest in, engagement with and reflection on the past, and has resulted in something of a renaissance for the discipline of history in its broadest sense. The programme has included formal state occasions, local events, stamps and coins, exhibitions, television and radio documentaries, podcasts, re-enactments, walking tours, workshops, conferences, newspaper supplements, and books and articles; and has involved archivists, librarians, poets, playwrights, dramatists, visual artists, musicians, local history groups, as well as the national cultural institutions, local authorities, heritage offices, academic institutions and academic scholars. Commemorations have taken place nationally and locally, with an inclusive approach that embraces the shared history on the island of Ireland. Some of the important events commemorated have included the Ulster Covenant; the foundation of the Irish Volunteers; the Home Rule and land bills; the 1913 lockout; the suffrage movement; the First World War; the 1916 Rising; the War of Independence; the establishment of Northern Ireland; the Anglo-Irish Treaty; the Civil War; and the creation of the Free State. The role of law, legal processes and legal institutions in many of these key events is becoming increasingly evident.

It is therefore unsurprising that legal history too has enjoyed a growth in popularity in recent years. Membership of the Irish Legal History Society remains strong, and attendance at events (both virtual and in-person) is high.[2] In 2022 the Irish Legal History Society jointly hosted the British Legal History Conference with Queen's University Belfast, which saw hundreds of legal historians from Europe, North America, Asia and further afield convene for four days in Belfast.[3] April 2024 saw the Society jointly host a special event

1 See www.decadeofcentenaries.com.

2 Virtual events since 2020 have included Dr Lynsey Black, Dr Sparky Booker, Dr Coleman Dennehy and Dr Niamh Howlin, 'Researching and writing Irish legal history in the 21st century', Irish Legal History Society winter discourse 2020, 10 Dec. 2020. The spring discourse 2021 included three papers: J. Larkin, 'One Irish constitution, two Irish parliaments: the Government of Ireland Act 1920'; Dr Bláthna Ruane SC, 'The "so-called Treaty": the implications of legal form for achieving settlement'; and Thomas Mohr, 'What did Irish people think of the Free State constitution in 1922?' All of these can be watched on the Society's YouTube channel at www.youtube.com/@irishlegalhistorysociety6890.

in Dublin Castle to mark the centenary of the establishment of the Irish courts system.[4] The Society also participated, for the first time, in the Dublin Festival of History, with an event in the former House of Lords on College Green in October 2024.[5] The Irish Legal History Society's doctoral and postdoctoral bursary schemes continue to make funds available for students and academics who need to travel in order to conduct their research. The annual Osborough composition prize remains open for entries, and the student essay prize is now in its fourth year.[6] The Society has also administered a prize for the best paper presented by a doctoral student at the British Legal History Conferences in 2022 and 2024.[7]

All of these initiatives are extremely encouraging, as are the wider trends in Irish legal history. There is a growing number of academics from different disciplines actively researching and publishing in the broad field of legal history. Aside from the Irish Legal History Society's book series with Four Courts Press, with which our readers will be familiar,[8] books and articles on Irish legal history are increasingly being published – and not only in Ireland, but also in Great Britain and the United States.[9] Scholarship on Irish legal

3 See J. Cairns, 'British Legal History Conference, Belfast, 6–9 July 2022', *Edinburgh Legal History Blog*, www.elhblog.law.ed.ac.uk/2022/07/15/british-legal-history-conference-belfast-6-9-july-2022/.

4 This event was jointly hosted by the Irish Legal History Society, the Courts Service and University College Dublin; see N. Howlin (ed.), *A century of courts: the Courts of Justice Act 1924* (Dublin, 2024).

5 The Dublin Festival of History is an initiative of Dublin City Council, which aims to preserve, share and promote the history and heritage of Dublin and Ireland and to encourage and facilitate historical research. See https://dublinfestivalofhistory.ie/event/centenary-of-the-irish-courts-1924-2024/.

6 See www.ilhs.eu for information about the various scholarships and prizes.

7 This is the Sir Anthony Hart Doctoral Paper Prize.

8 The full series can be viewed at www.fourcourtspress.ie/books/browse/law-and-legal-history/irish-legal-history-society-series/.

9 Recent examples include D.M. Doyle, 'Unlawful carnal knowledge in the Irish Free State, 1924–35', *The Historical Journal*, 1 (2024) 1; R. McMahon, 'Sir John Ross Bt: the last lord chancellor of Ireland 1921–1922' in N. Dawson, D. Capper and C. McCormack (eds), *Law and constitutional change: essays in legal history* (Cambridge, forthcoming); L. Cahillane and D.K. Coffey, *The centenary of the Irish Free State constitution; constituting a polity?* (London, 2023); M. Coen, 'Through a narrow window: women's jury service in Ireland, 1921–1927', *law&history* 9:2 (2022) 34; C. Dennehy, 'Crime, criminal policy, and law reform in seventeenth-century Irish parliaments', *Journal of Legal History*, 44:1 (2023), 2; T. Mohr, 'The "Provisional Period" – law and the birth of the Irish Free State, 1921–1922', *Irish Jurist* 70:345 (2023); T. Mohr, 'Irish newspapers and the creation of the 1922 constitution of the Irish Free State', *Comparative Legal History*, 11:2; O. Breen and N. McGrath (eds), *Palles: the legal legacy of the last Lord Chief Baron* (Dublin, 2022); C. Kenny, '"It is notorious that a lawyer cannot draft his own will clearly": framing the boundary commission in the Anglo-Irish Treaty 1921', *Irish Jurist,* 68 (2022), 1; G. Hogan, 'The Count Plunkett habeas corpus application and the end of the Dáil supreme court', *Irish Jurist,* 68 (2022), 25; A. Ó Hiorlaithe, 'Changes in scholarly approaches to early Irish law in the period since the publication of D.A. Binchy's *Corpus Iuris Hibernici*', *Irish Jurist*, 67 (2022), 170; K. Costello

history is also being disseminated through podcasts,[10] documentaries,[11] conferences[12] and workshops,[13] and legal history research projects continue to receive significant funding from the state and other bodies.[14] Encouragingly, legal history approaches are also increasingly being incorporated into broader historical and legal scholarship.[15] The reflective approach continues beyond the decade of centenaries; in 2025, for example, the establishment of both the Law Reform Commission and the Director of Public Prosecutions are being marked with publications, conferences and other initiatives. Recent years have seen four posthumous presidential pardons awarded on the basis of expert reports informed by Irish legal history.[16] Academics and legal

and N. Howlin (eds), *Law and religion in Ireland, 1700–1970* (London, 2021); T. Mohr, 'Natural law in early twentieth-century Ireland – *State (Ryan) v. Lennon* and its aftermath', *Journal of Legal History*, 42:1, 2021, 1; T. Mohr, 'Religious minorities under the constitution of the Irish Free State, 1922–1937', *American Journal of Legal History*, 61:2 (2021), 1; M. Coen, '"The work of some irresponsible women": jurors, ghosts, and embracery in the Irish Free State', *Law and History Review*, 38:4 (2020), 777; T. Mohr, 'Law journals and Irish history, 1922–1939', *Comparative Legal History*, 7:2 (2019), 1; A. Fallon, 'The foundational legislation of the Garda Siochana (1922–1926)', *Irish Jurist*, 62 (2019), 119; D.M. Doyle and L. O'Callaghan, *Capital punishment in independent Ireland: a social, legal and political history* (Liverpool, 2016); D.K. Coffey, *Drafting the Irish constitution, 1935–1937: transnational influences in interwar Europe* (London, 2018); M. Coen and N. Howlin, 'The jury speaks: jury riders in the nineteenth and twentieth centuries', *American Journal of Legal History*, 58:4 (2018), 505; D.K. Coffey, *Constitutionalism in Ireland, 1932–1938: national, commonwealth, and international perspectives* (London, 2018); N. Howlin and K. Costello (eds), *Law and the family in Ireland, 1800–1950* (London, 2017); L. Cahillane, *Drafting the Irish Free State constitution* (Manchester, 2016); K. Costello, 'The shopkeeper and the Irish law of bankruptcy 1860–1930', *Irish Jurist*, 56 (2016); A. Lyall, *The Irish House of Lords: a court of law in the eighteenth century* (Dublin, 2014); and L. Cahillane, 'An insight into the Irish Free State constitution', *American Journal of Legal History*, 54:1 (2014), 1.

10 See, e.g., the Green Street lecture series, available as a series of podcasts from the Bar Council of Ireland (www.lawlibrary.ie/podcast); the Irish Courts podcast series by the Courts Service (www.courts.ie/podcasts), as well as occasional episodes of other Irish legal and historical podcast series such as the Fifth Court (www.thefifthcourt.com).

11 E.g., F. Dwyer, 'Murder at Mother Mountain', documentary series, available at www.irishhistorypodcast.ie/murder-at-mother-mountain-1.

12 E.g., the 1922 centenary of the constitution conference, Shelbourne Hotel, Dublin, 6 Dec. 2022, organized by Dr Donal Coffey and Dr Laura Cahillane.

13 E.g., the UCD Legal History Research Group has hosted roundtable workshops on 'Law and the Family in Ireland' and 'Law and Religion in Ireland' in 2016 and 2018.

14 E.g., Dr Lynsey Black of Maynooth University was recently awarded an Irish Research Council (IRC) Starting Laureate worth €378,292 for a project examining issues of criminal justice and security at the Northern Irish border since its creation a century ago. Dr Fangzhe Qiu at the School of Irish, Celtic Studies and Folklore at UCD has received both Irish Research Council and Horizon Europe support for his work on the medieval law tracts, totally almost €2 million in funding.

15 Recent examples include M. Coen, *The Offences Against the State Act at 80: a model counter-terrorism Act?* (Oxford, 2021) and C. O'Riordan, P. Burns and C. O'Connor (eds), *Ireland's court houses* (Dublin, 2019).

16 See N. Howlin, *Report on the trial of Myles Joyce, 1882* (June 2017): https://ipo.gov.ie/eJELR/Report_by_Dr_Niamh_Howlin_Maamtrasna_Murders.pdf/Files/Report_by_Dr_

professionals continue to collaborate on projects examining Irish legal history from various angles. The chapters in this volume are representative of the rigorous and original Irish legal history scholarship that has emerged over the past decade.

Many of the chapters have their origin in discourses delivered to the Irish Legal History Society over more than a decade. These discourses take place twice a year, with the Dublin and Belfast members of the Society's council taking turns to host. The papers were delivered in a variety of venues in Dublin and Belfast, including the Regents House and the Graduates Memorial Building at Trinity College Dublin; Christ Church Cathedral in Dublin; the Law School at Queen's University Belfast; the Royal Courts of Justice in Belfast; and the Ulster Museum in Belfast. Undoubtedly, in the written format we miss the ambiance of those venues, the conviviality, the dramatic oratory and the visual aids and props. Nevertheless, even without the bells and whistles of a live presentation, the rigour and meticulousness of the research are clearly evident, as is the authors' enthusiasm for their subject-matter.

In *Poetry, politics and the law in modern Ireland*, Hanna has written that 'their deep connections with memory are what give both poems and laws what status they have as valued shared possessions'.[17] Law and history likewise have 'deep connections with memory'. The word 'confluences' in the title of this volume refers to these connections; it also refers to the relationship between legal theory – rooted, of course, in history – and the law in practice. Legal history or 'law and history' is, by its very nature, interdisciplinary, and it can extend into other disciplines too. The Irish Legal History Society has always taken a broad interpretation of 'legal history'. In our view, it includes such sub-disciplines as law and literature;[18] legal biography;[19] law and material

Niamh_Howlin_Maamtrasna_Murders.pdf; N. Howlin, *Report on the trial of John Twiss, January 1895* (April 2021): www.gov.ie/pdf/?file=https://assets.gov.ie/212463/23827554-4c1c-44bf-99ba-62e86947081a.pdf#page=null. See also a report prepared for the working group to examine the disregard of convictions for certain qualifying offences related to consensual sexual activity between men: N. Howlin, *Convictions for homosexual acts in the Irish courts, 1922–1993* (May 2022); reporting on the pardons of Sylvester Poff and James Barrett: http://assets.gov.ie/261373/c1774da9-f781–4205-831c-00ec54c3911a.pdf and https://president.ie/en/media-library/news-releases/president-higgins-signs-presidential-pardons-for-mr-sylvester-poff-and-mr-james-barrett.

17 A. Hanna, *Poetry, politics and the law in modern Ireland* (Syracuse, NY, 2022), p. 9. In their introduction to a cognate essay collection, Hanna and McNulty quote Ronner's linking of law and literature as 'spheres that have been and always will be confluent', A. Hanna and E. McNulty (eds), *Law and literature: the Irish case* (Liverpool, 2022), p. 1; A.D. Ronner, *Law, literature and therapeutic jurisprudence* (Durham, NC, 2010), p. 6.

18 See, e.g., W.N. Osborough, *The Irish stage: a legal history* (Dublin, 2015); A. Hardiman, 'Law, crime and punishment in Bloomsday Dublin' in F.M. Larkin and N.M. Dawson (eds), *Lawyers, the law and history: Irish Legal History Society discourses and other papers, 2005–2011* (Dublin, 2013); W.N. Osborough, 'The lawyers of the Irish novels of Anthony Trollope' in D. Hogan and W.N. Osborough (eds), *Brehons, serjeants and attorneys: studies in the history*

culture;[20] comparative legal history;[21] microhistories of law; local history; constitutional history,[22] bibliographic history;[23] political history;[24] architectural history;[25] parliamentary history;[26] and the histories of doctrinal law, legal procedure[27] and legal institutions.[28]

That broad interpretation of 'legal history' is reflected in this volume. The contributors include both legal practitioners and academics with a range of different specializations and expertise who are actively engaged in legal history scholarship. The time frame of the volume extends from the early seventeenth century right up to the end of the twentieth. It is the fifth collection of discourses that the Irish Legal History Society has published since its establishment in 1988. Although it is not a thematic volume, in editing the papers for publication the editors were struck by a number of shared themes that became apparent.

The scene where justice is administered and where members of society are most likely to interact with law is the courtroom. Chapters in this volume take

of the Irish legal profession (Dublin, 1990); N. Malone, 'Henry Burnell's Landgartha: family, law and revolution on the Irish stage' in C. Dennehy (ed.), *Law and revolution in seventeenth-century Ireland* (Dublin, 2020); and A. Carpenter, 'Lawyers and the circulation of scurrilous verse in Restoration Dublin', ibid.

19 See, e.g., D. Hogan and P. Maume (eds), *The reminiscences of Ignatius O'Brien, lord chancellor of Ireland, 1913–18: a life in Cork, Dublin and Westminster* (Dublin, 2021); J.C. Sweeney, *The life and times of Arthur Browne in Ireland and America, 1756–1805: civil law and civil liberties* (Dublin, 2017).

20 E.g., J.A.H. Martin, 'Reflections on judicial dress, with particular reference to the county and circuit courts' in Larkin and Dawson, *Lawyers, the law and history.*

21 E.g., C. Passarella, 'The juries' wisdom in the administration of criminal justice: Irish jurisdiction and the Italian justice system in the late nineteenth and early twentieth centuries', *Comparative Legal History,* 7:2 (2019), 157. The research for this paper was partly enabled through an Irish Legal History Society bursary.

22 E.g., G. Hogan, 'Some thoughts on the origins of the 1937 constitution' in Larkin and Dawson, *Lawyers, the law and history.*

23 E.g., C. Kenny, 'On lawyers, their obligations and the Cicero collection at King's Inns library' in Larkin and Dawson, *Lawyers, the law and history.*

24 E.g., I. Campbell, 'Magna Carta and political theory in seventeenth-century Ireland' in P. Crooks and T. Mohr (eds), *Law and the idea of liberty in Ireland from Magna Carta to the present* (Dublin, 2023); J. Kelly, '"Our civil rights and liberties": the politics of Protestant liberty in the eighteenth century', ibid.

25 E.g., C. Kenny, 'The Four Courts at Christ Church, 1608–1796' in W.N. Osborough (ed.), *Explorations in law and history: Irish Legal History Society discourses, 1988–1994* (Dublin, 1995).

26 E.g., J. McEldowney, 'Dicey and the sovereignty of parliament: lessons from Irish legal history' in N.M. Dawson (ed.), *Reflections on law and history: Irish Legal History Society discourses and other papers, 2000–2005* (Dublin, 2006) and B. McGrath, *The operations of the Irish House of Commons, 1613–48* (Dublin, 2023).

27 E.g., D. Greer, 'A security against illegality? The reservation of crown cases in nineteenth-century Ireland' in Dawson, *Reflections.*

28 See, e.g., K. Costello, *The court of admiralty of Ireland, 1575–1893* (Dublin, 2011); J.G. Crawford, *A star chamber court in Ireland: the court of castle chamber, 1571–1641* (Dublin, 2005); B. McGrath, *The operations of the Irish House of Commons 1613–48* (Dublin, 2023); and N. Howlin (ed.), *A century of courts: the Courts of Justice Act 1924* (Dublin, 2024).

us from local manor courts and recorders' courts right up to the permanent court of international justice, via the queen's bench and the supreme court. Kevin Costello, in 'Imprisonment for debt in early nineteenth-century Ireland, 1810–48', compares debt imprisonment in England and Ireland, and finds that the early establishment of civil bill courts in Ireland made imprisonment for small debts more prevalent in Ireland. Donnell Deeny, in 'The trials of Arthur Donnelly: a *cause célèbre* of the 1870s', brings us to the petty sessions courts in counties Armagh and Down. Robert Marshall, in 'Lisnafana: a townland in crisis on the Headfort Cavan estate, 1879–95', traces several sets of related proceedings through both the local and the superior courts. Sir Anthony Hart, in 'The law in action in Ulster in July 1898', examines a number of courts and judicial bodies operating in Ulster at the close of the nineteenth century, including the Land Commission, the petty sessions, the assizes and the county courts. Thomas Mohr's chapter, 'Dismantling the Anglo-Irish Treaty: removing the oath and the repugnancy clause from the constitution of the Irish Free State', considers proposals to refer a Treaty dispute to the permanent court of international justice in 1933.

Several authors focus on aspects of pre-trial and trial procedure, including Hart, Deeny and Jane Ohlmeyer in her chapter, 'Lords, the law and litigation in early modern Ireland'. The criminal law is a focus in these chapters, as in Patrick Geoghegan's 'Investigating Jack the Ripper and Parnellite crime: Sir Robert Anderson and the writing of history' in which he explores the reliability of Anderson's memoirs and their value as a historical source. Geoghegan's chapter provides new perspectives on the Ripper case and on the 'Parnellism and crime' articles published in the London *Times* in 1887.

Law-making could be a complicated business in Ireland, and contributors to this volume scrutinize different parliaments and law-making bodies, including the Westminster parliament, the Irish Free State parliament and earlier Irish parliaments. Ohlmeyer, in her chapter, considers the position of peers in the Irish parliament and looks at how patronage and influence operated in early modern Ireland. William Molyneux's *The case of Ireland's being bound by acts of parliament in England, stated* – the subject of Patrick Kelly's chapter 'Ambivalent patriot: William Molyneux and the art of rhetoric' – presented a claim for Irish legislative independence, while Marion Röwekamp's chapter, '"Suffrage first" or "suffrage as a crown": conditions for women's suffrage in Germany, Ireland and England', emphasizes the importance of women's votes in elections to parliament and other law-making bodies as a necessary prerequisite for advancing women's rights in every sphere.

In Ireland as elsewhere, legal institutions, processes and personalities were never entirely divorced from the political arena. Daire Hogan, John Larkin, Bláthna Ruane and Tom Mohr each examine areas where law and politics overlap. Hogan's 'James Henry Mussen Campbell QC, MP: a life in law and unionist politics' demonstrates how law and politics could intermingle with personal ambition. Campbell served as both lord chief justice of Ireland 1918–21 and chairman of the Senate of the Irish Free State, 1922–8, among other appointments. His career is indicative of the efforts made in the early years of the Free State to accommodate the southern unionist minority and also, perhaps more importantly, of the minority's acceptance of the new dispensation and co-operation with its government. John Larkin's 'The Irish Convention 1917–18: centenary reflections' considers that doomed attempt to bring together the various political forces in Ireland at that time to draft a Home Rule constitution for the island, while Ruane, in 'The "so-called Treaty": the implications of legal form for achieving settlement of the Irish War of Independence,' analyses how the British government's strategy of settlement by treaty was critical to a settlement being reached in 1922. Mohr's chapter on 'Dismantling the Anglo-Irish Treaty' considers the political as well as the legal ramifications of the abolition of the parliamentary oath contained in the 1921 Anglo-Irish Treaty and the related issue of the 'repugnancy clause' that placed all sources of Irish law in a subordinate position to the provisions of the 1921 Treaty.

Religious tensions also underlie some of the chapters in this collection; for example, in Deeny's 'The trials of Arthur Donnelly', we see jury packing in attempts to control the religious composition of juries, while Ohlmeyer, in 'Lords, the law and litigation', analyses the changing religious composition of the Irish peerage in early modern Ireland. Religious tensions also hover in the background in Marshall's chapter, while Mohr's chapter touches on the position of southern Protestants in the Free State of the 1920s.

The Irish land question provides the backdrop to several chapters. Paul Bew, Robert Marshall and Perry Curtis each approach land ownership and land use from different perspectives, making use of various sources to create an increasingly nuanced picture of the land war. Bew, in 'Parnell and the law', looks at the dynamics of the Irish land war of 1879–82 and argues that the Parnellite strategy was to exploit the limits of the law. Curtis, in 'Exploring the dynamic of the Irish land war, 1879–90', argues that as well as the political, social, economic and meteorological causes of the land war, there were also epistemological causes. He applies a Foucauldian analysis to the legal and political developments of this period, examining where power and knowledge lay. Marshall's 'Lisnafana: a townland in crisis' is a microhistory of an area of Co. Cavan within the Headfort estate. It illustrates not only how boycotting operated in practice, but also how the lives of the inhabitants were defined by *de jure* law and by the operation of a subaltern code – with church law also a factor.

This interplay of the national (or international) with the local is also evident in those chapters that examine the law and legal institutions in a comparative or transnational context. Both Mohr and Röwekamp consider the comparative or transnational aspects of their chosen topics. Mohr locates

1920s Ireland within the British commonwealth, while Röwekamp compares suffrage movements in Germany, Ireland and England in the context of the centenary of the granting of the vote to women – or at least to *some* women – in these countries. While acknowledging the importance of this reform, she notes that 'women's votes and voices still don't count the same as male ones, and the power positions are still overwhelmingly filled by men who are still almost as hesitant to grant more rights to women as one hundred years earlier'. John Larkin's chapter, like Röwekamp's, marks a centenary – that of the Irish Convention.

In addition to Röwekamp's comparative analysis of suffrage movements, other chapters also examine some of the ways in which women interacted with law and legal processes across different time periods. Bew, in 'Parnell and the law', focuses on an individual woman, Anna Parnell. Other contributors take a broader view of women and the law. Geoghegan, in writing about Jack the Ripper, looks at women as victims of crime, while Hart, Costello and Ohlmeyer consider the active roles of women as litigants, landowners, moneylenders and borrowers.

A common theme running through many of the chapters is that of law in times of transition. Chapters by Marshall, Curtis, Bew, Mohr, Ruane and Hogan take in the land war, the Home Rule movement, the Irish rebellion and the early years of the Free State. As well as high politics, law affects and is affected by social change. Costello, for example, traces some of the consequences of the economic depression following the end of the Napoleonic wars, while Röwekamp analyses the impetus behind the suffrage movements of the early twentieth century. Felix Larkin's chapter, 'The asinine law: Irish legal cartoons', considers how lawyers and the law were portrayed in political cartoons against the backdrop of social and political change over more than two centuries. While it is notoriously difficult to assess the impact of what appears in print, whether in the press or elsewhere, there is no doubt that images such as those discussed by Felix Larkin helped shape public perceptions of the legal world – and not in a positive way.

Charismatic personalities and persuasive writers appear in several essays. In his chapter, Patrick Kelly, whose new edition of William Molyneux's *The case* was published by the Irish Legal History Society in 2018,[29] revisits this work and analyses how Molyneux adopted the medium of forensic rhetoric as the vehicle through which to present the claim for Irish legislative independence. Hogan's analysis of the career of J.H.M. Campbell puts a spotlight on a particularly eloquent and dominant early twentieth-century Irish lawyer and politician, while Ruane's chapter highlights the impact of the wily Lloyd George on the negotiations that led to the establishment of the Irish Free State. The equally wily Éamon de Valera looms large in Mohr's

29 W. Molyneux, *The case of Ireland's being bound by acts of parliament in England, stated* [Dublin, 1698], ed. P.H. Kelly (Dublin, 2018).

chapter, while the impact of Charles Stewart Parnell on his times is evident in the chapters by Curtis and Bew.

The contributors to this volume have drawn on a range of different sources. Many, unsurprisingly, make use of primary legal sources such as legislation and official case reports. Papers consulted in the National Archives of Ireland, the Public Record Office of Northern Ireland and the National Archives in the United Kingdom include cabinet minutes, police reports and correspondence. Collections of papers in other libraries and archives also feature in the various chapters, with unpublished manuscripts, personal correspondence and estate records providing additional context. Marshall's chapter, for example, showcases the wide range of manuscript sources available to researchers pursuing estate histories. Parliamentary debates and reports are also used to good effect, and Costello makes extensive use of House of Commons parliamentary papers to produce a chapter on insolvent debtors which is firmly grounded in official statistics. Newspapers and periodicals have long been acknowledged as useful sources for the legal historian, and Deeny's chapter, for example, demonstrates how newspaper reports can be used to supplement surviving official documentation regarding high-profile prosecutions and trials. Hart's chapter is based largely on research in newspaper archives.

We have also been struck by the range of methodologies employed by the contributors. Hart and Marshall's approaches complement one other; Hart looks at the range of legal issues emerging in a specific place on a specific date, while Marshall focuses on a discrete group of actors across a number of years. Both demonstrate the 'law in action' in the late nineteenth century and incidentally provide us with vignettes of everyday life in Ireland in that period. John Larkin and Kelly engage in close reading and analysis of individual documents; the former considers the report of the Irish Convention, the latter Molyneux's *The case*. Felix Larkin explores the wealth of allusions in the cartoons that he references.

Readers will no doubt uncover further confluences and points of departure in these meticulously researched and richly detailed essays. The Irish Legal History Society's mission is to encourage the publication of original scholarship in the field. The chapters in this book undoubtedly further this. They make use of a wide range of hitherto unpublished primary sources from archives around Ireland and abroad. Several also delve into contemporary published material, including parliamentary papers, newspapers and periodicals, and legal treatises and manuals prepared for those working in the legal professions. The fact that our contributors also build upon existing scholarship is a sure indication of the evolving maturity of the field of Irish legal history.[30]

30 See W.N. Osborough, *An island's law: a bibliographical guide to Ireland's legal past* (Dublin, 2013).

Lords, the law and litigation in early modern Ireland

JANE OHLMEYER*

On 11 June 1628, Edmund Butler, third Baron Dunboyne, stood trial in the court of king's bench in Dublin Castle, accused of manslaughter. An extant account captured the proceedings, along with the ceremony of the occasion. The 'Lord high stewarte of Ireland came [to the king's bench] on horse from the White friares, attended by the peeres and judges' and preceded by the sergeant at arms 'with his Mace and two ushers'. The anonymous observer continued that inside the court was 'a chaire and a cloath of state, and other places for the nobilitie, peers, judges, the King's counsell, and common people to behold and see'. The bar, where Dunboyne stood, was covered in green cloth and his chair with a rich carpet.[1]

The baron was tried, with due formality, before thirteen of his peers. Rank determined arrangements in the court. The two Protestant earls, Londonderry and Meath, came first despite being newcomers to the peerage, thereby outranking the five viscounts, including those of more ancient lineage. The Catholic viscounts – Gormanston and Netterville – hailed from old English noble families, while the three others, Valentia, Moore and Baltinglass, were more recent new English, Protestant elevations. The six barons comprised four established old English lords – Howth, Dunsany, Upper Ossory and Louth – alongside two recent creations, Charlemont and Esmond. Francis Aungier, Baron Aungier of Longford, presided as lord steward. Of legal stock, Aungier had moved to Ireland in 1609 to take up a prominent position in the colonial administration as master of the rolls and later served as a member of the Irish privy council.[2]

The court heard the evidence against Dunboyne. The baron and some of his followers had travelled to Cahir Castle in Co. Tipperary to collect a legacy

* I am grateful to the members of the Irish Legal History Society and especially the then president, Sir Donnell Deeny, for inviting me to give this discourse. That evening I had the pleasure of sitting next to the late Sir Anthony Hart during dinner. I would like to dedicate this chapter to his memory. I would also like to thank Daryl Hendley Rooney for his assistance in preparing this chapter for publication.

1 HMC, *Report 15, app. 1, part ii* (London, 1897), pp 292–3. J. Kingston, 'Lord Dunboyne', *Reportum Novum: Dublin Diocesan Historical Record*, 3:1 (1961–2), 62.

2 These men are discussed in detail in J. Ohlmeyer, *Making Ireland English: the Irish aristocracy in the seventeenth century* (New Haven, 2012).

of plate from his late father-in-law, Thomas Butler, third baron of Cahir, who had died in 1627. James Prendergast, the keeper of the castle and a close kinsman (married to the sister of Lord Cahir), refused to hand the plate over and a heated argument followed. James Butler, the local justice of the peace, tried to keep order but one of Dunboyne's men goaded Prendergast telling him that Dunboyne 'was a better man than he or any in the house, except the two lordes'. Prendergast gave Dunboyne 'the lie' and Dunboyne punched him; Prendergast then drew his sword and Dunboyne 'suffered him not'. In the ensuing *mêlée*, Prendergast died of stab wounds. In his own defence Dunboyne agreed with most of this account. However, he denied delivering the fatal blow and suggested that FitzWilliam Butler had done so. Dunboyne added that Prendergast was 'deare and dearer to him then any man in the house present'. The jurors accepted Dunboyne's account and returned a non-guilty verdict. In so doing they overturned the ruling of the Tipperary grand jury, which had found Dunboyne guilty of manslaughter. When he heard the verdict Dunboyne 'satt downe upon his knees, and praied for the king, and afterwards arose and thanked his peers'.[3]

This brief account of Dunboyne's trial provides a number of invaluable insights into the operation and significance of the law in early modern Ireland. First, it highlights the privileged legal position that lords enjoyed: their right to be tried by their parliamentary peers. Second, it illustrates how, by the early seventeenth century, the courtroom acted as an important forum where a peer's reputation could be defended and his honour restored. Third, it demonstrates how a hybrid group of Irish lords of mixed ethnic and religious backgrounds collectively exercised justice. Finally, it was a very public and carefully choreographed display of royal justice reinforcing the authority of the Stuart dynasty and English law. The significance of this and of Dunboyne's public submission to the king and his peers would not have been lost on the 'common people' who witnessed it and those who later heard of it. This chapter explores these issues further and examines how English law shaped the worlds of the Irish peerage and how these lords and their kin used the law both to protect – and where possible to enhance – their status, dynasty, and estates.

THE LEGAL LANDSCAPE

In early modern Ireland the crown largely replicated the English judicial hierarchy. The high court of parliament sat irregularly in Dublin. The four central courts – exchequer, chancery, king's bench and common pleas – functioned effectively in Dublin Castle, along with the court of castle

3 HMC, *Report 15, app. 1, part ii*, pp 292–3.

chamber, which was the judicial arm of the Irish privy council. The crown set up assize circuits along with prerogative courts familiar from England, including the court of wards and admiralty courts.[4] More distant and troublesome regions fell under the jurisdiction of a lord president and provincial council, akin to the English councils of the Marches of Wales and of the North of England.[5] In concert with the crown, a lord deputy appointed key judges and bureaucrats. Where possible, these officials were Protestants (or at least willing to take the oath of supremacy) and ideally from England. Though little is known about the operation of manor courts, where local lords exercised justice, they were widespread and were only abolished in 1859.[6] Equally opaque were the ecclesiastical courts, based on the English model, which appear to have functioned in Ireland since the twelfth century. It was not uncommon for Catholics to seek redress in the Protestant ecclesiastical courts, especially when Catholic clergy were not forthcoming in addressing and accepting marriage litigation, for instance.[7]

So much for the courts, what of their archives? Sadly, most are lost. Many of the records for the central courts were destroyed in 1922; those that survived are in poor condition thanks to fire, smoke and water damage.[8] This misfortune, combined with the fact that the bulk of these extant records have never been systematically catalogued and are organized according to the stage of a particular case, perhaps explains the reluctance of all but the most persistent researchers to use them.[9] There are, of course, exceptions – most

4 T.C. Barnard, 'Lawyers and the law in later seventeenth-century Ireland', *IHS*, 28:111 (1993), 256; J.G. Crawford, *A star chamber court in Ireland: the court of castle chamber, 1571–1641* (Dublin, 2005).

5 M. Curtis Clayton (ed.), *The council book for the province of Munster,* c.*1599–1649* (Dublin, 2008).

6 R. Gillespie, 'A manor court in seventeenth-century Ireland', *Irish Economic and Social History*, 25 (1998), 81; T.C. Barnard, 'Local courts in seventeenth- and eighteenth-century Ireland' in M. Brown and S.P. Donlan (eds), *The laws and other legalities of Ireland* (Farnham, 2001), pp 33–46; N. Howlin, *Juries in Ireland: laypersons and law in the long nineteenth century* (Dublin, 2017); and R. McMahon, 'Manor courts in the West of Ireland before the Famine' in D.S. Greer and N.M. Dawson (eds), *Mysteries and solutions in Irish legal history: Irish Legal History Society discourses and other papers, 1996–1999* (Dublin, 2001), pp 115–60.

7 W.N. Osborough, 'Ecclesiastical law and the Reformation in Ireland' in R.H. Helmholz (ed.), *Canon law in Protestant lands* (*Comparative studies in continental and Anglo-American legal history* II) (Berlin, 1992), pp 223–52; H.A. Jefferies, 'The Armagh registers and the re-interpretation of Irish church history on the eve of the reformations', *Seanchas Ardmhacha: Journal of the Armagh Diocesan Historical Society*, 18:1 (1999/2000), 81.

8 For a great overview, see W.N. Osborough, *An island's law: a bibliographical guide to Ireland's legal past* (Dublin, 2013).

9 H. Wood, 'The public records of Ireland before and after 1922', *Transactions of the Royal Historical Society*, 13:4 (1930), 17. For a detailed listing of the extensive amount of chancery material that survived until 1922, see H. Wood, *A guide to the records deposited in the public record office of Ireland* (Dublin, 1919), pp 1–44. For a rough guide to the original records and later transcripts that survived the fire and chancery material donated, usually by solicitors,

notably, the pioneering and exhaustive research of Kenneth Nicholls. Quite rightly, Nicholls has alerted historians to the significance of these legal records and of the importance of basing any conclusions about the law and Irish legal systems on actual local situations rather than generalized principles.[10]

This is particularly true for the equity court of chancery, especially the pleadings, proofs, bill books and decree rolls (currently housed in the National Archives), together with the entry books of recognizances entered in the court of chancery (housed in the British Library).[11] In 1999 I undertook a detailed examination of chancery recognizances, dating from 1627 to 1634, which are housed in the British Library. The Irish Legal History Society kindly funded this research and the high-level findings were published in 2001 in Greer and Dawson (eds), *Mysteries and solutions in Irish legal history*. Given that the recognizances for 1627–34 represent only a very small percentage of the total number of suits pursued in chancery during these years, it seems clear that Ireland, like seventeenth-century England, was a highly litigious society and one in which the legal profession flourished.[12] The fact that a disproportionately large number of Catholic Gaels appear in these legal records is particularly significant and indicates, as O'Dowd has noted in her own work on the Irish chancery, that during the early modern period the chancery acted as 'a mediator between English common law and Gaelic customary law'.[13] English chancery records, which are extant in the National

to the National Archives after 1922 see *The fifty-fifth report of the deputy keeper of the public records and keeper of the state papers in Ireland* (Dublin, 1928), pp 114, 125–7; and *The fifty-sixth report of the deputy keeper of the public records and keeper of the state papers in Ireland* (Dublin, 1931), pp 34–6, 203–4, 213–308.

10 See, for instance, K.W. Nicholls, 'Some documents on Irish law and custom in the sixteenth century', *Analecta Hibernia*, 26 (1970), 105 where the court procedures are explained and a selection of salved chancery pleadings are printed in full; K.W. Nicholls, 'A calendar of salved chancery pleadings concerning County Louth', *Journal of the County Louth Archaeological Society*, 17:4 (1972), 250 and K.W. Nicholls, 'A calendar of salved chancery pleadings concerning County Louth, continued', ibid., 18:2 (1974), 112 where the salved pleadings are calendared; K.W. Nicholls 'Irishwomen and property in the sixteenth century' in M. MacCurtain and M. O'Dowd (eds), *Women in early modern Ireland* (Dublin, 1991), pp 17–31; and K.W. Nicholls, *Land, law and society in sixteenth-century Ireland* (Dublin, 1976), p. 3.

11 Material associated with chancery cases was documentary; witness statements, e.g., were recorded by designated local officials for future use. Therefore, the evidence generated in the course of a chancery suit was more likely to survive than in a common law action where oral testimony was given before a jury and rarely recorded. The legal material generated by a given suit was organized according to the type of document (recognizances, pleadings and answers, decrees etc.). The pleadings and proofs in particular provide a wealth of detail about the nature of the dispute and often include supporting documentation – witness statements, wills, marriage settlements, household inventories, leases and bonds. Given the paucity of personal estate archives, especially for the gentry, professional and merchant classes, these supporting documents are particularly interesting. Also see https:voicesproject.ie/impact/blog-3-from-the-ashes-locating-women-in-irish-chancery-court-records/.

12 J. Ohlmeyer, 'Records of the Irish court of chancery: a preliminary report, 1627–1634' in Greer and Dawson (eds), *Mysteries and solutions*, pp 15–50.

13 M. O'Dowd, 'Women and the Irish chancery court in the late sixteenth and early seventeenth centuries', *IHS*, 31:124 (Nov. 1999), 470.

Archives in London, also require further examination since they include cases that involved Irish people resident in England, along with others that relate directly to Ireland.[14] Though the scale remains to be determined, what is very clear is that much more material, albeit incomplete, dispersed and difficult to interrogate, appears to have survived the disaster of 1922 than was once thought, something that Peter Crooks' pioneering project – 'The Virtual Record Treasury of Ireland' – is confirming.[15]

The Irish Legal History Society has played an important role in helping to make available legal records that have survived in archives and libraries in Ireland and beyond. For example, it generously supported, through a postgraduate bursary to Margaret Curtis Clayton, research into the presidency of Munster, 1570–1672, which facilitated the publication of *The council book for the province of Munster,* c.*1599–1649*.[16] The Irish Legal History Society has sponsored a range of publications that have enriched our understanding of the law, litigation, legal personnel and the judiciary in the early modern period. For example, Crawford's *A star chamber court in Ireland: the court of castle chamber, 1571–1641* (Dublin, 2005) recovers over a period of seventy years some of the records of the court of castle chamber (the Irish equivalent to the court of star chamber) extant in the British Library, Trinity College Dublin and Sheffield Public Library. In this, along with *Anglicizing the government of Ireland* (Dublin, 1993), Crawford demonstrates how the court of castle chamber became central to policy making in pre-1641 Ireland.

This brings me back to the subject of this chapter: 'Lords, the law and litigation in early modern Ireland'. What do extant court records tell us about the legal worlds of the Irish aristocracy? In order to answer these and related questions, legal sources need to be consulted alongside extant estate papers and correspondence. A remarkable amount has survived for relatively few high-profile families; virtually nothing for the majority. For example, the Kildare letter book provides a wonderful insight into the legal wrangling in Dublin and London of George FitzGerald, sixteenth earl of Kildare, during the 1630s and particularly details on his infamous dispute with his kinswoman, Lady Offaly.[17] The earl of Clanricarde's letter books are equally revealing.[18] The archives of the Boyles, earls of Cork and of Orrery, the

14 J. Ainsworth, 'Some abstracts of chancery suits relating to Ireland', *Journal of the Royal Society of Antiquaries of Ireland* 9:1 (1939), 39; and P. Little, 'Select document. Providence and posterity: a letter from Lord Mountnorris to his daughter, 1642', *IHS,* 32:128 (Nov. 2001), 556.

15 https://virtualtreasury.ie.

16 This formed the basis for Clayton (ed.), *The council book for the province of Munster.*

17 A. Clarke and B. McGrath (eds), *Letterbook of George, 16th earl of Kildare* (Dublin, 2013).

18 B. Cunningham (ed.), 'Clanricard letters: letters and papers, 1605–1673, preserved in the National Library of Ireland, manuscript 3111', *Journal of the Galway Archaeological and Historical Society,* 48 (1996), 162; J. Lowe (ed.), *Letter-book of the earl of Clanricarde, 1643–1647* (Dublin, 1983); and John Smyth, *The memoirs and letters of Ulick, marquess of Clanricarde, and earl of Saint Albans* (London, 1758).

O'Briens of Thomond and the Brownes of Kenmare, are remarkably intact and bristle with materials relating to their legal cases, their lawyers and their attitudes towards the courts.[19] Eighteenth-century disputes over the estates of the Plunketts, barons Louth, contain much retrospective material that illuminates their seventeenth-century legal affairs.[20] In short, while the evidence may be scrappy and at times difficult to interpret, enough survives to allow us to begin to reconstruct the legal worlds of the Irish peers: their legal experiences; their legal teams and networks; their contacts with the inns of court; the nature of their litigation; and the scale and cost of their law suits.

LEGAL WORLDS

In the early decades of the seventeenth century, the crown's chronic shortage of cash resulted in the brazen sale of titles to the highest bidder. This resulted in a dramatic increase in the size of the Irish peerage from 29 lords in 1603 to 99 in 1640. From 1640 the numbers of peers remained remarkably constant at around one hundred. Thus, the crown created a new generation of ambitious and avaricious peers, usually Protestant and largely of English and, to a lesser extent, Scottish extraction who were determined to make their fortunes in Ireland and to secure public reward and social recognition. In 1603 the vast majority (*c.*90 per cent) of Irish peers were Catholic and included the great Gaelic lords of Tyrone and Tyrconnell. By 1640 the religious composition of the peerage had changed very dramatically indeed: roughly half were Catholic and the other half Protestant. Proportions remained fairly constant throughout the seventeenth century, though by 1690 the percentage of Catholic peers had increased. In short, the crown, lacking a paid bureaucracy, had effectively created a 'service nobility' of mixed religions and ethnicities to implement anglicizing policies.[21]

Three examples illustrate the direct link between a prominent legal career and social advancement. First, Adam Loftus, first Viscount Loftus of Ely (created 1622), was 'new English'. He had attended Lincoln's Inn and continued his legal studies in London becoming a bachelor in civil law, before coming to Ireland in 1597 where he then accumulated an array of public and legal offices, including that of lord chancellor of Ireland. Second, Dominick

19 E. MacLysaght (ed.), *Calendar of the Orrery papers* (Dublin, 1941); E. MacLysaght (ed.), *Kenmare manuscripts* (Dublin, 1942); F.W. Steer and N.H. Osborne (eds), *The Petworth House archives: a catalogue*, 4 vols (Chichester, 1968), i; and A.B. Grosart, *The Lismore papers, 1st [and second] series. Autobiographical notes, remembrances and diaries of Sir Richard Boyle, first and 'great' earl of Cork. Edited, with introductions and notes and illustrations by Alexander B. Grosart. From the original MSS. belonging to the duke of Devonshire, preserved in Lismore Castle*, 4 vols (London, 1886–8).

20 D. Mac Iomhair, 'The house of Louth in the seventeenth and eighteenth centuries', *Journal of the County Louth Archaeological and Historical Society*, 16:2 (1966), 67.

21 Discussed at length in Ohlmeyer, *Making Ireland English*, ch. 2.

Sarsfield, from Cork, was of old English stock. He served as attorney general, chief justice for Munster, judge of the king's bench and finally chief justice of the common pleas, before taking the title Viscount Kinsale in 1625.[22] Using the law to secure social advancement continued after the restoration of the Stuarts, and this brings us to our third example. In 1661 James Barry became Lord Santry. The son of a prominent Dublin merchant family, he was educated at Trinity College Dublin and called to the English bar at Lincoln's Inn in 1628 and to the King's Inns two years later. He enjoyed an illustrious legal career and was appointed prime sergeant in 1629, baron of the exchequer in 1634 and chief justice of king's bench in 1660. His political experience was also extensive, and he sat as an MP in the 1634, 1641, and 1661 parliaments and in the Convention of 1660. Socially, Lord Santry, like the other legal lords, was upwardly mobile and he serves as an excellent example of a man who used his office and influence to acquire wealth and status. His merchant background, however, remained something of an obstacle to his integration into the wider peerage and the earl of Barrymore took umbrage when his heir married Santry's daughter.[23]

The social engineering that occurred during this period was part of a wider agenda to 'civilize' and to 'anglicize' colonial Ireland.[24] The law was another key plank in the strategy. From the late sixteenth century a revitalization of central and provincial government occurred in Ireland and this facilitated the piecemeal reintroduction of English common law, something that the state believed was a critical prerequisite to the 'civilization' of Ireland.[25] Legislation that promoted the English language, dress and culture became law in 1537.[26] The need to reform 'uncivil' natives and to anglicize their 'barbarous' customs led to the prohibition of Gaelic cultural practices and attempts to remove Irish-speaking 'tympanours, poets, story-tellers, babblers, rymours, harpers, or any other Irish minstrels'.[27] The Kingship Act 1542 accorded Irish subjects 'the same rights as those of English origin'.[28] The Shiring Act 1569[29]

22 J. McCavitt, '"Good planets in their several spheares" – the establishment of the assize circuits in early seventeenth-century Ireland', *Irish Jurist*, 24:2 (1989), 248.

23 W.N. Osborough, 'Barry, James, first Baron Barry of Santry (1603–1673)' in *Oxford DNB*.

24 J. Ohlmeyer, 'Conquest, civilization, colonization: Ireland, 1540–1660' in R. Bourke and I. MacBride (eds), *The Princeton guide to modern Irish history* (Princeton, 2016), pp 21–47; J. Ohlmeyer, '"Civilizinge of those rude partes": the colonization of Ireland and Scotland, 1580s–1640s' in N. Canny (ed.), *The Oxford history of the British empire*, 5 vols (Oxford, 1998), i, pp 124–47; and J. Ohlmeyer, 'A laboratory for empire? Early modern Ireland and English imperialism' in K. Kenny (ed.), *Ireland and the British empire* (Oxford, 2004), pp 26–60.

25 R. Bolton (ed.), *The statutes of Ireland, beginning the 3rd yeare of k. Edward III until the … 13th yeare of k. James I* (Dublin, 1621), preface.

26 Act for the English Order, Habit and Language 1537 (28 Hen. VIII, c. 26).

27 E. Curtis and R.B. McDowell (eds), *Irish historical documents, 1172–1922* (London, 1943), p. 55.

28 The Crown of Ireland Act 1542 (33 Hen. VIII, c. 1); B. Bradshaw, *The Irish constitutional revolution of the sixteenth century* (Cambridge, 1979), pp 231–57.

29 An Act for turning of Countries that be not yet Shire Grounds into Shire Grounds 1569 (11 Eliz. sess. 3, c. 9).

signalled the arrival of English property law, the primacy of primogeniture, and the introduction of a culture of 'improvement'.[30] Other legislation proscribed the collection of tribute, cattle-raiding and the maintenance of armed retainers, and mandated that all law suits be settled by English common law, in an attempt, as one contemporary put it, to bring the people to 'the obedience of English law and the English empire'.[31]

Ever on the make, Irish peers were quick to use the legal system to their best advantage. To begin with, many became directly involved in the administration of justice and used local courts to strengthen their authority, especially on their own and neighbouring estates. They sought, as Barnard notes, 'to annex the legal system to their own interests' and to secure the appointment of local justices of the peace, commissioners, and sheriffs.[32] In other words, the peers sought to control not simply their own manorial courts but also the local operation of the law. No doubt the first earl of Antrim had an ulterior motive for asking that the quarter sessions of the assize be held on his estates at Oldstone, near Glenarm, rather than requiring his tenants to travel to the assizes held at Carrickfergus.[33] In 1627 the earl refused to let judges of the assize take cattle from his land, put bailiffs in stocks for trying to execute writs in the county, and fined – in his own manorial courts – those who had turned for justice to the local sheriff.[34]

Antrim's actions were not untypical, prompting disgruntled tenants or business associates to complain that baronial influence made it impossible for them to secure justice or to receive a fair trial. One charge regularly raised against the Protestant planter, Richard Boyle, first earl of Cork, outlined his ability to drag out law suits (and thereby impoverish his suitors), bully local sheriffs, intimidate witnesses and, as a result, prevent his opponents from enjoying a fair hearing.[35] In May 1634 Lord Deputy Wentworth summoned Lord Balfour of Glenawley in Co. Fermanagh before the court of castle chamber to account for the outrages he had allegedly committed while he served on an assize circuit. 'I do not think there is such another tyrant in the king's dominions', wrote Wentworth, 'who [is] utterly drunk with the vice of violence [and] hath with unequal and staggering paces trod down his majesty's people on every side'.[36] With the passage of time baronial sway over the administration of justice became entrenched, especially among the Protestant

30 J.P. Montaño, '"Dycheyng and hegeying": the material culture of the Tudor plantations in Ireland' in F. Bateman and L. Pilkington (eds), *Studies in settler colonialism: politics, identity and culture* (Basingstoke, 2011), pp 47–62; J.P. Montaño, *The roots of English colonialism in Ireland* (Cambridge, 2011).

31 R.P. Mahaffy (ed.), *Calendar of state papers, Ireland, 1625–1632* (London, 1900), p. 58.

32 Barnard, 'Lawyers and the law', p. 272.

33 R.P. Mahaffy (ed.), *Calendar of state papers Ireland, 1625–1632*, p. 490.

34 Crawford, *A star chamber court in Ireland*, p. 349.

35 Mahaffy (ed.), *Calendar of state papers Ireland, 1625–1632*, pp 549, 626.

36 Crawford, *A star chamber court in Ireland*, p. 390; W. Knowler (ed.), *The earl of Strafforde's letters and dispatches: with an essay towards his life*, 2 vols (London, 1739), i, p. 245.

peers. Well-placed recusants were quick to manipulate it as best they could. For example, in a letter back to Rome, dating from 1670, Oliver Plunkett, Catholic archbishop of Armagh, noted how he had cultivated many of the local Protestant lords so that 'I would be able to avail myself of the good will of these powerful men, upon whom all depends, whenever I should be summoned before a Protestant tribunal'.[37]

Equally important was the ability of Irish Catholics to use the law to protect family estates, especially in an era of increased and intensive colonization. That said, while expropriation brought tenurial insecurities, it also created opportunities for acquiring lands and thus local influence and political power. A knowledge of English law could well increase a family's chances for political and economic survival and enhancement. A variety of initiatives, dating back to the 1540s, allowed many to acquire a legal title to their lands. In a process known as 'surrender and regrant', land held by a non-English title or tenure was surrendered to the crown and re-granted to its holder with title and tenure good in English law. The various plantation schemes of the late sixteenth and early seventeenth centuries allowed many of the native peers to expand their existing holdings as well as enabling the newcomers to acquire vast patrimonies.[38] Thus a peer's knowledge of the law, his access to experienced lawyers and officials of the central courts on both sides of the Irish Sea, combined with access to the patronage networks around the king, the centre of power and influence, often determined his ability to acquire additional acres or to protect from greedy speculators lands which his lineage had traditionally held.[39]

Hardly surprisingly then, the peers – Protestant and Catholic alike – appreciated the importance of acquiring some knowledge of the law, no doubt in order to outwit it, and of cultivating contacts with the wider legal community in Dublin but especially in London. Thus peers like Jenico Preston, fifth Viscount Gormanston, who had sat as juror in Lord Dunboyne's trial in 1628, left in his will (dated 1629) £40 per annum for his son Robert should he wish to attend the inns of court.[40] The sons, kinsmen and factors of peers spent time at the inns of court in London.[41] For a few it provided a

37 J. Hanly (ed.), *The letters of Saint Oliver Plunkett 1625–1681, archbishop of Armagh and primate of all Ireland* (Dublin, 1979), p. 127.

38 D. Edwards, 'Collaboration without anglicization: the Macgiollapadraig lordship and Tudor reform' in P. Duffy, D. Edwards and E. FitzPatrick (eds), *Gaelic Ireland: land, lordship and settlement,* c.*1250*–c.*1650* (Dublin, 2001), pp 78–96.

39 Ohlmeyer, *Making Ireland English*, ch. 4 and 11.

40 Anon., 'A seventeenth-century will', *The Irish Builder*, 33:763 (1891), 218. I am grateful to Bríd McGrath for bringing this reference to my attention.

41 D.F. Cregan, 'Irish Catholic admissions to the English inns of court, 1558–1625', *Irish Jurist* 5:1 (Summer 1970), 95; J. Ohlmeyer, 'Irish recusant lawyers during the reign of Charles I' in M. Ó Siochrú (ed.), *A kingdom in crisis: the confederates and the Irish civil wars* (Dublin, 2000), app.; B. McGrath, 'Ireland and the third university: attendance at the inns of court, 1603–1649' in D. Edwards (ed.), *Regions and rulers in Ireland, 1100–1650: essays for Kenneth*

gateway to a career in the common law as barristers, attorneys, solicitors, accountants, brokers, entrepreneurs and land agents. For example, Archibald Hamilton of Ballygally, nephew of the Scottish planter, James Hamilton, first Viscount Clandeboye, was 'bred' at the inns and later managed Clandeboye's affairs at court.[42] His east Ulster neighbour, Viscount Montgomery, did likewise. Montgomery's younger son, James, attended university and travelled in France, Italy and Holland before spending time at the inns of court in London and from there 'sollicited his Father's business at the royal court, at the council table, at the parliament and prerogative in England, and before the government and Four Courts in Ireland'.[43] Sir Nicholas Plunkett, son of Lord Kileen and brother of the earl of Fingal, went on to become one of the leading lawyers in seventeenth-century Ireland and consistently guarded the interests of his kinsmen, together with other Catholic (and Protestant) lords. Toby Mathews of Thurles, the Catholic half-brother and trusted agent of James Butler, later duke of Ormond, entered Gray's Inn in 1640 but presumably the outbreak of war cut short his training. In short, the investment a family made in education, especially that of a younger son, helped to secure his future and was of wider benefit to the lineage, helping to secure the survival of some Catholic dynasties.

However, for the majority the inns of court served as an exclusive finishing school where young men 'may learn qualities fit for a gentleman'.[44] For those who attended the inns in their capacity as the 'third university of the realm', this did not necessarily mean, as Prest has convincingly argued, that the entrant received a legal education or had any genuine familiarity with the theory and practice of the common law.[45] The popularity of the inns lay in the fact that they were 'schools of civility and chivalry, as well as law. For the country gallant is here principled to his after improvement … he after becomes a luminary in the counterey firmament, an oracle of the justice bench, a worthy representative to parliament'.[46] From a base at one of the inns, young Irish lords could explore London, a dynamic metropolis that

Nicholls (Dublin, 2004), pp 217–36; and C. Kenny, '"Badge of servitude"? The Irish at England's inns of court', *Proceedings of the Royal Irish Academy*, 119C (2019), 199.

42 G. Hamilton, *A history of the house of Hamilton* (Edinburgh, 1933), p. 906.

43 W. MacIlwaine, 'Notice of hitherto unpublished portion of the "Montgomery manuscripts"', *Ulster Journal of Archaeology*, 9 (1st series, 1861–2), 154.

44 R.J. Fletcher (ed.), *The pension book of Gray's Inn, 1569–1669*, 2 vols (London, 1901), i, p. 295. In this respect the inns were typical of comparable institutions throughout contemporary Europe, see F. Ranieri, 'From status to profession: the professionalization of lawyers as a research field in modern European legal history', *Journal of Legal History*, 10:1 (1989), 184; and W.R. Prest (ed.), *Lawyers in early modern Europe and America* (London, 1981).

45 W.R. Prest, *The inns of court under Elizabeth and the early Stuarts (1590–1640)* (London, 1972); W.R. Prest, 'Legal education of the gentry at the inns of court, 1560–1640', *Past & Present*, 38 (1967), 20.

46 E.Waterhouse, *A discourse and defence of arms and armory* (1660), p. 134 (quoted in Prest, *The inns of court*, p. 40).

offered a wide range of exciting intellectual and cultural pursuits; forge excellent contacts at court and among the upper echelons of English society; and secure the patronage of political powerbrokers. In the process they might acquire some legal knowledge, especially in relation to property and inheritance law, enabling them to deal with suits involving troublesome tenants and avaricious neighbours.[47] It also afforded them with an ideal opportunity to forge contacts with the Irish and English legal communities.

For generations the Catholic Nettervilles of Dowth had attended the inns. Nicholas, first viscount, sent at least two (of his eight) sons to London: in 1629 Patrick entered the Middle Temple and in 1638 Robert entered Gray's Inn. The Protestant Aungiers were a legal dynasty that exercised influence across the seventeenth-century English empire. Though the first of his family to live in Ireland, Baron Aungier who presided over Dunboyne's 1628 manslaughter trial was descended from Henry Aungier, chief justice and lord chancellor to Edward II. Baron Aungier attended Gray's Inn (1577), as did his sons, Gerald and Francis (1614 and 1628). It is not clear if Francis ever practised but he did inherit his father's legal library, which suggests a continued interest in the law.[48] Baron Aungier's grandson, Gerald, later governor and president of Bombay and Surat (1669–77), was credited as being the 'architect of the judicial system' in Bombay.[49] An inventory of the library at Surat includes legal books, namely 'Boltons workes'.[50] Sir Richard Bolton (d. 1648), lord chancellor of Ireland, would have been a colleague of Baron Aungier who published *The statutes of Ireland* (1621) and *A justice of peace for Ireland* (1638).[51]

Gray's Inn attracted most of the aristocratic entrants (see table 1 and the appendix).[52] It was the largest of the inns, the most fashionable, the most open to the court and seems to have been the most tolerant of recusants (hence the remarkably high numbers of Catholic entrants). After 1625 the sons of the earl of Cork; the sons of Viscounts FitzWilliam, Mountgarret, Ikerrin, Dowth, and Ranelagh; and the heir of baron of Upper Ossory were admitted to Gray's

47 Much more work needs to be done on the nature and extent of litigation in early modern Ireland. For litigation arising out of outstanding obligations on the statute staple see J. Ohlmeyer and É. Ó Ciardha (eds), *The Irish statute staple, 1596–1687* (Dublin, 1998), pp 29–33. For fascinating insights on the nature of economic litigation in England, see C. Muldrew, 'Credit and the courts: debt litigation in a seventeenth-century urban community', *Economic History Review*, 46:1 (1993), 23; and C. Muldrew, 'The culture of reconciliation: community and the settlement of disputes in early modern England', *The History Journal*, 39:4 (1996), 915.

48 Anon., 'Testamentary records', *Irish Genealogist*, 2:6 (1948), 180.

49 J. Foster (ed.), *The register of admissions to Gray's Inn, 1521–1889* … (London, 1889), pp 186, 318.

50 'Acco[un]tt of Bookes Remayning in the Library of Surratt July 31st Anno Domini 1673', BL, India Office R/E/3/34 f. 86.

51 R. Bolton, *The statutes of Ireland* … (Dublin, 1621); R. Bolton, *A justice of peace for Ireland, consisting of two bookes; whereunto are added many presidents of indictments of treasons, felonies* … (Dublin and London, 1683).

52 Cregan, 'Irish Catholic admissions', p. 99.

Inn. The aristocratic connections with the three other inns were more limited but Lincoln's Inn and the Inner and Middle Temples nevertheless attracted some prominent figures, including Mark Trevor, later Viscount Dungannon; Arthur Annesley, later earl of Anglesey; and the recusant sons of Lords Cahir, Athenry and Kerry. What is striking is how few peers sent their sons to the inns after 1660. There is no clear explanation for this, but it might be attributed to the 'professionalization' of the inns and to the increased attraction of alternative institutions (especially the military academies) as training grounds for young lords.[53]

Table 1: Irish peers and their relatives admitted to the inns of court, 1602–41[54]

Inn of Court	Catholic	Protestant	Total
Gray's Inn	13+1H	7+1H	20+2H
Inner Temple	3	3	6
Lincoln's Inn	1H	3+2H	3+3H
Middle Temple	4	0	4
Totals	20+2H	13+3H	33+5H

H = Honorary admission

Whatever the explanation for this declining attendance at the inns, some of the families who spent time at them during the late sixteenth and early seventeenth centuries clearly used the law as a vehicle for social and political advancement. The Catholic FitzWilliams of Merrion, elevated to the peerage in 1629, owed their rise to prominence, together with their wealth and landed estates, to an able late fifteenth-century lawyer, Thomas, whose successors all attended the inns.[55] Arthur, later earl of Anglesey, attended Lincoln's Inns where, according to a friend, he 'with unwearied steps [his] diligence it seems overcame the craggy ascent of the study of the common law of England'.[56] Anglesey used this knowledge with great effect and became one of the most influential figures in Restoration Ireland and England, where he was lord treasurer. Interestingly, as his diary entries reveal, the earl retained very close

53 H. Maynard, 'Irish membership of the English inns of court, 1660–1699: lawyers, litigation and the legal profession' (PhD, UCD, 2006).

54 See appendix to this chapter (pp 28–30) for a list of names.

55 J. Kingston, 'Catholic families of the Pale', *Reportum Novum: Dublin Diocesan Historical Record,* 2:1 (1957–8), 88. Also see C. McAsey, 'Booterstown', *Dublin Historical Record*, 21:3 (1969), 81; and MacLysaght, *Kenmare manuscripts*.

56 P. P[et], *The happy future state of England: or, a discourse by way of letter to the late earl of Anglesey, vindicating him from the reflections of an affidavit published by the House of Commons Ao. 1680 by occasion whereof observations are made concerning infamous witnesses* (London, 1688), Bodleian, 599 k18, p. 3.

links with the profession, regularly dining at Lincoln's Inn and attending sermons there. Moreover, he drew on his legal knowledge throughout his life, drafting marriage settlements for friends and family, and preparing legal briefs and court cases.[57] His diary even records how on 12 April 1684 he 'drew a bill' against his own recalcitrant daughter!

Earlier in the century Adam Loftus had secured the key post of lord chancellor (1619–38) by offering the cash-strapped duke of Buckingham £1,000. He later sat as an MP in the 1613 parliament and as a lord justice (1622–5, 1629–33, 1636) before becoming a viscount in 1622. Well-connected though he undoubtedly was, Loftus of Ely also made powerful enemies and during the later 1630s fell foul of Lord Deputy Wentworth who had him imprisoned and dismissed from office.[58] Wentworth maintained that Loftus was unfit for his post of lord chancellor 'both in respect of the weakness of his understanding, as also of his indirect, oppressive, and corrupt proceedings in the execution thereof'.[59] In fact, it appears to have been more complicated than this. The earl of Clarendon later noted that Wentworth had had an affair with Loftus's daughter-in-law, Eleanor Rushe, citing as evidence 'certain letters of great affection and familiarity from the earl to that lady … others of passion'.[60] Whatever the detail, litigation over the settlement Loftus had made on his son's family dragged on from 1627 until 1680 and even came before the English House of Lords.[61]

While a handful of peers were professional lawyers, the bulk were not and had no alternative but to retain a legal team. For instance, the Catholic earls of Clanricarde surrounded themselves with prominent lawyers, including James Donellan, Patrick Darcy, Richard Martin, Garret Moore, Geoffrey Brown and Roebuck Lynch who acted for them in Dublin and London.[62] Interestingly, Catholic peers rarely instructed Protestant lawyers while Protestant peers regularly used Catholic ones. Thus, during the early decades of the seventeenth century, Patrick Darcy, a lawyer from Galway, represented the Catholic earls of Clanricarde and Antrim as well as the Protestant earls of Cork, Kildare and Ormond and Viscount Sarsfield of Killmallock. While after

57 Annesley's diary, 9 May 1671–2 Oct. 1675, BL Add MSS 40860, continued at BL Add 18730.

58 Crawford, *A star chamber court*, pp 29; 99–102; W.N. Osborough, 'Loftus, Adam, first Viscount Loftus of Ely (1568–1643)' in *Oxford DNB*. See e.g. HMC, *Report on manuscripts in various collections*, vol. iii (London, 1904), pp 156–212; HMC, *Ninth report. Part II. Appendix* (London, 1884), pp 292–316.

59 HMC, *Ninth report*, part II, p. 298.

60 Ibid., p. 299.

61 R.P. Mahaffy (ed.), *CSPI, 1669–1670* (London, 1910), pp 434–6, 453; HMC, *Ninth report. Part II. Appendix*, pp 294–300.

62 L. O'Malley, 'Patrick Darcy, Galway lawyer and politician, 1598–1668' in D. Ó Cearbhaill (ed.), *Galway: town and crown, 1484–1984* (Dublin, 1984), pp 90–109; Cunningham, 'Clanricard Letters'; K. Nicholls, 'The Lynch Blosse Papers', *Analecta Hibernia,* 29 (1980), 115; and G. Talon (ed.), *Court of claims: submissions and evidence, 1663* (Dublin, 2006).

1660, Nicholas Plunkett, the leading recusant legal mind in Restoration Ireland, provided legal services to Lord Lieutenant Ormond and other Protestant peers, together with his Catholic kinsmen and friends.

LITIGATION AND LEGAL WORK

So much for the lawyers, what was the nature of their work for the peers? The bulk of lawsuits in early modern Ireland concerned land and tenurial issues. Whether as contested mortgages, landlord-tenant disputes, remedies for defective transfer, or for performance of leases – failure to pay rents, to improve or build property or deforestation – these highlight the centrality of land to the political, economic and social fabric of early modern Ireland.[63] For example, squabbles over estates in Co. Limerick bedevilled the Butlers, barons of Cahir, and Bourkes, barons of Brittas, throughout the 1630s and all attempts at arbitration failed.[64] Similarly, the Hamiltons of Clandeboye and the Montgomerys of the Ards were at loggerheads for decades over disputed lands in east Ulster; only the outbreak of war in 1641 brought the two families together.[65] Litigation between the Conways and the Langfords of Langford Lodge, over the boundary of four Ulster townlands, dragged on for sixty years.[66]

Closely linked to disputes over land were others that concerned marriage settlements and maintenance for wives (as in the case of Loftus and Eleanor Rushe) or for widows. Lady Offaly's vendetta with the earl of Kildare during the early decades of the seventeenth century over her jointure is well documented. It ran for over thirty years and almost bankrupted Kildare.[67] Similarly, the earldom of Ormond was quite literally torn asunder by the bitter suit between Walter Butler, eleventh earl of Ormond, and the royal favourite, Richard Preston, earl of Desmond, who had married the only daughter and heiress of his uncle, the tenth earl of Ormond. When Ormond refused to co-operate with the division of his vast patrimony, he was imprisoned in 1619 in the Fleet, where he languished for the next eight years.[68]

63 Ohlmeyer, 'Records of the Irish court of chancery'.
64 HMC, *Twelfth report, app. 1* (London, 1888), pp 306 and 436; HMC, *Twelfth report, app. 2* (London, 1888), p. 116.
65 J. Stevenson, *Two centuries of life in Down, 1600–1800* (Belfast, 1920), pp 35, 40; R.P. Mahaffy (ed.), *CSPI 1647–1660* (London, 1903), pp 156–7.
66 M. Beckett, *Sir George Rawdon, a sketch of his life and times* (Belfast, 1935), p. 19.
67 C.W. Russel and J.P. Prendergast (eds), *CSPI 1606–1608* (London, 1874), pp 363, 393–4 and 436–7; C.W. Russel and J.P. Prendergast (eds), *CSPI 1611–1614* (London, 1877), p. 182; V. Treadwell, *Buckingham and Ireland, 1616–1628: a study in Anglo-Irish politics* (Dublin, 1998), pp 115–20.
68 T. Barnard and J. Fenlon (eds), *The dukes of Ormonde, 1610–1745* (Woodbridge, 2000), pp 60–3; Treadwell, *Buckingham and Ireland*, pp 115–29.

Marital and domestic disputes also proved costly. In the 1620s James, Lord Balfour of Glenawley, Co. Fermanagh, 'though an ancient man of great adge', married Anne, the fifteen-year-old daughter of Lord Blayney. After the wedding 'which was done on both sides with more haste than good speed', Balfour reneged on the marriage settlement on the grounds that another man 'had abused his wife both before his marriage with her and after'. Under duress, Anne confessed to her infidelities and a lengthy and humiliating lawsuit ensued that threatened to bankrupt her father, Lord Blayney – something that Balfour had fully intended.[69] Later in the century Clarendon and Ormond agreed that Lady Ranelagh had married 'the worst man in the world' who had left her without 'one shilling' for three years.[70] The acrimonious marital spats of the second earl of Orrery and his estranged wife reduced the entire family to emotional despair and financial embarrassment during the later decades of the seventeenth century and left their young offspring vulnerable to manipulation from all parties.[71] Other disputes related to the execution of wills, namely the payment of legacies, the administration of a trust, and provision for minors, especially the issue of a mixed marriage.[72]

A few peers were involved in criminal cases. In 1628 Lord Dunboyne was, as we have already noted, tried – and acquitted – for manslaughter.[73] In 1666 Viscount Mountgarret's son, Edmund, killed a man in a pub brawl, allegedly in self-defense. Found guilty of manslaughter, the court ordered that his hand should be burned. Edmund appealed to the king who pardoned him.[74] Particularly brutal was the attack in 1579 by Nicholas, eight Baron Howth, against his fifty-year-old wife and his twelve-year-old daughter, Jane, one of his fourteen children. Records of Howth's lengthy trial outlined in chilling detail how he repeatedly beat his wife 'so that she could not abide clothing next to her skin for many days thereafter', how he assaulted any servant who attempted to bring her food or water, and how he almost killed a butler who allegedly had been overly familiar with the unfortunate woman. The domestic abuse continued but this time against Jane. He stripped her naked and he then assaulted her thirty or forty times 'with sally rods'. She died twelve days later as a result of these wounds. But even her final days were ones of torment as

69 G.A. Little, 'Hungry Hamilton, Fellow of Trinity', *Dublin Historical Record* 11 (1930–40), 7; G.A. Little, *The Spottiswoode miscellany: a collection of original papers and tracts, illustrative of the civil and ecclesiastical history of Scotland*, 2 vols (Edinburgh, 1844) , i, pp 96–164; C.W. Russel and J.P. Prendergast (eds), *CSPI 1615–1625* (London, 1880), pp 352, 354; *CSPI 1625–32*, pp 18, 256–7, 292; R. Gillespie, 'The trials of Bishop Spottiswood 1620–40', *Clogher Record*, 12:3 (1987), 323.

70 Clarendon to Ormond, 30 Jan. 1666, Bodleian, Carte MSS 47, f. 104.

71 MacLysaght, *Calendar of the Orrery papers*.

72 E.g., Mac Iomhair, 'The house of Louth' and Ohlmeyer, *Making Ireland English*, ch.6.

73 J. Kingston, 'Lord Dunboyne', *Reportum Novum: Dublin Diocesan Historical Record,* 3:1 (1961–2), 62; HMC, *Fifteenth report, app. 1, part ii* (London, 1897), pp 291–3.

74 *CSPI 1669–1670*, p. 685; and HMC, *Tenth report, app. 5* (London, 1885), pp 81–3.

her father removed 'her from her accustomed bed to a rawe coulde place' where she died alone. In the subsequent manslaughter investigation, the child's mother was too terrified to testify, as were the battered servants. Nevertheless, Howth was called to account. On 8 July 1579 the court of castle chamber fined him £1,100 for wife beating, £300 for servant beating, £500 for daughter beating and ordered him to provide his abused wife with an income and an alternative home where she could raise her unfortunate brood. Howth's excessive use of violence transgressed codes of noble behaviour and resulted in the denigration of the baron as 'a dishonourable brute who frequented whores and kept mistresses and failed to uphold English civility'.[75]

By abusing his position as a husband and father, Howth threatened the stability of his household in much the same manner that the earl of Castlehaven later did. The trial in London and subsequent conviction and execution in 1631 of Castlehaven, whose principal estates were in Ireland, for being party to the rape of his own wife and for sodomizing his servants, caused a sex scandal throughout the three kingdoms and left the family honour severely tarnished.[76] A less salacious case dating from 1670 concerned Mark Trevor, Viscount Dungannon, who was indicted for the rape of a woman called Sarah. Henry Hamilton, earl of Clanbrassil, was charged for aiding and abetting Dungannon. In the event, Dungannon was acquitted, but only the king's direct intervention finally cleared Clanbrassil of any role in the alleged rape.[77] The king also restored Clanbrassil's good name, something critically important in an age where family honour and reputation underpinned the social order. As in early modern England and Scotland, the courtroom had effectively replaced the battlefield as the forum whereby a peer's reputation could be defended and his honour restored. The number of slander cases or suits over protocol and precedency also highlight that 'Honour and reputation, no less than avarice, drew some litigants into the lawyers' clutches'.[78]

Defending one's honour, suing for lands or resolving a disputed marriage settlement all proved costly. Understandably, the amounts spent on legal expenses and legal and court fees, together with endless bribes to lesser officials, varied from peer to peer. Suffice to say that all Irish lords incurred some legal costs, with some expending very considerable sums depending on the nature and the length of the litigation.[79] Lady Moore's account book

75 Crawford, *A star chamber court*, pp 152, 223–5, 228, 442–5; V. McGowan-Doyle, *The book of Howth: Elizabethan conquest and the old English* (Cork, 2011), pp 28–33.

76 C. Herrup, 'The patriarch at home: the trial of the 2nd earl of Castlehaven for rape and sodomy', *History Workshop Journal*, 41 (1996), 1; C. Herrup, '"To pluck bright honour from the pale-faced moon": gender and honour in the Castlehaven story', *Transactions of the Royal Historical Society*, 6 (1996), 137; and C. Herrup, *A house in gross disorder: sex, law and the second earl of Castlehaven* (Oxford, 1999).

77 *CSPI, 1669–1670*, pp 217; also pp 74, 195.

78 Barnard, 'Lawyers and the law', 270.

79 Ibid., pp 268–9.

reveals that between 1602 and 1604 she and her husband pursued cases in the courts of chancery, exchequer and king's bench and in the court of wards. In all £1259 11*s*. 5*d*. was 'layed out… [in] the suete in law' including 'fees to councellors and attorneys' and related expenditure.[80] By 1637 the second earl of Antrim owed Patrick Darcy over £1,600, presumably for legal services rendered.[81] Seeing a single case through the court of chancery cost George Rawdon, the Ulster factor to Lord Conway, £500 in legal fees alone.[82] In some instances litigation almost bankrupted some of Ireland's leading families. The legal expenses of Walter, eleventh earl of Ormond, for a twelve-month period (October 1630 and 1631) amounted to well over £5,000.[83] After the Restoration, the earl of Carlingford's kinsman and agent, Sir John Bellew, busied himself bribing and befriending key officials and coordinating the efforts of an array of legal counsels to ensure that Carlingford's estates were not only restored to him but increased in size. Bellew recorded in a notebook every bribe he paid out: a piece of gold to Sir William Domville, the attorney general 'to befriend my lord [Orrery]'; and payments to lawyers (including Sir Nicholas Plunkett) and the clerks to the commissioners of the court of claims.[84]

Litigation also set husband against wife; mother and father against son; brother against brother; and so on.[85] During the early seventeenth century, the mother of Nicholas, Lord Howth, recorded in her own will the heartache that litigation with her son had caused her:

> And although my son, Nicholas St Lawrence, Lord Baron of Howth, hath much grieved me, in putting me in suit, for the performing of a bargain, which I never concluded with him, yet I do hereby freely forgive him, and do leave with him, his wife and children, my prayers and blessing.[86]

In 1634 the Dublin court of chancery required Patrick, Lord Kerry and Lixnaw, to pay his three sisters their marriage portions of £500, together with '20 markes sterling on the feast of Easter and Michaelmas by equal portions'.[87] This stemmed from an earlier dispute between Patrick and his

80 Lady Moore's account book, 1602–4 (NLI MS 9739, f. 37).
81 PRONI D301/1.
82 M. Beckett, *Sir George Rawdon, a sketch of his life and times* (Belfast, 1935).
83 D. Edwards, *The Ormond lordship in County Kilkenny, 1515–1642: the rise and fall of Butler feudal power* (Dublin, 2000) pp 128–31.
84 NLI, MS 31,994, f. 7.
85 Little, 'Select document', pp 556–64.
86 J. Lodge (rev. Archdall Mervyn), *The peerage of Ireland or a genealogical history of the present nobility of that kingdom*, 7 vols (Dublin, 1789), iii, p. 200. Will of Elizabeth, wife of Sir Christopher, 22nd Baron Howth. She remarried Sir Robert Newcomen and died in 1627.
87 BL Add MS 19,842, ff. 138, 140, 141. At this point only Maria was married.

father over Patrick's own marriage, which attempts at arbitration had failed to resolve satisfactorily.[88] The Montgomery family historian recorded how financial worries during the 1650s forced Viscount Montgomery to sue his brother-in-law, Viscount Moore, for his wife's portion. This delighted the 'usurpers' (i.e., Cromwellians) who encouraged 'the king's friends [to] worry one another at law … for they encouraged privately animositys among the loyalists, and publicly let loose upon them all their creditors like fierce mastives, whom the wars had for some years chained up'.[89] In the event, Lords Mount Alexander and Moore reached a compromise but this example highlights the cost of litigation on familial relationships. In short, by the end of the seventeenth century English law permeated every aspect of the private and public lives of Ireland's aristocracy.

CONCLUSION

This chapter began with an account of the ceremony and public display associated with Lord Dunboyne's 1628 manslaughter trial, which was overseen by the lord steward, Baron Aungier. The spectacle began when Aungier, the peers and judges, paraded from White Friars, where Aungier lived, to Dublin Castle, the seat of English power in Ireland. Over 40 years later his grandson, Gerald, oversaw the opening of the Bombay law courts with a colourful procession, which perambulated through the town, from the fort to the court, the physical embodiments of English rule on the island.[90] 'Never was there a joy fuller day', wrote a Bombay judge on 8 August 1672, adding 'the whole island is become English, we are incorporated, and our interest is alone'.[91] Clearly the law was a central element in the wider 'civilizing' agenda in Bombay, as much as it was in Ireland.[92] Whether Gerald Aungier, born after his grandfather's death in 1632, was even aware of Dunboyne's trial or his grandfather's colonial policies is unknown but the coincidence is intriguing. One thing for sure, the law was at the heart of anglicizing initiatives in both regions of the English empire.

88 R.P. Mahaffy (ed.), *CSPI 1647–1660*, pp 69–70; and R.P. Mahaffy (ed.), *CSPI 1633–1647* (London, 1901), p. 119.

89 G. Hill (ed.), *The Montgomery manuscripts (1603–1706). Compiled from the family papers by William Montgomery of Rosemount* (Belfast, 1869), p. 204.

90 K. MacMillan, *Sovereignty and possession in the English new world. The legal foundations of empire, 1576–1640* (Cambridge, 2006), p. 178; J. Ohlmeyer, 'Eastward enterprises: colonial Ireland, colonial India', *Past & Present*, 240:1 (2018), 83.

91 'Narratiue of the establishment of the law on the Island Bombay', at the Governor's command, by George Willcox, 30 Dec. 1672, f. 46 (BL, Add MS 39,255E).

92 J. Ohlmeyer, R.J. Ross and P. Stern, 'Anglicization of and through law: British North America, Ireland, and India compared, 1540–1800', forthcoming.

APPENDIX. IRISH PEERS AND THEIR RELATIVES ADMITTED TO THE INNS OF COURT DURING THE SEVENTEENTH CENTURY[93]

(Protestants are indicated in *italics.* s=son; h=heir)

GRAY'S INN

DATE OF ADMISSION	NAME OF ENTRANT	ADDRESS	HONORARY MEMBERSHIP	FAMILY
3 Aug. 1602	Thomas Fitzgerald	London		brother of Gerald, earl of Kildare
26 Feb. 1608	*Charles Lambert*	*Pinchbeck, Co. Lincoln*		*s/h of Sir Thomas*
6 Mar. 1610	Richard, earl of Clanricarde		yes	
13 Aug. 1611	Edward Butler	Monehore		s/h of Peter, 2nd s of Lord Mountgarret
9 Mar. 1615	*Gerald Aungier*			*s/h of Francis, Lord Longford*
6 Aug. 1615	Thomas Purcell	late of Barnard's Inn		s/h of Richard, Baron Loughmo of Tipperary
2 Feb. 1619	James Butler			2s of earl of Ormond
2 Feb. 1620	*Charles, Lord Lambert*		*yes*	
15 May 1622	Nicholas Plunkett			s of Christopher, Lord Kileen
5 Aug. 1628	Oliver Fitzwilliam	Dublin, Merrion		s/h of Thomas, knight, later Viscount Merrion
5 Aug. 1628	Richard Fitzwilliam	Dublin, Merrion		s/h of Thomas, knight
19 Oct. 1628	*Francis Aungier*			*s of Francis, Baron Longford*
3 Aug. 1629	*James Butler, Lord Thurles*	*Kilkenny, Kilkenny*		
3 Aug. 1629	Walter Butler, earl of Ormond	Kilkenny, Kilkenny		
3 Aug. 1629	Barnaby Fitzpatrick	Queen's Co., Upper Ossory		s/h of Barnaby, baron of Upper Ossory
17 Mar. 1635	*Lewis Boyle, Lord Kynalmeaky*			*s of Richard, earl of Cork*

93 Hon. Society of Lincoln's Inns, *The records of the honourable society of Lincoln's Inn: admissions from AD 1420 to AD 1799*, 4 vols (London, 1896) i; H.A.C. Sturgess (ed.), *Register of admissions to the honourable society of the Middle Temple from the fifteenth century to the year 1944*, 3 vols (London, 1949) i; J. Foster, *The register of admissions to Gray's Inn, 1521–1889* (London, 1889); and *Students admitted to the Inner Temple 1547–1660* [ed. W.H. Cooke] (London, 1877); and Inner Temple Library, 'Admissions to the Inner Temple to 1659' (typescript by L. Rees Lloyd, [1954]).

DATE OF ADMISSION	NAME OF ENTRANT	ADDRESS	HONORARY MEMBERSHIP	FAMILY
17 Mar. 1635	*Roger Boyle, Lord Broghill*			*s of Richard, earl of Cork*
13 Oct. 1637	Robert Hussey	Meath, Galtrim		3s of Patrick, esq [baron of Galtrim]
24/3/1638	James Butler	Tipperary		s/h of Peter, Viscount Ikerrin
13 Aug. 1638	Robert Netterville	Meath		3?s of Nicholas, viscount of Dowth
20 Feb. 1640	Mathews, Tobias	Tipperary, Thurleigh [Thurles]		s of George, esq, dec'd [Ormond's stepbrother]
6 Mar. 1641	*Arthur Jones*			*s/h of Lord Ranelagh*
14 Nov. 1660	*James, marquess of Ormond*		*yes*	
14 Nov. 1660	*Thomas, Earl of Ossory*		*yes*	*s/h of earl of Ormond*
14 Nov. 1660	*Richard Butler*			*2s of earl of Ormond*
14 Nov. 1660	*John Butler*			*3s of earl of Ormond*
10 Mar. 1674	*Richard, earl of Burlington*		*yes*	
10 Mar. 1674	*Francis, Lord Longford*		*yes*	
2 Aug. 1675	*Charles, Lord Clifford*			*grandson/h of earl of Burlington*

INNER TEMPLE

DATE OF ADMISSION	NAME OF ENTRANT	ADDRESS	HONORARY MEMBERSHIP	FAMILY
7 Mar. 1615	John Le Power	Curraghmore, Wexford		
6 Jan. 1621	*John Trevor*			*3s of Sir Edward*
6 Jan. 1621	*Mark Trevor, later Viscount Dungannon*			*3s of Sir Edward*
31 Oct. 1638	Callaghan O'Callaghan			3s of Caher
23 Oct. 1669	Thomas Butler			nephew of earl of Ormond
13 Aug. 1677	*Chamber Brabazon*			*s of earl of Meath*

LINCOLN'S INN

DATE OF ADMISSION	NAME OF ENTRANT	ADDRESS	HONORARY MEMBERSHIP	FAMILY
7 Aug. 1628	*Adam, Viscount Loftus*		*yes*	
7 Aug. 1628	*Francis, Lord Mountnorris*		*yes*	
2 Oct. 1633	*Arthur Annesley*			*s/h of Lord Mountnorris*
2 Oct. 1633	*Robert Annesley*			*s of Lord Mountnorris*
20 Oct. 1637	*Toby Caulfield*			*s/h of William, Baron Charlemont*
1 Mar. 1640	Ulick, earl of Clanricarde		yes	

MIDDLE TEMPLE

DATE OF ADMISSION	NAME OF ENTRANT	ADDRESS		FAMILY
7 Aug. 1628	Richard Bermingham			s of Lord Athenry
22 Dec. 1629	Patrick Netterville	Meath, Dooth [Dowth]		2s of Nicholas, Viscount Dowth
4 May 1633	James Clotworthy			
1 Apr. 1640	Robert Fitzmaurice	Kerry, Linnam [Lixnaw]		5s of Thomas, late baron of Linnam [sic]

Ambivalent patriot: William Molyneux and the art of rhetoric

PATRICK HYDE KELLY*

In recent years commentators on William Molyneux's *The case of Ireland's being bound by acts of parliament in England, stated* (1698) have been increasingly preoccupied by what they see as serious shortcomings in his credentials as a pioneer of the Irish patriot tradition that flourished in the eighteenth century in the writings and speeches of Swift, Lucas, Grattan, Wolfe Tone and others. The main issues have been his apparent marginalization of the 'Antient [or native] Irish'; his seeming enthusiasm for union with England; his unreflecting assumption that the constitution that Henry II granted to the Irish princes in 1171–2 had seamlessly transferred to the Protestant colonists, who had ousted the former's descendants from both their property and the benefits of that constitution; and finally, and most notably, the startling contrast between Molyneux's founding his case on the universal rights of mankind and his failure to acknowledge that such rights should have extended to Irish Catholics.[1] Controversy over where Molyneux stood on these various matters is far from exhausted. Other commentators have objected to what they see as a tedious rehearsal of ancient precedents and dependence on questionable history, while yet others again have criticized him for, in effect, failing to write the book that they would have wished him to write.[2] In my recent edition of *The case* I sought to show that Molyneux,

* An earlier version of this paper was delivered at the 'William Molyneux of Dublin (1656–1698): life, work and legacy' conference at St Audeon's church, Dublin 8, on 23 Nov. 2019.

1 The marginalization of the 'Antient Irish' was raised by J.G. Simms in *Colonial nationalism, 1698–1776* (Cork, 1976), p. 41. The question of union was discussed by both sides in the debates over union in 1798–1800, when some of its opponents even denied that Molyneux had ever championed the cause of union. The third point was made by his contemporary critic Simon Clement in the anonymous *An answer to Mr. Molyneux his Case of Ireland's being bound by acts of parliament in England, stated … By reasoning from his own arguments and authorities* (London, 1698), Epistle dedicatory, [A3^{v}–A5^{r}], p. 163; while his failure to extend natural rights to Catholics was objected to by Catholic nationalists in the nineteenth century. Despite this, however, many nineteenth- and twentieth-century Catholic writers were still happy to accept Molyneux's claim to patriot status (as was the case for Swift): R. Mahony, *Jonathan Swift: the Irish identity* (New Haven and London, 1995), pp 68–80, 94, 105–6 passim.

2 See J.C. Beckett, 'Literature in English, 1691–1800' in *A new history of Ireland*, 9 vols (Oxford, 1986), iv, p. 457; N.L. York, *Neither kingdom nor nation: the Irish quest for constitutional rights, 1698–1800* (Washington D.C., 1994), p. 23; C. Brunstrom, internet blog on Irish philosophy, 11 Oct. 2017.

himself of course a lawyer, set out to present his arguments in a manner analogous to that in which a civil case would have been presented before the higher courts. This involved raising in succession a series of legal points which were then substantiated by detailed evidence, before moving on to consider the next point on the written pleadings, or state of the case, laid before the court before the commencement of the formal trial, each point being discussed afresh without reference to matters which had been raised previously.[3] While this method of presentation was largely responsible for the repetition to which modern critics have so frequently objected, it did allow for the advancement of arguments that were not necessarily compatible, in the hope that one or other of them might find favour with the 'jury' to whom Molyneux sought to appeal, in effect the members of the English parliament.

Though still convinced that interpreting the presentation of the pamphlet as analogous to that of a civil case is correct in as far as it goes, I have come to realize that there is another important dimension of the work which I had hitherto overlooked. That is, that the main text of *The case* (that is, what follows the Dedication to the King, and Preface to the Reader) constitutes a sustained and impressive exercise in forensic rhetoric, set out in accordance with the principles laid down by the ancient exponents of the art, Aristotle and his Roman followers, namely Cicero, the author of *Rhetorica ad Herennium* and Quintilian.[4] Consequently much of what Molyneux says is influenced by the techniques of argument and presentation which the rhetoricians taught would enable their pupils to persuade their audience, and in the case of forensic rhetoric particularly the jury, to agree with their presentation of the facts of the case.[5] In the rest of this chapter I wish to do two things, first to substantiate my claim that the pamphlet does indeed constitute an exercise in forensic rhetoric conducted in accordance with the art as taught by the classical rhetoricians, and then to examine what light viewing the work in this context throws on the 'anomalies' to which I began by referring.

***

3 See W. Molyneux, *The case of Ireland's being bound by acts of parliament in England, stated* [Dublin, 1698], ed. P.H. Kelly (Dublin, 2018), intro., pp 28–9. References to the text of *The Case* are to the 1698 pagination, printed at the top of the page in the 2018 edition.

4 The best-known ancient works on rhetoric were Aristotle, *The art of rhetoric* (ed. and trans. J.H. Freese (Cambridge, MA) 1926); Marcus Tullius Cicero, *De inventione* and *Topica* (ed. and trans. H.M. Hubbell (Cambridge, MA) 1936), *De oratore* (ed. and trans. E.W. Sutton (Cambridge, MA) 1942); the anonymous *Rhetorica ad Herennium* – once attributed to Cicero (ed. and trans. H. Caplan (Cambridge, MA) 1977); and Marcus Fabius Quintilianus, *Institutio oratoria* (ed. and trans. H.E. Butler, 4 vols (Cambridge, MA) 1920–2).

5 What opened my eyes to *The case* being a rhetorical treatise was re-reading Q. Skinner, *Reason and rhetoric in the philosophy of Thomas Hobbes* (Cambridge, 1996). Like the protagonist of Moliere's *Le bourgeois gentilhomme* (act 2, sc. 4), being amazed to discover he was speaking prose, I was astonished to realize that Molyneux had so clearly presented the case for Irish legislative independence in accordance with the precepts of classical forensic rhetoric.

To establish that William Molyneux's *The case of Ireland* drew heavily on the theory and techniques of classical rhetoric one need only look to the brief introduction on pages 1–4 of the text proper of the pamphlet, together with the even briefer conclusion on pages 171–4. These pieces, especially the introduction, can be shown to be textbook instances of the brief *exordium* and *peroratio* that ancient teachers of rhetoric recommended for opening and closing a rhetorical presentation. In the lengthier *exordium* Molyneux faithfully followed the advice as to how a speaker should begin to gain the confidence of a potentially hostile audience and render them receptive to being won over to his arguments, along the lines recommended by Cicero, the *Ad Herennium* and Quintilian, a process described as the establishing of '*ethos*'. The speaker was to start by introducing himself in terms that would promote his audience's confidence in what he had to say by speaking well of himself – though with a due measure of modesty; flatter his audience by pointing to their importance and general benevolence and draw attention to their meritorious conduct in the past; stress the importance and novelty of what he had to tell them, pointing out that what he advocated was not merely for their own benefit but for that of the community in general and, if possible, the wider world; and finally lead them to understand that their hitherto-differing opinion had been the result of people's having failed to bring to their attention the matters which he now wished to lay before them.[6]

In the opening pages of *The case* Molyneux covered almost all these points. He introduced himself as a public-spirited landowner and Irish MP who had only come forward to speak on his country's behalf in the absence of any better qualified figure; went on to claim that the English parliament had been misled into thinking that it had the power to legislate for Ireland – '[which] is no Defect in the Parliament of *England*, but is highly Blameable in the Persons whose Affair is Transacting, and permit that Illustrious Body of Senators to be Mis-informed'; flattered the members as defenders of liberty and rights, who 'could [n]ever think of making the least breach in the *Rights* and *Liberties* of *their Neighbours*, unless they thought they had *Right* so to do'; and exalted the cause which he spoke for by claiming to speak for the liberty of all mankind, not just the rights of Irish Protestants, since

> 'tis the Cause of the whole Race of *Adam* that I argue: *Liberty* seems the inherent Right of all *Mankind*; and on whatsoever Ground any one Nation can Challenge it to themselves, on the same Reason may the Rest of *Adam's* Children Expect it.[7]

6 See Skinner, *Reason and rhetoric*, pp 120–1, 129–32. B. Vickers, *In defence of rhetoric* (Oxford, 1988), p. 69, speaks of the winning of the audience's goodwill as *captatio benevolentiae*.

7 *The case*, pp 1–3 passim.

Then, in an instance of what rhetoricians termed *parrhesia,* Molyneux obsequiously claimed that 'if the Great Council of *England* Resolve the contrary' he would 'believe myself to be in an Error, and with the lowest Submission ask Pardon for my Assurance', going on to express a (as it turned out to be) mistaken confidence that he should 'not be hardly Censur'd by them … especially when … I declare my Intention of a Submissive Acquiescence in whatsoever they Resolve for or against what I Offer'. By the later eighteenth century such rhetorical conventions had, however, sufficiently fallen out of use for one indignant reader to comment in the margin of a copy of the 1770 edition of the book: 'Was it for Molyneux to use such language?'[8] Such dutiful adherence to the classical precepts for writing an *exordium* may in part have been intended to alert readers to the fact that the work was being presented in the form of a rhetorical treatise, and was seemingly picked up as such by Simon Clement who referred, albeit somewhat sarcastically, to Molyneux's 'abundance of Well chosen Words and Fine Rhetorical Turns'.[9]

Similar instances of following rhetorical conventions are to be found in the *peroratio*, or conclusion.[10] Here Molyneux relied on the tactic of deliberately affronting the prejudices of his hearers, to provide *ornatus* (that is, variation of tone and pace in order to maintain the attention of the audience) to round off his presentation.[11] Referring first to the '*Great Wisdom, Honour* and *Justice*' of the parliament of England, he then drew what one critic regarded as a highly offensive parallel between the English parliament's overriding 'the Rights and Liberties' of the 'People of *Ireland*' and Louis XIV's revocation of the Edict of Nantes, an act that had outraged Protestant Europe.[12] He went on to warn that '*Advancing* the Power of the Parliament of *England*' by trampling on the rights of Ireland may in time have 'ill Effects' even on England itself.[13] The book's final paragraph, however, returned, as Cicero recommended, to a calmer and more modest approach by reminding his hearers that they had the opportunity to defend 'the *Rights* of *Parliament* … [a] kind of Government, once so *Universal* over *Europe* … [but] now almost *Vanished* from amongst the Nations thereof', and urged them to protect this 'noble *Gothick Constitution*', which – other than in our own 'King's Dominions' – was now only to be found in Poland.[14]

8 RIA shelfmark HP 360/18.

9 [Clement], *Answer to Mr. Molyneux* (London, 1698), p. 166.

10 *The case*, pp 171–4

11 See Skinner, *Reason and rhetoric*, pp 127–31, 143–4. See Cicero's precept that it was the third duty of an orator to excite and agitate the minds of his audience: *De inventione*, Bk i, § 98.

12 *The case*, p. 172. See J. Cary, *A vindication of the parliament of England, in answer to a book, written by William Molyneux of Dublin* (London, 1698), pp 125–6.

13 Ibid., pp 173–4: a remark interpreted by [Clement], *Answer to Mr. Molyneux*, p. 161, as an implicit threat.

14 *The case*, p. 174. This brief reference to the 'noble *Gothick Constitution* … once so universal over Europe' (probably based on his friend Robert Molesworth's *Account of Denmark*

As well as employing the customary *exordium* and *peroratio* for opening and closing *The case*, Molyneux laid out the intervening material in a typical *dispositio in partes orationis* (ordering the parts of a rhetorical presentation), of *divisio, narratio, confirmatio, refutatio* and *conclusio*.[15] The *divisio* set out the question at issue, namely 'How far the Parliament of *England* may think it Reasonable to intermeddle in the Affairs of *Ireland*, and Bind us up by Laws made in their House', and indicated the headings under which he proposed to examine it.[16] The *narratio*, or presentation of facts, described Henry II's expedition to Ireland and the establishment of the ancient Irish constitution up to the issuing of the Irish Magna Carta in 1216, including the crucial grant of Ireland as a 'Separate and Distinct Kingdom' to Prince John in 1177.[17] The *confirmatio* (the proofs) listed numerous English statutes re-enacted in Ireland, from the Statutes of Merton and Marlborough in 1320 to those in the most recent Irish parliament of 1697,[18] while the *refutatio* (answer to objections) refuted 'the Objections and Difficulties ... that may seem to prove the contrary' from the *Statutum Hiberniæ* (case of coparceners) of 1229 through to the current issue of appeals to the English king's bench, followed by consideration of various points raised in the English pamphlets calling for the prohibition of Irish woollen exports in early 1698.[19] The *conclusio* summed up the foregoing case in ten numbered points,[20] which also introduced some additional proofs, drawn from natural and common law, leading on to the brief *peroratio*[21] already alluded to.[22]

***

Having shown how closely the structure and layout of *The case* conformed to the precepts of the ancient writers on rhetoric, it remains to examine how Molyneux followed their teachings in a more general way throughout the pamphlet and to illustrate some of the more salient examples of his use of

(London, 1694), pp 42–3) would seem scarcely sufficient to establish Molyneux as a serious exponent of the theory of the ancient Gothic constitution, *pace* the views of those referred to in C. Kidd, *British identities before nationalism* (Cambridge, 1999), pp 155–7.

15 Even in antiquity the recommended number of parts had varied, with Cicero favouring a fivefold division and Quintilian a sevenfold one. See further Skinner, *Reason and rhetoric*, pp 47, 53.

16 *The case*, pp 4–6.

17 Ibid., pp 6–54.

18 Ibid., pp 56–77.

19 Ibid., pp 77–149.

20 Ibid., pp 150–71.

21 Ibid., pp 171–4.

22 To have an extended recapitulatory *conclusio* as well as the normal brief *peroratio* was somewhat unusual, though Cicero, *de Oratore*, I, 143, recommended a *conclusio* replying to the objections, summing up the speaker's arguments, and ending by an appeal to the emotions of the audience.

specific rhetorical techniques. By the later sixteenth century, forensic rhetoric, or judicial rhetoric as it was sometimes termed, had come to differ from the two other main branches of rhetoric – the demonstrative, concerned with establishing praise or blame, and the deliberative which dealt with urging how people should act in a given situation – in that forensic rhetoric had a more readily identifiable source of 'invention' (that is the process of finding out arguments to support one's case) available to lawyers in the form of printed statutes, year-books, law reports, and the works of respected jurists, all of which Molyneux would resort to in the writing of *The case*.[23] Given that, as is well known, Molyneux drew on three major manuscript sources for the composition of *The case* – namely, in descending order of importance, 'A disquisition touching that great question, whether an act of parliament made in England shall bind the kingdom and people of Ireland', written by his father-in-law, Sir William Domvile, in 1660; Sir Richard Bolton's 'A declaration setting forth how, and by what means, the laws and statutes of England, from time to time, came to be of force in Ireland' of 1644; and the anonymous 'That the legislative power in Ireland doth belong to the king by the advice of his parliament of Ireland, not of his parliament of England' of 1697 – the task of 'invention' in the sense of finding out specific arguments, had largely been accomplished for him by others. He was left to focus on *dispositio* and *elocutio*, that is the processes of organizing and of setting forth these arguments in the fashion most conducive to persuading his audience. Arguably, it was in the way Molyneux adapted this earlier material for publication in 1698 that his debt to the ancient techniques of forensic rhetoric is most apparent, and constituted an obvious difference from these earlier sources couched in the guise of supposedly-straightforward legal opinions rather than a rhetorical performance intended to convince a potentially hostile audience. In contrast to the 'plain style' of these earlier legal opinions, Molyneux adapted his material to the 'grand style' displayed in *The case*: the first instance of which, as Quintilian said, being deployed to enable us to teach; the second to teach, delight, and move an audience to accept our point of view.[24] It was the art of rhetoric that enabled Molyneux to bring together the disparate material from these three manuscript sources in an intellectually compelling and emotively effective manner – and subsequently enhance it with further arguments, mainly drawn from Locke's *Two treatises of government* (1690). Interestingly, it was not until the twentieth century that the complaints over *The case*'s being burdened with antique precedents and questionable history came to the fore, even though the conventions of rhetoric as practised in the sixteenth and seventeenth centuries were, as the adverse

23 See Sir John Dodridge, *The English lawyer: describing a method for managing the lawes of this land* (London, 1631), pp 149–50.

24 Quintilian also identified a 'middle style', intended to 'teach and delight', which is not, however, pertinent to the distinction made here (see Skinner, *Reason and rhetoric*, pp 84–5).

comment in the 1770 copy (cited above) indicated, no longer familiar to many readers.

This reference to the changed practice of the eighteenth century raises the question of where and how Molyneux acquired his knowledge of rhetoric and makes necessary a brief digression on this topic – brief because information as to what Molyneux knew of the subject is more readily inferred from what he wrote than from direct information on the curriculum that he studied at school, at university, the three years he spent as a student for the bar in London at the Middle Temple (1675–8), or from the contents of the Molyneux family library. Unfortunately, his time both at Trinity College Dublin and at the Middle Temple coincided with a period of transition from a well-established syllabus and set of educational practices to a more modern and less formal structure, evidence about the evolution of which is in both instances disappointingly sparse.[25] Teaching the elements of rhetoric was an essential part of grammar school education in England and Ireland from the early sixteenth century, and Molyneux would presumably have studied elementary rhetoric at the grammar school attached to St Patrick's Cathedral, which he attended.[26] It would also have constituted a significant part of the first year of his arts course at Trinity in the form of Porphyry's *Isagoge*, and been studied in greater detail in his second and third years through analysis of classical texts. Though up to the middle 1630s the Trinity textbook for rhetoric was that written by the puritan Ramist provost William Temple, this was rejected in the syllabus laid down in the Laudian statutes of 1637, and rhetoric divorced once more from dialectic was studied primarily in the works of the ancient writers such as Aristotle, Cicero and Quintillian.[27] What little is known of the post-Restoration Trinity curriculum suggests this emphasis on the writings of the classical rhetoricians continued and that there was no backsliding towards Ramism, whose Calvinist connotations were unlikely to have appealed to Molyneux's orthodoxly-Anglican tutor, William Palliser.[28]

25 Ironically, Molyneux himself played a significant role in hastening his university's abandonment of the traditional rhetoric curriculum by persuading Provost Ashe to adopt Locke's *Essay concerning human understanding* as a logic textbook. For what replaced the old system, see Jean Dietz Moss, 'Discordant consensus: old and new rhetoric at Trinity College Dublin', *Rhetorica: a Journal of the History of Rhetoric*, 14 (1996), 383–411.

26 For Molyneux's schooling and university career, see J.G. Simms, *William Molyneux* (Dublin, 1982), pp 18–20, and for rhetoric in contemporary education, P. Mack, *Elizabethan rhetoric: theory and practice* (Cambridge, 2002), chs 2–3. Thanks are due to the latter for further guidance on early modern rhetoric, as also to Lorna Hutson and Kathy Hannah Eden.

27 See R.B. McDowell and D.A. Webb, *Trinity College, Dublin: an academic history, 1592–1952* (Cambridge, 1972), pp 7–9.

28 Three works on rhetoric are listed in the surviving Trinity student notebook from the period (that of Josias Haydocke matriculated 1677), namely Quintilian's *Institutio oratoria*, Cicero's *De oratore*, and a *Formula oratoriae*, TCD MS 2642, ff. 104–9. The last was probably John Clarke's highly-popular *Formulae oratoriæ, in usum scolarum* … [Rules of rhetoric, for the use of schools], published in 11 editions, 1630–72.

The other possible indicator of what Molyneux might have studied, the famous 'Provost's logic' written by Narcissus Marsh, was not published until 1679, the year Marsh commenced teaching at Trinity, and five years after Molyneux had graduated.[29]

Turning to what he might have learned at the Middle Temple, Perry's study of English printings of legal works such as directions for the study of law and pleading handbooks from 1660 to 1700 suggests that while rhetoric still influenced the practice of advocacy to a considerable extent, despite the abandonment of the old system of teaching through moots, readings and case-watchings at the inns of court, formal rhetorical presentation of a legal case, such as we find in *The case,* would have owed more to prior study at university than any teaching at the inns. While the latter still placed emphasis on the importance of *inventio*, *dispositio* and *elocutio* for the practice of advocacy, the inclusion of a formal *exordium* and *peroratio* – such as are found in *The case* – was almost unknown.[30] Thus it appears unlikely that whatever formal teaching Molyneux received at the Middle Temple had any significant impact on the rhetorical format of *The case*.

The sole rhetorical work that Molyneux revealed direct familiarity with in his book was Aristotle's *Art of rhetoric*, as shown by a deleted reference in the autograph manuscript to Aesop's fable of the horse and the stag (cited in the *Rhetoric* as a warning against giving irrevocable power to dictators).[31] The catalogue of the Molyneux library as sold in 1730 listed more than one edition of the collected works both of Aristotle and of Cicero, whose publication dates indicated that they might have belonged to William. There were also two editions of Quintilian's *Institutio oratoria*; the earlier was the work of the Parisian printer, Michel de Vascos, in 1542 (mistakenly listed as 1642), while the more recent was edited by the Strasburg professor of rhetoric, Ulrich Obrecht, in 1698, and thus less likely to have been acquired by William.[32] Rather surprising is the absence of any English sixteenth- or early seventeeth-century general rhetorical text such as Thomas Wilson's frequently reprinted *Arte of rhetorique* (1554) or Henry Peacham's *Garden of eloquence* (1593), let alone one specifically directed to lawyers such as Abraham Fraunce's *Lawier's*

29 [Narcissus Marsh], *Institutiones logicae: in usum juventutis academiae Dublinensis* (Dublin, 1679); M. McCarthy, 'Narcissus Marsh' in *DIB*.

30 See L.A. Perry, 'Legal handbooks as rhetoric books for common lawyers in early modern England' in J.A. Bush and A. Wijffels (eds), *Learning the law: teaching and the transmission of the law in early modern England* (London, 1999), pp 295–302 and W. Phillips, *Studii legalis ratio, Or, directions for the study of the law* ([1660], London, 1675), pp 31–7.

31 See *The case of Ireland* (2018 edn), p. 111, app. crit. and explanatory notes.

32 *A catalogue of the library of the Honble Samuel Molyneux, deceas'd* … (London, 1730), p. 44. On the library and what items may have belonged to William, see Kelly, 'The one that got away, or almost: the Molyneux family library and Trinity College, Dublin' in W.E. Vaughan (ed.), *The Old Library, Trinity College, Dublin, 1712 –2012* (Dublin, 2013), pp 94–101. Aristotle's *Works* are folio item 5, and octavo 29; Cicero's *Works* quarto 106, and octavo 313; and Quintilian's *Institutio* folio 503, and quarto 314.

logicke (1588), William Fulbeck's *Directive, or preparative to the study of the lawe* (1620), or the *Studii legalis ratio, or, Directions for the study of the law* by William Phillips (1660), reprinted many times to 1700 – including 1675, the year Molyneux began his studies at the Middle Temple. The only late seventeenth-century law manuals listed are *The young clerks guide* (1689) and *The clerk's tutor in chancery* (1695).[33]

Although Molyneux's presentation of the arguments in *The case* is a clear example of forensic rhetoric as influenced by classical models, there were two significant differences imposed on him by the circumstances under which he wrote. The first is that the bulk of ancient writing relating to forensic rhetoric involved criminal trials, where it was easier to apply rhetorical techniques such as exaggeration or diminution, depending on whether one was prosecuting or defending, than it would be in a civil case where matters rarely lent themselves to being presented in such simple black and white terms.[34] The second relates to the question of whom Molyneux envisaged as his intended audience. The answer is provided by the manuscripts of *The case*, which show that he originally conceived the work as a remonstrance addressed to the English parliament, though of course also having a wider readership in mind.[35] Addressing the English parliament put Molyneux in a somewhat ambivalent position in that those whom he sought to persuade were not only, as it were, the jury who would deliver the verdict on Irish legislative independence but at the same time to a significant extent also the adversaries whom he sought to refute. We are fortunate in that light is thrown on the effectiveness of some of Molyneux's arguments and how his use of rhetorical techniques struck his readers in the three answers to the pamphlet published by Whig critics in the summer of 1698, especially Simon Clement's anonymous *Answer to Mr. Molyneux*.

***

In persuading the English parliament that it was mistaken as to the nature of its authority over Ireland, the first challenge that faced Molyneux was to convince his hearers that their right to legislate for Ireland did not derive from Henry II's 'conquest' of the country in 1171. This had long been the predominant view in England, and had received its classic formulation in

33 *Molyneux library catalogue* (London, 1730), octavo items 1064 and 1085. The former probably denoted the 1689 reprint of T. Hawkins, *The young clerks tutor* (see L.A. Perry, *Legal rhetoric books in England, 1600–1700* (e-book, 2013), biblog.), while the latter was perhaps acquired as a result of Molyneux's 1695 appointment as a master in chancery.

34 See Cicero, *Topica*, §§ 91–6. Quintilian, however, had more to say about civil cases, see *Institutio oratoria*, Bk 4 *passim*, though much of this dealt with authenticating documents and other technical issues relating to evidence.

35 See *The case of Ireland* (2018 edn), pp 14, 103.

Coke's report on Calvin's case of 1608.[36] This celebrated case concerned the right of a Scots subject to inherit land in England after James I's accession to the English throne. As counsel for the plaintiff, Robert Calvin, Coke successfully argued (*inter alia*) that though English law precluded aliens from inheriting land, Calvin could not be adjudged an alien as he had been born into the ligeance of James as King of Scotland. Since ligeance was due to the natural person of the king, rather than severally to the crown of England or of Scotland, as a Scots subject Calvin could not therefore be accounted an alien, or *inimicus* to James, in his capacity of king of England. Discussion of the nature of ligeance in the kingdoms of England and Scotland naturally brought in the status of James's third kingdom, Ireland, where Coke took the rights of the English crown and parliament to derive from the Henrician conquest, leading him to assert (as Molyneux expressed it in *The case*):

> That tho' Ireland be a Distinct Dominion from England, yet the Title thereof being by Conquest, the same by Judgment of Law might by Express Words be bound by the Parliaments of England.[37]

Molyneux's rhetorical strategy in countering this claim was two-fold: first a re-examination of the factual circumstances of Henry's expedition to Ireland intended to show that, far from being the hostile conquest claimed by Coke, what occurred in 1171–2 was the voluntary submission of the Irish princes to the English king in return for the grant of English laws and liberties; and second, by redefinition of the key concepts of *conquest* and *consent* in such a way as to deny the validity of the consequences which Coke drew from *his* interpretation of these terms.[38]

Molyneux's initial move was to establish a 'narrative' of events by examining the historical evidence for what had happened when Henry came to Ireland in 1171. Focusing primarily on the work of the contemporary historian who had most clearly depicted Henry's expedition as a peaceful one, namely the *Expugnatio Hibernica* of Giraldus Cambrensis, Molyneux (or rather his father-in-law William Domville from whom he appropriated the bulk of this material) carried out a classic example of rhetorical diminution. In place of the hostile conquest that Coke and English opinion in general considered Henry's expedition to have been, Molyneux claimed that there was no violence on either side in 1171 and that the Irish had freely and willingly

36 Sir Edward Coke, *Les reports: la septieme part* (London, 1608), ff 1–23. It was corroborated and extended by Croke's verdict in *Ramsey v. Crawe* (1673) – indirectly alluded to in *The case*, p. 117. See further *The reports … of Sir John Vaughan* (2nd edn, 1714), pp 91–4.

37 *The case*, p. 117. See Coke, *7th report*, ff 17r–v. Molyneux's further reference to Coke's second mention of Ireland in this report in *The case*, p. 118, spoke of it as '[Coke's] Parenthesis' (ibid., f. 22r).

38 Coke was not mentioned by name at this stage; identifying him was deferred to a long and vituperative attack in *The case*, pp 116–22. See further pp 41–3 below.

submitted to the English king in the person of Roderick O'Conor, 'King of *Connaught* and *Monarch* as it were of the whole Island', in return for receiving English laws and liberties, including their own parliament.[39] As well as following his father-in-law in mitigating the historical record in this fashion, Molyneux resorted to the rhetorical technique of *redescription*, which he applied to the key term *conquest* in such a fashion as to deny Coke's claim that Ireland was subject to the adverse consequences that were held to flow from a hostile military conquest.[40] He asserted that 'we are to understand by *Conquest*, an *Acquisition of a Kingdom by Force of Arms*', adding crucially '*to which Force likewise has been Opposed*, if we are to understand Conquest in any other sense, I see not of what Use it can be made against *Irelands* being a Free Country',[41] further appealing to Spelman's *Glossary* as evidence *conquest* could be understood in a pacific as well as a hostile sense.[42] Since Henry's 'conquest' had not been a

> violent Subjugation of this Kingdom ... [the] Easie and Voluntary Submissions [of the Irish] Exempt them from the Consequents of an *Hostile Conquest* ... where there is no Opposition, *such a conquest* Can take no place.[43]

Molyneux proceeded to bring home this redescription of '*conquest*' by resort to the tactic of affronting the prejudices of his audience, recommended by Quintilian as a means of making an audience see things in a new moral light, by asserting that there was far more evidence of William of Normandy's having conquered England in 1066 than for Henry II's conquering Ireland in 1171.[44] 'For we all know with what Violence and Opposition from *Harrold*, K. *William* obtain'd the Kingdom, after a Bloody Battel nigh *Hastings*'.[45] Claiming that what had happened in England in 1066 amounted to a hostile conquest was, however, very much a red rag to a bull, since such an interpretation was seen as sundering continuity with the free institutions of

39 *The case*, pp 8–12. Though Molyneux/Domville described Henry's expedition as even more exclusively peaceful and comprehensive than the printed text of Giraldus did (e.g., in having O'Conor submit in person to Henry at Dublin), an almost identical account of the Henrician invasion (also based on Giraldus) is found in the 1569 Act of Attainder of Shane O'Neill (11 Eliz. sess. 3, c. 1). See further *The case* (2108 edn), intro. p. 55.

40 For the consequences of hostile conquest, see H. Grotius, *De iure belli ac pacis, libri tres*, 3 vols (London, 1625), Bk iii, ch. 8.

41 *The case*, p. 12.

42 See Quintilian, 'you must try to show that the action in question does not have the character alleged'; cited in Skinner, *Reason and rhetoric*, p. 144. H. Spelman, *Glossarium archaiologicum* ... (London, 1687), s.v. conquestus, a work for whose status as a recognized legal authority see T. Blount, *Nomo–Lexikon: a law dictionary* (London, rev. edn 1691), pref.

43 *The case*, p. 13.

44 See Skinner, *Reason and rhetoric*, p. 145.

45 *The case*, p. 14.

the Saxon past, a continuity that was such a fundamental pillar of the English doctrine of the ancient constitution.[46] Molyneux completed his rebuttal of the claim that the events of 1171 amounted to a hostile conquest of Ireland by resort to another rather similar rhetorical technique, namely *redefinition*.[47] He defined the agreement between Henry and the Irish princes as the '*Original Compact*' of the English government in Ireland – that is, an act of renaming (or, as we might say in modern parlance, a rebranding) a historical event as opposed to redescribing a concept such as *conquest* in such a way as to deny one's opponent the advantage that he hoped to derive from his own description of the concept.[48] Renaming Henry's agreement with the Irish princes as Ireland's '*Original Compact*' was particularly apposite in serving to assimilate what happened in Ireland in 1171 to the language of 'revolution principle' as articulated in the English debates over the settlement of the throne in 1688–90. '[T]is not possible to shew a more fair *Original Compact* between a *King* and *People*, than this between *Henry* the Second, and the *People* of *Ireland*.'[49] The term '*Original Compact*' furthermore resonated with the notion that the foundation of government must have derived from an original act of popular consent, a rhetorical move than can also be seen as an example of flattering the prejudices of one's audience – again as recommended by Quintilian.[50]

A parallel instance of redescription is found in the more morally acceptable sense in which Molyneux redescribed '*consent*' in order to counter the conquest-theorists' claim that consent in the form of the submission of the conquered was essential for achieving the completion of conquest.[51] Following

46 See J.G.A. Pocock, *The ancient constitution and the feudal law: … a re-issue with a retrospect* (Cambridge, 1987), pp 397–409. The uncomfortable parallels between what happened in England in 1066 and in Ireland in 1171–2 presented a challenge to those who looked to conquest as the basis of England's title. Discussing the matter earlier in the century, Chief Justice Hale had sought to distinguish between what he termed a conquest *in regem* in 1066 and a conquest *in populum* in 1171–2, only the latter of which involved the consequences of a hostile conquest: Sir Mathew Hale, *Prerogatives of the king*, ed. D.C. Hale (London, 1976), pp 4, 32–5, 129–31. [Clement], *Answer to Mr. Molyneux* , pp 21–2, asserted that, while at Hastings, William had merely warded off a challenge to his lawful succession, in 1171 Henry II effected a complete conquest of Ireland, even though the Irish had only been terrified into submission rather than defeated in battle.

47 The distinction between these rather similar strategies was that *redescription* related to things or concepts, while *redefinition* related to words, what rhetoricians termed *rem pro re* and *verbum pro verbo;* see Skinner, *Reason and rhetoric*, pp 144–50 passim.

48 The vulnerability of such a move to direct refutation can be seen from the straightforward counter-claim in [Clement], *Answer to Mr. Molyneux*, p. 22, which also made the corroborative point (citing the practice of the Romans) that giving laws to the conquered was crucial evidence that a conquest had taken place.

49 *The case*, pp 37–8.

50 See Skinner, *Reason and rhetoric*, pp 138–9.

51 For the conquest theorists' claim, see further P. Kelly, 'Conquest versus consent in Molyneux's *Case of Ireland*' in C. Brady and J. Ohlmeyer (eds), *British interventions in early modern Ireland* (Cambridge, 2005), pp 336, 339–40.

the example of Locke's *Second treatise of government*,[52] Molyneux asserted that to claim that the consent of the conquered was needed to complement and complete military victory was nothing but an admission that conquest alone could never provide an adequate title for the acquisition of new territory, and thus by implication an acceptance that legitimate government must rest on the consent of the people rather than on military power. Such consent, moreover, must not be forced but be entirely voluntary, and he went on to query

> whether Promises Extorted by *Force* without *Right*, can be thought *Consent*, and how far they are *Obligatory*. And I humbly conceive they *Bind not at all* ... for the *Law* of *Nature* obliges us only by the *Rules* she prescribes, and cannot therefore oblige me by the *Violation* of her Rules.[53]

This redescription of *consent* as necessarily being free and voluntary, if it were to carry its proper moral and legal authority, was of key importance for Molyneux's central argument in *The case*, as it cleared the way for the fundamental principle that he adduced for Ireland's right to legislative independence (what in the language of forensic rhetoric would be called 'the *status* of the case'), namely that England's legislating for Ireland violated the natural law principle that the law-making process required the explicit consent of the governed, given either in person or through their elected representatives.[54]

Another striking example of Molyneux's resort to the technique of agitating and exciting his audience is found in his consideration of '*The Opinions of the Learned in the Laws*', where in a remarkable instance of what rhetoricians termed *indignatio* he identified Sir Edward Coke as the person primarily responsible for misleading the English parliament into believing that it had the right to legislate for Ireland.[55] Coke's parenthetical assertion in his report on Calvin's case that Ireland '*by Judgment of Law might by Express Words be bound by the Parliaments of England*' was, Molyneux claimed, a flagrant contradiction of the verdict in the Merchants of Waterford's case that Coke had transcribed from the year books.[56] Since the verdict had been that

52 J. Locke, *Two treatises of government* (London, 1690), Treatise ii, s. 175.

53 *The case*, pp 25–6.

54 '[T]hat Universal *Law* of *Nature* that ought to prevail throughout the whole World, *of being Govern'd only such Laws to which they give their own Consent by their Representatives in Parliament* ... which *England* so justly Challenges [i.e. claims], and all *Mankind* have a *Right* to' (*The case*, pp 48, 56).

55 *The case*, pp 116–22. See Quintilian, *Insitutio oratoria*: 'the orator's aim is to jolt his audience into seeing things in a new light'; cited in Skinner, *Reason and rhetoric*, pp 141–2. For *indignatio*, see Cicero, *De inventione*, Book i, § 53, where it is described as arousing great hatred, or contempt, against some (prominent) person.

56 See Coke, *7th report*, ff 17r–v, f. 22r.

the Irish were not obliged by the 1324 Staple Act on the ground they were not represented in the English parliament, how could merely naming Ireland in a subsequent English statute make up for the lack of Irish consent which Coke himself had so emphatically stated was needed to make such an act binding here in Ireland? Such an assertion flew in the face of reason and violated the principle that such consent was the basis of legal obligation: to say nothing of the fact that Coke also failed to specify the record in which this supposed 'Judgment of Law' was to be found. Molyneux went on to accuse Coke of expounding the law on his sole authority as a judge without regard to the intentions of parliament, 'as if his *Plain Assertion*, without any *other Reason*, ought to prevail'. Finally, and perhaps most offensively, he claimed that Coke was ignorant of any other law than the common law, asserting that if he had studied 'the *Laws of Nature* and *Nations*' as diligently as he had the common law, 'he could never have been Guilty of such an Erroneous Slip'.[57] This vituperative and sustained attack on the figure known to contemporaries as the 'Father of the law' was all the more astonishing in that Coke's *Institutes* and *Reports* were probably Molyneux's most frequently cited legal authorities apart from statutes.[58] Molyneux's remarks excited the indignation of Simon Clement who devoted more than a dozen pages of his *Answer* to a refutation focused mainly on the Merchants of Waterford's case, while John Cary's riposte ran to four pages.[59]

Immediately prior to the attack on Coke, we find the most notable instance in *The case* of another important rhetorical technique: namely, appealing directly to the emotions of the audience rather than their reason, a tactic recommended by Quintilian for moving the hearts of an audience so they are not only persuaded by what is said, but come to desire that such a state of affairs should in fact be so.[60] Molyneux contrasted what he claimed was the unbroken record of no English statute having been pleaded in the Irish courts without prior re-enactment by the Irish parliament between the issue of the Irish Magna Carta in 1216 and the English Adventurers' Acts 1642, with examples of English legislation for Ireland in the Restoration period and since the Revolution, and ended by apostrophizing the English parliament as follows:

57 *The case*, pp 116–20. A gross injustice to Coke whose extraordinarily wide learning is attested by his library catalogue; see R.J. Schoek, 'Lawyers and rhetoric in sixteenth-century England' in J.J. Murphy (ed.), *Renaissance eloquence; studies in theory and practice of renaissance rhetoric* (Berkeley, CA, 1983), p. 278.

58 As recently emphasized by I. McBride, '*The case of Ireland* (1698) in context: William Molyneux and his critics', *Proceedings of the Royal Irish Academy*, 118 (2018), 203. For the sobriquet 'Father of the Law', see A.D. Boyer, 'Sir Edward Coke' in *Oxford DNB*.

59 [Clement], *Answer to Mr. Molyneux*, pp 89–102; Cary, *Vindication of the parliament*, pp 109–12. See also W. Atwood, *The history, and reasons, of the dependency of Ireland upon the imperial crown of the kingdom of England. Rectifying Mr. Molyneux's state of the case of Ireland being bound by acts of parliament in England* (London, 1698), pp 53–4, 211.

60 See Skinner, *Reason and rhetoric*, pp 138–9.

> And shall *Proceedings only of Thirty-Seven Years standing*, be urg'd against a nation, to deprive them of the *Rights* and Liberties which they Enjoy'd for Five Hundred Years before, and which were Invaded without and against their *Consent* … ? Let any English Heart that stands so *Justly* in Vindication of his own *Rights* and *Liberties*, answer this question, and I have done.[61]

Examining how Molyneux handled the major themes of conquest and consent, together with the other examples considered above, has shown how skilfully he utilized the resources of forensic rhetoric to make the case for Irish legislative independence. Although some of his moves – such as the astonishingly-outspoken attack on Coke – may strike us today as potentially counterproductive, it is to be remembered that for the classical exponents of rhetoric, resort to offense had an important role to play in what they termed *ornatus*. That is maintaining the interest of one's audience through varying pace and approach, including sometimes soothing and flattering their prejudices, while at other times shocking and affronting them.[62] What is remarkable is how Molyneux seamlessly matched the rhetorical treatise format which he adopted for his book with the six headings that he set out in the *divisio*[63] – so seamlessly indeed that it has taken until now for this underlying structure to be discerned.[64] Furthermore, Molyneux's reliance on the rhetorical treatise format in *The case* raises broader questions both about his general intellectual position and about the relevance of this format for the discussion of fundamental political and constitutional issues at the end of the seventeenth century. Resort to the formal features of classical forensic rhetoric does not, on the face of it, sit altogether easily with the image of Molyneux the scientific pioneer and author of *Dioptrica nova: a treatise on opticks, in two parts* (1692) with its dependence on geometrical argument, or the friend who exercised such influence over the revisions in the second edition of Locke's *Essay concerning human understanding* (1694). Nor at first sight would the

61 *The case*, p. 105. Such a claim was itself a notable piece of rhetorical exaggeration, as can be seen from the extensive list of English statutes applied here without re-enactment in Ireland, attested in Atwood, *Dependency of Ireland* (London, 1698), pp 167–89, which also referred to the passage cited above as Molyneux's 'terrible [i.e. outrageous] expostulation'

62 See p. 62 and nn 46 and 55 above. A more extensive consideration of Molyneux's use of rhetorical figures and tropes than there is room for here may throw further light on the tactics that he adopted in *The case*.

63 *The case*, pp 4–6.

64 Namely (1) the circumstances of Ireland's original annexation to the English crown under Henry II; (2) whether Henry's expedition, or any subsequent suppression of rebellions there, could properly be claimed to have been a conquest of Ireland; (3) what title a conquest would have conveyed to England; (4) what subsequent concessions had been made to Ireland by her English rulers by way of grants of laws and liberties; (5) various judicial decisions, and the opinions of distinguished jurists on the matter; (6) a summary of the main arguments for and against legislative independence, leading to some general conclusions on Ireland's behalf. See further p. 35 above.

format of the classical rhetorical treatise seem a promising vehicle for persuading members of the English parliament to refrain from legislating against what many saw as an ungrateful colony undercutting the main staple of the English economy at the end of a devestatingly expensive war, through competitive export of cheap woollen cloth.[65] Yet clearly Molyneux must have believed that resort to such a format did have the potential to induce the parliament to change their minds, or he would presumably not have chosen it. Significant though such questions are, they go, however, well beyond the scope of the present chapter and seeking answers to them must be for another time.

***

To come finally to the question of what light an appreciation that Molyneux presented his *The case* as a sustained exercise in forensic rhetoric throws on the chief 'anomalies' which critics have pointed to in the pamphlet (namely, the apparent marginalization of the 'Antient Irish'; the advocacy of union with England; the assumption that the present day Anglo-Irish were the legitimate heirs of the constitution granted to the Irish people in 1171–2; and the failure to consider the position of Irish Catholics in the light of the universal natural rights to which he appealed on behalf of the Protestant people of Ireland).

The anomaly that awareness of Molyneux's reliance on rhetorical technique most readily helps clarify is the question of union with England. Having referred to instances in which Irish representatives had attended the English parliament in medieval times, Molyneux continued (in a much cited passage):

> If from these last mention'd Records, it be concluded that the Parliament of *England* may *Bind Ireland*; it must also be Allow'd that the People of *Ireland* ought to have their *Representatives* in the Parliament of *England*. And this, I believe we should be willing enough to embrace; but this is an Happiness we can hardly hope for.[66]

Consideration of the context – particularly what immediately follows relating to the admission that such a practice had only prevailed when war or rebellion made it impossible to hold parliaments in Ireland, together with the reflection that sending representatives to England had proved 'troublesome and

65 As far as I can discover, no other late seventeenth-century political pamphlets opted for the forensic rhetoric format, an impression kindly confirmed by Mark Goldie, Ian McBride and Quentin Skinner. Professor Skinner interestingly suggested that, given its Ciceronian five-part *dispositio* and additional proofs in the *conclusio,* Milton's *The tenure of kings and magistrates* (London, 1649) might have provided a model for Molyneux's work. See further J. Milton, *Political writings*, ed. Martin Dzelzainis (Cambridge, 1991), intro. x–xi.

66 *The case*, pp 97–8.

inconvenient' – suggests that Molyneux's characterization of the Irish being allowed to have their representatives in the English parliament if it were to legislate for Ireland as 'an Happiness we can hardly hope for' could hardly be other than ironic. That is an application of the stock rhetorical technique of saying something, which is to be understood in a sense contrary to the literal meaning of the words employed. The view that the passage was intended ironically is corroborated by the original version of the phrase 'an Happiness we can hardly hope for' – as deleted in the autograph manuscript – namely the Latin tag '*non nobis licet esse tam beatis*', which in my edition I rather loosely translated as 'we should be so lucky'.[67] An ironic reading of Molyneux's call for union would seem further justified by the emphasis placed throughout the book on Ireland's status as 'a Separate and Distinct Kingdom' from England (deriving from its grant to Prince John in 1177).

Concern over the marginalization of the 'Antient Irish' is a relatively recent matter, owing its origin to objections raised by J.G. Simms in 1976 and taken further in his pioneering biography of Molyneux in 1982.[68] Once raised, it gained widespread support, though, as Hill has pointed out, the belief that the majority of the Irish population were of mixed British and Irish descent was not uncommon in both England and Ireland throughout the seventeenth century.[69] Examples can be found from Camden's *Britannia* of 1600 to Sir Richard Cox's *Hibernia Anglicana* of 1689. Clarification of what Molyneux sought to convey by this remark is provided by looking at the context in which it was raised, namely the assertion that the adverse consequences of Henry's conquest would only affect the '*Antient Race* of the *Irish*' not the '*English* and *Britains*' that came over and 'conquered' with him, who retained the 'Freedoms and Immunities of *Freeborn* Subjects; they *nor their Descendants* [my italics] could not in reason lose these'. Molyneux went on to say that since 'the great Body of the present People of *Ireland*, are the Progeny of the *English* and *Britains*', and those descended solely from the 'Antient Irish' are 'but a meer handful … So that if I, or any body else, claim the like Freedoms with the Natural Born *Subjects of England*, as being Descended from them, it will be impossible to prove the contrary'.[70] This apparent marginalization of the native Irish was thus in intention wholly benign in seeking to establish that no

67 This classical sounding phrase was used by a number of seventeenth-century writers, including Grotius, Milton, and Jeremy Taylor (more than once). It would seem to be an adaptation of Martial's epigram: '*Nobis non licet esse tam disertis qui musas colimus severiores* [We who cultivate more austere muses cannot be so clever]'. See Martial, *Epigrams*, ed. and trans. D.P.S. Bailey, 2 vols (Cambridge, MA, 1963), ii, Bk 9, ch. 11, lines 16–17.

68 See n. 1 above, and Simms, *William Molyneux*, p. 105.

69 See J.R. Hill, 'Ireland without union: Molyneux and his legacy' in John Robertson (ed.), *A union for empire: political thought and the union of 1707* (Cambridge, 1995), p. 181. For a similar claim as to the small number of people remaining of exclusively Irish descent, see *The present state of Ireland* (London, 1673), Epistle to the reader, [A3^{v}].

70 *The case*, pp 19–20.

one in Ireland could be denied the rights of freeborn English subjects on the grounds they were not of (at least partial) English descent. Lest such a reading may seem too indulgent to Molyneux, comparison should be made with Locke's *Second treatise*,[71] where a very similar argument was made on behalf of all inhabitants of England in relation to the Norman conquest.[72] Though this clarification owes little to Molyneux's direct deployment of rhetorical technique, stressing the common origins of the British and Irish should perhaps be seen as an instance of flattering one's audience, for even Sir Edward Coke had spoken of the Irish as great lovers of justice and 'the more indeared to us' because of their common ancestry with the 'Britaines'.[73]

The third and fourth anomalies are to some extent linked, since Molyneux's failure to recognize that 'the Universal Rights of Mankind' should apply to Irish Catholics can loosely be seen as a corollary of his assertion that the Protestants had now become 'the People of Ireland' and as such heirs to the constitution that Henry II granted to the Irish princes and people in 1171–2. What justified the Catholics' loss of their lands and the benefits of Henry II's constitution had been their frequent rebellions, particularly those in the seventeenth century when Irish Catholics had been guilty of rising against the king and the Irish Protestants in 1641 and again in 1689.[74] Arguably such jeopardy had been implicit in the original agreement to which the Irish committed themselves (and their descendants) in accepting English laws and liberties on submission to Henry II, which perforce included death and forfeiture of property (to be understood in seventeenth-century terms as covering both lands and political rights) as the penalty for rebellion.[75] The further step whereby the Irish Protestants of the seventeenth century acquired the morally privileged status of 'the People of Ireland' in place of the descendants of the original recipients of the Henrician constitution was something that Molyneux found himself unable to account for in detail. He resorted therefore to the technique recommended by both Cicero and Quintilian for handling such gaps in one's evidence, namely passing rapidly over the matter in question, though not so rapidly as to appear to evade the issue.[76] This weakness in Molyneux's argument did not, however, escape the eyes of his English critics, Simon Clement and Charles Davenant, both of whom queried why he should have simply assumed that the benefits of the Henrician constitution had seamlessly transferred to the 'English Irish'.[77]

71 Locke, *Two treatises*, Treatise ii, s. 177.

72 Consulting Locke for further clarification of the implications of conquest was expressly recommended in *The case*, pp 26–7.

73 Sir Edward Coke, *The fourth part of the institutes of the lawes of England* (London, 1644), p. 349.

74 *The case*, pp 106, 142–54.

75 See *The case*, pp 21–3.

76 See extracts from Cicero and Quintilian cited in Skinner, *Reason and rhetoric*, p. 135.

77 For Clement, see n.1 above; also Charles Davenant, *An essay upon the probable methods of making the people gainers in the balance of trade* (London, 1699), p. 112.

This sleight of hand in redescribing the key term, 'the People of Ireland', so as to refer exclusively to Irish Protestants was much of a piece with Molyneux's more egregious failure to acknowledge that the universal natural rights which he claimed on behalf of the Irish Protestants should equally have applied to Catholics. The latter contrast becomes the more glaring when we consider that Molyneux's case as a whole rested on the natural law principle that the consent of the governed was an essential part of a valid law-making process. Recognizing that *The case* was an exercise in forensic rhetoric does, however, provide an explanation – although a far from morally satisfactory one – as to why Molyneux should have failed to allude to the position of the Irish Catholics in his book. It would have been plain to Molyneux that in seeking to persuade the English parliament that it did not have the moral or legal right to legislate directly for Ireland, alluding to the rights of Irish Catholics would, to say the least, have been highly counterproductive. Given the virulence of anti-Catholic feeling in England following what was seen as James II's illegal attempt to place Catholics on equal terms with members of the established church, together with the continuing military threat from France, urging rights for Irish Catholics, could only have undermined the cause which Molyneux so determinedly sought to advance.

Although Simms was incorrect in asserting that Molyneux's claim that the 'Antient Irish' did not amount to 'one in a thousand' of the population was intended to 'relegate the majority of the people to the status of non-persons', such in broader terms was arguably the overall effect of his pamphlet.[78] For all his privileging of 'the Irish People' as the source of moral and legal authority in the law-making process, Molyneux was no proponent of nationalism in the sense understood since the French revolution, or even the more limited concepts of nationalism current in the eighteenth century and before. Shorn of the rhetorical flourishes of the *exordium*, the liberty for which he argued was in effect a dressing-up of the cause of 'the British Protestants of Ireland' (as he had originally termed them, before saving his future reputation by a fortunate last minute deletion of 'British' from this phrase throughout the printer's copy) in the rhetoric of universal natural rights.[79] In reality therefore Molyneux was little more than an advocate for a limited form of political liberty for a restricted and privileged group, though he himself would probably not have seen his position in such stark terms.[80] What can also be scarcely doubted is that the Molyneux of *The case of Ireland* was far from

78 Simms, *William Molyneux*, p. 105.

79 See P. Kelly, 'The printer's copy of the MS. of Molyneux's *The case of Ireland …*', *Long Room* 18–19 (1979), 13.

80 Quite how limited Molyneux's call for Irish liberty actually was is apparent from his earlier failure to support the demand voiced in the 1692 parliament for the Irish commons to control the introduction of financial legislation (the 'Sole Right' movement). See further *The case of Ireland* (2018 edn), intro. pp 6–8.

being an exponent of any form of patriotism that embraced an emotional commitment to fatherland and love of country such as was already manifested by his Catholic contemporaries, the historians of the Jacobite war, Nicholas Plunkett and Charles O'Kelly.[81] For better or worse, adopting the medium of forensic rhetoric as the vehicle through which to present the claim for Irish legislative independence in *The case of Ireland* served to render even more opaque what the author really felt and believed, and to establish the near impossibility of getting behind the text and discovering what the 'real' Molyneux may have thought about such an apparently fundamental question as where Irish Catholics stood in relation to the universal rights of mankind.

81 P. Kelly, 'Nationalism and the historians of the Jacobite war in Ireland' in M. O'Dea and K. Whelan (eds), *Nations and nationalism: France, Britain and Ireland in the eighteenth-century context* (Oxford, 1995), pp 95–9. Although commentators have pointed to the fact that Molyneux actually used the term *patriot* in *The case*, p. 170, he did so only in the now unusual sense of 'a supporter, or champion of a cause' (see *Oxford English dictionary*, s.v. 3), with no hint of its more familiar use.

Imprisonment for debt in early nineteenth-century Ireland, 1810–48

KEVIN COSTELLO*

In 1817 the chief secretary for Ireland, Robert Peel, left Dublin Castle in order to view for himself the conditions in Dublin's debtors' prisons. Peel seems to have been genuinely affected by what he witnessed: 'ten miserable human beings' detained in a cell that was no more than twelve feet by seven.[1] What Peel had seen was the consequence of the surge in the numbers in Ireland's debtors' prisons which had occurred in the economic depression following the end of the Napoleonic Wars. In May 1817 Peel's secretary warned him that unless something was done 'some dreadful fever may be the consequence during the summer'.[2] But the government's room for manoeuvre was restricted. There were two options. One way of dealing with the problem would have been to build new prisons. But Peel had vetoed a plan to spend money on the construction of a new debtors' prison.[3] The alternative was to moderate the law relating to the imprisonment of debtors. This was legally and commercially problematic. The chief justice of the Irish court of king's bench, Downes, had warned Peel that he could not soften the law without destroying the system of credit that the power of arrest sustained. The threat of imprisonment was a necessary support to creditors: 'abolishing imprisonment for debt' would, he warned, 'destroy our mercantile credit'.[4]

The mercantile credit that Downes CJ had in mind was consumer credit: the credit offered, particularly by shopkeepers and merchants, to their customers. Ultimately, it was these creditors' interests that were sacrificed. In 1819 Peel took the first of a number of measures that would dismantle creditors' traditional power to use imprisonment against their debtors. Further steps in the process would unfold between 1813 and 1872. Underlying this process was a conflict of interest: between law reformers on the one hand, and merchants and shopkeepers on the other.

* An earlier version of this paper was delivered as the Irish Legal History Society's winter discourse at Queen's University Belfast in Nov. 2011. The author would like to thank Brian Donnelly, senior archivist, National Archives of Ireland, for his assistance in the research for this article.

1 *Hansard's Parl. deb., 2nd series*, vol. 35, col. 1277 (28 Mar. 1817).
2 W. Gregory to R. Peel, 10 May 1817, BL Add MS 40,204, f. 133.
3 Ibid.
4 Downes CJ to W. Gregory, 22 May 1817, BL Add MS 40, 204, f. 163.

THE RATE OF IMPRISONMENT FOR DEBT IN EARLY NINETEENTH-CENTURY IRELAND

The powerful remedy of arrest resulted, particularly before 1848, in the imprisonment of thousands annually. In the early nineteenth century debtors made up about one-third of the entire prison population. In the year 1818, for instance, 13,000 persons were committed in the criminal process.[5] In the same year 6,600 were committed for debt.[6]

This process of imprisonment for debt was overwhelmingly used against debtors owing small debts; sums under ten or twenty pounds. In 1820, out of the 1,783 prisoners in Dublin prisons, 1,127 had been imprisoned for debts under £20.[7] This pattern had not changed greatly by the early 1840s. In March 1844 the general Irish debtor prison population included 711 imprisoned for sums under £10; as opposed to 267 for sums greater than £10.[8] This was one of the comparative differences between the Irish and English experience of imprisonment for debt. In England in the 1840s the highest number in prison tended to have been imprisoned for debts in the region of £50. In Ireland, by contrast, debtors owing less than £10 were the most vulnerable to imprisonment.[9] This had been the case since the beginning of the century. In 1829 the reforming MP Joseph Hume noted that while the numbers detained for small debts in England was not as large as he had expected it to be, in Ireland the reverse was the case. In Ireland 'the evil was more severely felt'.[10]

This comparatively higher rate of imprisonment for the recovery of small debts in Ireland was enabled by the extensive small debt judicature that operated in nineteenth-century Ireland. The Irish legal system provided a more advanced system of small claims courts. First, there were the civil bill courts. Creditors in the Irish countryside had access to the civil bill courts, which had been instituted in 1697 for 'the recovery of small debts'[11] and which heard claims for debts under £20. In 1851 this maximum was increased to £40.[12] In 1847 a group of imprisoned debtors petitioned the government to consider introducing a power to order debts to be paid in stages.[13] This

5 *The inspector general's report on the state of the prisons in Ireland for the year 1818*, HC 1819 xii.453 (534), p. 31.
6 Ibid., p. 29.
7 NAI CSORP/1820/71/B.
8 *Imprisonment for debt. Abstract of a return of the number of persons confined for debt in the prisons of London, Middlesex and Surrey … and for Ireland*, HC 1844 xxxviii.613 (292), p. 55.
9 Ibid.
10 *Hansard's Parl. deb., 3rd series*, vol. 20, col. 432 (19 Feb. 1829).
11 An Act for the more easy and speedy securing and recovery of small debts 1697 (9 Will. III, c. 15 [Ir]), preamble.
12 Civil Bill Courts (Ireland) Act 1851 (14 & 15 Vict., c. 57), s. 45.
13 Memorial by prisoners in Monaghan prison, 14 Apr. 1847, NAI CSORP/1847/G5143.

suggestion was adopted in 1851 when the Civil Bill Act 1851 empowered an assistant barrister to direct the payment of civil bill decrees by instalments.[14]

Second, and more widely used than the system of county civil bill courts, were the 43 local courts of request. This was a collection of courts of conscience, manor courts, courts baron, courts of record, tholsel courts, corporation courts and mayoralty courts with jurisdiction to hear small claims. These courts also had power to commit for non-payment of debt.[15] Courts of request were far cheaper – about half the price – and less formal than civil bill courts, and creditors pursuing their debtors flocked to them. Where available these courts tended to do more business than the civil bill courts. In the city of Limerick, where creditors had access to both a court of request (the mayor's court) and a civil bill court, creditors preferred the mayor's court. In 1844, eighty-four debtors passed through Limerick prison. In the vast majority of these cases – fifty-eight – the warrant had been obtained from the mayor's court.[16] In Dublin, creditors for small sums overwhelmingly preferred the court of conscience as opposed to the civil bill court. In 1830, 2,765 warrants of arrest for non-payment of debts under 10*s*. were issued by the court of conscience. The following year, the Dublin civil bill court issued just sixty-one commitments for non-payment of debt.[17]

Shopkeepers were the major users of the process. In 1844, the most common occupation of those who used the Dublin court of conscience to arrest their debtors was the retailer. Out of forty-seven arrests, twenty were carried out by provision dealers, druggists, tailors, grocers or spirit merchants.[18] The profile of detaining creditor in Limerick in 1844 is fairly similar: out of fifty-six committals, seventeen of the detaining creditors were grocers, drapers, publicans, coffee house proprietors, tailors, or shoe makers.[19]

Merchants and suppliers made up a second constituency that heavily relied on the power of arrest to recover debts. Merchants were participants in the same vicious chain of credit as shopkeepers. Merchants supplied goods to shopkeepers on credit; and shopkeepers supplied produce to customers on credit. Merchants relied on the process to enforce debts owed by trade customers like publicans, drapers, shopkeepers, builders and artisans. In early 1840, the debtors seeking release from the court of insolvent debtors included

14 Civil Bill Courts Act 1851 (14 & 15 Vict., c. 57), s.112.

15 *Courts of request. An abstract return of the number of courts of law in England, Wales and Ireland under the name courts of request, 1826–27*, HC 1830 xxiii.217 (23).

16 Register of debtors, Limerick prison 1835–1850, NAI PRIS 1/24/02; mf GS 51/085.

17 *Civil bill commitments (Ireland). A return of the number of persons committed to each prison in Ireland during the last five years under civil bill decrees, and the amount for which every such decree was obtained*, HC 1836 xlii.459 (184), pp 1, 3; *Court of conscience, Dublin. Returns of the number of summonses issued, and decrees made, by the court of conscience, in Dublin, in each of the last three years*, HC 1830–1 viii.57 (170), p. 2.

18 Dublin court of conscience minute book 1845; DCA, MS GI/10/02.

19 NAI PRIS/24/02.

twenty shopkeepers, twenty publicans and six tailors.[20] In 1849 an imprisoned debtor explained how he had guaranteed loans made to his sons who had opened a drapery in Westport and who had obtained goods on credit from some 'houses in the drapery trade' in Dublin. The drapery business had failed and the Dublin merchants, pursuing the debt which he had guaranteed on behalf of his sons, had imprisoned him.[21] In 1866 the inspector of prisons described how the Four Courts Marshalsea in Dublin was full of 'small shopkeepers and tradesmen', many, presumably, detained by their merchant supplier creditors.[22]

A third user group was the landlord. Landlords of urban tenements used imprisonment as an oblique means of ejectment. Non-payment of rent generated, of course, a debt. A defaulting tenant could then be arrested for non-payment of this debt by his landlord. A landlord in the parish of St Nicholas in Dublin described how he made a rental income from houses 'consisting of two to three apartments, each apartment paying from six pence to upwards of one shilling'.[23] The problem was that Irish landlords did not have a measure equivalent to the simple justices' eviction process established by English Small Tenements Recovery Act 1838.[24] In the absence of such a measure, Irish landlords were resorting to imprisonment as a means of forcing tenants to leave.[25] Arrest could be used as a form of ejectment. It would be made a condition of settling the debt, and of the debtor's release from prison, that the debtor tenant should vacate the premises. In 1821 the chief commissioner of the insolvent debtors court recorded an order: 'J Grogan discharged; will deliver up land to his landlord within a week... landlord undertaking to release him from all arrears of rent'.[26] In 1844 an editorial in the *Freeman's Journal* complained that the process of imprisonment for debt 'is now become a more certain process of ejectment than even that which the landlord law provides'.[27]

Moneylenders and bill discounters also relied on the threat of imprisonment to recover the loans that they provided. In 1840, an Irish judge observed that the void caused by the absence of a banking system in nineteenth-century Ireland was being filled by disreputable underground operations: 'the result', he said, 'has naturally contributed to call into existence those bill-brokers and money-jobbers who now unfortunately infest the city'.[28]

20 *Dublin Gazette,* Jan. to Mar. 1840.
21 NAI CSORP/1849/G7040.
22 *Forty-fifth report of the inspectors general on the general state of the prisons of Ireland, 1866*, HC 1867 xxxv.1 (Cmnd. 3915), p. 523.
23 E. Barry to W. Somerville, 6 June 1848, NAI CSORP/1848/Z5633.
24 1 & 2 Vict., c. 74.
25 Barry to Somerville, 6 June 1848, NAI CSORP/1848/Z5633.
26 14 Sept. 1821, TCD MS 3919.
27 *Freeman's Journal,* 30 Mar. 1844.
28 Ibid., 24 Jan. 1840.

Moneylenders and bill discounters provided the credit that was not being provided by the banks. Larger moneylenders were operating as full-scale loan offices. There were at least eight of these in Dublin in 1844.[29] As an alternative to the moneylender, persons in need of credit turned to their neighbours. These private lenders were also forced to resort to imprisonment when the arrangement broke down. In 1843 the marshal of the Marshalsea described how one of the debtors in his custody had 'contracted a debt for support with a poor woman in Drogheda'. He had neglected to repay her, and 'she had to sue him in the civil bill court there where she obtained a decree for £4'. She was eventually forced to imprison him when she discovered that he was in receipt of a military pension.[30]

IMPRISONMENT FOR MEDIUM OR LARGER DEBTS

Before 1851 the civil bill courts had no jurisdiction to hear claims for sums greater than £20.[31] Accordingly, committals for sums over £20 followed judgments obtained in one of the three superior courts of common law in Ireland. Creditors who went to the Four Courts went either to the court of exchequer or to the court of queen's bench; the court of common pleas was the least used creditors' court.[32] Originally, the court of exchequer had been the overwhelmingly preferred court of creditors. This had been accounted for by the ability of the exchequer to operate in default of the appearance of the debtor. This facility had been extended to the king's bench by the Process (Ireland) Act 1803.[33] Thereafter the king's bench caught up with the exchequer. In 1819 the chief justice of the king's bench attributed the 'increased business of the court' to the Process Act 1803.[34] By the 1840s that gap was narrowing further. The prison register for Kilmainham prison in Dublin for 1844 shows that the king's bench was about to overtake the court of exchequer (13 executions were issued by the court of exchequer; and 10 by the court of queen's bench) and by the late 1840s the queen's bench was imprisoning more debtors than the exchequer.[35]

29 Ibid., 16 Nov. 1843.
30 J.D. Mullen to Elliott, 3 Oct. 1843, NAI CSORP/1843/G13580.
31 Civil Bill Courts (Ireland) Act 1851 (14 & 15 Vict., c. 57), s. 45.
32 *Returns of the total amount of law fund duty received in or yielded by the court of common pleas*, HC 1850 li.323 (316).
33 43 Geo. III, c. 53. *The sixth report of the commissioners appointed to enquire into the duties, salaries and emoluments of the officers, clerks and ministers of justice in all temporal and ecclesiastical courts in Ireland*, HC 1819 xii.287 (6), p. 50.
34 Ibid.
35 NAI prison registers, Pris 1/10/1.

THE PROCESS OF IMPRISONMENT; ARREST ON MESNE PROCESS

Arrest for debt took two forms: a pre-trial process and a post-trial process. The pre-trial process was mesne process. The post-trial process was arrest in execution. Mesne process, or arrest on a 'marked writ', enabled a creditor to arrest in advance of the trial. The writ of mesne process was purchased over the counter from one of the three courts of common law. It usually did not require a judge's fiat. This lack of judicial oversight was one of the principal grounds of objection to the process. The radical MP Joseph Hume said that to 'imprison an Englishman, except on the verdict of a jury, was a disgrace to the law'.[36] The creditor's attorney would simply swear, and file, an affidavit asserting that the plaintiff had a cause of action valued at over £20. He would then complete a standard form containing the details of the amount of the debt.[37] The writ was signed by the prothonotory, or clerk of the rules, and sealed.[38] It was then delivered to the sheriff of to the plaintiff's bailiff for execution.

The defendant, when presented with the writ, was given a choice: either submit to arrest and go to prison, or give bail to the sheriff to guarantee his appearance. This early taste of prison might pressurize the debtor into settling his debts before he could waste or conceal his assets. As a result, mesne process was the preferred choice of the early nineteenth-century Irish creditor who was pursuing larger debts. The occupants of the Four Courts Marshalsea in 1826 were mainly debtors owing between £20 and £50. The process which was used to detain them was overwhelmingly mesne process: there were sixty-nine mesne process prisoners as opposed to thirty-two final process prisoners.[39] In 1828, 262 mesne process arrested debtors passed through the Four Courts Marshalsea; there were just fifty-six committals under final judgment.[40]

REFORM AND ABOLITION OF MESNE PROCESS

There was considerable political unease about a process that enabled a person to be arrested with no prior judicial scrutiny, and accounts of abuse of mesne process circulated. Daniel O'Connell MP told the House of Commons that

36 *Hansard's Parl. deb., 2nd series*, vol. 22, col. 268 (9 Feb. 1830).

37 Process (Ireland) Act 1803 (43 Geo. III, c. 53). W.D. Ferguson, *A treatise on the practice of the queen's bench, common pleas, and exchequer of pleas in Ireland,* vol. i (Dublin, 1841), p. 126.

38 Ibid., p. 129.

39 *A return of the number of prisoners imprisoned for debt [on the 19th April 1826] in the king's bench, Fleet, Marshalsea … also a similar return for Ireland*, HC 1826–7 xix.201 (108). See Plate 4.1.

40 *Debtors, Ireland. Return of the number of prisoners committed for debt in Ireland, in the years 1827 and 1828*, HC 1829 xxii.379 (93).

he had seen a client arrested for £100,000 at the suit of a total stranger.[41] This power of casual imprisonment was, it was alleged, commonly used for extortionate purposes. In 1810 a resident of Castletownsend in Co. Cork, who was involved in a dispute with a partner over ownership of a boat, was arrested on mesne process. The arrest, he complained, was not for the purpose of debt recovery but in order to pressurize him into yielding up his interest in the vessel.[42] In 1840 the National Trades Political Union alleged that mesne process was being used for improper political purposes 'against trades people and artisans to debar and prevent the due exercise of the elective franchise'.[43]

In 1829, the Irish chief secretary, Francis Leveson-Gower, promoted a measure to abolish the use of mesne process against debtors owing merely small sums.[44] The remedy of mesne process was withheld from creditors pursuing debtors owing less than £20. More than one quarter of those committed to prison in the 1829 had been arrested on mesne process for amounts less than £20.[45] The inspector general of prisons anticipated that the reform 'must diminish to a considerable degree the number of persons confined in our pauper class'.[46] However, the reform entirely failed to accomplish this objective of clearing the prisons; indeed, the number of committals rose slightly.[47] There were at least two reasons for this. First, the legislation was not retrospective. Prisoners already detained on mesne process were not 'relieved by it and still languish in confinement'.[48] Second, creditors simply substituted arrest on final process for arrest on mesne process. After 1829 creditors for small debts postponed imprisonment until after the judgment had been issued, and then proceeded by final process.

In 1838 the mesne process was totally abolished in England. Similar legislation was introduced in Ireland in 1840.[49] In the end, the reform attracted little opposition. The judges of the superior courts in Ireland were consulted in advance of the measure in 1839; they appear to have indicated no opposition.[50] Irish mercantile interests were also content to let the measure pass; the English measure had not badly damaged creditors' interests. The Dublin Chamber of Commerce stated that 'the principle of the bill had been

41 *Hansard's Parl. deb., 2nd series*, vol. 24, col. 228 (29 Apr. 1830).

42 Petition of Joseph Broadley, 6 Oct. 1818, NAI OP/3018.

43 *Freeman's Journal*, 22 Apr. 1840.

44 84 *Commons Journals* 301 (15 May 1829). The measure was enacted as the Arrest on Mesne Process (Ireland) Act 1829 (10 Geo. IV, c. 35).

45 Of the 2,036 committed to prisons in Dublin in 1829, 645 had been committed for sums under £20. *Eighth report of the inspectors general on the state of the prisons in Ireland*, HC 1830 xxiv.719 (48), p. 22.

46 Ibid.

47 From 5,429 in 1828 to 6,898 in 1831. *Imprisonment for debt. Ireland. A return of all persons imprisoned for the three years last past,* HC 1833 xxix.361 (356).

48 William Segrave to the marquis of Annesley, 21 May 1831, NAI CSORP/1831/1269.

49 Debtors (Ireland) Act 1840 (3 & 4 Vict., c. 105).

50 NAI CSORP/1839/632 (1 Mar. 1839).

acted on previously in England and had met with very little opposition when proposed to be extended to Ireland'.[51] However, the measure did little to relieve the size of the prison population. The numbers of debtor prisoners, instead of halving, remained fairly stable.[52] The explanation may be that creditors were simply substituting post-judgment process for mesne process, postponing imprisonment until after they had obtained judgment.

ARREST ON FINAL PROCESS: *CAPIAS AD SATISFACIENDUM* AND EXECUTION AGAINST THE BODY

In the case of a decree from the civil bill courts, the creditor would indicate whether he wanted it executed 'against the body' or 'the goods' of the creditor. The decree would contain this provision when drawn up. The process of arrest under a judgment obtained in one of the superior courts began with the plaintiff obtaining the writ of capias from the court offices, where it was sealed and signed by the clerk of writs.[53]

The decree or writ would then be taken to the sheriff. Arrest under process of the superior courts was formally entrusted to the sheriff or sub-sheriff. However, the sheriff was entitled to delegate the function to one of his bailiffs.[54] Bailiffs were regarded as 'persons of low description',[55] and their behaviour could be thuggish. In 1841 a female debtor alleged that the bailiff had 'ordered her out of bed … [although] she had only her petticoats on' and had 'kicked and cuffed her down the street'.[56] There were complaints about the inertia of the official bailiff.[57] In 1837 the judge of the Kilkenny civil bill court informed the Irish secretary that he had been forced to dismiss his sheriff for 'not executing a great number of decrees entrusted to him by one of the suitors in my court'.[58]

In the superior courts, the alternative to the sheriff's bailiff was the special bailiff, a person nominated by the plaintiff and granted a warrant by the sheriff.[59] A version of the special bailiff operated in the civil bill courts until

51 Dublin Chamber of Commerce: *Report of the council of the chamber of commerce 1841* (Dublin, 1841), p. 1.

52 *Return of the number of prisoners confined for debt in the different gaols of Ireland on the first day of January in each of the years 1837 etc*, HC 1847 lvi.175 (354), p. 1. On 11 Jan. 1840 there were 850 persons in custody for debt; in 1843 that figure had increased to 946 (ibid., p. 1).

53 *Report of the commissioners appointed to inquire and report with a view to the revision of the offices of the superior courts of common law in Ireland*, HC 1842 xxiii.1 (Cmnd. 378), p. 46.

54 *(Ireland.) The fifteenth report of the commissioner appointed ot inquire into the duties, salaries and emoluments of the officers, clerks and ministers of justice, in all temporal and ecclesiastical courts in Ireland. Office of sheriff*, HC 1825 xvii.29 (310).

55 Ibid., p. 7.

56 *Browne v. Sir Nicholas Brady*, *Freeman's Journal*, 2 Dec. 1841.

57 (1867) 1 *ILTSJ*, 105.

58 NAI CSORP/1837/1264.

59 Ibid., p. 10.

it was suspended between 1836 and 1851. Although formally the sheriff executed that decree, he could, at the request of the creditor, issue a warrant for the execution of the writ 'to some friend [of the creditor] of his nomination'.[60] The creditor's right to use his own personal bailiff was temporarily abolished in 1836, when the power to execute the decrees of civil bill courts was transferred from the sheriff to a new officer: the civil bill bailiff.[61] Policy on the creditor's right to use his own bailiff chopped and changed. In 1851 the creditor was given the power to execute his arrests by this own private special bailiff; in 1864 execution was again restricted to the sheriff and his staff.[62] This reform was not well received. The *Irish Law Times* alleged that the transfer of the power of arrest to the sheriff had 'rendered [debts] irrecoverable'.[63]

The sheriff or bailiff did not always succeed in accomplishing arrest. In the case of about one-third of the arrests entrusted to the sheriff of Wexford in the late 1860s and early 1870s, there was an entry of 'not found'.[64] The principal techniques available to debtors for frustrating arrest were either flight, or not venturing out of their home. Debtors' domiciliary asylum derived from the common law rule that the sheriff executing civil process could not break into or forcibly enter a house.[65] The sheriff could, on the other hand, enter through an unlocked or open door. The sheriff could also trick his way inside. The Strabane writer, John Gamble, includes a story in his 1818 *Northern Irish tales* of entry by deceit. The tale involved a debtor who was keeping to his house but who was undone when the sheriff of Dublin 'assuming the shape of a gentleman' persuaded the debtor's servant to admit him. Entering the parlour 'with great politeness', he informed the debtor that he was a prisoner.[66] The one relief from self-imposed detention came on Sunday. Sunday was a *dies non* on which a writ of arrest could not be executed, [67] and debtors known as 'Sunday Promenaders'[68] were free to re-join social life for a day. The debtor in the reported case *White v. Browne* was a fellow of Trinity College Dublin who was keeping to his rooms.[69] He left college on Sunday and was returning to Trinity College that night. The

60 *State of Ireland. Minutes of evidence taken before the select committee appointed to inquire into the disturbances in Ireland in the last session of parliament, 13 May–18 June 1824*, HC 1828 vii.1 (129), p. 426.

61 Civil Bill Courts Act 1836 (6 & 7 Will. IV, c. 75), s. 41.

62 Civil Bill Courts Act 1851 (14 & 15 Vict., c. 57), s. 145; Civil Bill Courts Procedure Amendment Act (Ireland) 1864 (27 & 28 Vict., c. 99), s. 4.

63 (1867) 1 *ILTSJ*, 59.

64 NAI 1C/43/44.

65 The classical authority was *Seyman v. Gresham* (1601) Cro Eliz 908; 78 ER 1131.

66 J. Gamble, *Northern Irish tales* (Dublin, 1818), p. 40.

67 Sunday Observance Act 1695 (Ir) (7 Will. III, c. 17, s. 7).

68 J. White, *Mansions of misery: a biography of the Marshalsea debtors' prison* (London, 2016), p. 6.

69 *White v. Burrow* (nd) Rowe's Reports 431.

factual contest was whether it was past midnight when he was arrested. The bailiffs swore that 'as they proceeded down Sackville Street they heard the clock strike twelve and the watchmen call it several times'. They waited, however, until 'they came to the House of Lords and there arrested him as he was going to the college'.[70]

The alternative – and, in practice, more common – means of evasion was flight. Some moved abroad. The Execution Act 1848 contained a provision for the arrest of debtors about to quit Ireland.[71] This was most commonly executed against debtors who had purchasing tickets for the emigrant ship to America.[72] Others chose Europe. In 1842 an Irish debtor called Maginn had fled to France to join the French army in Algiers.[73] The majority, of course, did not flee. For these, the sight of the bailiff was usually enough to induce rapid settlement of the debt. In 1867 in Wexford out of 16 arrests, 12 debtors settled.[74] It was probably only a minority of debtors who underwent an extended period of imprisonment.

Assuming that imprisonment was executed, sometimes – though very rarely – the prisoner was able to use the courts to obtain his release. An application for discharge could be made on a motion in court establishing the illegality of the arrest. It was a condition to the legality of the detention that the prior legal process have been correctly administered. Where the process was defective, the prisoner might enter a rule in the court requiring the detainer to justify the arrest. Occasionally, such applications were successful. Discharge might be ordered where the prisoner had not been taken directly to prison,[75] or where the affidavit grounding the mesne process arrest was insufficiently detailed,[76] or where the plaintiff had not proceeded to trial within three terms after delivering the declaration.[77]

More usually, imprisonment for debt only ended either when the prisoner paid the debt or when the prisoner was discharged by the insolvent debtors court. Friends and family sometimes helped prisoners to raise funds to settle with the creditor. The marshal of the Four Courts Marshalsea used a small

70 Ibid.

71 11 & 12 Vict. c. 28, s. 7.

72 *O'Brien v. Moore*, *Freeman's Journal*, 20 Feb. 1847; *Tyrell v. Sullivan*, *Freeman's Journal*, 17 June 1851; *Bannatyne v. Gorman*, *Freeman's Journal*, 7 Nov. 1851; Petition of James Johnston, NAI CSORP/1851 & 1852/G6661.

73 *Freeman's Journal*, 11 Apr. 1842.

74 NAI 1C/43/44.

75 *Deering v. Palmer*, *Freeman's Journal*, 3 June 1842.

76 The Process (Ireland) Act 1803 (43 Geo. III, c. 53), s. 5 required that the plaintiff, on obtaining the arrest, file an affidavit specifying the cause of action and the sums claimed. Failure to comply with s. 5 was a regular ground of discharge: *O'Doherty v. Fox* (1833) 1 Law Rec (ns) 36; *Shelburne v. Burke* (1833) 1 Law Rec (ns) 115; *Tighe v. Abraham* (1833) 2 Law Rec (ns) 35; *Scott v. Doyle* (1833) 2 Law Rec; *Dowd v. Cunningham*, *Freeman's Journal*, 26 Sept. 1842.

77 *Codd v. Hyde* (1833) 1 Law Rec (ns) 90.

fund derived from rents to assist the discharge of poor prisoners.[78] Private individuals sometimes lent charitable assistance, and bequests for the release of debtors were common.[79] In 1801 a testator called Elizabeth Fletcher left £100 to each Marshalsea in the city of Dublin for the release of prisoners confined for small debts.[80] Large public subscriptions for the discharge of debtors were collected in Armagh and Cork 1809 to celebrate the jubilee of the George IV.[81] Dublin Castle was routinely petitioned by debtors and sometimes senior officials were persuaded to provide private assistance. When the lord lieutenant was tempted to help a female prisoner who was confined in the Four Courts Marshalsea, he was advised to maintain complete discretion since 'if such a transaction came to the knowledge of the public it would open door for imposition and endless trouble to the government'.[82]

Some prisoners managed to use their time in prison to open negotiations for a settlement or composition of the debt. In 1845 it was reported that prisoners in the Four Courts Marshalsea were engaging in negotiations with their creditors 'conducive to the advantage of both'.[83] But not all creditors were willing to compromise: in 1848, at the height of the Famine, one female debtor was found to have been in custody for three years. Although the debt was only for £12, the detaining creditor would 'not accept any less'.[84] The procedure for obtaining discharge following the settlement of the debt was made more efficient by a reform introduced in 1853. Prior to 1853, the process of release after settlement of the debt was indirect. The debtor would repay the creditor or his attorney.[85] The creditor would then instruct the sheriff to discharge the debtor. The time involved in this process was reduced by the Common Law Procedure Act 1853, which provided that a prisoner was entitled to simply settle the debt with the sheriff or the gaoler without having to engage with the creditor.[86]

Up to the early 1820s release could be frustrated by the requirement that the prisoner pay a gratuity to the sheriff for his release. In 1820 a prisoner in

78 In 1837 the marshal of the Marshalsea paid for the release of five debtors out of the room rents, NAI CSORP/1837/1550.

79 In 1830 the doctor in the city Marshalsea reported that he had used £20 'received from some ladies in Denzil Street' to compromise the debts of 42 prisoners who were then released, *Freeman's Journal*, 19 Feb. 1831.

80 'List of charitable donations and bequests, registered in the prerogative and consistory offices of Dublin, Jan. 1801 to close of 1804', NAI CHAR/1.

81 NAI OP/288.

82 Logan to Gossett; 21 Apr. 1831, NAI CSORP/1831/912. In 1837 the marshal of the Marshalsea paid for the release of five debtors out of the room rents, NAI CSORP/1837/1550.

83 23 Jan. 1845, NAI CSORP/1845/G4106.

84 Re Bridget McDonnell, 7 July 1848, NAI CSORP/1848/G10381.

85 *Woods v. Finnis* (1852) 7 Exch R 363. *English and Irish law and chancery commission. First report of her majesty's commissioners appointed to inquire into the superior courts of common law and courts of chancery of England and Ireland*, HC 1863 (Cmnd. 3238), p. 18.

86 16 & 17 Vict., c. 113, s. 139.

Ennis prison, who had managed to raise enough money to discharge the debt complained that the sheriff would not release him because he had not paid the release fees. Parliament responded to this abuse by enacting the Prisons Act 1821 abolishing 'all prison fees whatsoever'.[87] However, the chief justice of the king's bench, in an informal opinion in 1821, held that the 1821 Act did not extend to prisoners confined for debt. This ruling caused considerable irritation. The inspector of prisons, complained to the chief secretary that the chief justice had 'misunderstood [the law] to the injury of persons confined for debt'. He knew 'the intention of the member of parliament who was active in framing the act that debtors' fees are included'.[88] Parliament was forced to sort out the problem in the following sessions, enacting in the Prisons Act 1822 a provision that 'the abolition of such fees extends to persons confined for debt'.[89]

CONDITIONS IN DEBTORS' PRISONS

In 1828 there were forty-six debtors' prisons in Ireland – six in Dublin and forty outside Dublin.[90] Within those prisons, a division was made on class lines: between master debtors, on the one hand, and pauper debtors, on the other. At the top of this hierarchy were the master debtors who could afford to rent the most comfortable rooms. At the bottom, were the destitute debtors segregated in the pauper building. In the largest of the debtors' prisons, the Four Courts Marshalsea, there was a middle class. This was made up of those who could not afford to rent the master apartments but could afford their upkeep. This intermediary group were held in the common hall.[91] Prison officers – or hatchmen – made a profit on renting furniture for the debtors rooms,[92] and according to one sheriff's prison inmate, even charged '2 shillings for liberty to place a leg of mutton before the fire'.[93] The English custom of debtor prisoners singing 'welcome welcome brother debtor' to new arrivals was practised in Irish debtor prisons in the mid-nineteenth century.[94]

The more lenient administration in the debtors' prison was justified by its non-punitive objective. The marshal of the Four Courts Marshalsea explained that its governance was 'framed in a spirit of indulgence and in the principle that a debtors prison is for safe custody, not punishment'.[95] In the largest of

87 1 & 2 Geo. IV, c. 57.
88 23 Apr. 1822, NAI CSORP/1822/909.
89 Prisons (Ireland) Act 1822 (3 Geo. IV, c. 64), s. 51.
90 *Debtors, Ireland, 1827–28*, pp 4–6.
91 NAI/CSORP/1838/2058.
92 H. Hitchins to T.A. Larcom, 19 Apr. 1853, NAI CSORP/1853/ 6663.
93 *Freeman's Journal*, 18 Nov. 1839, p. 4.
94 W. Meyler, *St Catherine's bells: an autobiography*, 2 vols (London, 1870), ii, p. 120.
95 Report by J.D. Mullen, 12 Jan. 1843, NAI CSORP/1843/G792.

the debtors' prisons, prisoners for debt enjoyed liberties not granted to criminal convicts. Debtors were allowed to receive family and friends and to use a tennis court.[96] They held assemblies and exercised rights of petition.[97] The king's bench operated a supervisory jurisdiction over the Four Courts Marshalsea, and the court would hear prisoners' complaints of excessive punishment.[98] Prisoners expected to be treated courteously by the governor 'as one gentleman to another'.[99] John Dillon MP recollected, in the House of Commons in the 1890s, balls being held in the Marshalsea in the mid-nineteenth century.[100] Alcohol was prevalent. Until the 1850s the Four Courts Marshalsea even contained a bar, or 'tap room'.[101] A new arrival at the City Marshalsea in 1843 described how he was treated to biscuits and three glasses of sherry by the governor.[102] Although the prison rules forbade the sale of spirits, high alcoholic drink was smuggled into the prison.[103] In 1812 it was reported that 'strong wire lattrices' had been affixed to the windows of the sheriff's prison to obstruct the importation of spirituous liquors. However, the authorities failed to prevent friends and relatives smuggling drink into the prison.[104] In 1822 a former prisoner described the sheriff's prison in Dublin as a 'constant scene of drunkenness, riot and disorder'.[105] A number of inmates in the Marshalsea were diagnosed as suffering from 'whiskey fever'[106] and a 'member of one of Ireland's oldest most aristocratic families' was to be found 'in the face of day raging drunk, mad'.[107] Under the influence of the temperance movement, Marshalsea alcohol consumption dropped in the middle of the nineteenth century. In 1840 the tapster in the Four Courts prison noted the influence of the temperance movement on debtors who had 'taken a serious change from their former habits to total abstinence ... drinking water at their repast instead of beer'.[108]

In Dublin, unlike London, imprisonment meant confinement. Prisoners in the Dublin Four Courts Marshalsea were not allowed the privilege afforded

96 Rules of the Marshalsea 1838, NAI CSORP/1838/2058; *Prisons of Ireland. Twenty-sixth report of the inspectors general of the prisons on the general state of the prisons of Ireland*, HC 1847–8 xxxiv.253 (Cmnd. 952), p. 43.

97 For a newspaper account of a meeting of debtors in the sheriff's prison, see *Saunders' Newsletter*, 25 Nov. 1839.

98 Reddish to Graham, 12 May 1846, NAI CSORP/1846/G9336.

99 12 Feb. 1859, NAI CSORP/1859 & 1860/1608.

100 *Hansard's Parl. deb., 4th series*, vol. 63, col. 85 (27 July 1898).

101 Rules of the Four Courts Marshalsea, 1 Mar. 1852, shut down the tap room. In place of the tap room, wealthier debtors were entitled to one pint of beer at lunch time (Rule 9), NAI CSORP/1887/14726.

102 Meyler, *St Catherine's bells*, ii, p. 119.

103 Rules of the Four Courts Marshalsea, NAI CSORP/1838/2058.

104 Report by H. Hitchins, 21 May 1853, NAI CSORP/1853/6663.

105 NAI CSORP/1822/1418.

106 Benson to Logan, 4 Nov. 1837, NAI CSORP/1837/2173.

107 21 May 1853, NAI CSORP/1853/6663.

108 Memorial of Thomas Walpole, Dec. 1840, NAI CSORP/1840/G16830.

to debtor prisoners in London of living outside the prison but within the neighbourhood known as 'the rules'.[109] In 1812 it was recommended, as a means of reducing the pressure on space, that an equivalent 'day rules' measure be introduced in Dublin:

> a clause empowering the marshal to grant a licence to prisoners to go out at certain times within day time, during term, within certain limits, as is the practice in the Kings Bench and Fleet prison in London.[110]

Although the recommendation was never implemented, prisoners were, in practice, sometimes allowed temporary release in the company of a warder. But there was no legal basis for this. If the prisoner made off while released, the marshal was liable to an action by way of escape. It was, as the governor explained to the chief secretary, 'doubtful whether in point of law the marshal has the power of giving day liberty'[111] and the governor was liable to an action in escape if – as did happen on occasion[112] – the prisoner decamped.

Until the mid-nineteenth century debtor prisoners were, at the discretion of the prison governor, allowed to have family members reside in the prison with him.[113] There are accounts of wives and daughters living in nineteenth-century Irish prisons.[114] William Dorritt, the debtor in Dickens's novel *Little Dorritt*, was looked after by his devoted daughter in the Marshalsea in London; forty years earlier the Irish novelist, Maria Edgeworth, in her 1814 novel *Patronage*, had explored a similar relationship.[115] A combination of the desegregation of sexes, and the sociable regime enjoyed by master debtors, facilitated extra-marital affairs in the Four Courts Marshalsea. In 1822 the chief justice of the court of king's bench alerted the lord lieutenant to the fact that prisoners in the Marshalsea were engaging in sexual relations. He had

109 Irish insolvent debtor legislation commonly referred to the absence in Ireland of the right of debtor prisoners in Dublin to live outside prison, in 'the rules', as in London: Insolvent Debtors Relief (Ireland) Act 1809 (49 Geo. III, c. 54); Insolvent Debtors (Ireland) Act 1810 (50 Geo. III, c. 47); Insolvent Debtors Relief (Ireland) Act 1811 (51 Geo. III, c. 123); Insolvent Debtors Relief (Ireland) Act 1812 (2 Geo. III, c. 163).

110 Oireachtas Library MS Report on gaols in Ireland, 1812.

111 Marshal of the Marshalsea, Dublin to T. Drummond, 19 Oct. 1839, NAI CSORP/1839 56/8915.

112 Opinion of the attorney general, Maziere Brady, 12 Feb. 1837, NAI CSORP/1837/315.

113 'If it shall appear to the marshal that the wives and children of prisoners may be accommodated consistently with the health and convenience of the other prisoners, such persons may be permitted to remain'; Rules of the Four Courts Marshalsea 1831, (NAI/CSO/1838/2058). Where overcrowding was acute this might be withdrawn: Logan to Gossett, 21 Dec. 1831, NAI CSORP/1831/3356. The discretion to allow family members live with the debtor was abolished by the 1851 Rules of the Four Courts Marshalsea, NAI CSORP/1887/14726.

114 Petition of T. Owen, NAI GPO/1851/carton 1/253.

115 M. Edgeworth, *Patronage* (London, 1814).

heard a trial for an adultery committed in the Marshalsea during which 'profligate transactions were disclosed'.[116] In 1859 another scandal forced the authorities to introduce a rule preventing prisoners of different sex visiting each other.[117]

At the other end of the social band were the pauper prisoners. Pauper debtors could not pay for their own upkeep; accordingly, food, fuel and bedding had to be provided for them from the county rates. Grand juries, however, were reluctant to burden ratepayers with this expense. It was reported that the 'grand juries of the several counties object to allow diet to such poor debtors as are confined and cannot provide it for themselves'.[118] This reluctance was corrected by the requirement in section 6 of the Prison Act 1822, which positively required grand juries to raise presentments to fund the subsistence of poor prisoners.[119] The burden of looking after pauper debtors imposed on ratepayers by section 6 of the 1822 Act became a political grievance. In 1843 the cess payers of Cork complained of the charge on the city of having to provision poor debtors.[120] Section 6 of the 1822 Act only applied to county prisons. The most important debtor prison in Ireland – the Four Courts Marshalsea in Dublin – was a *government*, not a county prison. In order to alleviate hardship in that prison, the lord lieutenant, the Marquess Wellesley, 'as an act of benevolence' made available bread and milk to pauper prisoners.[121] The statutory 'gaol allowance' reduced the dependence of poor prisoners on charity.

The detaining creditor usually paid nothing towards the upkeep of the prisoner from whom he was attempting to compel payment. In 1822 a measure was enacted to distribute the financial burden of financing imprisonment from the county ratepayer to the detaining creditor. Section 5 of the Prisons (Ireland) Act 1822[122] gave the court the power to direct the creditor of a prisoner owing less than £10 to make a payment of not more than four shillings per week. But there was no obligation to make such an order. The seneschal of the manor court of Bridgestown, Skibbereen, who had seen a notice in a Cork newspaper which suggested that he was obliged to direct the creditor to pay the expenses of committal, was sharply instructed to read the actual legislation. The provision, it was explained, was purely discretionary:

116 Bush CJ to the Marquess of Wellesley, 19 Aug. 1822, NAI CSORP/1822/1489.
117 N. Caulfield to Lord Naas, 11 Feb. 1859, NAI CSORP/1859 & 1860/1608.
118 J. Palmer to H. Goulborn, 21 Sept. 1822, NAI CSORP/1822/1527/2.
119 3 Geo. IV, c. 64.
120 NAI CSORP/1843/G10536.
121 J. Palmer to H. Goulborn, 21 Sept. 1822, NAI CSORP/1822/1527.
122 3 Geo. IV, c. 64. The power was re-enacted in section 83 of the Prisons Act 1826 (7 Geo. IV, c. 74).

> the court is only to order the allowance if they think proper, in the circumstances of the case, to do so, and … such allowance can in no case exceed the rate of four shilling per week but may be as much less as the court shall think proper.[123]

The discretionary character of section 5 was its principal weakness. Its existence was said to have been ignored by one of the most active debtor-committing courts in the 1820s, the Dublin court of conscience.[124] By 1847 the inspectors general of prisons in Ireland concluded that the power had become a dead letter: the discretion 'not being imperative is ... exceedingly inoperative'.[125]

A society 'for the relief and discharge of persons confined for small debts' was established in Cork in the 1770s.[126] The Cork initiative coincided with developments in Dublin where a Debtors' Friend Society was established in 1775. A second association, the Marshalsea Society, was founded in Dublin in 1795.[127] The Debtor's Friend Society continued to be active in Dublin prisons into the 1820s.[128] Even after the introduction of the gaol allowance in 1822, charity continued to be the only support for pauper debtors held in prisons that were not subject to the Act. Prisoners in the Dublin City Marshalsea were supported through the 'benevolence of charitable societies and individuals [were] supplied with coals and straw for bedding'.[129] Bequests for the relief of poor debtors were common in early nineteenth-century Dublin wills. A bequest by Charles Powell provided for celebratory dinners at Christmas and Easter. When this charity was found to be abused by prisoners exchanging their supply of beef for whiskey, it was decided to bring these 'annual scenes of intoxication to an end'.[130] The middle-class tradition of providing charity for imprisoned debtors was the subject of a scene in the 1840s Dublin-based

123 Opinion of J.S. Townsend, 12 Sept. 1822, NAI CSORP/1822/880. On the other hand, the use of this provision was said to have emptied one debtors' prison, that attached to the manor court of St Sepulchre in central Dublin. Its use by the civil bill court in Mayo had 'proved to have been of great advantage', while one inspector claimed that the 83rd section is attended to at every quarter session'. *Eighth report on prisons of Ireland*, p. 22. *Twenty-fourth report of the inspectors general on the general state of prisons*, HC 1846 xx.257 (Cmnd. 697), p. 42; NAI CSORP/1847/G3754.

124 *Prisons of Ireland. Eleventh report of the inspectors general on the general state of the prisons of Ireland*, HC 1833 xvii.307 (67), p. 17, *Prisons of Ireland. Fourteenth report of the inspectors general on the general state of prisons*, HC 1836 xxxv.431 (118) p. 17.

125 *Prisons of Ireland, twenty-sixth report*, p. 7.

126 M.V. Conlon, 'Debtors in Cork gaols, 1705–1872', *Journal of the Cork Historical and Archaeological Society*, 47 (1942), 9.

127 NLI, LO folder 8(37); G. Wright, *An historical guide to the city of Dublin* (London, 1825), p. 123

128 Ibid.

129 NAI CSORP/1835/2512.

130 Report by H. Hitchins, inspector general of government prisons, 29 Dec. 1853, NAI GPO/1853/Carton 4/346; *Freeman's Journal*, 19 May 1855.

novel *The freaks of cupid* in which a Dublin gentleman and his daughter visited the Four Courts Marshalsea and were admitted to the pauper dormitory where they provided one of the inmates with a couple of shillings with which to settle his debts.[131]

Friends, family and fellow prisoners also helped out. John Temple Finn (who, before insolvency, held the franchise for providing dinners to barristers dining at the King's Inns) relied upon the assistance of friends who paid his rent and provided some furniture.[132] A desperate prisoner in 1847 wrote that his 'wife was obliged to pawn her wearing apparel to procure him food'.[133] Begging from wealthier prisoners was also effective. A debtor in 1838 reported that 'but for the humanity of fellow prisoners in lending a few shillings from time to time' he would have been forced to sleep sitting up.[134] In 1832, Dublin prisoners acknowledged that the charity of fellow prisoners had prevented them dying from starvation.[135] Others supported themselves through the 'internal economy' of the prison: acting as servants to wealthier prisoners; or waiting on the attorneys who visited the prison.[136]

For the desperately poor, a stay in the Marshalsea offered a form of social protection. In 1831 it was reported that there were prisoners who had been making an asylum 'of the [Four Courts Marshalsea] for years on end'.[137] It was alleged in the House of Commons in 1847 that family members, by taking fictitious debt actions against relatives, were using debtors prison to provide for family members.[138] Throughout the 1830s inspectors general of the prisons in Ireland drew attention to the problem of poor prisoners using debtors' prisons as an alternative to the workhouse. A reform (originally suggested by the deputy marshal of the Four Courts Marshalsea in 1837)[139] was taken up by the government and implemented in the Four Courts Marshalsea Act 1842.[140] The 1842 Act made it a condition to access to the gaol allowance that the prisoner should make an application to the court for the relief of insolvent debtors. Release by the court would automatically follow unless – which was unlikely in the case of an asset-less pauper debtor – the detaining creditor entered an opposition to the prisoner's liberation.[141] When, in 1842, the first

131 C. Abbot, *The freaks of cupid* (London, 1845), p. 158.
132 Memorial of John Temple Finn, Sept. 1848, NAI CSORP/1848/G 9023.
133 W. Corry to the inspector general of prisoners, 29 Mar 1847, NAI CSORP/1847/G3754.
134 The petition of Michael Rogers and report of Monck Mason, 4 Oct. 1838, NAI CSORP/1838/2596.
135 NAI CSORP/1833/2721.
136 Staveley to W. Pole, 16 Sept. 1811, NAI OP/347/23.
137 H. Logan to W. Gregory, 26 Nov. 1830, NAI CSORP/1831/2804.
138 *Hansard's Parl. deb., 3rd series*, vol. 90, col. 1109 (10 Mar. 1847).
139 Memorial of deputy marshal, Four Courts Marshalsea, NAI CSORP/1837/315.
140 5 & 6 Vict., c. 95.
141 There remained a gap in the legislation. Discharge was suspended if the creditor opposed the prisoner's release. Once a creditor entered opposition, the prisoner could maintain this suspension in being indefinitely by not advancing his application for release. In 1854 it was

batch of pauper prisoners were thrown out of the Four Courts Marshalsea, it was calculated that their release had saved the exchequer £1,000.[142] However, this pauper debtor clearance measure was never extended beyond one prison: the Four Courts Marshalsea. Despite appeals to extend the 1842 Act, county gaols continued to be inhabited by a constituency of persons who preferred the local Marshalsea as a means of poor relief.[143]

Although the 1822 Act ensured that poor debtors were fed, the physical conditions in the paupers' wings in Irish Marshalseas remained a source of humanitarian concern. In the 1830s the Marshalsea in Dublin was holding six prisoners in each cell.[144] In 1832 a public meeting in the sheriff's prison drew attention to the fact that pauper prisoners slept on 'straw and damp floors … and worse than any condemned cell'.[145] A passage in *The freaks of cupid* described the paupers' rooms as 'crowded with prisoners, and in some cases with their wives and children … in a state of the most disgusting filth'.[146] A prisoner in 1853 complained of the squalor of a 'bucket or tub [being] placed in the sleeping apartments'.[147] Overcrowding became especially intolerable during the Famine of the late 1840s. Roscommon prison was reported to be 'crowded to suffocation'; contagion and fever were making 'awful ravages'.[148] For the middle-class debtor, conditions in the pauper wing were particularly intolerable; an insolvent business owner complained of being forced to live with persons of 'the lowest order and society to whose habits and manners he was quite unaccustomed'.[149]

Poor prisoners were also discriminated against in respect of privileges. Master debtors were allowed alcohol; pauper prisoners were not.[150] Pauper debtors' rights of access to their solicitors were also more limited. An attorney in Clare complained that, while master debtors enjoyed an unrestricted right to consult their solicitors, pauper prisoners were only allowed to consult on two days a week. This privilege resulted in wealthier prisoners being more successful in reaching composition with their creditors; 'equal privileges should be extended to the rich as to the poor'.[151]

reported that one pauper prisoner called O'Toole had failed to further his application for release 'in consequence of which he continues in the Marshalsea as long as he pleases, retains his pension, cheats his creditors, and lives at the expense of the government', NAI GPO/1854/carton 6/FCM 1.

142 *Freeman's Journal*, 1 Oct. 1842.

143 J.D. Mullen to E. Cottingham, 29 Jan. 1847, NAI CSORP/1847/G1421.

144 T. Duggan to E.G. Stanley, 4 Dec. 1832, NAI CSORP/1832/6051.

145 25 Apr. 1832, NAI CSORP/1832/1841.

146 Abbott, *The freaks of cupid*, p. 148.

147 NAI CSORP/1853/66632.

148 Memorial of Patrick Bartley, 10 July 1847, NAI CSORP/1847/G8155.

149 Memorial of J. Temple Finn, Sept. 1848, NAI 1848/CSORP/G9023.

150 Report by deputy marshal, Four Courts Marshalsea, 26 Apr. 1852, NAI GPO/1852/Carton 2/1662.

151 Complaint by Michael McNamara, 1 May 1846, NAI CSORP/G83461.

INSOLVENT DEBTORS' LEGISLATION

The traditional eighteenth-century means of dealing with the problem of overcrowded debtors' prisons had been the enactment of a temporary Insolvent Debtors Act. This temporary legislation enabled a court to order the discharge of a debtor in return for the debtor prisoner yielding up his property for distribution among the debtor's creditors. This continued into the nineteenth century: occasional Insolvent Debtors Acts for Ireland were passed at Westminster in 1809,[152] 1810,[153] 1811[154] and 1812.[155] There measures were purely temporary; relief was not available to debtors after the legislation had expired. There was resistance from creditors to the weak investigation of debtors' means exercised under these acts. The creditor's principal interest was in ensuring that none of the debtor's assets were being concealed. A simple motion before quarter sessions under an Insolvent Debtors' Act did not provide much opportunity for investigation of the schedule of assets submitted by the debtor. It was far from the thorough asset-discovery process of bankruptcy. The chief justice of the Irish king's bench concluded that the Insolvent Debtors Acts 'produced little else than fraud and perjury and have relieved those who little merited it'.[156]

In England, in 1813, Baron Redesdale (the former lord chancellor of Ireland) introduced a measure designed to professionalize the insolvent relief judicature. The English Insolvent Debtors Act 1813 established a dedicated court for the relief of insolvent debtors.[157] A proposal for the extension of Redesdale's reform – a dedicated insolvent debtors' court – to Ireland was vetoed by a jealous Irish judiciary. Downes CJ said that, while he had no problem with the 'generous principle of the bill', he was concerned with the means proposed to accomplish that object: the creation of a specialist court.[158] The quantity of prisoner applications did not justify such an innovation. England was different: 'It may very probably be necessary in England to ease the superior courts of the cases of insolvent debtors on account of the vast numbers of such applications as would probably arise out of the operation of the bill.' But in Ireland the 'quantity of such business will not be likely for a considerable number of years to be so great as to require a special court for that business alone'.

In the face of the judges' discomfort, Peel let the matter drop and instead introduced a revised measure designed to maintain the status of the courts of

152 49 Geo. III, c. 54.
153 50 Geo. III, c. 47.
154 51 Geo. III, c. 123.
155 52 Geo. III, c. 163.
156 Downes CJ to R. Peel, 22 May 1817, BL Add MS 40204, f. 163.
157 53 Geo. III, c. 102.
158 Downes CJ to R. Peel, 22 May 1817, BL Add MS 40 204, f. 163.

common law. There was to be no specialist insolvent debtors court. Instead the petition was to be adjudicated upon 'by the court from whence such process issued'; in other words, the petition would be heard by court which had originally authorized the detention of the debtor. This proposal maintained the status of the common law courts. Where the writ of *capias* had been issued from the court of exchequer, it was the court of exchequer who the prisoner petitioned for release.

The Irish compromise measure was not a success. The superior courts did not have the time to properly attend to this insolvent debtor relief. The function was delegated to the junior judge of the court.[159] Debtors suffered through not being able have their applications heard promptly and during the long vacations between court sittings. In 1814 an amending measure was introduced requiring the courts to hear applications in vacation.[160] The judges, however, remained reluctant to waste their vacation travelling into the Four Courts to hear insolvent debtor business. 'The truth', wrote the Irish attorney general, 'is that during their vacations [the judges] are loath every day to be called on to discharge an insolvent'.[161]

Creditors also distrusted the legislation. It was alleged by Dublin mercantile interests that the Act was being exploited by dishonest debtors who were concealing their assets. The courts did not, they complained, have the time to properly scrutinize the statement of affairs or the creditors' objections. The Dublin Chamber of Commerce alleged that the administration of the legislation by the judges 'at intervals of leisure … necessarily admitted of little enquiry, and of a very imperfect examination into the conduct and affairs of the insolvent'.[162] Observers of the system alleged that prisoners could suppress the quantity of their assets, and thereby squirrel away money for their own use. One described how during his visits to prisons

> he had seen the insolvent surrounded by prisoners of the worst character who it has been whispered are counselling him what part of his effects to return and what to withhold from his schedule.[163]

The over-use of the power of adjournment was said to weary out creditors from pursuing objections:

159 Judge Jebb to W. Gregory, 4 July 1820, NAI CSORP/1820/734.

160 Insolvent Debtors (Ireland) Act 1814 (54 Geo. III, c. 114) provided that a debtor could apply in vacation.

161 W. Saurin to R. Peel, 28 Apr. 1815, BL Add MS 40211, f. 105.

162 *Report of Dublin chamber of commerce respecting the court of insolvent debtors 1833*, NAI CSORP/1833/3248.

163 R. White to C. Grant, 30 Apr. 1819, NAI CSORP/1819/1008.

> when the case is re-called some of the creditors were absent, and by that means affect their discharge. This I believe frequently occurs in vacations when the parties are absent from town.[164]

Overcrowding in Dublin prisons was one of the unintended by-products of the 1813 Act. Prisoners removed themselves from country prisons to the Dublin Marshalseas in order to make their petitions in the Four Courts. This further added to the pressure on the prisons. Downes CJ acknowledged that 'the cause of the extreme crowded state of the Dublin gaols is one which was intended to empty the gaols, that is the Act for relief of insolvent debtors'.[165] Nonetheless, Peel's Act did accomplish its function of reducing the number of debtors in the prisons: in 1816, 1,425 debtors were discharged under Peel's Act (there had been 6,891 committals in total); in 1817, 2,217 were released under Peel's Act (8,266 debtors had been committed); in 1819, 984 debtors were discharged (there were 5,506 committals).[166] In 1820, 1,121 were discharged under Peel's Act; 5,735 had been committed.[167]

THE ESTABLISHMENT OF THE INSOLVENT DEBTORS' COURT IN 1821

Peel's Act – which had been designed as a temporary measure – eventually lapsed. The mess caused by entrusting so much of the process to the superior courts was eventually brought to an end in in 1821 when leave was given to the chief secretary to bring in a new insolvent debtors bill.[168] A full-time court for the relief of insolvent debtors was established. The Catholic emancipationist activist, Peter Burrowes, was appointed the chief commissioner of the new court.

The accessibility of the court to imprisoned debtors was improved. The court was required to sit continuously throughout the year. There were to be no superior court-like vacations.[169] The court was required to undertake circuits throughout the country.[170] Like its English equivalent, the court

164 Ibid.

165 Downes CJ to W. Gregory, 22 May 1817, BL Add MS 40204, f. 163.

166 *Prisons. Ireland. Extracts from the inspector general's reports on the state of the prisons in Ireland, 1815–1820*, HC 1821 xx.159 (620).

167 Report by Foster Archer, 22 Feb. 1821, NAI CSORP/1820/71. A paper in 1861 estimated that 5,000 persons had been released during the eight years that the 1813 Act was in operation; this seems to be under-estimation: J.C. Heron, 'Bankruptcy and insolvency statistics in 1861', *Journal of the Statistical and Social Inquiry Society of Ireland*, 3 (1862), 198, at 205.

168 Enacted as the Insolvent Debtors Act 1821 (1 & 2 Geo. IV, c. 59). 76 *Journal of the House of Commons*, 390 (28 May 1821).

169 Insolvent Debtors Act 1821, s. 2.

170 Ibid., s. 31.

contained some of the features of a bankruptcy court. Debtors were required to hand over all of their real and personal estate to the court. The 1821 Act envisaged the appointment of assignees to collect the estate.[171] A chief clerk was appointed with power to examine the accounts and schedule submitted by the prisoner.[172]

The commissioners – when not on circuit – sat in premises on Ormond Quay ('in the very path of the trading community').[173] Designed by the government architect, Francis Johnston, its plain brick exterior attracted criticism ('a dismal block house'). Its architect defended the building saying that it had been designed 'without any useless architectural decoration' in order to avoid unnecessary expense.[174] The Northern Union Commercial Hotel, which was near the court premises, marketed itself as providing accommodation for country creditors opposing discharge in the insolvent debtors court.[175]

Three Insolvent Debtor Acts were enacted: in 1821, in 1840 and in 1857. All three followed the same three-part structure. First, the procedure was initiated by the prisoner making a summary petition seeking discharge.[176] The submission of the petition would activate the second stage: the prisoner filing a schedule containing a 'full, true and perfect' account of his estate.[177] The schedule was a seven-page form in which the prisoner listed each of his debts and his assets. The list of assets might typically include items like household furniture and cash.[178] Even this exercise could prove beyond the capacity of some debtors. There was no provision for legal aid to assist debtors in drawing up this schedule. In 1842, the law offices had decided that the government should not provide a solicitor.[179] In the absence of professional assistance, gaol house lawyers and charlatans preyed upon vulnerable petitioners. In 1844 contempt proceedings were taken against an unqualified attorney who had been 'in the habit of visiting the gaol at Mullingar and obtaining money from the prisoners on the pretence of acting professionally in their behalf'.[180] In

171 Ibid., s. 11.
172 Ibid., s. 21.
173 James Russell to Goulburn, 7 Oct. 1825, NAI CSORP/1825/1290.
174 Ibid.
175 *Freeman's Journal*, 13 Nov. 1840.
176 Insolvent Debtors Act 1821 (1 & 2 Geo. IV, c. 59), s. 8; Insolvent Debtors (Ireland) Act 1840 (3 & 4 Vict., c. 108), s. 18; Bankrupt and Insolvency Act 1857 (20 & 21 Vict., c. 60), s. 178.
177 Insolvent Debtors Act 1821, s. 10; Insolvent Debtors Act 1840, s. 57; Bankrupt and Insolvency Act 1857, s. 179.
178 A number of these debtors' schedules survive, including the schedule of Lawrence Mathews, a Marshalsea prisoner who attributed his ruin to his 'property being destroyed by the Whiteboys in year 1817' (22 Oct. 1825); the schedule of Michael White, detained in St Sepulchre's prison (18 Aug. 1828); and the schedule of John Frew (30 Sept. 1839), NAI 2/482/14.
179 NAI CSORP/1842/G14072.
180 *Freeman's Journal*, 15 Feb. 1844.

1845 an unqualified lawyer named Darley managed to collect £11 from gullible prisoners.[181] Discharge was also being delayed by the serious problem of court officers taking unauthorized leave. Monday was always a 'holy day'. The chief clerk left for his weekend retreat in the country on Friday and did not return until Wednesday.[182]

The third step in the process was for the court to direct that the prisoner be brought up to be examined. At the same time, the creditors would be notified. One of the main concerns underlying the procedure was to ensure that the full amount of the prisoner's assets was not suppressed. The safeguard against this was to secure the participation of the prisoner's creditors in the process. The court would place a notice in the *Dublin Gazette* advertising the hearing, and each of the debtor's creditors would be specially notified.[183] Compliance with this requirement was treated as indispensable. In 1836 Commissioner Curran refused to continue proceedings at Downpatrick when it emerged that affidavits of service on the creditors of the hearing had been mislaid.[184] Once notified of the debtor's application, a creditor could go to the court office in Ormond Quay and enter notice of his intention to make objection to the prisoner's discharge in the 'opposition book'.[185]

A well-established abuse involved debtors trying to wear out their creditors by having the hearing heard away from their creditors' place of residence. Country prisoners would have themselves removed to the Four Courts Marshalsea in order to have their petition heard in Dublin away from their creditors' base. This strategy could be effective. The insolvent debtors' court was told in 1838 that the reason that 'no other creditors appeared in opposition [to the debtor's discharge] was on account of the insolvent coming up to Dublin to be discharged instead of remaining in the country'.[186] The over-use by the court of its power to adjourn proceedings was also said to wear our creditors:

> when the case is re-called some of the creditors were absent, and by that means affect their discharge. This I believe frequently occurs in vacations when the parties are absent from town.[187]

Most applicants were unopposed, and received a free discharge. The 1824 notebook of the chief commissioner of the court, Peter Burrowes, recorded that he travelled on circuit to Lifford in the winter of 1824 where there were

181 Ibid., 10 July 1845.
182 Minutes of the inquiry into the insolvent debtors' court, Apr. 1833, NAI CSORP/1833/2284.
183 Insolvent Debtors Act 1821, s. 21; Insolvent Debtors (Ireland) Act 1840, s. 10; Bankrupt and Insolvent Act 1857, s. 206.
184 W.H. Curran to the earl of Mulgrave, 24 Mar. 1836, NAI CSORP/1836/902.
185 Insolvent Debtors Act 1840 (3 & 4 Vict., c. 107, s. 62).
186 *Freeman's Journal,* 16 July 1838.
187 R. White to C. Grant, 30 Apr. 1819, NAI CSORP/1819/1008.

thirteen applications, only two of which were opposed; he then moved on to Enniskillen where there were eight applications and no oppositions; then to Sligo where there were eight applications and no oppositions.[188] The new court did at least accomplish its objective of more efficiently clearing the county prisons of their debtors than the previous arrangement. In the year 1820, 1,002 were released under the old insolvent debtors' legislation.[189] In 1831 the specialist debtors' court managed to release 2,530 prisoners.[190]

In the case of contested applications, the theory was that the insolvent debtors' court should act like a court of bankruptcy – discovering and yielding up funds and dividends to creditors. In fact, the sums collected were far lower than the court of bankruptcy. Aggrieved creditors regularly accused the court of being over-innocent. One furious Dublin creditor described the judge, Burrowes, as 'this old idiot, or rather this old knave'. He accused the court of issuing free discharges to 'fraudulent scoundrels' who practised 'fraud, villainy and perjury in direct opposition to law and to the ruin of thousands of poor creditors and their families'.[191]

There appears to have been grounds for the charge that the court was under-recovering. Between 1840 and 1857 creditors received a dividend from the assignees in only 1.2 per cent of cases.[192] Part of the problem was the ineffectual system of asset collection. The collection and liquidation of the debtor's property for distribution to the creditors was entrusted to the provisional assignee. However, 'the provisional assignee was slow and debtor's property [was] wasted before the assignee [took] possession'.[193] It was alleged that the under-performing provisional assignee had become 'a merely passive recipient' and was not actively collecting or searching out assets.[194] Real improvement came in 1857 when the collection of assets was taken out of the hands of the old ineffective provisional assignee. The Bankruptcy Act 1857 transferred the function from the provisional assignee of the insolvent debtors' court to the more purposeful official assignee of the bankruptcy court, and his staff.[195] By comparison with the inactive provisional assignee of the debtors' court the official assignee of the court of bankruptcy was purposeful and 'realized all that it is possible to realize'. By 1860 the number of cases in which dividends were made had risen to 17 per cent.[196] Debtors'

188 Judicial notebook of P. Burrows, 17 July 1824–2 Feb. 1825, TCD, MS 3922.
189 MS Report on prisons in Ireland by Foster Archer, NAI CSORP/1820/71.
190 *Insolvent debtors' court Dublin. Return of the number of persons discharged by the court of insolvents in Dublin and the several counties of Ireland during the last three years*, HC 1831–32 xxxv.119 (530), p. 3.
191 T. Dunne to Littleton, 20 Nov. 1834, NAI CSORP/1834/4829.
192 *Insolvent debtors' court Dublin*, pp 205–7.
193 *Report of the Chamber of Commerce of Dublin 1833*.
194 Heron, 'Bankruptcy and insolvency', p. 205.
195 Bankruptcy and Insolvency (Ireland) Act 1857 (20 & 21 Vict., c. 60), s. 56.
196 Heron 'Bankruptcy and Insolvency', p. 207.

under-valuations were being successfully exposed. In 1861 the total amount of property which debtors admitted to possessing was £20,636; the amount actually realized by the official assignee was £23,655.[197]

THE ABOLITION OF IMPRISONMENT FOR SMALL DEBTS

The pressure on prisons intensified – probably doubled – during the Famine crises of the late 1840s.[198] By 1847 the inspectors general of prisons were reporting that all of the debtors' prisons in Ireland were seriously overcrowded.[199] A debtor in Roscommon gaol reported that twenty-one inmates per week were dying.[200] The small debtor arrest power now threatened a humanitarian disaster, and in 1848 the government introduced the Execution Bill 1848 which proposed to abolish the power of imprisonment for debts under £10.[201]

The 1848 measure abolishing imprisonment for small debts was the hardest fought of the nineteenth-century imprisonment for debt reforms. The proposal met with strong opposition from sections of mercantile community – particularly shopkeepers who claimed that the measure was an attack on the 'industrious middle classes'. The Mercantile Guardian Association of Dublin, which had been established as a rival to the Dublin Chamber of Commerce in order to advance the interests of smaller businesses was represented in parliament by the Dublin Conservative MP, Sir Edward Grogan.[202] Opposition was particularly strong in the North-East of Ireland. Petitions against the measure were presented to the House of Commons by the corporation of Drogheda,[203] and from traders in Killyleagh,[204] Fermanagh[205] and Coleraine.[206] The continued existence of imprisonment was said to be justified by the difficulties in successfully executing judgments against property. A Dublin merchant tailor despaired that he 'might as well shut up shop' if the measure was enacted. It was impossible to execute judgment by seizing these persons' goods: the majority of his 'customers [were] respectable clerks in public offices, most of whom stop in furnished lodgings and have no property'.[207] The threat of arrest was the only remedy. The Dublin Mercantile

197 Ibid., p. 208.
198 *Twenty-fourth report on prisons in Ireland*, p. 18.
199 *Prisons of Ireland, twenty-sixth report.*
200 NAI CSORP/1847/ G8155 (10 July 1847).
201 The bill was enacted as 11 & 12 Vict., c. 28.
202 *Hansard's Parl. deb., 3rd series*, vol. 99, col. 681 (15 June 1848); *Freeman's Journal*, 11 May 1848.
203 *Hansard's Parl. deb., 3rd series*, vol. 47, col. 1019 (27 Mar. 1848).
204 Ibid., vol. 97, col. 926 (12 May 1848).
205 Ibid., vol. 98, col. 1212 (19 May 1848).
206 Ibid., vol. 99, col. 85 (30 May 1848).
207 NAI CSORP/1848/23.

Protection Society rehearsed the same argument that the ineffectiveness of distress required the continued existence of a process against the person:

> the traders of Dublin are constantly obliged to give credit to persons who have respectable situations but no tangible property which could be taken in execution and unless enabled to execute decrees against the person of the debtor they have in such cases no means of enforcing payment.[208]

But the chief secretary, Sir William Somerville, who was determined that 'these poor debtors might have the privilege of spending their Christmas out of prison', declined to give way.[209] The measure instantly emptied the debtors sections of the county prisons. The Act came into force in November 1848; within weeks about half of the debtor prisoner population had been discharged.[210]

IMPRISONMENT FOR DEBT IN IRELAND; AN ASSESSMENT OF ITS EFFECTIVENESS

The Execution Act 1848 changed the character of the Irish debtors prison. The number of committals to prison fell. In 1847 the number of committals for debt was 4,521.[211] By 1857 the figure had dropped to 789.[212] The severe weakening of the process in 1848 enabled its virtual abolition in 1872. Arrest and imprisonment for mere inability to pay off debts (as opposed to refusal to pay) was eventually brought to an end by the Debtors (Ireland) Act 1872.[213]

The reform was the outcome of the victory in argument of abolitionists over small business interests. The dispute was perceived by the small business community in terms of social class. It was a contest between the legal and political elite, on the one hand, and the lower-middle-class business interests on the other. It was, as Irish traders saw it, 'the upper ten thousand' – the professional and political elite – against the 'mercantile interests of Ireland'.[214]

208 16 Mar. 1848, NAI CSORP/1848/345.
209 *Freeman's Journal*, 12 June 1848.
210 NAI CSORP/1848/G10811.
211 *Abstract of returns of the persons confined for debt in each gaol in Ireland, in each of the years ending the 1st day of May 1843, 1844, 1845, 1846 and 1847*, HC 1847 lvi.177 (565).
212 *Thirty-sixth report of the inspectors general on the general state of the prisons of Ireland, 1857*, HC 1857–8 xxx.1 (Cmnd. 2394), p. x.
213 Debtors Ireland Act 1872 (35 & 36 Vict., c. 57), s. 5(1). Imprisonment was never entirely abolished. The 1872 Act abolished the imprisonment of those who could not pay. After 1872 imprisonment continued to apply to the most recalcitrant debtors, those who had means to pay the debt but had refused to discharge it: Debtors Act 1872, s. 6(2).
214 J. Ganly, 'The new Irish bankruptcy amendment act', *Freeman's Journal*, 15 May 1871.

Abolitionists, on the other hand, argued that private imprisonment indulged vindictive creditors who could use the existence of a debt as a means of tormenting their enemies.[215] The abolitionists' principal argument was that the process was ineffective in achieving its objective. Imprisonment did not work as a means of recovering unpaid debt. Most imprisoned debtors were too poor to settle with their creditors; most had to be discharged by the insolvent debtors' court. The overall outcome was 'no benefit to the creditor'; imprisonment was 'ineffectual in its results'; indeed the 'creditor suffer[ed]'.[216]

The claim that the system was 'no benefit' to creditors requires evidence that most debtors were released by the insolvent debtors' court without settling their debts. The evidence seems to contradict this. Most debtors imprisoned (or threatened with imprisonment) did not use the insolvent debtors' court. Most debtors responded to imprisonment, or the threat of imprisonment, by settling their debts. Imprisonment was actually an effective means for businesses to recover debts. The mere issue of a warrant was often sufficient to induce a settlement. In the first three quarters of 1829, the Dublin court of conscience issued 2,756 warrants of arrest; in the entire year there were just 732 committals.[217] This very high rate of non-enforcement may be explained by the fact that debtors preferred to settle with their creditors when as soon as they heard that a warrant was out. In 1826 the coroner of Dublin, Edward Brett, said that it is 'one writ in one hundred that the coroner ever hears of its execution'. The reason for this was that 'the debt is generally arranged by the plaintiff taking some new security'.[218]

Even when the issue of the warrant did not induce a settlement and there was an arrest, most imprisoned debtors settled with their creditors. In 1820, 468 prisoners were discharged under the insolvent debtor system. However, the vast majority – 1,124 – were released by the creditor on settling the debt.[219] There were 168 committals to Sligo in 1844;[220] 128 settled. Sheriffs'

215 *Forty-fourth report of the inspectors general on the general state of the prisons of Ireland, 1865*, HC 1866 xxxiv.235 (Cmnd. 3690), p. 523.

216 *Copy of the fourth report made to his majesty by the commissioners appointed to inquired into the practice and proceedings of superior courts of common law*, HC 1831–2 (239), p. 40; Anon., 'Bankruptcy legislation' (1869) 3 *ILTSJ* 193; 'Imprisonment for debt' (1868) 2 *ILTSJ* 1.

217 *Return of the number of prisoners committed for debt to the custody of the keepers of the Four Courts Marshalsea, city Marshalsea, and other prisons in Dublin, and to each of the other prisons in Ireland, in the year 1829*, HC 1830–1 xxiii.209 (118); *Court of conscience, summonses issued*, p. 2.

218 *(Ireland). The sixteenth report of the commissioners appointed to enquire into the duties, salaries, emoluments of the officers, clerks, and ministers of justice, in all temporal ecclesiastical courts in Ireland. Crown office*, HC 1826–7 xi.163 (341), p. 152.

219 Report by Foster Archer, 22 Feb. 1821, NAI CSORP/1820/71. A study of debtors' prisons in eighteenth-century England has found that debtors' prisons worked as a practical means of debt recovery. Alexander Wakeham, *Credit and debt in eighteenth-century England: an economic history of debtors' prisons* (London, 2021), pp 88, 97–8, 108–9,

220 Register of Sligo debtors' prison 1843–1878, NAI PRIS/1/34/03.

books also indicate the extent to which the issue of a writ was an effective means of forcing a settlement. In 1865 – when imprisonment for debts over £10 remained – the sheriff of Longford arrested eight debtors; five either immediately, or subsequently, settled with the creditor.[221] The sheriff of Wexford arrested sixteen debtors in 1868; twelve settled with the creditor.[222]

The losing class in this debate was the Irish retail constituency. Their defeat by what they considered the elite – the 'upper ten thousand' – continued to be a grievance. In 1868 a public meeting of shopkeepers in Coleraine passed a resolution noting that the 'that the Act [of 1848] taking away the power of arresting the body of a defendant for amounts not exceeding £10 has enabled many persons to defraud their creditors and petitioned for the restoration of the power of arrest for small debts'.[223] The dismantling of the system of imprisonment for debt removed the second most common cause of imprisonment in the early nineteenth century legal system. But this adjustment in favour of personal liberty necessarily entailed costs. Those costs fell principally on one class. This was the class represented at meetings like that in Coleraine in 1868: the small business class; and, in particular, small retailers.

221 Longford process book, NAI 1C/58/53.
222 Wexford sheriff's decree and order book, NAI 1C/43/44.
223 (1867) 1 *ILTSJ* 781.

The trials of Arthur Donnelly: a *cause célèbre* of the 1870s

DONNELL DEENY*

In 1872 Arthur ('Attie') Donnelly was 59 years of age.[1] In the prosperous town of Lurgan, Co. Armagh, where he lived, he was not only a publican, grocer, grain merchant and shoe manufacturer but a property developer and licensed arms dealer. When Lurgan was granted its own local government in 1855, he was one of the first fifteen commissioners elected alongside the town's patron and principal landlord, Lord Lurgan. In time Donnelly's own properties were to exceed, at least in number, those of the Lurgan estate. Bassett, writing in 1888, says that '[w]ith the single exception of Belfast, no town in Ireland has increased in population and wealth so rapidly as Lurgan. The population in 1851 was 4,561. In 1881 it was 10,135 and there is good reason to believe that it is now far on the way to 15,000.'[2] It seems that Donnelly both contributed to and benefitted from this rapid expansion. He was the epitome of the successful Victorian paterfamilias and entrepreneur. It is therefore rather startling to learn that he was accused of murder and returned for trial not once but three times for firing on passers-by with intent to kill or wound.

To set the scene for this rather extraordinary set of circumstances it is necessary to consider the historical context. The absence of political movement in the 1860s – when, of course, Ireland was governed from London – had contributed to the rise of the Irish Republican Brotherhood, commonly known as the Fenians, who had mounted a small and abortive rising in 1867. A Liberal government had come to power in the United Kingdom under W.E. Gladstone in 1868. He declared his mission to be 'to pacify Ireland'. He proposed to address the principal grievances of Irish Catholics and

* This chapter is a slightly revised version of my presidential discourse to the Irish Legal History Society delivered at the Graduates Memorial Building, Trinity College Dublin, on 23 Nov. 2018. With the assistance of the late Gregory O'Connor, I was able to locate a series of relevant documents in the National Archives of Ireland: NAI CSORP/1872/16620. These consist of a very interesting series of newspaper reports and the Dublin Castle file relating to the early stages of this affair, including letters from the lord lieutenant, Earl Spencer, and the chief secretary for Ireland, the marquess of Hartington MP (his second cousin). I have quoted from these documents in this chapter.

1 That is his age as indicated by his headstone although his O'Neill descendants believe from notes they have that he was born in 1807. If born in 1813, he would only have been 24 when he got a licence from the court to open his spirit grocers business in 1837.

2 G.H. Bassett, *The book of County Armagh: a manual and directory* (Dublin, 1888), p. 324.

nationalists, of whom Arthur Donnelly was undoubtedly one. The slowness of substantive reform, however, left a wide section of Irish society dissatisfied and contributed to the foundation of the Home Government Association. In 1873 Isaac Butt QC MP became the leader of the movement and renamed it the Home Rule League. In the 1874 general election it returned some 59 MPs to Westminster in support of the principle of securing again some kind of parliament in and for Ireland. This rise in strength of the Irish Party was assisted by the introduction of secret voting under the Ballot Act 1872.[3]

As before and since, Ulster had significant peculiarities compared to the rest of Ireland. Ulster tenant right had ensured that the conditions of the rural peasants were somewhat more secure than elsewhere on the island; but against that, sectarian conflict was more prominent. In particular, the Orange Order had been founded in Co. Armagh in 1795. It had been banned several times by government earlier in the nineteenth century and by the 1870s was still prohibited by law from conducting marches or processions. This did not prevent persons of one view or another parading about the towns and villages of the county and sometimes coming into conflict with one another. There had been quite severe sectarian riots in Lurgan in 1870.

Lord O'Hagan KP in a debate in the House of Lords in 1873 denied that the state of Ireland was worse than five years before, as Earl Grey had said; he considered it better but he was, of course, a supporter of the Liberal government.[4] He also rebuked Lord Russell, several times, *inter alia* with regard to the state of Ireland, pointing out that for its population it had the fewest crimes of any country in Europe. This relative quietude may explain why the incidents involving Arthur Donnelly attracted considerable attention. Lord O'Hagan was a Belfast Catholic who rose to be lord chancellor of Ireland, perhaps helped and not hindered by his education at the Royal Belfast Academical Institution.

What were the events that led this middle-aged businessman to find himself in the dock on a charge of shooting with intent to kill and murder, or to do grievous bodily harm? Arthur Donnelly, or Mr Donnelly as he is referred to in all the newspaper accounts, had substantial premises at 50 Church Place. He had recently ceased to live above his premises and had built himself another house nearby. The allegation against him arose from the fact that on Friday, 16 August 1872, a party of Good Templars, a temperance association active in the north of Ireland and Scotland, had returned from a day out at Shane's Castle in Co. Antrim by train and had proceeded from the railway station in William Street up to Mr Donnelly's premises at 50 Church Place. When, prosecuting counsel Dr Elrington QC subsequently submitted at the first trial, a small portion of them passed Donnelly's house he

3 35 & 36 Vict., c. 33.

4 George Teeling (ed.), *Selected speeches and arguments of the right hon. Thomas, Baron O'Hagan* (London, 1885), p. 366ff.

> appeared at the door, and, raising his hand to about the middle of his body, fired two shots into that crowd. That was, in fact, the charge they had to try. He was not able to tell them what was the motive or what was the reason of that most extraordinary act on the part of Mr Donnelly. Unquestionably, almost immediately after that occurrence a very serious riot occurred in Lurgan.[5]

Remarkably, if this allegation was true, Donnelly was not immediately arrested on 16 August, although Mr William Hancock JP was present close by with sub-inspector Gardner of the Royal Irish Constabulary and forty police. He was only arrested on 17 August, after Captain Henry Keogh RM arrived in Lurgan and was confronted by an angry crowd demanding Donnelly's arrest. Keogh was told that a young man named Bell had been shot and seriously wounded by Donnelly. The *Belfast Telegraph* of 20 August reported its correspondent as follows: 'I understand that the young man Bell, who was shot by Mr Donnelly on Friday evening last in the Good Templar party, is this morning in a very critical condition.'[6]

Donnelly, despite his means and age, was refused bail at the magistrates' court on 20 August. The *Belfast Telegraph* of the following day reports its correspondent as follows:

> I have just learned that the prisoner Arthur Donnelly has been removed to Armagh jail under a large escort of constabulary to await his trial for shooting at the Lurgan crowd. Bail had been refused and, perhaps only for the escort, Donnelly would have received severe treatment. Bell lies in a very precarious and uncertain state.[7]

Curiously, there had been another incident in Lurgan on 15 August, the day before Donnelly allegedly fired into the Good Templar crowd, and that may be seen as throwing light on Donnelly's character. The aforementioned William Hancock JP wrote to Thomas Henry Burke about this incident for the information of the lord lieutenant. Burke was the under secretary for Ireland. He was of a landed family in Co. Galway and was effectively the permanent head of the Irish executive from May 1869 until his murder on 6 May 1882 by the Invincibles. It will be remembered that he was walking in Phoenix Park with the newly arrived chief secretary, Lord Frederick Cavendish, when they were attacked with knives and murdered. (Richard Piggott famously forged a letter in the name of C.S. Parnell expressing the opinion that 'Burke got no more than his desserts'.) Hancock was the agent to Lord Lurgan as well as a JP. He was at the very heart of the events of 16 and

5 *Newry Reporter*, 22 July 1873.
6 *Belfast Telegraph*, 21 Aug. 1872.
7 Ibid., 20 Aug. 1872.

17 August but, unlike two resident magistrates who were also involved, an account of his actions does not seem to have been sought. Apart from Captain Keogh, the other RM involved was Mr McSheehy, the resident magistrate based in Portadown. It was he who had called for police reinforcements for the town in anticipation of events on 15 August – a day associated with Catholic nationalist marches and demonstrations in Ulster – and he was in Lurgan on 17 August.

What Hancock reported to Dublin Castle on the incident on 15 August was that a 'Roman Catholic party assembled in large numbers in the Mall and thence marched to the railway station. About 250 of the processionists accompanied by a band of music proceeded by train to Scarva. Many of them wore green and white scarves and had green rosettes.'[8] Apparently some stones were thrown at them on the way to the station. When they got to Scarva, 'the Excursionists' were told that a severe riot had occurred at the place of meeting and they would not be allowed to proceed. They then returned peacefully to Lurgan by train and on arrival, and headed by their band and their banner, sought to march through the town. In the meantime a large crowd of Protestants had gathered, Mr Hancock reported. He filed the party of forty constabulary under his command across the main street and 'went to the leaders of the procession and begged of them to disperse. They were not unanimous on this point, they were likely to quarrel among themselves but ultimately they furled their banner and dispersed themselves amongst the public houses.'[9] No collision took place.

In the subsequent report to the lord lieutenant by Captain Keogh RM, generally hostile to Hancock, we find this: 'He described himself as a Socinian[10] in religion and a radical in politics. He has always shown the greatest sympathy with the Roman Catholic party and their political aims.' I take from this that he is conveying that Hancock was neither a good Protestant nor politically sound. But Captain Keogh, despite his hostility, acknowledges that Hancock dissuaded the Catholic party from marching into the middle of the town 'with the help of Arthur Donnelly. He used his influence to induce the crowd to furl their banners and return to the Pound.'[11] The Pound is now called Edward Street and remains part of the Catholic part of the town. This peace-making role might seem inconsistent with the course Donnelly is alleged to have taken the following day.

It is appropriate to pause at this point to say a word about justices of the peace and resident magistrates. The JPs were lay and unpaid and drawn from the nobility, gentry and other supposedly respectable classes of the

8 NAI CSORP/1872/16620.
9 Ibid.
10 The Socinians were members of a sect founded by two 16th century Italian theologians who denied the divinity of Christ.
11 Confidential report of Captain Henry Keogh RM, NAI CSORP/1872/16620.

community. While later in the century Liberal governments did appoint Catholics and nationalists to the magistrates' bench, this would appear not to have been the case in the 1870s. The appointment of resident magistrates, who were paid was intended to stiffen the lay magistrates' bench rather than to replace it. That did not happen until after partition – and indeed justices of the peace still serve in Northern Ireland, albeit in a limited range of functions. Most readers will be aware that in the United Kingdom the superior judges can only be removed for misconduct by a joint resolution of both houses of parliament, subject to some recent legislative change. A similar position applies in the Republic. But the RMs were dismissible by the lord lieutenant. It is relevant to recall in this context these words of Sir Christopher Lynch-Robinson:

> magistrates in Ireland were appointed by, and held office during the pleasure of the lord lieutenant as titular head of the executive. The conception of anyone exercising judicial functions being subject to instant dismissal by the executive is, of course, quite foreign to British theory and practice which protects the courts from executive interference by establishing the complete independence of judicial officers who hold office during the pleasure of parliament.[12]

Consistent with that position of service to the executive was the magistrates' role regarding the police. Until the early nineteenth century, magistrates – that is, justices of the peace – were laymen responsible for law and order in their own district. They could swear their own servants and others in as special constables and seek to maintain the rule of law. They could call upon military power to assist them if military were available and it was appropriate. This was not a very efficient system. Sir Robert Peel, as chief secretary for Ireland in the first decade of the nineteenth century, created the Royal Irish Constabulary. This force of full-time constables did much to restore Ireland to order after the long-running disturbances that followed the bloodshed and terror of 1798 and the crushing of the rebellion. It seems, however, that the constabulary continued to be subject to the direction of JPs and later of RMs when these were appointed. The reports of, for example, Inspector St Leger of the local RIC to Dublin Castle, showed that he had views on the matter but that he was outranked by the RM and JP as to the execution of those views.[13]

Hancock's employer is not without interest and has earned a place in the *Dictionary of Irish biography*.[14] He was the second Lord Lurgan and is perhaps most famous as the owner of the greyhound Master McGrath. But he was also

12 C. Lynch-Robinson, *The last of the Irish RMs* (London, 1951), p. 95.
13 NAI CSORP/1872/16620.
14 L. Lunney, 'Charles Brownlow, 2nd Baron Lurgan' in *DIB*.

a lord-in-waiting to Queen Victoria from 1869 to 1874 and was lord lieutenant of Co. Armagh from 1864 until his death in 1882. McAtasney reports that he was a generous donor to relief funds during that period and his death was widely regretted by both sections of the community.[15] An ancestor had helped found the Orange Order, but he and his successor adopted a much more even-handed and tolerant policy towards the people of the town.

Undoubtedly significant disturbance did occur in Lurgan on 16 August whether or not because of the firing from Donnelly's house. His house was attacked. A claim for compensation included one for the loss of seventy-two pairs of shoes. This might suggest that the attackers who broke his windows and his shutters, for which he also claimed, were, if not *sans-culottes*, at least *sans-chaussures* – or perhaps Donnelly's shoes were particularly elegant and fashionable and so highly desirable. Although Hancock was present on 16 August with his forty police close by, as he had been on the previous day, he made no attempt to arrest Donnelly. The confidential memorandum of Captain Keogh to the lord lieutenant, clearly written after consulting Hancock, says that Hancock and the police 'took refuge' in Black's Court near the house of a Mr Geddis, which was also attacked. According to Keogh, Hancock refused to let the police break into Donnelly's house. When Donnelly sent to Hancock to ask for protection from the crowd, Hancock responded by sending two police officers to ask him to stop firing at the crowd. He was found 'with revolver in his hand and a number of country looking people with pitch forks around him'. It was then reported as follows: 'An effort was made to charge and disperse the men throwing stones at or breaking into Donnelly's house'.

At this point, it should be noted how a newspaper sympathetic to Donnelly, the *Nation*, perceived the events of 16 and 17 August:

> Amongst the various establishments of Catholic proprietors attacked was that of Mr Arthur Donnelly, a respectable merchant of large means and social influence. Mr Donnelly attempted to scare off the wreckers by a discharge of firearms from the window, but the mob of ruffians outside were not so easily deterred from their coveted plunder, and Mr Donnelly's premises were sacked and gutted after the orthodox Orange fashion. This, however, was not deemed sufficient punishment. He had committed the enormity of attempting to protect his property and his life, and Orangemen howled for vengeance. He had fired, it was pretended, on an unoffending crowd. The Orange press took up the cry and shrieked for Mr Donnelly's arrest. 'Volley after volley', it was declared had been fired from his house; but the magistrates, though by no means unwilling to act, found that, much as was spoken of the

15 G. McAtasney, *Lurgan and the Famine* (Belfast, 1997), p. 48.

'carnage', no wounded were forthcoming … [They demanded] that an information should be lodged showing that he had injured someone, but for all the cry about the 'murderous fusillade', no one with a gunshot would could be discovered. In this extremity the Orangemen brought forward a boy named White, suffering from a wound in the head. There would be no difficulty, it appeared, about swearing that he had been shot by Mr Donnelly; but there was this difficulty about the case, that the doctors declared the cut was not a gunshot wound at all, and that, in fact, it had, beyond all question, been caused by a stone. But the Orange party were not to be baulked by such trifles. Again they summoned in their legions from the country districts, and on Saturday [17th] they entered Lurgan armed, says the report, 'with sticks and bludgeons', intent on compelling the authorities to obey their behests. They were met, not as they should have been met, at the bayonet's point, but with honed speeches and conciliatory promises. Lord Lurgan was there, and the gentle Mr Hancock (who is accused of having torn down a green flag two days before with his own hand), and Captain Keogh RM and policemen in strong numbers. But the rowdies who assembled to overawe the authorities and over-ride the course of justice received no threatening order for dispersion. They were mildly reasoned with by the Revd Mr Black, and gently expostulated with by Lord Lurgan and the amiable Hancock. They demanded, as the only conditions of dispersion, the liberation of one of their own bludgeon men, who had by some chance been taken into custody, and the arrest of Mr Donnelly. Will it be credited? Their demands were on both points acceded to. Amidst peals of Kentish fire the captured bludgeon man was set free on the spot, while Mr Donnelly – another lad with a cut head about which the doctors could not speak so positively having been found – was thrown into prison. And then the Orangemen, having dictated terms to the Government and trampled on the executive power, marched homewards in triumph. The days of ascendency had come again.[16]

It would be easy to dismiss this as a partisan view, but one finds an interesting passage in the reports of these events in the *Irish Times*. The newspaper was neither Catholic nor nationalist in its sympathies at that time. A succinct summary from their special correspondent reads as follows:

Lurgan, 10.00 o'clock
A most desperate riot has been raging here for the last hour and a half. The excursion party of the Good Templars, who left for Shane's Castle, returned to this station at half past eight. They were met by a band and

16 *Nation*, 18 Aug. 1872.

> a crowd of between 3,000 and 4,000 men of the Orange party who headed the Temperance procession up William Street flourishing bludgeons, cheering and shouting 'no Home Rule'. When they arrived opposite the grocery establishment of Mr Arthur Donnelly, Church Place, it is alleged that a shot was fired from one of the upstairs windows. The procession immediately broke up and the yells of the crowd in consequence were terrific. The cry was raised 'wreck Donnelly's' and no sooner said than done. Stones rattled in volumes on the shutters and broken glass fell down upon the pavements. A volley of pistol shots followed from nearly all the windows of the three-storey house of Donnelly. The crowd drew off on either side, but, having raised the paving stones, they returned to the assault amid cheers and a shower of missiles were hurled with a view of effecting a breach. Another volley of shots from the windows, and another withdrawal of the enraged mob succeeded; this continued for nearly an hour. Apparently the party in Donnelly's were firing merely blank cartridge at first, but someone shouted out of the windows 'keep off, or we will shoot some of you'; but the attack continued at intervals. I fear ball cartridges were used for I heard that a young man was killed and young girl badly hurt, but the excitement is so great that it is impossible to learn accurately. The shop of Donnelly has been wrecked, and a few others, while some houses occupied by Protestants in the Pound district have been similarly injured in retaliation. Mr Hancock, a Magistrate, and Mr Gardner, Sub-Inspector [RIC], as promptly as possible adopted measures for dispersing the rioters, and so far succeeded as to break them into small parties, thus destroying their power for further mischief and at this hour the town is comparatively quiet.[17]

Note the reference to three to four thousand men of the Orange party, but this does not seem to have been included in the papers sent to prosecuting counsel. Moreover, commenting on riots in Belfast in the same week, the *Times* of London was very critical of the Orange interest:

> Unhappily it is the party which most professes to be the party of order that on the face of it is the first and worst offender. The Orangemen were allowed to have their procession without interruption but they interrupted the Roman Catholic procession, not only with offensive gestures and cries but with brick bats and pistol shots.[18]

The Dublin Castle file containing 'particulars of damage done to property during the riots in Lurgan on 16 and 17 August 1872 in cases for which

17 *Irish Times*, 17 Aug. 1872.
18 Quoted in the Dublin *Evening Telegraph*, 20 Aug. 1872.

compensation is being claimed of the county' is extant. The entry for Arthur Donnelly of Church Place reads: 'A quantity of plate glass, window frames and blinds, shop goods, articles of furniture, 74 pairs of boots, window shutters.' It is a little sad to note that the religion of the various claimants is noted by the resident magistrate or his clerk who compiled this list.[19]

There are other documents in the National Archives of Ireland relating to the Lurgan riots.[20] The first indication on file of possible trouble is dated 13 August when McSheehy, the RM based in Portadown, calls for fifty infantry to attend on 15 August, at the behest of Lord Lurgan. On 14 August there is a further request from another party asking for fifty extra police. As already stated, some forty police did arrive on 15 August and acted under the directions of Hancock JP. On 17 August Lord Lurgan telegrammed to the under-secretary, Burke: 'Serious rioting last night – please send a RM.' McSheehy then arrived in Lurgan with forty more policemen. As McSheehy later reported to the lord lieutenant, he had a meeting with Hancock and Lord Lurgan and on the advice of the two magistrates Lord Lurgan addressed the crowd that had gathered again in Lurgan and assured them that a close enquiry would be made into the events of the previous day, including any shooting by Donnelly, when the magistrates' court sat on following Tuesday, 20 August. (One observes that that was a somewhat unrealistic promise to make.) This seemed to satisfy the crowd which dispersed. For whatever reason, however, Lord Lurgan telegrammed Dublin Castle pointing out that McSheehy was really needed in his home base of Portadown and that another RM should be sent. Captain Keogh then arrived from Dublin Castle.

In a subsequent memorandum for the lord lieutenant, Captain Keogh RM claimed that there was 'a mass of evidence' to say that Donnelly had fired on the passers-by before a pane of glass was broken. Keogh claimed that it was for that reason that he ordered his arrest. His report understandably caused a concern in Dublin Castle when it was read. It was noted that the order for arrest only seemed to have been made by Captain Keogh after the first Protestant crowd had dispersed and another crowd had arrived at about 6 p.m. That body was described by Robert Wilson, secretary to Captain Keogh, in a letter to the Castle of 26 August, as 'the Orange mobs from the country'. Inspector Leger in a later report describes them in similar terms. The impression was, and the allegation was, that Keogh had in fact only ordered the arrest of Donnelly to appease the Orange mob rather than dispersing them.

The report was read by the then attorney general. That was no less a person than Christopher Palles, not only an alumnus of Clongowes Wood College and a distinguished graduate of Trinity College Dublin but one of the

19 Report of Henry Keogh RM, 6 Sept. 1872, NAI CSORP/1872/16620.
20 NAI CSORP/1872/16620.

greatest judges ever to sit on the Irish bench. Palles was only forty at the time and was having an active time as law officer, complicated by his defeat in the Londonderry by-election so that he had no seat in the House of Commons. He commented on the unfortunate impression being created that the arrest was only ordered to quieten the mob. He trusted 'that no effort will be spared to make the missing "leaders" [of the Orange mob] amenable. Have warrants been issued?'[21] Captain Keogh later provided the names of six persons said to be leaders of that crowd but there is no report of any prosecution of them. On 28 August, Lord Spencer, the lord lieutenant, echoed Palles' comments but he was obviously concerned about the failure to arrest Donnelly at an earlier stage and directed further reports to be obtained.

The first of these reports was from McSheehy RM who vigorously defended his own conduct in not arresting Donnelly on the morning of 17 August. (He offered to stand over his account on oath.) He pointed out that it was he who had called for the police to come to the town in his earlier telegram of 13 August. He said that Captain Keogh was in an excited fashion and that if he had consulted McSheehy, Dublin Castle would never have been troubled about this matter. He pointed out that he had some 80 police under his command on the Saturday, but Captain Keogh wanted to bring in troops as well. He denied that Sub-Inspector Webb or anyone else from the RIC had urged him to arrest Donnelly. He was obviously not an admirer of Sub-Inspector Webb. He wrote to the Castle that 'an old man called Toner, a Roman catholic, was grievously assaulted. His life was in danger for several days.' The evidence of the extent of his assault which McSheehy gave was that his treatment had cost twelve guineas to the county. This same Sub-Inspector Webb had then asked to be substituted as the prosecutor of a man called Ellis for the assault on Toner. This was done and when the case was called he withdrew it!

One would think that the answer to the questions about the delayed arrest of Donnelly on which puzzled not only the attorney general, Palles, but the lord lieutenant and the chief secretary – the marquess of Hartington, later leader of the Liberal Unionists who broke with their party over Home Rule – would be to ask for a statement from Hancock as to what the position was, he having been on the ground. But this was not done. The determination after all these reports came in was that an inquiry should certainly be made – but not at this time, as the attorney had recommended, as there would be an inevitably tendency 'to go back upon the facts of Donnelly's case'. That was the view of Lord Spencer on 26 October and a note of two days later, apparently from an official in his office, was to like effect because such an inquiry must not prejudice Donnelly's case 'as upon it his guilt or innocence depends'.[22]

21 Ibid.
22 Note signed R(?) Down, NAI CSORP/1872/16620.

The prosecution continued. But a prosecution for what? The young man called Bell, despite all the rumours, did not die. Furthermore, although Captain Keogh thought that he had been shot with a pistol loaded with ball and not just powder or shotgun cartridge, a short medical note on the man, again for the purposes of payment of fees, refers only to a 'cartridge wound'. Where he got it and when remained quite uncertain. The suspicion of the nationalists was that this was, in fact, an attempt to frame Donnelly and that Bell had not been wounded at all, or at least not by Donnelly. Some of his employees were also firing from the windows. Clearly, the attorney general was not satisfied of the strength of the wounding case, because the ultimate prosecution was not for attempted murder or wounding with intent but for discharging a firearm with intent to kill or cause grievous bodily harm.

The usual fortnightly petty sessions were held on 20 August in Lurgan. Resident Magistrate McSheehy and Mr Watson JP presided. Hans McMordie of Belfast applied for bail for Donnelly, who was then in Armagh jail, but the court said it was a matter for Captain Keogh. The solicitor pointed out that Donnelly 'was a gentleman owning a large amount of property in the town – some thousands of pounds – and that if he was admitted to bail he was not a person likely to run away and leave it behind him'. Second, he could now produce any amount of bail for appearance. Captain Keogh said he had always made it a rule not to admit any person to bail while the life of the person injured by him was in imminent danger. Such was the case at present and he was reluctantly obliged to refuse McMordie's application. Nevertheless, Donnelly was released later in September. The *Nation* of 28 September contains the following report:

> Mr Arthur Donnelly of Lurgan, who, it will be remembered, was committed to prison under such curious circumstances a few weeks since, has been released and reached his home from Armagh on Tuesday night. It is stated in the daily papers that on his arrival at the railway station in Lurgan he was received by quite a crowd of sympathizers with him in his unmerited persecution by the Orange faction in that town, and that again on arriving at his residence there was another crowd who heartily cheered him.[23]

After the events in August, one would have expected the trial to proceed at the winter assizes in Armagh. This did not happen. Later file notes indicate two things. First, the attorney general had 'adjourned the prosecution for health'. (Presumably that was the health of Donnelly, and not of the attorney.) Second, on 28 January 1873 it was noted that Donnelly would apply for a change of

23 *Nation*, 28 Sept. 1874.

venue.[24] This came up in the queen's bench court before the lord chief justice on 17 April 1873. The prosecution had been moved by *certiorari* into the queen's bench court. Donnelly, 'the traverser', was described by the reporter in the *Freeman's Journal* on that occasion as 'a respectable looking middle-aged man, who stood at the side bar. He pleaded not guilty and gave advance sureties in the sum of £500 each.'[25] The matter was adjourned to 1 May and then to 15 June. Isaac Butt QC MP had come in to lead for Donnelly, but, one suspects, counsel had been speaking behind the scenes because on this occasion the solicitor general announced that the crown moved to transfer the venue to Downpatrick from Armagh, and such an order was then made.

The case finally came on for trial at Downpatrick on 21 July 1873. It was called over by Keogh J, once an MP and leader of a group of MPs after O'Connell's demise. They were known by some as the 'Pope's brass band'. His decision to take office was regarded as selling out by his supporters. Indeed, it largely explains why nationalist MPs never later took office, an attitude that continued in Northern Ireland after partition – see, for example, the controversy about Thomas Campbell KC accepting a judgeship late in life and the refusal of the McSparrans, father and son, to serve on the bench. Keogh J passed the case to Lawson J. It was widely reported not only in the local but in the Dublin papers, albeit in abbreviated form. Dr Elrington QC appeared for the prosecution. The newspaper reports agree that Donnelly's junior was called Donnell and his solicitor McMordie, but his silk is described in one report as Porter QC and in another as Falkiner QC. It may be that he had two senior counsel. Certainly it will be seen that Falkiner was acting for him at this stage. His trial came on on the same day as the third trial of Sub-Inspector Montgomery of the RIC for the murder of a bank official in Newtownstewart – a more famous *cause célèbre*.

The least bad account that I have found of the hearing was in the *Newry Reporter* of 22 July 1873. Having recorded the appearances, it noted that Donnelly answered to his bail and the paper proceeded to list the names of all the jurors who were challenged on the part of the prisoner. Their surnames seemed to suggest that they were probably of planter stock. It then listed the persons who were stood down by the crown, only some of whom appeared to be of native Irish stock. It then proceeded to list the jury as actually sworn, all but one or possibly two appearing to be of planter stock.

I have already quoted the opening of Elrington accusing Donnelly of firing from body height with a loaded pistol. He referred to a model of the town. Indeed, the Dublin Castle file has a neat map of the town to explain it to those unfamiliar with that locality. Dr Elrington's opening is reviewed in full but maddeningly it is followed by this brief passage:

24 NAI CSORP/1872/16620.
25 *Freeman's Journal*, 17 Apr. 1873.

> A number of witnesses were examined and cross-examined, after which Mr Porter summed up the evidence. Dr Elrington replied on the part of the crown. His lordship commenced to sum up about half past five o'clock.[26]

I pause here to point out two matters of legal interest. First of all, Elrington closed for the crown after the defence. The defence in Northern Ireland did not, in fact, get the last word until the 1970s in criminal trials. Note also the absence of any reference to what Donnelly said. An accused person did not have the right or option of giving evidence on his own behalf at that time.[27] A prisoner did have the right to make an unsworn statement from the dock but we do not know if Donnelly did so.[28] Oral tradition has it that Donnelly treated the proceedings with contempt, reading and signing business papers while sitting in the dock.

The newspaper quotes the judge's summing up as follows:

> His lordship instructed the jury that the law was that, if a man fired a loaded pistol into a crowd he was guilty of firing with intent to do bodily harm to someone in that crowd unless either the pistol were fired by accident or over the heads of the people or fired in defence of the person's own life and property.[29]

The judge then proceeded to review the evidence very minutely and concluded his charge at half past six. The jury retired but returned at 7.40 p.m. to say that they were satisfied as to the firing of the shot but disagreed as to the intention with which it was fired. The judge replied that if they believed the shot was fired in a direction that would do injury, they were bound in point of law to impute the intent. If he fired over the heads of the crowd, the case was different. The jury were then locked up and at half past ten were called out again. When the foreman stated they could not agree, they were discharged. At that time, verdicts had to be unanimous.

The next day Lawson J announced that he was ready to retry Donnelly there and then. He seemed keen to do so. But the crown merely asked that the case be adjourned to the first day of the Michaelmas term in the queen's

26 *Newry Reporter*, 22 July 1873.

27 An accused person only gained that right or option in Northern Ireland by section 1 of the Criminal Evidence Act (Northern Ireland) 1923. The equivalent legislation in the Irish Free State was section 1 of the Criminal Justice (Evidence) Act 1924. It had been introduced in England and Wales in 1898.

28 That right survived in Northern Ireland also into the 1970s. I recall it discussed as a possibility by counsel but I do not remember ever hearing one actually made. It may conceivably have been done by a prisoner who was refusing to recognize the court as some republicans did in the 1970s.

29 *Newry Reporter*, 22 July 1873.

bench division on the same terms as before, i.e., Donnelly's own bail of £1,000 and two sureties each of £500. A cabinet minister's salary at this time was £5,000 per annum and a judge's about £2,000, so these were substantial sureties.

It is sad to report that Donnelly's granddaughter in the last year of her life burnt all the family papers. She did so over the protests of her nephew, on the basis that they were just reminders of 'the bad old times'. This was in 1958, ironically, given the worse times yet to come. But a few documents have survived and one of them is a letter written by or on behalf of Donnelly on the day the jury disagreed, 21 July 1873, to James O'Flinn of Castlewellan.

> On my return once more to my family I take the earliest opportunity of thanking you for the great interest you took in my case and that it is partly due to your exertions that I am a free man to-day. You were the means of bringing forward one or two honest men to stand between me and a legion of enemies.
>
> I was most unfortunate in having Falkiner for my counsel. He is a bitter Orangeman and either through prejudice or not reading his brief he made a sad mess of my case. I had nearly 25 witnesses and he only produced about 4 leaving 20 of the best ones unexamined. If they had been produced I have every reason to believe I would have been creditably acquitted. The judge is a barefaced partisan and his charge was very hostile to me. He made the best possible use of everything against me and glossed over anything that was in my favour.
>
> However from the unfavourable position I was placed in I have every reason to be thankful for the issue which seems to have been a mercy of providence.
>
> For your warm hearted interest allow me once more to thank you from my heart.
>
> I may never expect to repay your kindness, but if it be ever in my power to make even a feint acknowledgment be assured I won't miss the opportunity.[30]

Counsel or former counsel will smile at the complaint of the client that counsel failed to call all his witnesses. Laypersons tend to think that more is better. But the more you call the more opportunity there is for damaging inconsistencies to emerge in their evidence. It is obviously impossible to say now whether Falkiner's course was justified or an unwise course. Frederick Falkiner has the distinction of being mentioned in Joyce's *Ulysses* – in a neutral way, in his capacity as recorder of Dublin.[31] He was indeed later

30 In private possession.
31 See V. Igoe, *The real people of Joyce's* Ulysses*: a biographical guide* (Dublin, 2016), p. 100.

knighted after twenty-nine years in office, possibly to induce him to retire from that office.

Judges may also smile at the allegation that the judge was 'a bare-faced partisan'. Disappointed litigants often come out of court complaining about the judge. However, here it may be that Donnelly was not so very far off the mark. Ball records that Lawson 'escaped assassination in 1882 by a hair's breadth for his firmness in upholding the supremacy of the law' during the land troubles.[32] McDowell, in his history of the Kildare Street and University Club, mentions this incident, which took place outside the club.[33] Apparently the judge was saved by the efforts of his detective. He had the unusual honour of receiving a doctorate of civil law from the University of Oxford and was a member of the Royal Irish Academy, having been in the past a professor of political economy in Trinity College Dublin, in succession to Isaac Butt. The *Dictionary of Irish biography* records that he was an able man but 'noted anti-nationalist', imprisoning the editor of the *Freeman's Journal* for three months at one point.[34] Certainly the reporter suggested a surprising keenness to immediately retry Donnelly.

After the jury disagreed, it was hoped and expected by Donnelly's family that he would not be retried but the decision on that would be one for the prosecution – ultimately the attorney general, Palles. In the days before mobile phones, he might not have been accessible. But a strange delay now takes place. One might have expected a trial to take place in Dublin to where it was adjourned, but that did not happen. Was Donnelly's health again a factor? Or did Palles show some hesitation to retry him, having heard presumably from prosecuting counsel or someone attending them as to the evidence at the trial in Downpatrick? In any event, he was appointed lord chief baron on 16 February 1874 and his Conservative successor, John Thomas Ball, had no hesitation. Donnelly was told to attend at the winter assizes in Downpatrick on 2 March 1874. Donnelly was unable to attend for health reasons.

A further family document that has survived is a second letter to Mr James O'Flinn of Castlewellan, this time from Arthur's son Andrew ('Andy') Donnelly. It is dated 8 March 1874. This passage is relevant:

> It was providential that he did not go to Downpatrick. He was most anxious about going himself. He is not yet able to be out of bed, but I expect in a fortnight he will be all right again with God's help.

That letter also contains the only extant account of Donnelly's view of the matter according to his son:

32 F. Elrington Ball, *The judges in Ireland, 1221–1921* (New York, 1921), p. 312.
33 R.B. McDowell, *Land and learning: two Irish clubs* (Dublin, 1993), p. 77.
34 D. Murphy, 'James Anthony Lawson' in *DIB*.

> The mob came purposely into the town to wreck the Catholic houses. They fired shots in at him and broke his windows before he returned it – then he only fired over their heads to scare them. If he had intended to kill he could not have missed them, the crowd was that large and numerous. The fellow Bell being wounded is only a concoction and a swindle.

Happily, a number of letters of Donnelly's son-in-law and partner, Charles O'Neill, have survived.[35] From these we learn that the family were dismayed when they were given notice to appear on trial at Downpatrick on 2 March. Two things then followed. Donnelly fell ill and to his condition 'two doctors were prepared to testify in court. Judge Keogh reluctantly postponed the hearing until 17 July.' The second thing that was happening was a feverish examination of the jury list for Co. Down. Donnelly came from Co. Armagh but the trial was in Downpatrick. Fortunately, Charles O'Neill was from Co. Down as was Mr James O'Flinn, twice thanked by the Donnellys. They apparently contacted the 'leading clergy and laity in Co. Down' to evaluate all the prospective jurors (Catholic and Protestant). Charles O'Neill developed a secret code of annotating the list, which in those days was entirely public. He divided the potential jurors into six categories: Catholic, liberal Protestant, Protestant, Orangeman, bigoted or bitter Orangemen, and easy-going soft Protestants that could be easily led. One reads of this with a mixture of dismay and humour, but you will recall that the future Lord O'Brien of Kilfenora won his reputation as 'Peter the Packer' by taking such steps to ensure that juries brought in favourable verdicts for the crown. Indeed, after Donnelly's trial in July 1874 Mr Verner MP asked a question in the House of Commons regarding the crown solicitor standing by all the potential Catholic jurors in Donnelly's case. According to an O'Neill letter of 11 July 1874, there were only Protestants on the jury at the July 1874 trial.

Keogh J opened that assize but passed the case to Fitzgerald J. John David Fitzgerald was a former Liberal attorney general who had been appointed to the queen's bench division of the high court in 1860. He had the unique distinction of being appointed straight from the high court to the judicial committee of the House of Lords in 1882, in which he sat until his death in 1889. (The only persons who have followed him in this step were Michael Morris, later Lord Killanin, and Lord MacDermott, later the lord chief justice of Northern Ireland. Fitzgerald has the added distinction of being the ancestor of Jonathan Powell, Tony Blair's chief of staff who was greatly involved in the Northern Ireland peace process at the end of the 1990s.)

35 I am grateful to Mrs Patricia McKaigue of Belfast who has kindly provided me with an unpublished document by her uncle, Father Edmund S. O'Neill, titled 'The beginnings of a family history: letters of my grandfather, Charles O'Neill (1835–1886)'.

The *Belfast Weekly News* account records that Arthur Donnelly of Lurgan was indicted for having, on 16 August 1872, fired a pistol loaded with powder and leaden balls against a person unknown, with intent to kill and murder. On another count he was indicted for having fired the pistol with intent to do grievous bodily harm. The newspaper records the jurors who were sworn. It mentions the fifteen jurors who were challenged on behalf of the prisoner but does not mention how many were stood by.[36]

Dr Elrington QC, who was the senior crown prosecutor for Co. Armagh, led for the prosecution with Dr M'Blaine and Dr Kaye. (Kaye later became assistant secretary in Dublin Castle and was also knighted.) Mr Falkiner QC was no longer leading counsel for Mr Donnelly; Mr Porter QC led Mr Hamill QC and Mr Donnell BL for the prisoner. Porter was Andrew Marshall Porter, later master of the rolls and a baronet.[37] He was unusual in the judiciary of the period in having been educated not in Trinity College Dublin but at the Queen's University Belfast. He sent his sons to TCD but one, not long after, died in the Boer War.[38]

Elrington's opening is covered extensively in press reports. He said that the incident happened between 7.00 and 8.00 in the evening of 16 August 1872:

> At that time a procession of persons called Good Templars passed through the street, coming from the railway into the town. At the time that the procession was passing through Church Place there was a band of music accompanying them ... The procession passed through Church Place, and some of them were opposite Donnelly's house, others being past it, and the remaining portion being behind, not having yet come up to the house. At this time two shots were fired, which unquestionably were fired by the prisoner. After that, unquestionably a riot took place. Many shots were fired. Shots came from Mr Donnelly's house and a great number of stones were thrown, so that the town of Lurgan was the scene of the utmost riot and confusion during the whole evening ... a man named William Bell, who was standing near some of the houses, saw the first shot being fired and heard Mr Donnelly make use of such words as 'boys, fire'. He heard the report of the second shot and it would be described to them [the jury] that he was struck; and respecting the wound which he unquestionably did receive medical evidence would be produced to show that it had been inflicted by a bullet. He would be exceeding his duty if he did more than state what he would produce in evidence, medical gentlemen who would prove to them what he had stated – that the wound was decidedly by a bullet.[39]

36 *Belfast Weekly News*, 25 July 1874.
37 George Smith, *The North-East bar* (Belfast, 1910), p. 109.
38 There is a large memorial window to him on the first landing of the Graduates Memorial Building in Trinity College Dublin.
39 *Belfast Weekly News*, 25 July 1874.

William Bell was called and in reply to Dr Kaye, the crown junior, gave evidence in accordance with the opening. He saw Donnelly reaching out his arm and firing. 'Witness then proceeded up the street a few perches when he heard a second shot. It struck witness on the head.' The allegation therefore was that not only was Bell not doing anything but that he had walked on past Donnelly's house some fifteen or twenty yards when he was shot. Dunlop Crawford also saw Donnelly fire a shot, indeed two shots. 'Then saw a lot of firing out of Donnelly's houses – both old and new. Heard the sound of glass breaking; but that was after the firing commenced.' John Wilks and George Davidson gave similar evidence. Head Constable Wilson said he arrested Donnelly on 18 August.[40] He had a pistol and a box of ammunition in his pocket. In cross-examination, he acknowledged that on 15 August he saw Donnelly causing a Catholic party to furl a banner to prevent a row. Dr Alfreds deposed to dressing the wound and Bell's head. 'He believed it to be a gunshot wound.' Dr Palmer, assistant surgeon and Dr Robinson, surgeon, Armagh Infirmary, gave similar evidence.

Hamill QC in opening the case for the defence said:

> he felt confident that when the case had been fully investigated by the jury and when the witnesses for the defence had given their evidence the accused would leave the courthouse without a stain upon his character. He would prove by witnesses that the accused was struck with a stone while standing at the front of his own house and that other persons were at the same time struck and injured. Mr Donnelly's family on that day consisted, he believed, of his wife and of an interesting young woman of about 22 years of age who was labouring under the fatal illness of consumption for eighteen months previous. They would take into consideration his great anxiety to protect the young woman from injury. It would be proved that but a short time previous to the arrival of the procession at the house this young girl was in one of these rooms, the windows of which were broken with stones from the mob outside. The accused, to show these persons that he was armed, fired the pistol in the air in order to warn them not to proceed further in their molestations. If the jury believed that the accused fired the pistol in the air with this object he claimed a verdict and asked to have Mr Donnelly discharged.[41]

Arthur's daughter Catherine died on 26 April 1873, eight months after these events.

40 It is unclear whether this date was stated in error or if the arrest on 18 Aug. relates to a different charge.

41 *Belfast Weekly News*, 25 July 1874.

Rather disappointingly the *Belfast Weekly News*, which was a unionist paper, does not report any of the evidence for the defence but concludes succinctly:

> Evidence for the defence having been given, His Lordship summed up, and the jury retired, and, after about 10 minutes absence, returned into court with a verdict of not guilty.

Thus ended the trials of Arthur Donnelly arising from the Lurgan riots of August 1872. He was acquitted. He was free to return to his home. But the account remains a very curious one. If the crown was calling Bell to say he had been shot by Donnelly and calling three medical witnesses to prove it was a gunshot wound, it is rather surprising that Donnelly was not charged with wounding with intent. It may be that there was some doubt as to whether it was he who had fired the shot.

Donnelly's employees or 'shopmen' were also firing – for between fifteen minutes and an hour according to conflicting accounts. Oral tradition is that one of these men fired a shot which may have hit Bell, but Donnelly declined to 'name or blame' him. He left the county the same night. Clearly the jury, predominantly unionist to all appearances and stated so to be by Charles O'Neill, had little trouble in concluding that Donnelly was not guilty of firing with intent. It may be that the charge from Fitzgerald J was more sympathetic to the prisoner than that of Lawson J the previous year, or the defence better conducted, or both.

One would like to say that the gentleman returned to his home and lived happily ever after. Unhappily, almost exactly the same thing happened in 1886.[42] Donnelly, by now in his 70s, was alleged to have fired on persons outside his house in Church Place who were quietly walking by and to have hit one of them with a bullet from his gun. The newspaper accounts of the incident, however, show that the doctor is very sceptical as to whether a shot had, in fact, hit the complainant. Nevertheless, Donnelly's solicitor had considerable difficulty in avoiding his being remanded in custody again when he was returned for trial, but finally bail was granted by the magistrates. There was no trial on this occasion as Donnelly died before the winter assizes came on and the issue could be tested further. These allegations and his return for trial – for the third time – were the subject of public attention and questions in parliament as well.

In the centre of the Dougher graveyard in the townland where Arthur Donnelly was born, there stands a fine funerary monument in the high Victorian style. The inscription on it reads as follows:

42 See D.S. Cook, 'Playing games with history: Arthur Donnelly first elected Catholic representative in Lurgan', *Familia: Ulster Genealogical Review*, 29 (2013), 123.

> Erected by Andrew Donnelly of Lurgan in loving memory of his mother Margaret Donnelly who died on 10 May 1885 aged 78 years and his father Arthur Donnelly a native of this townland who died on 19 November 1886 aged 73 years. He was a good parent, a sincere Catholic, honest and honourable during a long and active business life of 50 years. Proud of his country and her struggle for liberty, he was an ardent supporter of the National cause and *fearlessly withstood the local bigots of his time*. (author's emphasis).

It may be that this rather aggressive conclusion is understandable in the light of the events described in this chapter. There was then as now, and almost always, a tension between decent people trying to do their best, from both communities, and those whose actions or judgment are motivated or influenced by hostile or improper factors.

'Attie' Donnelly, as he was known, is remembered in Lurgan not only by his gravestone but by a street named after him, Donnelly Gardens, and several plaques of his own erection over houses in Church Place and passing references in a number of published works about the town and county. One hopes his shade rests in peace but if it survives in some form it may have derived some slight satisfaction from an occasion in 2006 when his great-great-grandson sat as a judge of the high court in Downpatrick courthouse – where he had twice been tried and thrice returned for trial. He may have secured further pleasure from the fact that sitting beside the judge on the bench was his great-great-granddaughter, the high sheriff of Co. Down, Mrs Fionnuala Cook.

Exploring the dynamic of the Irish land war, 1879–90

L. PERRY CURTIS, JR*

> There is nothing which so generally strikes the imagination, and engages the affections of mankind, as the right of property; or that sole and despotic dominion which one man claims and exercises over the external things of the world, in total exclusion of the right of any other individual in the universe.
>
> Sir William Blackstone

INTRODUCTION

Ever since the publication of John E. Pomfret's classic narrative, *The struggle for land in Ireland, 1800–1923*,[1] historians have wrangled over the causes of the land wars that erupted in 1879 and continued into the early 1900s. According to Pomfret most landlords were predators who charged high rents and eventually inspired their increasingly politicized tenants to mobilize through the auspices of the Irish National Land League that aimed to lower rents, achieve security of tenure and eventually abolish landlordism altogether. Since Pomfret's work, most historians of the land wars have chosen one of four causes for that country-wide rebellion.

According to the *political* causation school, Irish nationalists led by Charles Stewart Parnell, John Devoy and Michael Davitt forged a grand alliance under the New Departure of 1878–9 and embarked on a non-violent campaign to lower rents, guarantee security of tenure and repeal the Act of Union. In the long run they aspired to achieve occupier ownership and the abolition of landlordism. These ambitious goals were to be realized by means

* This essay originated in a talk to the Parnell Summer School held at Avondale in August 2014. For the invitation to attend, I am most grateful to Felix M. Larkin who was at that time the school's academic director. Since then extensive revisions have taken place with the help of Robert Marshall and Brian Casey. Besides the expert proof-reading of Dave Kay and Stephanie Dearmont, I owe a huge debt to Blake Perkins whose editorial skills and thorough readings have greatly enhanced the content. For the Pomfret thesis, see W.E. Vaughan's succinct summary in his rigorously revisionist monograph, *Landlords and tenants in mid-Victorian Ireland* (Oxford, 1994), pp v–x.

1 J.E. Pomfret, *The struggle for land in Ireland, 1800–1923* (Princeton, 1930).

of a two-front offensive waged by the more radical leaders of the Land League founded in October 1879 and the relatively moderate Home Rule parliamentary party led by Parnell. This incongruous alliance between physical force Fenianism and constitutional nationalism produced a political and social conflict that disrupted parliamentary debate and at times threatened the cause of law and order in Ireland.[2] Among the Land League's favourite tactics were mass protest meetings, civil disobedience, boycotting anyone who disobeyed its edicts, resistance to eviction and verbal as well as physical intimidation.

Those historians who opt for a primarily *economic* explanation of the outbreak of the land agitation lean heavily on both the rent nexus that embroiled landlord and tenant relations and the agricultural depression of the 1870s that lowered prices for cereal crops, store cattle, butter and livestock. In Connacht, partial failures of the potato harvest made matters much worse for cottiers or smallholders and labourers who relied heavily on this staple food source.[3] If better-off tenants enjoyed security of tenure so long as they paid their rent, they also depended on credit provided by shopkeepers and moneylenders whose interest rates were always high. Relying on multiple regression analysis, Andrew Orridge has concluded that 'the land war was an economically provoked movement of the poorest groups which gradually spread to much of the island, although it was always strongest in less prosperous areas'.[4]

On the other hand historians wedded to *social* causation have argued that the protest movement grew out of the age-old class conflict between the mostly Protestant landed elite and the mostly Catholic rural populace – known collectively as the peasantry – whose animosity stemmed from not only the huge disparity in wealth but also the deep sectarian divide given the Protestant faith of the largest landowners. In his pioneering if controversial book, *Social origins of the Irish land war,* the historical sociologist Samuel Clark took note of the agricultural depression and the resulting economic distress but denied that discontent arising from 'relative deprivation' triggered the tenants' uprising. Relying on mobilization theory and a social-structural approach, he emphasized instead the 'challenging collectivity' that evolved

2 For cogent contributions to the 'political school', see F.S.L. Lyons, *Ireland since the Famine* (London, 1971), as well as his biographies of John Dillon and Charles Stewart Parnell: F.S.L. Lyons, *John Dillon: a biography* (London, 1968) and F.S.L. Lyons, *Charles Stewart Parnell* (London, 1977). See also T.W. Moody, *Davitt and Irish revolution, 1846–82* (Oxford, 1981).

3 Lee contends that the post-Famine economy became more monetized, thereby accelerating the modernization of agriculture. See J.J. Lee, *The modernization of Irish society, 1848–1918* (Dublin, 1973), esp. pp 1–14, 36–41, 65–85, 92–105.

4 A.W. Orridge, 'Who supported the land war? an aggregate–data analysis of Irish agrarian discontent, 1879–1882', *Irish Economic and Social Review,* 12:3 (Apr. 1981), 203, esp. 203–4, 217–19 and 228.

from a latent into a manifest revolt. In the longer run, he maintained, the agitation mounted by agrarian activists became ever more militant and aimed at abolishing the hegemony of the landlords.[5]

Disagreeing with Clark's hypothesis, James Donnelly, the astute social and economic historian, has argued that larger farmers and townsmen had grown accustomed to rising income since the 1860s, and this 'revolution of rising expectations' made them more than 'unwilling to abandon their conviction that economic progress could and must be perpetuated' by challenging the landlord class.[6] An altogether different interpretation came from Paul Bew who, adopting a quasi-Marxist model, insisted upon the existence of class war between bourgeois or strong farmers and graziers on the one hand and poor plebeian smallholders on the other. What prevented the outbreak of a violent clash between these inherently rival classes was mutual hostility towards the landlords.[7]

Besides these arguments or explanations – each of which contains distinctly plausible elements deserving notice – we must add the *meteorological* factor or the harsh hand of nature. A prolonged spell of cold and wet weather during 1878–9 ruined harvests and caused potatoes to rot, especially in the cottier-dominated far west. These conditions dashed the 'rising expectations' of many poor tenant farmers and moved them to resist paying the full rent due in the autumn of 1879. Even if most landlords under-rented their lands, as Vaughan has alleged, the cry of 'down with rack rents' could soon be heard at protest meetings across the country.[8]

To this list of primarily empirical narratives we need to add a fifth hypothesis – one that deserves the label of *epistemological* for want of a simpler term. Within this category we encounter various cultural and ideological factors arising from ways in which the protagonists or actors in this conflict understood the lay of the land and the always litigious nature of the laws pertaining to the rights of property along with the growing collision between official and popular justice that came to a head during 1878–9.

5 'The underlying cause of the Irish land war was not the depression of the late 1870s, but rather the long–term evolution of this social group'. S. Clark, *Social origins of the Irish land war* (Princeton, 1979), pp 11 12, 245–304, 350–71.

6 J.S. Donnelly, Jr, *The land and the people of nineteenth-century Cork* (London, 1975), pp 251–86.

7 P. Bew, *Land and the national question in Ireland, 1858–82* (Dublin, 1978), esp. pp 74–114. See also D.S. Jones, *Graziers, land reform, and political conflict in Ireland* (Washington, DC, 1995) and D.S. Jones, 'The cleavage between graziers and peasants in the land struggle, 1890–1900' in S. Clark and J.S. Donnelly (eds), *Irish peasants: violence and political unrest, 1780–1914* (Manchester, 1983), pp 374–417.

8 For the origins of the Irish National Land League, see Moody, *Davitt*, esp. pp 271–4, 330–4; D. Jordan, *Land and popular politics in Ireland: County Mayo from the plantation to the land war* (Cambridge, 1994), pp 199–263; Donnelly, *Nineteenth-century Cork*, pp 256–86; and Bew, *National question*. The (revisionist) argument that Irish landlords consistently under-rented their property may be found in Vaughan, *Landlords*, pp 44–66.

Traditional landlord and tenant relations never recovered from the challenge posed by the Land League to the status quo. Since the 1850s, owners of estates of over 500 acres – whether Protestant or Catholic, Anglo-Irish or Irish – who let or leased their lands to a heterogeneous tenantry had grown accustomed to tenant-right associations that focused on lowering rents and ensuring security of tenure. The Land League, however, proved to be a far cry from these mostly moderate combinations of aggrieved tenants; and landlords as well as their agents soon grasped the gravity of what Clark has called the 'challenging collectivity' led by radical urban and rural organizers and orators who were determined to alter if not end the hegemony of the landlords. Ranging from prosperous strong farmers and graziers to impoverished cottiers, the rank-and-file members of the League were divided by the size, productivity and location of their farms as well as by the yawning sectarian gulf between church and chapel or parson and priest. The long simmering conflict between the landed elite that comprised over 6,500 owners of estates over 500 acres and the roughly half-million occupiers who worked those holdings came to a head in the autumn of 1879.

Following the unusually cold and wet weather of that summer and autumn, many tenants – especially those in western Connacht – heard the anti-landlord harangues of activist shopkeepers, tradesmen and newspaper proprietors, and began to resist paying the full rent due because it had now become exorbitant if not ruinous. Weighed down with loans and running low on credit, these occupiers demanded substantial abatements as well as an end to eviction for non-payment. This groundswell of protest culminated in the founding of the Land League of Mayo, which became the progenitor of the Irish National Land League launched on 21 October.[9] Inspired in large part by Michael Davitt's impassioned tirades against the 'feudal' tyranny of landlordism, this critical mass of tenant-right activists began to mobilize their communities against so-called rack renters and looked forward to the day when the land was restored to 'the people'.[10]

Needless to say the growing challenge to landlord hegemony caused alarm among aristocratic and gentry landowners whose chronic indebtedness and

9 For the rise of tenant–right activism after the Great Famine, see Clark, *Social origins*, esp. pp 209–20; Jordan, *Popular politics*, pp 209–29; G. Moran, 'Laying the seeds for agrarian agitation: the Ballinasloe Tenant Defence Association, 1876–80' in C. King and C. McNamara (eds), *The West of Ireland* (Dublin, 2011), pp 73–92; A. Shields, '"Serving the farmer": the tenant right movement in the West, 1847–57' in King and McNamara (eds), *The West of Ireland*, pp 51–72; B. Casey, 'Matt Harris and the Irish land question, 1876–1882', *Rural History* 25:2 (Oct. 2014), 183; B. Casey, 'Constructing political consciousness in the West of Ireland, 1876–79: the case of the Ballinasloe Tenant Defence Association', *New Hibernia Review* (Spring 2016), 58; and Moody, *Davitt*, pp 191, 271–3.

10 Moody spells out the Mayo Land League's aims and the founding of the Irish National Land League in his magisterial book, *Davitt*, pp 317–20, 325, 334–7. See also Bew, *National question*, pp 8–97; Jordan, *Popular politics*, esp. pp 199–229; and *Freeman's Journal*, 22 Oct. 1879.

heavy interest payments could turn any fall in rent receipts into a serious problem. If it took many months for them to organize effective counter measures, a minority of proprietors did resist the League's offensive, which forced them to spend much money and effort in defense of their vital interests. The growing tenant demand for estate-wide rent reductions of at least 15 per cent, accompanied by death threats posted around demesnes, caused many a sleepless night in the Big House outside north-east Ulster.[11] Moreover both police and civilian officials in Dublin Castle had good reason to worry about the mounting defiance of law and order manifested by dozens of attempts to murder owners and their agents as well as process servers, not to mention less lethal forms of agrarian violence.

The agricultural depression worsened in 1881, threatening the solvency of many landowners who contended that they could not afford to lower their rents significantly. Because so many tenants were paying only a portion of the rent owed, or withheld their rent, arrears soared and the number of actual or threatened evictions rapidly doubled or tripled. Fearing for the safety of their families, some of the richer proprietors closed down their mansions, laid off the indoor and outdoor staff, and fled to their London town houses or clambered on board their luxurious yachts in the Mediterranean until their agents, who had no choice but to face the dangers of staying behind, assured them that it was safe to return.

THE THEORETICAL CONTEXT

The various implications of this growing rebellion against the rent nexus require some kind of theoretical framework. In his radical 'analysis of the deep structure of the historical imagination', Hayden White pointed out how heavily historians have relied on not just empirical data but also 'a narrative structure for their presentation'. White went further by insisting that this kind of 'prefiguration' was both a linguistic and a 'poetic' process that forced historians to choose between 'the four tropes of poetic language' or master narrative modes.[12] Whether or not one accepts White's literary or interpretive straitjacket, his 'metahistorical' reflections afford unique insights into the nature of historical productions. Indeed, the title of his seminal essay – 'The fictions of factual representation' – goes far towards explaining how subversive his approach was to claims of truth or reality by historians.[13] For

11 For the 'fair rent' movement, see Moody, *Davitt*, pp 304–7, 320–2 and Bew, *National question*, pp 121–6.

12 These four tropes are metaphor, metonymy, synecdoche and irony. See H.V. White, *Metahistory: the historical imagination in nineteenth-century Europe* (Baltimore, 1973), esp. pp x–xii, 13–42.

13 See White, *Metahistory*, pp ix–xii, 1–42 as well as his fascinating *Tropics of discourse: essays in cultural criticism* (Baltimore, 1978), pp 1–25, 121–34.

White, the veracity or reliability of the empirical evidence seemed to matter less than the historian's choice of a master narrative needed to arrange and explicate the so-called facts. Not only does 'theory' come in all shapes and sizes its wonders to perform but it often sets off loud alarms in the minds of historians wedded to the sacrosanct evidence they have found in the archives. To quote that icon of English empiricism, Sherlock Holmes: 'It is a capital mistake to theorize before one has data. Insensibly one begins to twist facts to suit theories, instead of theories to suit facts.'[14] What the world's greatest 'consulting detective' should have perceived, of course, is just how inseparable theory and data are as they constantly inform and interact with each other in the historian's relentless pursuit of past realities.

THE POWER/KNOWLEDGE FACTOR

The defining line of argument in this essay follows neither Hayden White nor Conan Doyle but centres around the French philosopher, *philosophe*, historian and savant, Michel Foucault (1926–84). In the huge house that Foucault built there are many mansions; and the one chosen here comes closest to his more historical as distinct from philosophical reflections.[15] In particular, Foucault's approach to such subjects as discipline, surveillance and government efforts to control the citizenry have considerable relevance to landlord and tenant relations despite the obvious fact that tenants were not confined in prisons, hospitals or lunatic asylums. As part of his sustained assault on both empiricism and rationalism, he dwelled at length on the 'micro-physics' of state power. He also deplored the claims of the medical and psychological sciences to absolute truth or verifiable fact. His lofty ambition to enlist 'the will to knowledge' in the struggle against the efforts of the state and governing class to maintain their hegemony has even more relevance today than it did half a century ago.[16]

Foucault's concept of Power/Knowledge sheds much light on both the inherently frictional nature of landlord and tenant relations and the 'subjectification' of plebeians.[17] In his classic text, *Surveiller et punir* (1975),

14 A. Conan Doyle, 'A scandal in Bohemia' in *The adventures of Sherlock Holmes* (London, 1892), p. 11.

15 This essay draws heavily on *Discipline and punish* (1975), as well as on his thoughts on Power/Knowledge, rather than on *The order of things* (1966) or *The archaeology of knowledge* (1969).

16 See also P. Rabinow's introduction to *The Foucault reader* (New York, 1984), esp. pp 3–23.

17 According to Foucault, 'the body of the worker becomes a useful force only if it is both a productive and a subjected body'. For his more philosophical writings, see *Les mots et les choses* (1966) and *The archaeology of knowledge* (1969) wherein he revealed his deeply ironic skepticism about the 'thing called order' as well as Western epistemology. See also H. White 'Foucault decoded: notes from underground' in White, *Tropics of discourse*, pp 230–60.

loosely translated as *Discipline and punish,* he concentrated on the political and cultural forces designed to create submissive citizens or 'docile bodies'. Drawing on Jeremy Bentham's master plan of the panopticon or circular prison wherein the solitary governor observes every prisoner through peepholes inside an annular tower, Foucault pointed out that prisoners internalized surveillance because they could never know whether or not they were being watched.[18] In this way the enterprising prison governor enjoyed a near monopoly of Power/Knowledge while making a profit from the prison he owned.

If Irish tenants were far removed from eighteenth-century prisoners, they too knew the meaning of surveillance whenever land or sub-agents appeared on the scene to inspect the premises and recommend improvements to the holding. Of course, the primary function of the agent was to collect the rent, keep the account books in good order and reprimand any tenant who neglected his holding or piled up arrears of rent. Whether strong farmers or smallholders, most occupiers knew how to cope with the rules or customs of the estate if only to make their holdings more profitable. Unless they were caught breaking some covenant they enjoyed security of tenure so long as they paid the gale rent due and steered clear of the Land League.

Foucault regarded his concept of Power/Knowledge – hereinafter designated as P/K – as a force that circulates rather like oxygen through and around society. In other words, it is the essential ingredient of not just survival but also upward social mobility. To put this another way, P/K informs and facilitates every kind of interaction between the governors and the governed as well as between the so-called expert and the layperson. Thus 'power produces knowledge … power and knowledge directly imply one another … there is no power relation without the correlative constitution of a field of knowledge, nor any knowledge that does not presuppose and constitute at the same time power relations'.[19] Far from being an entirely repressive force flowing from the top down and stifling the ability of subaltern classes to promote their own interests, P/K 'produces reality' as well as 'domains of objects and rituals of truth'.

In Foucault's view both 'the individual and the knowledge that may be gained of him belong to this production'.[20] Conventional definitions of power

18 M. Foucault, *Discipline and punish: the birth of the prison*, trans. A. Sheridan (New York, 1977), p. 26.

19 'It is not the activity of the subject of knowledge that produces a corpus of knowledge, useful or resistant to power, but Power/Knowledge, the processes and struggles that traverse it and of which it is made up, that determines the forms and possible domains of knowledge.' Foucault, *Discipline and punish,* esp. pp 27–8. For further discussion of Power/Knowledge, see M. Foucault, *Power/Knowledge: selected interviews and other writings* (New York, 1980), esp. pp 87–96, 109–33, 146–65, 183–90, 198–209, 233–46.

20 Foucault, *Discipline and punish,* p. 194. For one of many overviews of Foucaultian theory, see White, *Tropics of discourse,* pp 230–60.

tend to emphasize the one-directional authority possessed by an army officer over a private, or a prison guard over a prisoner, or a schoolmaster over a student. By contrast Foucault argued that P/K can be affirmative and creative – even liberating. Pervasive, ubiquitous and multidirectional, it circulates throughout society and affects everyone in any given community or institution. The efficacy – indeed, beauty – of Foucault's concept is that it highlights the ability of the subaltern to challenge or resist the authority of his or her master without violence. To put this another way, P/K is far from being the exclusive preserve of the social and political elite – whether the wealthy, the bureaucracy or the educated classes. Even the lowliest plebeian – whether slave, serf, scullery maid or prisoner – possesses a quotient, however limited, of P/K that could be used to undermine or deceive the master or superior should the occasion arise.

BINDING COVENANTS

Turning to a rudimentary form of empiricism, we submit as evidence of official or juridical P/K two documents found in virtually every estate office. These printed forms epitomize the binding nature of the rent nexus by affirming the landowner's right to protect his or her interest or investment in the property to be let or leased. The first document consists of an indenture or contract for one year's occupancy of a holding. Printed on parchment-like paper and emanating from the Cork estate of Hayes St Leger, fourth Viscount Doneraile, it bears the title of 'Regulations' and contains blank spaces for the tenant's name, the location of the holding, and the date and the amount of rent. Besides reserving the right of the owner and his heirs to all mines, minerals, royalties, gravel pits, quarries, timber, fish and game, the deed sets forth the following terms of tenure: 'The demised premises must be kept in right, good, perfect order, repair and condition.' In addition, the tenant had to:

> well and sufficiently preserve, maintain and keep all houses, fences, ditches, drains, gardens, hedges, edifices, buildings, and all other improvements that now are or hereafter during this demise shall be made or erected upon the demised premises.

Needless to say, the emphasis on 'perfect order' gave any exacting landlord or agent a wide berth in ensuring that the lessee kept the premises 'in good order and repair'. If the latter failed to carry out or pay for the work deemed necessary, then his livestock or crops might be seized and sold to settle the account. The penalty for failure to pay the rent due was eviction.[21]

21 For the undated Doneraile indenture, printed on stiff parchment-like paper and measuring 28.5 by 21.5 inches, see Curtis MSS, North Pomfret, VT. A lease for thirty-one years on the

Although the second document bears the same title, it is not a formal lease but rather a printed notice containing six commandments. Addressed to the tenants of Charles H.B.C.S. Wandesforde on his Castlecomer estate in Co. Kilkenny and dated 8 July 1844, it reads:

1. No Grass Land within one mile of the town of Castlecomer, to be broken up; nor any Buildings whatsoever erected, nor drains made, nor Hedges cut, without receiving permission from the Office.
2. All Buildings and Yards to be kept in a proper state of repair and cleanliness.
3. All Hedges, other Fences, and Gates to be kept in order, and Ditches scoured out.
4. All Weeds to be rooted up or cut before they go to seed.
5. All Trees to be protected by those on whose farms they grow.
6. All private roads to be kept in repair, and the water tables and sewers kept free, by those whose lands adjoin them, or who make use of them.[22]

The provision requiring the tenant to keep his holding in 'a proper state of repair and cleanliness' left the occupier little room for neglect.

Both documents embody the kind of control that owners sought to maintain over their property; and if any of these covenants chafed or caused resentment to the tenant, that was the additional price of cultivating the holding and occupying the dwelling. For his part the owner or his agent had to maintain some degree of surveillance over the premises to avoid neglect or disrepair. After 1860 the legal rights of property owners were greatly reinforced by Deasy's Act,[23] which placed landlord and tenant relations on a firmer contractual footing, reinforced landlords' rights, and helped land agents and their subalterns to ensure compliance with the regulations.

In theory landlords could evict tenants-at-will – as distinct from leaseholders – cheaply and promptly. In most cases, however, after the Famine clearances of the 1850s proprietors showed restraint not least because the threat of eviction usually drove the occupier to mend his ways. On some estates arrears of two or three years were tolerated during hard times, especially if the occupier was industrious but had endured a family health crisis. Because reliable tenants were in somewhat short supply, they usually were allowed to remain undisturbed pending payment of arrears so long as they showed no sign of defiance. In the words of Vaughan, 'the threat of

estate of Lt Col. Charles Smyth Vereker (1818–85) in Parkroe, Co. Limerick, dated 20 Feb. 1851, authorized the owner to seize and sell the tenant's stock as compensation for unpaid rent and allowed him to evict the lessee by court order if necessary. NLI deed 26,829; see facsimile 1 in NLI, historical documents, *The land war, 1879–1903* (Dublin, n.d.).

22 Curtis MSS, North Pomfret, VT.

23 Landlord and Tenant Law Amendment (Ireland) Act 1860 (23 & 24 Vict., c. 154).

eviction was not decisive. At most it could be used to control stragglers, but not against concerted opposition from tenants who had made up their minds.'[24] An important exception to this rule was membership in the Land League. Thus several tenants were evicted in 1882 on Lord de Vesci's estate in Queen's County for organizing an anti-rent campaign.[25]

Taken together these formal and customary covenants comprised a thinly veiled system of discipline and punishment designed to keep the property in good order and ensure a steady flow of rental income. On well-managed estates what might be labelled the landlord's writ covered every acre of tenanted land and could be enforced in a variety of ways.

LANDLORD AND AGENT P/K

The P/K enjoyed by landlords and agents operated within overlapping spheres that converged around rents and arrears, compliance with the custom of the estate and improvements to the holding. As Vaughan points out, 'the working of the land system was remarkably visible' and local newspapers tended to report any untoward incidents relating to estate matters. Within the political sphere, we find newsworthy items ranging from local and parliamentary elections to concerted efforts by both the police and landlord organizations to combat the Land League. In addition, both the provincial and national press carried reports of the futile campaign of landlords to obtain compensation for all the rental income they claimed to have lost through the fair rent clauses of Gladstone's land legislation.

On every estate the letting contracts or leases prioritized keeping the farm in 'good repair' and forbade the sale of the tenant's interest or goodwill in his holding without permission. The penalties for any violation of these covenants might include denial of access to turf (turbary), timber or gravel. For serious violations of covenants there was always the dreaded possibility of ejectment.[26]

After 1879 the hunger of landlords for cash to pay their bills – not least the quarterly interest due on their burdensome mortgage loans – grew more acute and often resulted in urgent requests to their agents to press tenants harder for the gale rent due. Thus in the spring of 1882, when faced with a rent strike and in sore need of cash, Lord Annesley, who was cruising on his yacht in the Mediterranean after receiving a threatening letter, told his agent that he could not decide whether to sell the tenants' interest in their holdings, cut off their

24 Vaughan, *Landlords*, p. 33.

25 Four years later two of these evicted tenants were living in huts built by the Land League; see the fourth Viscount de Vesci to Gladstone, 20 Feb. 1886, Gladstone papers, BL Add MS 44.495, ff. 3–4.

26 'The notice to quit … was an administrative maid-of-all-work, offering a quick, effective means of settling disputes'. Vaughan, *Landlords*, pp 29–31.

water supply, forbid access to the quarry or execute ejectment decrees with costs.[27] Although we do not know the course he chose and whether or not the agent executed his order, this range of options says much about the extent of landlord P/K and the punitive measures available to the owner.

Ample proof of the agent's command of P/K may be found in the out-letter books containing copies of correspondence with tenants, trustees, family members, solicitors, accountants, local merchants and other creditors. This rich source, copied onto onion-skin paper, reveals endless insights into the daily operations of the estate as well as the financial condition and personal problems of the proprietor and his immediate family. For example, the thousand-page out-letter book ranging from 1857 to 1886 of James and Henry Crossle, who managed the affairs of Sir William Verner in counties Armagh, Tyrone and Monaghan, deals with everything from leases and arrears of rent to livestock and local elections. It also includes Lady Verner's frantic quest for a loan of £400 in 1881.[28]

Another classic example of agent P/K appears in a warning sent by Crossle to a trouble-making tenant: 'I will put you off the estate' should he or any member of his family bother a neighbouring tenant over a new road built at Cranlorne.[29] Growing resistance to rent placed Sir William in a financial bind; and he urged his agent to find a short-term loan of £60,000 at no more than 5 per cent interest. He also ordered Crossle to lean harder on tenants who were demanding abatements of up to 30 per cent. The possibility of eviction, he made clear, remained on the table.[30] Caught in a classic bind, Crossle informed Lady Verner that 'our duty is, whilst endeavouring to treat the tenants with every kindness and fairness, yet to try and protect the landlord's interest'.[31]

In Co. Meath, Gilbert Hodson, the agent for his brother, Sir Robert Hodson, warned a tenant mired in steep arrears that she would lose much of the value of the interest in her holding if she neglected her farm. Should she fail to make a 'substantial payment of rent', he warned, an ejectment writ would reduce that value even more. He also rebuked another tenant for

27 'If you are against doing anything, tell me how to get the arrears and what you do advize [*sic*].' Annesley to W. Moore, 12, 18 May 1882, Annesley papers, PRONI D1854/5/8 and folio VIII, pp 12–13.

28 See J. Crossle to Lady Verner, 11 Aug. 1881 and Crossle to A.R. Jackson (solicitor), 13 Aug. 1881, Out-letter books of James and Henry Crossle (1857–1886), p. 218, PRONI D236/488/1.

29 J. Crossle to J. Donnelly of Cranlorne, 26 June 1868, ibid., p. 326. Emphasis in the original. For another example of an agent's micromanagement, see the out–letter books and correspondence of Samuel M. Hussey et al. in the Kenmare papers, PRONI D/4151/G/1–33.

30 The county court judge postponed all these petitions for ejectment decrees without any request from the defendants. Crossle to Jackson, 29 Dec. 1881 and 12 Jan. 1882, PRONI D236/488/3/ pp 323, 359.

31 Crossle to Lady Verner, 5 Jan. 1882, ibid., p. 346. For Maria Edgeworth's definition of 'a good agent', see *The absentee* (New York, 1976), p. 212.

disobeying his order not to extract any more gravel from the pit on his holding. If this practice continued, then 'I will institute proceedings against you'.[32]

On the sprawling Kilkenny and Tipperary estates of the 3rd Marquess of Ormonde, his brother and agent, Lord Arthur Butler, was besieged with requests for abatements in the autumn of 1879. Backed by Ormonde, who was aboard his yacht in the Mediterranean, Lord Arthur denied these petitions. But he did distribute some kindling and seed potatoes to tenants in serious distress. Ormonde saw no reason to reduce rents on account of one bad season if only because his tenants had profited from the run of good harvests. One year later, he changed his mind and approved modest abatements and allowances on the next gale rent due.[33] Unfortunately, these out-letter books reveal little or nothing about the feelings of those tenants burdened by the rent nexus.

Occasionally agents were asked to intervene in the quarrels of tenants embroiled in family squabbles or feuds. In particular a few wives requested protection of their rights (and bodies) from allegedly abusive husbands. Long-running disputes over money owed, dowries, land usage rights and inheritance prompted these women to plead for 'justice' from the estate office. Such appeals for help increased the agent's already considerable reserve of P/K concerning the lives of tenants.[34]

Besides the land agent, members of the legal profession obviously enjoyed a fund of P/K pertaining to estate management. Well versed in the arcane world of land laws, including proprietorial rights, solicitors knew how to use technicalities and obscure legal terms to defend the interests of their clients. Presumably terms like *fieri facias* (or *fi. fa.*), trover, corporeal hereditament, writ of replevin, entail, estovers, emblements, *custodia legis*, habendum and reddendum were bound to bewilder most tenants. In any event such legal arcana served as potent weapons in the hands of agents and solicitors whenever property rights were disputed.

Conscientious or efficient landlords, whose numbers increased after the Great Famine, also deployed their P/K to enforce discipline among their tenants. Thus the semi-absentee Sir John Benn-Walsh inspected his larger

32 G. Hodson to M. Scott, 5 Aug. 1896, NLI Hodson papers, MS 16,501, ff. 135–7 and Hodson to P. White, 31 Oct. 1891, ibid., f. 123.

33 See the out-letter book of Lord Arthur Butler, NLI Ormonde papers, MS 23,578, esp. pp 629–31, 669, 692–700, 721–5, 732–3, 783–4, 793–4, 813–14, 854–8 and MS 23,801. Evidently, by 1884 Lord Ormonde had lost upwards of £1,805 in arrears under Gladstone's Arrears of Rent (Ireland) Act 1882 (45 & 46 Vict., c. 47). Ibid., MS 23,801.

34 On the Shirley estate in Co. Monaghan, tenant petitions during the 1840s ranged from sibling and marital disputes to the grievances of vulnerable widows, unwed daughters and abused wives who had no other recourse. R.A. Harris, 'Negotiating patriarchy: Irish women and the landlord' in M. Cohen and N.J. Curtis (eds), *Reclaiming gender: transgressive identities in modern Ireland* (New York, 1999), pp 207–25.

farms and interviewed the occupiers during visits to his Cork and Kerry estates between 1821 and 1864. The fallout from the Famine had enabled his agent to 'weed out' paupers and 'bad tenants'. However, the owner worried lest the agent fall into 'very slovenly & negligent' habits. So he personally supervised all the improvements for which he had paid. Over the course of forty years he managed to double his rental income.[35]

The ever-vigilant landlord William Bence Jones of Lisselan, near Clonakilty, Co. Cork, forced his leaseholders to sign leases for thirty-one years and forbade them to make improvements. He also inspected every building, fence, drain and ditch for which he had paid. This micromanager went so far as to spell out the five types of manure that tenant farmers should spread on different fields. Any tenant caught subdividing his holding faced summary eviction. In the long run, this keen wielder of P/K made the property profitable by attending to proper drainage, embankments, crops, livestock and new roads, and by getting rid of both middlemen and 'slothful … weak and wayward' tenants. He also consolidated small holdings and rewarded industrious tenants with new leases, albeit at higher rents. Like many other landlords he 'exploited every possible loophole' in the Landlord and Tenant Amendment (Ireland) Act 1870[36] and refused to lower rents in 1880. When the local Land League branch retaliated by blocking the sale of his cattle in Ireland and imposing a stifling boycott, his anger boiled over and spilled onto the pages of a bristling memoir that accused the tenants of rank ingratitude for all his improvements and blamed the League for preventing covenants from being enforced. In his opinion Ireland's three greatest evils were lying, drink and debt; and he also denied that evictions were cruel.[37]

One of the most infamous wielders of landlord P/K was the third earl of Leitrim, whose countless enemies crossed class lines. This authoritarian owner of 95,000 acres in four or five counties was an obsessive improver who abolished rundale, squared tenancies, supervised farming, oppressed his tenants and personally collected rents. Fond of litigation, he would take a tenant to court over the slightest breach of contract. He also gave his superior landlord, Trinity College, a hard time. Adopting a 'regular system of espionage', he went so far as to keep his own agents under surveillance.[38]

35 Donnelly, *Nineteenth-century Cork*, pp 50–2, 63, 66, 118–19, 159–61, 194 and J.S. Donnelly, 'The journals of Sir John Benn-Walsh relating to the management of his Irish estates, 1823–64', *Journal of the Cork Historical and Archaeological Society* 79 (1974), 86 and 80 (1975), 15–43.

36 33 & 34 Vict., c. 46.

37 Convinced that landlords could no longer win any court cases for breach of contract because leases had become a game of 'heads I win, tails you lose', he declared that many tenants 'were hopelessly and incorrigibly bad as can be'. W. Bence Jones, *The life's work in Ireland of a landlord who tried to do his duty* (London, 1880), pp v–xii, 47–52, 162–3. For Jones' rants about the tenantry and his aversion to tenant right, see also Donnelly, *Nineteenth-century Cork*, pp 161–5, 206–9, 272–5.

38 Leitrim banned cutting bushes and trees and burning fields after the harvest. Any tenant who

Another vigorous wielder of P/K was the fifth earl of Annesley who took threatening notices seriously enough to abandon his Co. Down demesne in favour of a leisurely tour of the Italian Riviera. From that safe distance he urged his agent to evict any 'Hills men' who refused to pay rent or treated his employees with disrespect: 'I think a few sharp examples will do a world of good & will bring the people to their senses … You need not take any of the odium on yourself as I can get away & you can't.' 'Your business', he wrote from Corfu on 13 March 1882, 'is to fight my former tenants, but present enemies, by every means in your power, assisted by my lawyers; if you do your best, no man can do more.'[39]

In 1876, upon his father's death, Sir Henry Gore-Booth took over the management of the Lissadell estate in west Sligo where he introduced 'a very thorough system of accounts and book-keeping'. His passion for travel abroad, including the Arctic, did not prevent him from getting to know many of the tenants, their holdings and their needs. Evidently this benevolent wielder of landlord P/K kept rents low and supervised improvements.[40]

In Co. Mayo Charles Strickland, the Catholic agent of Lord Dillon, supervised the tenantry with due diligence and acted as 'their guide and counsellor'.[41] By way of contrast, the irascible third earl of Charlemont left his lavishly remodelled mansion, Roxborough, near Moy in Co. Tyrone, at the end of 1879 for the comforts and safety of London. After crossing the Channel, he took the healing waters at a German spa and then ventured to Florence where he fretted about all the rental income he was losing. Lashing out against tenants who supported the Land League and tenant right, he told his agent that Ireland was facing a 'Radical Revolution against all property, all law, all order'. He wanted to evict the 'surplus population' of smallholders and convert their acreage into pasturage. In addition, he issued orders to evict any Catholic who participated in processions: 'I say collect all the rents you can and buy arms and fortify your premises.'[42]

However selective, these examples illustrate the depth and breadth of landlord P/K even if we cannot know how many of the owner's orders were

sold the interest in his holding without permission faced eviction. His sworn enemies included not only local officials but also fellow landlords who accused him of giving them a bad name. A.P.W. Malcomson defends Leitrim in his deeply researched and revisionist biography, *Virtues of a wicked earl: the life and legend of William Sydney Clements, third earl of Leitrim (1806–78)* (Dublin, 2009). Vaughan deals with Leitrim's 'obsession with detail … unusual in a great nobleman' and his overbearing or arbitrary exercise of landlord authority in *Landlords*, pp 36, 76, 86, 97, 103–5.

39 Annesley to William [indecipherable], 8 Dec. 1881, PRONI D1854/6/8.

40 D. James, *The Gore-Booths of Lissadell* (Dublin, 2004), pp 56–68.

41 F. Dun, *Landlords and tenants in Ireland* (London, 1881), pp 190, 201–2.

42 Fearing a 'radical revolution against all property, all law, all order' Charlemont also wanted to charge some of his larger tenants more rent and blamed the 'Papist leaguers' for his 'exile' in Florence. Charlemont to Hugh Boyle, 17 Feb. 1879, Summer 1879, 11 Apr. 1880, 23 Sept. 1880, 5 Dec. 1880, PRONI D266/367/11a, 14, 37, 39, 55.

carried out. Unlike the personal or familial finances of proprietors, most estate disputes over rents and arrears earned notice in local papers as well as gossip in local pubs.

Combative proprietors like Arthur MacMurrough Kavanagh of Borris, Co. Carlow, made good use of their money and connections as well as P/K to launch and sustain such militant anti-League organizations as the Irish Land Committee, the Orange Emergency Committee, the Property Defence Association, the Irish Defence Union and the Land Corporation of Ireland. After 1887, the influential Irish Landowners Convention, backed by wealthy allies in the House of Lords, worked long and hard, if unsuccessfully, to win some compensation for all the rental income they had lost through the fair rent provisions of Gladstone's Irish land acts. Backed by prominent English plutocrats of Tory or unionist persuasion, these anti-League and anti-Plan of Campaign activists formed several syndicates that rescued several beleaguered estates from bankruptcy. Taken together these proactive landlord associations had spent well over £300,000 on their counteroffensive by 1900.[43]

Landlords and their agents also relied on P/K to draw up new leases designed to nullify those clauses in the complex Landlord and Tenant (Ireland) Act 1870[44] that compensated outgoing tenants for not just improvements to their holdings but also 'capricious eviction'. In Donnelly's view, this measure gave rise to 'a flood of new leases … some of which contained covenants that were doubtfully legal and positively damaging to the interests of the tenants'.[45] Vaughan dwells on the often costly litigation pursued by better-off tenants who applied to the courts for compensation for their disturbance as well as improvements.[46] All those lawsuits exemplify the readiness of better educated tenants to defend their interests after the 1860s. By the same token more vigilant proprietors or their agents supervised improvements in order to prevent tenants from making unwarranted claims for compensation for disturbance. In addition, on some estates leaseholders were compelled to sign stricter leases or risk non-renewal.[47]

43 For these landlord combinations, see L.P. Curtis Jr, 'Landlord responses to the Irish land war, 1879–1887', *Éire/Ireland*, 38:3&4 (Fall/Winter 2003), 169.

44 33 & 34 Vict., c. 46.

45 The ambiguous custom known as Ulster tenant right did not prevail on every estate in that province. Many landlords opposed it because it saddled the incoming tenant with heavy payments on the loan needed to buy the interest on the farm. According to Vaughan, the Landlord and Tenant (Ireland) Act 1870 (33 & 34 Vict., c. 46) 'was very complicated … ineffective or … not needed'. *Landlords*, pp 23–7, 93–102, 213–17. For Ulster tenant right and security of tenure, see also Donnelly, *Nineteenth-century Cork*, pp 204–5, 215–20; E.D. Steele, *Irish land and British politics: tenant right and nationality, 1864–70* (Cambridge, 1974), passim; and Moody, *Davitt*, pp 37–9, 191–2. For declining evictions after 1855, see L.P. Curtis Jr, *The depiction of eviction in Ireland, 1845–1910* (Dublin, 2011), p. 58.

46 See Vaughan, *Landlords*, esp. pp 93–102.

47 Tenants whose leases had expired were occasionally forced to sign new leases of thirty-one years or longer that 'debarred them from claiming compensation for disturbance'. Strong

Although the vast majority of non-League tenants enjoyed security of tenure, the threat of distraint or seizure of chattel and crops – not to mention a writ of ejectment for non-payment – hung over the heads of any occupier weighed down with arrears or guilty of violating some other covenant. In fact, agents often used asterisks in their annual rentals and accounts to identify tenants whose arrears exceeded two years.[48] Among the sanctions imposed on those who committed infractions was the *fieri facias* decree that authorized the sheriff to seize and auction off the errant tenants' livestock or livelihood.[49]

According to Foucault 'power … is the multiplicity of force relations immanent in the sphere in which they operate and which constitute their own organization'. In the context of the land war, landlord P/K did not reside exclusively inside the estate office or the Big House. On the national scene, after 1820 the British state undertook the formidable task of mapping Ireland under the auspices of the Army Ordnance Survey whereby scholars like Eugene O'Curry, George Petrie and John O'Donovan provided vital geographical and statistical data that aided and abetted the tightening control of the British state over the country. In this respect the slow but steady erosion of the Irish language and Gaelic-named topography that was greatly accelerated by the Great Famine played a crucial role in the expansion of imperial rule in Ireland.

As Brian Friel made clear in his brilliant play, *Translations*, the conversion of Irish into English place names was part and parcel of Britain's ambitious cultural campaign to dilute, if not purge, Ireland's Irish or Gaelic heritage. Apart from the decennial census and English instruction in schools, there could be no better example of the state's deployment of P/K to achieve greater control over the indigenous citizenry than in the realm of making English the vernacular language. In the words of the bilingual historian Gearóid Ó Tuathaigh, 'suppressing or expelling a language and replacing it with another … must have been sharply disruptive'. This far-reaching cultural movement reflects Foucault's argument that 'power is everywhere, not because it embraces everything, but because it comes from everywhere'.[50]

farmers with holdings valued at over £50 were able to 'contract out' of the Act. Among the large proprietors who tried to avoid compensating tenants for disturbance were the duke of Leinster and Lords Kenmare and Cork. Donnelly, *Nineteenth-century Cork*, pp 201–5. For the saga of the Leinster lease, see pp 123–4.

48 For security of tenure, see Donnelly, *Nineteenth-century Cork*, pp 200–5.

49 For the sheriff's sale by auction of livestock belonging to four tenant farmers on the estate of Sir Erasmus Borrowes in Kildare, see *Freeman's Journal*, 9 Jan. 1882. Further discussion of estate management may be found in Vaughan, *Landlords*, pp 103–37; Donnelly, *Nineteenth-century Cork*, pp 9–14, 52–72, 158–69, 173–210; and Curtis, *Eviction*, pp 15–21.

50 For the Ordnance Survey, see H.F. Mulvey, *Thomas Davis and Ireland* (Washington, DC, 2003), pp 229–32 and J. Sheehy, *The rediscovery of Ireland's past: the Celtic revival, 1830–1930* (London, 1980), pp 20–7. For the steady decline of the Irish language after 1845, see G. Ó Tuathaigh, *I mBéal an Bháis: the Great Famine and the language shift in nineteenth-century Ireland* (Hamden, 2015), esp. pp 35–40. See also M. Foucault, *History of sexuality*, vol. i: *The will to knowledge* (New York, 1976, 1978), pp 92–3.

TENANT P/K

Whether lowly cottiers or affluent strong farmers and graziers, many tenants made good use of their quotient of P/K to defend their interests – not to mention their homesteads. Only a small minority – notably the rural banditti or 'hillside men' known as Moonlighters – resorted to overt violence to achieve their goals. In the realm of political action, the increasingly radical tenant-right associations owed much of their inspiration to the agrarian populist and intellectual James Fintan Lalor, who deplored all the profound social, political and economic disparities in his country. A bitter enemy of landlordism, this misshapen son of a strong farmer was determined to teach smallholders how to make use of their 'moral power'. He invoked natural law to explain why the aristocracy and gentry had no right to the land that really belonged to the Irish nation or people. In vain he called for a general strike against rent at the height of the Great Famine.[51]

Yearning for a countryside filled with small farmers who owned their profitable holdings and resembled English yeomen, Lalor also was keen to promote light industry in urban areas. What Ireland needed in his opinion was a moral and social revolution among smallholders that would result in a 'productive and prosperous ... active and affluent husbandry', thereby generating both rural and urban prosperity. Plagued by poor health, he proved too much of a loner and utopian to foster enough support or create an effective organization. However, his strictures against landlordism left their mark on the next generation of radical agrarians, notably Michael Davitt.[52]

An iconic preacher and practitioner of tenant P/K, Davitt was born in 1846 into grinding poverty in Straide, Co. Mayo, where his family would suffer a traumatic eviction. Emigrating to Lancashire in his youth, he lost an arm in a factory accident. Sworn into the Fenian movement at nineteen, he was arrested for gun-running and suffered seven brutal years in prison. During 1878–9 his remarkable resilience, powerful intellect and political skills enabled him to emerge as a key player in the New Departure. By the end of 1879 he had become the driving force behind the newly formed Land League

51 'The occupying tenants of the soil of Ireland ought ... to refuse all rent and arrears ... beyond and except the value of the overplus of harvest produce remaining in their hands ... to refuse ALL rent to the present usurping proprietors until the people ... have, in national congress or convention, decided what rents they are to pay and to *whom* they are to pay them'. L. Fogarty, *James Fintan Lalor: patriot and political essayist* (Dublin, 1919), p. 95.

52 As Lalor's recent biographer writes, 'If his influence on the Fenians was slight, his influence on the land war ... was surely crucial'. In his insightful study, *James Fintan Lalor: radical* (Cork, 1990), D.N. Buckley contends that Lalor was neither a genuine nationalist nor a socialist. Davitt, however, did credit him with being 'the prophet of Irish revolutionary land reform'. See esp. pp 59–67, 84–92. As for the cause of independence, Lalor resorted to a railway metaphor. Repeal, he believed, could be achieved only by attaching it to the 'self-acting' steam engine of the land question that – once the fire was kindled – would pull this carriage along behind it. Fogarty, *Lalor,* p. 83.

that demanded the abolition of so-called rack rents.[53] To the growing dismay of Dublin Castle and Big House society Davitt thrilled League audiences around the country with his rants against landlordism 'weighed down with crimes of centuries, and clogged with the spoils of robbery and injustice ... supported by brute force'. Another firebrand, the veteran Fenian James J. O'Kelly, warned landlords in November 1885 that if they did not exercise restraint, the people would 'crush' them as 'completely as grapes in a wine press'.[54]

On the political front, a new feature in the later 1870s was the emergence of a gifted cadre of local agrarian activists. These able and energetic men who were mostly in their thirties and forties, and aided and abetted by a handful of militant women, soon proved their mettle as organizers and propagandists in the campaign to abolish landlordism. A prime example of radical tenant right, Matt Harris was born in Roscommon town, the son of a small farmer near Athlone, who championed Chartism and Fenianism and also deplored the poverty of urban as well as rural plebeians. In 1876 he founded the virulently anti-landlord pressure group known as the Ballinasloe Tenant Defence Association. His fierce hostility to landlords did not prevent him from condemning the grazier class for monopolizing so much fertile land and caring only about its profits from the lucrative cattle trade. Although he conceded that not all landlords were 'bad', he declared that on the whole they deserved to be shot like partridges. He also deliberately conflated moral and physical force on the grounds that they were as inseparable as the body and soul.[55]

Collective tenant P/K usually operated within three overlapping spheres – the private, the local and the national. By private is meant personal, intra-familial or neighbourly disputes; by local, community or parochial affairs; by national, membership in the Land League along with unswerving support of Home Rule.

After 1879 the countless requests of tenants for rent reductions gathered momentum. When landlords resisted these demands, enrollments in the local League branch increased dramatically. There was nothing new, of course,

53 For Davitt's career up to 1882, see Moody, *Davitt*, esp. pp 43–5, 69–79, 145–85.

54 Davitt was speaking at Borris, Co. Carlow, *Freeman's Journal*, 31 Jan. 1881. For O'Kelly's speech at Dysart, see *Freeman's Journal*, 2 Nov. 1885.

55 On one occasion Harris advised an audience against cutting off the tails of jackasses – 'and I don't mean a landlord when I speak of a jackass ... cut the tail off the landlords as soon as you like. Devil a much of a tail the landlords have left [*sic*].' Quoted in the *Special commission to inquire into charges and allegations against certain MPs in proceedings in action of O'Donnell v. Walter*, HC 1890 Cmnd. 5890, xxvii, 477, vol. i, p. 122. Harris also deplored the tight grip of landlords, shopkeepers, and gombeen men over everyone who owed them money. The land question could only be resolved by replacing landlordism with peasant proprietorship. See Casey, 'Matt Harris and the Irish land question', as well as B. Casey, 'Matt Harris and the Ballinasloe Tenant Defence Association, 1876–9' in B. Casey (ed.), *Defying the law of the land: agrarian radicals in Irish history* (Dublin, 2013), pp 90–9.

about either land hunger or the desire of tenants to own their holdings. During the rebellion of 1798, for example, the earl of Clare had recognized the growing hostility of tenants towards the Ascendancy, whose forebears had expropriated the best land. 'Confiscation', he observed, 'is their common title; and from their first settlement they had been hemmed in on every side by the old inhabitants of the island, brooding over their discontents in sullen indignation.'[56] By the same token, the bloody history of secret agrarian societies like the Houghers, Whiteboys, Rockites, Peep O' Day Boys, Thrashers and Ribbonmen also could be written in terms of a collective P/K that enabled the actors to express their penchant for violence and their intimate knowledge of the local terrain in order to terrify their enemies.

In Ulster, some agrarian agitators founded a Tenant League in 1847; branches soon spread south and west. A few years later, a number of strong farmers and graziers flexed their political muscles by forming Farmers Clubs that shared some of the Tenant Leagues' goals.[57] By 1880 some tenant-right combinations became radicalized, espoused Fenian goals and joined the Land League's war against so-called rack rents. Besides denouncing landlords who refused to lower their rent, some of the rougher Leaguers began to assault process servers, bailiffs and subagents who took part in evictions or distrained livestock. Drawing heavily on their quotient of P/K, and exploiting their tactical advantages, some rural communities vigorously boycotted or intimidated anyone who defied the League branch's edicts. In this way the age-old tactic of 'social ostracism' evolved into a highly effective form of communal action.[58]

Despite the deep internal divisions arising out of class, region, religion and ideology, the almost meteoric rise of the Land League – followed by the short-lived but equally aggressive Ladies Land League – attests to the strength and ubiquity of tenant P/K. Venturing well beyond the familiar conflicts between landlords and tenants over the terms of tenure, the League's demand for the 'Three F's' – fair rents, fixity of tenure and freedom to sell the tenant's interest in his holding – had a huge reservoir of support both at home and in North America where touring members of Parnell's parliamentary party

56 Quoted in P. Bull, *Land, politics, and nationalism: a study of the Irish land question* (Dublin, 1996), p. 78.

57 Besides the Ulster Tenant Right Association founded in Derry in 1847, equivalents appeared in Ballyclare and Ballymena. The more radical Ballinasloe Tenant Defence Association that emerged in 1876 was led by Matt Harris and other local townsmen with strong ties to the farming community. Most of the farmers' clubs and tenant associations called for an extension of Gladstone's Landlord and Tenant Act of 1870 and the 'Three F's' as well as Home Rule. For these tenant leagues and clubs, see Clark, *Social origins*, pp 211–20; and Vaughan, *Landlords*, pp 76–83.

58 One of the earlier instances of communal boycotting or Quaker-like 'exclusive dealing' occurred in Queen's County in 1832 during the anti-tithe agitation and involved the father of James Fintan Lalor. See Buckley, *Lalor*, p. 11.

raised thousands of pounds or dollars for the cause. More than a mere testament to collective P/K, the successes of the New Departure represented a giant leap forward in the mobilization of the Irish Catholic majority in both town and country.

The combined forces of the Home Rule and tenant-right movements – promoted by remarkable organizational and oratorical talent – put Dublin Castle as well as the landed elite on the defensive and cost the government vast sums of money. Heavily outnumbered and relatively isolated, gentry families dreaded having to abandon their beloved demesnes. Alarmed by sporadic attacks on land agents and a handful of landowners, they faced a stark choice between sporadic police protection and arming themselves whenever they left their grounds.[59]

No manifestation of collective tenant P/K proved more effective than the boycott. Ostracizing individual or communal offenders had a long history in Ireland, and this tactic gained momentum after Parnell's vigorous endorsement in a speech at Ennis in the autumn of 1880. The high-handed land agent on Lord Erne's Co. Mayo estate, Captain Charles C. Boycott, had antagonized numerous labourers and tenants with his harsh actions. In a petition to their landlord 38 tenants accused Boycott of vindictive and self-aggrandizing behavior that included hiring outside workers and failing to pay local labourers. Boycott then made matters worse by calling his Lough Mask tenantry 'Irish swine'. Refusing to pay their rent, they called on Lord Erne to fire his agent.[60] Parnell's declaration that Boycott deserved to be sent into 'moral Coventry' left the agent isolated and unable to harvest his crops. To save him from ruin, an Orange relief expedition marched from the north protected by over one hundred well-armed soldiers. Despite pouring rain and muddy fields, the Ulstermen rescued most of the harvest but could not break the boycott that crippled his income.

It took a fund of P/K to arrange and then enforce such collective action. Whether the victim happened be a landlord, agent, process server or land grabber, day and night surveillance was essential because the League branch had to punish anyone caught helping the offender and his family.[61] Because the ordinary criminal code contained no provisions for prosecuting those who withheld their services until parliament passed a coercion act in 1881,[62] the Land League enjoyed something of a carte blanche when dealing with its

59 Vaughan, *Landlords*, pp 177–83. See also D. Jordan, 'Merchants, "strong farmers" and Fenians: the post-Famine political elite and the Irish land war' in C.H.E. Philpin (ed.), *Nationalism and popular protest in Ireland* (Cambridge, 1987), pp 320–48.

60 See tenants' petitions to the earl of Erne, 12 Aug. 1879 and 15 July 1881, Erne papers, PRONI D1939/21/9/15 and 20.

61 For the origins of the boycotting tactic on Lord Erne's estate, see Jordan, *Popular politics*, pp 285–93. See also Vaughan, *Landlords*, pp 177–9; M. Davitt, *Fall of feudalism in Ireland* (London, 1904), pp 274–9; and Moody, *Davitt*, pp 418–19.

62 Protection of Persons and Property (Ireland) Act 1881 (44 & 45 Vict., c. 4).

enemies. Although the new statute authorized the arrest and prosecution of boycotters and intimidators, the League continued to tighten its grip on many communities and inflict untold hardship on its enemies by mobilizing the boycott.

A notable example of tenant P/K in action was the campaign waged by some League branches to disrupt fox hunting as a protest against the arrest and imprisonment of Davitt, Parnell and other leaders in the autumn of 1881. Infuriated by this action, some League branches decided to deprive the gentry of their favourite field-sport. Following the boycott of several hunts in the south and west, they sallied forth to disrupt meets. On the appointed day, local Leaguers would confront the riders, blow horns, shout insults and curses, and throw clods of grass as well as stones at the riders. Prominent among the protestors were tenant farmers who also resented this annual invasion of their fields and pastures. Some extremists went much further by scattering poisoned meat around fox coverts and masters of hounds' kennels to the disgust and outrage of the entire fox-hunting community.

On the sprawling estate of the fifth marquess of Waterford, disputes with tenants over non-payment of rent as well as threats of eviction culminated in attacks on the famed Curraghmore hunt. On 6 October 1881, some 300 men and women gathered at Newtown Wood near Faheen, Co. Waterford, and assaulted the hunt with sticks, stones and pitchforks, swearing that they would prohibit further hunting until their leaders had been released from prison. One hound died from its wounds and others were badly bruised. So incensed was Lord Waterford by these vicious assaults that he resigned as master of the hounds, closed down his hunting establishment, laid off his stable hands and took his best hunters to England. The fracas at Newtown Woods heralded similar protests around the country. By May 1882, at least thirty hunts had been disrupted while a dozen packs of hounds and harriers were forced to suspend activities for most of the season. Frank Dadd's dramatic print in the *Illustrated London News* of a hunt being obstructed by angry protestors captured this brazen but mostly non-violent form of tenant P/K (Plate 6.1). Adding insult to injury, several League branches organized raucous 'people's hunts' drawn from the village or townland. With gusto and shouts of encouragement, they chased hares and rabbits with sticks and a pack of mongrel dogs. On these festive occasions, boisterous crowds would curse the landlords' cherished pastime as duly reported in local papers.[63]

Landlords who underestimated the cleverness or craftiness of their tenants did so at their own peril or peace of mind. Some resident owners acknowledged this mental acuity and ability to outwit or dodge authority. Bence Jones, who accused tenants of flagrantly violating the terms of their

63 See L.P. Curtis, Jr, 'Stopping the hunt, 1881–1882: an aspect of the Irish land war' in Philpin (ed.), *Nationalism and popular protest*, esp. pp 353–86; and H. Laird, *Subversive law in Ireland, 1879–1920* (Dublin, 2006), ch. 3.

leases, insisted that the Irish peasantry were not just 'semi-barbarous' and full of vices but also clever wheelers and dealers. 'Scheming and falsehood', he wrote, pervade 'everything said and done in Ireland'. Irish tenants, he added, were 'the keenest and best bargainers' in Europe. These inveterate 'schemers' knew how to 'make personal gain out of everything'. His rant did not stop there. He went on to declare emphatically that 'Jews cannot live in Ireland. They have no chance.'[64]

Another landlord who recognized the crafty or wily nature of his tenants was John C. Delmege of Castle Park, Co. Limerick, who informed the Bessborough Commission in 1880 that 'perhaps in Europe there is not a cleverer or cannier set of people than the Irish peasantry; they are highly educated now, and are very well able to make their contracts and bargains'.[65]

Some enterprising League activists needed only a little money and a sharp lawyer to defend their interests or outsmart their enemies in cases ranging from alleged exorbitant rents, grazing rights, turbary and water rights to overholding or other breaches of contract – all faithfully recorded in agents' letter-books, judicial records and the provincial press. Plaintiffs often loved litigation for its own sake and knew how to use the land laws to their advantage – hoping to bankrupt their adversaries through legal expenses in the process.[66]

As Richard Edgeworth pointed out in a memorable endnote in his daughter's famous novel, *Castle Rackrent* (1798), contrary to popular beliefs many tenants were well versed in civil law procedures. No doubt he exaggerated when declaring: 'Almost every poor man in Ireland, be he farmer, weaver, shopkeeper, or steward, is, besides his other occupations, occasionally a lawyer. The nature of processes, ejectments, custodians, injunctions, replevins etc. is perfectly known to them and the terms as familiar to them as to any attorney. They all love law.'[67] Such a verdict, however, could hardly be applied to tenants at will or small holders west of the Shannon.

Take the case of an obstinate tenant named Michael Gartlaney, who held a four-acre farm in Co. Tyrone. In 1860 he fought against the agent's decision to evict his brother from a small farm as part of a consolidation scheme. Gartlaney managed to hire not one but three solicitors to argue his case for non-disturbance. This case dragged on for four years, embroiled the agent's whole family and eventually damaged his health. Although landlord P/K prevailed and the Gartlaneys lost their farm, they appealed this verdict at the

64 Bence Jones, *Life's work*, pp v–vi. For more rants against leaseholders, see also pp 47–52, 163–4.

65 *Report of her majesty's commissioners of enquiry into the working of the Landlord and Tenant (Ireland) Act of 1870 and the acts amending the same*, HC 1881 Cmnd. 2779, 2779-I, 2779-II and 2779-III, xvii.1, 73, xix.1m 825, vol. ii, p. 721.

66 Several English travellers in Ireland remarked on the Irish peasant's mastery of 'the technical niceties' of the law to an extent not found among the English peasantry. É. Hickey, *Irish law and lawyers in modern folk tradition* (Dublin, 1999), pp 21–39.

67 See M. Edgeworth, *Castle Rackrent* (New York, 1976), p. 75.

assizes and eventually received £70 for alleged improvements under the Land Act of 1870.[68] On the duke of Leinster's estate around Maynooth in Cos. Kildare and Meath, a parson sued his landlord in 1879 for compensation after the agent had ordered him to cut down some trees and remove a fence, allowing rabbits to consume his crops. To the duke's acute dismay, the Revd Mr Patterson not only won his case but inspired the presiding judge in the court of exchequer, Baron Richard Dowse, to question the legitimacy of the duke's title to the land. The judge also chided Leinster for banning the shooting or trapping of rabbits that were devouring Patterson's crops.[69]

One educated tenant who knew how to make good use of P/K lived on the Dromoland estate of the Baron Inchiquin. In spring 1885 a widow named Mrs Catherine Whelan of Ardsollus objected to the agent's plan to dig a 'water course' or deep ditch across her potato field in order to construct a water-wheel that would pump water into a reservoir above the castle. She held her ground and spurned the offer of compensation. On the advice of the estate solicitor as well as the agent, Lord Inchiquin doubled her rent in the vain hope that she would apply for a judicial rent in the land court. To her defence rushed the proactive parish priest, Father Corbett, along with his curate, Corry, whom Lord Inchiquin accused of being a 'firebrand' for having preached 'a violent sermon' against him in Quin chapel. Flatly denying this charge, Corry insisted that he would never profane 'our sacred edifice with allusions to temporal affairs'. This controversy roiled the estate office for months. In the end, the widow presumably prevailed because the agent ordered the ditch to be dug and the water-wheel erected further up the river aided and abetted by a loan from the Board of Works.[70]

Classic examples of effective mobilization of tenant P/K abounded in the myriad cases of collective resistance to eviction during the 1880s. Seeking to increase the expense of eviction to the owner and Dublin Castle, some League branches hired experts to teach tenants how to fortify their dwellings against the besieging forces of bailiffs and police. Tenants facing removal were taught how to blockade windows with furze and boulders, stockpile stones, pitchforks

68 Vaughan, *Landlords*, pp 39–43. Vaughan also cites the case of a tenant named Friel who bested Lord Leitrim in a dispute over tenant right and won on appeal in 1872. Ibid., p. 97.

69 The jury found the duke guilty of trespass and assessed damages at £576, 16*s*. This verdict provoked Lord Charlemont, who was taking the waters at Bad Ems, to complain bitterly to his agent, Hugh Boyle, that Irish judges seemed to believe 'the only way to retain their salaries is to bring the landlords into more and more hatred and contempt'. Charlemont to Boyle, 13 June 1879, PRONI D226/367/12. For another litigious tenant, see the case of *Gethings v. Cloney* (1915) cited in V.T.H. Delany, *Christopher Palles, Lord Chief Baron* (Dublin, 1960), pp 148–50.

70 Lord Inchiquin to R.V. O'Brien, 1, 28 Feb., 14, 12 Apr. 1885, 27 Mar. 1886; O'Brien to Fr D. Corbett, 7 Apr. 1885, and Corbett to O'Brien, 11 Apr. 1885; O'Brien to Fr Corry, 12 Apr. 1885, and Corry to O'Brien, n.d. [1885], Florence O'Brien papers, TCD MS 10048/21. I remain more than grateful to the late Professor T.W. Moody for having loaned me these letters back in 1970.

and long poles, and fill buckets or cauldrons with hot and filthy water to throw at the invaders. If these defensive measures avoided serious injuries and proved futile in the long run, they required a good deal of communal cooperation as neighbours and friends gathered to curse and jeer at the enemy armed with crowbars and pickaxes as well as the rifles and bayonets of the RIC. In short, Castle authorities had good reason to wonder about where the line should be drawn between moral and physical force during the land war.[71]

By far the most popular tactic classified as an outrage by Dublin Castle was the threatening letter or death notice posted around the demesne. Although these grim warnings rarely resulted in actual harm, they proved a useful tool in the League's arsenal of protest tactics and understandably alarmed the entire household of the presumed victim. Some of these leaflets contained crude sketches of daggers, pistols and nooses along with skulls and crossed bones. Whether or not inspired by personal – as distinct from political – grievances, they harkened back to the pre-famine era of secret agrarian societies. Here and there a witness to some outrage might have to flee abroad to avoid giving evidence to the authorities.[72]

A classic example of applying a violent form of tenant P/K occurred in April 1878 when the notorious earl of Leitrim and two servants were ambushed and brutally murdered near Milford in Co. Donegal. Bent on vengeance against a landlord with a reputation for harshness who had been accused – rightly or wrongly – of having raped the daughter of a tenant, the conspirators knew exactly when and where to strike. If any locals knew the identity of the perpetrators, whom they regarded as heroes or liberators, they were not talking.[73] Whatever the motives behind this ambush, the lethal assault and escape route required considerable advance planning.

All this intimidation, boycotting and resistance to eviction required much preparation as well as secrecy on the part of the resisters who sought to drain

71 Organized resistance to eviction is treated at length in Curtis, *Eviction* (Dublin, 2011), esp. pp 96–118, 194–223.

72 This conspiracy of silence goes far to explain how and why the murderers of five small landlords in 1868 as well as of Lords Leitrim and Mountmorres, Lord Clanricarde's agent, and two of Lord Ardilaun's bailiffs all eluded arrest. Vaughan, *Landlords*, pp 184–9. For the murder of the Ardilaun bailiffs and the recovery of their bodies in Lough Mask, see *Times*, 27 Jan. 1882.

73 Leitrim's young clerk and car-driver also died in the ambush. Incensed by all the accusations of lewd and lascivious conduct, a mob attacked his funeral procession outside St Michan's church in Dublin. The allegations of Leitrim's sexual misconduct – which were groundless according to Malcomson – pervaded local folklore and still persist today. Davitt stressed the suspicions about Leitrim's sexual 'debauchery' as well as the reputation of other landlords for this kind of 'unforgivable wrong'. Malcomson called this 'an act of war, a resort to retaliatory justice where no civic redress could be obtained by an appeal to the law'. Malcomson, *Wicked Earl*, pp 184–92. S. Mac Philib, 'Profile of a landlord in folk tradition and in contemporary accounts: the third earl of Leitrim', *Ulster Folklore*, 34 (1988), 26; and the *Times* and *Freeman's Journal*, 4–6, 13 Apr. 1878, as well as D. Thomson, *Woodbrook* (London, 1974), pp 196–202.

Dublin Castle's resources. The siege of fortified dwellings also imposed a burden on local rate payers who had to pay for at least some of the damage to property. In addition landlords had to shoulder some of the heavy costs arising from the presence of police and soldiers to protect the sheriff's eviction party.[74]

In the meantime, nationalist newspapers filled their columns with lengthy reports of speeches delivered by Parnellite or League leaders around the country. Often braving injury from missiles, the intrepid reporters attended banned rallies and sent detailed accounts of the proceedings to their copy-editors. One exemplar of this nationalist journalism was James Daly, who presided over the influential *Connaught Telegraph*.[75] Complementing these dedicated reporters and editors were such gifted comic artists as J.F. O'Hea, J.D. Reigh and Thomas Fitzpatrick, whose clever and colourful cartoons appeared almost every Thursday in the *Weekly Freeman* and *United Ireland*.[76]

Arguably the single-most effective possessor and wielder of tenant P/K was the local parish priest, especially if he belonged to the executive of the local League branch. His 'acute social antennae' (to use Casey's apt metaphor) provided him with all kinds of useful knowledge about disputes over tenurial rights and wrongs as well as the assorted problems – whether personal or financial – of his parishioners. Such knowledge came with the cloth and by way of the confessional. Defying Cardinal Cullen's orders to avoid involvement in politics, the more combative clerics rose to defend aggrieved members of their flock against landlord P/K and the police. They also provoked the ire of resident magistrates and Castle officials by chairing banned League rallies when and where evictions were pending. At the height of the harsh coercive policies imposed under the Irish chief secretary, Arthur Balfour, in 1887–90 well over a dozen of these defiant priests spent up to six months in prison for denouncing rack renters, evictors and land-grabbers.[77]

Proof positive of the inherent clash between landlord and tenant P/K arose on the 68,000 acre estate of the third duke of Leinster in counties Meath and Kildare. Although rents were reasonable and moderate arrears were tolerated, the duke and his agent, Charles Hamilton, drew up a restrictive lease in 1872

74 For the Land League's efforts to foil the forces of Dublin Castle, see Bew, *National question*, pp 115–44; Moody, *Davitt*, esp. ch. 11; and Donnelly, *Nineteenth-century Cork*, ch. 6. Forceful resistance to eviction is discussed at length in Curtis, *Eviction*, ch. 7–9 and Bew, *National question*, pp 91–3.

75 For the vital role of the *Connaught Telegraph* in the early stages of the land war, see Jordan, *Popular politics*, esp. pp 150, 207–309.

76 See R. Douglas, L. Harte, and J. O'Hara, *Drawing conclusions: a cartoon history of Anglo–Irish relations 1798–1998* (Belfast, 1998), esp. pp 79–126.

77 Vaughan, *Landlords*, pp 177–216. See also L.P. Curtis Jr, *Coercion and conciliation in Ireland, 1880–92* (Princeton, 1963), pp 231–6; Curtis, *Eviction*, pp 177–8, 180–1, 219–20; B. Mac Suibhne, 'Soggarth aroon and gombeen–priest: Canon James MacFadden (1842–1917)' in G. Moran (ed.), *Radical Irish priests, 1660–1970* (Dublin, 1998), esp. pp 157–70; and F.M. Larkin, 'Canon Keller of Youghal' in Casey, *Defying the law*, pp 154–63.

that forbade compensation for tenant improvements made without the owner's consent. This new contract effectively nullified key clauses in Gladstone's recent Land Act[78] that guaranteed departing tenants compensation on holdings valued under £50.[79] Leaseholders who refused to sign the new agreement ran the risk of eviction. Despite his reputation as a 'good' landlord who had spent thousands of pounds on improvements, the duke forbade the sale by outgoing tenants of the interest in their holdings. The refusal of several tenants to sign the new lease and the subsequent ejectment decree plunged the estate into turmoil.[80]

Enraged by the new lease and the eviction of a strong farmer near Athy who had spent £3,000 on improvements but refused to sign the new lease, some 'middle-class tenants' founded the Leinster Tenants' Defence Association and demanded revocation of the lease. Despite the agent's assurance that the evicted farmer would be reinstated upon signing, several other tenants soon faced the same fate for noncompliance.

After his father's death in October 1874, the fourth duke inherited this festering dispute. In 1880 a Land League branch was founded in Kildare town by John Heffernan, the son of a prosperous local merchant and Fenian sympathizer. At the end of December an angry crowd gathered in the town square of Athy to condemn the Leinster lease. At this torch-lit rally, the Irish-American League organizer Michael Boyton burned copies of the lease impaled on a rusty '98 pike – a stark reminder of open rebellion. Boyton's use of a pike from the 1798 Rising, with its direct link to Lord Edward FitzGerald and the United Irishmen, was a clever move. Frank Dadd's portrayal of this scene in the *Illustrated London News* provided graphic evidence of what League members could achieve by flexing their P/K (Plate 6.2). The new lease severely damaged the longstanding reputation of the FitzGeralds as benevolent landlords.[81]

Another classic example of tenant P/K was the anti-rent combination launched in 1886 known as the Plan of Campaign that called for tenants on estates in financial trouble to pay the rent due less the desired reduction to a trustee who would hold the money in escrow until the owner surrendered to their demands. By 1888 this aggressive agitation had caused serious turmoil

78 Landlord and Tenant Amendment (Ireland) Act 1870 (33 & 34 Vict., c. 46).

79 In the words of Dooley, the new lease 'required tenants to forego claims to compensation for disturbance or for improvements, except where the latter had been carried out with the written permission of the duke'. T. Dooley, *The decline and fall of the dukes of Leinster, 1872–1948* (Dublin, 2015), p. 40.

80 For the Leinster lease and the terms applying to farms valued above and below £50, see Dooley, *Decline and fall*, pp 39–49; Dun, *Landlords and tenants*, pp 20–9; Clark, *Social origins*, pp 177; and Bew, *National question,* p. 129.

81 For details of the struggle over tenant right on the Leinster estate, see Dooley, *Decline and fall of the dukes of Leinster*, pp 39–49. See also Dun, *Landlords and tenants*, pp 20–9; Bew, *National question*, pp 129, 269; Vaughan, *Landlords*, p. 1; and N. O'Sullivan, *Aloysius O'Kelly: art, nation, empire* (Dublin, 2010), pp 67–8.

on well over one hundred estates. Determined to thwart the Plan, Balfour recruited some rich landed magnates in England to organize syndicates that bought several estates teetering on the brink of insolvency. By this means the actual owner staved off surrender to the Plan. During this new anti-rent offensive hundreds of evictions and the fierce resistance they engendered had inflamed parts of the countryside in the south and west. Although the Plan resulted in hundreds of high-profile evictions, it also earned feature articles in the press as well as widespread sympathy for the evicted tenants.[82]

In the meantime, threatening letters or death notices continued to proliferate. The recipients were warned not to defy the League's will, let alone authorize notices to quit. On a few occasions the threat went beyond mere words or sketches. In the spring of 1879 someone sent a widow's cap – intended for the duchess of Marlborough – to her husband, then the lord lieutenant of Ireland.[83] While most resident landlords shrugged off these notices as the handiwork of idle or cowardly men, others worried about the safety of their families if not themselves and appealed for police protection or carried arms whenever they left their demesnes. Baron Richard Dowse of the court of exchequer and a former attorney general also was threatened with assassination 'if you convict any Land Leger [*sic*]'. Sent from Irishtown, Co. Limerick, in 1880, this note ended with the words: 'To hell with Victoria la Reine – Vive Parnell Notre Roi.'[84] Because the RIC classified threatening letters as agrarian outrages, the number of criminal offences rose exponentially after 1880, making the case for coercion much more compelling.[85]

Despite the solemn pledge of Davitt, Parnell and their cohorts in the New Departure to wage a non-violent or constitutional agitation for both Home Rule and radical land reform, the League's national leadership declined to restrain the violent defenders of tenant right and resistance to eviction. Ever since the launch of the New Departure, the executive leaders – notably Davitt and Parnell – had to contend with the physical force minority that ranged from drunken thugs to hired assassins and diehard Fenians. These 'hillside

82 Conceived and orchestrated by Tim Harrington, John Dillon and William O'Brien, the Plan called for tenants to deposit their rents less the desired reduction in the hands of a trustee, often the parish priest, until such time as the landlord granted their demands. By the early 1900s, most but not all of those evicted during this struggle had been reinstated. See Curtis, *Coercion and conciliation*, pp 147–60, 236–63; Curtis, *Eviction*, pp 159–93, Larkin, 'Canon Keller'; and L. Geary, *The Plan of Campaign* (Cork, 1986).

83 For this threat to the duke of Marlborough while residing in Co. Westmeath, see Lord Oranmore and Browne's speech in the House of Lords, *Hansard's Parl. deb., 3rd series*, vol. 247, col. 1687.

84 Irish Land Committee, *The land question, Ireland, II: The anarchy in Ireland* (Dublin, 1880), p. 48.

85 For examples of threatening letters, see Irish Land Committee, *The anarchy in Ireland*. E.P. Thompson ranged far and wide over English variants of this tactic in 'The crime of anonymity' in Douglas Hay et al. (eds), *Albion's fatal tree: crime and society in eighteenth-century England* (New York, 1975), pp 255–344.

men' or 'Moonlighters' scoffed at the concept of moral force and preferred fists, blackthorns, arson, livestock maiming and blunderbusses to cheap talk. Their readiness to punish offenders – especially informers – threatened at times to subvert the implicit pledge of Leaguers to adhere to the non-violent commitment of the New Departure.

From 1880 to 1882 the number of crimes against person and property rose dramatically – ranging from assaults and arson to shooting at landlords, agents, process servers, sheriffs and land-grabbers. After the outlawing of the Land League in 1881, however, the national leaders had moved swiftly to fill the vacuum with the National League that pursued a much more political or electoral agenda. Following his release from Kilmainham jail in early May 1882, Parnell and his lieutenants renewed their campaign for Home Rule instead of the land question and tightened the discipline of the parliamentary party.

By 1883, those developments along with the Gladstone government's strenuous efforts to curb agrarian crime by means of coercion acts, greater police protection, the creation of summary justice courts and the imprisonment of many alleged perpetrators all combined to lower the incidence of agrarian violence. Later, in 1887 the Tory regime passed a harsh 'perpetual' coercion act that included summary justice courts presided over by Castle-appointed magistrates bent on securing convictions.[86]

SUBVERTING THE BRITISH LEGAL SYSTEM

What came to be known as popular justice posed a grave threat to both the Ascendancy and Castle rule. In her groundbreaking study, *Subversive law in Ireland,* Laird posits a fundamental conflict between English or official law and old Irish or Brehon conceptions of legal legitimacy. In her view the English conquest and the forceful imposition of the king's or queen's writ across the country 'created a space for the establishment of alternative legal concepts and structures that monitored and regulated the behaviour of rural communities'. After 1870 more tenant-right activists invoked both the written and oral traditions of Brehon law to promote their claim to the land expropriated by Anglo-Norman and Welsh conquerors since the twelfth century. With the founding of the Land League some radical jurists and tenant righters combined forces to undermine English law along with its elaborate court structure upon which the Ascendancy (including Catholic landowners) depended for their privileges if not their very existence.

As Laird makes clear, Catholic tenant farmers could never forget – let alone forgive – the horrors of the Great Famine, searing memories of which

86 Criminal Law and Procedure (Ireland) Act 1887 (50 & 51 Vict., c. 20).

had mortally wounded the reputation of the landlord class. Several Victorian legal scholars, moreover, argued that ancient Gaelic laws and customs had not only enriched Irish culture but also fostered a system of justice characterized by 'the continued presence of an absence' thereby filling the space with 'popular justice' courts aimed at subverting the existing official or English legal system.[87]

According to Laird, the growth of farmers' mutual aid clubs and tenant-right leagues represented a growing opposition to landlordism and an embrace of the old Brehon code in order to adjudicate land disputes and put on trial those who defied the verdicts of these counter-courts. The new League courts applied supposedly ancient Irish legal practices to challenge English law, bringing into collision two rival forms of justice. Relying on an atavistic faith in Gaelic justice and inventing some convenient 'customs' along the way, these 'peoples' courts' posed a threat to the entire British legal system. In this way militant Land Leaguers hoped to challenge Castle rule and eventually abolish both landlordism and the Act of Union – all in the name of 'the unwritten law of the people'.

These new courts dispensed their own version of justice pertaining to rents, land tenure, improvements, eviction and land-grabbing. Roughly equivalent to the French revolutionary committees of public safety (minus the guillotine), they tried people accused of disobedience. If found guilty, the latter faced punishments ranging from public apologies and fines to boycotting.[88] In short, these 'communal tribunals' kept many locals fearful if not always submissive.[89] In March 1881 Dublin Castle declared such courts illegal and threatened to arrest and prosecute anyone involved in carrying out their orders to boycott or intimidate defendants found guilty. However, not even the stringent Protection of Persons and Property (Ireland) Act 1881[90] could suppress this challenge to official law and order. By October 1881, when

87 In *Subversive law*, esp. pp 13–24 and 103–7, Laird explores 'the extent to which the various practices and institutions that are incorporated within this category mimicked, paralleled, appropriated, parodied, subverted and displaced official law in Ireland'.

88 See D. Jordan, 'The Irish National League and the "unwritten law": rural protest and nation building in Ireland, 1882–1890', *Past & Present* 158 (Feb. 1998), 146, esp. 148–69.

89 S. Ball, *Policing the Irish land war: official responses to political protest and agrarian crime, 1879–91* (London, 2000), pp 222–32 and 246–50. There is one aspect of so-called popular justice that has eluded historians owing to its rarity and lack of documentation – namely, the seigneurial or manorial jurisdiction. On a small minority of estates, where the tenants trusted or approved of their landlord, the latter would hold a weekly ad hoc court to hear the alleged wrongs or problems of his tenants. The petitioner would state his or her case and the proprietor would then render his verdict – whether enforceable or not. Evidently every Saturday morning the widely revered owner of the Borris estate in Co. Carlow, Walter MacMurrough Kavanagh, who defied his father and converted to Home Rule, serving as a rural county councillor until his death in 1922, would sit under a big tree in the courtyard of his demesne, listen to the litigants and then render his verdict in such disputes. (Personal information from the late Mrs MacAlpine Downey, July 1969.)

90 44 & 45 Vict., c. 4.

the Land League was outlawed, Dublin Castle had recorded over one thousand cases of boycotting. And by 1890 hundreds of National League courts were flourishing across the country.[91] More to the point, this populist movement did not fade away. After 1898, organizations like the United Irish League, Sinn Féin and the Dáil sponsored their own courts to dispense what they saw as popular or Gaelic justice.

CONCLUSION

Foucault's concept of Power/Knowledge coupled with Laird's arguments about the 'subversive' nature of the League courts help considerably to explain the origins and dynamic of the land war. As we have noted, the founding of the Land League marked the culmination of long-standing grievances arising from the rent nexus and all those strict leasing contracts. Given the painful memories of the Great Famine and the growing dissatisfaction of those who survived that ordeal during the depression of the late 1870s, some kind of overt conflict between tenants and landlords and their allies was bound to occur.

Predictably, hardly any Big House owners shared Parnell's willingness to allow the state to interfere in the supposedly sacred rights of property – especially when it came to determining the rent. As a result they balked at the tenants' growing demand after 1880 for estate-wide rent abatements regardless of individual need.

Any significant reductions were bound to injure the landed elite's privileged way of life. Their refusal to grant voluntary abatements of more than five or ten percent gave the League's propaganda campaign all the more reason to proclaim the radical message that the land really belonged to the people. Invoking the cherished Brehon legal code, as Laird makes clear, a growing number of farmers, smallholders and labourers followed Davitt in condemning a system that allowed seven thousand scions of the Ascendancy to reap most of the profit from the toil of tens of thousands of tenants. If middle-class or strong farmers and their urban allies formed the spearhead of this growing revolt, they could not have prevailed without the support of countless poor small holders in the West.[92]

91 According to Captain Owen Slacke, divisional magistrate for the South-East, the number of League courts in his region alone grew from 165 in 1885 to 221 in 1886. See his testimony to the Parnell Commission on 24 Jan. 1888, *Report of the special commission,* vol. ii. See also Jordan, '"Unwritten" law', 159–68 and Ball, *Policing*, pp 246–50.

92 See Bew, *National question,* pp 55, 94 and Orridge, 'Who supported the land war?', 203–33. This could serve as an antidote to Clark's dismissal of tenant discontent as a cause of the land war. See also F. Lane, 'Benjamin Pelin, the knights of the plough and social radicalism, 1852–1934' in Casey, *Defying the law,* pp 176–200.

To his lasting credit Gladstone realized that most Irish Catholics had never fully 'embraced the idea of the occupation of land by contract'. And he designed his historic Land Acts of 1870 and 1881 as the best way to recognize 'the old Irish notion that some interest in the soil adheres to the tenant'.[93] If landlord P/K dwindled substantially after 1879, the owners of Big Houses still retained enough money and political clout to hold on to their estates until such time as the government could sweeten the terms of sale to their satisfaction. In addition, they had not lost all their power to evict despite all the adverse publicity.[94] On the other hand, the Land and National Leagues embodied 'a widespread refusal to recognize the absolute property rights of the landlord class'.[95] Drawing on a galaxy of gifted politicians – both national and local – the rebellious tenantry began to take legal matters into their own hands and even risked eviction in their efforts to abolish landlordism as well as the Act of Union by non-violent means.

Long after the land wars had ended, a retired Indian civil servant from Ennis summed up the historic conflict between landlords and tenants:

> The Irish Land League was founded for the protection of the Irish tenant against the rapacity of the Irish landlord. That such protection in particular cases was needed is indubitable … I think myself that there were landlords in Ireland who might have been shot to the great advantage of society. But not all landlords were bad; and the League warred alike on the just and the unjust … Landlord and tenant throughout the last half of the nineteenth century faced each other in a mood of embittered disgruntlement; and to the bitterness of both there contributed causes over which neither had control. Such causes were the working of economic processes, and the bungling, doubtless well-meaning bungling, of the English legislature.[96]

Ironically, a scathing criticism of the landlord class came from a member of the old Catholic gentry, William J. O'Neill Daunt, who had championed Repeal while serving as MP for Mallow. This moderate and thoughtful Home Ruler not only deplored the tactics and personnel of the Land League but also condemned the inequities of landlordism. Writing to his learned Liberal Unionist friend, the eminent historian W.E.H. Lecky, in September 1880, he declared:

93 Quoted by Laird in *Subversive law*, p. 106.

94 For one more example of that authority we find the earl of Charlemont instructing the agent on his Armagh estate in 1880 to threaten the Patterson family with eviction: 'I will not have the one widow and two young families there, so notice them at the proper time and let their claims go to the land sessions. I am sorry to do this but it must be. They have been bad to the land and no use to me beyond the rent.' Lord Charlemont to H. Boyle, 7 Jan. 1880, PRONI D266/367/1, 21 B.

95 Laird, *Subversive law*, p. 103.

96 J. Chartres Molony, *The riddle of the Irish* (London, 1927), pp 191–3.

> The present deplorable condition of matters is the fault of the atrocious landlords who have mercilessly scourged the unfortunate people by intolerable rents and capricious evictions. They confiscated the improvements effected by peasant-industry and they held aloof from, or actively opposed, the just and moderate demand for fixity of tenure and fair rents, as well as our most righteous demand for the restitution of the Irish parliament. By their greed, their cruelty and their degrading West Britonism they left the field open for such men as the present fraternity of anti-landlord agitators. They deserted the post they should have occupied as Irishmen, and it was accordingly seized upon by unprincipled spouters, whose wild and mischievous extravagance finds favour with multitudes who are maddened by a real undeniable grievance.[97]

In sum, the land war emerged out of a growing conflict between two worlds, two antithetical interests, two ways of looking at the world, two opposing concepts of justice, and of course two distinct religious cultures. The gifted comic artist John Fergus O'Hea captured this binary opposition brilliantly in his cartoon, 'Two Christmas Hearths', in the *Weekly Freeman* of 18 December 1886, wherein a shivering and wounded tenant farmer huddles with his family inside the ruins of their evicted hovel, staring across a frozen field at the Big House all aglow with Yuletide cheer (Plate 6.3).

As the Plan of Campaign faded away, the number of evictions fell rapidly; and by 1908 roughly one-third of the 5,700 registered evicted tenants had been reinstated under government auspices.[98] Beginning with the Ashbourne Act of 1885,[99] the subsequent land purchase measures culminated in the transforming Acts of 1903 and 1909[100] that taken together enabled well over 200,000 occupiers to buy their holdings by paying an annuity below the old rent to the British treasury – thereby eliminating the traditional rent nexus and reducing rural landlordism to a near nullity. Within twenty years the majority of tenant farmers outside north-east Ulster, sustained in large part by the Land League and its allies during the 1880s, had reached the promised land of peasant proprietorship in a bloodless revolution. In addition, twenty-six of Ireland's counties would win political independence from Westminster secured by a parliamentary system, if at a steep price in lives lost and property destroyed. Neither of these remarkable achievements could have been realized without the Irish National Land League, the *locus classicus* of tenant or subaltern Power/Knowledge.

97 W.J. O'Neill Daunt to W.E.H. Lecky, 21 Sept. 1880, TCD, Lecky papers, MS No. 203. See also D. McCartney, *W.E.H. Lecky: historian and politician, 1838–1903* (Dublin, 1994), esp. pp 95–9.

98 Laird, *Subversive law*, p. 103.

99 *Purchase of Land (Ireland) Act 1885* (48 & 49 Vict., c. 73).

100 Land Purchase (Ireland) Act 1903 (3 Ed. VII, c. 37); Irish Land Act, 1909 (9 Ed. VII, c. 42).

Parnell and the law

PAUL BEW*

Charles Stewart Parnell emerged in the mid-1870s as one of a new breed of non-deferential Irish nationalist politicians. He was impressed by the victory of the dying revolutionary John Mitchel at the polls in the 1870s. Soon after, Parnell won a seat in Meath. In this early phase, Parnell was always respectful to the militants of the Fenian movement who had launched a chaotic insurrection but whose members remained energetically involved in nationalist politics. Parnell never actually committed himself to Fenian strategies, but many observers believed that he had indeed done so.

It is possible to construct a picture of Parnell in which he is a scrupulous defender of legality. If the dynamics of the Irish land war of 1879–82 are properly analysed, we can see that the main, specifically novel, Parnellite elements of strategy were to exploit the limits of the law. But, of course, this interpretation requires some argument and evidence in its defence.

There are those accounts (often generally unsympathetic to the agitation) which emphasize the role of violent intimidation of landlords, landlord's agents and peasants who opposed the Land League's will. We are presented with a catalogue of shootings, mutilations and burnings. The role of agrarian violence (and its relationship to the progress of parliamentary nationalism) has been seen as one of the key suppressed problems in nationalist historiography. All that may be said here on this topic is that violent intimidation was, of course, a significant component of the peasant struggle. However, on its own in the pre-Land League period it had never achieved more than relatively limited success, and in the 1879–82 period itself murderous violence greatly increased in significance *after* the suppression of the League – in other words, in the absence of the characteristic Land League forms of struggle.

To modify the role of illegal violence in this way requires some elaboration. In 1879 and early 1880, the Land League paid for many legal interventions in the Connacht law courts, exploiting protections for the small tenants that had been on the statute book but lain dormant since 1870. In 1880 the Land League is famous for giving the word 'boycott' to the world after an unpopular land agent, Captain Boycott. Parnell himself used the term 'shun', not

* The original version of this chapter was delivered to the Irish Legal History Society at the Ulster Museum on 21 Feb. 2014.

'boycott', for those who failed to respect the peoples' will. By the end of the 1880s, it should be noted that Gladstone regarded the 'boycott' as equivalent to 'exclusive dealing' and thus entirely legal.

There is no doubt that the boycott did play a significant role, particularly as one of the methods of isolating backsliding tenants. In a more general sense the refusal to provide police with cars and other such actions are obviously part of the boycott tactic. But the 'boycott system', in so far as it operated in the main sense used by historians, appears to presuppose a landlord attack of some sort to which it is a response. To this extent it has fitted neatly with the traditional conception of the Land League as a *defensive* movement. This view is exemplified by Máire and Conor Cruise O'Brien in their *A concise history of Ireland*:

> Its policy was to select estates especially notorious for rack-renting and eviction; concentrate public attention on those estates by means of mass meetings; and then by pressure of social ostracism and refusal of services render a life as difficult as possible for the landlord (if resident), and especially for grabbers – those who rented land from which the tenant had been evicted and which the League had placed under a ban.[1]

In fact, the Land League was something very different: an *offensive* movement. During the crucial period of the Land League's offensive advance in 1880, the boycott played a minimal role in large areas of the country. It could only have played a larger role if there had been more evictions than the peasantry in many key areas were prepared to tolerate. It is impossible to estimate with total accuracy the role of the boycott, as we cannot know how many landlords were deterred from eviction or sale of an interest by its existence. Nevertheless, there is one significant fact to be noted. Despite its prominence in the rhetoric of this period – W.E. Forster was mesmerized by it – Bernard Becker, the journalist who had done most to bring the boycott to popular attention, was at the end of 1880 regarding it merely as a novelty whose full limitations were just beginning to appear.[2]

In reality, the *dominant* strategy was one that the textbook accounts have almost entirely omitted. It is now long overdue that its importance should be stressed. This strategy was denoted by the slogan 'rent at the point of the bayonet'. What this meant was that the peasantry delayed the payment of rent until the last possible moment, then paid the rent while the Land League defrayed the often hefty legal costs incurred by the delay. It is an incidental but important fact that it was here, rather than in financing outrage, where the

1 M. Cruise O'Brien and C. Cruise O'Brien, *A concise history of Ireland* (London, 1972), pp 190–10.
2 B.H. Becker, *Disturbed Ireland: being the letters written during the winter of 1880–81* (London, 1881), p. 326.

Land League's Irish-American dollars found their most significant use. The theory of massive League sponsorship of outrage first received widespread currency as a result of the obsessions of the Special Commission in 1888.[3] The low-risk nature of the strategy was, of course, objectively in the interests of the more substantial tenantry. But this very fact, plus also the high financial cost for the organization, made it unpopular with sections of the poorer tenantry and the agricultural proletariat. It is the conflict around the validity and political nature of this policy which, in conjunction with the better-known coercion-concession dialectic, punctuated the rhythm of the land war in the crucial period from February to October 1881.

At the end of May 1881 Anna Parnell went to Mayo to reassure the small farmers of the West that the rich farmers of Meath, Limerick and Cork were now prepared to fight 'your battles for you, it is not all left on your shoulders now'.[4] But was she sure? She noted the collapse of Col. Tottenham's tenants in Wexford in June 1881,[5] and even more dramatically senior Land Leaguer Andrew Kettle's surrender the same month with the full 'decorum of the law' preserved.[6] As late as July 1881, Anna Parnell publicly supported Land League methods, including rent at the point of a bayonet. 'I can only suppose', she wrote later, 'that I was wilfully shutting my eyes to the evidence before me, and refusing to see because I did not want to see.'[7] As the League spread across the country, it was clear that areas where larger farmers dominated were quite prepared to join the Land League alongside the small holders of the West. But it was also clear that they felt they had a lot to lose. They were exceptionally reluctant to be evicted just to be part of a process exercising pressure on the British government and the landlord class. They were prepared to engage in protracted legalistic conflicts. In particular, they were prepared to do so if the lawyers involved were paid, as they were, with Irish-American dollars. But the provisions of the law that might be exploited for the benefit of farmers mainly were limited to the rights of smallholders. In short, Ireland's middle and strong farmers already had a substantial effective property in their farms and the Land Act was clearly intended to enhance that property.

This was the crux for a revolutionary like John Dillon: how did he hold the bulk of the Irish farmers to a revolutionary line in such a context? On 12 July, Dillon wrote frankly to William O'Brien about the differences within the Land League executive on this very question. The militant wing of the Land

3 Established by the Special Commission Act 1888 (51 & 52 Vict., c. 35) to inquire into the charges made by the London *Times* newspaper against Parnell in a series of articles entitled 'Parnellism and crime'.

4 *Nation*, 28 May 1881; D. Jordan, *Land and popular politics in Ireland: County Mayo from the plantation to the land war* (Cambridge, 1994), pp 302–3.

5 *Wexford People*, 25 June 1881.

6 *Dublin Daily Express*, 20 June 1881.

7 J. McL. Côté, *Fanny and Anna Parnell: Ireland's patriot sisters* (Dublin, 1991), p. 181.

League executive – Dillon, Egan, Brennan and Davitt – were in serious disagreement with Parnell and the parliamentary section of the executive:

> I am not quite clear as to what course I shall take when I am set at liberty. But I am quite clear that I cannot allow the people to suppose that the course adopted by the Parliamentary Party towards the Land Bill is satisfactory … It is not unlikely that I shall retire from politics.[8]

O'Brien later said that John Dillon was now 'at the heart of the semi-revolt of the "Kilmainham" Party in 1881 against Parnell for even his very qualified dependence upon the Westminster parliament'.[9] O'Brien added:

> Mr Dillon was simply influenced by that lack of imaginative insight, which is the principal element of greatness wanting in his character, and which led him habitually to view any new line of action, in the constantly shifting circumstances of the Irish movement, with a suspiciousness, an indecision, a certain revolutionary Toryism of mind, which fails to perceive that old 'methods' cannot always continue to be the most effective ones.[10]

Parnell and Dillon were both interned in the autumn of 1881 and held in prison until May 1882. They issued a 'No Rent Manifesto' which Parnell (the moderate) was enthusiastic to sign and Dillon (the revolutionary) very reluctant. As Parnell's sister pointed out, the manifesto was sure to fail and it simultaneously rescued the League leadership from the heavy financial expenses of 'Rent at the point of the bayonet'.

After the 'Kilmainham treaty' with the UK government in 1882, Parnell broke with all forms of illegality. He ceased to walk, as his first great biographer Barry O'Brien put it, on 'the edge of treason felony'. He ceased to flirt with Irish withdrawal from the UK parliament. Parliament instead became the centre of Irish strategy. He no longer spoke of Fenianism as a world of high-souled patriots – rather, as he told Henry Labouchere, that it was a world of 'assassinations' and 'outrages'. When John Dillon attempted to revive agrarian agitation – the Plan of Campaign – in the late 1880s, Parnell told his lawyer Frank Lockwood that he was totally opposed to it as it alienated moderate Tories. Then when the efforts of the government and the *Times* to criminalize an entire popular movement failed spectacularly – with the demonstration that it had relied in Parnell's case on forged evidence – Parnell, in legal terms, at least remained entirely fragrant.

8 W. O'Brien, *Recollections* (London, 1905), pp 304–5.
9 W. O'Brien, *The Parnell of real life* (London, 1926), pp 71–2.
10 O'Brien, *Recollections*, p. 305.

But this discourse, while true, is not the whole truth. As Parnell admitted to the Special Commission, he had known that he led a movement which was likely to involve violent crime. When interned in 1881–2, he was well aware that the shadowy underground of Irish nationalism intended – as a form of revenge for internment – to attack the lives of senior British officials. When released from prison, as is well documented, Parnell wanted immediately to reach out to men of violence like Patrick Sheridan and Patrick Egan. The purpose was to assure them he had not sold out to gain his release and encourage them to remain loyal to the leadership. But he may, as Maume pointed out in *Irish Historical Studies* in 1995, have offered to take some sort of secret society oath as a confidence-building measure for the revolutionaries.[11] Shortly thereafter, the appalling Phoenix Park murders – the most dramatic political crime of the nineteenth century in the UK – took place. Parnell always remained fearful that Sheridan possessed *kompromat* on him and was capable of gossiping on the subject, as Sheridan certainly did. Parnell was particularly worried when the English press reported that Sheridan, for a price, was prepared to give evidence to the Special Commission in 1889. He was greatly relieved when this did not actually happen.

So which Parnell does the high legalist choose? The truth is Parnell was essentially a constitutional politician. But Barry O'Brien was also right: he had walked from time to the edge of 'treason felony'.

11 P. Maume, 'Parnell and the I.R.B. oath', *IHS*, 29:115 (May 1995), 363.

Investigating Jack the Ripper and Parnellite crime: Sir Robert Anderson and the writing of history

PATRICK GEOGHEGAN*

In the early hours of Friday, 31 August 1888, the body of Mary Anne ('Polly') Nichols was discovered on Buck's Row in Whitechapel in the East End of London. Her throat had been slashed and her body repeatedly stabbed.[1] Although she was the third woman to have been murdered in Whitechapel that year, because of the way she was killed she is considered by experts to be the first canonical victim of Jack the Ripper.[2] Later the same day, Robert Anderson was appointed head of CID – the criminal investigation department – at Scotland Yard, and found himself in charge of the investigation. Anderson would later write two volumes of memoirs about his involvement in the events of this period, including the Ripper investigation as well as previously unknown covert activities, and the most dramatic revelations were serialized in *Blackwood's Magazine* in 1910.[3]

One throwaway admission in an article in *Blackwood's* in April 1910 horrified the government of the day and caused a major political scandal. Anderson revealed that he was the author of the 'Parnellism and crime' articles in the *Times* in 1887, which attempted to link Parnell to violence and illegal activities. In the House of Commons, the prime minister, Asquith, attacked the publication as 'a gross breach of official confidence' and Anderson was forced to backtrack and downplay his involvement.[4] A year later, a new Official Secrets Act was passed making this kind of disclosure a

* This chapter is a slightly revised version of the presidential discourse to the Irish Legal History Society delivered in Belfast on 26 Nov. 2021.

1 H. Rubenhold, *The five: the untold lives of the women killed by Jack the Ripper* (London, 2019), p. 5.

2 There is a vast Ripper literature of varying degrees of quality. For a good introduction, see R. Davenport-Hines, 'Jack the Ripper' in *Oxford DNB*. See also P. Sugden, *The complete history of Jack the Ripper* (London, 1995) and D. Rumbelow, *The complete Jack the Ripper* (London, 1975).

3 R. Anderson, *Sidelights on the Home Rule movement* (London, 1907); R. Anderson, *The lighter side of my official life* (London, 1910); and *Blackwood's Magazine*, 187:1133 (Mar. 1910) and throughout the year.

4 *Hansard's Parl. deb., 5th series* (Commons), vol. 16, col. 893 (11 Apr. 1910).

criminal offence.[5] This chapter explores the reliability of Anderson's memoirs and their value as a historical source, and makes the case that they provide a startling new perspective on some of the most dramatic events of the 1880s – namely, the attempts to destroy the reputation of Parnell and the Whitechapel murders.

Born in Dublin in 1841, Robert Anderson was the son of the crown solicitor for Dublin, Matthew Anderson. His father was from Londonderry and Robert was proud to describe his ancestors as being 'among the Scotch colonists who made Ulster what it is'.[6] A Presbyterian, Robert Anderson was educated at Trinity College Dublin, and then entered the King's Inns, and was called to the bar. Later, he returned to Trinity and graduated with a doctorate in law.

In his two volumes of memoirs Anderson spends some time reminiscing about his student days, and especially his involvement in the College Historical Society, which he identified as 'the first and chiefest' of all the clubs and societies in Trinity.[7] Anderson took great pride in the fact that he was 'elected auditor (or president) of the society' in 1864, suggesting that it taught him the valuable lesson 'that a man can do what he makes up his mind to do'. Crediting 'any little capacity I possess for public speaking' to the experience he gained there, he believed that the great strength of Trinity in general, and the debating society in particular, was that everyone met 'on perfectly even terms, and learned not only to hear, but to respect opinions'.[8]

The nostalgic reminiscences are a good example of the Anderson style: self-regarding, self-promoting, and deliberately omitting anything that might undercut the narrative he was presenting. For example, Anderson neglects to mention that after his election he rarely turned up for meetings, and the society was forced to introduce a rule change requiring the auditor to attend at least two-thirds of events or relinquish the post.[9]

Instead of pursuing a career as a barrister, Anderson suddenly found himself involved in secret service work in 1865 when his father began showing him confidential documents on the Fenians. Anderson made himself an expert on the subject, and the following year the chief secretary, Lord Mayo, asked him to prepare a report on Fenian activities. This was the start of his involvement in intelligence work. Following the failed rising in 1867 and the attempted rescue of the prisoners at Manchester, he was asked to come to London, where he was attached to the Home Office as an 'adviser in matters

5 Official Secrets Act 1911 (1 & 2 Geo. V, c. 28).
6 B. Porter, 'Sir Robert Anderson' in *Oxford DNB*.
7 Anderson, *Lighter side*, p. 6.
8 Ibid., pp 4–5.
9 P. Geoghegan, *Oratory and debate: the College Historical Society, 1770–2020* (Dublin, 2020), p. 130.

relating to political crime'.[10] To justify his salary, he was also made secretary to various government enquiries, and he was appointed to the Prison Commission on its establishment in 1877.[11] His effectiveness as a counter-intelligence operative was questioned by some, but in 1887 he was appointed to work with James Monro, the head of the CID who was also in charge of intelligence work, on various secret service matters, also described as political matters to do with policing.

Monro resigned as head of the CID in 1888, and Anderson was chosen to succeed him, taking office on the day of the first Whitechapel murder. He was chosen not because of his detective skills but because of his political experience, and he was tasked with helping to make the case against Parnell at the Special Commission.

In the second volume of his memoirs, *The lighter side of my official life*, published in 1910 (the title itself fairly insensitive given some of the subject matter), Anderson made three distinct claims about the Whitechapel murders. The first was that it was as a direct result of the measures that he had taken that the killing spree was brought to an end. The second was that he and the police, in the course of its investigations, had discovered the identity of the murderer but had been unable to bring him to justice because of a conspiracy of silence and because British law was too concerned with a presumption of innocence. The third claim was that the correspondence from Jack the Ripper – which was published at the time – and which gave the murderer the name by which he is known throughout the world – was a hoax, the work of an unscrupulous journalist, out to sensationalize the crimes. If Anderson was correct, then 'Jack the Ripper' is a name the murderer never called himself and was purely a media invention.

Due to the significant role he played in charge of Scotland Yard throughout the course of the investigation, Anderson features prominently in the work of Ripperologists. Some believe he would not 'have lied on moral and ethical grounds as he was a devoutly religious man who believed in the second coming of Christ and wrote many theological books in his lifetime'.[12] One Ripperologist even calls him 'God's Detective'.[13] Others are more sceptical about his claims, and there continues to be huge interest in his life and work.

Anderson's writings on the Ripper investigation have certain distinct features. At every point he vindicates his own actions, while settling scores and criticizing the mistakes of others. Occasionally insightful, often prejudiced,

10 Porter, 'Sir Robert Anderson'.

11 Prisons Act 1877 (40 & 41 Vict., c. 21).

12 See, e.g., the description on the Jack the Ripper Casebook website, one of the most significant online resources, https://thejacktherippertour.com/casebook/police-investigation/robert-anderson/.

13 D.R. Stoke, 'Sir Robert Anderson' in *Baptist Bible Tribune* https://www.tribune.org/gods-detective/.

sometimes brilliant, always self-serving, Anderson was not afraid to embellish, and sometimes even to fabricate. Throughout he declines responsibility for anything that went wrong, while claiming credit for everything positive, and all the time teasing that he could say more – that he knows more – but unfortunately cannot. His writings are of a type familiar to us today, when we are used to seeing people who once occupied positions of influence, spending their time burnishing their own reputations at the expense of others.

Anderson's writings reveal him to be a reactionary with all of the prejudices and narrow beliefs of his time. From the outset he was unsympathetic to the victims, dismissing them as 'belonging to a very small class of degraded women who frequent the East End streets after midnight, in hope of inveigling belated drunkards, or men as degraded as themselves'.[14]

The first of many mistakes Anderson made over the course of the investigation was at the very start when he decided to go on a four-month holiday, claiming ill health and nervous exhaustion, and quoting his Harley Street doctor in support. The home secretary, Henry Matthews, refused to sign off on this, but Anderson was adamant that he could not take up his duties until he had at least a month's holiday in Switzerland. And so, on 8 September, Anderson left London, the same day that Annie Chapman was brutally murdered at Hanbury Street, becoming the second victim of the Whitechapel murderer. The absence of Anderson was soon noted by the press, and he was criticized for leaving the CID without leadership at a critical time. As the *Pall Mall Gazette* complained: 'The chief official who is responsible for the detection of the murderer is as invisible to Londoners as the murderer himself. You may seek Dr Anderson in Scotland Yard, you may look for him in Whitehall Place, but you will not find him.'[15]

The home secretary became increasingly frustrated as public hysteria grew and instructed Anderson to spend the final week of his leave in Paris so he could work remotely and keep in touch with the investigation back in London. Anderson arrived in Paris on 30 September 1888, just as news was breaking that the bodies of third and fourth victims had been found. Elizabeth Stride and Catherine Eddowes had both been murdered in Whitechapel within an hour of each other. That was it for the home secretary, and he sent a telegram to Anderson requesting his immediate return to London.[16]

During Anderson's absence the decision was taken to publish correspondence by someone alleging to be the murderer, creating the legend of 'Jack the Ripper'. Up to then, the press had given the murderer a number of names, including 'the Whitechapel Murderer', 'Leather Apron' and the 'Red Fiend'. On 27 September a letter was received by the Central News Agency in London, a news distribution service similar to Reuters and the

14 Anderson, *Lighter side*, p. 136.
15 Quoted in P. Sugden, *The complete history of Jack the Ripper* (London, 1994), p. 103.
16 Anderson, *Lighter side*, p. 135.

Press Association, written in red ink which began with the salutation, 'Dear Boss', and which was signed 'Jack the Ripper'.[17] The author boasted that he was 'down on whores and I shant [*sic*] quit ripping them till I do get buckled. Grand work the last job was. I gave the lady no time to squeal.'[18] Promising that they would hear more of his 'funny little games', he claimed to have kept some of his victims' blood to use as ink, but it got too thick, so '[r]ed ink is fit enough I hope ha'.

The author claimed that in his next job he would 'clip the ladys [*sic*] ears off and send to the police officers just for jolly wouldn't you' and he advised them to '[k]eep this letter back till I do a bit more work, then give it out straight'. The letter concluded: 'My knife's so nice and sharp I want to get to work right away if I get a chance. Good Luck. Yours truly Jack the Ripper.'

On 29 September the letter was passed on to the metropolitan police, who dismissed it as a hoax, but they were forced to re-examine it following the discovery of the bodies of Elizabeth Stride and Catherine Eddowes, especially as the ear-lobes of Eddowes had been mutilated. The letter was released to the press the next day and appeared in some publications such as the *Daily News* on the morning of Monday, 1 October. A second piece of correspondence, in similar handwriting, was received by the Central News Agency, that same day. It was a postcard, also written in red ink, and it read:

> I was not codding dear old Boss when I gave you the tip, you'll hear about Saucy Jacky's work tomorrow double event this time number one squealed a bit couldn't finish straight off had not the time to get ears for police. thanks for keeping last letter back till I got to work again.
>
> Signed 'Jack the Ripper'

The postcard was handed over to the police and was also cleared for publication and facsimiles of the letter and the postcard were put up in police stations across London. The publicity had the effect of creating a widespread hysteria, and in the days and weeks ahead over two hundred letters claiming to be from the murderer were sent to the police and to various news organizations. In the *Freeman's Journal* and the *Belfast News Letter*, as well as newspapers around the world, we see the name 'Jack the Ripper' beginning to appear, and it became synonymous with the murders in the public mind as a dark legend was created.[19]

Anderson was almost certainly correct that the 'Dear Boss' correspondence was a hoax, and this was also the view of the police at the time. Charles Warren, the commissioner of police, informed the Home Office on 10 October that he believed 'the whole thing a hoax' before adding 'but of course

17 For the full text and a detailed account see www.jack-the-ripper.org/dear-boss.htm.

18 Ibid.

19 *Freeman's Journal*, 8 Oct. 1888; *Belfast News Letter*, 9 Oct. 1888.

we are bound to try and ascertain the writer in any case'.[20] There are many reasons for believing that Anderson and the police were correct in their analysis. While it was possible the murderer may have written letters to taunt the authorities, it is suspicious that he decided to write to the Central News Agency, rather than to the police directly, or one of the major newspapers of the time, such as the *Times* or *Daily Telegraph,* or even to any of the more popularist morning or evening newspapers. The Central News Agency received massive publicity from being the recipient of the correspondence, and the other agencies were obliged to credit and reference them.

Suspicion has fallen on two main suspects, the first a journalist at the *Star,* Fred Best. Indeed Best is alleged to have confessed to co-authorship of the correspondence in 1931, but there are problems with this claim, including the fact that it was not made public until 1966 when Best was safely dead.[21]

The person Anderson suspected was Thomas Bulling, a journalist with the Central News Agency. John George Littlechild was the head of special branch in 1888 and he named Bulling as the chief suspect in a letter in 1913. Describing the correspondence as 'a smart piece of journalistic work', Littlechild revealed that it 'was generally believed at the Yard that Tom Bullen [*sic*] of the Central News was the originator'.[22] Anderson revealed in 1910 that: 'the "Jack the Ripper" letter which is preserved in the police museum at New Scotland Yard is the creation of an enterprising London journalist'.[23] He claimed he knew the identity of 'the pressman who wrote the letter', but did not reveal it as he believed 'no public benefit would result from such a course' and it would damage the reputation of the police force.

It was noted at the time by the perceptive journalist and playwright, George R. Sims, how curious it was 'that this maniac makes his communication to an agency which serves the entire press'.[24] He believed it revealed such a detailed knowledge of the working of the media that the author of the correspondence was either a journalist perpetrating a hoax, or that the murderer himself was a journalist or editor. It was indeed strange that the author knew enough to send it to a press agency, but not enough to send it to one with a more credible reputation, such as the Press Association or Reuters.

One historian has noted how the Central News Agency had a reputation among newsmen for 'underhand practices and stories of dubious veracity'.[25] In 2019 Andrea Nini, a lecturer in linguistics and English language at the

20 S.P. Evans and K. Skinner, *Jack the Ripper: letters from hell* (London, 2001), p. 43.

21 See the analysis on the Ripper casebook website, https://wiki.casebook.org/frederick_best.html.

22 K. Skinner and S. Evans, *The ultimate Jack the Ripper sourcebook* (London, 2013), p. 43.

23 Anderson, *Lighter side,* p. 138.

24 Evans and Skinner, *Jack the Ripper,* p. 52.

25 P. Begg, *Jack the Ripper: the definite history* (London, 2003), pp 219–22.

University of Manchester, analysed the correspondence and concluded that if it were written by a journalist, it was 'probably the most successful case of fake news in history'.[26]

Bulling was forty-one years old in 1888 and an alcoholic. As Littlechild later remembered, '[p]oor Bullen [*sic*] occasionally took too much to drink, and I fail to see how he could help it knocking about so many hours and seeking favours from so many people to procure copy'.[27] A popular but probably apocryphal story is that he lost his job in 1898 following the death of Otto von Bismarck, when he sent a telegram to his office announcing the news with the message 'Bloody Bismarck is dead', and was fired as a result.[28]

Evidence that the correspondence was a hoax, and that Bulling was directly involved, can be seen from the third and final item in the correspondence, what is known as the 'Moab and Midian' letter. This was a letter addressed to the Central News Agency dated 5 October, and it was sent to Scotland Yard by Bulling, but this time he only passed on the original envelope and instead gave them his own handwritten copy of the letter. The reason for this was never explained and the original has never been found. This letter included biblical quotes, and even more exaggerated taunts such as, 'I must get to work tomorrow treble event this time yes yes three must be ripped. will send you a bit of face by post I promise this dear old Boss.'[29] By this time the police had come to realize what a mistake it had been to publish the original correspondence and, believing the letters to be a hoax, they requested that it was not published. There were no murders the next day, never mind the promised 'treble event'. Because the letter was never made public at the time, it is not as well known and the credibility of the first two pieces of correspondence was not challenged.

In his book *Life and death at the Old Bailey,* published in 1935, Thurston Hopkins wrote that he believed that the letters were a hoax, and thought that if the handwriting had been identified 'it would have led to the arrest of a harmless Fleet Street journalist'.[30] The figure described closely resembles Bulling, who was reported as having a breakdown and becoming 'a whimsical figure in Fleet Street, only befriended by the staff of newspapers and printing works. He would creep about the dark courts waving his hands furiously in the air' and shouting 'Ha ha ha'. To anyone who would listen he would tell them the 'inner story' of the Whitechapel murders and '[m]any old Fleet Streeters had very shrewd suspicions that this irresponsible fellow wrote the famous Jack the Ripper letter'.

26 https://blog.oup.com/2019/10/journalist-created-jack-the-ripper/.
27 J.G. Littlechild to G.R. Sims, 23 Sept. 1913 (www.casebook.org/official_documents/lcletter.html).
28 A. Cook, *Jack the Ripper,* p. 97.
29 D.C. Gibson, *Jack the writer: a verbal and visual analysis of the Ripper correspondence* (London, 2013), p. 49.
30 R. Thurston Hopkins, *Life and death at the Old Bailey* (London, 1935).

It was in this feverish atmosphere that Anderson returned to London, with, as he described it, 'the Jack the Ripper scare in full swing'.[31] Anderson believed the whole country was overacting, suggesting that 'when the stolid English go in for a scare they take leave of all moderation and common sense', remarking that enough nonsense was talked and written about the murders to sink a Dreadnought.

Anderson later described how he devoted his time upon his return 'in reinvestigating the whole case' and was soon brought before the home secretary and the chief commissioner of police, Charles Warren. 'We hold you responsible to find the murderer' was the blunt message from the home secretary, prompting Anderson to decline responsibility for making a successful arrest. He put the blame on the existing police policy towards prostitutes, calling it 'wholly indefensible and scandalous', because he believed that 'these wretched women were plying their trade under definite police protection'.[32]

Without naming him, Anderson was criticizing the police commissioner, Charles Warren, who a year earlier had instructed the police not to arrest street walkers unless there was a public complaint.[33] This followed the failed prosecution of a respectable young woman, Elizabeth Cass, who had been arrested for soliciting, and there had been much embarrassment when the case collapsed. Arrests of sex workers declined dramatically, and the police largely ignored the open soliciting that took place in parts of London such as Whitechapel. Warren resigned as police commissioner on 8 November 1888, not because of the murders but rather because of a controversy over his concerns about the independence of the CID, and was replaced by Anderson's former boss, James Monro.

Anderson's preferred solution was to instruct the police to arrest every known prostitute found on the streets after midnight. This, however, was rejected as being 'too drastic'.[34] His alternative policy was to have the police issue a warning that 'street women' out late at night would not be protected by the police. Anderson's own belief was that the murderer was 'a sexual maniac of a virulent type' and 'that he was living in the immediate vicinity of the scenes of the murders'.[35]

The fifth murder – and what is considered the final canonical murder – of Jack the Ripper took place at Miller's Court on 9 November, and Anderson gloated that 'the circumstances of that crime disposed of all the theories of the amateur "Sherlock Holmeses" of that date'.[36] This was the murder of Mary Kelly, who was murdered in her home at Miller's Court. Anderson boasted

31 Anderson, *Lighter side*, p. 135.
32 Ibid., p. 136.
33 P. Stubley, *1888: London murders in the year of the Ripper* (London, 2012), pp 74–5.
34 Anderson, *Lighter side*, p. 136.
35 Ibid., p. 137.
36 Ibid.

that it was his harsh warning that ensured that 'no other street murder occurred in the Jack the Ripper series'.[37]

Because it didn't suit his narrative, especially his claim that he brought the killing spree to an end, Anderson does not mention the other four women who were killed in Whitechapel between December 1888 and February 1891. Rose Mylett's body was discovered on the morning of 20 December 1888 in Clarke's Yard on Poplar High Street in the East End. In his post-mortem examination, Dr Brownfield confirmed the cause of death as strangulation, and gave his expert opinion that she could not have done it herself, and this was supported by three other doctors.[38] Anderson, however, visited the scene himself and insisted that the death had been by natural causes, suggesting that Mylett had accidentally strangled herself while drunk. Dr Thomas Bond, who was assisting Anderson on the Whitechapel murders, was sent to review the scene and he also confirmed his belief that it was foul play. But Anderson refused to accept this and asked him to take a second look at the body, and this time Bond concluded that Mylett had fallen down while drunk and had accidentally choked herself on her stiff velvet collar. At the inquest the jury returned a verdict of 'wilful murder', but the police refused to investigate it any further.

Alice McKenzie was murdered on 17 July 1889 in Castle Alley, Whitechapel, and there was disagreement about whether this was a Ripper killing as the wounds were not as deep and a shorter knife had been used. It was the opinion of Dr Bond that it was the same murderer, but Anderson insisted it was an imitation killing.[39] Part of a woman's body was discovered at Pinchin Street in Whitechapel on 10 September 1889. The rest of the body was not discovered, and the woman was never identified, and the police suggested it was the work of a different serial killer.[40] Frances Coles was murdered on 13 February 1891 and a man called James Sadler was arrested and charged with her killing. However, there was a lack of evidence and he was released. Once again, the murder was not accepted by the police to be the work of the so-called Ripper.

As far as Anderson was concerned, there was no mystery to the identity of the Ripper, and in his 1910 memoir he said he was 'almost tempted to disclose the identity of the murderer'.[41] Exposing his anti-Semitism, Anderson insisted the murderer was a 'low-class Polish Jew', and suggested the only reason he has not been captured was because 'people of that class in the East End will not give up one of their number to Gentile justice'. This was

37 Ibid., p. 136.
38 S. Evans and D. Rumbelow, *Jack the Ripper: Scotland Yard investigates* (London, 2010), pp 245–6.
39 P. Begg and J. Bennett, *Jack the Ripper: the forgotten victims* (London, 2014), pp 177–8.
40 Ibid.
41 Anderson, *Lighter side,* p. 138.

dangerous talk and it was also untrue. There was no evidence at all for the theory, nor for Anderson's extraordinary claim that 'the only person who ever had a good view of the murderer unhesitatingly identified the suspect the instant he was confronted with him; but he refused to give evidence against him'.[42]

Anderson's comments provoked uproar and were criticized in the *Jewish Chronicle* as 'an aspersion upon Jews'.[43] Responding in a letter to the paper, Anderson defended his comments and claimed to have many Jewish friends. Anderson insisted that the term 'Polish Jew' was meant to 'specify race, not religion', and said that it 'would outrage all religious sentiment to talk of a religion of a loathsome creature whose utterly unmentionable vices reduced him to a lower level than that of the brute'.[44] In a follow-up, Anderson was again rebuked, not for saying that he believed the murderer was a Jew, but for claiming that he had been shielded from the police 'so that he could continue his horrible career'.[45] Anderson's belief that the killer was Jewish helped shape the investigation and it has been noted that a disproportionate number of the people questioned by the police over the killings were Jews.[46]

Although he is unnamed in the memoir, it is possible to identify Anderson's chief suspect from various pieces of evidence. In 1895 Major Griffiths, writing under the name Alfred Aylmer, first presented Anderson's theory in print that the murders had been committed by a homicidal maniac, who had then been committed to an insane asylum. Anderson also suggested this in an article published in 1901 and repeated the claim in 1904 and 1907.[47] In the serialized account in *Blackwood's Magazine*, Anderson suggests that the murderer 'had been safely caged in an asylum', though he left this description out of the version in the book.[48]

The name of the suspect was Aaron Kosminski, a Polish-immigrant who worked sporadically as a barber at Whitechapel. Kosminski had serious mental health issues and was briefly placed in a workhouse in 1890 and was forcibly readmitted in February 1891 and then transferred to Colney Hatch lunatic asylum. Chief Inspector Donald Sutherland Swanson co-ordinated the investigation when Anderson was in Switzerland and bought a copy of Anderson's memoir in 1910. On the margin of the page where Anderson considers naming his chief suspect, he wrote 'Kosminski'. While it is possible Kosminski was the killer, there are some problems with the solution, but it

42 Ibid., p. 138.

43 *Jewish Chronicle*, 4 Mar. 1910.

44 Ibid., 11 Mar. 1910; and R.M. Gordon, *Alias Jack the Ripper: beyond the usual Whitechapel suspects* (London, 2001), p. 142.

45 *Jewish Chronicle*, 11 Mar. 1910.

46 H.L. Malchow, *Gothic images of race in nineteenth-century Britain* (Stanford, 1996), p. 164.

47 R. Anderson, 'Our absurd system of punishing crime', *The Nineteenth Century and After*, 49 (Feb. 1901), 268.

48 *Blackwood's Magazine*, 187:1133 (Mar. 1910).

does explain why the killing of women in Whitechapel ended in February 1891.

The reality is that the police did not have just one main suspect, but three, and in the final official report sent to the Home Office it listed them as a Polish Jew who had been incarcerated in a mental asylum (that is, Kosminski); 'a Russian doctor of vile character' called Michael Ostrog; and an English barrister, Montague John Druitt, whose body was discovered in the Thames in December 1888.[49] Some of those who were senior in the investigation were highly critical of Anderson's posturing in 1910, and claimed that 'his statement went beyond established facts'.[50]

Anderson made one final attempt to vindicate his handling of the investigation. In a single sentence he suggested that 'if the police here had powers such as the French police possess, the murderer would have been brought to justice'. This idea was not developed, but it was a complaint Anderson had written about previously, in 1903, in an essay critiquing the fictional detective Sherlock Holmes. Anderson praised the French approach, where suspicion was 'sufficient to justify an arrest', while the 'necessary evidence was obtained at leisure', with the search aided by 'admissions extracted from the accused'. He contrasted this unfavourably with Britain where an accused person had to be brought without delay before a magistrate, and the crime and the grounds of the arrest had to be disclosed. Anderson also regretted that 'a prisoner is most jealously guarded against any attempt to obtain from him admissions to his prejudice'. In other words, it would have been easier to convict someone of the Ripper killings if someone had been arrested without charge, beaten to secure a confession, and then convicted.

While Anderson was almost certainly correct that the Ripper correspondence was a hoax, he bears responsibility for being missing in action when the decision was made to publish the correspondence, thus creating the very Ripper scare he was so quick to criticize. He offers no real evidence that his actions brought the killing spree to an end, and there is also a problem with his timeline. It is only hearsay that Kosminski was ever identified, and there is no evidence at all for the disgraceful claim that Jews in the East End knew who the killer was and refused to hand him over to 'Gentile justice', and this claim was heavily criticized by the metropolitan police as dangerous and dishonest upon publication.

Anderson retired from the CID in 1901 and from public life, and was knighted for his services. Turning now to his writing, he wrote a number of devout religious works, including *The coming prince* (1881) and *Human destiny* (1887), and he defended the bible as representing a literal truth. In his essay on Sherlock Holmes, published in 1903, he questioned the detective's

49 *The Referee,* 17 Apr. 1910.
50 Ibid.

approach to solving crimes and dismissed him as 'insufferably egotistical and tiresome'.[51]

Anderson's first volume of memoirs, *Sidelights on the Home Rule movement*, was published in 1906 and it is noted in the *Oxford dictionary of national biography* that it 'raised a storm over his secret-service methods and was acknowledged by Joseph Conrad to have been a source for his novel *The secret agent*, published a year later'. In his next book, *Criminals and crime,* Anderson shocked many contemporaries by suggesting that 'professional' criminals should be locked up for life and prevented from breeding in order to protect society.[52]

In April 1910 *Blackwood's Magazine* published the seventh in a series of articles by Anderson in advance of the publication of his second memoir, *The lighter side of official life.* In an otherwise unremarkable piece, Anderson made one statement that proved to be political dynamite, and it was this line which so incensed Asquith, the prime minister, and provoked furious scenes in the House of Commons. In between an anecdote about a lecture he had given on Grattan's parliament, and a discussion of the 'falseness of the Home Rule agitation', Anderson wrote the following:

> To the present hour I do not know whether the home secretary was then aware of my authorship of the *Times* articles of 1887 on 'Parnellism and crime' for in relation to that matter I acted with strict propriety in dealing with Mr Monro and not with the secretary of state. I made no secret, however, of the fact that in my Whitehall days I wrote for the press and this may have made the Home Office suspicious of me after I went to Scotland Yard.[53]

The first of the 'Parnellism and crime' articles was published in the *Times* on 7 March 1887, and over the next few months fourteen articles were published linking Parnell and various members of his party with agrarian violence as well as terrorist conspiracies, including bombing campaigns in England. As part of the series, on 18 April it published the facsimile of a letter purporting to be from Parnell showing some support for the Invincibles in the immediate aftermath of the killing of Cavendish and Burke, including the crucial line: 'though I regret the accident of Lord F. Cavendish's death, I cannot refuse to admit that Burke got no more than his desserts'. The British government, under Lord Salisbury, moved to investigate the charges, setting up a Special Commission where the *Times* was invited to prove its allegations.[54]

51 R. Anderson, 'Sherlock Holmes as seen by Scotland Yard', *T.P.'s Weekly,* 2 Oct. 1903.

52 Porter, 'Sir Robert Anderson'.

53 *Blackwood's Magazine*, 187:1134 (Apr. 1910), p. 517.

54 *Special Commission to inquire into charges and allegations against certain members of parliament and others,* 19 vols (London, 1899).

As Dungan has described so memorably, the case against Parnell collapsed when Richard Pigott was destroyed on the witness stand in February 1889, and it was revealed that he had forged many of the letters that were used as documentary evidence to support the articles.[55]

A second witness also threatened to reveal much about the inner workings. Thomas Maguire, the professor of moral philosophy at Trinity College Dublin – who was known to some as 'Professor Red-Headed Whiskey' – was a virulent opponent of Home Rule and it was revealed at the Commission that he had contributed £850 to pay Pigott for the letters. There was even some mystery about this, because Maguire was known to have no money, and he was called before the Commission to testify. However, on the morning of Tuesday, 26 February he was found dead in his lodgings. There were immediately rumours that he had been murdered, or had committed suicide, but the home secretary, Henry Matthews, was adamant that he had died of natural causes, 'of inflammation of the windpipe'. Afterwards, Parnell famously wondered aloud who had given Maguire the £850 to purchase the 'fabricated and perjured evidence', given that he 'was a pauper and died a pauper'.[56]

At the same time as the body of Maguire was being discovered, Pigott was due to return to the Special Commission and it looked like the entire conspiracy against Parnell would be exposed. When Pigott failed to return to the Special Commission on 26 February, a warrant was issued for his arrest. Anderson was now the head of the CID and he writes in his first memoir that the warrant 'was placed in my hands'. Anderson selected the officers to find Pigott, and he wrote about how they 'tracked him to Madrid, but on their arriving at the hotel in which he was staying, he shot himself'.[57] The *Times* was forced to pay for the costs of the Commission, almost bankrupting the newspaper, and Parnell received a hero's welcome when he next attended the House of Commons.

Oscar Wilde attended some sessions of the Special Commission and might well have wondered that to lose one critical witness was a misfortune, but to lose two looked like carelessness. The sudden deaths of Maguire and Pigott saved the government from much embarrassment, and from having to explain elements of the *Times* campaign against Parnell that made no sense. It also saved Anderson from any scrutiny of his own involvement in the events, or those of his superiors.

In Anderson's first memoir, *Sidelights on the Home Rule movement*, he discussed the Special Commission and the charges against Parnell. Twice he insisted that apart from the disclosures of his agent, Henri le Caron, he had 'nothing to do with the *Times* case'; le Caron's evidence, he reiterated, 'was

55 M. Dungan, *Conspiracy: Irish political trials* (Dublin, 2013), pp 219–63.

56 T.P. Foley, 'Thomas Maguire and the Parnell forgeries', *Journal of the Galway Archaeological and Historical Society*, 46 (1994), 173.

57 Anderson, *Sidelights*, p. 213.

my only point of contact'.[58] This was not only misleading; it was deliberately untruthful, and it masks and distorts Anderson's true involvement.

Questions about his role were asked at the time. When le Caron mentioned Anderson's name under cross-examination, his involvement was discussed in the newspapers, and there was criticism that he may have used his position as head of the CID to assist the case against Parnell. The Home Office papers do not shed light on this, though there are revealing documents in other collections. For example, Arthur Balfour, the chief secretary for Ireland, wrote to the home secretary on 24 March 1889 asking him to instruct Anderson to co-operate with some of the work against Parnell.[59] Anderson volunteered to testify before the Commission, but he was not called.

Anderson claimed that 'in private practice no competent barrister' would have called Pigott into the witness box because 'it was known that the other side had been tampering with him for months, and the obvious course would have been to treat him as a hostile witness'.[60] Denying that Pigott had forged the facsimile letter, he left the matter of whether it was genuine as 'an open question'.

Despite the collapse of the case against Parnell, Anderson never stopped asserting in public that the allegations had been correct, standing over the original 'Parnellism and crime' articles, and even the facsimile letter that claimed to prove that Parnell was sympathetic to the Invincibles. Anderson insisted that 'the real Parnell' was someone whose 'ruling passion of his political life' was 'intense, unreasoning hatred of England'. And he wondered: 'Did Parnell cherish the insane dream that with £200,000 of Fenian money, he could meet the military force of Britain?'[61]

In his memoirs, Anderson twisted the evidence to suggest Pigott was both innocent of the forgery and working against the government. He speculated that if it was a forgery it had been concocted, not by the *Times,* but by 'extremists among the Land Leaguers'.[62] Although Anderson conceded that Parnell's repudiation of the letter 'deserves weight', he balanced this by saying that 'some of his denials at the Special Commission were untruthful'. And he concluded by asserting that whether the letter was genuine or not, 'such was the bitterness of feeling in Ireland at the time, Parnell might have said, and probably did say' the contentious line in the letter that 'Burke got no more than his desserts'.[63]

Anderson's admission that he had authored the 'Parnellism and crime' articles caused an immediate sensation. It revealed that someone working at

58 Ibid., p. 149.

59 F.S.L. Lyons, 'Parnellism and crime, 1887–90', *Transactions of the Royal Historical Society*, 24 (1974), 137

61 Anderson, *Sidelights,* p. 143.

61 Ibid., p. 214.

62 Ibid.

63 Ibid.

the highest levels in secret service activities for the British government, with the authorization of his superior, had engaged in a public campaign to destroy the reputation of an Irish political leader. There was a big difference between the *Times* deciding to take on Parnell and a covert intelligence campaign, especially as it had been revealed so dramatically that some of the evidence was manufactured.

In the House of Commons on 11 April 1910 John Redmond, the leader of the Irish Parliamentary Party, discussed the revelations, describing Anderson as an adviser to the Home Office when the articles were published and noting that when he became head of CID in 1888 he put the resources of the police behind proving the allegations contained in the *Times*. Redmond asked if 'the government of the day were a party to this action; whether such conduct has any precedent; whether it is possible under existing conditions to-day; and whether he will cause inquiry to be made into this matter?'[64]

In response the prime minister, Asquith, denied that Anderson had ever been a political adviser to the Home Office, describing him as being in 1887 'secretary to the prison commissioners, and also employed by Mr Monro on secret service work'. In a strong denunciation, Asquith insisted that '[i]f Sir Robert Anderson wrote the *Times* articles, or any part of them, his action was contrary to the rules and traditions of the civil service, and, so far as I know, without precedent'.[65] A number of MPs had suggested setting up an inquiry, but Asquith argued that after a distance of twenty years it would serve no useful purpose.

Within hours, Anderson rushed to issue an important clarification, and he sent a letter to the *Times* that was published the next day. The letter only corrected one point, but it changed the significance of the entire revelation. This letter was also published in the appendix to his memoir – where, however, the paragraph referring to authorship of the 'Parnellism and crime' articles was excised completely. Anderson insisted that he had written in his manuscript the word 'May' before 1887, but that this had been left out of the published version because of an unfortunate error by the publisher of *Blackwood's Magazine*.[66] Anderson was adamant that he was responsible for only three of the 'Parnellism and crime' articles, the three with the heading 'Behind the scenes in America'. This correction was convenient, and it rescued the government from much of the difficulty it had found itself in. The three articles were relatively anodyne, they did not contain any of the most serious allegations against Parnell, and they were not the crucial articles of March which had prompted the establishment of the Special Commission.

James Monro, who had been Anderson's superior at the time and who he had claimed to have consulted on the letters, also issued a statement denying

64 *Hansard's Parl. deb., 5th series* (commons), vol. 16, col. 891 (11 Apr. 1910).
65 Ibid., cols 893–4.
66 *Times*, 12 Apr. 1910.

that he had been consulted about the writing of the 'Parnellism and crime' articles.[67] This statement was delivered to Winston Churchill, the home secretary, and read into the record of the house on Thursday, 21 April. Monro conceded he had talked to Anderson about the 'Parnellism and crime' articles, because they 'caused a sensation in London', and he admitted that he 'can quite imagine that I may have welcomed public interest being directed to the existence of a dangerous conspiracy'. But he insisted that 'such an expression of opinion was a very different thing from authorizing an agent of mine to give information to the public'. Today this might be called a non-denial denial, and it is certainly full of caveats and qualifications. Monro conceded that Anderson had informed him of his authorship at some later point, and that he had informed the Home Office 'in confidential talk, but as the incident had passed many months previously, and there was no object in reopening the question, I did not report it officially'. Upon hearing this, the nationalist MP Jeremiah MacVeagh joked that perhaps 'the statement of Sir Robert Anderson that he had the permission of his official superior to write these articles for the *Times* may be treated as another of 'Anderson's Fairy Tales'.[68]

The controversy reignited in the Commons later the same day. T.P. O'Connor of the Irish Parliamentary Party led the attack, denouncing Anderson as a man of 'strong violent political prejudices'.[69] These prejudices were so powerful he claimed, 'that they blind him very often to all the difference between what is right and what is wrong in the conduct of his fellow-creatures'. O'Connor reminded the House that Asquith had been a junior counsel during the Parnell Commission and had cross-examined the manager of the *Times* where he had attempted, and failed, to discover the identity of the author of the articles. He suggested that if it had been known that one of the writers was Robert Anderson, then the head of the CID, a very 'different complexion would have been placed on the matter'.

In response, the home secretary, Winston Churchill, noted that Anderson had now 'reduced his claim to three articles of minor importance dealing with the Fenian societies in America – [the] three of them which appeared in May 1887, two months after the important articles had appeared which led to the Parnell Commission'.[70] Churchill insisted that if anyone in the government at the time had known of Anderson's involvement he would have been dismissed at once. Dismissing the articles in *Blackwood's Magazine* as being 'written in a spirit of gross boastfulness' in the style of 'How Bill Adams Won the Battle of Waterloo', Churchill attempted to trivialize their significance.[71] At the same time, he revealed that he would not be using his powers to take away Anderson's pension, because the offences were in 'the distant past'.

67 *Hansard's Parl. deb., 4th series* (commons), vol. 16, col. 2323 (21 Apr. 1910).
68 Ibid.
69 Ibid., col. 2335.
70 Ibid., col. 2355.
71 Ibid.

Historians have accepted Anderson's clarification. In F.S.L. Lyons' ground-breaking article on 'Parnellism and crime', published in 1974, he accepted that Anderson was the author of the three 'Behind the scenes in America' articles, and believed that this involvement proved that 'what outwardly appeared to be a journalistic venture had much wider and more serious ramifications'.[72] The role of Anderson in the secret service activities of the day were also explored in Leon Ó Broin's book *The prime informer: a suppressed scandal*.[73]

At the time, many people believed that the author of the 'Parnellism and crime' articles was John Woulfe Flanagan, the son of an Irish judge, who had joined the staff of the *Times* in 1886 and wrote many of its editorials. This was certainly the view of Michael Davitt, who named Flanagan at the Special Commission. When Flanagan died in 1929, his obituary in the *Times* confirmed his authorship and this has been accepted by most historians.[74]

When Flanagan was proposed for membership of the Athenæum Club in 1890 by George Earle Buckle, the editor of the *Times*, his reputation as an 'infamous libeller' preceded him and 'the number of black balls deposited against him was the largest ever known against any person seeking admission'.[75] However, according to an Irish MP in the House of Commons, Buckle 'pleaded piteously' on Flanagan's 'behalf that he had not written all the articles in the *Times*, but only three of them, and those not by any means the worst'.[76]

There are some more obvious problems with accepting Anderson's clarification, and firm grounds for believing that his initial statement in *Blackwood's Magazine* was correct. Anderson's subsequent clarification does not really hold up. Anderson claimed that the word 'May' had been left out of the published version by mistake, meaning that the correct line should have been:

> To the present hour I do not know whether the home secretary was then aware of my authorship of the *Times* articles of May 1887 on 'Parnellism and crime' for in relation to that matter I acted with strict propriety in dealing with Mr. Monro and not with the secretary of state.

As it happens, two of the three articles were published in May (on 13 and 20 May) and the final one on 1 June. There were also other 'Parnellism and crime' articles published in May, so it would have been both inaccurate and

72 Lyons, 'Parnellism and crime', p. 128.
73 L. Ó Broin, *The prime informer: a suppressed scandal* (London, 1971).
74 *Times*, 18 Nov. 1929.
75 This was later discussed in the House of Commons. See *Hansard's Parl. deb., 5th series* (commons), vol. 342, col. 377 (10 Mar. 1890).
76 Ibid.

confusing to make reference to writing the articles of 'May 1887'. Given the relative unimportance of the articles, it is also not entirely clear why Anderson should have been wondering if the home secretary of the time had ever been aware of his authorship. It is revealing that rather than correct the error in the printed book – changing the date to May 1887 – Anderson chose to delete entirely the relevant passage in his letter of clarification as published in the book.

It is also notable that although Anderson claimed to have worked on the articles under the supervision of his secret service head, James Monro, Monro denied any knowledge at the time of this work – even the three articles entitled 'Behind the scenes in America'. Either Monro or Anderson was lying and, given that it was accepted by the government in 1910 that Anderson had written at least some of the articles, it seems more likely that it was Monro covering for himself and for the government.

It is my contention that Anderson wrote most, if not all, of the 'Parnellism and crime' articles, and admitted this openly in *Blackwood's Magazine,* almost as a throwaway remark, never expecting it to generate such controversy. Faced with a massive backlash, including an attack from the prime minister in the House of Commons, and criticism from his former colleagues, and fearing the loss of his pension, he rushed to issue an untrue clarification that lessened the impact of the revelation.

Anderson died in November 1918 of heart complications after having contracted the H1N1 virus – more commonly and incorrectly known as Spanish flu – during the great influenza pandemic of a little over a century ago. He was buried at Kensal Green cemetery in London and directions to his grave can be found on some Ripper websites for those who follow the case to an unhealthy degree. After his death he was praised as 'one of the men to whom the country, without knowing it, owes a great debt'.[77]

Winston Churchill had the measure of Anderson when he suggested that he was 'so anxious to show how important he was, how invariably he was right, and how much more he could tell if only his mouth was not what he was pleased to call closed'. Nonetheless, we learn much from these accounts. Re-reading his memoirs, and treating them like any other primary source, to be evaluated and critiqued, provide valuable insights into the political and criminal world of the 1880s. We learn much about the covert attempts to destroy the reputation of Charles Stewart Parnell, as well as the mistakes and failures that bedevilled the investigation into the Whitechapel murders. Anderson believed that he was a patriot, serving a higher cause at all times, and was always able to justify every action taken. Read today, his memoirs remind us of just how dangerous it is to lack any self-doubt or self-awareness, and the high cost that comes with such certainty.

77 *Times,* 18 Nov. 1918.

Lisnafana: a townland in crisis on the Headfort Cavan estate, 1879–95

ROBERT D. MARSHALL*

INTRODUCTION

This chapter reviews events that took place in the townland of Lisnafana on the marquess of Headfort's Cavan estate, near Virginia, between 1879 and 1895.[1] Over that period of sixteen years, Lisnafana experienced the contested change of ownership of two holdings, the trauma of the Plan of Campaign and a boycotting and its consequences. Civil and criminal proceedings were involved: civil to enforce payment of a judgment debt through a court sale, and criminal arising from breaches of the peace and the subsequent killing of John Reilly of Curraghmore by Hugh Moore in 1895. These events will be used to examine the extent to which an alternative or 'subaltern' legal code then operated in the Irish countryside distinct from the official rule of law.

Laird argues that the subaltern code determined what was acceptable behaviour between landholders, and that the code included sanctions to secure compliance.[2] Her proposition is based upon the observations of experienced and middle-ranking administrators transferred to Ireland following service in India and Africa, and the works of Somerville and Ross, William Carleton and, principally, Emily Lawless's novel *Hurrish*. Laird sets her proposition in a wider imperial context by drawing on the work of a school of mainly Indian subaltern scholars. She recounts Clifford Lloyd's opinion

* A shortened version of this chapter was delivered as the author's presidential address to the Society on 27 Nov. 2015 at the Public Record Office of Northern Ireland. The author is grateful for the support received at PRONI, at TNA and in Dublin at the NLI and NAI; the assistance of the late Gregory O'Connor in the NAI was indispensable. Felix M. Larkin was a patient chauffeur on the visit to Virginia and Lisnafana in August 2015.

1 The nature of the events was such that they were reported in the local press or sometimes ignored to accommodate the politics of the proprietor and readership. It has been possible to supplement those reports and create a larger picture with detail from the papers of the Headfort estate office in the NLI; the Registry of Deeds; the Valuation Office; county and divisional police reports; Chief Secretary's Office papers; and surviving court records and papers in the NAI and TNA. Together they build a picture of the lives of individuals and their circumstances. Lisnafana is spelt also as Lisnafanna and, in older Headfort records, as Lisnafanny, standardized in this chapter as Lisnafana.

2 H. Laird, *Subversive law in Ireland, 1879–1920: from 'unwritten law' to Dáil courts* (Dublin, 2005).

that land resistance had established a polity capable of replacing the colonial state and was, in fact, accepted by many as the legitimate political authority. From contemporary accounts, Laird demonstrates how boycotting became an administrative arm of an alternative state run by the Land League. The official law was powerless to sanction people for doing things collectively which they had every right to do individually. In the competition between the two, the unwritten law was powerful because punishment was sure to follow its infraction. Intimidation, cattle rustling and maiming were the tools to enforce the boycott as individuals declared to be obnoxious were ostracised.[3]

The statutory legal code was the Landlord and Tenant Amendment (Ireland) Act 1860,[4] known as Deasy's Act.[5] This provided that the basis of the relationship of landlord and tenant was contract, with land held by one party from another at a rent with other terms being expressed or implied. The landlord's position was secured by three ejectment remedies: 'on the title' (where a condition of the letting was breached); for 'overholding' (where the leasehold term had expired); and for 'non-payment of rent' (where rent of one year or more was in arrear). Ejectment for non-payment of rent was the most common form of proceeding and was subject to the restriction that a tenant could redeem the tenancy and re-enter the property by paying the arrears and costs within six months of the actual ejectment.[6] This created uncertainty for a landlord in whose hands the recovered property was temporarily moribund. For a tenant, whose whole business and home had been lost, redemption was extremely difficult. The tenant was entitled to raise all his defences at law or in equity in the course of the proceedings.

The interest of a tenant in his lease could be valuable. If a judgment was granted against a tenant in the superior courts or a county court, it could be attached to the land by a judgment mortgage. Such mortgages were in statutory form and registered in the Registry of Deeds in Dublin. Thus, a shopkeeper advancing credit to a tenant could obtain judgment for the amount owing, secure it upon the land and in due course have the debtor's interest sold by the court. After enquiry the court would then divide the proceeds of sale net of costs between the secured parties according to established rules of priority. Of course, the creditor of a tenant was exposed to a landlord determining the tenancy for due cause and destroying the security.

The Headfort estates in Meath and Cavan adjoined one another and were so extensive that the marquess of Headfort could journey from his home at Kells to his shooting lodge at Virginia, a distance of almost fourteen miles, without leaving his own land. The Cavan estate had been purchased in the late

3 Ibid., ch. 1 and D.G. Boyce, *Nineteenth-century Ireland* (2nd edn, Dublin, 2005), p. 179.
4 23 & 24 Vict., c. 154.
5 R.R. Cherry, *The Irish land law and Land Purchase Acts, 1860–1891* (2nd edn, Dublin, 1893).
6 Deasy's Act, s. 71.

1730s. It was let in a multiplicity of small lots whereas the Meath estate was let in large holdings. The 'Ulster custom' of tenant right prevailed on the Headfort Cavan estate, but not upon the adjoining Meath estate.[7] When a tenant died or a farm changed hands within the Cavan estate it was revalued: this revision was categorized as a fair rent known to the parties from the outset. Where an outgoing tenant desired to sell, he requested leave to do so (which was invariably given where the party was respectable), but not by way of auction. The procedure operated by surrender and new agreement, giving the landlord privity with the incoming tenant and direct control of the process. It did not necessitate solicitors, because no assignment was required.[8] The amounts paid for tenant right were very large, the average on the old rent being twenty years purchase. The new rent generally increased by 10 per cent, so a purchaser paid eighteen times the revalued rent.[9]

Aside from Hugh Moore, referred to above, this study will encounter several Lisnafana tenants – all with the surname Reilly, some but not necessarily all related to one another. Their holdings to which reference is made are identified in the accompanying map at Plate 9.1 by the numbers 1, 3, 4 and 5.

A COURT SALE ON THE HEADFORT CAVAN ESTATE

The first of the contested changes of ownership was a protracted business. Peter Reilly (the tenant of Farm 1), along with Patrick Reilly and Michael Reilly (possibly his brothers), owed Con Reilly (the tenant of the adjoining Farm 3) £70 on a bill of exchange. In September 1879, Con Reilly entered judgment against them in the exchequer division of the high court for £77 10*s.* plus costs of £7 8*s.*[10] He swore an affidavit on 2 March 1880 to register the judgment mortgage[11] which carried interest at 4 per cent per annum and affected thirty-one statute acres in Lisnafana. It was filed at exchequer the next day and registered in the Registry of Deeds later that afternoon.[12]

7 For an analysis of the Headfort estate, see J. Mooney, *The changing fortunes of the Headfort estate, 1870–1928* (Dublin, 2012). See also Plate 9.5.

8 Consequently the provision introduced by Deasy's Act of endorsing consent to assignment on the lease or assignment was not relevant.

9 *Report on the select committee on the working of the Irish Land Act, 1870 with minutes of evidence and appendix* (1877) HC 328 xii.1, evidence of Major Dalton, pp 153–63. Dalton was Headfort's elder half-brother and land agent. Dalton gave evidence of a number of transactions but no further evidence of the procedures or the terms of letting was given and what Dalton meant by 'respectable' was not explored. For the examples see q. 2574.

10 He proceeded in Dublin because the limit of the county court jurisdiction was £50.

11 Pursuant to the Judgment Mortgage (Ireland) Act 1850 (13 & 14 Vic., c. 29), s. 6. See J.C.W. Wylie, *Irish land law* (3rd edn., Dublin, 1997), para. 13.163 *et seq.*

12 Registry of Deeds, 1880, Bk. 11, no. 237. The procedure for registration of a judgement mortgage and subsequent court sale is outlined by Wylie in ch. 13. The procedures had not changed significantly since they had been established in the 1850s.

Con's decision to take this step may have resulted from an action by Lord Headfort to recover £38 11*s*. 8*d* rent owing by Peter Reilly as tenant from year to year.[13] Peter Reilly had been a tenant of this farm for upwards of twenty years. The previous tenant, possibly his father, held the farm since 1828. Peter missed the November gale of 1874, but his troubles really began with the gale accruing on 1 November 1877 due by 30 April 1878. Thereafter, Peter carried the half year's rent in arrear until the gale accruing on 1 May 1879 which he had not paid by 31 October 1879. Following referral to Headfort's solicitor in Kells,[14] the ledger records Peter as paying a year's rent net of county rates, and 10*s*. for costs. It kept the wolf from the door, but when he made no payment in October 1880 against a full year's rent due an undated entry in the rental for May 1880 records a decree in the sheriff's hands. It was not executed: the rental for May 1881 records that a year's rent net of county rates with costs of £2 0*s*. 6*d*. had been paid.[15]

Nothing in the countryside goes un-noticed, and the story became one of the marquis against Con as the former sought his rent while the latter sought his mortgage debt. Unsurprisingly, Con issued an equity civil bill seeking an order for sale of Peter's farm which came on for hearing before Judge Waters at the October 1880 quarter sessions in Cavan. An application was made for foreclosure and sale,[16] and the sum of £91 17*s*. 2*d*. was ascertained to be due to Con for principal, interest and costs. The usual decree for sale and enquiry as to other encumbrances was made, but no date fixed for the sale. Lord Headfort's estate office could see the complications. Peter Reilly was now a risk with debts to the estate and his neighbour totalling £149 14*s*. 8*d*.

The clerk of the crown and peace dated his certificate of debts 19 March 1881 and it was confirmed at the Easter sessions on 7 April 1881 when the defendants were represented by a solicitor named Kennedy. A further affidavit by Con Reilly was opened to the court and an order made that the lands be sold by public auction at Virginia on 11 May 1881, the sale to be conducted by Phillip McEnroe. Con's solicitor, John Lynch, was to have conduct of the sale and prepare conditions of sale for approval by the clerk of the crown and peace.[17] A date was fixed for the submission of biddings to the judge. A stay was agreed upon to the June sessions when a date for the sale was fixed as 1 December 1881. All of this must have been difficult between neighbours, although the making of the order seems to have been *in terrorem* to secure payment rather than force a sale. The situation became more

13 M.W. O'Connor (agent) to T. Lynch (solicitor, Kells), 7 Feb. 1880, Headfort papers, NLI MS 25,429(2).
14 O'Connor to Lynch, 7 Jan. 1880, NLI MS 25,429(2), instructing institution of proceedings against several tenants.
15 Headfort estate rentals, NLI MS 25,410 (14, 16).
16 *Cornelius Reilly v. Peter Reilly, Patrick Reilly and Michael Reilly*, Equity civil bills, Cavan 1881, NAI 1C.1.44. Bk 67, p. 36.
17 Ibid., p. 43.

complex when Peter died at Lisnafana on 21 December 1881, four months after the passing of the Land Act 1881.[18] He was buried in the imposing family plot at Lurgan churchyard beneath a headstone erected by the Revd Cornelius Reilly of Phillipsburg, New Jersey.[19]

The matter came on again on 19 May 1882 when the surviving defendants, Patrick and Michael Reilly, undertook to pay £50 on or before 12 October 1882. Peter's death had not been registered and seems not to have been mentioned to the court.[20] The estate rental for May 1882 records a reduction in arrears of 18 months rent comprising a payment of 9 months rent and an allowance of the same amount by the landlord: nevertheless, a full year's rent remained outstanding. Taken together, these two payments look like an interim settlement with 50 per cent of the debt due to each creditor being paid. A further hearing took place at the December 1882 sessions when an order was made to pay out £50 to Con Reilly and that a sale fixed for April 1883 should not proceed if the sum of £40 was paid into court before 24 March 1883. A further order was made at the October 1883 sessions directing payment into court of £38 19*s*. 8*d*.

At this point two-and-a-half years rent was owing. A note in the Headfort estate rental for November 1883 simply states 'evicted', which may mean that a court order had been obtained but not executed. The rental for the following half-year carried the arrears forward without mention of a caretaker agreement and Peter Reilly continued to be noted as the tenant. The total amount for rent and arrears carried forward was £96. 14*s*. It seems likely Patrick and Michael Reilly continued in possession, but the ejectment proceedings book does not survive to record the detail of the proceedings.

Despite two sets of proceedings in the county court, no grant of administration had been taken out to the estate. In April 1884 Judge Waters ordered that the defendant Patrick Reilly be appointed as administrator of Peter Reilly deceased for the purpose of the suit.[21] Presumably the court was satisfied that the gross assets of Peter Reilly excluding leasehold land did not exceed £500 and that the annual value of his lands did not exceed £30. No payment having been made by May 1884, the court fixed the auction for 3 July in Virginia.[22]

Giving evidence to the Morley Committee in 1895 on the workings of the Land Acts, Lord Justice Fitzgibbon noted:

18 Land Law (Ireland) Act 1881 (44 & 45 Vict., c. 49).

19 Pastor at the Roman Catholic church of St Phillip and St James, Phillipsburg, diocese of Trenton 1861–1885: W.T. Leahy, *The Catholic church of the diocese of Trenton* (Princeton, 1906).

20 *Cornelius Reilly v. Peter Reilly, Patrick Reilly and Michael Reilly*, NAI 1C.1. 44. Bk 67, p. 75.

21 Equity civil bills, Cavan 1881. NAI 1C.1.44 Bk 68, pp 31 and 31A.

22 Ibid., p. 31A.

> A very usual thing in Ireland, the appellant before the court had not taken out administration, and had no legal title; but we do not question those things in Ireland; it is for the revenue to look after that.[23]

The revenue had not looked after it in this instance, with the result that both Con Reilly and the surviving defendants were caught off guard when on 3 July, the day fixed for the sale, a grant of administration intestate to the estate of Peter Reilly was issued to his daughter, Bridget Reilly of Ballyjamesduff (wife of Andrew Reilly).[24] The intervention of Bridget Reilly may reflect a family dispute, suggesting that the assumption made at the time of the judgment mortgage as to the interests of the then defendants went un-queried and that the title to the leasehold interest in the farm had not yet been produced. A copy of the eviction order with the sheriff's return on it would have set out all of the title detail required to sell a yearly tenancy under the 'Ulster custom' or the Land Act 1881 at the time. Much of the detail would have been available in the ejectment book as a matter of public record. A rent receipt at completion would, of course, be crucial. This suggests that Con Reilly's then intention was not to force a sale of the farm but to secure repayment.

Following the grant of administration, the suit was stood over twice until 9 January 1885 when no rule was made.[25] Bridget Reilly sought the fixing of a judicial rent, which she was entitled to do at any time until the right to redeem the tenancy had lapsed. Having made the application she was in a position to apply to the court, as distinct from the Land Commission,[26] to stay the ejectment proceedings until a fair rent had been fixed. Cherry comments that such a stay would be granted in ejectment proceedings only upon condition of a substantial payment of rent within a short time.[27] A Land Commission order was made on 24 March 1885 by consent fixing the rent at £31, being £2

23 *Report from the select committee on Land Acts (Ireland) 1894*, HC 1894 xiii.1, 13 p. 183 (*Morley committee*).

24 This reference to her husband was a hangover following the passing of the Married Women's Property Act 1882 (45 & 46 Vict., c. 75), which allowed Bridget to administer her father's estate herself and her delay may have been to gain the benefit of the independence afforded to her under the act. Previously it would have been administered by her husband on her behalf. See Probate and Letters of Administration Act 1857 (20 & 21 Vict., c. 79), ss 31 and 47. The rental for Nov. 1884 records the tenant of the farm as 'Reps. Peter Reilly', NLI MS 25,410 (23).

25 Equity civil bills, Cavan 1881, NAI 1C.1.44 Bk 68, p. 69. John Reilly, a second creditor, brought separate proceedings seeking to have payment of several charges or a sale of the lands. His suit, at which Bridget Reilly (Kennedy Solicitor), Michael and Patrick Reilly (Fowler Solicitor) and Con Reilly (Lynch Solicitor) all appeared, was dismissed without costs. No rule was then made on Con Reilly's proceedings which must have been seen to be incorrectly framed following the intervention of Bridget Reilly.

26 See Hart's chapter in this volume, 'The law in action in Ulster in July 1898'.

27 Land Act 1881, s. 13 (3) and Cherry, *The Irish land law*, p. 362.

above the annual rateable valuation and a reduction of £7 11*s.* 8*d.* The rental for the half year to 30 April 1885 records a payment of £106 5*s.* 7*d.* and an allowance for rates of £9 9*s.* 5*d.* Bridget Reilly was now noted as tenant of the farm and entered as such in the rental for the half year commencing 1 May 1885.[28]

What, therefore, emerges is that Lord Headfort and Con Reilly were both using the courts as a mechanism to procure payment and with some success, despite the inaccuracies in the constitution of the various proceedings. Neither appears to have wished to terminate the interest of Peter Reilly or later of his family in the farm.

When Con Reilly issued fresh proceedings in 1886 to recover the money due to him, everything had changed. Then he sued Bridget Reilly as administrator, as well as one John Reilly whose interest it has not been possible to establish: perhaps John had been the source of the large sums of money paid to the Headfort estate and Con Reilly following the death of Peter. Matters proceeded apace and on 12 October 1886 the court fixed the date of the sale for 24 January 1887, some days after the January sessions.[29] This time the auction took place and on 26 March 1887 at the spring sessions the court confirmed the sale to Con Reilly for £290, directing the purchase money be lodged forthwith and authorizing the sheriff to put him into possession.[30] The court record contains no reference to the service of statutory forms upon Lord Headfort under the 1881 Act, nor any acceptance by the estate of Con Reilly as tenant.[31] It would not be until 10 May 1889 when the storm of the Plan of Campaign had largely passed, that a deed of assignment would be made to Con Reilly.

The surviving papers disclose a dispute but not its detail between the defendants, Bridget Reilly and John Reilly, over the division of the proceeds of sale. They appealed the certificate prepared for the court by the clerk of the crown and peace, dividing the net proceeds of sale, which may account for the refusal of Bridget Reilly to execute the deed, ultimately done on her behalf by the clerk of the crown and peace.[32]

THE PLAN OF CAMPAIGN ON THE HEADFORT CAVAN ESTATE

John Dillon's speech expounding the Plan of Campaign at Woodford, Co. Galway, was reported in the *Freeman's Journal* on 18 October 1886. On 22 October Lord Headfort received a deputation of his tenants seeking an

28 NLI MS 25,410 (23, 24).
29 Equity civil bills, Cavan 1881, NAI 1C.1.44 Bk 68, p. 165.
30 Ibid., p. 192.
31 Land Act 1881, s. 2. See e.g. *Headfort v. Cochrane* (1892) 26 ILTR 112.
32 Memorial, 10 May 1889, Registry of Deeds, 1889, Bk 23, no. 36.

abatement of the gale rent then payable in accordance with the Plan. The meeting was not directly reported, apart from a statement by the parish priest of Virginia who had accompanied the deputation that Headfort took careful notes during the speeches before replying that there was no distress at all and that the season was a better one than for years past. The marquess agreed however to consider the matter and wrote the following day that the condition of the country did not call for a general abatement but any cases of exceptional distress would have his careful consideration.

A meeting chaired by the parish priest was later held at the Virginia courthouse when 'nearly all the tenants on the estate were present or represented'.[33] A series of resolutions was proposed by speakers from across the community, generally condemning Headfort's actions. None of the resolutions referred to Home Rule or other nationalist aspirations. Revd Aitken, the Presbyterian minister at Munterconnaught, was reported as proposing the key resolution:

> That payment of the full rent is now an impossibility, a fact admitted by the present government, as reductions are now universal on the part of neighbouring landlords and as all consideration has been refused us, we hereby bind ourselves to withhold payment of our rents pending the grant of a general reduction and we now start a defence fund to which each tenant should subscribe 1*s*. in the £ on his valuation.

This was carried unanimously. The *Anglo Celt* reported that a committee was then formed comprising the two Catholic priests, the Presbyterian minister, a justice of the peace, a solicitor and three farmers – Joseph Whitley, William Strong and John Brady. It remarked on how the Catholic clergyman, the Presbyterian minister, the Protestant farmer, magistrates and professional men had joined together in a movement of charity, mercy and justice.

The estate's reaction was swift. Its first step was to break up the coalition that had been assembled. The agent, Matthew Weld O'Connor JP, wrote to the moderator of the Presbyterian church complaining that 'the position Revd Aitken had assumed had brought great discredit (in his opinion) upon the highly respectable order to which he belongs and forced him [O'Connor] … to bring this conduct under the notice of his superiors'. He quoted Revd Aitken's words as follows:

> Ireland could never thrive until the landlord and agents were in their coffins and securely screwed down and that he would do his level best to see them securely screwed down.

33 See *Freeman's Journal*, 29 Oct. 1886; *Anglo Celt*, 30 Oct. 1886: and *United Ireland*, 6 Nov. 1886. The key word was 'represented' given that there were some 430 tenants and the size of the courthouse (See plate 9.2).

He noted that, although Aitken had not joined the deputation to the marquess nor had he written asking for an abatement for his co-religionists, he nevertheless considered himself 'justified in making use of such expressions which even the lowest of the tenantry on the estate have confirmed themselves shocked at'.[34] Given that response to the words of the Presbyterian minister, we may assume the pressure applied to the Protestant farmers was considerable. Aitken himself wrote to the *Freeman's Journal* denying he had proposed or seconded a motion but confirming that he had 'made some remarks of a general character'.[35] O'Connor also wrote to the press confirming that the tenants were paying steadily and well, adding that 'most of the respectable tenants had already paid and cheques were coming in daily.'[36]

Arrears of rent, which in October 1886 amounted to £66 12*s.* 8*d.* in Lisnafana and £1,786 on the estate as a whole, climbed to £183 in Lisnafana and £4,203 on the estate, slightly in excess of a half year's rent. These figures mask the fact that many tenants paid their rent. At no point did the estate income drop below 60 per cent of the rents due. While the receipts included some arrears, they suggest that a majority of the tenants by rental value, if not in number, elected not to tangle in the Plan of Campaign with the wealthy marquess. What did Con Reilly do? He had a closer relationship with the estate than most for he had a mare serviced by it annually.[37] Aside from personal liability for his own rent, he was dependent on the consequences of unpaid rent on the farm over which he had a judgment mortgage. On 31 October 1886, rent would be due on both farms. The court sale was ordered for January 1887. Con played the ends against the middle: along with other tenants in Lisnafana he did not pay his rent to 31 October 1886, something he had never done before. Though he left that gale outstanding, he was the first of the Lisnafana tenants to resume payment.[38] A quiet visit from the bailiff may have been sufficient because of the stakes involved in purchasing the adjoining farm. Except for Con, the rents out of the Lisnafana townland were not well paid.

The Plan of Campaign on the Headfort estate was then subsumed into a struggle that stretched beyond Ireland to Westminster and the Vatican. Chief Secretary Balfour embarked upon a policy of coercion in Ireland. The passage of the Criminal Law and Procedure (Ireland) Act 1887[39] presaged a new

34 M. Weld O'Connor to Revd Robert Ross (moderator of the general assembly), 30 Oct. 1886, NLI MS 25,429 (2).

35 *Freeman's Journal,* 1 Nov. 1886.

36 *Dublin Daily Express*, 24 Nov. 1886. See also further correspondence from Fr Patrick Fitzsimons CC, Virginia, in *Dublin Daily Express*, 1 Dec. 1886 and *Freeman's Journal,* 2 Dec. 1886.

37 Stallion book, Headfort papers, NLI MS 25,410.

38 Headfort estate rentals 1 Nov. 1885–1 May 1887, NLI MS 25,410 (25–28).

39 50 & 51 Vict., c. 20.

approach to boycotting, while the Land Law (Ireland) Act 1887[40] addressed the civil side of the struggle. Characterized by nationalists as 'the eviction made easy act', the latter reduced eviction for non-payment of rent to a bureaucratic process. Service of notice by registered post and the posting of a summary notice on the courthouse or police barracks constituted the person in occupation a caretaker, so commencing the six-month period for redemption.[41] The notice publicized the particulars of rent and costs as set out in the judgment. This procedure answered press criticism and adverse public opinion in England.[42] Hard information on evictions was also gathered by the RIC whose monthly reports formed the basis of returns made to parliament by the lord lieutenant. The act created some breathing space for the police and army charged with keeping order at evictions by reducing and postponing the number of occasions upon which they were required to attend. Its effect upon the cash flow of landlords would depend upon how willing tenants were to settle on the posting of the notice rather than await the arrival of the sheriff to terminate their occupation as caretakers.

To further undermine the subaltern code underpinning the Plan of Campaign, the government sought and obtained papal condemnation of the practices of the Plan.[43] The investigations of Archbishop Persico in Ireland in the winter of 1887–8 and the mission to the Vatican of the duke of Norfolk and John Ross of Bladensburg culminated in the publication of the Papal Rescript of April 1888. Its timing was important. Norfolk left Rome in early April and the Rescript was finalized some days later. The covering letter to the bishops was dated 23 April 1888 and reports began to appear in the press, commencing in the *Times*, in advance of the gale day of 1 May.[44] It is inconceivable that the importance of the gale day was not mentioned by Norfolk and Ross when lobbying at the Vatican. The question posed in the Rescript was:

40 50 & 51 Vict., c. 33.

41 Cherry, *The Irish land law*, summarizes the procedure at pp 384–5 and provides the text of the applicable high court and county court rules.

42 For an analysis of Balfour's policy and of the press coverage of evictions see L.P. Curtis, Jr, *Coercion and conciliation in Ireland* (Princeton, 1963) and L.P. Curtis, Jr, *The depiction of eviction in Ireland* (Dublin, 2011). The Act also facilitated the introduction of the battering ram as a landlord could not demolish a house in which a tenant had an unexpired equity of redemption.

43 For analyses at a high political level see T.J. Morrissey SJ, *William J. Walsh, archbishop of Dublin* (Dublin, 2000), ch. 5–7 and A. Macaulay, *The Holy See and the Plan of Campaign in Ireland, 1885–93* (Dublin, 2002).

44 Rentals opened on 1 May or 1 Nov. for each half year. Rent falling due on those dates was not paid for six months. While the rent was legally payable in advance, in practice it was paid in arrear. The effect of this was that a tenant was always within a single rental payment of being in arrear for 1 years rent and so liable for eviction for non-payment of rent. This practice was known as 'the hanging gale.'

> In disputes between letters and holders of farms in Ireland, is it lawful to have recourse to those means known as the Plan of Campaign and Boycotting? – and their Eminences having long and maturely weighed the matter have unanimously replied in the negative.[45]

Unusually some sentences of explanation were added. These were perceived as inaccurate in Ireland and formed the basis for rejection of the decree by both politicians and almost all of the bishops. The final explanation in the decree read:

> It is altogether foreign to the nature of justice and Christian charity that a new form of persecution and of proscription should ruthlessly be put in place against persons who are satisfied with and prepared to pay the rent agreed on with their landlord or against persons who in the exercise of their right take vacant farms.

The Vatican, lobbied by Norfolk and Ross, took the side of formal law. Archbishop Walsh's 70,000-word thesis put the alternative case; but it came too late, was too lengthy and probably was not read by the committee of cardinals and theologians who took the decision. The reaction of nationalist leaders showed how much they feared the effect of the Rescript. Similarly, the reaction of the bishops showed their appreciation of the competing loyalties and pressures on their people. On 28 April the *Freeman's Journal* carried a report from its Rome correspondent reporting the view that the document had been obtained by misrepresentation and intrigue. This was not wholly inaccurate given Norfolk's promise that the government would gladly embrace any opportunity to establish diplomatic relations with the Vatican. Norfolk had said:

> Nothing could be more helpful to the government in carrying out those proposals than some action by the Holy See which showed that the Pope had the power to set right the course taken by too many of the clergy and that he was actually making use of that power.[46]

Whatever the controversies surrounding it, all of the pieces were now in place to enable the landlords to counterattack should they wish to do so.

Headfort did so wish. He offered an abatement of 3*s*. in the £1 (15 per cent) on the timely payment of the rent accruing on 1 May 1888.[47] That rental

45 The quotations from the Rescript are taken from Macaulay, *The Holy See*, pp 172–3, upon which this section heavily relies.

46 Ibid., p. 146.

47 This 15 per cent abatement on the gale was more generous than the 10 per cent abatement similarly accorded tenants in the May 1881 rental.

records allowances to tenants of £377 4*s*. 10½*d*., representing timely payment of some £2,500 of the accruing rent of £4,100. Total receipts were £5,547 so that arrears were reduced by some £2,000.[48] The marquess also commenced legal proceedings against ninety-eight of the 432 tenants on the estate; sixty-two small cases were referred to Richard Allen in Cavan and thirty-six larger cases to Barrington in Dublin.[49] The result was that of the 434 tenants, 385 made payments; 228 were paid up to date; 206 were in arrear and forty-nine tenants (less than 9%) made no payment. In seven townlands, all of the tenants paid and in a further nine only one tenant was in arrears. No payment did not necessarily mean support for the Plan as, apart from the usual rhythm of the estate, there were tenants who had introductory rent-free periods. Of eighteen tenants in Ballydurrow, twelve paid, five were rent free, leaving one default.[50]

Lisnafana stands out. All tenants were in arrear at the opening of the rental for 1 November 1887. At the close of the following rental four farmers remained in arrear. It was the only townland where over half of the tenants were in this position. The nearest rivals were in Lurganboy where five of twenty-one tenants and Cornaslieve where five of twenty-four tenants were in that position. The payment of rents on the estate continued to improve, although interrupted in May 1890. Arrears settled in the early 1890s at just over £950, skewed by events in Lisnafana which will be considered in the next section.

Con Reilly paid his own rent regularly, withholding payment only once in thirty years – the rent due to 31 October 1886 – and he still had his court sale to complete. He was the only tenant in the townland to receive the 15 per cent abatement. As already noted, it was not until May 1889 that an assignment was made in his favour. Astutely or through happenstance, Con had negotiated his way through ten years of turmoil to purchase an additional farm through a court sale against the wishes of the former tenant.

THE BOYCOTTING OF HUGH MOORE

The second of the contested changes of ownership involves Farms 4 and 5 held by Patrick Reilly – not, it may be assumed, the same Patrick Reilly against whom (with Peter Reilly and Michael Reilly) Con Reilly had entered

48 Headfort estate rental to 1 May 1888, NLI MS 25,410(30).

49 Mooney, *The changing fortunes*, p. 37 charts the legal costs incurred by the estate peaking in Nov. 1886 at almost £600. This figure would have included costs of enforcement proceedings and on the fixing of rents under the Land Act 1881 before the land commissioners.

50 This outcome was not publicized at the time, the third marquess being too discreet to claim victory. The information only became available with access to the Headfort papers at the NLI.

judgment in the exchequer division of the high court in September 1879. The rent on these farms had been judicially reduced[51] in August 1882, and in May 1884 Patrick Reilly secured advances from the commissioners of public works to fund drainage works on his farms.[52] Between then and the opening of the Plan of Campaign in October 1887, Patrick failed to establish a regular rhythm of half-yearly payment. When the rental opened on 1 May 1887, Patrick owed just over £80. Subsequent to the Papal Rescript, eviction decrees were obtained against him in January 1888. By November 1888 Patrick owed two years' rent.[53] Patrick reduced his arrears in October 1889, but the estate's patience was exhausted and the rental for November 1889 notes that the case had been referred to Barrington, the Dublin solicitor. The £82 10*s.* due by Patrick accounted for approximately 5 per cent of the rent arrears due on the estate.

His arrears increased further in the following years. When the gale on 1 May 1892 was missed, the decision to eject was noted in the November 1892 rental. An eviction notice was posted. No payment having been made, the decree was lodged with the sheriff in April 1894. The date of the caretaker eviction is not recorded in the rental. Why had things gone so wrong with Patrick? Old age does not seem to have been a factor and the pattern of non-payment of rent having begun before the Plan of Campaign excludes political radicalism. Patrick left for America *c.*1893 leaving behind a wife and children. Local information in 2015 suggested that the demon drink was the problem.

In October 1893, County Inspector Rodgers recorded in his monthly report for Cavan that:

> Of late a much better feeling seems to have grown up between the landlords and the tenants. This may be partly attributed to the reduction in rents but principally I think [illegible] owing to the nationalist party having withdrawn very much of late from interference in the affairs of the farming classes.[54]

The county inspector's report for Cavan for September 1894 stated that there were no cases of boycotting or intimidation and the prospects for the harvest were generally favourable so that the people would be 'in a good way of living

51 NLI MS 25,410 (18–19).

52 Patrick Reilly to commissioners for public works, 2 May 1884, registry of deeds, 1884 Bk 25, no. 21.

53 The detail in this and succeeding paragraphs is to be found in the Headfort rentals papers, NLI MS 25,410 (28–39).

54 District inspector's report, police reports, Midland Division, TNA CO 904/61 and 62. The divisional and county inspector's reports in CO 904 are available at the National Archives of Ireland: NAI MFA 54. The reason for the change on the part of the 'nationalist party' was Gladstone's pending second Home Rule bill and a desire by the party for quietness in the countryside while it made its passage through parliament.

the coming winter' with the prospect of 'every man being able to pay his rent'.[55] However, the report disclosed a hundred evicted farms in the county, of which seventy-four were derelict.

Sir David Harrell[56] in a memorandum for John Morley, who was considering how the difficult issue of evicted tenants might be resolved, wrote:

> It is to be remembered that the planter acquired possession without having paid for the former tenant's interest and could never have regarded himself as quite free from some obligation to do so.[57]

A more nuanced position was taken by Canon Gibbons of Bala, before commencing his sermon on 26 September 1897:

> Where a poor person is unjustly evicted from his holding because he cannot pay his rent, and some other person takes advantage of his necessitous position while he the former tenant has any hope of regaining it – that in my opinion is land-grabbing. But on the other hand if a person who has been evicted from a holding, has no desire or hope of regaining it, and leaves the place, it would be a loss to the whole country and absurd that it should be left waste.[58]

The fact that Patrick Reilly had abandoned his holding, with 'no desire or hope of regaining it', did not mitigate how events played out in Lisnafana between October 1894 and July 1895.

In December 1893 Lord Headfort's elder son died. When the marquess died the following July, the title passed to his surviving son, Lord Geoffrey Taylour, then aged 16. Accordingly, the estate was held by Henry Crichton and Lord Arthur Hill as trustees for an infant leaving them less room for manoeuvre than a life tenant of full age.[59]

Hugh Moore had come to Billis, a short distance from Lisnafana, to assist his widowed sister and her six young children on a farm leased on the Sankey Dunlop estate. Not content with assisting his sister, Moore began to negotiate a lease from the Headfort estate. He had not completed the formalities before

55 Divisional inspector's report, Sept. 1894, monthly confidential reports Northern, TNA CO 904/50 (hereafter divisional or county inspector's report).

56 Sir David Alfred Harrell, commissioner DMP 1883–92, under-secretary for Ireland 1893–1902.

57 Harrell to Morley, Morley papers, Bodleian, MS Eng C 7071.

58 The case commented upon was on the Pringle estate where grazing on an evicted farm was taken for 6 months. The former tenant had left for America before the eviction and the farm had been derelict since 1889. TNA CO 903/6 no 26. Oct. 1897.

59 Settled Land Act 1882 (45 & 46 Vict., c. 38), s. 60. See further Wylie, *Irish land law*, para. 8.028.

the thunderclouds started to rumble. At a meeting of the Virginia branch of the Irish National Federation (INF), the anti-Parnellite wing of the Irish Parliamentary Party, on 13 October 1894 land-grabbing was condemned and the people of the parish exhorted to earnest and energetic action so that 'the land grabber would have no place in Irish life and that together with the shopkeepers and tradesmen they would make the position of the land-grabber one that is not to be desired.'[60]

Notwithstanding the INF branch meeting in Virginia, Moore paid a deposit of £100 to the agent Matthew Weld O'Connor JP, and took Farms 4 and 5 from which Patrick Reilly had been evicted.[61] Moore was given possession on 24 October 1894 by bailiff John Nugent. His first year was rent free. The lease was not perfected until 4 February 1895. The annual rent payable was £30.[62]

In November and December, shortly after taking possession, Moore's cattle were driven off the land at night, and he and his brother were turned back by the same Con Reilly of Farms 1 and 3 when passing between Con's fields. Con told them that he would not get leave to live in the country if he allowed them to do so; Moore replied that if that was the case, he was long since shot – to which Con answered there was time enough for that.[63]

The INF did not delay in taking action. A meeting was called for 6 December. The county inspector's monthly report stated that Hugh Moore was the object of the meeting, that 'the owner of the farm was absent in America and that his wife was willing to take money for her interest in the holding'.[64] While the subaltern code might demand money for the wife's consent to Moore's occupation, the official law saw the matter differently. However harsh it may seem, the wife had no standing to justify the payment. Trustees for a minor had no discretion to pay following an eviction.

The meeting in Virginia on 6 December was attended by over three thousand people, three bands, a host of clergy and, contrary to the county inspector's expectations, three members of parliament: William O'Brien (Cork), James Gibney (Meath) and Samuel Young (East Cavan). Joseph Devlin, a civic delegate from Belfast, was also present.[65] O'Brien's object in

60 *Weekly Freeman,* 13 Oct. 1894.

61 The homestead is marked 'A' on the map (Plate 9.1). The rental for May 1892 records a decision to eject the following Nov. when £152 19*s*. 2*d* was owing on annual rents totalling £55. The rental of May 1893 notes 'eviction notice 6 June 1893' and 'decree sent to Allen' (solicitor) on 3 Mar. 1894 with 'possession given by the sheriff on 3 Apr. 1894'. The rental of Nov. 1894 noted the rent payable by Patrick Reilly as 'unrecoverable', NLI MS 25,410 (38, 39).

62 The reduction of £25 compared to the evicted yearly tenant's rent reflected the weakness of the position of the Headfort estate. The title of the Headfort estate has not been examined as at the time of writing. The original title is not yet accessible in the NLI.

63 Moore memorandum.

64 County inspector's report, 4 Dec. 1894, TNA CO 904/50.

65 See the *Anglo Celt*, 8 Dec. 1894. Divisional Commissioner Captain Owen R. Slacke also reported on the meeting: report of 8 Jan. 1895, TNA CO 904/50.

coming to Virginia was to reach out to northern farmers seeking their support for a land bill. In acknowledging the address presented to him, O'Brien said:

> The Protestant farmers of the North are in the matter the absolute masters of the situation. It is the first time, the only time, that Ulster will have it in its power to decide the fate of a land bill and I would remind the Protestant farmers of the North of this that they are infinitely more deeply concerned in the passing of the Land Bill than the nationalists of the South for if the worst comes to the worst the nationalists of Ireland are pretty well able to regulate these matters for themselves with bad landlords by combination and by passing a little rough and ready legislation of our own (cheers) whereas the Protestant farmers of the North have absolutely nothing to look for except what they can gain from within the four corners of an act of parliament.[66]

A proposal was made to the meeting to adopt some such 'rough and ready legislation' by resolutions which condemned land-grabbing as destructive of the best interests of the tenant farmers and of the national cause. To cheers of 'Down with the grabbers', Revd Fr Francis McKiernan said:

> The real enemy of the tenant farmer is the man who grabs an evicted farm. If you adopt the resolutions like men, the landgrabber could not live in your midst for three months. You can meet him in the fairs and markets and see that he cannot buy or sell goods. If you had a horn and blow it after him, there is not a man in the town but will know him. It is only by a combination like this that you will obtain a good land act.[67]

And so it turned out for Moore in the New Year with the boycott commencing between 3 and 8 January.[68] Mud was thrown at Moore as he left 'mass'. James McManus, a miller with whom Moore was having oats ground, advised him to take them away as people were talking about his grinding them.[69] On 24 January 1895, he brought his sister's colt to Virginia Fair, but being hooted and abused was unable to sell it. He sheltered with police under

66 See the *Anglo Celt*, 8 Dec. 1894. The interest of the Northern farmers in the land bill was reviewed by Slacke in his report of 8 Jan. It appears tenant concern that rights proposed to be accrued under the land bill might be lost prior to its enactment heightened tension and led to increased public disturbance across the Northern Division.

67 Ibid.

68 The district inspector's report of 3 Jan. 1895 stated that the speeches of 6 Dec. 1894 had had no effect, and nor was it expected they would. The Northern divisional inspector's report of 8 Jan. 1895, which also outlined the meeting of 6 Dec. 1894, recounted the emerging public order problem. TNA CO 904/50 and NAI MFA 54/17.

69 Ibid. In including the most recent information not included in the district inspector's report, Slacke included mistaken detail on the religious affiliation. Moore's family were Church of Ireland, his eldest brother sometime a rector in the diocese of Ossory.

an archway before being followed by a crowd out of the town.[70] He had difficulty bringing hay to Lisnafana on 2 February after he had bought three cartloads of hay from Peter Brady of Murmod, who was also boycotted. There was some disorder before leaving Murmod. A disorderly crowd assembled, stones and sods of turf were thrown, and Moore drew his revolver, firing two ineffective shots in the air.[71] Moore and his three men, accompanied by Brady, were met at Lisgrey crossroads by another crowd, which abused them and frightened the horses.[72] The first horse fell and the tethers were cut on the third cart. The crowd defied Moore to shoot as they continued shouldering and shoving him: he again fired in the air. Knocked to the ground, the crowd tried to take Moore's revolver until one of Moore's men, John James Cox, drew his revolver, whereupon Moore was released and he and his party continued the journey leaving the crowd, alleged to number some two hundred, to do as they pleased with the upset horse and cart. Some of the crowd cut across the fields to get to the farm first but a police patrol from Ballyjamesduff was there and brought the situation under control. When they returned to rebuild the upset load accompanied by the police, Moore and his men were again annoyed by the crowd. Two days later they were the object of further abuse when they brought the carts back to Billis.[73]

At the petty sessions on 7 February, Alexander William Sankey JP remarked in the course of a case that the INF was not going to rule the place yet and he hoped it never would. A meeting of the INF on 10 February condemned such outbursts of passion and the conduct of Sankey which, it was alleged, 'invariably outrages the feelings of the people'.[74] John Ross MP queried in the House of Commons whether the chief secretary was aware of the boycotting of Moore and the incident in February and that boycotting notices had appeared in the *Drogheda Independent*. John Morley confirmed that the facts stated in the question, including the boycotting of Moore's sister, were correct and that the government had directed the prosecution of the ringleaders.[75]

70 Moore memorandum; and divisional commissioners' reports, Jan. and 9 Feb. 1895 TNA CO 904/50.

71 Moore memorandum. Peter Clerkin, an evicted tenant, in retaliation against proceedings brought against him for assault by Brady, alleged that Brady fired these shots and prosecuted Brady, but it was dismissed. Clerkin was bound to the peace on Brady's charge. The divisional commissioner's report of 8 February 1895 put the crowd in Virginia at 200 and noted that a special report (not found) had been submitted previously. It recorded that '[s]ince then he had been followed along the public road by crowds blowing horns etc.' TNA CO 904/50 and NAI MFA 54/17.

72 Lisgrey Crossroads, marked 'B' on the map.

73 Moore memorandum; police crime division special, monthly confidential report, 2 Jan. 1895; and divisional commissioner's report, 9 Feb. 1895, TNA CO 904/50.

74 TNA CO 903/4, M series, no. 35, p. 23, quoting *Weekly Freeman,* 12 Feb. 1895.

75 *Hansard's Parl. deb., 4th series,* vol. 30, cols 966–7 (18 Feb. 1895).

Moore brought some of his sister's flax to the mill of Thomas Kellett JP in Curraghmore[76] to have it dressed. While there, a brother of the evicted Patrick Reilly whose farms Moore had taken came in and told the head scutcher that the mill would be boycotted if he attempted to scutch the flax. The man who issued the warning was Con Reilly, likely the same man who held Farm 3 and to whom Farm 1 had been assigned in 1889 (though this has not been confirmed). So, although Moore had been told that the mill would scutch the flax this was not done.[77]

Two days before the prosecutions were due to be heard, William Ellison-Macartney MP enquired what action the lord chancellor proposed to take against two of the local magistrates, Fitzsimons and Tierney, given their involvement in the meeting of 6 December, and what steps would be taken to prevent them from participating in the court at which the proceedings were pending. Morley replied that neither had taken part in any illegality concerning the events giving rise to the prosecutions that would take place at the March sessions where Fitzsimons and Tierney were entitled to sit. Morley added that they were persons of respectability and fit for the post.[78]

When the petty session bench assembled in Virginia on 7 March, Sankey was in the chair.[79] Objection was taken to the presence of Fitzsimons and Tierney on the grounds already noted, namely that they had taken part in the meeting that gave rise to the proceedings. The solicitor for the accused objected to O'Connor, Headfort's agent, and to the chairman owing to the political views he had expressed. O'Connor, Fitzsimons and Tierney withdrew. Sankey chaired the court, sitting with Olphert RM.[80] Among those prosecuted[81] was Peter Clerkin, whom Moore identified as the ringleader at Virginia Fair and as being in the front rank of the crowd on 2 February. Peter Brady and John James Cox gave corroborative evidence, Cox admitting his membership of the Property Defence Association, indicating that he was an 'emergency man' brought in by Moore to break the boycott. Bernard Reilly

76 Thomas C. Kellett JP held 62 acres on the small estate of Samuel and Alex Hunter, comprising a house, a flax mill, two other houses, out offices, land and water having an annual value for the buildings £12 and the land £37. Lurgan Lodge coloured mauve and mill marked "C" on the map. The description of the mill as a 'Corn Mill' on the Ordnance Historic map is corrected manually to 'Flax Mill' on the Valuation Office map.

77 Moore memorandum. The fact of the incident and the boycotting of Moore's sister is also recorded in the district inspector's report of 3 Mar. 1895, TNA CO 904/50.

78 *Hansard's Parl. deb., 4th series*, vol. 31, cols 388–9 (5 Mar. 1895).

79 Those on the bench included Olphert RM, M. Weld O'Connor, L. Fitzsimons and J. Tierney.

80 *Anglo Celt*, 9 Mar. 1895.

81 Moore and Hamilton DI prosecuted. It was necessary for Moore to prosecute pursuant to 36 Ed. III, c. 12 (1362) as an order to bind a person to the peace could only be made at the suit of the aggrieved party. Moore had to prove he was in fear of a corporal hurt. Clerkin was also prosecuted by Brady. See Richard Burn, *Justice of the peace and parish officer* (30th edn, London, 1869), p. 743. For a subsequent view of the law see J. O'Connor, *Justice of the peace* (Dublin, 1911), ch. 4.

and John Reilly, sons of Con Reilly,[82] were similarly charged. The outcome was that four of the accused were bound to the peace, but the case against Bernard Reilly was dismissed and one other case was withdrawn.[83]

Meanwhile, Dublin Castle had been dealing with Fr McKiernan. He had drawn attention to himself by entering the controversy over the magistrates. He asked Samuel Young MP to raise a question with Morley in the House of Commons but Young, discreetly, forwarded the correspondence to Morley on 15 February 1895 seeking a suitable reply so that he need not raise the question formally.[84] When Captain Owen Slacke, then divisional commissioner at Dundalk, saw the query on 26 February, he regarded it as extraordinary that McKiernan should complain through Young of that which he himself had been the cause. He also noted that Young, who had forwarded the query, was also present at the meeting of 6 December in Virginia and must have heard what was said. Slacke left at the bishop of Kilmore's residence a copy of the *Anglo Celt* reporting McKiernan's remarks. Two weeks later, Slacke returned and had a long discussion with the bishop about McKiernan and reported his satisfaction that McKiernan had seen the error he had committed and was unlikely to cause further trouble. The report went all the way to Morley, via Harrell, indicating the potential for the case to cause further embarrassment. From personal investigation, Slacke was satisfied the police were doing all in their power to keep things quiet, notwithstanding which the annoyance to Moore and Brady was daily increasing.[85]

Unionist politicians did not let go of the opportunity to harry Morley over his magistrates. Macartney returned to the issue on 11 March to ask Morley what the lord chancellor intended to do about Fitzsimons and Tierney. Morley replied that the lord chancellor had been informed that neither took any part in the proceedings on 7 March and, after enquiry, found that neither had taken part in any illegality on the occasion out of which the prosecutions of 7 March arose, and no further action was proposed.[86]

At the end of March, the northern division report noted that since the prosecutions, there had been an improvement, as the demonstrations had not been as hostile nor the disturbances so daring as formerly. This improvement did not survive the failure of a prosecution against one Peter Carroll arising from an incident at Bailieborough. In late May, a drumming party assembled on a hill about half a mile from Moore's house and drummed for half an hour cheering and groaning, and the police reported that the local press left nothing undone to keep the sore open.[87]

82 1901 census return by Cornelius O'Reilly, Lisnafana.
83 See Plate 9.3. The prosecutions and their outcomes were noted in the divisional and district inspectors' police reports of Mar. 1895. TNA, CO 904/50
84 NAI CSO 756/0, 27 Feb. 1895.
85 NAI CSO 893/0, 27 Feb. and 23 Mar. 1895 (marked 'confidential').
86 *Hansard's Parl. deb., 4th series*, vol. 30, cols 966–7 (18 Feb. 1895).
87 District commissioner and county inspector's report, 4 June 1895.

THE EVENING OF 22 JUNE 1895 AND ITS CONSEQUENCES

When Moore left Billis on the evening of 22 June 1895 he was followed as he took the back road to Lisnafana. Cheering by Michael McCabe and Patrick Mulvanney caused numbers to increase and when Moore reached a fork where he could take the pass to Lisnafana through the farm of one Hugh Reilly in Cleggan, he saw people waiting on the hill beside the lane. He chose instead to 'go straight the road to Mr Kellett's field'. As he did, Moore passed people on the road. He recognized John Reilly and his brother Bernard from Lisnafana, sons of Con Reilly, joining the crowd. He wrote afterwards that the crowd followed him, some with horns made for the purpose. Others were annoying him, and 'he could see the road before him lined with people of the same class and, fearing to keep the road, [he] entered into Frank Corrigan's corn field at the foot of which [he] only had to jump into his own land'.[88]

What happened after Moore entered Corrigan's cornfield was the subject of a police investigation, a coroner's inquest and a magisterial investigation, with the latter two being widely reported in the nationalist *Anglo Celt*, *Cavan Weekly News* and the *Drogheda Independent* and the unionist *Meath Herald and Cavan Advertiser*. The investigations followed the pattern identified by Vaughan,[89] and what follows is a compilation of the reported evidence resulting from the three enquiries. Unfortunately, neither the record of the inquest nor the crown prosecution file have been found, presumed removed, or lost in 1922.

Frank Corrigan, returning home from Lisgrey, saw Moore in his field with people walking after him. He challenged Moore to go back and not trample his oats. Moore presented his revolver and told Corrigan to keep back or 'I will do you'. The taunting of Moore continued but it was maintained at the inquest by Patrick Mulvaney, who with Michael McCabe had followed Moore from Billis, that no stones or clay were thrown at him. These appear to have missed their target as Constable John Curtin could find no marks on Moore when examining him later that evening. McCabe, who was a couple of yards from the hedge, said that the people in the field had no weapons.

Moore stumbled on jumping into his own land. The evidence was that no attempt was made to follow him. Two minutes after he crossed the ditch, he fired a shot in the direction of the crowd. Bernard Reilly deposed that the shot was fired towards him and that he heard the whizz of the bullet pass his ear, but no one was hurt. Some of the children ran away but Mulvaney, Bernard Reilly and another John Reilly, a youth of 18 years from the neighbouring townland of Curraghmore, remained some thirty feet away from the hedge. Moore said nothing. Crouching, Moore moved closer to the ditch where the

88 Moore memorandum. Pass labelled 'D' and Corrigan's field labelled 'E' on the map.
89 W.E. Vaughan, *Murder trials in Ireland, 1836–1914* (Dublin, 2009), ch. 2 & 3.

hedge was uncut, took aim and fired a second shot through the hedge. John Reilly fell, shot in the head. He was carried to the road where he died shortly afterwards and was then carried home on a door taken from his parents' house above the field. Moore went up his field in Lisnafana and back to his own place. He was alleged by Michael McCabe to have answered the charge that he had shot John Reilly with the words 'Well, there is one of you gone anyway', but Frank Corrigan said Moore made no reply. The police arrived quickly and having inspected the scene District Inspector Hamilton arrested Moore, cautioned him, and charged him with the offence. A fully loaded revolver, smelling as if it had recently been fired, but no ammunition was found in Moore's house.

The *Cavan Weekly News* reported that in Virginia 'the greatest excitement prevailed with large and angry crowds pacing the streets crying "blood for blood", "down with the grabbers" and "lynch them".'[90] The police managed to deliver Moore to the barracks through the large crowds by disguising him as a policeman. The following day Moore was remanded to Bailieborough Bridewell.

Dr G.J. Bourke JP, the coroner for East Cavan, held the inquest on 24 June in the victim's home at Curraghmore. It was very much a people's proceeding.[91] The coroner was an official elected on the parliamentary franchise and the jury comprised householders with a valuation greater than £4.[92] The jurors' names were published, twelve names mentioned by the *Anglo Celt* and fourteen by the *Drogheda Independent*.[93] They appear to have come from nearby townlands and at least one was from a modest cottage.[94] Family apart and excluding representatives of the press, at least twenty-three people were present: the coroner, and his jury, the county and district police inspectors, four witnesses, Dr McDaid, and Dr Caldwell and two solicitors representing Moore. The jurors viewed the body and Dr McDaid, assisted by Dr Caldwell performed the autopsy in the victim's home.

County Inspector Rogers and District Inspector Hamilton were present to watch the case on behalf of the crown but the police gave no evidence to the inquest. The coroner requested that Moore be produced, but Hamilton

90 *Cavan Weekly News*, 29 June 1895.

91 For a summary of the law concerning inquests during the nineteenth century, see Vaughan, *Murder trials*, pp 40–53.

92 The Coroners (Ireland) Act 1846 (9 & 10 Vict., c. 37), ss. 8 & 23. The franchise was last revised under the Representation of the People Act 1884 (48 & 49 Vict., c. 3). For a recent study of the work, life and background of a coroner, see M. McGoff-McCann, *The Irish coroner: death, murder and politics in Co. Monaghan, 1846–78* (Dublin, 2023).

93 At least 12 jurors were required for a valid verdict. Coroners (Ireland) Act 1881 (48 & 49 Vict., c. 35), s. 6.

94 Much detail can be gained by checking the names against the heads of household recorded in the 1901 census 5 years later. The juryman franchise can be cross checked against the Valuation Office records. One Andrew Rock lived in Curraghmore in a house rated at £4.

objected, saying Moore was in Bailieborough Bridewell, and neither the coroner nor the jury had power to compel his attendance. After hearing evidence from the victim's father, four other witnesses and two doctors, the coroner charged the jury, saying that the young man died of a gunshot wound inflicted by Moore but they had to determine if it was murder or manslaughter. After a short deliberation the jury replied that Hugh Moore 'did on 22 June wilfully, maliciously and of malice aforethought kill and slay John Reilly' adding the rider 'that Moore should not have been allowed to carry firearms as he had police protection and had threatened to shoot down people in the road'. The death was subsequently registered, the death certificate stating the cause of death as: 'Laceration of brain. About 10 minutes. Caused by revolver shot inflicted by Hugh Moore (homicidal).'[95]

Getting Moore from Bailieborough to the Virginia courthouse for the magisterial investigation on 28 June again required some care. He was brought in a brake escorted by 25 constables, with the *Drogheda Independent* reporting the additional precaution of six patrols of police placed along the road at different locations. The bench comprised Irwin RM and the recently appointed Tierney who had withdrawn from hearing the March prosecutions. Sankey, Kellett, Olphert and O'Connor were all absent, as was Fitzsimons, the prominent member of the INF. Cavan crown solicitor Hugh Kennedy prosecuted. Bird BL represented Moore and solicitor W.H. Halpin watched the case on behalf of the executors of the Headfort estate. Kennedy agreed to an adjournment.[96]

When the investigation resumed on 10 July, Starkey RM joined the bench and all of the inquest witnesses (except the father) were examined, along with a further six witnesses. Kennedy objected to all reference to the boycotting in the cross-examination of Michael McCabe. The chairman allowed the questions saying it would be relevant if Moore had been apprehensive of danger. Kennedy need not have worried for no one admitted to knowing that Moore was boycotted. Moore maintained in his memorandum that, apart from cheering, horns had been blown to draw out an increased crowd. The evidence to the magistrates was contradictory however, partly because the questions were not framed consistently: some by Kennedy in his examination in chief and others by Bird BL for Moore in cross examination. For example, McCabe did not have a horn and did not see any horns; John Brady heard no horns; but both Frank Corrigan and Bernard Reilly heard a horn blown. The district inspector produced the six-chamber revolver. When the depositions were complete, they were read over again, and the chairman of the court again read the charge followed by a short statement from Moore who was returned for trial at the next Cavan assizes. Bail was refused and he was removed to

95 General register of death, superintendent's district of Oldcastle, registrar's district of Virginia, April–June 1895, entry no. 495, General Registrar's Office, Dublin.
96 *Anglo-Celt*, 29 June and 13 July 1985; *Drogheda Independent*, 29 June and 13 July 1985.

Armagh jail.[97] The murder charge against Moore was recorded in the printed prosecutions record for July 1895.[98] For some reason and despite the finding at the inquest, the charge was reduced to manslaughter before the end of July. The trial was automatically transferred to the winter assizes in Londonderry.[99]

On 13 August 1895 Moore was granted bail by Murphy J at the queen's bench, in the sum of £200 on two sureties of £100 each.[100] On 17 August, a police protection post was established on his farm comprising an acting sergeant and two constables. Moore was accompanied everywhere by two armed policemen.[101] The *Anglo Celt* fanned the flames. In a leader on 14 September 1895 entitled 'Provoking the people' it wrote:

> Is it not enough that Moore, the emergency man, has been liberated on bail though the coroner's jury found him guilty of the murder of the boy John Reilly and should at will under the protection of policemen's rifles saunter about the spot where the unfortunate lad fell; is not gratification sufficient to the Tory and extreme Orange section of the community that the father of the dead boy must in the course of his daily work see the man who admitted to having done the deed – how or in what circumstances it is for a jury to decide.

The publication of resolutions passed by the Virginia branch of the INF was referred to Dublin Castle in September. The resolutions were clearly in contempt of court but it was felt no useful purpose would be served by a prosecution, an opinion with which the attorney general Cecil Atkinson concurred.[102]

97 Moore was committed for trial by the magistrates following his arrest by the constabulary and not by the coroner. Under the Coroners (Ireland) Act 1881 (44 & 45 Vict., c. 35), ss 7 & 8, the coroner or two justices of the peace before whom the inquest was held could grant bail in cases of manslaughter, but not murder. The justices had no power to admit to bail a person committed by a coroner's warrant. Although a committal for trial on a coroner's verdict was not unknown, Napier AG was of the view that coroners' inquisitions obstructed rather than promoted the ends of public justice. See Vaughan, *Murder trials*, p. 107.

98 Virginia Petty Sessions, District Court Order Book, Co. Cavan, Virginia. Aug. 1894–Feb. 1896, TNA Court Service Petty Sessions S 1/10399 and NAI MFGS 58/3011.

99 Winter Assizes Act 1876 (39 & 40 Vict., c. 57) (extended to Ireland by the Supreme Court of Judicature (Ireland) Act 1877 (40 & 41 Vict., c. 57), s. 63.

100 *Drogheda Argus*, 17 Aug. 1895. See also the *Ulster Gazette*, *Drogheda Independent* and the *Meath Herald and Cavan Advertiser*. The sureties were two of Moore's brothers. Moore's counsel was John Ross MP, son of the Presbyterian Moderator to whom Matthew Weld O'Connor had written in 1886.

101 TNA CO 903/5 (B series, 11) p. 43, citing NAI CSO 15782 (not found). The crown may have opposed the bail application in an endeavour to ameliorate reactions against the downgrading of the charges and the expense of the protection post.

102 NAI CSO 15768, 25–8 Sept. 1895. The text of the resolutions is not among the papers.

1.1 Samuel Wooley, 'The House of Lords portico, Dublin', 1797, NGI.2652

2.1 James Malton, 'The Upper Yard, Dublin Castle', NGI.11568

3.1 James Black, 'William Molyneux (1656–1698), philosopher and M.P. for Trinity College, Dublin', 1813, NGI.3692

4.1 Andrew Reid, 'The main courtyard of the Four Courts Marshalsea (Debtors) Prison, Thomas Street, Dublin', 1860, NGI.2641

4.2 Thomas Sautelle Roberts, 'The Four Courts, Dublin', NGI.11912

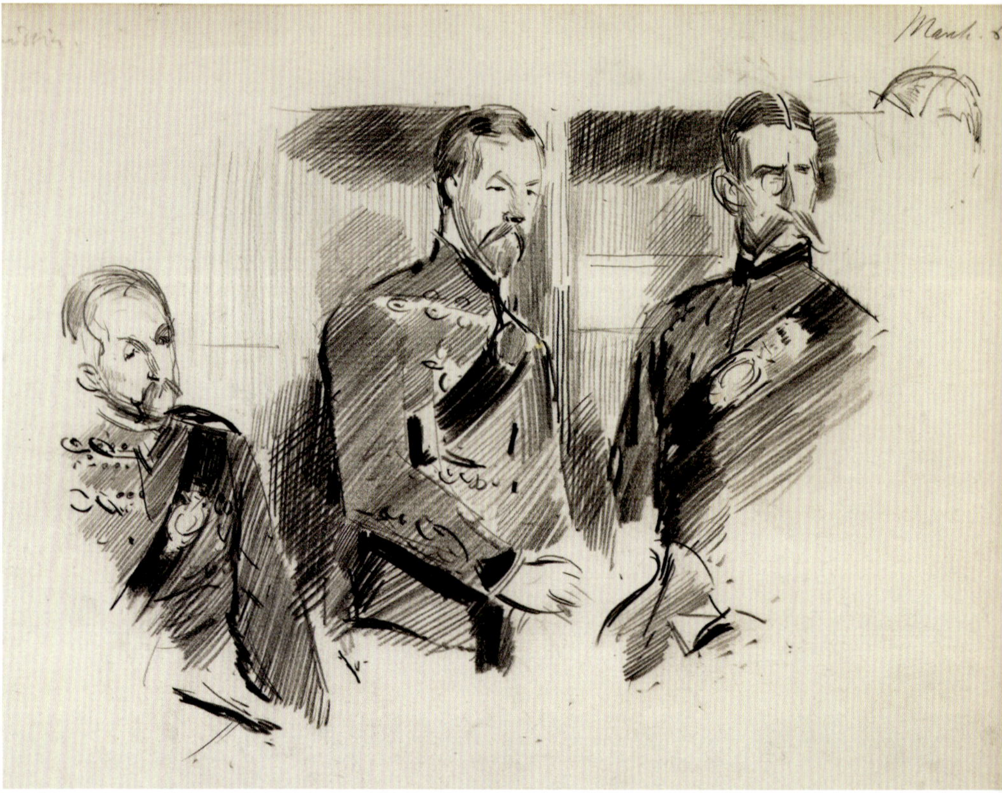

5.1 Sydney Prior Hall, 'Three members of the Royal Irish Constabulary', 1889, NGI.2813

6.1 Frank Dadd, 'The state of Ireland: stopping a hunt', *Illustrated London News*, 24 Dec. 1881

6.2 Frank Dadd, 'The Irish Land League: Mr. Boyton burning the Duke of Leinster's leases on a '98 pike in the Market Place of Kildare', *Illustrated London News*, 8 Jan. 1881

6.3 John Fergus O'Hea, 'Two Christmas hearths', *Weekly Freeman*, 18 Dec. 1886

7.1 Sydney Prior Hall, 'Charles Stewart Parnell in the House of Commons', NGI.2835

7.2 Howard Helmick, 'News of the Land League', 1881, NGI.4507

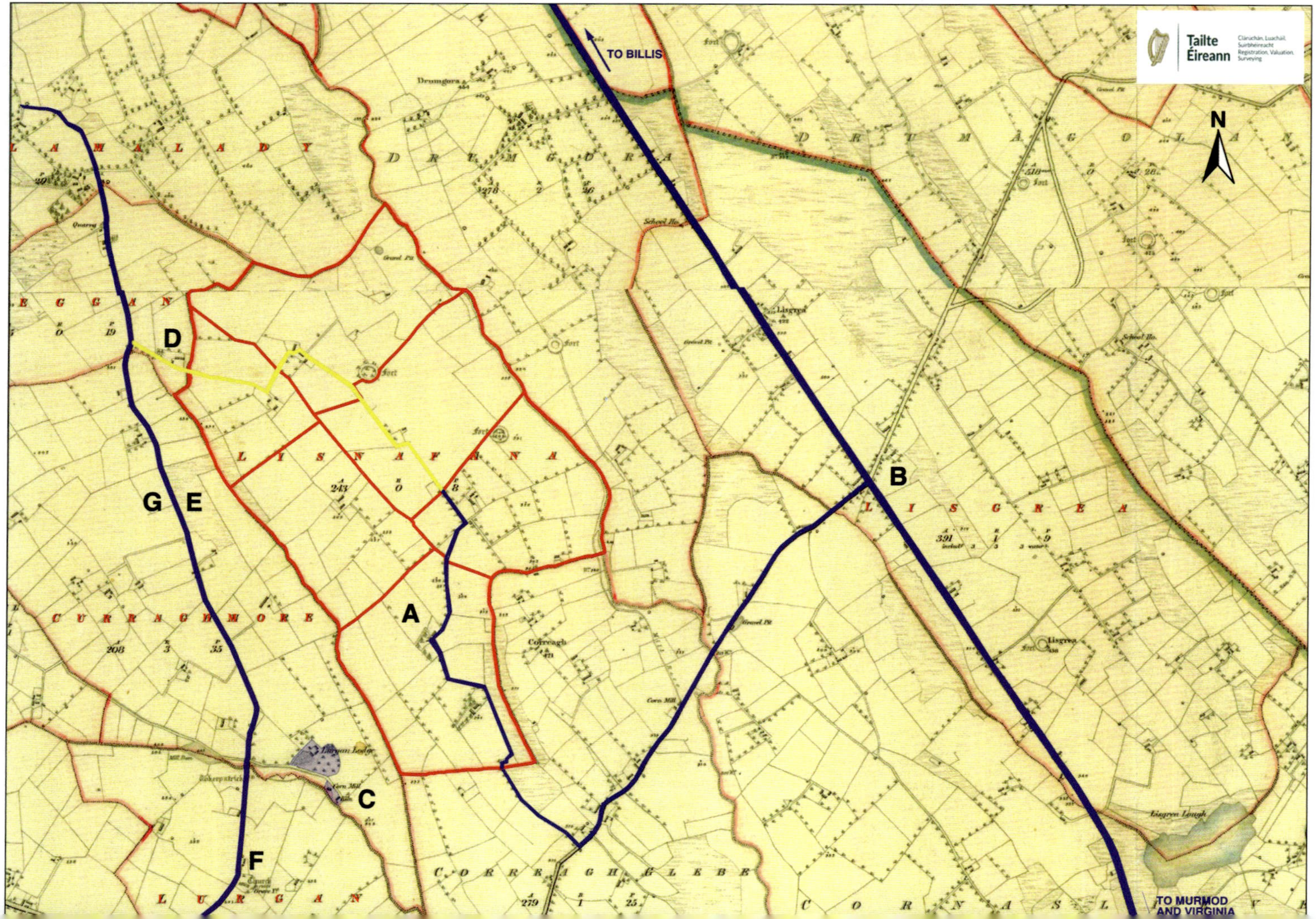

TO BILLIS
Táilte Éireann
Clárúchán, Luacháil, Suirbhéireacht
Registration, Valuation, Surveying
N
LAMMALADY
DRUMGORA
DRUMAGOLAN
EGGAN
LISNAFANNA
LISGREA
CURRAGHMORE
CORRAGHGLEBE
CORNASLEAN
LURGAN
A
B
C
D
E
F
G
TO MURMOD AND VIRGINIA

9.1 (*opposite*) Historic map CN033/039 of Lisnafana, Co. Cavan, surveyed 1836. © Tailte Éireann/Government of Ireland. Cartography and key drawing courtesy of Leanne R. Martin, B. Arch., MRIA.

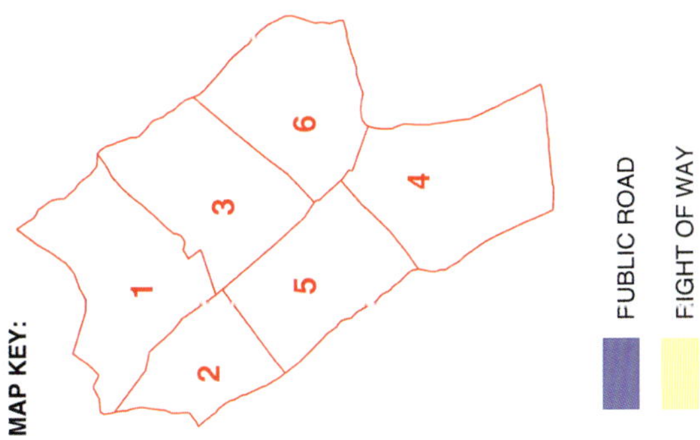

Farm 1 Peter Reilly, acquired by Con Reilly
Farm 2 Margaret Reilly
Farm 3 Con Reilly
Farm 4 & 5 Patrick Reilly evicted; reset Hugh Moore
Farm 6 Garrett Reilly

A Moore's Farmstead
B Lisgrey Crossroads
C Kellet's Mill
D Pass To Con Reilly's Farm
E Corrigan's Cornfield
F Old Lurgan Church & Graveyard
G Memorial Stone

9.2 Virginia Court House, Co. Cavan, 2015, courtesy of Robert Marshall

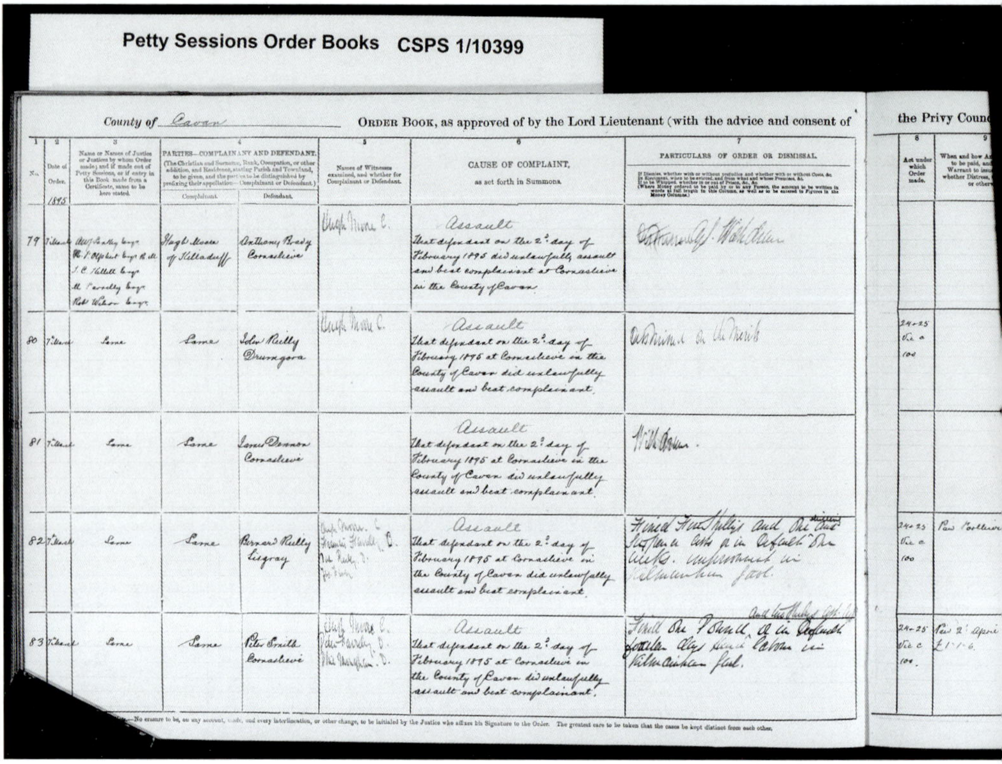
Petty Sessions Order Books CSPS 1/10399

County of Cavan — ORDER BOOK, as approved of by the Lord Lieutenant (with the advice and consent of the Privy Council

No.	Date of Order. 1895	Names or Names of Justice or Justices by whom Order made	Complainant	Defendant	Names of Witnesses examined, and whether for Complainant or Defendant	CAUSE OF COMPLAINT, as set forth in Summons	PARTICULARS OF ORDER OR DISMISSAL
79	7 March	[illegible]	Hugh Moore of Killaduff	Anthony Brady Cornaslieve	Hugh Moore C.	Assault That defendant on the 2nd day of February 1895 did unlawfully assault and beat complainant at Cornaslieve in the County of Cavan	[illegible] Withdrawn
80	7 March	Same	Same	John Reilly Drumgora	Hugh Moore C.	Assault That defendant on the 2nd day of February 1895 at Cornaslieve in the County of Cavan did unlawfully assault and beat complainant	Dismissed on the merits
81	7 March	Same	Same	James Brennan Cornaslieve		Assault That defendant on the 2nd day of February 1895 at Cornaslieve in the County of Cavan did unlawfully assault and beat complainant	Withdrawn.
82	7 March	Same	Same	Bernard Reilly Lisgray	[illegible]	Assault That defendant on the 2nd day of February 1895 at Cornaslieve in the County of Cavan did unlawfully assault and beat complainant	[illegible]
83	7 March	Same	Same	Peter Smith Cornaslieve	[illegible]	Assault That defendant on the 2nd day of February 1895 at Cornaslieve in the County of Cavan did unlawfully assault and beat complainant	[illegible]

No erasure to be, on any account, made, and every interlineation, or other change, to be initialled by the Justice who affixes his Signature to the Order. The greatest care to be taken that the cases be kept distinct from each other.

9.3 Five prosecutions by Hugh Moore for assault at Cornaslieve on 2 Feb. 1895, at Virginia. Photograph by Robert Marshall; reproduction of the original under Open Government Licence V3.0.

9.4 Vernacular memorial stone in the wall at Curraghmore opposite the entrance to Corrigan's corn field, courtesy of Robert Marshall (photographed in 2015)

9.5 Leslie Ward ('Spy'), 'An Irish property', caricature of Thomas Taylour, 3rd Marquess of Headfort (1822–94), *Vanity Fair*, 31 Mar. 1877

10.1 J. Newman & Co., 'Court House, Belfast', NLI 10TA

11.1 Hanna Sheehy Skeffington [1902], NLI

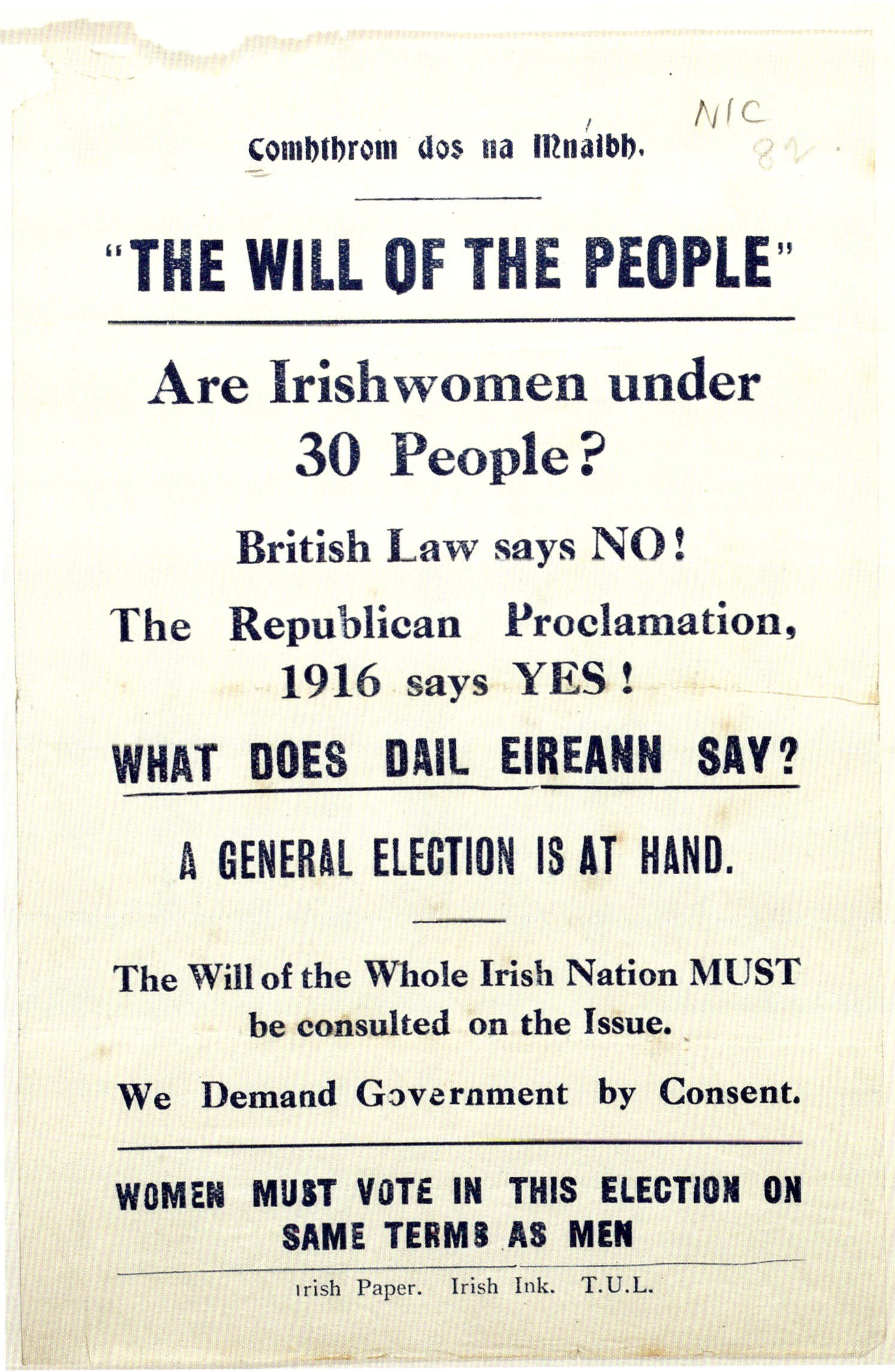

Comhthrom dos na Mnáibh.

"THE WILL OF THE PEOPLE"

Are Irishwomen under 30 People?

British Law says NO!

The Republican Proclamation, 1916 says YES!

WHAT DOES DAIL EIREANN SAY?

A GENERAL ELECTION IS AT HAND.

The Will of the Whole Irish Nation MUST be consulted on the Issue.

We Demand Government by Consent.

WOMEN MUST VOTE IN THIS ELECTION ON SAME TERMS AS MEN

Irish Paper. Irish Ink. T.U.L.

11.2 'The will of the people', handbill urging suffrage for women under thirty years [1918?], NLI D151/82

13.1 Walter Paget, 'The Irish Convention, 1917–1918, in full session at Trinity College Dublin', NLI PD E16

13.2 Harry Jones Thaddeus, 'Portrait of John Redmond (1856–1918), Parliamentarian', 1901, NGI.889

14.1 John Lavery, 'The ratification of the Irish Treaty in the English House of Lords, 1921', NGI.1736

When Moore came to trial routinely at the winter assizes in Londonderry, on 3 December 1895, the assize judge was Murphy J, who had granted Moore bail. He charged the grand jury,[103] remarking:

> It appears that Reilly was undoubtedly shot by a revolver bullet that was fired by Moore, and the question of finding a bill – if they did find a bill – before the court and the petty jury would be whether, under the circumstances that will be detailed, the prisoner Hugh Moore, was legally justified in doing the act committed by him. It had arisen out of that very terrible and pernicious form of persecution known as boycotting.

Murphy had clearly carefully read the depositions and after summarizing the evidence he continued:

> If Moore from the conduct pursued towards him or from any reasonable apprehension – not merely the apprehension of a timid man, but the apprehension that might occur to a man of firm judgment – if he were reasonably apprehensive that his life was in danger and that he considered the only means of preserving it was by showing that he was armed and by firing from the revolver, then Moore would be justified in the action he had taken for the preservation of his own life. But if it should occur to the jury the alarm under which he fired or the fact of his firing was not done under fairly reasonable apprehension that his own life was in danger and that it was essential for him for the preservation of his own life that he should fire, then they would find the bill for manslaughter that would be sent before them.

By convention the judge charged the grand jury in the absence of the lawyers. The grand jury then considered the case, with the six crown witnesses required to go through their evidence again privately.[104] That done, the grand jury found no bill. [105] Unexpectedly, Moore was free to go. When the report on the case by the *Derry Journal* was circulated at Dublin Castle, it was accompanied by the annotation:

103 The foreman was Sir Henry Harvey Bruce, and the jury of 23 included 4 deputy lieutenants and 14 justices of the peace.

104 For a discussion of grand jury procedure, see N. Howlin, *Juries in Ireland: laypersons and law in the long nineteenth century* (Dublin, 2017), pp 36–42 and W.G. Huband, *A practical treatise on the law relating to the grand jury in criminal cases, the coroner's jury and the petty jury in Ireland* (Dublin, 1896), ch. 1 & 2.

105 Crown Book, indictment and pleas, Ulster winter assizes, 1895, PRONI LOND/1/3/1/1. The district inspector was informed by wire on the following day and he anticipated that this was 'apt to cause a strong feeling'. District inspector's report, 4 Dec. 1895, TNA CO 904/50

> The grand jury found no bill against Moore, and though no reasons were, of course, given for their decision, there can be no doubt that they formed the conclusion that Moore fired the shots in self-defence. In so concluding they were doubtless influenced to some extent by the drift of the judge's observations.[106]

This view was also taken by the *Londonderry Sentinel*, which opined:

> It may even be that with a feeling of subtle sympathy for the sentiments of their co-religionists some Londonderry jurors also entertained more than an ordinary amount of curiosity in the Cavan case. But Mr Justice Murphy's carefully weighted charge hardly left the grand jury any alternative except to take the course they did of throwing out the bill on the ground that on the law as stated by the judge Moore acted in self-defence.[107]

A chance interview at Lisnafana in the research for this paper suggested that Moore had intended to target the ringleaders and not shoot the 'garsoon'. The identity of the ringleaders was not disclosed but it is possible that one was Bernard Reilly of Lisnafana, son of Con Reilly and nephew of the evicted tenant Patrick Reilly, who had been unsuccessfully prosecuted the previous March and who deposed that the first shot was fired at him. Whoever were the ringleaders, the point could not have been made for the prosecution. It carried the risk of incrimination and prosecution for conspiracy notwithstanding that establishing such a motive would have considerably improved the chances of convicting Moore.

A vernacular stone in the wall opposite Corrigan's oat field records the death of John Reilly who was buried nearby in the Old Lurgan churchyard looking south-westwards over east Cavan. A headstone notes that 'John Reilly 18 years was shot by Hugh Moore the Landgrabber on June 22nd 1895'.[108] Moore, who himself was just 22 years old, returned to his farm but he was not free. He was protected by four police living on the farm and while not interfered with he could not leave 'his own place' nor visit beyond which the District Inspector believed 'he would be shouted at and have horns blown at him from the back of houses'.[109] The boycott was lifted against his sister when

106 TNA CO 903/5 (B series), p. 5.

107 *Londonderry Sentinel*, 7 Dec. 1895. The full piece was biased, including a statement that Moore dealt generously with the wife of the former tenant – something Moore did not assert in his own memorandum. The inaccuracy highlights the need to carefully consider the readership of newspapers of the time when weighing their reportage.

108 See Plate 9.4. The ruined Old Lurgan church coloured green and marked 'F' and memorial stone marked 'G' respectively on the map.

109 The district inspector's monthly reports (Cavan 1896–1900) report the position until the protection post was broken up, TNA CO 904/50.

she remarried but it persisted against him.[110] The Property Defence Association supported him, but there was correspondence indicating difficulties between it and the estate. Apparently, Fowler, O'Connor's successor as agent, suggested to Moore that they were a slippery organization – to which the Association's committee duly took exception.[111] The estate supported Moore supplying timber and purchasing corrugated iron for roofing in November 1898, the cost being amortized as additional rent. An arrangement for Moore to graze cattle for the estate was not renewed and the RIC protection hut continued to be manned. In February 1900 Moore called it a day and enlisted for short service in South Africa with the 74th Imperial Yeomanry battalion.[112] The farm was advertised for sale by public auction fixed for 21 April, but it did not sell. Valuation Office records confirm that in 1911 the farm had been sold to Fr Gaffney, the industrious parish priest of Lurgan.

CONCLUSIONS

This chapter has demonstrated the application of the subaltern code in nationalist east Cavan at the end of the nineteenth century and suggests the various 'institutions' involved in its application were an embryonic state.

In east Cavan, rents on the Headfort estate declined gradually from 1879, particularly following the Plan of Campaign, as the tenants engaged with the procedures established by the 1881 and 1887 Land Acts. However, there was no general abatement of rent on the estate as a result of the Plan of Campaign. The haste with which the Plan was adopted following Dillon's speech at Woodford and the involvement of the Presbyterian minister and of Protestant farmers suggest there was some advance planning in the locality stemming from an underlying discontent. Those who proposed the Plan appreciated the necessity for cross-community support for its success while the Headfort estate, which was well run by a wealthy resident landlord, appreciated the necessity to break that consensus.

At policy level, government intervention in Rome to obtain the Papal Rescript was an attempt to amend the subaltern code by removing the

110 District inspector's monthly reports, TNA CO 904/51–52, and NAI CSO Index 1896 ref. to RP/1896/9974 (not found).

111 Filgate to Fowler, June 1898, NLI MS 48,953/4.

112 Moore enlisted voluntarily at Newbridge on 1 Mar. 1900 for service in South Africa. He served with the 74th Imperial Yeomanry battalion, 3rd Dublin (trooper 15177) for 14 months: TNA WO 128 Box 46, no. 61. The *Anglo Celt* reported on 23 June 1900 receipt at Ballyjamesduff of a letter stating that Moore had died of a fever on his way to the front. Actually, he was discharged on 21 May 1901 to work for De Beers Mines at Kimberly. He qualified for the Queen's South Africa medal with clasps for Cape Colony and Transvaal 1901, TNA WO 128, roll 127.

sanction of boycotting and the associated limitations it imposed on freedom to contract. The timing of the Rescript in April 1888 and Headfort's immediate campaign for payment of rent falling due on 1 May 1888 saw the protest wither on his estate, but revealed the difficulties faced by some farmers which the struggle had concealed. In the short term, individual rents were inflexible, and the entire farming risk remained with the tenants. The fittest survived the downturn but, as in 1879, the elderly, those in ill health, the less-than-competent and the profligate struggled. The system was inherently incapable of coping with these difficulties and depended upon family solidarity locally or remittances from abroad. The alternatives were death, the workhouse, a cabin by the roadside or emigration. Rent should have bound the farming classes together, but this chapter has revealed that their common identity was divided by class and religious affiliation, which the estate exploited to retain control. Unusually, the estate had the strength to face down the Plan of Campaign.

The subaltern code operated in east Cavan but not in a vacuum. It drew legitimacy from the 'rough and ready legislation' adopted at a large nationalist public meeting. Banners, local bands, and the presence on the platform of members of parliament and local clergy created a sense of dignity and occasion to enhance that legitimacy.

There was still a nationalist willingness in east Cavan to engage with the *de jure* law where it provided a remedy. Con Reilly engaged over ten years with the official law to recover a debt due to him by his neighbour resulting in the ownership of his neighbour's farm being changed through the county court without consent of the tenant or objection from the community. Further, participants in the boycotting of Hugh Moore willingly went to the Londonderry winter assizes as prosecution witnesses against Moore. Such participation would have lasting significance for the continuation of the legal system when the Irish Free State retained the statute book and the common law.

The Presbyterian church was lobbied by the Headfort estate. The Roman Catholic church was subjected to pressure from the state and from its flock. On one side the state obtained condemnation of the subaltern code from the Vatican during the Plan of Campaign and assurances as to the activity of Fr McKiernan following his speech at Virginia in December 1894. On the other side, the church was informally influenced by the laity, when during the Plan of Campaign the bishops had to finesse the terms of the Papal Rescript to maintain their political influence. Sankey's observation from the bench as to the INF not ruling the place yet expressed his awareness of the code and his insecurity when confronted by it, notwithstanding that he regarded it as illegitimate. The problem seen from the bench was that the court could only penalize what was illegal, not people doing collectively what they could do individually within the law. The nationalist provincial press also supported the subaltern code both in the events covered and in the tenor of editorials. While the police recognized 'the local press in each case leave nothing undone to keep the sore open',[113] that press had to avoid any accusation of publishing seditious material.

The clashes between the subaltern state and the *de jure* state come most clearly into focus in the conflicting verdicts of the coroner's jury in Curraghmore and the grand jury in Londonderry. That was a clash between two perspectives that could not be reconciled. Both sides agreed that Hugh Moore shot John Reilly, but they could not agree on the validity of the defence. The refusal of the grand jury to find a bill precluded the practices and procedures of the subaltern code being examined in court by the defence, for the grand jury's decision implied that the operation of the code justified Moore's action which had cost a young man his life

113 Cavan county inspector's report, 4 June 1895, TNA CO 904.

The law in action in Ulster in July 1898

ANTHONY HART*

This chapter draws upon research I carried out some years ago in the Belfast Central Library into newspaper reports of court cases in July 1898. That period was chosen because I discovered a printed dinner list of the North-East circuit for the summer assizes of July 1898, and was attempting to identify the number of members of the North-East circuit who were appearing on circuit at that time. I was struck by the number of reports of legal proceedings of all sorts routinely carried in the Belfast and provincial newspapers of the day. While these reports are not law reports in the sense that a lawyer uses that term, nevertheless they constituted a significant proportion of the content of all newspapers. I have referred to some of that material elsewhere,[1] but in this chapter I want to consider the everyday work of the courts at all levels as they dealt with cases of Ulster interest. These reports provide an excellent insight into the everyday work of the Irish courts, and something of life in general throughout Ulster near the end of the Victorian era.

By Ulster I mean the nine counties of the historic province of Ulster, which at that time formed the bulk of the area covered by the North-East and North-West circuits of the Irish bar. In July 1898 the North-East circuit consisted of counties Meath, Louth, Monaghan, Armagh, Down and Antrim. Carrickfergus and Drogheda were also assize towns. Counties Westmeath, Longford, Cavan, Fermanagh, Tyrone, Donegal and Londonderry made up the North-West circuit. Lord Chief Baron Palles[2] and Lord Justice Fitzgibbon[3] were the going judges on the North-East circuit, and Mr Justice Kenny and Mr Justice Madden went on the North-West circuit.

* An earlier version of this paper was delivered to the Irish Legal History Society at the Ulster Museum, Belfast, on Saturday, 22 Feb. 2014. Editorial note: This chapter touches on a number of different areas of law. Since the discourse was delivered in 2014, more scholarship on these areas has been published. The untimely death of our friend Tony Hart in 2019 meant that he did not have a chance to engage with this new material. Knowing his enthusiasm for keeping abreast of developments in the field, the editors have taken the decision to add references to recent scholarship where this would be of use to the reader.

1 A.R. Hart, *A history of the bar and inn of court of Northern Ireland* (Belfast, 2013), pp 74–7.

2 See O. Breen and N. McGrath (eds), *Palles: the legal legacy of the last lord chief baron* (Dublin, 2022).

3 See P. Maume, 'Fitzgibbon, Gerald' in *DIB*.

Apart from Belfast and Londonderry (which had also become a thriving commercial and industrial centre with its shirt factories and other industries)[4] and the towns of the Lagan Valley with their linen factories, Ulster was still predominantly a rural, agricultural community of county and market towns surrounded by estates with tenant farmers paying substantial rents to their landlords. Although the transformation of rural society by Wyndham's Land Act 1903,[5] which provided government loans to enable tenants to buy out their landlords and repay the purchase price to the government over many years, was still in the future, nevertheless Gladstone's Land Act 1881[6] had already brought about considerable change to the structure of rural society. Lyons described the 1881 Act as 'extremely complicated and after it became law led to an immense amount of tedious and vexatious litigation'.[7] However, it legalized the 'three F's'; that is, fixity of tenure, a fair rent, and free sale of the tenant's interest in his holding, as well as compelling the landlord to compensate the tenant for disturbance and for improvements he had made to the holding. The 1881 Act and subsequent acts also made provision for advances to tenants to purchase their holdings.[8]

The Land Commission was responsible for carrying these changes into effect. Presided over by a high court judge who was part of the queen's bench division, assisted by two judicial commissioners and many sub-commissioners, the Land Commission was empowered to fix a 'judicial' rent for a tenant, and we see several illustrations of its work in this period. At the end of the month Meredith J (sitting with Gerald Fitzgerald QC) gave a lengthy judgment in the Land Commission court on the issue of fair rents and tenant right (the so-called Ulster custom), before giving judgment in 36 cases from counties Antrim, Louth, Monaghan and Donegal which had been heard in Belfast.[9] We find sub-commissioners sitting in Strabane, Co. Tyrone,[10] earlier that month, and in Armagh at the end of June, with significant reductions being imposed in virtually every case in Armagh. For example, the rents payable by four tenants of the countess of Dartry were reduced by 23¾ per cent in total.[11]

Other signs of the financial strains faced by many landlords can be glimpsed in the proceedings of the land judges' court. This was also presided over by a high court judge, in this case Ross J. The land judges' court was part of the chancery division and was the successor to the landed estates court set

4 J. Bardon, *A history of Ulster* (Belfast, 1992), pp 394–6. See the image of Belfast Courthouse at Plate 10.1.

5 Land Purchase (Ireland) Act 1903 (3 Ed. VII, c. 37).

6 Land Law (Ireland) Act 1881 (44 & 45 Vict., c. 49).

7 F.S.L. Lyons, *Ireland since the Famine* (2nd edn London, 1985), p. 172.

8 C.F. Kolbert and T. O'Brien, *Land reform in Ireland* (Cambridge, 1975), pp 34–9.

9 *Belfast News Letter*, 27 July 1898.

10 *Londonderry Sentinel*, 7 and 9 July 1898.

11 *Armagh Guardian*, 1 July 1898. The 1881 Act provided for 15-year rental periods, and these may have been examples of the second round of judicial rents.

up by the Encumbered Estates Act 1849[12] which had been designed to facilitate sales of estates burdened with debt, such as the 30,000 acres of the third marquess of Donegall.[13] Although the number of land judges had been reduced to one by 1898, it would seem that there was still a need for a mechanism for the sale of such estates, at least to judge by the advertisement that appeared on 18 July of the forthcoming sale of an estate of 593 acres with a net annual rental of £1,748 11*s.* at Ballinvalley, eight miles from Newry and seven miles from Rostrevor in Co. Down.[14] This is not the only mention of the land judges' court, because on 30 June, Ross J heard an application to fix the rent of a house, demesne and lands at Ringdufferin, Co. Down.[15] On 26 July it was reported that he had dealt with applications to fix the rents on a Co. Tyrone estate, and for the payment out to a life tenant of part of the funds held in court where another estate had been sold.[16]

Given that so many depended upon the land for their livelihood, it is unsurprising that many of the cases before the county courts, and on appeals to the assizes, were disputes about issues involving rights to land, such as licences to cross neighbouring farms. The *Fermanagh Times* of 7 July carried a report of three cases at Newtownbutler quarter sessions, two of which were trespass cases, and the third involved the obstruction of a 'pass' to a well. That such disputes were a substantial part of the civil business of county courts is confirmed by the reports in the same newspaper[17] of the cases heard at the Fermanagh assizes a few days later when ten out of twenty-one civil bill appeals involved matters of title. Another report reminds us of the now-extinct hiring fairs that were a major feature of Ulster country life well into the twentieth century. Hiring fairs were gatherings of people who congregated in country towns seeking employment as agricultural labourers or domestic servants. Naturally such gatherings also attracted large crowds of people with money to spend. The plaintiff, who alleged that the defendant took money from her, said they met at hiring fairs at Trillick, Co. Tyrone, and Lisbellaw, Co. Fermanagh. She alleged that she had lent the defendant £4, which he had said at first that he would keep for a fortnight and that he was going to marry her, but the minister was sick! She later laid an information against him for theft, but the charge was dismissed by the magistrates, and she lost in the county court as well.[18]

Naturally, court reports were not confined to cases involving landlord and tenant, and newspapers carried reports of a wide range of matters before different courts. What would now be called 'family' cases came before the

12 Encumbered Estates (Ireland) Act 1849 (12 & 13 Vict., c. 77).
13 Bardon, *A history of Ulster*, p. 317.
14 *Belfast News Letter*.
15 Ibid.
16 Ibid.
17 *Fermanagh Times*, 14 July 1898.
18 Ibid., 7 July 1898.

courts at various levels, and demonstrated the precarious position of women at the time.[19] A deserted wife could apply to the petty sessions for a maintenance order, an example being a case heard at Markethill petty sessions. The *Armagh Guardian*[20] carried a detailed report of the proceedings in which the wife said she had been forced to go to the workhouse. She admitted she had not been on good terms with her husband because of his 'fancy woman', but denied her husband's allegations that she had been misappropriating farm produce. The magistrates found in her favour, and awarded her 5*s*. a week. Claims for the maintenance of illegitimate children could also be brought, and we find the recorder of Belfast hearing a claim for maintenance by the mother of an illegitimate child against the father of the child, presumably on appeal from the petty sessions.[21] Actions for seduction are also to be found, two civil bill appeals coming before Fitzgibbon LJ at the Antrim assizes.[22] At the same assizes, Fitzgibbon also tried two breach of promise actions. In one of them, Serjeant Dodd described his client, the plaintiff, as 'a young lady of irreproachable character, and a very handsome girl' from Galway who had risen to be manager of the King's Arms hotel in Larne. The defendant, a widower who was a retired policeman aged 72 with a pension of £69 a year, denied promising to marry her, saying that she had refused to marry him. The report is punctuated with 'laughter', and in one case 'great laughter'. The plaintiff was successful, but although she had claimed £500 the jury only awarded her £45. The other action was undefended. The plaintiff, a weaver from Portadown, gave evidence that the defendant, a master mechanic, also from Portadown, had seduced her and she had a child. Without leaving the box the jury awarded her £75.

Divorce in the form of a dissolution of the marriage was only possible in Ireland by a private act of parliament,[23] and the *Belfast News Letter* of 5 July carried a report of the hearing in the House of Lords before the lord chancellor and three law lords of a bill brought by one Captain Vigors of Limerick seeking a divorce on the grounds of his wife's adultery. Realistically this was a course only open to the wealthy. However, it was possible to obtain a judicial separation in the form of a divorce *a mensa et thoro*, and at the Co. Down assizes a decree was granted by Fitzgibbon LJ to a doctor in an undefended suit where the evidence showed that the wife had run off to London with her lover. This was described as being the first occasion such an application was heard on circuit following a recent change in the law.[24]

19 See generally N. Howlin and K. Costello (eds), *Law and the family in Ireland, 1800–1950* (London, 2017).
20 *Armagh Guardian*, 1 July 1898.
21 *Belfast News Letter*, 8 July 1898.
22 Ibid., 29 July 1898.
23 See D. Urquhart, '"Divorce Irish style": marriage dissolution in Ireland, 1850–1950' in Howlin and Costello (eds), *Law and the family*.
24 *Down Recorder*, 16 July 1898.

Cases where the custody of children were in dispute also came before the courts in the form of *habeas corpus* applications, two such cases being mentioned in this period. The first came before the queen's bench divisional court consisting of Sir Peter O'Brien LCJ, Palles CB and Madden J. The father successfully sought custody of his son who had been in the care of his brother-in-law since the death of his mother.[25] The second concerned two children and came before Boyd J, also sitting in the queen's bench division.[26]

Individuals were just as anxious to defend their reputations in the courts as in more recent times, at least to judge by the number of libel or slander actions.[27] Some were trivial, such as the slander action for £500 that had been transferred to the assizes, and was tried by Palles CB in Downpatrick. The chief baron was clearly unimpressed by the whole matter, saying: 'Why this wretched action had gone on when there was no justification filed was not clear.' He wondered 'that the respected gentlemen who acted for the defendant had not tendered 10*s.* or £1 in court'. The jury were clearly of the same view and awarded two guineas to the plaintiff, although, as the paper observed, the verdict 'carries costs'.[28] One case in Belfast that was settled was brought by Francis Curley, 'merchant tailor', who sued one Patrick Teevan for trespass and conversion, Teevan counter claiming for libel and slander.[29]

In the days before legal aid the defendant in person was a familiar figure in the criminal courts, but in Belfast we find an unrepresented defendant successfully resisting two seniors and a junior in another slander action. The defendant was 'a flesher carrying on a good business on the Crumlin Road', and according to Serjeant Dodd 'was more or less a sporting man'. The significance of the 'sporting man' description became clear when the plaintiff, who was a publican in Crown Entry where there was a billiard room and a club, admitted that he had been a bookmaker, but denied being one now. The defendant said the plaintiff's son was a bookmaker, and that he (the defendant) 'was one of the mugs who backed horses' with the son. That may well have prejudiced the jury against the plaintiff, because they did not accept his allegation that the defendant said the plaintiff had robbed a drunk of two £50 notes that had been among the money deposited by the drunk with the plaintiff, the defendant's case being that it was the drunk who alleged that the plaintiff had robbed him.[30]

25 *Belfast News Letter*, 2 July 1898.

26 Ibid., 27 July 1898.

27 See L. Calvert, '"I am friends wt you & do entertain no malice": discord, disputes and defamation in Ulster Presbyterian church courts, *c.*1700–1838' in K. Costello and N. Howlin (eds), *Law and religion in Ireland 1700–1970* (London, 2021).

28 *Down Recorder*, 16 July 1898.

29 *Belfast News Letter*, 28 July 1898. Until quite recently Francis Curley's shop in High Street was one of the city's leading gentleman's outfitters.

30 Ibid., 23 July 1898.

Defamation actions were not confined to individuals. Two of the other cases reported during this period involved newspapers, although not quite in the manner we are familiar with today because both were brought by the editors of local newspapers. The libel action by the editor of the *North Down Herald* against the chairman of Bangor town commissioners was adjourned to the next assizes because essential witnesses were unavailable, so we do not know what angered the editor of that paper.[31] However, we can follow the proceedings reported by the *Armagh Guardian* as 'the Armagh Eatonswills'. The report more than justified the reference to the famous disputes between rival newspaper editors described by Charles Dickens in *The Pickwick papers*. The action, heard by O'Brien J and a special jury in Dublin, involved a claim for libel by a writer for the *Armagh Standard* against the proprietors of the *Ulster Gazette*, and a counterclaim for libel by the publisher of the *Gazette* against the *Standard*. Involving as it did allegations of betrayal of his principles by an Orangeman who was both county grand secretary of the Orange Order and town clerk of Armagh, space does not permit a lengthy description of this case. A flavour of the bombastic and vituperative language used by writers on both newspapers about each other can perhaps be gathered from the following extracts from the respective libels. The article in the *Ulster Gazette* contained this passage:

> The proprietor of the *Armagh Standard*, who could not himself write a leader counting two dozen lines, and the workhouse cad hireling dubbed 'editor' have been doing this dirty thing. It has been a matter of surprise to some why these two dirty birds pursue this dirty course. It need not, however, surprise anyone, as it is alleged that the workhouse editor would bear false witness against the highest and purest in the land for the mess of pottage.

That of the *Armagh Standard* was in no less trenchant and abusive terms:

> On the same night a meeting of the town commissioners was held, at which the [election of the town surveyor] was discussed. It was evident from the remarks of several of the commissioners that they had been 'got at' by the town clerk … During a number of days prior to the election representatives of the nationalists proceed to canvass on behalf of their clergy … In this they were assisted by the town clerk, and one or two unionist commissioners, over whom the town clerk is a bearded cardinal … In expressing the barefaced conduct of Mr Parkinson's unprincipled canvassing opponents, we cannot overlook the contemptible behaviour of the county grand secretary of the Orange

31 Ibid., 22 July 1898.

> Society and our versatile town clerk. We are determined at all risks to thoroughly expose his high-handed, un-gentlemanly and shabby conduct.

The *Armagh Guardian* did not stint itself in its report of this dispute between two of its local rivals, giving a full account of the proceeding over three-and-a-half pages. The jury took forty minutes to find that the articles in the *Gazette* were libellous and not justifiable comment on matters of public interest, awarding damages of £100 against the publisher and £5 each against the proprietors of the *Ulster Gazette*, while awarding £5 on the counterclaim for the article in the *Armagh Standard*.[32]

Although the county courts (often referred to as quarter sessions) dealt with small civil claims, the most frequent courts were, of course, the petty sessions. Unlike the present day when such courts have been drastically reduced in number in recent decades to improve efficiency, courts were held in many different places in the same county. [33] So, we read of courts being held in Enniskillen, Lisnaskea and Derrylin, in Co. Fermanagh as well as in Ballyconnell in Co. Cavan and Fivemiletown in Co. Tyrone. Usually the local resident magistrate (RM) presided accompanied by a number of other magistrates, although there seems to have been no fixed number. Two or three are common, occasionally one or four would sit with the RM, but in one case the RM sat on his own. In Belfast it seems the RM sat on his own in the custody cases, and other magistrates would deal with minor civil cases. The composition of the magistracy was a matter of great controversy for many years. John Morley as the Liberal chief secretary for Ireland in Gladstone's government of 1892–4 appointed many magistrates with liberal or nationalist sympathies, diluting the representation of the predominantly unionist landed gentry. However, many gentry were still to be found sitting on the magistrates' bench, as at Enniskillen petty sessions when Mr R.G. Bull RM was accompanied by Viscount Corry and E.M. Archdale, both members of leading Fermanagh Protestant and unionist families and deputy lieutenants, and Mr Patrick Crumley, who, to judge by his name, was likely to be a Roman Catholic.

Among the cases reported are minor assaults and thefts, one of dress material reported in the *Armagh Guardian* that resulted in the defendant being sentenced to three months for the theft and one month for not reporting his presence to the police as he was what the report terms 'a returned convict'.[34] Cases of drunkenness and unmuzzled dogs were common, as at Lisnaskea where the reporter referred in passing to '[a] few simple drunks and three or four cases for allowing dogs to go unmuzzled, were

32 *Armagh Guardian*, 1 July 1898.

33 See C. O'Riordan, P. Burns and C. O'Connor (eds), *Ireland's court houses* (Dublin, 2019).

34 15 July 1898.

disposed of'.[35] Drunk in charge of a vehicle is not a new phenomenon, because courts also dealt with charges of being drunk in charge of a horse and cart, as at Fivemiletown where two such cases came before the same court, the fines being 2*s.* 6*d.* in one case but 7*s.* 6*d.* in the other, in both cases plus costs.

As the judges went round their circuits in each assize town they were preceded by a meeting of the grand jury for the county. The grand jury was still responsible for the administration of local government in each county, for fixing the cess or rates for the county, and deciding what should be spent on roads and bridges. They also dealt with a variety of other problems of the day, such as the Armagh county analyst reporting that he had found samples of whiskey and buttermilk to be adulterated, and two samples of water from Portadown unfit for drinking.[36] Grand jurors also performed a quasi-judicial role when deciding what amounts should be awarded for malicious injuries, what we now call criminal damage claims, and deciding what geographical area should have to pay the award.[37] Thus we find the Co. Armagh grand jury awarding £15 to an applicant whose brother had taken a farm whose previous occupant had been evicted and whose shed was set on fire, destroying the shed and a horse (ironically named 'Home Rule'), a collar and a cart.[38] These tasks would soon be swept away when the local government bill going through parliament at that time set up a system of county, rural and urban district councils.

As the assize judges on the North-East circuit made their way towards Belfast where, as we shall see, they finished their circuit, we see the first signs of some of the effects of the industrialization of North-East Ulster. By the end of the nineteenth century Belfast had grown from a small town of around 20,000 people to a great industrial city of almost 350,000, and one of its greatest problems was an acute shortage of water. 'As late as the 1890s there were serious water famines, and people were driven to pump water from the Lagan, a last resort considering the rudimentary disposal of sewage.'[39] In 1893 it was decided to tap the Mourne mountains, but the first water did not reach Belfast until 1901. Compulsory purchase was necessary, and in 1898 a large number of decisions by the arbitrator relating to compensation were appealed to the Downpatrick assizes, where they were decided by a jury. Such was the number of cases that Fitzgibbon LJ had to return to complete the list at the end of the circuit, a task that occupied him for a further day-and-a-half.[40] The Belfast water commissioners did not confine their search to the Mourne

35 *Fermanagh Times,* 14 July 1898.

36 *Armagh Guardian*, 8 July 1898.

37 See N. Howlin, 'Compensation for criminal injuries: *Palles* at the intersection of civil and criminal law' in Breen and McGrath (eds), *Palles.*

38 Ibid.

39 E. Jones, 'Late Victorian Belfast: 1850–1900' in J.C. Beckett and R.E. Glasscock (ed.), *Belfast: the origin and growth of an industrial city* (London, 1967), p. 115.

40 *Down Recorder,* 16 July 1898, and *Belfast News Letter*, 3 and 4 Aug. 1898.

mountains because similar appeals to the Co. Antrim assizes show they acquired land at Woodburn, Carrickfergus, Co. Antrim for the same purpose.[41]

Railways were the main means of communication and of transport, both of people and goods, including animals. At the Donegal assizes in Lifford, Madden J heard an appeal from the county court in which the plaintiff claimed that his horse had been left for four hours in a siding at Omagh on its journey to Donegal town from Dungannon via Omagh and Strabane. The horse, which was returning from the November horse sales at The Moy, Co. Tyrone, thereby missed its connection at Strabane, and developed laryngitis. Madden J affirmed the decision of the court below, awarding £20 against the Great Northern Railway (GNR).[42] However, the GNR was more successful at Lisburn quarter sessions where the owner of a quantity of hay unsuccessfully sued it for destruction of the hay due to sparks from a GNR engine.[43] The interaction between steam and rural life was further illustrated when plaintiffs claimed damages for what was presumably a thatched dwelling house set on fire by the sparks from a traction engine. They were more successful, the decree given at the county court being affirmed on appeal to the assizes in Downpatrick.[44] However, it would be wrong to infer that industrialization was confined to the cities or larger towns. As many of us will recall, one of the features of many Ulster towns was the local gasworks, and Ballinahinch, Co. Down, was one such town. Palles CB heard an appeal from a dismissal in the county court in a case where two labourers were injured in an explosion in a barber's shop in the town caused when the manager of the company was searching for the leak with a light. The light is not described, but was presumably a lamp with a live flame. Palles CB allowed the appeal, saying that the manager had exercised very little care.[45] An interesting aspect of the case, which had been remitted to the county court, was that it was tried by a judge and jury in the county court, and not, as now, by the judge alone.[46]

As one might expect given its size as a major industrial city there was a considerable amount of commercial litigation to be dealt with by the judges when they arrived in Belfast to sit at the Co. Antrim assizes, which at that time included Belfast. Carrickfergus still had its own assizes, and Fitzgibbon LJ took the opportunity of his address to the Carrickfergus grand jury to deal at length with complaints about the burden of jury service and the volume of work at the Antrim assizes. In this he referred to the volume of civil work, saying that there were already 108 civil bill appeals, and although ten had been

41 *Belfast News Letter*, 29 July 1898.
42 Ibid., 16 July 1898.
43 Ibid., 2 July 1898.
44 *Down Recorder*, 16 July 1898.
45 See S. Hedley, 'Christopher Palles and tort' in Breen and McGrath (eds), *Palles.*
46 Ibid.

settled more could still be lodged, and he anticipated about one hundred would remain to be heard. The printed list of cases contains twenty-two common jury records (or writs): two breach of promise,[47] one slander, one wrongful dismissal, one assault and battery, one ejectment, one probate, one trespass and injunction, one breach of a charterparty, one libel, one interpleader, one withdrawal of support, as well as various claims for breach of contract, or for goods sold and delivered or work done. There were also seven special jury cases,[48] two for personal injuries, one for return of title deeds, one wrongful dismissal, one for trespass and conversions with the defendant counter claiming for libel and slander. Finally, there were two non-jury cases; one for seduction and one for possession of land.

Most of the records were settled, although the charterparty case ran into a third day. While many of these causes of action are what one might expect of a major industrial city with an agricultural hinterland, others were somewhat unusual and merit some notice, although one was heard by the recorder of Belfast and not at the assizes. The telephone was now a feature of life in the city. A blind plaintiff tripped over a telephone box erected by the National Telephone Company on the public footpath at Mill Street in Belfast and was awarded £6 by the recorder of Belfast.[49]

Throughout the Victorian era the city expanded enormously in size to house the ever-increasing population. The prosperous middle and upper classes sought to build new and grander homes on the outskirts of the city, but on at least some occasions were anxious not to be too close to the rows of terrace houses that had sprung up to house the workers in the mills and factories that contributed so much to the wealth of the city. That at least became clear in *Chapman v. Marlborough Park Co Ltd*,[50] an action tried by Fitzgibbon LJ and a special jury. The plaintiff bought a plot in one of Belfast's grandest developments, lying between the Malone and Lisburn Roads, upon which he erected a villa. He claimed that it had been rendered worthless by the erection of artisan dwellings by the defendant company in the immediate neighbourhood, 'the privies of which were within 50 feet of [the plaintiff's] drawing room windows'. Opening the case for the plaintiff, Serjeant Dodd described the owners of the company in somewhat unflattering terms, say that they 'had the reputation of being very close-fisted, but honest gentlemen, but he was afraid that that case, whatever might be the result in point of law, would not redound to their honour and integrity as gentlemen'. When pressed by Fitzgibbon LJ if the plaintiff was suing in contract, Serjeant Dodd

47 See M. Sinnott, 'The action for breach of promise' in Howlin and Costello (eds), *Law and the family*.
48 See N. Howlin, *Juries in Ireland: laypersons and law in the long nineteenth century* (Dublin, 2017), ch. 4.
49 *Belfast New Letter*, 9 July 1898.
50 Reported in the *Belfast News Letter*, 19 July 1898.

said that he relied upon an implied term, and the jury would be asked to decide whether the plaintiff acted on foot of a binding representation by the defendants upon which they knew he would act. The case was adjourned to allow the jury to view the premises, and then adjourned to the next day because a witness was unavailable. When the case was called the next day, it was announced as settled for £450 and costs.[51]

Political issues were sometimes aired in court, or, as we shall see, at least the consequences of political unrest resulting in rioting and civil disorder, features of Belfast life then as now. In an era of limited suffrage the revision of voters' lists was closely scrutinized and contested in the courts. At the beginning of the month we see the lord chief justice hearing an application for taxation resulting from an appeal to the queen's bench division against a decision by the recorder of Londonderry (a closely contested constituency) admitting 65 voters to the freemen's roll.[52] A different aspect of political activity was also scrutinized in the queen's bench division a fortnight later when Boyd J set aside a judgment marked by a solicitor against the plaintiff for £65 for a bill of costs. The defendant alleged that the plaintiff had agreed to act for him for £10, and had entered judgment while negotiations over the bill were continuing. The unusual feature of the case is that the costs related to the plaintiff acting for the defendant in his unsuccessful campaign to be elected to Belfast corporation for the Ormeau ward. The judge remarked that some of the items seemed rather startling, such as attending at Ballynafeigh Orange hall at a public meeting between eight p.m. and eleven p.m. 'and as conducting agent making a speech in favour of the [defendant's] candidature, engaged upwards of three hours, £3 3*s*.' There was laughter in court when the judge said he 'did not know whether it was the custom of solicitors to make speeches at three guineas a day'.[53]

Much of the business of the assizes was, of course, concerned with criminal cases, and it was the function of the grand jury to decide whether there was a sufficient case against each defendant on a bill of indictment that was fit to go to trial.[54] If there was, then the jury found a 'true bill'; if not, it returned 'no bill'.[55] In some counties there was little or no criminal work, as in Fermanagh[56] and Carrickfergus where there were no bills and the crown judge received the traditional gift of white gloves from the high sheriff. Where there were cases to be tried, it was the practice for the crown judge for that county to describe

51 Ibid.
52 Ibid., 2 July 1898.
53 Ibid., 14 July 1898.
54 See Howlin, *Juries in Ireland*, ch. 3.
55 It was not until 1969 that the grand jury was finally abolished in Northern Ireland by the Grand Jury (Abolition) Act (Northern Ireland) 1969. The task was transferred to the crown court judge, and it remains a significant judicial function at the present day. See J.A.C. Valentine, *Criminal procedure in Northern Ireland* (2nd ed. Belfast, 2010), pp 173–4.
56 *Fermanagh Times*, 14 July 1898.

the evidence on each bill of indictment to the grand jury in open court. To judge by the remarks of Palles CB in Armagh, he explained the significance of the evidence and how they should approach each case, saying in one case of manslaughter that the grand jury should not find a true bill unless they believed that upon the evidence given they would themselves convict if they were on a petty jury. He said that in his view, while there was grave suspicion, there was no evidence upon which they could find a true bill[57] – and the jury found no true bill.[58] In a case where the defendant faced two bills, one for the manslaughter of her child, the other for concealment of the birth of the child whose body had been found in the river, he left open the manslaughter bill but told them to find a true bill for concealment of birth.[59] The grand jury duly found a bill on that charge only.[60]

Not only did the crown judge deal with the bills of indictment in his remarks or 'charge' to the grand jury; it was also the practice for the judge to comment on the report made by the county inspector of the RIC on the level of crime in the county since the last assizes. In Fermanagh, Kenny J commented that whereas there had been nine cases of crime reported at the summer assizes for the previous year, there were only three this year, and the number of cases of intoxication had fallen by 75 compared with the previous year.[61] At the Co. Antrim assizes in Belfast, Palles CB was informed by the county inspector that there had been a significant reduction in the number of specially reported cases from thirty-four to twenty in the past half year, whereas the commissioner for Belfast (a higher ranking officer) had to report that the number of such cases in the city had risen from 24 to 126, a figure that would not be significantly changed even if the riots were left out of consideration.[62]

A number of features of the criminal process of the day are of interest. Not all defendants were professionally represented, although many were, presumably because they or their family and friends were able to find the money. However, where the defendant was charged with murder, the judge would assign counsel at the request of the defendant's solicitor, and the crown would meet the cost of the defence.[63] Palles CB did so in two cases in Belfast, and Kenny J assigned junior counsel in a case at the Donegal assizes where the defendant was charged with the murder of his wife on Tory island. There was a preliminary issue whether the defendant was fit to plead, and when the jury found him incapable of pleading he was ordered to be kept in custody at

57 *Armagh Guardian*, 8 July 1898.
58 *Belfast News Letter*, 7 July 1898.
59 See E. Farrell, 'Interrogating the charge of concealment of birth in nineteenth-century Irish courts' in Howlin and Costello (eds), *Law and the family*.
60 *Armagh Guardian*, 8 July 1898.
61 *Fermanagh Times*, 14 July 1898.
62 *Belfast News Letter*, 15 July 1898.
63 W.E. Vaughan, *Murder trials in Ireland, 1836–1914* (Dublin, 2009), p. 220.

Her Majesty's pleasure. The defendant had been discharged from Letterkenny asylum two years before on recognizance, even though the medical superintendent refused to certify that he was sane. Kenny J strongly condemned as 'a deplorable state of the law' the practice he described whereby inmates in an asylum could be released on recognizances entered into by relatives, one way that – then as now – society struggles to deal with the release of individuals suffering from mental disorder.[64] An assigned counsel had little time to prepare the case to judge by a murder tried by Palles CB in Belfast where he assigned counsel on Thursday and fixed the case to start on Saturday.[65]

Once the defendant was arraigned, the next stage was to empanel a jury.[66] It seems that on occasion it was suggested that the parties accept a jury that had already been sworn in an earlier case, something that was common in civil cases, though not in criminal cases, until recent times in Northern Ireland. In a riot case in Belfast the defendant, who was unrepresented, agreed to take the jury in the previous trial. The crown refused, and a new jury was sworn in which the crown stood by five jurors. Standing jurors by on behalf of the crown was a common practice, although one that had long been highly contentious in Ireland.[67]

Once the trial started, most trials were conducted very quickly, and even murder cases rarely went into a second day. A three-day private prosecution for fraud of several people, including some of their employees, by the Great Northern Railway was a notable exception. By this time the practice of the police administering a caution to the defendant had become well established, as in a case of wounding with intent where the defendant was cautioned and replied 'all right, I did it'. He was convicted.[68] Palles CB was particularly sceptical of alibi defences, saying to a Belfast jury in a riot case that

> from the evidence for the defence the jury were afforded an opportunity of seeing how an alibi was capable of being manufactured in that city, just as they had been manufactured for the last one hundred years in the south and west and lower parts of the east of Ireland.

Not surprisingly, perhaps, the jury returned a verdict of guilty.[69] However, lest it be thought that Palles was not being even-handed in his concerns, he was alert to the risk of the unreliability of uncorroborated admissions made by a defendant while in police custody. In one case in Belfast where an unrepresented defendant was acquitted despite an alleged admission, his

64 *Belfast News Letter*, 16 July 1898.
65 Ibid., 15 July 1898.
66 See Howlin, *Juries in Ireland*, ch. 8.
67 Vaughan, *Murder trials in Ireland*, pp 147–60; Howlin, *Juries in Ireland*, ch. 10.
68 *Belfast News Letter*, 15 July 1898.
69 Ibid., 22 July 1898.

brother having accepted full responsibility and pleaded guilty, Palles stated that 'he never ceased expressing his disapprobation of verdicts given on the wholly uncorroborated statements made to policemen'.[70] This was not the only occasion when he displayed his concern about the voluntariness of admissions made in custody, as can be seen from the following extract from a report of the Armagh case of concealment of birth referred to earlier:

> Evidence then being given of a statement made by the prisoner when arrested. It however appeared that when she was in the barracks her mother and sister pressed her to tell the truth as to the father of the child so that an innocent man should not lie under the blame. Const. Cullen the orderly was appealed to, and he also advised her to tell the truth. She then began to tell her story, and he went for Sgt. O'Donnell, who cautioned her. His lordship elicited from Const. Cullen that that prisoner did not send him for Sgt. O'Donnell, but that he went on his own accord, and told the sergeant, as she was making a statement, it was better he should come down. His lordship declined to receive the statement, as the woman did not make the statement of her own free will, and the jury accordingly found a verdict of not guilty.[71]

In Belfast, many of the cases arose out of one of the city's periodic explosions of sectarian violence. Serious rioting took place in the city on 6 and 7 June. There were sectarian clashes between a nationalist procession returning to the Falls Road after celebrating the 1798 rebellion, and crowds gathered behind police lines at Percy Street, Dover Street and Northumberland Street on the Shankill Road. The details of the subsequent trials have a depressing familiarity. The RIC faced heavy stoning for several hours, and although mounted police charged the crowd, such was the severity of the rioting that cavalry were called in to assist the police, and a force of three officers and 80 dragoons carried out several charges to clear the streets. About thirty police officers subsequently received medical treatment for wounds that could have been caused by stones.[72] Of the fifty-eight defendants indicted for offences connected with the rioting, twenty-three were convicted and twenty-six acquitted, the grand jury threw out two cases, the crown withdrew four indictments, and one case was adjourned to the next assizes. Two men convicted of wrecking a public house received five years penal servitude, and one who injured a policeman two years' imprisonment. Those convicted of riot received eighteen months, and those of unlawful assembly, twelve months imprisonment.[73]

70 Ibid., 18 July 1898.
71 *Armagh Guardian*, 8 July 1898.
72 *Belfast News Letter*, 19 July 1898.
73 Ibid., 28 July 1898.

At this time a defendant could not give evidence on his or her own behalf, although considerable latitude was extended to unrepresented defendants, some of whom asked questions and were apparently allowed to make unsworn statements from the dock.[74] It was ironic that the Criminal Evidence Act 1898,[75] which provided for a defendant to give evidence on his own behalf and be cross-examined, and which became law on 12 August of that year, did not apply to Ireland, and the law was not changed in the same way until 1923 in Northern Ireland and 1924 in the Irish Free State.[76]

While the rioting of July 1898 has many depressing parallels with the rioting of more recent times, I would like to end by referring to a happier comparison. Among the many firms of solicitors appearing in cases reported in the papers of the day are names that are, or were until recently, still to be found among those firms practising in Belfast or Co. Antrim. Carson & McDowell, C. & J. Black, Crawford & Lockhart, L'Estrange & Brett, Martin H. Turnbull, Joseph Donnelly, J.W. McNinch and O'Rourke & McDonald are all to be found in the papers during this month, demonstrating the continuity that is one of the strengths of the legal profession.

74 Ibid., 18 July 1898.

75 Criminal Evidence Act 1898 (61 & 62 Vict., c. 36).

76 See the account of the opposition from both nationalist and unionist MPs to this measure being extended to Ireland in C. Jackson, 'Irish political opposition to the passage of reform, 1893–98: the Criminal Evidence Act 1898' in J. McEldowney and P. O'Higgins (eds), *The common law tradition: essays in Irish legal history* (Dublin, 1990).

'Suffrage first' or 'suffrage as a crown': women's suffrage in Germany, Ireland and England

MARION RÖWEKAMP*

INTRODUCTION

When women in Germany attained suffrage in November 1918, they received congratulations from women all over the world. Isabella Ford, one of the leaders of the English suffrage movement, wrote:

> I write to send you my warmest congratulations on your brilliant political liberation, which is so much more far-reaching than ours. I am so very, very happy about it, because I am sure that the world needs the help of all women of all nations to rebuild Europe and the whole world.[1]

This illustrates some points that characterize the women's suffrage movement and the research on it.

First, English women were engaged with the developments in Germany and vice versa. That was no exception, but the rule – at least as far as countries of the western hemisphere or the global north were concerned. Women informed each other, they collected and compared knowledge, they used the information to pressure their own governments and they developed common solutions in their common struggles. Suffrage was not only a struggle within each country, but also an international or transnational struggle; neither the English nor the German struggle can be understood without the other.

Second, it is clear that suffrage in different countries did not necessarily mean the same thing. As Ford pointed out, German suffrage was much more extensive than English women's suffrage,[2] which in 1918 was limited to women over 30 who were registered property owners, who were married to registered property owners, or who were university graduates voting in a university constituency.[3] It is not easy to judge which country was 'first',

* A version of this paper was delivered to the Irish Legal History Society in the School of Law at Queen's University Belfast in Feb. 2018 to mark the centenary of women's suffrage.

1 As reported *in Die Staatsbürgerin* 12 (1919), 102.

2 Ibid.

3 Representation of the People Act 1918 (7 & 8 Geo. V, c. 5), s. 4.

because, as Gisela Bock points out, suffrage rights came in different degrees and thus only have a limited comparability.[4] It was not until 1928 that full suffrage was achieved in England,[5] whereas women in Germany had received equal suffrage with men in 1918.[6] Irish women received limited suffrage in 1918[7] in parallel with women in Britain, and gained full suffrage in 1922.[8] In the US white women received suffrage in 1920,[9] but many black women could only exercise their suffrage rights after 1965.[10] So which date is the one that really counts as being the 'first'? When the first group of women received suffrage or when all women became equal citizens? This illustrates the general difficulties of the 'first' and 'last' concept, as well as the challenges of comparative history in general.

Finally, the quotation from Ford points to the understanding, shared by many of the movements, that women were needed 'to rebuild Europe and the whole world'. This reinforces the idea that the women's suffrage movement is not only national, but also transnational.

To understand the impact of female suffrage in England, Ireland and Germany, we must look at the history of women's movements, electoral history, party histories and the history of universal suffrage. It is also important to consider the history of democracy in general, of which women's suffrage and women's equal rights are an important, though often-neglected, part.[11] Both democracy and law change over time and in line with cultural norms. Law is a political tool in the context of women's rights, particularly family law and suffrage. In fact, these two legal areas worked together to hold women in a double bind; as Bock has defined it, to have women tied legally down. The strong relationship between these two areas will be one of the

4 G. Bock, 'Frauenwahlrecht. Deutschland um 1900 in vergleichender perspektive' in M. Grütter et al. (eds), *Geschichte und Emanzipation. Festschrift für Reinhard Rürup* (Frankfurt am Main, 1999), pp 95–136; G. Bock, '100 Jahre Frauenwahlrecht: Deutschland in transnationaler Perspektive', *Zeitschrift für Geschichtswissenschaft* 66:5 (2018), 395.

5 Equal Franchise Act 1928.

6 'Germany has the honour to be the first republic founded on true principles of democracy, universal and equal suffrage for all citizens and all men and women,' marvelled German feminist Marie Stritt: M. Stritt, 'Germany: victory for woman suffrage', *International Women's News* 13:4 (1919), 44.

7 Representation of the People Act 1918.

8 Constitution of the Irish Free State, art. 3.

9 United States constitution, 19th amendment.

10 Voting Rights Act, 6 Aug. 1965; R. Terborg-Penn, *African American women in the struggle for the vote, 1850–1920* (Bloomington, 1998); and M. Jones, *Vanguard: how black women broke barriers, won the vote, and insisted on equality for all* (New York, 2020).

11 B. Bader-Zaar, 'Politische Partizipation als Grundrecht in Europa und Nordamerika. Entwicklungsprozesse zum allgemeinen, gleichen, geheimen und direkten Wahlrecht für Männer und Frauen vom späten 18. bis zum frühen 20. Jahrhundert' in M. Grandner, M. et al. (eds), *Grund- und Menschenrechte: historische Perspektiven - aktuelle Problematiken* (Vienna, 2002), pp 203–56; and H. Richter and K. Wolff (eds), *Demokratisierung der Demokratie in Deutschland und Europa* (Hamburg, 2018).

interwoven parts of this chapter. The history of suffrage cannot be written without taking the interdependence of family law and suffrage into account;[12] even when women gained suffrage, they did not escape discrimination within the family.

Women's movements in England, Ireland and Germany had very different perceptions of the 'tool' of suffrage. The Anglo-American model was 'suffrage first' and the German model was 'suffrage as a crown'. Most English-speaking women assumed that suffrage was the basis for all achieving equal rights. For most women in Germany, suffrage was supposed to be the peak of the pyramid; in other words, it would be achieved once other rights had been granted.

Another difference was the method chosen in the fight for suffrage. In Great Britain a small group among the movement resorted to violence and the state answered in kind. In this regard, the British (and Irish) case with militant suffragettism was one of the hardest of the struggles. As German feminist Regine Deutsch claimed: 'The storm-centre of the warfare which waged from East to West, from Lapland to Italy, from Canada to South Africa was England, in the throes of the revolutionary suffragette movement.'[13] This led to an unbalanced view of the importance of the British suffrage movement in the history of the international movement.

This chapter builds on comparative studies for Germany and England,[14] comparative studies in general,[15] and particular studies on England,[16]

12 G. Bock, *Women in European history* (Oxford, 2002), pp 132, 138 and M. Röwekamp, '"The double bind": von den Interdependenzen des Frauenwahlrechts und des Familienrechts vor und nach 1918' in H. Richter and K. Wolff (eds), *100 Jahre Frauenwahlrecht. Kampf, Kontext, Wirkung* (Hamburg, 2018), pp 99–121.

13 R. Deutsch, *The International Woman Suffrage Alliance: its history from 1904–1929* (London, 1929), p. 15.

14 B. Bader-Zaar, 'Zur Geschichte des Frauenwahlrechts im langen 19. Jahrhundert. Eine international vergleichende Perspektive', *Ariadne* 40 (2001), 6–13; B. Bader-Zaar, 'Frauenwahlrechtsbewegungen und Verfassungsstaat: Deutschland, Großbritannien und Österreich im Vergleich, 1866–1918' in M. Kirsch et al. (eds), *Der Verfassungsstaat vor der Herausforderung der Massengesellschaft. Konstitutionalismus um 1900 im europäischen Vergleich* (Berlin, 2002), pp 231–53; C. Wickert (ed.), *Heraus mit dem Frauenwahlrecht: die Kämpfe der Frauen in Deutschland und England um die politische Gleichberechtigung* (Pfaffenweiler, 1990); H. Schröder, *Widerspenstige, Rebellinnen, Suffragetten: feministischer Aufbruch in England und Deutschland* (Aachen, 2001); and D.L. Teele, *Forging the franchise: the political origins of the women's vote* (Princeton, 2018).

15 I. Sulkunen, S.L. Nevala-Nurmi, and P. Markkola (eds), *Suffrage, gender and citizenship: international perspectives on parliamentary reform* (Cambridge, 2009); J. Hannam, *International encyclopedia of women's suffrage* (Santa Barbara, 2000); C. Daley and M. Nolan, *Suffrage and beyond: international feminist perspectives* (Auckland, 1994); and B. Rodríguez-Ruiz and R. Rubio-Marín, *The struggle for female suffrage in Europe: voting to become citizens* (Leiden, 2012).

16 E.g., E. Crawford, *The women's suffrage movement: a reference guide* (London, 1999); C. Eustance et al. (eds), *A suffrage reader: charting directions in British suffrage history* (London, 2000); I. Fletcher et al., *Women's suffrage in the British empire: citizenship, nation and race* (Abingdon, 2000); H.L. Smith, *The British women's suffrage campaign, 1866–1928* (London,

Ireland[17] and Germany.[18] This chapter will not chronicle the different events that led to suffrage rights for women, but will contextualize the women's movements and their attitudes towards suffrage in the three countries before 1918. It will focus on feminists' words and arguments, as well as on the linkages between the women's battles in England, Ireland and Germany.

CONDITIONS FOR THE DEVELOPMENTS OF WOMEN'S MOVEMENTS IN ENGLAND, IRELAND AND THE GERMAN EMPIRE

Common to all three countries was the societal norm of women belonging in the private sphere and men in the public. It was as much part of the German idea of the middle class as it was in England. In 1909 the English-German feminist Alice Zimmern characterized the status of a woman in Germany 'as the home-maker and *Hausfrau*' and this was 'so firmly established and the intellectual superiority and absolute predominance of man so much taken for granted by both sexes' that there was not much desire to revolt against this subjection.[19] Women developed different strategies to overcome the boundaries set for them. They sought to transcend the boundary between the private and the public through education, thereby gaining access to the public sphere. They stressed the special qualities that women might bring to the public sphere. Arguments based on equality of access to education, professions and law were used at the same time, such arguments being common in all three countries.[20]

Democracy versus monarchy: two different institutional set-ups

The struggles for equal rights took place in different political, social and legal contexts. The struggle for suffrage by the English women's movement has a

1998); B. Caine, *English feminism, 1780–1980* (Oxford, 1997); and M.L. Shanley, *Feminism, marriage, and the law in Victorian England* (Princeton, 1989).

17 E.g., E. Crawford, *The women's suffrage movement in Britain and Ireland: a regional study* (London, 2006), L. Ryan and M. Ward (eds), *Irish women and the vote: becoming citizens* (Newbridge, 2018); L. Ryan, *Winning the vote for women: the* Irish Citizenship *newspaper and the suffrage movement in Ireland* (Dublin, 2018); and S.B. Watkins, *Ireland's suffragettes: the women who fought for the vote* (Dublin, 2014).

18 There are still only two works on the subject: U. Rosenbusch, *Der Weg zum Frauenwahlrecht in Deutschland* (Baden-Baden, 1998) and J. Sneeringer, *Winning women's votes. propaganda and politics in Weimar Germany* (Chapel Hill, 2002). There are also several edited books, including H. Richter and K. Wolff (eds), *Frauenwahlrecht: Demokratisierung der Demokratie in Deutschland und Europa* (Hamburg, 2018).

19 A. Zimmern, *Women's suffrage in many lands* (London, 1909), p. 79.

20 Some examples include U.L. Davidoff and C. Hall, *Family fortunes: men and women of the English middle class, 1780–1850* (Chicago, 1987); U. Frevert (ed.), *Bürgerinnen und Bürger. Geschlechterverhältnisse im 19. Jahrhundert* (Göttingen, 1988); and R. Habermas, *Frauen und Männer des Bürgertums: eine Familiengeschichte (1750–1850)* (Göttingen, 2000).

far longer history than the German one. Great Britain had a longstanding liberal political background, which allowed broad public agitation and debate, encouraging strong suffrage movements. The starting point in Britain was the first major suffrage reform in 1832. This period also saw the high-profile cases of Henriette Greenhill and Caroline Norton, who both sought custody of their children.[21] Greenhill lost, but Norton succeeded in getting the law changed. The treatment of these cases in the press, courts and parliament shows that justice and moral sentiments were shaped by a rising public awareness of legal discrimination against women.[22] Besides, Queen Victoria ascended the throne in 1837, and it was not long before women argued that if a woman can reign over the empire, a woman should also be able to vote.[23]

The *International Woman Suffrage News* reported in 1923 that '[t]he suffrage movement in Ireland began rather late, because the interest of those who cared for political questions was always so much absorbed by the pros and cons of the nationalist movement'.[24] Irish women's suffrage history was indeed strongly intertwined with the fight for independence. This made women's situation in Ireland very different from that in England or Germany, not in the sense that nationalism didn't play a role in England or Germany – it did – but both countries, unlike Ireland, were already geographically and constitutionally formed states. The Irish women's movement situation can, therefore, be better compared to that in the later states of Poland, Czechoslovakia or the Baltic Republics. There, as in Ireland, women fought on the side of men for independence and argued for their rights as part of their common fight. In Ireland, the political situation was polarized. Women either chose nationalism or unionism to pursue their claims, or else fought independently of these other political movements. Some moved between these modes, and it is therefore much more difficult to generalize for Ireland than it is for England and Germany, where women followed some clear patterns.

Irish women had the same rights and suffered the same discrimination as their British sisters. They were governed by the same law, and they often chose to cooperate closely with their British/English counterparts. But the situation of Irish women was different in many respects, and not only because of the large shadow of the Irish independence question; Irish women were less well educated, the country was poorer and the suffrage organizations were led by a smaller group of women. In general, it was a much more conservative society, strongly influenced by the Catholic and Protestant churches with their ideas of marriage and family, in which the role of women – especially

21 J. Wroath, *Until they are seven: the origin of women's legal rights* (Winchester, 1998).

22 G. Bäumer, 'Die Geschichte der englischen Frauenrechtsbewegung' in H. Lange and G. Bäumer (eds), *Handbuch der Frauenbewegung I. Teil: die Geschichte der Frauenbewegung in den Kulturländern* (Weinheim, 1980), pp 241–6.

23 M. Garrett Fawcett, *Woman's suffrage: a short history of a great movement* (London, 1912), p. 13.

24 'Ireland: Miss Dora Mellone', *The International Woman Suffrage News* 18:11 (1923), 167.

within the family – was firmly set. Still, the movement shared the idea of the English: 'Suffrage first – before all else'.[25]

As in Ireland, in Germany the women's movement formed decades later than in England. The militarization of society and a new authoritarianism led to a new ideal of masculinity that was reflected in the family and family law, as Marianne Weber has argued.[26] The militarization of society and the state's theory of the 'male sex' were conditions that German women's movements had to deal with.[27] Thus, when the first German women's voices for voting rights and equality in the family and society were raised around 1848, they were quickly silenced. The consequences were a lack of free speech, censorship and limited rights of assembly for women in most German states.[28] Everything which was deemed political was shut down. The German highest court had defined the scope of the 'political'. It was everything which is related to 'constitution, administration, legislation of the state, the civil rights of subjects, and the international relations of states to each other'.[29] Thus any public or organized advocacy for more rights for women was punishable. Feminist Helene Lange recorded in 1898 how the first claims for women's suffrage were formulated in the 1860s and what they learned about the public reaction to these claims:

> When the representatives of the women's movement began their struggle 33 years ago, they understood the ultimate goal had to be the acquisition of women's suffrage. They openly expressed this view at several women's congresses at that time, but their experience was that they had thereby severely damaged their other undertakings. Thus, it was decided to postpone the discussion of this most important topic for some time, but, as soon as the opportunity arose, to state openly that without gaining the right to vote, women would never be able to achieve the development of their powers they were striving for.[30]

When in 1888 the International Council of Women (ICW) was founded in Washington, the Allgemeiner Deutscher Frauenbund (ADF) replied to the call to join the founding congress by trying to explain their difficulty:

25 M. Ward, 'Suffrage first – above all else. An account of the Irish suffrage movement', *Feminist Review*, 19 (1982), 21–36; Ryan and Ward (eds), *Irish women and the vote*; Ryan, *Winning the vote for women*; and Watkins, *Ireland's suffragettes*.

26 M. Weber, *Ehefrau und Mutter in der Rechtsentwicklung. Eine Einführung* (Aalen 1971, n.p. 1907), p. 411.

27 Bock, *Women in European history*, pp 133–4.

28 U. Gerhard, 'Grenzziehungen und Überschreitungen. Die Rechte der Frauen auf dem Weg in die politische Öffentlichkeit' in U. Gerhard (ed.), *Frauen in der Geschichte des Rechts. Von der Frühen Neuzeit bis zur Gegenwart* (München, 1997), pp 509–46.

29 Reichsgericht decision in criminal case, 10 Nov. 1887, Entscheidungen des Reichsgerichts in Strafsachen (RGSt), vol. 16, 383.

30 H. Lange, 'Über das Frauenwahlrecht', *Neue Bahnen*, 33:7 (1898), 68.

> In Germany we have to work with great tact and by conservative methods … The difference between our position and that of our American sisters is largely due to the fact that you live in a republic, we in a monarchy – you in a young country where everything is new, we in a land centuries old, where the ideas and habits of thought are, so to speak, encrusted in the people.[31]

Auguste Schmidt, co-founder of the ADF, gave a lecture on 'the aims of the German women's movement' in 1875. She compared 'the German women's movement with that in other countries, namely in England and America', where one already strives 'for political rights' and 'strives for the farthest goals and skips the middle links, while here one pays homage to the mode of progress as organic development, i.e., strives for further education, and first considers work and associated matters'.[32] Therefore, it does not come as a surprise that German women chose to focus on topics that were not as openly political as 'voting rights' but were in line with the traditional 'female sphere' of influence: education and welfare and later the family.

The limitations of male suffrage

Another important factor in the greater effectiveness of women's rights political activities in Britain and Ireland was that an elected parliament already existed in the United Kingdom as an addressee for legislative petitions. Furthermore, the government was answerable to this parliament. In Ireland, however, depending on the political stance people took, a vote for a parliament that was considered not to be its own could be regarded as lacking value. For example, the first Irish female parliamentarian, Constance Markievicz, when elected to the Westminster parliament, chose not to take her seat and exercise her voting rights there. 'I would never take an oath of allegiance to the power I meant to overthrow', she wrote.[33]

The political value of even the male vote in the German Reichstag was limited, because under the 1871 constitution the parliament had no right to form the government.[34] Prussia and other states had an election law that was not universal for men. This was the case in Great Britain as well, but the government was answerable to parliament.[35] German feminist Charlotte Pape

31 *Report of the International Council of Women. Assembled by the National Woman Suffrage Association, Washington, DC, March 25 to April 1, 1888* (Washington, DC, 1888), p. 220.

32 Anon., 'Die VII. Generalversammlung des Allgemeinen, deutschen Frauenvereins (VIII. Frauentag) in Gotha vom 2. bis 5. Oct. 1875', *Neue Bahnen*, 22, 23 (1875), 169.

33 A. Marreco, *The rebel countess: the life and times of Constance Markievicz* (London, 1967), p. 241.

34 M.L. Anderson, *Lehrjahre der Demokratie. Wahlen und politische Kultur im Deutschen Kaiserreich* (Stuttgart 2009).

35 Until 1867 only 20% of men were allowed to vote and until 1918 only around 60%. J. Rendall, 'Citizenship, culture and civilization' in Daley and Nolan (eds), *Suffrage and beyond*, pp 129–50.

mused that considering that political rights in general for men were so new, it would be better for women to wait:

> Many of the best and most experienced friends of the women's cause in Germany nevertheless consider that the time has not yet come to begin the practical struggle for women's suffrage there, and they are most probably right. Political rights are still so new, so little appreciated, and of such limited practical value in the recent history of Germany, that to demand them now for women would probably only harm the success of other efforts for their better position.[36]

This meant that suffrage would be of less value to women in Germany than in England and Ireland. Thus, German women gave more weight to areas other than suffrage law, such as family law reform, which became the centre of women's attention. This is the reason the women's movement reunited rapidly and strongly within the context of the codification of the new civil law in the last quarter of the nineteenth century. So, Gertrud Bäumer claimed in 1901 that 'the main area in which the women's question appears as a legal issue is that of marriage'.[37] Women believed they were more likely to gain equal rights in the family than political rights. How mistaken they were, as history would soon prove.

Foundations of the history of ideas for general and women's suffrage

There is another ideological rationale for the right to vote. To understand the discourses and the strategies of the English and the Irish women's movement, the close link between property and voting rights must be considered. According to Anglo-Saxon tradition, the right to vote was not based on a natural law argument as in the continental discourse, but on the historical privileges of landowners and household heads. Women were understandably indignant that while their property was taxable, they had no civil rights and no right to vote. These are some of the reasons why women fought mainly for their property rights in the nineteenth century.[38] After the publication of Anna Wheeler's and William Thompson's *Appeal* in 1825,[39] Henry Hunt, a member of the House of Commons, submitted the first known petition for women´s suffrage to parliament in 1832. Mary Smith, an unmarried landowner, was

36 C. Pape, 'Briefe' *Neue Bahnen,* 11:15 (1876), 119.

37 G. Bäumer, 'Die Geschichte der Frauenbewegung in Deutschland' in Lange (eds), *Handbuch der Frauenbewegung*, p. 70.

38 J. Rendall, 'Recovering lost political cultures: British feminisms, 1860–1890' in Sylvia Palatschek and B. Pietrow-Ennker (eds), *Women's emancipation movements in the 19th century* (Stanford, 2004), p. 38.

39 A. Wheeler and W. Thompson, *Appeal of one half the human race, women, against the pretensions of the other half* (London, 1925).

behind the petition and claimed the right to vote based on land ownership, with reference to the right of male landowners to vote. The result was that parliament expressly limited voting rights to 'male persons'.[40] The same happened when one-quarter of German states abolished suffrage limitations after 1900: they changed the word 'person' to 'male person' thus making suffrage clearly limited to the male sex.[41] This is a reaction that we can observe all over Europe to the first demands of women for equal rights in almost all areas. As soon as these rights were demanded, the laws were changed to make it clear that the privileges applied only to men.

The connection between property rights and suffrage also becomes clear in the struggles to improve the position of married women in property law. The campaigns around the Married Women Property Acts of 1870[42] and 1882[43] led to a slight improvement in married women's situation in private law. Another immediate success of these campaigns was that women taxpayers were granted municipal suffrage in England and Wales in 1869; in Ireland this applied only to women in Belfast and two other towns. Women elsewhere in Ireland were not granted municipal suffrage until the Local Government (Ireland) Act 1898.[44] In all three countries they were admitted to various offices in school administration and poor relief after 1870. Ireland also lagged behind here; the Women's Poor Law was not enacted until 1896.[45]

Women within the suffrage movement acknowledged the connection between property and the vote. Thus, when feminist Lydia Becker organized the union of local groups in 1867 and co-founded the London and Manchester National Society for Women's Suffrage, it was under the motto 'no taxation without representation'. From 1870, she published the *Women's Suffrage Journal*. This link between property rights and voting rights was also evident in the original fight of single women to keep or gain communal suffrage in Germany.[46] However, this fight was soon forgotten and the strong link between the vote and property was more coherently and consistently advanced as an argument in England.[47]

40 *Hansard's Parl. deb., 3rd series*, vol. 14, col. 1086 (3 Aug. 1832).
41 Bock, *Women in European history*, p. 133.
42 Married Women's Property Act 1870 (33 & 34 Vict., c. 93).
43 Married Women's Property Act 1882 (45 & 46 Vict., c. 75).
44 61 & 62 Vict., c. 37.
45 A. Haslam, 'Irishwomen and the Local Government Act', *The Englishwoman's Review of Social and Industrial Questions*, 29:239 (1898), 221; 'The Irish Local Government Act of 1898', *Women's Suffrage Calendar* (1899), 53; K. Costello, 'Married women's property in Ireland, 1800–1900' in K. Costello and N. Howlin (eds), *Law and the family in Ireland, 1800–1950* (London, 2017); and A.A. Burt, 'Reforming the married state: women and property after the Married Womens' Property Acts, 1870–1935' (PhD, 2020, Boston University).
46 Anita Augspurg gave an overview of the existing possibilities in her report for the third IWSA conference, *Report of the second and third conferences of the IWSA*, Berlin, Germany, 3–4 June 1904; Copenhagen, Denmark, 7–11 Aug. 1906 (Copenhagen, 1906), pp 79–81. See also Rosenbusch, *Wahlrecht*, pp 85–131.
47 The Manchester Society for Women's Suffrage, Manchester Archives and Local Studies

Women's vote and centres of power

Analyzing how the different women's movements referred to the methods of other women's movements also sheds light on the different societal and political contexts in which they developed. Charlotte Pape, who lived in London, tried to explain the English focus on suffrage to feminists in Germany in 1876:

> When I moved to England three years ago, and moved into the centre of the women's movement in beautiful Edinburgh, I thought as well: Why the heck do these strange British women focus with all their might on women's suffrage? It is after all not that important! Let's first get into the professions, open schools and universities for us! That makes much more sense. But very soon I understood that in England women cannot enter any profession, school or university, they cannot break free from barbarian laws, they cannot protect themselves at all, if they don't have influence on the parliament.[48]

She explained that in England, laws passed by the parliament ruled every institution, and so women needed to focus on suffrage. According to her, the decision to focus on suffrage stemmed from the setup of the English parliamentary system: 'There is no government here, no departments and authorities, separate from the parliament. And the only possibility to influence the parliament and the legislation is to share in the election of a member of parliament, the political vote.'[49] This was also the case for women in Ireland – with the complication, of course, that the Westminster parliament was across the Irish Sea. Political power was located in London, so Irish feminists had to travel there to lobby Irish MPs and work with the British feminists, while doing basic propaganda work in Ireland.

In Germany, on the other hand, the centres of power were more diverse. Parliament had less influence and other governing institutions such as the executive and especially the administration had to be reckoned with. To focus on parliament made less sense than in England. To put it the other way around, English women had no other option but to focus on suffrage and on petitioning parliament to gain change. Thus, Pape explained how successful the tool of petitions to parliament was and encouraged German women to do the same:

> This abolition of a sinful law is not as impossible as it may seem to German women. Surely women in Germany are allowed to send petitions to the Reichstag or the parliaments of the individual states.

M50/1; Lydia Becker papers, GB 106 7LEB, Women's Library Archives, London School of Economics.

48 Pape, 'Briefe', p. 117.

49 Ibid.

> And if such petitions are repeated steadily, year after year, with an ever-increasing number of signatures, public opinion and parliaments cannot continue to disregard them.[50]

Accordingly, the board of the ADF was instructed to prepare a legislative petition against the adoption of the *Bürgerliches Gesechtsbuch* (BGB), or Civil Code, and to collect signatures throughout Germany. But, reflecting the lesser position of parliament within the power structure in Germany, the ADF did not send the petition to the Reichstag, but to the first commission drafting the BGB.[51] They learned from the methods of their British sisters, but adapted that knowledge to the German situation as they saw it.

Women's treatment and men's support in parliament

Due to the lack of direct suffrage, women in all three countries were only able to exert direct influence on legislation if they had male allies within the parliaments who would present their petitions to parliament. Petitions from women were read aloud in English parliament, so there was some hope that these petitions could lead to a change. In comparison, while the German women's movement also used the instrument of petitions (and later they also directed them to parliament), they never were read or discussed and usually refused 'under sharp rebuke of the content'.[52]

Another difference between the German and British suffrage campaigns, as the German activist Minna Cauer pointed out to her German readers in 1899, related to the more parliamentarian and democratic system in Britain. The English women's movement was based on a notion of personal freedom that was a basic feature of the English system, so English women had strong male supporters:

> Hence the position of women, their work, and their struggles are entirely different from here in Germany or in other countries. English women find support for their struggles in the aristocracy, in the church, in public opinion and in parliament; with real English humour they ponder the pros and cons of women's questions and are amused about the brave fight their women are putting up even though the fights might be strongly criticized and counteracted. But everybody understands that English women do have a right to fight for their rights, and this is the big difference for the German women's movement.[53]

50 C. Pape, 'Rechte der Mutter über ihre Kinder', *Neue Bahnen* (1876), 12.

51 T.C. Riedel, *Gleiches Recht für Frau und Mann. Die bürgerliche Frauenbewegung und die Entstehung des BGB* (Cologne, 2008), p. 123.

52 *Motive zu dem Entwurfe eines Bürgerlichen Gesetzbuchs für das Deutsche Reich*, vol. IV (Berlin 1896), p. 136; Riedel, *Gleiches Recht*, p. 122.

53 M. Cauer, 'Gedanken über den Internationalen Frauenkongress in London', *Die Frauenbewegung* 14 (1899), 122.

Cauer spoke about England, but this was also the case for Ireland. In fact, women in England usually had the help of male parliamentarians – for example, in the case of Norton in her struggle for a change of custody law and in the early married women property rights reforms in the nineteenth century. The first petition for the Married Women's Property Act 1870[54] was followed by the establishment of a Special Commission dealing with the question of the legal situation of married women in terms of property law. The debates in the commission and parliament showed that the question was taken seriously, and it gave the women's movement a certain respectability. In 1856, Henry Brougham, lord chancellor, also supported women in their first petition to the Westminster parliament for the right to vote. Many parliamentarians – such as John Stuart Mill, Russell Gurney, Jacob Bright and George Shaw Lefevre, for example – had strong links to the women´s movement. Mill, Gurney and Bright were married to members of the women's movement. In 1866 Mill introduced the first petition of women to parliament for equal suffrage with men, which meant the census suffrage based on their wealth. This petition was supported by the Langham Place circle, including Barbara Leigh Smith Bodichon and Bessie Rayner Parkes who had published two important works on women's equal rights: Bodichon's *Brief summary in plain language of the most important laws of England concerning women* and Parkes' *Remarks on the education of girls*.[55] Mill himself had published together with his wife, Harriet Taylor Mill, the influential book *The subjection of women* in 1869 which influenced the women's movements all over the world.

While Irish women, subject to the same regime as English women pre-independence, worked along the same lines, the general feeling towards women's suffrage in Ireland was more negative than in England. The grudging support the English gave their women was not evident in Ireland – partly because the political priority in Ireland was winning Home Rule. When in 1912 the Irish Party voted en bloc against the Conciliation Bill, many women on both sides of the Irish Sea concluded that Irish men would not support women's suffrage and so resolved to fight for their own interests ignoring the usual political divides. Militant feminists began violent protests also in Ireland. When Hanna Sheehy Skeffington was imprisoned as a result of one such protest, she received little support from the public. 'Not only were we enemies of Home Rule,' she explained, 'but rebels as women.'[56] So, while in theory Irish women could use the same patterns of collaboration with men as English women, the general support for their fight was low.

In Germany, on the other hand, the kind of collaboration with men as described in England was generally not available to women; advocates for

54 Married Women's Property Act 1870 (33 & 34 Vict., c. 93).

55 C.S. Lacey, *Barbara Leigh Smith Bodichon and the Langham Place Group* (New York, 1987).

56 H. Sheehy Skeffington, 'Reminiscences of an Irish suffragette' in A.D. Sheehy Skeffington, and R. Owens (eds), *Votes for women: Irish women's struggle for the vote* (Dublin, 1975), p. 20. See Plates 11.1 and 11.2.

women's causes worked in isolation.[57] While women shared ideas about suffrage with the socialists, the women's movement hesitated to side with them, as their position in the imperial regime was as unfavourable as that of the women. In the end, the German parliamentarian discourse did not consider interests of women because they were felt to be not in line with bigger ideas for the institutions of the state. Like the Irish Party at Westminster, German parliamentarians had other priorities.

How common law and the court system influenced women's suffrage claims

The final difference we must keep in mind when comparing the actions of German feminists with their British and Irish counterparts is the legal difference. The respective legal cultures strongly shaped the fights women waged and their approaches to legal struggles. Common law in the United Kingdom and Ireland is based on case law, which means individual women could construct strong cases that carried consequences for other women. An example in the area of family law was Caroline Norton: she pushed for the first changes in English custody law, the Custody of Infants Act 1839,[58] as an individual – a wronged wife – rather than as a representative of the broader women's movement.[59] Common law provided a framework within which individual women were able to obtain decisions which then had a wider impact on women's rights. This was not the case in Germany – first, because married women could not file in court; and second, because an advantageous individual court ruling created no precedent whatsoever for other women, even in similar cases. That meant married women could not use the courts to change the law.[60]

But there is another side to this argument about legal culture. While the position of married women in common law may have had a positive influence on women's rights, nevertheless British and Irish married women did not possess any individual legal personality but fused theirs with that of their husbands. They legally did not even exist anymore, and their legal position was in this sense even weaker compared with all other European countries. Only the access to the vote could give women the chance to get laws passed that would give them full legal capacity.

57 There were individual male supporters in Germany, see K.E. Hubler, 'Man's duty to woman: men and the first wave of German feminism, 1865–1919' (PhD, Boston College, 2012).

58 Custody of Infants Act 1839 (2 & 3 Vict., c. 54).

59 R. Probert, 'Family law reform and the women's movement in England and Wales, 1830–1914' in S. Meder, and C-E Mecke (eds), *Family law in early women's rights debates: western Europe and the United States in the nineteenth and early twentieth centuries* (Cologne, 2013) and Caine, *English feminism*; Shanley, *Feminism, marriage, and the law in Victorian England*, pp 22–39.

60 M. Röwekamp, 'Frauen vor und im Gericht' in P. Collin (ed.), *Handbuch zur Geschichte der Konfliktlösung in Europa*, vol. IV (Heidelberg, 2021).

In summary, the claims for 'suffrage first' and 'suffrage as a crown' are in both cases a decision born out of necessity and not from choice, and not a sign of a more liberal and progressive attitude of English woman as compared to the German ones, as contemporaries and later research judged it. British and Irish women had no option but to focus on suffrage as a means of advancing women's rights, whereas the suffrage in Germany would not have guaranteed the same benefits for women; German women would have to seek their rights in other ways.

TIT FOR TAT: EACH JUDGING THE METHODS OF THE OTHER

While the women's movements internationally were in contact with each other and were broadly well-informed about what was happening in other countries, they also had their misgivings about each other. German women, for example, felt hurt by the demeaning representation of them by English women as being conservative, moderate, backward and tame, and by English women's positioning themselves as pioneers when it came to enlightening the women of other nations. They were amazed by the misinformation on the situation of women in other countries and the contexts of their fights that influenced their choices in their fights for women's rights – as suggested in a comment by the German feminist, Marie Stritt, in her report on the ICW congress in London in 1899:

> The naive ignorance of the state of women's endeavours outside England and America, which was supplemented by false reports and distortions with regard to Germany, put us in the pleasant position that our reports were received with great interest and even astonishment. I don't think though that our gracious English and American sisters in spirit will deduce any kind of obligation on their part to be better informed about the work of their like-minded sisters in the future. The pleasant knowledge of having brought the 'late-comers' onto the right way is enough for them.[61]

Moreover, the German women's movement was split in how they judged the English suffragette movement when it started to radicalize under the leadership of the Pankhursts.[62] The *Bund Deutscher Frauenvereine* (BDF), or National Council of German Women, rejected their methods strongly; its president wrote:

61 M. Stritt, 'Der Internationale Frauenkongress in London', *Die Frau*, 6 (1899), 644.

62 J. Marcus (ed.), *Suffrage and the Pankhursts* (London, 2013) and P. Bartley, *Emmeline Pankhurst* (London, 2002).

> We are convinced that the use of violent means is in fundamental contradiction to the nature and aims of the women's movement and therefore cannot be justified in principle either by external political circumstances or by the loyalty to conviction and readiness to sacrifice demonstrated in the process ... Women who use revolutionary means of struggle not only deny their own feminine nature, they also ultimately harm the interests of the women's movement.[63]

Success was thought to come only from 'the uplifting power of women's positive achievements, not from the bitter and internecine struggle of the sexes for external power'.[64]

The radical wing of the BDF protested immediately against this statement. Anita Augspurg and Lida Gustava Heymann responded in an open letter, complaining that 'German women were stabbing their English sisters in the back on behalf of the entire German women's movement'.[65] This split between the radical and moderate wing of the movement demonstrated how limited the space to act for women in Germany was in 1912. It was the different contexts of the English and German movements manifesting itself: German women were afraid to relate to the suffragettes because it would have greatly harmed their cause. Hedwig Dohm, who had famously claimed suffrage in 1876 in her book *Women's nature and law*, expressed understanding for the suffragettes but also said clearly: 'The transplantation of the suffragettes on German soil would be misguided propaganda for the right to vote'.[66] Feminist Lucia Dora Frost explained:

> The English national spirit is more brutal than the German, more straightforward and more tolerant of the will of the individual. This must be kept in mind to understand the actions of the suffragettes. In our country, such a terrorist act would never have occurred … German public opinion obliges the leaders of the women's movement to put greater emphasis on persuasion and to be more reserved. This makes their tactics more subtle, perhaps more effective.[67]

63 Declaration of the General Board of National Council of German Women, Helene Lange Archiv (HLA) B Rep. 235–01, Nr. 44, 8–11, Landesarchiv Berlin (LAB) reprinted: G. Bäumer, 'Zur Kampfesweise der Suffragettes. Erklärung des Gesamtvorstands des Bundes Deutscher Frauenvereine', *Die Frauenfrage* 15:3 (1913/14), 17–8 and H. Lange, 'Die Taktik der Suffragettes' in H. Lange, *Kampfzeiten. Aufsätze und Reden aus vier Jahrzehnten*, 2 vols (Berlin, 1928), ii.

64 Ibid.

65 L.G. Heymann and A. Augspurg, 'Offener Brief', HLA B Rep. 235–01, Nr. 44, 4–5, Landesarchiv Berlin; re-printed in *Die Frauenbewegung* 19:11 (1913), 88; K. Schirmacher, *Die Suffragettes* (Weimar, 1912). There are a number of documents about this conflict in the Helene Lange Archive, B Rep. 235–01, Nr. 44, Landesarchiv Berlin.

66 Anonymous, 'Deutsche Frauen über die Suffragetten', *Berliner Lokal-Anzeiger*, No. 372, 24 July 1912.

67 Ibid.

In other words, if German women wanted to be recognized by society, they needed to convince men of the rightness of their demands through arguments and to find a consensus with the central institutions and the state.[68] They had little other option in the oppressive climate of imperial Germany. Indeed, the strong reaction in the German press to the suffragettes' struggle showed once again how little room for manoeuvre there was in society. Women were equated with hyenas, and urgent warnings were issued against the work of the German suffragists on the grounds that they ultimately wanted to overthrow the natural order.[69] At the same time, even by 1918 not all member organization of the BDF agreed on suffrage as a common claim of the BDF; some argued suffrage was a political claim and inconsistent with the character of the BDF as a non-political organization.[70]

The Irish suffrage movement was not perceived in Germany as different from the English one. If Ireland was mentioned at all separately in the German-speaking women's press, it was to mention the beauty of the landscape and the striking poverty.[71]

In reviewing the German reaction to the suffragettes in Great Britain, it is important to remember that the suffragettes also constituted only a radical minority alongside many suffrage societies in Britain. The majority of these were united since 1897 in the National Union of Women's Suffrage Society (NUWSS) and used methods not unlike the ones the BDF favoured. In 1914, the organization included about 500 local chapters.[72] Its president for more than twenty years was Millicent Garrett Fawcett, a liberal democrat who had been involved in the women's movement since the 1870s.[73] She wrote:

> Women's suffrage will not come, when it does come, as an isolated phenomenon. It will come as a necessary corollary of the other changes which have been gradually and steadily modifying during this century the social history of our country. It will be … based upon social, educational, and economic changes which have already taken place … The revolution has been quietly taking place.[74]

68 There are a number of letters to the general board of the National Council of German Women expressing this sentiment: HLA B Rep. 235–01, Nr. 44, Landesarchiv Berlin (LAB).

69 Anonymous, 'Eine deutsche Verteidigung der englischen Stimmrechtsweiber', *Berliner Neueste Nachrichten* Nr. 637, 14 Dec. 1912.

70 See, e.g., Reifensteiner Verband to BDF, 6 Apr. 1918, HLA B Rep. 235–01, Nr. 44, 140, LAB as well as the fact that the Protestant Women Organization left the BDF in 1918 as a protest against the claim for women's suffrage.

71 E.g., M. Knapp, 'Erlebnisse und Eindrücke in Irland', *Die Frau* 21:7 (1914), 407.

72 L.P. Hume, *The National Union of Women's Suffrage Societies, 1897–1914* (New York, 1982).

73 D. Rubinstein, *A different world for women: the life of Millicent Garrett Fawcett* (Ohio, 1991).

74 M. Garrett Fawcett, 'The appeal against female suffrage: a reply', *Nineteenth Century,* 19 (1886), 746.

She attempted to achieve women's suffrage by peaceful and constitutional means through legislative reform in shifting coalitions with the Liberals or with the Labour Party. The NUWSS protested against the violent methods the suffragettes used.

In all cases – England, Ireland and Germany – the radical wings mastered media strategies better than the conservative women. They came to dominate the contemporary perception of the struggles of the women's movements,[75] and seemed to be more effective by operating outside mainstream feminist organizations.[76] They thus manage to catch the attention of historians and researchers, with the result that their story is more often told.

AFTERMATH: DID SUFFRAGE MATTER?

Suffrage for women came in all three countries in 1918 (though only partially in Great Britain and in Ireland at first), and it seems like neither the 'suffrage first' model nor the 'suffrage as a crown' model was more successful. In Germany, women had received the 'suffrage-crown' without having won the other citizenship rights; they had to accept that the 'crown' was only one part of the great struggle for equal rights of women and that all the rights they wanted to have before gaining the 'crown' were still very far away. In Britain and Ireland, the concentration on suffrage had the advantage that 'all our force' was concentrated 'upon a single, narrow front', which had 'immensely simplified the women's movement.'[77] So, the movements had to regroup around a more complex set of issues.[78] Measured by the timing, when women in Britain, Ireland and Germany received suffrage, it seems like the different goals and methods in the struggle for suffrage had not mattered greatly.

Arguing throughout this chapter for the importance of the differences between the women's movements and closing with the remark that in the end none of that seems to have mattered may seem like a contradiction. It is not so, however, because the means the women chose (or were forced to adopt) were not as important as the fact that they did succeed and that the ideas of

75 S. Schraut, 'Internationale Konferenzen, Publikationen und die Stiftung von Erinnerung: Mediale Strategien in den Richtungskämpfen der bürgerlichen Frauenbewegung im Kaiserreich', *Feministische Studien*, 35:1 (2017), 61–75; U. Wischermann, *Frauenbewegung und Öffentlichkeiten um 1900. Netzwerke, Gegenöffentlichkeiten, Protestinszenierungen* (Königstein, 2003).

76 S.L. Weldon, *When protest makes policy* (Ann Arbor, 2011).

77 Anonymous, 'The second round', *Woman's Leader,* 12 Mar. 1920, 1125.

78 J.V. Gottlieb (ed.), *Feminism and feminists after suffrage* (New York, 2016); C. Beaumont, *Housewives and citizens: domesticity and the women's movement in England, 1928–64* (Manchester, 2013); and M. Röwekamp, '"Männer und Frauen haben grundsätzlich die gleichen staatsbürgerlichen Rechte". Weimar – Meilenstein auf dem Weg zur Gleichberechtigung der Geschlechter?' in Friedrich-Ebert-Stiftung (ed.), *Die Weimarer Verfassung, Wert und Wirkung für die Demokratie* (Erfurt, 2009).

equality were discussed and negotiated in different ways. After all, they fought for a common idea that found only a different expression in each country.

Besides, there are other factors which might explain this contradictory result. Some scholars, such as Gisela Bock and Dawn Teele, point to the interconnection with male suffrage. Men did not possess universal suffrage in Germany, Britain or Ireland.[79] If a small group of elite women were granted suffrage, how long could the male elite keep out poor men and women? This was the case in all three countries where pressure was mounting for universal male suffrage. Just as Helene Lange had predicted in 1896: if women were enfranchised it would hardly be due to a 'sudden attack of justice frenzy in our parliaments', but 'men will not give women the suffrage until it serves their own interest'.[80] Parties came to adopt women's suffrage in the hope of gaining women's votes. Interestingly, conservative parties often came around to the idea sooner than liberal parties because they assumed women would tend to vote conservative. In Germany, the social democrats needed the female votes – and they got them. Female voters, whose turn out rate at the polls in 1919 was 89 per cent, voted for the Weimar coalition of the Social Democrats, the Democratic Party and the Catholic Centre Party.[81]

Moreover, the common timeline between Britain, Ireland and Germany shows that the history of women's suffrage is not just a national story.[82] Legally electoral laws are a national matter, but the pathway to suffrage in case of women was decidedly global. It was part of an international and transnational movement, which fought at the same time for the same rights. Women's national struggles were accompanied by women's efforts to find a common global solution, and to support each other with arguments and information for the individual national struggles. There were personal contacts at regular conferences; there were exchanges of ideas via books, newspapers and letters; and then there were the transnational organizations such as the International Council of Women and, in terms of suffrage especially, the International Women's Suffrage Association (IWSA). Feminists kept each other informed of the developments in suffrage and other citizenship rights of women globally. This transnational flow of knowledge was part of the national struggles, and these national struggles cannot be analyzed without considering the influence the transnational movement might have had within individual countries. We can see the influence the British movement had on Germany; methods used in one country were also used in

79 In Germany they did at the federal level but not at state level and in many states, such as in Prussia, it was unequal because it was related to the census.

80 H. Lange, 'Wahlrecht' in H. Lange (ed.), *Kampfzeiten. Aufsätze und Reden aus vier Jahrzehnten*, vol. 1 (Berlin, 1928), p. 190.

81 Bock, *Women in European history*, pp 146–56; Teele, *Forging the franchise*, pp 177–94.

82 L. Rupp, *Worlds of women: the making of an international women's movement* (Princeton, 1997) and E.C. Dubois, 'Woman suffrage around the world: three phases of suffragist internationalism' in Daley and Nolan (eds), *Suffrage and beyond*.

the other or they were rejected – but any case they were well informed about the methods. The British probably adopted less from the Germans, but they learned about ideas and arguments from women who travelled abroad, especially in connection with the IWSA. But at the same time England was also 'too imbued with an imperialist hauteur, too fiercely embattled in its own national struggles, *and* spoke with too many suffrage voices, to match the internationalist spirit of Holland, Denmark and Sweden' for example.[83] The internationalism of Germany was also limited in other ways, but the German women were open to learn.[84]

Not only were women in Great Britain, Ireland and Germany granted suffrage at the same time; but women were enfranchised in fourteen other European countries between 1915 and 1931, with most of them receiving full suffrage rights. This curious coincidence led to an attempt to explain the coming of women's suffrage in a comparative way. Many scholars have stressed the war efforts of women and their patriotism and dedication to the war effort as one of the reasons for women's suffrage. While the war certainly served as a catalyst of change, some scholars believe that it postponed women's suffrage.[85] For all European countries, 1918 was a time of instability. In Germany and Ireland especially, suffrage was granted at a time of revolutionary change and was seen as indicative of a new democratic impetus.

In the aftermath of women's suffrage, this initial attempt at granting women equality ended when the period of instability and transition ended. Perhaps men felt that granting the vote had come too hastily, and further change should be more carefully considered and possibly avoided. Thus, in all three countries – England, Ireland and Germany – women came to realize that suffrage was only valuable insofar as their voices counted, and they found that their voices counted for less than they had expected after finally receiving suffrage. On one hand, suffrage meant little in everyday life compared to issues such as who has the last word in decisions about the children, or whether a married woman could work without the consent of her husband, or could manage her property the way she chose to. These equality rights were not gained with suffrage, but were often much more meaningful to women in daily life.

Women fighting for equal rights in the interwar period soon found out that their votes had only a limited value. As most female voters did not vote for the

83 J. Liddington, 'Was the suffrage campaign truly international? Votes for women in Edwardian England, 1903–1914' in E. Schöck-Quinteros et al. (eds), *Politische Netzwerkerinnen. Internationale Zusammenarbeit von Frauen, 1830–1960* (Bremen, 2007), p. 330.

84 I. Remme, *Die internationalen Beziehungen der deutschen Frauenbewegung vom Ausgang des 19. Jahrhunderts bis 1933* (Berlin, 1955); Schöck-Quinteros et al., *Politische Netzwerkerinnen.*

85 Bader-Zaar, 'Frauenwahlrecht', 2001, 6–13; Bock, 'Frauenwahlrecht', 95–136; A. Schaser, 'Zur Einführung des Frauenwahlrechts vor 90 Jahren am 12. Nov. 1918', *Feministische Studien* 27:1 (2009), 97–110; and A.S. Fell and I. Sharp (eds), *The women's movement in wartime: international perspectives, 1914–19* (London, 2007).

parties who wanted to grant women equal rights but for the conservative parties, so women's votes changed politics and the idea of women's place in society to a smaller extent than was hoped for.[86] Women did not manage to change the laws with their votes, despite the new equality rights that at least German women were granted in the Weimar constitution of 1919. In all their attempts to change laws that discriminated against them, they kept running up against barriers. In Ireland, women soon discovered that men did not mean them to have more than the voting rights granted by Article 14 of the 1922 constitution. When the drafters of the constitution set out a clear equality clause, the provisional government realized that this would mean eventually absolute equality for women, so they watered the clause down. When women protested strongly and a group of them even pointed towards the equality formulation in the Weimar, Polish and Czech constitution, the legislators could only agree on a very weak formulation that would have negative consequences for women's struggle for equal rights for decades. The Irish Free State set out into freedom with unfree women. The 1937 constitution with its notorious Article 41.2. sealed the constitutional situation, sending women back to the home.[87]

'Under the 1916 Proclamation, Irishwomen were given equal citizenship, equal rights and equal opportunities. Subsequent constitutions have filched these or smothered them in mere "empty formulae"', complained Hanna Sheehy Skeffington in 1943.[88] 'Is the constitution a scrap of paper as far as women are concerned?' asked Emmy Beckmann, a teacher, and head of the General German Teachers' Association, in 1931.[89] The answer came from Anita Augspurg and Lida Gustava Heymann. Equality 'was in the constitution, was there on paper, but that was all. The economy, finances, administration, the entire state apparatus, which is a decisive factor in revolutions and upheavals, was in the hands exclusively of men.'[90] Augspurg

86 K. Heinsohn, 'Ambivalente Entwicklungen. 150 Jahre Frauenbewegung, Politik und Parteien', *Ariadne* 67:68 (2015), 40; H.M. Lauterer, *Parlamentarierinnen in Deutschland* (Königstein, 2002); and B.v. Hindenburg, *Die Abgeordneten des Preußischen Landtags 1919–1933: Biographie- Herkunft- Geschlecht* (Frankfurt am Main, 2017).

87 'Women's position in Ireland', *Equal Rights,* 11:49 (1925), 389; H. Sheehy Skeffington, 'Women in the Irish Free State', *Equal Rights,* 23:12 (1937), 96; T. Mohr, 'The rights of women under the constitution of the Irish Free State', *Irish Jurist,* 41 (2006), 20; and M. Valiulis, *The making of inequality in the Irish Free State, 1922–37: women, power and gender ideology* (Dublin, 2019).

88 H. Sheehy Skeffington, General election manifesto 1943, quoted in C. Beaumont, 'Women, citizenship and catholicism in the Irish Free State, 1922–1948', *Women's History Review* 6:4 (1997), 563.

89 Emmy Beckmann, Brochure of the Allgemeiner Deutscher Lehrerinnenverein, 'Fight against dual incomes and the dismissal of married female teachers, ca. 1930–31', Marie Elisabeth Lüders papers, Bundesarchiv Koblenz, BA N/1151/154, 3.

90 L.G. Heymann and A. Augspurg, *Erlebtes, Erschautes: deutsche Frauen kämpfen für Freiheit, Recht und Frieden 1850–1949* (Frankfurt, 1992), p. 187.

and Heymann realized that suffrage by itself was not enough to make a full change but only a very beginning as the English had claimed: 'The vote alone is valueless, but it is the key to citizenship. It unlocks the door to real equality.'[91]

While it was a necessary tool for the fight for equal rights for women, women had to look far beyond the vote and consider how major social institutions and especially the law helped to perpetuate women's oppression. Solving the women's question meant reorganizing society, changing laws and enabling women to become full members of the human community. Suffrage granted women a formal right but without substantive representation and real inclusion. Without these real changes suffrage threatened to become a farce when it was countered by the patriarchal marriage and family law and other legal areas with its overhanging privileges, customs and power. German women would learn a short time afterwards how empty those voting rights were when they could only vote for one party after 1933.

At the same time, suffrage was a milestone for women's struggle for equal rights. It offered a better opportunity for women to challenge male domination and it was a substantial step on the way of ending the subordination of women. Women had forced men in the years after suffrage to defend their views, and women's reform ideas were now out in the open in the political arena to be realized much later, but realized eventually.[92]

We should be aware that the celebration of the centenary of women's suffrage is also a smokescreen for the fact that women's voices still don't count as much as male ones, and that positions of power are still overwhelmingly filled by men who are still almost as hesitant to grant more rights to women as they were one hundred years earlier. The fact that we can celebrate the great achievement of having gained suffrage should not distract us from the fact that men and women are still far from taking the same responsibility for the family; and that in a crisis such as the Covid pandemic, the first rights which were limited were women's rights. We should be aware at this time of celebration that a democracy is only a democracy when in reality all voices and the interests of all citizens count the same.

91 NUSEC, *The case of equal franchise*, Elisabeth Macadam 1924 TUC Library, quoted in V.C. Law, 'The women's cause: feminist campaigns, 1918–1928' (PhD, University of London, 1993), p. 439.

92 Suffrage also mattered for the development of the welfare state. Women's suffrage increased social spending in Europe, as women in the parliaments were especially interested in social politics and were to the fore in making demands for social reform. G. Bock and P. Thane (eds), *Maternity and gender politics* (London, 1994) and Bock, *Women in Europe*, pp 181–9.

James Henry Mussen Campbell QC, MP: a life in law and unionist politics

DAIRE HOGAN*

James Henry Mussen Campbell (1851–1931), the first Baron Glenavy, was successively lord chief justice (1917–18) and lord chancellor of Ireland (1918–21). He was subsequently nominated as a member and elected to be the first chairman (1922–8) of the Senate of the Irish Free State, and held a prominent social position in Dublin, particularly in golf and tennis circles. Obituaries published on his death in 1931 were conventionally respectful. The *Irish Times* said of him that 'he had no personal enemy … He was a man of singularly dignified and noble bearing and presence, and his manners conveyed the impression of straightforwardness, candour and genuine kindness of heart.'[1] His grandson, Patrick Campbell, the third Baron Glenavy, wrote to the same effect that 'he was extremely good-looking, in a most distinguished and autocratic way, with silvery white hair and an elegantly drooping white moustache'.[2]

An imposing, perhaps even intimidating, presence in court is suggested by a reported exchange with Chief Baron Palles in which Campbell asked that his protest at a procedural ruling that had been given be formally noted, to which Palles retorted: 'Indeed I will not. There is a certain discretion allowed to a judge, and a worm must turn some time.'[3] Campbell was a prominent lay member of the Church of Ireland, being variously and at different times a member of the Representative Church Body and of the General Synod, chancellor of the United Dioceses of Dublin, Glendalough and Kildare and an advocate and subsequently a lay judge in the court of the General Synod, and was remembered as 'a commanding figure' with strong opinions.[4] The clerk (and historian) of the Senate, Donal O'Sullivan, described him as 'a man of very strongly marked, and even dominating, personality … [whose] clarity

* This chapter is a modified version of the spring discourse delivered to the Irish Legal History Society at Trinity College Dublin in 2013. The author wishes to acknowledge the permission granted by the Parliamentary Archive to use the Bonar Law and Lloyd George papers.

1 As republished in the *Irish Times*, 23 Mar. 1931.

2 P. Campbell, *My life and easy times* (London, 1967; pbk ed., 1968), p. 67.

3 *Law Times*, 106 (8 Apr. 1899), 523.

4 *Church of Ireland Gazette*, 28 Mar. 1931. See also R. Marshall, 'The constitution of the Church of Ireland in action; ritualist litigation in a disestablished church, 1871–1937' in K. Costello and N. Howlin (eds), *Law and religion in Ireland, 1700–1970* (Cham, Switzerland, 2021), pp 298 and 315.

of mind and his power of expression remained in their full vigour, and in the legal examination of a case and its subsequent exposition he had no superior'.[5] It was such qualities and force of personality, as thus still notable in later life, rather than any geniality that brought him to the front rank of the bar and of politics, and ultimately to high judicial office.

Campbell was born in 1851 in Dublin. He had a long connection with Trinity College, where he had a distinguished academic record and was elected auditor of the College Historical Society. He was subsequently an MP for Dublin University (1903–16) and its vice-chancellor[6] (1919–31). He was called to the bar in 1878 and joined the North-East circuit, becoming a QC in 1892, and a bencher of the King's Inns in 1894. Members of the bar were subject to what used to be known as the 'cab rank' rule, an obligation ordinarily to accept instructions from any prospective client who (through a solicitor) might approach them. That he had an uncomplicated approach to this practice is suggested by the fact that in the space of a couple of months at the end of 1895 and the New Year of 1896 he appeared both for and against the Pharmaceutical Society of Ireland in cases under the Pharmacy Acts (Ireland) 1875–90.[7] He had extensive experience in criminal law and was appointed crown prosecutor for the winter assizes in Belfast in 1898 and 1899.[8] His ability and his involvement in Conservative Party politics led to other legal patronage appointments, succeeding George Wright QC in each case, as senior crown prosecutor at Green Street in Dublin in 1900,[9] and then as solicitor general in October 1901[10] following Wright's appointment as a judge. He was criticized in 1902 for inattention to the duties of that office while representing a private client.[11] Maurice Healy in his memoir of the Munster circuit wrote of Campbell's prosecuting address to the jury in a murder trial in Cork in or about 1905:

> I learned afterwards that he had left the House of Commons at 8 o'clock the night before, not having opened the brief; he read and mastered it before his trip across on the night mail, which reached Cork at 10.35 next morning; and at 11 o'clock he began a masterly statement of the case to the jury. Admittedly it was an easy case; but few counsel would today treat a prosecution for murder so cavalierly.[12]

5 D. O'Sullivan, *The Irish Free State and its Senate* (London, 1940), p. 244.
6 That office was abolished in 1964; its functions are now discharged by pro-chancellors.
7 *R (Cleland) v. Pharmaceutical Society of Ireland* [1896] 2 IR 368; *Pharmaceutical Society of Ireland v. Boyd & Co.* [1896] 2 IR 394.
8 *ILTSJ*, 32 (12 Nov. 1898), 516; *ILTSJ*, 33 (18 Nov. 1899), 483.
9 *Law Times*, 108 (3 Feb. 1900), 315.
10 *Law Times*, 111 (26 Oct. 1901), 577.
11 *Hansard's Parl. deb., 4th series* (commons), vol. 108, cols 381–3 (15 May 1902); *ILTSJ*, 36 (31 May 1902), 206
12 M. Healy, *The old Munster circuit* (Dublin, 1939), p. 218.

He was briefly attorney general in December 1905, replacing John Atkinson QC who was appointed as a lord of appeal in ordinary ('law lord'), on the eve of the Conservatives going out of office. The Liberals won a landslide victory in the general election of January 1906, marking the start of what seemed likely to be a long period in opposition for the conservatives, during which Campbell would have no prospect of judicial promotion. He had been called to the bar in England in 1899, by Gray's Inn,[13] of which he became a bencher in 1901, and after 1905,

> Campbell for some time essayed to follow in the footsteps of, and indeed under the patronage of, [Sir Edward] Carson at the English bar. In this country [England], however, he was not a success at the bar. The vigour of his methods of cross-examination and of his speeches to juries, which were in contrast with the conversational style characteristic of forensic addresses in this country, failed to gain him the ear of the judges or of the juries.[14]

Healy noted that members of the Irish bar rated Campbell much above Carson, acknowledging that 'Carson was quiet, sarcastic and imperturbable; Campbell was flamboyant, hectoring and excitable … [and] well known as about as tough-skinned a man as ever wore wig and gown.'[15]

He was first elected to the House of Commons as a Unionist MP at a by-election in 1898 for the St Stephen's Green constituency in Dublin, which covered a much larger area of the city than its name might suggest. The sitting member, William Kenny QC, a Catholic Liberal Unionist, had been appointed as a judge. Campbell emerged as the Conservative candidate after a short internal party contest with, among others, Arthur W. Samuels QC.[16] It was a marginal constituency, and Campbell won a narrow victory over the Nationalist candidate, Count Plunkett (3,525 votes to 3,387, a 51/49 per cent division). He lost the seat at the general election in 1900, his small majority being changed by a lower unionist turnout into a nationalist majority of 556 (2,873 votes to 3,429).[17]

In 1902 the ill-health of the eminent historian W.E.H. Lecky, one of the sitting members for the Dublin University constituency, led to speculation that he would soon resign, and Campbell announced that he would not stand again in St Stephen's Green and would contest any vacancy in the university.[18] When Lecky retired at the end of 1902 Campbell won the by-election in

13 *Law Times*, 107 (6 May 1899), 3.
14 *Times*, 23 Mar. 1931.
15 Healy, *Old Munster circuit*, pp 95 and 253.
16 *Irish Times*, 17, 18 and 20 Dec. 1897.
17 A. Jackson, 'The failure of unionism in Dublin, 1900', *IHS*, 26:104 (Nov. 1989), 377–95.
18 *Irish Times*, 22 Apr. 1902.

March 1903, receiving 1,492 votes to 1,421 for his opponent, Samuels. There were boisterous scenes in the university, in College Green and in the law library at the Four Courts after the declaration of the poll.[19] That was the last contested election that he fought, and, with Carson, he was returned unopposed for the university at the next general election in 1906 and at the two general elections in 1910. Between 1832 and 1922 the university was represented by 21 MPs, of whom 17 were barristers, only one of whom was not eventually appointed as a judge,[20] a pattern of the representation of the university being used almost as a matter of course as a stepping stone for legal promotion that occasioned some discontent. Between 1903 and 1905 both of the university MPs held office as solicitor general, Campbell in Ireland and Carson in England.

Campbell was a diligent constituency MP, alert to protecting the status of the university throughout his parliamentary career, initially to prevent any modification of its position in the course of the reforms, discussed for decades, to provide a more extended system of third-level education acceptable to Catholic opinion.[21] The Irish Universities Act 1908[22] established the National University of Ireland and Queen's University Belfast as independent universities. He proposed an amendment to the first Home Rule bill in 1912 to exclude the intended new domestic Irish parliament from having any power to make laws relating to Trinity College,[23] which would have been a form of extra-territorial status going further than general opinion in the college was comfortable with.[24] That principle was accepted in subsequent legislation, which provided not for an absolute prohibition on any such legislation but for the consent of the college being necessary. The Government of Ireland Act 1914,[25] as re-stated in the subsequent 1920 legislation,[26] provided that '[n]o law made by the Irish parliament shall have effect so as to alter the constitution, or divert the property of, or repeal or diminish any existing exemption or immunity enjoyed by the University of Dublin, or Trinity College Dublin or the Queen's University of Belfast, unless and until the proposed alteration,' etc. had been approved by a number of specified internal college governance bodies.

He accepted a brief for a newspaper publisher in the defence of a libel action in England in 1913 taken by the attorney general and others. This arose out of allegations of supposedly corrupt dealings in shares of a Marconi

19 Ibid., 7 Mar. 1903.
20 R.B. McDowell, 'Trinity College Dublin and politics' in his *Historical essays, 1938–2001* (Dublin, 2003), p. 82.
21 Ibid., p. 80.
22 7 Edw. VII, c. 38.
23 *Hansard's Parl. deb., 5th series* (commons), vol. 42, cols 1763–70 (21 Oct. 1912).
24 R.B. McDowell, *Crisis and decline: the fate of the southern unionists* (Dublin, 1997), p. 36.
25 4 & 5 Geo. V, c. 90, s. 42.
26 Government of Ireland Act 1920 (10 & 11 Geo. V, c. 67), s. 64.

company with the benefit of government inside information. The details were complicated,[27] but the allegations, some of which related to Lloyd George, the chancellor of the exchequer, gave rise to a major political controversy. The fact that not only Campbell but also two of the other principal unionist lawyer MPs – Carson and F.E. Smith – had accepted professional engagements to represent various parties in the episode, thus disqualifying themselves from joining in parliamentary debate about it, appalled Andrew Bonar Law, the party leader, and was resented by many of their colleagues.[28]

A new career vista for Campbell opened in May 1915, when growing criticism of the war effort, in light of recent military setbacks such as the tenuous landing at Gallipoli in April, led to consensus on a reconstruction of the government on a broader basis, with the Unionists joining a coalition government with the Liberals. Campbell immediately showed great anxiety for advancement, writing to Bonar Law that

> If there is going to be a 'reshuffle' I want the Irish chancellorship. *You* can get it for me and I think that I have earned it by much longer and harder service than others whose names I see mentioned.[29]

Nationalist opposition frustrated his ambition then, and three anxious years of campaigning and solicitation would pass before he succeeded in being appointed.

When the new cabinet was announced on 25 May there was widespread Liberal and nationalist dismay at the appointment of Carson as attorney general for England,[30] and also (among Liberals) at the removal from office of the lord chancellor of Great Britain, Haldane, an episode that 'reflects discredit on everyone involved except Haldane himself.'[31] Carson was the leader of the Ulster unionist resistance to Home Rule, exemplified by the Ulster Covenant in 1912. John Redmond, the Nationalist leader, had told the prime minister, Asquith, at the outset both that he was not prepared to accept an invitation to join the government, and that Carson should not join it.[32] His appointment as principal legal adviser to the government seemed incongruous to many, in light of his challenge or defiance of the authority of parliament to legislate for Home Rule, and the proclamation by the Ulster Unionist Council

27 F. Donaldson, *The Marconi scandal* (London, 1962).

28 R. Blake, *The unknown prime minister: the life and times of Andrew Bonar Law, 1858–1923* (London, 1955), p. 143; and R.J.Q. Adams, *Bonar Law* (London, 1999), p. 120.

29 Campbell to Bonar Law, 19 May 1915, quoted in R.F.V. Heuston, 'Legal history and the author: some practical problems of authorship' in W.N. Osborough (ed.), *The Irish Legal History Society: inaugural addresses* (Dublin, 1989), p. 29.

30 An office which, as it transpired, he held for a few months only, resigning in Oct. 1915.

31 R.F.V. Heuston, *Lives of the lord chancellors, 1885–1940* (Oxford, 1964), p. 221.

32 Redmond to Asquith, 19 May 1915, quoted in Denis Gwynn, *The life of John Redmond* (London, 1932), p. 423.

in September 1913 of intent to set up a provisional government 'for taking over the government of the province [of Ulster] in trust for the British nation' if Home Rule were enacted.[33]

Campbell had his own role in resisting Home Rule as a leading southern unionist, and was associated with the Ulster provisional government. The prospect of not one but two of such leading unionist legal figures now being given responsibility for the rule of law and the administration of justice, in England or Ireland, provoked 'a feeling in Ireland of the most intense character.'[34] Nationalist opinion rallied to the defence of the sitting lord chancellor, Ignatius O'Brien, not so much for his own merits but because he was not (and was an obstacle to) Campbell.[35] Asquith told Redmond that Bonar Law had raised Campbell's position

> in the very early stages of the negotiations, before even the composition of the new cabinet was settled. The Tories ... wanted some kind of recognition both in Ireland and in Scotland ... [and] expressed themselves satisfied if Campbell could be given the great seal. Both Lloyd George and I (though we were too preoccupied with other things to give the matter very careful attention) thought that this would not be a bad bargain. The chancellor in Ireland does not appoint the judges, is not necessarily involved in or even consulted about the course of administration, and is, and increasingly ought to be, a mere judicial officer; a post for which every lawyer in Ireland would agree that Campbell has special qualifications. The result was that, with our authority, they offered the position to him, and he accepted it.[36]

Birrell, the chief secretary for Ireland, had sought in similar fashion to explain the circumstances to Redmond, saying that there was to be a 'coalition all through', including in the administration of Scotland and Ireland, and that in dealing with the unionists 'it was a little difficult to close the doors altogether in their ugly faces ... [T]he result is that Campbell has (I have no doubt, though I am not formally apprised of the fact) effected a lodgement as lord chancellor.'[37]

When Bonar Law was told by Asquith, mindful of nationalist goodwill, that Campbell's appointment could no longer proceed he replied that

33 'Proclamation of provisional government within the province of Ulster', 24 Sept. 1913.
34 Redmond to Asquith, 7 June 1915, quoted in Gwynn, *John Redmond*, p. 430.
35 D. Hogan, 'Ignatius O'Brien and the law' in D. Hogan and P. Maume (eds), *The reminiscences of Ignatius O'Brien, lord chancellor of Ireland, 1913–18* (Dublin, 2021), p. 44.
36 Asquith to Redmond, 6 June 1915, quoted in J.A. Spender and C. Asquith, *The life of H.H. Asquith, Lord Oxford and Asquith*, 2 vols (London, 1932), ii, p. 169.
37 Birrell to Redmond, 29 May 1915, quoted in Gwynn, *John Redmond*, p. 427.

> it is not merely a question of disappointing Campbell, though that is serious to me after I had told him that he would receive the appointment; but it means that we have no voice in the Irish Administration and therefore no knowledge of what is being done … If Campbell's appointment is impossible then we must press either for the chief secretary or the lord lieutenant.[38]

He also approached Lloyd George, saying that:

> I was very surprised to hear from the PM today that he had any doubt about Campbell's appointment. You were present when I spoke to him about this and I regarded it as absolutely settled. In consequence Carson and I both told Campbell that he was sure of the appointment, and in view of the fact that at present we have no one in the Irish office at all I do not know what would happen if there were any hitch in this appointment. I do hope therefore that you will use your influence with the PM to make sure that this appointment goes through.[39]

What had initially seemed to be an item of local judicial patronage was escalating into a more fundamental issue of inter-party goodwill and understanding.

Bonar Law was in contact again with Lloyd George on 4 June:

> I am really greatly alarmed about the Campbell business. Of course if it comes to the breaking point we may have to give way but I think the pressure of our party will be so strong that some of those in the cabinet would resign and at the best even if we feel, and I think that this may be the case, that we cannot resign we shall start with very little prospect of doing useful work together. In addition to this, is not the whole object of the coalition to be strong enough to do what we think right and are we to begin by going back on the definite arrangement made by the prime minister on the first breath of hostility? In other words, are the nationalists to exercise a veto on everything that we do and play the same game as they played in regard to drink. I do not think I need to tell you that I have as little bitterness against the nationalists as any unionist can have but you must show as a government we are not afraid of them, and if the PM simply says I have done it there may be a little fuss but it will come to nothing. I am writing to you instead of taking it up with the PM because I have known you better personally and I feel the position will be very serious if there is further delay.[40]

38 Bonar Law to Asquith, 28 May 1915, Bonar Law papers, PA 53/6/12; Blake, *The unknown prime minister*, p. 284.

39 Bonar Law to Lloyd George, 27 May 1915, Bonar Law papers, PA 53/6/8.

40 Bonar Law to Lloyd George, 4 June 1915, ibid., 53/6/22.

A few days later the wider crisis was defused, but on a basis that was to leave Campbell complaining for the next three years that he had been let down. Asquith told Redmond that

> the whole Campbell business has given me an infinity of trouble ... The claim of the chancellorship for Campbell has now been withdrawn, subject to suitable provision (which I have undertaken) being made for him, and to a place of minor importance being found for a unionist in the Irish administration. Naturally, before agreeing to the new suggestion I insisted on knowing who was proposed and for what office. The answer is John Gordon (who, I imagine, is from our point of view the least objectionable of their lawyers) for the attorney generalship, the present attorney general ([Jonathan] Pim) receiving the vacant judgeship in the king's bench.[41]

Gordon was a QC and had been MP for South Londonderry since 1900. The *Freeman's Journal* reported this arrangement under the headline 'The attorney general raised to the Bench to make room for Mr Gordon'.[42]

Difficulties arose in finding an appointment for Campbell either in Ireland or in England. The initial plan was that he would be appointed as lord chief justice of Ireland, to replace R.R. Cherry, or as a lord of appeal in ordinary, but both Cherry and one sitting law lord who it was thought might have been prepared to retire were unwilling to do so.[43] There was no shortage of persons eligible to sit on appeals to the House of Lords, and there was no appetite for changing the law to permit the appointment of an additional law lord, and adding to the expense of government in wartime. Talk of Campbell being appointed to a judicial position in England was resisted by the lord chancellor of Great Britain. Shortly before Campbell was appointed as attorney general in April 1916, a few days before Easter, while still maintaining his claims for a higher position, Redmond had been asked by Bonar Law whether it was 'really worthwhile to persecute Campbell', a characterization Redmond strongly rejected.[44]

The arguments that Campbell used in extensive correspondence with Bonar Law and with Asquith to advance his claims are an indication of how articulate he could be – perhaps especially in his own behalf – as an advocate, changing tack and re-ordering his arguments to meet changing circumstances. One theme was his sense of financial insecurity, and Bonar Law was

41 Asquith to Redmond, 9 June 1915, quoted in Gwynn, *John Redmond*, p. 432. The letter is misdated as 9 May in the authorized biography of Asquith; Spender and Asquith, *H.H. Asquith*, ii, p. 169.
42 *Freeman's Journal*, 11 June 1915.
43 Heuston, *Lord chancellors*, p. 273.
44 Gwynn, *John Redmond*, p. 467.

reportedly 'pained, and indeed shocked, by the avidity of his old friend'.[45] Campbell stressed his friendship and comradeship with Bonar Law in the service of the Unionist Party, and made various political points, initially in May 1915, on the necessity for unionist participation in the government of Ireland, and subsequently saying that if conscription into the army was not extended to Ireland, having regard to nationalist opinion, then his appointment could be insisted upon as a concession to unionist opinion. He thought that more ought be made of the breach of faith by the Liberals in his abandonment in 1915, and that his colleagues should stand by him later on more firmly than they were doing. He thought that there would be no real problem in just making the appointment, that there might be a little fuss but it would die down, and that privately many of his colleagues at the bar in Ireland would have welcomed his appointment, as strengthening the court of appeal. He floated the idea of accepting a lower salary for a time as lord chancellor, so that the salary, when taken with the pension that would become payable to the incumbent lord chancellor, Ignatius O'Brien, would not, in wartime, give rise to a net increase in public expenditure.

In the first week of November 1916 Cherry indicated his intention to retire and Asquith offered his position to Campbell. A number of elements combined to delay this appointment for some weeks. Campbell requested confirmation that the arrangement for further promotion, as lord chancellor or as lord of appeal in ordinary, would not be prejudiced by acceptance of the office of lord chief justice, and he was greatly affected by the death in action in France at this time of his third son, Philip.[46] Asquith was replaced by Lloyd George early in December, before the appointment had been finalized. It was announced on 21 December, the last day of the Michaelmas law term, coupled with the honour of a baronetcy.[47] Soon afterwards at the request of Campbell (and of Carson)[48] Bonar Law reminded the new prime minister that

> when the coalition was formed Mr Campbell was offered the lord chancellorship of Ireland and this had to be waived. After a lapse of time the late prime minister offered him the lord chief justiceship but at the same time gave him a pledge that the first vacancy of lord of appeal in the House of Lords would be offered to him. Campbell wishes to have this formally confirmed by you. I am sure that you will think this right and perhaps you would either send him a note or authorize me to do so in your name.[49]

45 Blake, *The unknown prime minister*, p. 254.
46 *Irish Times*, 11 Nov. 1916.
47 Ibid., 22 Dec. 1916.
48 Carson to Bonar Law, 13 Dec. 1916, Bonar Law papers, PA 81/1/56.
49 Bonar Law to Lloyd George, 22 Dec. 1916, ibid., 84/6/20.

Campbell was given this assurance a fortnight later.[50] He was formally sworn in as lord chief justice on 11 January 1917, and in a change from recent practice took his oath of office in open court, in 'a public function of a really impressive character',[51] which also perhaps obviated any awkwardness that might have existed if the ceremony had taken place in the chambers of the lord chancellor whom he had been trying to oust and replace.

He was a judge for four-and-a-half years, for some seventeen months (to June 1918) as lord chief justice and the balance (to June 1921) as lord chancellor, thus sitting both as a common law judge as the head of the king's bench division of the high court and in chancery and as head of the court of appeal. Presiding over a divisional court he dealt fairly briskly with motions seeking orders for a new trial and suchlike, saying for instance that 'we do not find it necessary to hear any further argument in this case',[52] that 'we do not think it necessary to allow this case to stand over for consideration because we have come to a clear conclusion',[53] and that 'we do not think it necessary to call upon counsel for the crown as we are satisfied that the application is wholly untenable'.[54] A new trial was ordered in a case in which he remarked that the conduct of the impugned trial 'was not at all satisfactory', since the notes of the judge (Dodd J) did not fully describe the evidence.[55] He heard two difficult cases as to the custody of a child, under the Custody of Children Act 1891, in one of which the parties had different religious beliefs, and hence were in dispute as to the religion in which the child might be brought up.[56]

His judgments in the court of appeal included careful reviews of whether compensation payable for the felling for military purposes of trees on an estate (as contrasted with trees felled by accident or wind) was the property of the tenant for life or of the trustees of a settlement,[57] and of the nature of an easement of a right of way by necessity.[58] He presided over the court for crown cases reserved in a case as to whether a jury had sufficient evidence of death, on foot of confession of the defendant, where the body of a deceased person had not been found, in which the court upheld the decision of the trial judge at assizes not to withdraw the case from the jury and affirmed a conviction.[59] Campbell's judgment rejected forcefully arguments put forward by defence counsel, based upon some previous observations by Palles CB limiting the reliance that could be placed upon a confession in a case of murder:[60]

50 Bonar Law to Campbell, 6 Jan. 1917, ibid., 84/6/37.
51 *Law Times*, 142 (20 Jan. 1917), 203; *Irish Times*, 12 Jan. 1917.
52 *R (Futter) v. Justices of Co. Cork* (1917) 2 IR 430, at 435.
53 *Town and County Advance Company v. Provincial Bank* (1917) 2 IR 421, at 425.
54 *R (McMorrow) v. Fitzpatrick* (1918) 2 IR 103, at 107.
55 *Coughlan v. Monks* (1918) 2 IR 306.
56 *In re Boyd* (1918) 2 IR 98; *In re Connor* (1919) 1 IR 361.
57 *Gage and Roper v. Pigott and de Jenner* (1919) 1 IR 23.
58 *Maguire v. Browne* (1921) 1 IR 148.
59 *R v. McNicholl* (1917) 2 IR 557; *ILTSJ*, 51 (29 Dec. 1917), p. 311.
60 *The Queen v. Sullivan* (1887) 20 LR Ir. 550, at 570.

> I confess to the greatest difficulty in following the reasoning of Palles CB … I have asked in vain and searched in vain for any decision which supports, much less establishes, the proposition that, in the absence of the finding of the body, the confession of the accused cannot supply proof that the act was done … I therefore express in the clearest and strongest way the unqualified dissent of every member of this court from the proposition that the case of murder is an exception to the general and accepted principle of our common law that the confession of the accused may be the highest and most satisfactory proof of guilt, and our refusal to give any countenance to the proposition that in a charge of murder, in which the accused has made a full and free confession of the commission of the crime … the case can never go to the jury unless there is proof of the finding of the dead body.[61]

The *Irish Times* had remarked in 1917 that on his appointment Campbell 'now leaves the exciting arena of politics for the cooler atmosphere of the judicial bench,'[62] but his new status as a judge did not end his participation in political life nor his ambition. His involvement in various informal discussions aimed at securing a compromise settlement over Home Rule

> led more hard-line unionists to regard him as an opportunistic lawyer who had used them to secure office for himself, while nationalists continued to cite his 1912–14 Ulster speeches as setting precedents for the Easter Rising and as treasonable utterances which should have disqualified him from public office.[63]

In the spring of 1918, as a major German offensive on the Western Front threatened to break the military deadlock, he was invited to attend a meeting of the war cabinet in Downing Street[64] in the context of an impending change in the law that would raise the age of conscription in Britain from 41 to 51, and would permit, by order of the privy council, its extension to Ireland.[65] With Carson, he advised the cabinet against the possible extension of conscription to Ireland, the prospect of which led to a very widespread opposition in Ireland: 'apart from the unionists all groups in Ireland co-operated against conscription, and not since the days of O'Connell had Catholic Ireland been so united'.[66]

After Lloyd George decided at the end of April on a new political initiative in Ireland, perhaps combining the introduction of Home Rule with

61 *R v. McNicholl*, at 588, 589 and 592.
62 *Irish Times*, 11 Jan. 1917.
63 P. Maume, 'James Campbell' in *DIB*.
64 Minutes of meeting of War Cabinet 376, 28 Mar. 1918, TNA CAB 23/5/68.
65 Military Service (No. 2) Act 1918 (8 Geo. V, c. 5), ss 1 and 2.
66 M. Laffan, *The resurrection of Ireland; Sinn Fein, 1917–23* (Cambridge, 1999), p. 134.

conscription, Campbell was asked if he would take a political office, as one of a triumvirate of persons who, as lords justice, would replace the lord lieutenant of Ireland.[67] That did not interest him, but he brought up again the prospect of being appointed lord chancellor, and Bonar Law told him that 'if there is a vacancy I feel sure that [Lloyd George] will offer it to you and I shall certainly do my best to make sure of that', counselling him at the same time to accept the office if invited to do so without attempting to negotiate any changes in its functions or responsibilities.[68] As weeks passed without any appointment being made Campbell became apprehensive that, as had happened three years before, the appointment might not be made and pressed Bonar Law on the subject. He received a reply that 'there has been no intentional delay in this case. The PM has been away so much that it has been impossible to get an opportunity of talking to him about it but I saw him today and he is arranging to take the necessary steps.'[69] Within a week O'Brien had been dismissed, consoled with a peerage as Lord Shandon,[70] and Campbell appointed. He was unable to take his seat in court for some three weeks, having trouble with his sight.[71]

His relations with the government transpired afterwards not to be as warm as might have been expected. He expressed frustration at a lack of consultation on the appointment in August 1918 of James O'Connor as a member of the court of appeal in succession to Thomas F. Molony, who had replaced him as lord chief justice.[72] He then referred publicly to conscription as a 'danger and disaster', adding that he was not responsible for government policy.[73] Some two years later he stated that he had not been for many months associated with the executive.[74] He took an active part in encouraging the erection of war memorials, for the bar,[75] as a national memorial,[76] and for Trinity College.[77]

He retired as lord chancellor on 27 June 1921, that being the day on which, pursuant to the Government of Ireland Act 1920, the office of lord chancellor ceased to have any executive functions and became a purely judicial office.[78]

67 Diary of Field Marshal Sir John French (Lord French of Ypres), 29 and 30 Apr. 1918, Imperial War Museum, London, PP/MCR/C32, JDF 1, vol. R.
68 Bonar Law to Campbell, 8 May 1918, Bonar Law papers, PA 84/7/29.
69 Bonar Law to Campbell, 27 May 1918, ibid., 84/7/33.
70 Lloyd George to O'Brien, 30 May 1918, Lloyd George papers, PA LG F/45/5/1; D. Hogan, 'Ignatius O'Brien and the law', p. 46.
71 *Law Times*, 145 (29 June 1918), 170.
72 Campbell to Bonar Law, 3 July 1918, Bonar Law papers, PA 83/5/2, and 8 July 1918, ibid. 85/5/7.
73 *Irish Times*, 24 Aug. 1918; *Law Times*, 145 (24 Aug. 1918), 327; (31 Aug. 1918) 343.
74 *Law Times*, 150 (4 Sept.1920), 149.
75 *ILTSJ*, 53 (31 May 1919), 132.
76 *ILTSJ*, 53 (30 Aug. 1919), 209.
77 *ILTSJ*, 53 (8 Nov. 1919) 268.
78 Government of Ireland Act 1920 (10 & 11 Geo. 5, c. 67), s44; Government of Ireland (lord chancellor of Ireland) Order 1921, S. R. & O. 1921/ 1130 (27 June 1921).

He was raised to the peerage in October 1921, and took his name from (having previously named his mansion in Milltown, in the Dublin suburbs after) the village of Glenavy, Co. Antrim, with which there had been some family connection. Patrick Campbell wrote that 'when he became the first baron he took his title from Glenavy more because he liked the sound of it than because of landed estates in the area. I doubt, in fact, if he'd ever been in the village in his life.'[79] The benchers of Gray's Inn in London congratulated him, and commissioned a portrait of him, by Sir William Orpen RA, for the hall of the inn, which was exhibited at the Royal Academy summer exhibition in 1923.[80]

In the early years of the Irish Free State Campbell became a prominent symbol of unionist acceptance and co-operation with its government, not only as a member and the first chairman of the Senate but also as chair of a committee established to recommend the basis of restructuring of the judicature.[81] The committee, which included Hugh Kennedy and Timothy Sullivan, who were subsequently appointed to be, respectively, the first chief justice and the first president of the high court of the new state, and Charles A. O'Connor, the master of the rolls, sat between February and May 1923. Its recommendations, published in June, formed the basis of the reforms that were legislated for in the Courts of Justice Act 1924. Before this engagement in the governance of an independent Ireland, however, he had inquired whether, as a member of the House of Lords, he might sit on the hearing of appeals from lower courts in the United Kingdom, since he was eligible (but not entitled) for such a function.[82] The lord chancellor, Lord Birkenhead (his former colleague, F.E. Smith), rebuffed these inquiries, as did Bonar Law, who 'sent a thunderous rebuke.'[83] He had been introduced into the House of Lords in November 1921,[84] and contributed (as his only speeches in the House) to the debates in December 1922 on the statutes that gave effect under the law of the United Kingdom to the Treaty that had been signed twelve months before, the Irish Free State Constitution Act 1922 and the Irish Free State (Consequential Provisions) Act 1922. He spoke warmly of the leaders of the Irish government, saying that he had followed their progress for the last two months and was 'bound to say that I have been tremendously impressed, not only by their courage and sincerity, but also by the qualities of statesmanship and moderation which they have displayed'.[85] This tribute drew a sarcastic comment from Carson which, ignoring the bitterness behind

79 Campbell, *My life and easy times*, p. 76.
80 *Irish Times*, 23 July 1921; *ILTSJ*, 57 (19 May 1923), p. 124.
81 *ILTSJ*, 57 (3 Feb. 1923) 33; (23 June 1923), 154; *Report of the judiciary committee* (Dublin, 1923).
82 Appellate Jurisdiction Act 1876 (39 & 40 Vict., c. 59), ss. 5 and 25.
83 Heuston, 'Legal history and the author', p. 30.
84 *Hansard's Parl. deb., 5th series* (lords), vol. 47, col. 217 (9 Nov. 1921).
85 Ibid., vol. 52, col. 192 (1 Dec. 1922).

it, Campbell turned away by describing it as good-natured banter.[86] A couple of days later, on 6 December, W.T. Cosgrave, the president of the executive council of the Irish Free State, announced that he would be a member of the new Senate, and he was elected as its chairman at the first meeting, on 11 December,[87] being re-elected annually until he stepped down in 1928.

Campbell left a very substantial estate on his death in 1931, which was valued for probate purposes in England at over £90,000, somewhat belying his earlier financial worries. His will established a complicated family trust, of which his elder son, Charles Gordon Campbell, the second baron (1885–1963), would speak with reverence to his son Patrick, the third baron (1913–80), referring to 'the monies' held in the Glenavy Trust, 'probably with the intention of giving them the sacrosanct and untouchable quality of the Crown Jewels'.[88]

86 Ibid., cols 197–8, 203.
87 O'Sullivan, *The Irish Free State and its Senate*, pp 90 and 117.
88 Campbell, *My life and easy times*, p. 40.

The Irish Convention 1917–18: centenary reflections

JOHN F. LARKIN*

The Irish Convention first met on 25 July 1917 and adjourned *sine die* on 5 April 1918. Its purpose, as expressed by David Lloyd George, was 'that Irishmen of all creeds and parties might meet together in a Convention for the purpose of drafting a constitution for their country'.[1] That constitution was, again in Lloyd George's words, to 'secure a just balance of all the opposing interests, and finally compose the unhappy discords which have so long distracted Ireland and impeded its harmonious development'.[2] We cannot even pretend, like Oscar Wilde translating one of the Passion narratives,[3] not to know how this ends. A single constitution for this island, justly balancing all of its opposing interests and composing its unhappy discords, has still not been achieved. If the Irish Convention failed to draft such a constitution – and it did fail in that herculean task – no other assembly has since succeeded in it.

In this chapter I raise the curtain by looking at one version of the technocratic case for Home Rule as it was articulated shortly before the First World War. This is followed by a look at the two main primary sources for the Irish Convention, being, first, the official report, and, second, the confidential report produced by Sir Horace Plunkett. I then explore the immediate constitutional context of the Convention, the task of the Convention, the two main schemes of government discussed at the Convention, and the tangible legacy of the Convention.

* This chapter is based on a lecture given to the Irish Legal History Society in Regent House, Trinity College Dublin, on 17 Feb. 2017 to mark the centenary of the Irish Convention. Editorial note: In this chapter the term 'Dominion' (with a capital 'D') is used to avoid confusion with the wider term 'his majesty's dominions', which refers to the British empire as a whole; there were five Dominions in 1917: Canada, Australia, New Zealand, South Africa and Newfoundland.

1 *Report of the proceedings on the Irish Convention* (Dublin, 1918), p. 9. See Plate 13.1.

2 Ibid.

3 Two different versions of the narrative are cited by H. Gardner, *In defence of the imagination* (Cambridge, MA, 1982), p. 124.

TECHNOCRATIC DEVOLUTION

As an expression 'Home Rule' had an emotional impact that 'devolution' could (and does) not possess. A technocratic case for devolution – that is, an argument for devolution as a means by which better government could be delivered for Ireland – was made by Lord MacDonnell of Swinford in an address to the Literary and Scientific Society of Queen's University Belfast in February 1911. Both the man and the location matter. MacDonnell had a brilliant career in the Indian administration and a shorter – controversially shorter – career in the Irish administration. MacDonnell was not a party politician and a nationalist argument for Home Rule would be unlikely to fall on sympathetic ears among many students of QUB in 1911. McDonnell is important because he remained at the centre of the technocratic debate about improving the government of Ireland before the Convention, as a member of the Convention and after the Convention.

In his Belfast paper, MacDonnell made it clear that not only did he support 'the delegation or devolution of parliamentary powers to subordinate assemblies for local purposes' in Ireland but also 'general federation … or devolution all round'.[4] The phrase 'general federation' is not now regarded as having the same meaning as the phrase 'devolution all round', but this tendency to equate devolution with federation was not peculiar to MacDonnell. He explored three topics: how an Irish legislative assembly would be constituted; the relations between this assembly and parliament; and Irish financial arrangements. The single transferable vote model of proportional representation was proposed as a basis of election to the assembly.[5] The relations between parliament and the Irish assembly, MacDonnell thought, 'must be one of subordination on the part of the latter and plenary control on the part of the imperial parliament'.[6] Having 'examined the constitutions of our great self-governing colonies of Australia, South Africa and Canada', MacDonnell considered that greatest assistance could be obtained from the Canadian model on the assumption 'that what we have in view is the establishment between the United Kingdom and Ireland of some such relations as exist between the Dominion government and its component provinces'.[7]

There could in MacDonnell's scheme be no place for Dominion status for Ireland: 'I reject at once the idea, if anyone entertains it, that the relations between the United Kingdom and the Dominion government should be reproduced in Ireland. Such an arrangement as that might lead to Ireland's

4 A.P. MacDonnell, *Some suggestions concerning the future welfare of Ireland* (Dublin, 1911), p. 9.
5 Ibid., pp 10–13, 29–30.
6 Ibid., p. 13. Such a model of subordination and control remains the pattern for devolution in the United Kingdom. See, e.g., s. 5(6) of the Northern Ireland Act 1998.
7 Ibid., p. 14.

entering into relations with foreign states which, though suitable and perhaps inevitable in the case of such a colony as Canada, would, in the case of Ireland, lying as she does at the empire's heart, directly lead to numberless embarrassments'.[8]

MacDonnell concluded his analysis of the financial relationship between Ireland and Britain by observing that 'the most urgent duty which will lie upon the Irish legislative assembly will be the duty of effecting economy in the public expenditure and ordering her public expenditure for the future on the lines befitting a comparatively poor country with undeveloped resources'.[9]

THE OFFICIAL REPORT AND THE CONFIDENTIAL REPORT

While an exploration of the Convention will still often begin through the prism of McDowell's enduringly important monograph, *The Irish Convention, 1917–18*,[10] the two main primary printed sources for the Convention are the published official report which appeared as a command paper in 1918 and the printed, but unpublished, confidential report finalized by the chairman late in 1918 or early 1919. The *Report of the proceedings of the Irish Convention* enables the formal proceedings of the Convention to be followed; it included various reports and notes by participants in the Convention as well as an appendix that included the Convention's division lists and sub-committee reports.

By any reckoning, Plunkett's *Confidential report to his majesty the king* is an intriguing text.[11] From the preface, dated Christmas 1918, it appears that Plunkett supplied the king with regular notes about the Convention and he expresses the hope that the *Confidential report* would give any government resuming the search for an Irish settlement a clearer understanding of the work done in the Convention than that afforded by the published report.[12] He adds that '[t]o the historical student it may also be of value'.[13] The *Confidential report* extends beyond the active life of the Convention. Plunkett, in a section tellingly entitled 'The wreck of the Irish Convention in the British parliament', exposes the consequences of the extension of conscription to

8 Ibid.
9 Ibid., p. 27.
10 R.B. McDowell, *The Irish Convention, 1917–18* (London, 1970). McDowell's monograph on the Irish Convention remains an indispensable treatment. Not only was it based on a wide range of printed and manuscript sources but he was able to discuss the Convention with Dr Edward MacLysaght, a member of the Convention, and with Lord Southborough who had served on the Convention secretariat (see p. ix). I have benefitted too from T. Irish, *Trinity in war and revolution, 1912–1923* (Dublin, 2016).
11 H. Plunkett, *The Irish Convention: confidential report to his majesty the king* (Dublin, 1918), available at https://digitalcollections.tcd.ie/concern/works/bk128k22t.
12 There is, however, no evidence available to me that demonstrates the realization of this hope.
13 Plunkett, *Confidential report*, p. ii.

Ireland: 'the political consequences would be ruinous [while] the military advantage would be nil'.[14] He wrote: 'I seemed to see the Convention ship, after its stormy voyage, torpedoed at the harbour's mouth'.[15]

As far as the proceedings of the Convention are covered in the *Confidential report*, Plunkett considered that '[t]he narrative is, I believe, truthful. Where I express my own views I have tried to be fair; but I do not pretend to maintain the impartiality I observed in the chair'.[16] Plunkett's decision to set aside the austere impartiality of the chair – or, at least, its appearance – makes for a vivid and entertaining read. He does not appear to have struggled unduly with any conflict between the obligation he had assumed to write confidentially to the king and his belief that his often colourful and always interesting thoughts on the Convention merited a wider readership.[17] Throughout the confidential report it is clear that Plunkett had an eye for the small but illuminating details, as, for example, when he notes that 'the Protestant and Roman Catholic bishops simultaneously sought adjoining seats'[18] – a good sign, he thought.

Yet Plunkett often appears a little too pleased with himself and disdainful of Convention participants. Referring to his speech from the chair on 26 February 1918, which dealt with an important letter from Lloyd George, he writes: '[w]hen I sat down, I had spoken for over an hour. I am not often guilty of cruelty to dumb animals'.[19] A contrast with this gracelessness is the impish beginning to the sixth section of the *Confidential report*, 'The chairman's summing up': '[h]aving now sat in judgment upon the different sections and leading individuals in the Irish Convention, none of whom (with the exception of the chairman) I have found altogether satisfactory.'[20]

Plunkett considered that a presentational mistake had been made by the vote in favour of a narrative report without any in-depth defence of the majority position, while permitting each section to put in its own notes and reports (a permission amply enjoyed, for example, by the Ulster unionists).[21] The result was, in his view, that '[i]n effect, the majority had won the battle and instructed me to allow their opponents to write the dispatches and the press reports'.[22]

14 Ibid., p. 130.
15 Ibid.
16 Ibid., p. ii.
17 Apart from the general desire for a wide readership, it is clear that the *Confidential report*, as it then stood, was shared in January 1918 with 'a known authority upon the period of American history which included the story of the Philadelphia Convention, whose proceedings probably came nearest to furnishing useful analogies for the Dublin Convention'. Plunkett, *Confidential report*, p. 126.
18 *Confidential report*, p. 6.
19 Ibid., p. 88.
20 Ibid., p. 125.
21 See their report at *Report of proceedings*, pp 30–4.
22 Plunkett, *Confidential report*, p. 116.

If the Convention had decided to adopt a colourless report, this did not stop Plunkett from prefacing it with a vivid letter of transmission.[23] This letter of transmission annoyed the Ulster unionists who characterized it, in the words of H.M. Pollock, as 'written in defiance of the unanimous and specific instructions of the Convention', as 'the final proof of his unsuitability for the position of an impartial chairman', and which, as a summary, 'grossly misrepresented the conclusions arrived at'.[24] Of these characterizations, the first is untrue but understandable,[25] the second is arguably plausible,[26] but the third will scarcely seem honest to anyone who reads the official report.

THE CONSTITUTIONAL CONTEXT OF THE CONVENTION

Plunkett might have exaggerated the complexities and anomalies of the constitutional context in which the Convention was established but it was, nonetheless, strikingly odd and anomalous. Ireland was in 1917 operating under a system of government 'which', as Plunkett put it, 'survives only because the Act abolishing it[27] cannot, consistently with ministerial pledges, be put into operation without further legislation no less difficult and controversial than that which it has to amend'.[28] The Government of Ireland Act 1914[29] had received royal assent and was a full programme for legislative and executive devolution. The operation of that Act was suspended by section 1(1) of the Suspensory Act 1914[30] until such later date 'not being later than the end of the present war' as might be fixed by order in council.[31] This nature of the suspension effected by the Suspensory Act 1914 added a further twist to the constitutional context as it stood in 1917. Section 1(1) appeared to provide a clear outer limit ('the end of the present war') so that the provisions of the Government of Ireland Act 1914 and the Welsh Church Act 1914[32]

23 *Report of Proceedings*, pp 3–7.
24 Belfast Chamber of Commerce, address of the president (Mr H.M. Pollock) on the Irish Convention at the annual meeting of the Chamber, 21 May 1918, p. 2, PRONI D627.436.18.
25 'But when it was decided that everybody was to be free to express their own personal opinions, was I to be the only member of the Convention from whom this privilege was withheld?' Plunkett, *Confidential report*, p. 126.
26 'Perhaps, had I been appointed to the chair by the Government ... I might have hesitated to write the letter which will be found at the beginning of the official report.' Plunkett, *Confidential report*, p. 126.
27 The Government of Ireland Act 1914 (4 & 5 Geo. V, c. 90).
28 *Report of proceedings*, p. 7.
29 4 & 5 Geo. V, c. 90.
30 4 & 5 Geo. V, c. 88.
31 This was superseded by section 1(1) of the Termination of the Present War (Definition) Act 1918 (8 & 9 Geo. V, c. 59). The Great War did not end until midnight on 31 Aug. 1921 by virtue of an order in council made under the 1918 Act on 10 Aug. 1921. See *London Gazette*, 12 Aug. 1921, p. 6289.
32 4 & 5 Geo. V, c. 91.

would come into effect when the war ended even if no Order in Council were made.

The Convention met just over a year after the Easter Rising. Sinn Féin had nothing to do with the Rising but it retrospectively became Sinn Féin's Rising. This required certain adjustments: a republican Rising could not readily be appropriated by a party whose central platform in 1916 was a dual monarchy on the pattern of the Austro-Hungarian *Ausgleich*.[33] It has been suggested relatively recently by Loughlin that 'Griffith's argument [in favour of a dual monarchy] was open to criticism on the grounds of the historical debasement of Ireland's status by English monarchs, and of being a disguise for continued subjection given the transformation in the role of the monarchy over the nineteenth century'.[34] This dual criticism is difficult to understand: first, if one assumes 'the debasement of Ireland's status by [unnamed] English monarchs', there is no evidence that such debasement would have occurred or been possible in the early twentieth century. Second, 'the transformation in the role of the monarchy over the nineteenth century' was to reduce the political and constitutional power of the monarch making 'subjection' even less likely. George V did not have the power of George III.

While Laffan has detected a weakening in Griffith's support after 1916 for a constitution based on the King, Lords and Commons of Ireland, observing only two references throughout 1917 to the traditional Sinn Féin platform,[35] it was not until October 1917 that the Sinn Féin ard fheis dropped its monarchist policy in favour of a republic[36] and even then with the proviso that when the republic had been obtained the Irish people were free to choose either a monarchy or republic as a form of government. Although this change in its constitutional policy came after the Convention had begun its work, the Sinn Féin attitude towards the Convention was, nonetheless, hostile: '[s]he [England] proposes a convention to smooth out the differences previously created by her agents and general policy; also in the hope of discovering the minimum Ireland could be induced to accept, for nobody would now tolerate the Act on the statute book.'[37] Sinn Féin declined to attend the Convention.[38]

33 [A. Griffith], *The resurrection of Hungary: a parallel for Ireland* (Dublin, 1904).
34 J. Loughlin, *The British monarchy and Ireland: 1800 to the present* (Cambridge, 2007), p. 306.
35 M. Laffan, *The resurrection of Ireland: the Sinn Féin party, 1916–1923* (Cambridge, 1999), p. 242.
36 A. Ó Snodaigh, 'Remembering the past: the rebirth of Sinn Fein', *An Phoblacht*, 6 Apr. 2000.
37 *Ireland's appeal to America 1917* ([Dublin], n.d. [1917]), p. 5. L.S. Amery's view expressed in a letter of 17 May 1917 to Carson was that 'the Home Rule Act is now dead as mutton', PRONI D1507/A/23/36.
38 *Report of proceedings*, p. 9; *Confidential report*, p. 5. At p.18 of the *Confidential report*, Plunkett indicates that a prominent leader of Sinn Féin told him 'that he regretted the refusal of the Sinn Féiners to take part in the Convention. They would, I gather, probably not have abstained but for the fact that their counsels were, for the present, dictated by a committee of extreme men more interested in physical force than in constitutional methods'.

In 1917 Plunkett's judgement was that '[t]he tendency of recent political thought among constitutional nationalists has been towards a form of government resembling as closely as possible that of the Dominions'.[39] This seems to give a measure of support with the Sinn Féin judgment about universal dissatisfaction with the suspended Government of Ireland Act 1914 and, as we shall see, the constitutional parameters available to the Convention were wider than would have been thought possible in 1914.

Dissatisfaction with the 1914 Act did not, of course, come from one direction only. According to Hugh Barrie, the chairman of the Ulster unionist delegation to the Convention, 'northern unionists had come to the Convention to find a compromise between the Act of 1914, which had been accepted as a final settlement of the nationalist demand, and the partition proposals of 1916'.[40] While acknowledging that nationalism had moved beyond the 1914 Act, Barrie thought that the mean should still be sought 'between the two extremes of the Home Rule Act on the one hand and the partition of Ireland on the other.'[41]

Finally, in terms of constitutional context, it should be remembered that the suggestion of a Convention in Lloyd George's letter of 16 May 1917 was offered as an alternative to a four-part proposal consisting among other things of a bill providing for the immediate application of the 1914 Act to Ireland, with the exclusion of the six counties of north-east Ulster initially for a period of five years – although a Council of Ireland comprising all of the Westminster MPs from the excluded area and a delegation equal in number from the Irish parliament[42] could agree to the inclusion of the excluded area, subject to a majority of voters in the excluded area voting for inclusion.

When Lloyd George wrote to Redmond on 16 May 1917, the bill amending the Government of Ireland Act 1914 had already been prepared by a committee of the war cabinet chaired by Lord Curzon. Although the bill had been drafted and was ready for introduction, Curzon's committee did not see the bill as a straightforward alternative to some larger discussion of Irish government. On the contrary, Curzon's committee had

> drawn up this draft bill in the belief that, should it be fortunate enough to receive a second reading in the House of Commons, it will then be referred, along with the Home Rule Act of 1914, to a commission or conference, with instructions to draw up a new bill, as already promised, in amendment of that Act for submission to parliament. The fortunes of the draft bill will in our opinion depend very much upon the terms in which any such reference is made. If the draft bill were referred alone

39 *Report of proceedings*, p. 5
40 Plunkett, *Confidential report*, p. 62.
41 Ibid.
42 The letter is reproduced in *Report of proceedings*, p. 50, app. I.

> without the concession of a power to propose amendments in the Home Rule Act, much disappointment would probably be caused, and it is doubtful if any practical result would ensue. If, on the other hand, the Act be referred, together with the draft bill, there would seem to be a fair chance of evolving a reasonable and acceptable scheme.[43]

Curzon's suggestion was duly embodied in Lloyd George's letter to Redmond. Lloyd George suggested that:

> the bill embodying the above proposals, together with the Home Rule Act, should be forthwith considered by a conference to be constituted on the lines of the speaker's conference on electoral reform, though not consisting exclusively of members of parliament, and meeting under the chairmanship of someone commanding the same general confidence in his impartiality and judgment as Mr Speaker himself. The conference would, of course, have full power to suggest any alterations in the Government scheme which it might decide.[44]

In McDowell's summary of Lloyd George's letter there is no reference to the conference; the alternatives are presented as Home Rule with exclusion or a convention.[45] The alternatives were much less starkly opposed than that: the conference, not confined to members of parliament, would consider the new bill and the Government of Ireland Act 1914 together; the Convention, 'the secret conference in the Regent House',[46] would produce by itself a constitution for Ireland.

THE TASK OF THE CONVENTION

Lloyd George's letter of invitation addressed to members of the Convention quoted from his remarks in the House of Commons and summarized the object of the Convention as 'to submit to the British government a constitution for the future government of Ireland within the empire'.[47] This was a remarkable assignment for the 94 representatives and nominees[48] at the Convention. The criterion of acceptability as far as the United Kingdom government was concerned was that Ireland would remain within the empire. The plain implication was that Ireland need no longer remain part of the

43 TNA CAB/24/89.

44 *Report of proceedings*, p. 50.

45 McDowell *Irish Convention*, pp 76–7. There is a similar summary (omitting the conference) in A. Jackson, *Home Rule: an Irish history, 1800–2000* (Oxford, 2003), p. 177.

46 Plunkett, *Confidential report*, p. 130.

47 *Report of proceedings*, p. 9.

48 The list of members is at *Report of proceedings*, pp 52–3.

United Kingdom. Yet the dissident minority nationalists were in part inaccurate to note that '[t]he terms of reference given to the Convention contained the single limitation that the constitution must be within the empire';[49] that was to ignore the initially implied and then later quite explicit limitation that the constitution secure the support of all Irish parties.[50]

It was also to ignore that ground – especially ground laid by Lloyd George – could shift. On 25 February 1918 Lloyd George wrote to Plunkett and gave it as the government's view 'that the only hope of agreement lies in a solution which, on the one side provides for the unity of Ireland under a single legislature with adequate safeguards for the interests of Ulster and the southern unionists, and, on the other, preserves the well-being of the empire and the fundamental unity of the United Kingdom'.[51] Plunkett did not appear to note the shift or accept its significance,[52] but it did not escape analysis by the bishop of Raphoe: '[t]he terms of reference to the Convention had laid down but one limitation. The prime minister's letter laid down many.'[53] Rather most robustly, the letter was 'denounced as a gross breach of faith' by nationalists outside the Convention.[54]

Writing a constitution is difficult. Plunkett realized early that '[f]ar the most important part of the initial work was what can be quite accurately (though not without danger of giving offence) be described as the education of the Convention'.[55] There were two reasons for this. Plunkett had no high regard for any Convention participant except himself[56] and thought that '[p]robably less than a dozen of the members have given any close attention to the details of the subject they have to discuss. Even professional politicians are seldom constitutional architects, and, in any case, they were but a small minority.'[57] Secondly, there was the inherent difficulty of the task: '[t]he particular constitution now to be built up,' Plunkett said, 'has inherent

49 *Report of proceedings*, p. 37.

50 See the letter of 21 Jan. 1918 from Lloyd George to Plunkett reproduced in *Confidential report*, p. 76: 'they [Government] are prepared to do anything in their power to assist the Convention finally to reach a basis of agreement which would enable a new Irish constitution *to come into operation with the consent of all parties* [my emphasis].'

51 Plunkett, *Confidential report*, p. 85.

52 He comments in the *Confidential report*, p. 87, that the letter 'represents the most generous concession ever made by a British Government to the wishes of the majority of the Irish people'. In his letter of 9 Mar. 1918 to Convention members, Plunkett says: 'We are charged to produce a scheme of Irish self-government within the empire', ignoring Lloyd George's reference to the fundamental unity of the United Kingdom. Plunkett, *Confidential report* p. 95.

53 Plunkett, *Confidential report*, p. 90.

54 Ibid., p. 99. The Lloyd George letter gave rise to a proposed amendment to the draft report of the Convention condemning what the proposer of the amendment (William M. Murphy) saw as the letter's baleful effects. The proposed amendment was defeated by 41 to 16 votes (ibid., pp 117–18).

55 Ibid., p. 6.

56 Ibid., p. 126.

57 Ibid., p. 6.

complexities of extreme difficulty, as anyone may realize by a perusal of the Home Rule Act on the statute book.'[58]

When an unnamed correspondent contrasted the Convention with the Philadelphia Convention to the former's distinct disadvantage, referring to 'the slip-shod, unworkmanlike, less-than-half-thought-out schemes ... submitted to the Dublin Convention', comparing these with 'the extraordinary grip on practical constitutional construction ... shown ... at the Philadelphia Convention',[59] Plunkett's response was to acknowledge that 'most of the members of the Irish Convention had little, if any, technical equipment for their formidable task' although as the Convention proceeded 'there was a steady improvement in the grasp of constitutional principles and in the practical sense needed to apply them.'[60] Plunkett's response to his unnamed correspondent, which is less a defence of the substantive work of the Convention than a defence of the Convention as advanced training in sound constitutionalism, prepares the way for the acknowledgement (or excuse) in the chairman's letter of transmission that '[w]hile technically it was our function to draft a constitution for our country, it would be more correct to say that we had to find a way out of the most complex and anomalous political situation to be found in history – if not in fiction'.[61]

In his letter to Convention delegates of 17 August 1917 Plunkett had assured them that the grand committee[62] or an *ad hoc* committee would draft a bill that would be introduced in the Convention 'where it would go through the usual stages of a bill in the House of Commons'.[63] Quite apart from the failure to reach a consensus that would embrace Ulster unionism, the Convention failed to produce anything resembling a draft bill.[64] The production of a scheme was entrusted in October 1917 to the bishop of Raphoe.[65] His 'heads of scheme' 'formed the basis of discussion throughout the constructive part of the debates' within the Convention.[66]

While the chairman cannot be faulted for the failure of the Convention to find an elusive or inexistent consensus, he can be faulted for failing to ensure that the Convention produced a draft bill. Plunkett claimed that the Convention had presented the government with a plan for a settlement that was 'reasonable and workable'[67] (and this is a bold claim as respects

58 Ibid., p. 6.
59 Ibid., p. 127.
60 Ibid.
61 *Report of proceedings*, p. 7.
62 A committee composed of twenty members of the Convention. See Plunkett, *Confidential report*, p. 7.
63 Plunkett, *Confidential report*, p. 9. Agreement on procedure is confirmed at pp 10–11.
64 While there are twenty-one paragraphs in the statement of conclusions, these could not be regarded as sufficient even as instructions to legislative drafters. *Report of proceedings*, pp 24–9.
65 Plunkett, *Confidential report*, p. 38.
66 Ibid., p. 61.
67 Ibid., p. 129.

'workable') but the Convention was asked for a constitution, bound itself to produce a draft bill and managed to do neither. And yet it is difficult to withhold sympathy from a chairman who, along with everything else, had to put up with a good deal of unhelpful waffle. In the joint note by the provost of Trinity College and the archbishop of Armagh, they said '[w]e have more than once put forward a federal scheme based on the Swiss or Canadian precedent, which might ensure a united Ireland with provincial autonomy for Ulster, or any other province that desired it'.[68] Insofar as the archbishop's speech of 14 March 1918 may be said to contain his own contribution towards such a scheme, then it is quite empty of substance and structure. Together with a good deal of hand-wringing, it does little more than point to Canada as an example and remind his hearers that the provost had pointed to Switzerland and had offered suggestions based on his knowledge of that country.[69]

THE SCHEMES OF GOVERNMENT

While there is much in the work of the Convention of great interest, including the arrangements for the composition of the Irish House of Commons and the Irish Senate,[70] the focus here will be on the form of the main schemes of government discussed at the Convention. Consistent with Lloyd George's invitation, the first two schemes of government introduced for discussion at the Convention were 'both based upon the Dominion principle of self government'.[71] Edward Lysaght said that Sinn Féin 'would accept a bold and far-reaching settlement within the empire'.[72] When the Convention met in Belfast, John Redmond while emphasizing that '[t]he proposal before them was called Dominion Home Rule' denied that this implied an independent parliament: 'there was only one sovereign parliament; every other parliament was subordinate.'[73] Reviewing matters as they stood at the end of the presentation stage of the Convention, Plunkett considered that of the seven schemes presented 'five … proposed to give Ireland a status like that of the Dominions, while the authors of the two remaining schemes, though aiming at the federal type, have both felt themselves free to depart from every known model of that type by giving Ireland fiscal autonomy'.[74] For the Dominions there was no Westminster representation. In a federal model, the existence

68 *Report of proceedings*, p. 35.
69 'Irish Convention: a speech delivered by the Lord Primate of All Ireland, 14 Mar. 1918', pp 9–10, PRONI D989.C.1.24.
70 *Report of proceedings*, pp 26–7.
71 Plunkett, *Confidential report*, p. 11.
72 Ibid., p. 18.
73 Ibid., p. 21. See portrait at Plate 13.2.
74 Ibid., p. 35.

of a state or provincial legislature sat readily with, indeed required, representation at the federal legislature. In November 1917, on a discussion of possible Irish representation at Westminster, nationalists opposed such representation as inconsistent with Dominion status. On being informed by Ulster unionists that 'this was to them a *sine qua non*',[75] nationalists agreed not to break negotiations on the issue.

Lord MacDonnell appears to have been the main driver of what emerged as the Convention's majority position. Hugh Barrie reported to Carson on 5 March 1918:

> I can see MacDonnell is angling for the support of the bishops and their friends, but I think he will succeed. The bishops' following, however, has weakened, and is not put at higher than twenty tonight. On this basis MacDonnell will carry by a considerable majority, and his proposal is a very plausible one.[76]

Dawson Bates reported to Carson that 'the south of Ireland unionists … are voting steadily for Lord MacDonnell'.[77] With the exception of Lord Londonderry's muted expression of support for federalism, the Ulster unionist members of the Convention did not engage in the construction of any scheme for the government of Ireland within the empire. Federalism appears as, at least impliedly, desirable for Ulster unionism towards the end of the report of the Ulster unionist delegation to the Convention in which it is said that '[o]ne of the many objections to the scheme presented in the [official] report is that it would make the future application of federalism to the United Kingdom impossible'.[78] Plunkett, correctly, saw this as false: '[W]hen the majority set up a local parliament in one unit of the United Kingdom, provided for continued representation of that unit in the central parliament, and put no real obstacle in the way of future extensions of the federal system, they went as far in the direction of federation as it was possible to go in the circumstances.'[79]

In their report to the Convention, the Ulster unionists claimed that the bishop of Raphoe's scheme included 'a sovereign independent parliament for Ireland co-equal in power and authority with the imperial parliament'.[80] This is simply untrue and refuted by paragraph 1(2) of the Convention's statement of conclusions: 'notwithstanding the establishment of the Irish parliament or anything contained in the Government of Ireland Act, the supreme power and

75 Ibid., p. 43.
76 Barrie to Carson, 5 Mar. 1918, PRONI D1507/A/26/56.
77 Bates to Carson, 13 Mar. 1918, PRONI D1507/A/26/59.
78 *Report of proceedings*, p. 34.
79 Plunkett, *Confidential report*, p. 128.
80 *Report of proceedings*, p. 31.

authority of the parliament of the United Kingdom shall remain unaffected and undiminished over all persons, matters and things in Ireland and every part thereof.'[81]

Plunkett criticized the minority nationalists within the Convention (whose scheme had been based, he believed, on the earlier work of Squadron Observer Erskine Childers RN, a member of the Commission secretariat)[82] for 'fathering a scheme of government, without any recognition of the fact that nine-tenths of the provisions had been agreed by the majority of the nationalists and the labour representatives, and by all the southern unionists' – an action 'calculated … to discredit the majority in the eyes of all men who looked to the Convention to give to the world the fullest possible measure of agreement'.[83] This had the effect of playing into the hands of the Ulster unionists 'whose chief concern was … to prove that there was no agreement at all'.[84] As a judgment on the overall presentational difficulty created by the division in nationalism within the Convention, this seems fair, but the minority nationalists' report merits attention for its constitutional flexibility. Although claiming Dominion status, these nationalists acknowledged that national defence would remain outside the competence of an Irish parliament and that 'in the matter of trade there is room for a special arrangement'.[85] While these nationalists believed emphatically 'that the nearer the Irish constitution approaches to that of the Dominions, the better will be its prospects',[86] there was no explicit rejection of federalism – rather a claim that even under a federal system Ireland could still have control over customs.[87]

Plunkett complained that 'the federal idea had never been fairly argued in the Convention'[88] and while he asserted that '[t]here was only one federalist of note in the Convention, Lord Dunraven; and the scheme he presented was … an unworkable compromise between a Dominion and a federal status',[89] there was a late (February 1918) expression of support by Lord Londonderry for federalism – although this was not developed.[90] When the nationalist MP

81 *Report of proceedings*, p. 24. The bishop of Raphoe voted for this: see ibid., p. 143 (division no. 6). Lord MacDonnell referred to this part of the Ulster unionist report as 'complete delusions' and said that such a claim 'was never made': *Hansard's Parl. deb., 5th series* (lords), vol. 35, col. 593 (15 July 1919).

82 Plunkett, *Confidential report*, p. 123.

83 Ibid., pp 123–4.

84 Ibid., p. 124.

85 *Report of proceedings*, p. 37.

86 Ibid., p. 37.

87 Ibid., p. 38: 'Federation is not in view. Even if it were, and Ireland were still intent on retaining control of her customs, her sea boundary and her distinct national character and economic interests would give her a claim in that respect which no member of a federation anywhere else can advance.'

88 Plunkett, *Confidential report*, p. 91.

89 Ibid., pp 53–4.

90 Ibid., p. 91.

Stephen Gwynn observed on 5 March 1918 that 'Home Rule, as outlined by Butt, Parnell, and Redmond assumed federation as the ultimate end',[91] the Ulster unionist, H.M. Pollock, riposted that '[t]he claim for federation might have been made from the Ulster Unionist benches'.[92]

If Plunkett appeared sincerely to regret the flaw in Lord Dunraven's scheme, that it gave Ireland 'complete control of taxation, including customs – a power possessed by no province in any existing federation',[93] he had visibly less patience with Archbishop Crozier and Provost Mahaffey and mocked their contribution in the *Confidential report*:

> [They] claim for their discovery that it 'would be capable of being adapted to some larger scheme of imperial federation for the whole British empire'. It will create surprise that neither in these pages nor in the official report is there any mention of this important contribution to the deliberations of the Irish Convention. I must, therefore, defend both its members and its staff from the charge of neglecting to give the most careful consideration to a proposal of such importance coming from the heads of an ancient seat of learning and of a yet older Church. But the fact is, through some accident, the scheme of these distinguished members never came before the Convention in such a form that it could be practically discussed.[94]

It is all the stranger that federalism did not get the hearing that Plunkett would have wished for it, since Lord Midleton (leader of the southern unionists), Lord Londonderry (secretary to the Ulster unionist delegation), Sir Edward Carson, and Plunkett himself had all been sent copies of F.S. Oliver's confidential memorandum *A method of constitutional co-operation: suggestions for the better government of the United Kingdom*.[95] This printed memorandum, dated 12 June 1917, to which Lord Selborne contributed, ran to forty pages and is a cogent and coherent statement of the federalist case. It appears to have been accompanied by a draft bill, but I have not seen this – though some idea of its precision can be gained from the memorandum.[96] The Oliver/Selborne scheme was not adopted by any member of the Convention and was not discussed at it.

91 Ibid., p. 92.
92 Ibid.
93 Ibid., p. 36.
94 Ibid., p. 125. For the thinness of Crozier's 'scheme', see p. 242 above ('Irish Convention: a speech delivered by the Lord Primate of All Ireland, 14 Mar. 1918').
95 A copy of Lord Selborne's letter of 13 Oct. 1917 to Carson enclosing the memorandum, together with a copy of the memorandum, is in PRONI D1507/A/24/20.
96 Fn. 1 on p. 40 of the memorandum sets out the text of clauses dealing with each kingdom's powers over income tax, PRONI D1507/A/24/20.

In 1917 and 1918 federalism was much discussed but as J.R. Fisher, later one of the Irish Boundary Commissioners, observed in May 1918: 'They [younger unionist MPs] are all out for federalism, but when tackled as to what they exactly mean by that they are all at sea.'[97] In the Convention all of the parties appeared to have a kind word for federalism. Only the majority nationalists and the labour representatives make no reference to it in the official report, and there is no suggestion that theirs is a hostile silence. The note by southern unionists included in the official report, plainly open to some as yet unformed scheme, insisted that 'Ireland occupy the same position as other parts of the United Kingdom in any scheme for the federation of the empire or the United Kingdom'.[98] As already noted, the report of the minority nationalists contained no explicit rejection of federalism. The minority nationalists would, consistent with an openness to federalism, have preferred that representation at Westminster would cease 'until such time as a parliament is created in which all parts of the empire or the realm could be properly and equitably represented'.[99]

The report of the Ulster unionist delegation specifically included among its objections to the majority scheme 'that it would make the future application of federalism to the United Kingdom impossible'.[100] Lord Dunraven enthusiastically supported federalism and expressed 'regret … that the Convention did not proceed on more definite federal lines', but he considered that the scheme arrived at was 'not incompatible with a federal system'.[101]

Although, as we have seen, Plunkett was accused of grossly misrepresenting the conclusions of the Convention in his letter of transmission,[102] this was unfair and perhaps even dishonest. The Convention's two difficulties were, indeed, as Plunkett described them in his letter, 'Ulster and customs'.[103]

FEDERALISM IN THE AFTERMATH OF THE CONVENTION

Two significant developments occurred during the first half of 1918 in the work of the committee on the Government of Ireland bill established by the cabinet to respond to the work of the Convention. The first was a letter of 18 April from Walter Long to the prime minister which began by reporting that preparation of a bill was proceeding 'very well', but that Long considered

97 Fisher to Montgomery, 4 May 1918, PRONI D627/434/9.
98 *Report of proceedings*, p. 48.
99 Ibid., p. 40.
100 Ibid., p. 34.
101 Ibid., p. 47.
102 See fn. 25 above.
103 *Report of proceedings*, p. 5.

> that if we could make a commencement towards the establishment of a federal system for the United Kingdom, we should make the passage of the bill much easier in the House of Commons, make it far more acceptable to the mass of people in Great Britain and, I believe, make it easier for nationalist Ireland to accept provisions which, if intended solely for an Irish parliament, might seem to them not to be sufficient for the purpose, and certainly it would make the position of Ulster infinitely easier.[104]

As far as the committee was concerned 'opinion … has hardened in the direction of a federal system, and the further one goes in the preparation of the bill, the more evident it is that once you adopt the federal system, the drafting of the bill becomes much easier'.[105]

Second, and more importantly, the interim report of the committee dated 14 June 1918 expressed the committee's view that 'it is useless to proceed with the drafting of the bill until the cabinet as a whole have considered the general question'.[106] This view was influenced by the judgment that

> the immediate enforcement of conscription is impossible … The lawlessness which prevents conscription is itself the strongest argument against the establishment of a government dependent on the support of a population so utterly out of hand, whilst the effect of the agitations of the last few weeks has been to increase the hostility of Ulster and to strengthen the Ulster case, to alienate the moderate unionists of the south and west and to destroy the prospect of their support and finally to leave the nationalists without influence or authority and at the same time in open resistance to the measures which the Government declare necessary for the conduct of the war.[107]

Here is government confirmation of the accuracy of Plunkett's assessment of the effect of extending conscription to Ireland.[108]

The committee suggested two possible courses of action: the cabinet could instruct the committee to resume its consideration of the draft bill 'in order that the government may be in a position to prove their *bona fides* by showing that they have a bill upon the stocks'.[109] Alternatively,

104 Long to Gladstone, 8 Apr. 1918, TNA CAB/24/49. Among the advantages indentified by Long was that it would be possible to 'devise a title for the bill which would get rid of the words "Home Rule for Ireland" … [T]he words "No Home Rule" have become a sort of sacred creed in Ulster.'

105 Long to Gladstone, 8 Apr. 1918, TNA CAB/24/49.

106 Interim report, 14 June 1918, TNA CAB/24/54.

107 Ibid.

108 Plunkett, *Confidential report*, p. 130.

109 Interim report, 14 June 1918, TNA CAB/24/54.

> some of our number are of opinion that the question cannot be satisfactorily resolved, and indeed that the draft bill cannot be effectively proceeded with, except by considering the case of Irish government as part of the wider problem of a federal constitution for the United Kingdom as a whole; and they would prefer that the case of Ireland and an Irish bill should be postponed for the present, but only on the understanding that a commission be set up to investigate the federal solution in its possible application to every part of the United Kingdom.[110]

By September 1919 the cabinet had received from Walter Long's committee what was described as a draft of a bill for a federal system for the United Kingdom.[111] While this draft bill was incomplete, with provision being made for the constitution of each local national parliament to be settled by commissioners or conventions and then included in the first schedule, a flavour of the bill's scope and ambition is given by clause 1(1) which provides:

> On and after the appointed day there shall be established in each of the following countries, that is to say, England, Scotland, Ireland and Wales, local national parliaments consisting in each case of His Majesty the King and one or two chambers as provided in the First Schedule to this Act.[112]

Although this fascinating draft bill was described as providing for a federal system, the description is at best ambiguous and perhaps merely inaccurate. By clause 1(2) 'the supreme authority of the parliament of the United Kingdom shall remain unaffected and undiminished over all persons, matters and things in the United Kingdom and every part thereof'.[113] In the absence of some limitation on parliament respecting matters within the competence of the local national parliaments, the bill is better described as providing for devolution or 'Home Rule all round'.

By December 1919 it was clear that federalism or 'Home Rule all round' would not be pursued and the scheme prepared by a committee of the war cabinet chaired by Lord Curzon in 1917 had been modified to provide for a parliament of Southern Ireland and a parliament of Northern Ireland and a Council of Ireland.[114] In July 1919, dismayed by events in Ireland and by the government's failure to bring forward its response to the Convention, Lord MacDonnell moved in the House of Lords '[t]hat in the opinion of the House

110 Ibid.
111 Draft bill, Sept. 1919, TNA CAB/24/89.
112 Ibid.
113 Ibid.
114 TNA CAB/24/94.

it is of the utmost importance that the policy of his majesty's government in regard to Ireland should be declared forthwith'.[115] He set out his own position:

> I am at the same time bound to tell the House that the political atmosphere in Ireland to-day is not precisely what it was fifteen months ago. The feeling of Irish nationalists has hardened much upon the question of control of customs revenue, so much so that they attach to the enjoyment of customs revenue the term of the Dominion status, an absolutely inaccurate misnomer which has become almost a shibboleth in Ireland. It has come to this, that if one does not regard the Dominion status as the least of her demands, you are considered not to be a nationalist. Personally I adhere to the Convention nomenclature, and consider Dominion status to be an incorrect and an inaccurate term.[116] Dominion status means that Ireland shall have her own army and navy. The Convention has repudiated any such intention. Dominion status means that Ireland should make no contribution to the imperial revenues. The Convention has accepted the obligation of making a contribution to the imperial expenditure; and for the purpose of determining what the amount is to be, this inquiry is to be held under the prime minister's instructions. I think that a very great injury is being done to the Irish cause in this country by the misuse of the term Dominion status.[117]

Lord MacDonnell in 1919 was as clear-sighted and exact as he had been in 1911 but these were less marketable virtues in 1919 and by that date the Convention's scheme of government had itself ceased to be marketable.

THE CONVENTION'S LEGACY

It may be asked if the Convention has left anything approaching a permanent legacy apart from what one might learn from or about it. In the removal of religious disabilities, it can be said that the work of the Convention has had an enduring effect. A decision taken at the Convention provided a pathway to the final removal of laws imposing civil disabilities on Catholics that was achieved by section 5(2) of the Government of Ireland Act 1920.[118]

115 *Hansard's Parl. deb., 5th series* (lords), vol. 35, col. 585 (15 July 1919).

116 Here MacDonnell echoes Plunkett in the *Confidential report*, p. 127: 'Dominion Home Rule having become a shibboleth, its advocates naturally did not realize that it was a misnomer.'

117 *Hansard's Parl. deb., 5th series* (lords), vol. 35, cols 589–90 (15 July 1919).

118 10 & 11 Geo. V, c. 67.

The first matter treated in the fourth head of the bishop of Raphoe's scheme (dealing with the legislative competence of the Irish parliament) was 'prohibition of laws interfering with religious equality'.[119] This referred back to section 3 of the Government of Ireland Act 1914, which prohibited the enactment of laws by the Irish parliament that (to use the modern shorthand expression) discriminated on the ground of religious belief. Section 3, while containing a limitation on the future legislative competence of the new Irish parliament, would have left intact any extant provisions that discriminated on the ground of religious belief. These existing disabilities were addressed by an important note in the bishop's scheme. This contemplated that 'a sub-section should be framed to annul any existing legal penalty, disadvantage or disability on account of religious belief'.[120] This aspect of the bishop's scheme was welcomed by the sub-committee of nine[121] in its provisional conclusions: 'the provision for equal treatment of religious denominations in future must proceed from a basis of equal treatment at present. That is, the disabilities etc remaining under the Act of 1829 should be annulled.'[122] The view of the sub-committee of nine found expression in the fourth majority conclusion of the Convention.[123]

The effect of those disabilities is still observable in the 1919 case of *Moore v. His Holiness Pope Benedict XV*[124] in which the judge of the chancery division of the high court of justice in Ireland, Mr Justice Powell (who, as John Blake Powell KC had served as a southern unionist delegate to the Convention) held that a legacy to the Pope 'to use and apply at his sole and absolute discretion in the carrying out of the sacred office' purported to create a trust but that this was not a valid charitable trust not least because of the Pope's role in the governance of certain religious orders which were then still illegal (but flourishing) in Ireland. Counsel for the residuary legatees submitted '[t]his money might be devoted to the support of orders illegal in Ireland, such as Benedictines, Dominicans, Franciscans, which are charitable but not legal'.[125] Counsel was, in fact, confused: these orders were not then charitable because they were not lawful by reason of section 26 of the Roman Catholic Relief Act 1829.[126]

Section 5(2) of the 1920 Act, which gave effect to the decision of the Convention, had no equivalent in the 1914 Act. Section 5(2) provided that any existing provision under which any penalty, disadvantage or disability is

119 *Report of proceedings*, p. 12.
120 Ibid.
121 A sub-committee of the grand committee whose formation is described in Plunkett, *Confidential report*, p. 38.
122 *Report of proceedings*, p. 12.
123 Ibid., p. 25.
124 [1919] IR 316.
125 Ibid., p. 317.
126 10 Geo. IV, c. 7.

imposed on the ground of religious belief or on a member of a religious order shall cease to have effect in Ireland. This included section 26 of the Roman Catholic Relief Act 1829, which penalized the wearing of Catholic ecclesiastical vestments or habits outside places of worship; sections 28–36 of the 1829 Act penalized members of male religious orders. Curiously, section 37 expressly exempted female members of religious orders from any analogous penalty.

CONCLUSION

Turning from one Plunkett to another, that is, from Sir Horace to Count Plunkett, the latter in the debates on the 1921 Anglo-Irish Treaty,[127] speaking on 19 December 1921 against the resolution to ratify the Treaty, referred to the Convention in unfair and inaccurate terms as follows:

> The schemes put forward at the Convention called by the English government were rejected with scorn, for no broad-minded Irishman would enter that assembly. It was a manufactured assembly and did not express the views of the Irish people; but to-day by a side-wind you are told that the only thing for you to do is to accept these rejected things.[128]

'[T]hese rejected things' were also denounced in the same debates by Erskine Childers TD – who, as we have seen, had served on the Convention's secretariat[129] and who had provided 'the clearest and ablest statement of the case for the Dominion status for Ireland' on which the minority nationalist scheme was 'obviously' based.[130] In his dismissal of the Convention, Count Plunkett was echoing what de Valera was reported to have said in 1919. In what Lord Chancellor Birkenhead described as a 'contemptuous reference to the proposal in the direction of Dominion Home Rule', de Valera is said to have asserted that '[w]e do not want anything of the Plunkett character'.[131]

Dominion status was how what is often referred to as the War of Independence was concluded. The gap between the Government of Ireland Act 1914 and the constitutional settlement of 1921 is considerable. The gap between what was offered in 1917 and what was agreed in 1918 on one hand and what was conferred in 1921 on the other is not. Indeed, if partition is

127 What was actually at issue in these debates was 'the articles of agreement for a Treaty'. Regarding the use of the term 'Treaty' in this context, see B. Ruane's chapter in this volume, 'The "so-called Treaty": the implications of legal form for achieving settlement of the Irish War of Independence'.

128 *Dáil deb.*, vol. T, no. 6 (19 Dec. 1921).

129 *Report of proceedings*, p. 53.

130 Plunkett, *Confidential report*, p. 123.

131 *Hansard's Parl. deb., 5th series* (lords), vol. 35, cols 608–9 (15 July 1919).

viewed as a significant detriment (and it was so viewed by all of the parties at the Convention), it may reasonably be said that much less was obtained in 1921 than had been agreed by a large majority of Convention members in 1918. It should be remembered that it was not until the enactment of section 4 of the Statute of Westminster 1931 that the United Kingdom parliament bound itself not to enact laws for any Dominion (including the Irish Free State) except with the consent of the relevant Dominion.[132] Here, as often, constitutional law was catching up with political reality, the Statute of Westminster giving legal effect to the political declaration of the Imperial Conference of 1926 on the definition and effect of Dominion status.[133]

Early in his *Confidential report* Plunkett had written that 'all serious men, North and South alike, realize that, if the Convention fails to work the miracle, there is nothing before us but chaos and revolution'.[134] In this Plunkett, for all his faults as a chairman, was a reasonably well-sighted prophet. We know there was no 1918 'miracle at Regent House' but are we not entitled today – over a hundred years later – to wish that there had been such a miracle and ought we not to reflect earnestly on what its contemporary equivalent might be?

132 This Act is a striking example of one parliament, contrary to the constitutional truism, appearing to bind its successors. There would, of course, be no legal obstacle to a later parliament repealing the 1931 Act.

133 Sir William Anson, *The law and custom of the constitution*, vol. ii: *the crown, part 2*, ed. A.B. Keith (4th edn, Oxford, 1935), pp 83–4.

134 Plunkett, *Confidential report*, p. 5.

The 'so-called Treaty': the implications of legal form for achieving settlement of the Irish War of Independence

BLÁTHNA RUANE*

The ground-breaking agreement known as the Anglo-Irish Treaty[1] was signed in London on 6 December 1921 by the British and Irish delegations to the peace negotiations that had commenced in early October. The agreement was the culmination of negotiations to end the War of Independence that broke out in January 1919, in which radical Irish nationalists sought to end centuries of British rule in Ireland. The British delegation was led by Lloyd George, British prime minister and leader of a Conservative-Unionist and Liberal coalition. The Irish delegation was led by Arthur Griffith, then deputy president of the radical nationalist party Sinn Féin and minister for foreign affairs, who represented the Irish parliament or Dáil. In the 1918 British general election, Sinn Féin had won most of the Irish seats. They boycotted Westminster and formed a rival parliament, Dáil Éireann, and also established a Dáil ministry. The Dáil issued a declaration of Irish independence in 1919 and proclaimed a republic. The Dáil was not recognized by the British, who had attempted to suppress it.

The settlement reached in December 1921 provided for the creation of the new Irish Free State, which was to have Dominion status within the British commonwealth of nations (Articles 1 and 4). Dominion status was a restricted form of statehood within the British empire, whereby the self-governing Dominions had incomplete sovereignty, with certain powers being retained by the United Kingdom, such as the conduct of foreign relations. There were then five Dominions: Canada, Australia, New Zealand, South Africa and Newfoundland. Self-government for the Dominions was legally rooted not in

* An earlier version of this chapter was delivered to the Irish Legal History Society on 26 Mar. 2021. Editorial note: In this chapter the term 'Treaty' (with capital 'T') refers to the 'Articles of Agreement for a Treaty between Great Britain and Ireland' signed on 6 December 1921 and the term 'Dominion' (with a capital 'D') is used to avoid confusion with the wider term 'his majesty's dominions', which refers to the British empire as a whole.

1 The full title was 'Articles of Agreement for a Treaty between Great Britain and Ireland'. See Plate 14.1.

treaties but in British statutory grants of rights.[2] Dominion powers had however evolved considerably over time, particularly following the important support they had given the British empire during the First World War. By 1920 the prominent Conservative-Unionist, Bonar Law, told the House of Commons that Dominions could secede from the empire.[3] However, the formal status of the Dominions remained undefined until the Balfour Declaration in 1926.

Ireland was given Canadian-style Dominion status.[4] The members of the Irish Free State parliament had to swear true faith and allegiance to the constitution of the Irish Free State and fidelity to the king.[5] In addition to the restrictions associated with Canadian Dominion status, there were extra restrictions on Irish sovereignty, such as an obligation to make an Irish contribution to the public debt,[6] retention of British access to Irish ports in time of peace and war,[7] restriction on the maintenance of an Irish army,[8] and the right of Northern Ireland to opt out of the Irish Free State within one month of the legislative ratification of the Treaty[9] and thus to retain its devolved status under the Government of Ireland Act 1920.[10] Under the latter there were to be two parliaments, one for Northern Ireland and one for Southern Ireland, but that of Southern Ireland had been repudiated by the majority radical nationalists.

Instead of looking at the individual provisions of the Treaty, which have been examined frequently elsewhere, the focus here is on the achievement of settlement through the legal mechanism of a treaty. Since the Acts of Union 1800,[11] passed by the British and Irish parliaments to establish the Union, under British legal theory Ireland was an inherent part of the sovereign state known as the United Kingdom of Great Britain and Ireland. Despite repeated Irish nationalist demands for Home Rule during the nineteenth and early twentieth centuries, there was no separate Irish parliament. Ireland's elected representatives were members of the British parliament in Westminster. The monarch was represented in Ireland by the viceroy. The chief secretary for Ireland, who spent much of his time in London and was frequently a member of the British cabinet, ran the administration in Ireland.

2 See, e.g., Commonwealth of Australia Constitution Act 1900 (63 & 64 Vict., c. 12 [Aus.]); the British North America Act 1867 (30 & 31 Vict., c. 3 [Canada]).
3 *Hansard's Parl. deb., 5th series* (commons), vol. 127, col. 1125 (30 Mar. 1920).
4 Art. 2.
5 Art. 4.
6 Art. 5.
7 Art. 7.
8 Art. 8.
9 Arts. 11, 12.
10 10 & 11 Geo. V, c. 67.
11 Union with Ireland Act 1800 (39 & 40 Geo. III, c. 67 [G.B.]) and the Act for the Union of Great Britain and Ireland 1800 (40 Geo. III, c. 38 [Ir.]).

Since the late nineteenth century, previous efforts at achieving a political settlement in Ireland had been treated as a purely internal constitutional matter, to be addressed by legislative proposals for devolving powers to a Home Rule parliament. These proposals were to be implemented by Westminster legislation, providing a statutory grant of limited powers to an Irish parliament.[12] In 1921 Lord Sumner, the Conservative-Unionist law lord, described the process of the earlier attempts at Home Rule as follows: '[e]very Home Rule Bill has been announced long beforehand – introduced as a bill, discussed line by line, and week after week, in the House of Commons and in Your Lordships' House, and, with whatever ultimate result, it has been hammered out in the ordinary way of legislation.'[13]

A major distinguishing but largely ignored factor between those earlier unsuccessful attempts at settlement and the more successful effort of 1921 was the change in the legal form of settlement adopted in 1921, namely the use of a treaty. According to constitutional practice in Britain, parliament had no formal role in treaty-making, as the power to do so was vested in the crown acting through the executive. Treaty-making was by means of the exercise of a royal prerogative power, acting on the advice of the cabinet.[14] Following the truce agreed in early July 1921, there had been talks in London between Lloyd George and Éamon de Valera, the Sinn Féin president of Dáil Éireann, about whether there could be settlement negotiations. Sinn Féin insisted that settlement by 'treaty' was 'an essential element in the negotiations'.[15] That demand was consistent with Sinn Féin's view of Ireland's legal status as being that of an independent republic, and so already having the legal capacity to enter into an international agreement with the United Kingdom. That was the antithesis of the British view of Ireland's legal status then, namely that since 1800 it was an inherent part of the United Kingdom of Great Britain and Ireland.

Following evolving international consensus, the legal mechanism of settlement of disputes by means of a treaty was well understood by 1921 as meaning an agreement made between two states that are separate and distinct. The then British lord chancellor, Lord Birkenhead, the author of a text on international law, had written that '[t]reaties form the contract law of *states* [emphasis added] … The right to make treaties is an inherent element in national independence, and is, perhaps, the most decisive test of the existence of sovereignty'.[16] Thus, for the British government to offer settlement by treaty would have major implications for Ireland's status and negotiating

12 See Government of Ireland bills 1886 and 1893; Government of Ireland Act 1914 (4 & 5 Geo. V, c. 90) and Government of Ireland Act 1920 (10 & 11 Geo. V, c. 67).

13 *Hansard's Parl. deb., 5th series* (lords), vol. 48, col. 166 (16 Dec. 1921).

14 See E.W. Ridges, *Constitutional law of England* (London, 1905), p. 424.

15 See minutes of cabinet meeting, 20 July 1921, p. 148, TNA CAB 23/26/15, 60 (21).

16 F.E. Smith, *International law* (2nd ed., London, 1903; repr. London, 2015), p. 84.

position. It would imply acceptance by Britain that Ireland was already an independent state and a republic. Even if negotiations broke down, Sinn Féin would be able to argue that Britain's willingness to negotiate towards a treaty constituted acceptance of that status.

By July 1921 there was pressure on Lloyd George to grant Dominion status to Ireland, which he had hitherto resisted.[17] As it happened, a meeting of the Dominion prime ministers in London had begun on 20 June which indirectly brought Dominion attention to the Anglo-Irish war. The South African prime minister Jan Smuts, who had led the Boers in their fight against the British and was interested in Irish claims for self-rule, promoted the desirability of an Irish settlement. He was instrumental in shaping the king's speech given at the opening of the devolved parliament of Northern Ireland under the Government of Ireland Act 1920 in June 1922 towards reconciliation. Smuts also exerted influence on Lloyd George to offer Dominion status.[18]

Towards the conclusion of his talks with de Valera, Lloyd George decided to give de Valera a letter setting out the British government's offer. That was inevitably going to be a very important moment for the direction of any future negotiations. Any concessions made at this stage would be difficult or impossible to retract later. A draft letter setting out the proposed terms was discussed by the British cabinet on 20 July 1921.[19] It had been prepared by Lloyd George who had consulted some cabinet colleagues.[20] Broadly, the terms were an offer of Dominion status with additional obligations and restrictions imposed on Ireland and provision for separate treatment for Northern Ireland if it so wished.

Referring to the legal mechanism for how the settlement could be reached, the draft used the term 'Treaty', as well as references elsewhere to a 'Pact'. The cabinet queried 'the expediency of using the word "Treaty" on page 5' of the draft. The cabinet minutes recorded that '[i]t was suggested that the word "Pact" would be preferable, on the ground that the use of the word "Treaty" would furnish *a precedent fraught with danger, involving recognition of an existing Irish Republic* [emphasis added] and which it might prove impossible to resist in the case of India. On the other hand reference was made to the treaty of Limerick.' Lloyd George 'assured' the cabinet that Sinn Féin regarded the word 'treaty' as an 'essential element in the negotiations', and the attorney general, Sir Gordon Hewart, assured them 'that there was no essential difference between a treaty and a pact from the point of view of

17 See T.L. Crosby, *The unknown Lloyd George* (London, 2014), pp 299–301.

18 Ibid., p. 300–1, fn.17.

19 Minutes of cabinet meeting, 20 July 1921, pp 148–9, and attachment, pp 154–9, TNA CAB 23/26/15, 60 (21). See also letter sent 20 July 1921, with attached proposals, from Lloyd George to de Valera in Official Correspondence relating to the Peace Negotiations, June–September, 1921 at https://celt.ucc.ie/published/E900003-007/text001.html.

20 See editorial commentary in T. Jones, *Whitehall diary, vol. III Ireland, 1918–1925*, ed. K. Middlemas (London, 1971), pp 89–90.

the position which would arise should the negotiations break down'. The cabinet then agreed that 'the words "in the form of a Treaty"' could be used.[21]

Further insight into the anxiety caused by that usage of the word 'treaty' and the cabinet mood emerges from an account of it given two days later by the then principal assistant secretary to the cabinet, Thomas Jones. Jones revealed the considerable controversy created over the use of the term 'treaty'. He recounted that

> [a]n instrument 'in the form of a Treaty' is proposed. This caused a lot of heart-burning inside and was only got through by the passionate pleading of the P.M. and his references to South Africa, Scotland, Sarsfield and the Treaty of Limerick, etc.[22]

It is thus clear that cabinet members were very perturbed that using the term 'treaty' would connote acceptance that Ireland was already a separate state and an independent republic and that such acceptance would be detrimental if no settlement was achieved. They were also afraid that they might have to make a similar concession to India, which was still ruled directly but was becoming restive for independence.

In arguing in favour of the term 'treaty', Lloyd George had referred to South Africa, Scotland, Sarsfield and the treaty of Limerick. However, these examples were legally not analogous to the context of negotiations he was considering with de Valera because the status of Ireland in 1921, in British legal theory, differed very significantly from the status of the other negotiating parties in the situations he cited.

The reference to South Africa was to what was known as the treaty of Vereeniging, made in 1902 to end the second Boer War. The British government reached peace terms with representatives of the 'Government of the South African Republic' and the 'Government of the Orange Free State', which had been annexed by Britain as colonies in 1900. Those Boer republics had earlier asserted their independence, but had also functioned under varying degrees of British suzerainty. They manifestly had never formed an inherent part of the United Kingdom of Great Britain and Ireland.

Up to 1707, Scotland and England were two separate kingdoms. In 1603 the existing king of Scotland succeeded to the English throne, so that the same king ruled both separate states, resulting in the creation of a personal union of crowns. However, full political union of the kingdoms was only achieved over a century later in 1707 by means of a treaty negotiated by the representatives of both states, the terms of which were then embodied in acts of both the Scottish and English parliaments. It was thus the treaty of 1707

21 Minutes of cabinet meeting, 20 July 1921, pp 148–9, TNA CAB 23/26/15, 60 (21).
22 Jones to Bonar Law, 22 July 1921, in Jones, *Whitehall diary*, p. 91.

between two separate states that created the single state of the United Kingdom of Great Britain. That was very different from, and offered no precedent for, the offer of a treaty in July 1921 to one part of what was, in British legal theory, the existing state of the United Kingdom of Great Britain and Ireland.

Lloyd George had also cited the treaty of Limerick of October 1691, made in much more complex circumstances. At that time, Ireland and England were separate kingdoms, although Ireland was subordinate to England.[23] Pursuant to an act of the Irish parliament of 1542, James II had become king of Ireland by virtue of his having become king of England in 1685.[24] Since 1685 James II had been king of the three separate kingdoms of England, Scotland and Ireland. James, a Catholic, was deposed in 1688 and replaced by the Protestant Dutch king William of Orange and his wife Mary. James resisted and war ensued. James was defeated in England and Scotland. The English parliament recognized William and Mary as king and queen of England and Ireland,[25] and they became king and queen of Scotland in 1689. The Irish Jacobite parliament, however, supported James as the lawful king of England and of Ireland, a view widely shared among the Catholic majority population, and it also declared that Ireland 'is and hath always been a distinct kingdom from that of his majesties realm of England'.[26] War between the Jacobite Catholic army and the Protestant army of William and Mary commenced in Ireland in 1689 and ended with the treaty of Limerick 1691.[27]

That treaty[28] consisted of two sets of articles of agreement, one military and one civil, which were signed by the Irish Jacobite general, Patrick Sarsfield and his officers on 'behalf of the Irish inhabitants' of the city of Limerick and six named counties on the one hand and by William's general, Baron de Ginckle, commander in chief of the English army, and two lords justices of Ireland, both of whom had been Williamite appointees,[29] on the other.

The Jacobite signatories actually represented the main Jacobite leadership in Ireland (as James had fled to France for help), and in consequence critically

23 Under Poynings Law 1495 (10 Hen. VII, c. 4), Irish parliament bills required prior approval from the king's lieutenant and Irish privy council under the great seal of Ireland, and approval from the English king and English privy council. The executive was already controlled by the king.

24 The Crown of Ireland Act 1542 (33 Hen. VIII, c. 1).

25 The Crown and Parliament Recognition Act 1689 (2 Will. and Mary, c. 1).

26 An act of recognition of the just and most undoubted rights of his majesties imperial crown (no. 1) 1689 and an act declaring that the parliaments of England cannot binde Ireland, and against writs of error and appeals, to be brought for removing judgments, decrees and sentences given in Ireland into England (no. 10) 1689. See J. Bergin and A. Lyall (eds), *The acts of James II's Irish parliament of 1689* (Dublin, 2016), pp 3–6, 54–7.

27 The war in Ireland was part of the European Nine Years War.

28 Text available at https://celt.ucc.ie/published/E703001–010/text001.html.

29 J.G. Simms, *Jacobite Ireland* (repr. Dublin, 2000), pp 188–9.

important civil articles giving certain religious rights to Catholics were included.[30] This gave the treaty the characteristic of an agreement with very widespread application. In return, the treaty required the Irish Jacobite rebels and those seeking to exercise those rights to take an oath swearing fidelity and allegiance to William and Mary, being king and queen of both England and Ireland, a status which the Irish Jacobite parliament had earlier refused to recognize.

William and Mary ratified the treaty in February 1692 in Westminster – notably, under the great seal of England, and not that of Ireland.[31] The treaty was also partially ratified by an English statute under the great seal of England in 1691.[32] Because Ireland was then a separate kingdom, separate Irish parliamentary steps were also to be taken to ratify and implement the treaty. Under the civil articles the lords justices and general had undertaken that William and Mary would ratify the articles within eight months and would 'use their utmost endeavours' that the articles would 'be ratified and confirmed in parliament'.[33] The king and queen also said in their ratification that for any parts for which 'an Act of Parliament shall be found to be necessary, We shall recommend the same to be made good by Parliament, and shall give Our Royal Assent to any Bill or Bills'.[34] Despite this, because the Irish parliament had by then became dominated by Williamite Protestants who opposed the concessions made to Catholics, the treaty was ultimately only partially ratified in Ireland in 1697 by the Williamite Protestant parliament.[35]

From the English Williamite legal perspective, the status of William and Mary in 1691 was that, as king and queen of England, they were also king and queen of Ireland. The treaty settled with the majority Irish Catholic population William and Mary's disputed claim to recognition of that status by affording recognition of them as lawful monarchs of Ireland by virtue of being lawful monarchs of England. Unlike the dispute in 1921, where, under British legal theory, there was only one state involved, in 1691 there were two states involved.

So the legal reality was that Lloyd George's offer of a treaty in 1921 was unprecedented, indeed maverick. On the one hand, as his cabinet colleagues feared, his offer to settle by means of a treaty would arguably recognize

30 Arts. 1, 2, 9 of the civil articles, at fn. 28 above.

31 In their ratification instrument, the *Inspeximus,* William and Mary ratified and confirmed the articles. Text available at https://quod.lib.umich.edu/e/eebo2/B08779.0001.001?rgn=main;view=fulltext.

32 An Act for the Abrogating the Oath of Supremacy in Ireland and Appointing other Oaths 1691 (3 & 4 Will. and Mary, c. 2).

33 Art. 12 of the civil articles, at fn. 28 above.

34 See *Inspeximus*, at fn. 31 above.

35 An Act for the Confirmation of Articles made at the Surrender of the City of Limerick 1697 (9 Will. III, c. 2).

existing Irish independence. On the other hand, if he still denied that independence, then he would be changing the internal constitutional British arrangements and, as opponents would later argue, his method would be unconstitutional as it would lack proper parliamentary consideration. The records do not record his reasoning, apart from the reference to de Valera's 'essential' demand for a treaty. It is clear, however, that Lloyd George's choice, albeit legally risky, afforded him the negotiating benefits of the treaty mechanism and simultaneously gave what de Valera had demanded, thereby improving Lloyd George's chance of securing agreement. Lloyd George did not restrict his strategy by formal legal constraints, and he proceeded firmly and opportunistically on the basis that he was negotiating a treaty. As his opponents later argued, a 'treaty' meant that parliamentary scrutiny of the arrangements was far less than for the earlier four attempts at settlement. When the terms of the Treaty were later brought to parliament, it was on a 'take it or leave it' basis, so parliament had little real chance to amend the terms.

For Sinn Féin, settlement by means of a treaty which could not be altered unilaterally by later British legislation and which implicitly recognized Ireland's independent statehood was a breakthrough. In all the other Home Rule negotiations, Ireland was never recognized as a separate state, and there had always been the risk of statutory alteration. Even if the anticipated negotiations broke down, Sinn Féin could argue that Britain had already conceded Ireland's independent status by making such an offer. The sting for Sinn Féin was that they could only achieve their goal of a settlement by treaty by accepting terms involving the simultaneous downgrading of Irish independence to a restricted form of Dominion status. Another problem was that even if other Dominions could later secede from the commonwealth, Britain might argue that Ireland might be prevented from doing so by virtue of their having accepted additional obligations under the Treaty.

De Valera's formal response by letter of 10 August 1921 to Lloyd George's offer was negative. In correspondence that ensued, notwithstanding his offer to settle by treaty, Lloyd George tried to diminish the legal significance of his offer to negotiate a treaty by rejecting Ireland's claim to independent status.[36] Eventually, however, both sides agreed pragmatically to maintain their positions but allowed the negotiations to proceed.

In preparation for the negotiations, on 14 September the Dáil ratified Irish delegates as plenipotentiaries[37] and they were appointed by de Valera on 7

36 See de Valera to Lloyd George, 10 Aug. 1921; Lloyd George to de Valera, 13 Aug. 1921; de Valera to Lloyd George, 12 Sept. 1921; Lloyd George to de Valera, 15 Sept. 1921; Lloyd George to de Valera, 18 Sept. 1921; and Lloyd George to de Valera, 29 Sept. 1921 in Official Correspondence referred to at fn. 19 above.

37 *Dáil Éireann deb.*, vol. S, no. 10 (14 Sept. 1921).

October as president of the Dáil.[38] Plenipotentiaries are frequently appointed by states to negotiate treaties, and so this designation was consistent with Sinn Féin's claim that Ireland was a sovereign independent state. However, they were not formally recognized as such by the British, whose formal records referred to them as the 'Irish representatives'.[39] Immediately after the settlement was reached however, during the Commons debates in December 1921, Lloyd George referred to the 'various plenipotentiaries'.[40]

The negotiations commenced on 11 October 1921. The tactical advantages for Lloyd George of offering a treaty proved to be immense, as previously mentioned. It enabled negotiations to be conducted directly with the Irish representatives by the representatives of the British government alone, to the point of a concluded agreement, rather than through a parliamentary process of debate with the opposition and revision of draft legislation.[41] That allowed the parties to negotiate in secret, rendering the negotiating process politically far more manageable for Lloyd George. During the negotiations Lloyd George was subjected to strong attacks in the Commons in late October from the extreme unionist wing of the Conservative-Unionist Party over the handling of the negotiations and the failure to inform parliament.[42]

An overall agreement very similar to what Lloyd George had originally offered in his letter of 20 July 1921 was reached on 6 December 1921. The British government was then obliged to go to parliament to disclose the terms reached, so as to get approval and ratification in accordance with Article 18 of the instrument. The agreement was signed by what were described as the members of the British and the Irish 'Delegations'. There was no reference to 'plenipotentiaries'. Article 18 provided that the instrument had to be approved in Britain by the Westminster parliament and in Ireland at 'a meeting summoned for the purpose of the *members* [emphasis added] elected to sit in the House of Commons of Southern Ireland, and if approved shall be ratified by the necessary legislation'. It was made clear in the immediate aftermath of the signing that the Irish would draft their own constitution, subject to the Treaty and pledges to the minority, meaning that the British government would have to approve it.[43]

38 Ibid., vol. T, no. 17, Appendix 5 (10 Jan. 1922).

39 There was confusion on the Irish side about the presentation of credentials. They were not formally presented but were apparently seen by Lloyd George. See *Dáil Éireann deb.*, vol. T, no. 2, cols 11–14 (14 Dec. 1921); vol. T, no. 3, col. 147 (15 Dec. 1922). British official records do not record the presentation of the Irish delegates' credentials (see Irish Conference 1921, Record of Negotiations, pp 10–12, TNA CAB 43/4).

40 *Hansard's Parl. deb., 5th series* (commons), vol. 149, col. 43 (14 Dec. 1921).

41 W. Anson, *The law and custom of the constitution*, 2 vols (3rd ed., Oxford, 1907), ii, part 1, pp 53–4; A. Berriedale Keith, *The constitution, administration and laws of the empire* (London, 1924), pp 55–7.

42 *Hansard's Parl. deb., 5th series* (commons), vol. 147, col. 1367 (31 Oct. 1921).

43 Lloyd George to Griffith, 13 Dec. 1921, NAI DE 4/5/10; Meeting Lloyd George with the Southern Unionists, 7 Dec. 1921, TNA CAB 43/1 (57–60).

The Treaty had then to go through an approval and ratification process on either side. Legal issues regarding the treaty mechanism itself arose immediately on both sides in the efforts to have the agreement approved. There was confusion in the immediate aftermath of the signing because the title on the Irish delegation's signed version did not contain the word 'treaty' but read 'Articles of Agreement'. That was clarified with the British subsequently[44] and adjusted to 'Articles of Agreement *for* a Treaty between Great Britain and Ireland [emphasis added]'. Despite referring to a 'treaty', that amended wording itself was somewhat ambiguous in that it suggested that there was not yet a treaty in existence. The use of the word 'for' in all likelihood was due to the fact that, under Article 18, the agreement had yet to be ratified on both sides and in that sense it was not a finalized deal until ratification occurred. Under international law, a treaty that required ratification was, once ratified, regarded as taking effect from the date of its signing.[45] If no ratification occurred, the agreement would have collapsed. Despite that requirement, from the outset, it was described by Lloyd George and others in Westminster as a 'treaty'.[46]

On 14 December, Lloyd George's government presented the signed agreement to parliament with a 'take it or leave it' choice over whether to accept the terms. While acknowledging their power to criticize then and on the future ratification legislation, Lloyd George indicated that if parliament wanted changes, they would require Irish consent, with a strong risk of the collapse of the agreement and indeed of settlement prospects.[47] Using a treaty thus enabled him to stifle disruptive hard-line unionist opposition.

The motion on which the Commons and Lords voted was that each house was '*ready* to confirm and *ratify* [emphasis added]' the 'Articles'.[48] 'Ratification' is a term associated with giving effect to treaties, and thus its usage was consistent with British acceptance that the settlement was indeed being processed as a treaty. Legislative ratification would follow later if the motions were passed.

Initially in Westminster substantial legal issues of principle relating to the legal form of the settlement by means of a treaty were raised as serious obstacles to ratification. On 14 December very senior legal figures in parliament, mainly in the Lords,[49] challenged the constitutional validity of making a 'so-called treaty' with what was, in British legal theory, a part of the

44 *Dáil Éireann deb.*, vol. T, no. 2, col. 135 (14 Dec. 1921).

45 Smith, *International law*, p. 87.

46 *Hansard's Parl. deb., 5th series* (commons), vol. 149, col. 26 (14 Dec. 1921), Lloyd George; vol. 149, col. 174, Winston Churchill; col. 139, Herbert Asquith (15 Dec. 1921).

47 *Hansard's Parl. deb., 5th series* (commons), vol. 149, cols 126–7 (15 Dec. 1921).

48 Ibid., col. 305 (16 Dec. 1921), *Hansard's Parl. deb., 5th series* (lords), vol. 48, col. 10 (14 Dec. 1921).

49 See also *Hansard's Parl. deb., 5th series* (commons), vol. 149, cols 90–2 (14 Dec. 1921).

United Kingdom. The objection was that the United Kingdom could not make a 'treaty' with a part of itself.

The Liberal Lord Bryce, a leading British jurist, diplomat and former chief secretary for Ireland, referred to the agreement as the 'so-called Treaty' and the 'constitutional difficulties' as 'a sort of *coup d'état*'.[50] Lord Sumner attacked the suggestion that the agreement could be a 'treaty'. He pointed out that Ireland was not a foreign country or a Dominion but was an integral part of the United Kingdom and that a treaty could not have been made with the Isle of Wight or Wales. He argued that likewise under British constitutional theory a treaty could not be made with Ireland. He also claimed that any arrangement regarding its government ought to have been made by statute in the normal way, rather than by executive negotiation with only final approval being sought from parliament. Suspicious of Lloyd George's strategy, he claimed that 'a deliberate attempt has been made to convey, as far as the negotiators dared, that Ireland was what the Sinn Féiners have claimed that Ireland always has been, an independent and separate country'. He suggested two reasons for this. First, that the description of it as a 'treaty' was hoped to 'appease the negotiators [that is, Sinn Féin]'. Second, it was 'foreseen' by the British government to be a way to avoid the type of detailed parliamentary scrutiny that had been given to the Home Rule bills. Characterizing the agreement as a treaty 'would be a very convenient way of introducing it into the Legislature when it had to be introduced at long last, and would save the Government a world of trouble'.[51] Another menacing legal view from the government's perspective was that taken by the staunchly unionist law lord, Lord Carson. He likewise questioned whether it was a 'treaty' and the constitutionality of the government's strategy of regarding it as a 'treaty'.[52] These were especially powerful attacks from Conservative law lords who might possibly have to adjudicate on the Treaty or aspects of it later and therefore their legal doubts had to be taken very seriously.

Despite the serious legal protestations, Lloyd George prevailed and on 16 December 1921 both the Commons and the Lords voted strongly that they were ready to confirm and ratify. Legislative ratification would follow later. The political reality was that once an agreement had been reached that could only be unravelled with huge political consequences, and once it got past the first vote, these issues never captured political momentum. Having got through that crucial first hurdle in December 1921, the momentum thereafter lay with ratification of the Treaty. The British government's strategy of settlement by treaty, on a 'take it or leave it' basis, was critical to settlement being reached. The December vote represented the first British parliamentary recognition of existing Irish sovereignty and the first parliamentary

50 Ibid. (lords), vol. 48, col. 104 (15 Dec. 1921).
51 Ibid., cols 165–6 (16 Dec. 1921).
52 Ibid., cols 39, 46 (14 Dec. 1921).

acceptance of the derivation of Dominion status from a treaty.[53] The British political reverberations were softened because it was simultaneously accompanied by an Irish acceptance of restricted Dominion status.

The Dáil debates were far more prolonged and bitter. The Treatyites also adopted a 'take it or leave it' approach.[54] A wider range of legal points against the Treaty's acceptance was argued (along with other legal issues such as the nature of the oath and of the Dominion status obtained), but some legal issues relating to its status as a treaty arose during the private sessions.

Very briefly, initially failure to refer to the word 'treaty' in the title of the document was raised as indicating that it was not a treaty.[55] However, when the circumstances were clarified,[56] and with Lloyd George having described it as a 'treaty' and Westminster later voting for readiness to approve and ratify it, that point receded and other legal issues received more attention.

The anti-Treatyites challenged the validity of the agreement on an Irish constitutional point, arguing that the plenipotentiaries appointed by Dáil Éireann were not entitled to sign without reverting to the Dáil cabinet.[57] They also argued that the Dáil members, who had been elected as guardians of the independent Irish state, which had declared itself to be a republic, could not accept the Treaty which was inconsistent with the republic. They claimed that the members, who had sworn oaths of allegiance to the republic, could not ratify the agreement: it was *ultra vires* the second Dáil,[58] which was bound to uphold the republic.[59] De Valera wanted to renegotiate with the British based on an alternative proposal, for an association external to the commonwealth.[60]

The Treatyites countered by arguing that the plenipotentiaries were responsible to the Dáil,[61] that they were not obliged to revert to the cabinet in the circumstances,[62] and that de Valera had accepted that they were entitled to sign the agreement.[63] They could not revert to the cabinet because of Lloyd George's demand for an immediate decision with 'immediate'[64] war in the event of a rejection, but the plenipotentiaries had left the Dáil free to reject it.[65] They asserted that the agreement was an international settlement between

53 See also comments of Berriedale Keith, the leading authority on Dominion law, quoted in L. Kohn, *The constitution of the Irish Free State* (London, 1932), p. 57.

54 *Dáil Éireann deb.*, vol. T, no. 2, cols 121, 138 (14 Dec. 1921).

55 Ibid., no. 3, col. 142 (15 Dec. 1921).

56 Ibid., no. 2, col. 135 (14 Dec. 1921).

57 Ibid., no. 2, cols 8–118 (14 Dec. 1921); no. 8, cols 97, 124 (21 Dec. 1921).

58 Ibid., no. 2, cols 122–4 (14 Dec. 1921); no. 7, cols 53, 81 (20 Dec. 1921). The second Dáil was elected in 1921.

59 Ibid., no. 6, col. 25 (19 Dec. 1921).

60 Ibid., no. 2, col. 122 (14 Dec. 1921); no. 3, cols 150–1 (15 Dec. 1921).

61 Ibid., no. 8, col. 97 (21 Dec. 1921).

62 Ibid., no. 2, cols 104–9 (14 Dec. 1921); no. 8, col. 97 (21 Dec. 1921).

63 Ibid., no. 2, cols 104, 108 (14 Dec. 1921); no. 9, col. 129 (22 Dec. 1921).

64 Ibid., no. 2, col. 109 (14 Dec. 1921).

65 Ibid., no. 8, col. 97 (21 Dec. 1921).

states;[66] that Ireland itself, as a separate state already, was conferring Dominion status on itself;[67] and that it was a stage on the road to achieving a republic.[68] They argued that conscience and responsibility required the Dáil members to act in Ireland's best interests, notwithstanding an oath.[69] They also asserted that the anti-Treatyites' absolutist construction of the oath as requiring an absolutist republic was untenable and inconsistent with the decision to negotiate the terms of the Treaty and the claim for external association.[70]

Another important legal issue that did not touch directly on the legal validity of the Treaty but which directly affected its ratification concerned how the proposed constitution was to be adopted. Lloyd George had indicated on 13 December 1921 that the Irish were to draft the constitution 'subject to the terms of the Agreement'.[71] The anti-Treatyites attacked that arrangement because they said that the constitution would not be a true Irish constitution, but would be determined by the British and would derive from a British act.[72] The Treatyite argument was that it would be drawn up by the Irish government for the approval of the Irish people; that it would be the duty of the framers to frame it in accordance with the wishes of the Irish people; and that the constitution would 'derive, not from this Treaty, not from any Act of the British Parliament, but from the Irish people'.[73]

Despite the range of legal arguments on both sides, but because of political support for the settlement in Ireland and Britain, those legal issues were not resolved at the time of the historic parliamentary votes on the Treaty. Future events were determined by political reactions rather than by judicial determination of legal disputes. Legal issues did not prevent approval on both sides, in Britain by large majorities and in Ireland on 7 January 1922 by a small majority, 64 votes to 57.[74]

The Dáil had been asked to vote on whether to 'approve' the Treaty or not,[75] reflecting the language of Article 18 of the Treaty, which referred to 'approval'. While its vote was crucial politically, and was required to satisfy the Sinn Féin view of national status at that time, it was actually the approval of the members of the House of Commons of Southern Ireland that the Treaty required. After the split vote on the Treaty, on 9 January de Valera resigned

66 Ibid., no. 2, col. 108 (14 Dec. 1921).
67 Ibid., no. 9, col. 151 (22 Dec. 1921).
68 Ibid., no. 6, col. 32 (19 Dec. 1921).
69 Ibid., no. 9, cols 151–2 (22 Dec. 1921); no. 10, cols 192–3 (3 Jan.1922).
70 Ibid., no. 2, cols 106–7 (14 Dec. 1921); no. 3, cols 147–8 (15 Dec. 1921); no. 10, cols 192–3 (3 Jan. 1922).
71 Lloyd George to Griffith, 13 Dec. 1921, NAI DE 4/5/10.
72 *Dáil Éireann deb.*, vol. T, no. 6, cols 38–9 (19 Dec. 1921); no. 8, col. 100 (21 Dec. 1921).
73 Ibid., no. 8, col. 86 (21 Dec.1921); vol. T, no. 9, col. 130 (22 Dec. 1921).
74 Ibid., no. 15, cols 345–6 (7 Jan. 1922).
75 Ibid., no. 6, col. 20 (19 Dec. 1921).

and an attempt to re-elect him failed.[76] On 10 January de Valera and the anti-Treatyites walked out of the Dáil and Griffith was elected president of Dáil Éireann. Six ministers, whom he chose, were nominated and ratified by the remaining members and together they formed the Dáil ministry.[77]

On 14 January there was a meeting of the members of the ill-fated House of Commons of Southern Ireland, which had never met before as it had been scorned by Sinn Féin. The membership of the Commons and Dáil was very similar except that the Commons included four unionist members and did not include representatives of the Northern Irish constituencies. By having the members vote, there was some deference to the Government of Ireland Act 1920.[78] Only pro-Treatyites and the four unionist members attended and they voted unanimously to approve the Treaty and they also elected the provisional government,[79] to be led by Dáil minister for finance, Michael Collins. A substantial overlap between the members of the Dáil ministry and the provisional government facilitated transitional dual government and compliance with Irish and British requirements.

Although British legislation was now needed, its form had not yet been clarified.[80] However, even without British legislation there was an immediate transfer of powers from the British government to the provisional government.[81] The provisional government was the only executive recognized by the British but because its status derived from the Treaty, the anti-Treatyites did not recognize its legitimacy. It could only continue until the constitution and the parliament and government of the Free State were established in accordance with the Treaty. That limitation required that a constitution would be adopted by then and there was also an outer limit of a maximum of twelve months from the date of the Treaty.[82]

The first step in Britain's legislative ratification process was in March through the Irish Free State (Agreement) Act 1922.[83] During the debates on the bill, Lloyd George's legal tactics were attacked again by the Conservative-Unionist hardliners claiming he invalidly categorized the agreement as a treaty, illegally altered internal constitutional arrangements without proper parliamentary scrutiny and prevented parliamentary scrutiny. Some self-serving justifications for using a 'treaty' emerged from senior legal figures. Birkenhead, the lord chancellor, claimed that even if there were not two international parties involved in the agreement, they 'occupy a position …

76 Ibid., no. 16, cols 378–9 (9 Jan. 1922).

77 Ibid., no. 17, cols 410–11 (10 Jan. 1922).

78 'The official record of members present at meeting, 14 Jan. 1922', NAI DE 4/7/2.

79 'Agenda and minutes of meeting, 14 Jan. 1922', NAI DE 4/7/1 and D/T S.1.

80 *Hansard's Parl. deb., 5th series* (commons), vol. 149, col. 127 (15 Dec. 1921).

81 NAI D/T S 11, Heads of working arrangements for implementing the Treaty agreed between British and Irish ministers, 24 Jan. 1922.

82 Art. 17.

83 12 Geo. V, c. 4.

quite comparable to that'.[84] The Liberal former lord chancellor, Viscount Haldane, claimed that '[w]henever you settle a civil war in that way the instrument by which you settle it is more analogous to a Treaty than it is to a contract between private persons or to any Statute'.[85]

Churchill, however, provided a rather more frank explanation. On 2 March he acknowledged the political pragmatism behind the usage of the term 'treaty', claiming that it had a 'great sentimental advantage' and that '[t]his is one of the occasions when one should go out of one's way to employ a term like this when you are seeking, without concessions, without additional concessions in substance, to invest your legislation and action with the greatest amount of acceptability in the eyes of those with whom you are trying to effect a friendly reconciliation'. He claimed that the same approach had been used in the settlement with the Boers at Vereeniging.[86]

None of these explanations, however, addressed how a treaty could be appropriate in British legal theory, when the 'other party' was an integral part of the United Kingdom itself, and where existing constitutional procedures applied for variation of those constitutional relationships. Benefitting from the elasticity of an unwritten constitution, pragmatism prevailed and the 'take it or leave it' 'treaty' policy continued, and the bill duly passed.

While the Act gave the agreement the immediate force of law,[87] it was 'not to be deemed to be the Act of Parliament for the ratification of the Articles of Agreement … from the passing whereof' the 'Ulster month' was to run.[88] The effect was that the 'Ulster month' during which Northern Ireland could opt out (which, it will be recalled, was provided for in the Treaty) did not yet start to run.[89] The delay was because neither the British nor the Irish negotiators had adequately appreciated that Northern Ireland would otherwise be asked to vote before seeing the Free State constitution which had not yet been adopted. The Act also provided for the legal transfer of powers to the provisional government provided for under the Treaty. It also required that the existing parliament of Southern Ireland would be dissolved within four months and elections held for a new parliament, which was intended to adopt a constitution, although the constitution was not actually mentioned.[90]

The parliament of Southern Ireland was dissolved on 27 May and an election was called for a provisional parliament. Meanwhile the Treatyites had prepared a draft constitution that they hoped would curtail British incursions on Irish freedom caused by the British formal requirements regarding

84 *Hansard's Parl. deb., 5th series* (lords), vol. 49, col. 686 (21 Mar. 1922).
85 Ibid., vol. 49, c. 552 (15 Mar. 1922).
86 *Hansard's Parl. deb., 5th series* (commons), vol. 151, col. 602 (2 Mar. 1922).
87 S. 1(1).
88 S. 1(5).
89 The 'Ulster month' was inaccurate shorthand as the provision for opting out applied only to the six counties of Northern Ireland and not to the nine counties of Ulster.
90 S. 1(2).

Dominion status. However, during acrimonious negotiations in London in May and June, the British rejected the Irish draft as a 'negation' of the Treaty,[91] and threatened 're-occupation'.[92] It was hurriedly redrafted to render it consistent with Dominion status in British eyes. Most of the revised constitution was made public, for the first time, immediately before the election of 16 June. The election result strongly favoured the Treatyite candidates and was regarded by many as signifying the electorate's support for the Treaty, but it was not actually a plebiscite on the Treaty or the constitution.

Meanwhile republican opposition to the Treaty had become more militant and the termination of their months-long occupation of the Four Courts led to the outbreak of Civil War in late June. In August Griffith died and Collins was assassinated. W.T. Cosgrave became the new Treatyite leader. In September and October the draft constitution was debated in what the Treatyites called the third Dáil and the British called the provisional parliament sitting as a constituent assembly. On 25 October it passed the Constitution of the Irish Free State (Saorstát Éireann) Act 1922 to enact a constitution and to implement the Treaty. The Act's introductory recitals and proclamation asserted an indigenous Irish authority for its adoption. However, section 2, required by Britain, arguably undermined that by providing that the constitution was to be construed in accordance with the Treaty. The Act enscheduled both the constitution and the Treaty. It also gave the Treaty 'the force of law' and was therefore later regarded as being the Irish legislative ratification of the Treaty, but under Article 83 it would not come into effect until British legislation was passed in December and a royal proclamation issued.

The final British legislation was not passed until early December and even at a very late stage concern arose about whether that legislation would proceed. Lloyd George fell from power in October and was replaced by a Conservative-Unionist government, with the stridently unionist Bonar Law as prime minister. In the event, British public opinion was such that the Conservative-Unionists, satisfied that the constitution complied with the Treaty, decided not to unpick the Treaty that parliament had approved twice already and which had by then also been passed by the third Dáil or provisional parliament. With Civil War raging in Ireland, the legislation was given the final imprimatur on the strict basis that it was a Dominion-type constitution within the scope of the Treaty.[93] The British statute, the Irish Free State Constitution Act, was passed by the Westminster parliament on 5 December 1922.[94] That Act deemed it to be the act of ratification of the Treaty

91 'Conference on Ireland, Aide Memoire, 27 May 1922', TNA CAB 43/3 (240).

92 *Hansard's Parl. deb., 5th series* (commons), vol. 154, col. 2128 (31 May 1922).

93 The constitution was re-examined by the new law officers. See *Hansard's Parl. deb., 5th series* (commons), vol. 159, col. 329 (27 Nov. 1922).

94 12 & 13 Geo. V, c. 1.

for the purposes of the commencement of the 'Ulster month',[95] thus completing the statutory requirements for British ratification. The last step was taken the following day when the royal proclamation was issued.

From the standpoint of Anglo-Irish negotiations, settlement by treaty hugely facilitated getting a deal approved by Westminster on what was the fifth attempt to settle the 'Irish question'. Lloyd George's stage management of the early approval and ratification process went through the motions of parliamentary oversight but in reality prevented unionist hardliners from disrupting the settlement. The Treaty settlement came before parliament as a done deal, appearing in schedules to the Acts, rather than set out in the main text where its detailed provisions might more readily be assailed by opponents. The scheduled Treaty could not be renegotiated line-by-line in parliamentary debates without risking the collapse of the settlement, and perhaps even the British government. The choice of taking it or leaving it was a very different process to the lengthy parliamentary trench battles over detailed legislation of earlier settlement attempts. It ensured that the agreement did not get snarled up in unionist amendments and opposition, despite the forceful criticisms of Lloyd George's legal strategy. The negotiating dynamic in 1921 had also been different because Sinn Féin refused to participate in Westminster parliamentary debate. The process also benefitted significantly from the great change in the public mood, which by then favoured peace.

Sinn Féin also benefitted from being able to negotiate directly with the British government, rather than having to battle through Westminster parliamentary processes, as their predecessors had to endure. The limited choice of having to take it or leave it, cast against British military threats, while provoking a long-lasting Civil War, ironically assisted the Treatyites in the Dáil by preventing anti-Treatyite attempts at re-opening negotiations to address the objections of hard-line republicans. Negotiations between the two parliaments, as occurred before the Union in 1800, would not have worked in the far more fraught circumstances of 1921.

Apart from facilitating the reaching of a settlement, the treaty mechanism also boosted the Treatyite characterization of the Free State's indigenous root of title. It bolstered their assertion that Ireland was already independent and that its prior independence had been recognized by the legal instrument used. That was a symbolically important achievement, despite the incursions into the sovereignty of the Irish Free State. The trophy of a treaty was an important part of their legal narrative. Settlement by treaty did not, however, avoid British legislation but it did at least fix the terms of the agreement unless alteration was jointly agreed.

95 S. 5.

Although they were compelled to have their constitution approved by the British in order to take effect, the Treatyites sought to ensure that the various legal steps required for the approval and ratification of the Treaty and the adoption of the constitution were carried out as far as possible in a manner that was consistent with their assertion of pre-existing independent statehood. While Britain (and the anti-Treatyites) could claim that the Free State and the Irish constitution were creatures of a British act of parliament, the Treatyites could plausibly counter argue that the settlement was by treaty and the constitution was actually adopted by the third Dáil whose legal legitimacy derived from the Declaration of Independence of 1919 made by the first Dáil.[96] The Treatyites could thus argue that the state's root of title was not based on British legislation. Their argument was that it was an independent Ireland that accepted the Treaty, and the compromise of restricted Dominion status gave them extensive internal control and the path for evolution into full sovereign independence. That it was an international treaty was recognized by its implementation by the process of approval and ratification. Ultimately the Irish succeeded in having the Treaty registered as a treaty with the League of Nations in 1924, despite protests from the British on the grounds that the registration arrangements did not apply to commonwealth agreements among members *inter se*, but Britain at least did not deny that it was a treaty.[97]

Lloyd George's strategy was maverick, opportunistic, legally inconsistent and unprincipled in many respects, but it proved to be a very important element in allowing negotiations to take place and reaching a settlement. De Valera's successful demand for a treaty proved pivotal to reaching a settlement, but ironically as Sinn Féin split over the substantive terms, it was ultimately to prove disadvantageous to him and his supporters and contributed to his fall from power.

It may very briefly be noted that de Valera revisited the legal dispute over the Treaty later in the 1930s in a very different political context, when he returned to power as president of the executive council. He gradually dismantled many of the Treaty's constitutional impacts. By then the Statute of Westminster had been passed allowing Dominions to amend British acts applicable to them. There had also been several Irish judicial considerations of the legal effects and roles of the Treaty and British statutes in the adoption of the Irish Free State constitution. The conclusions were somewhat diverse but included some strong affirmations of the indigenous basis for the adoption of that constitution.[98] However, a decision in 1935 of the judicial committee of the privy council firmly rooted the authority for the adoption of

96 The third Dáil did not, however, include representativeness from Northern Ireland.

97 See Berriedale Keith's comments, quoted in Kohn, *The constitution of the Irish Free State*, p. 57.

98 See particularly the views of Kennedy CJ in *Re Reade* [1927] IR 31 and *The State (Ryan and others) v. Lennon and others* [1935] IR 170.

that constitution in the (British) statute, the Irish Free State Constitution Act of December 1922.[99] These cases were instrumental in shaping de Valera's determination to introduce the new constitution, Bunreacht na hÉireann, in 1937. That constitution was adopted on foot of a plebiscite on its provisions, thus removing any British role in its origins. By the end of the decade, de Valera had substantially emasculated the Treaty and had a republic in all but name.

99 *Moore and others v. Att Gen* [1935] IR 472.

Dismantling the Anglo-Irish Treaty: removing the oath and the repugnancy clause from the constitution of the Irish Free State

THOMAS MOHR*

INTRODUCTION

The parliamentary oath contained in the 1921 Anglo-Irish Treaty dominated Irish political life from the time of its creation to its abolition in the 1930s. The long and difficult dialogue that produced this oath has been examined in accounts of the British-Irish negotiations that preceded the signing of the Treaty, which have further proliferated since the centenary of that important document.[1] The oath is often presented as a root cause of the Irish Civil War and the debate continues as to whether the popular name 'oath of allegiance' is an accurate term.[2] This chapter outlines the background to this controversial oath, and attempts to explain why Irish governments in the early years of the self-governing Irish state failed to abolish it. It offers detailed consideration of the legal arguments relating to the final removal of the oath from the constitution of the Irish Free State in the early 1930s.

* This chapter was originally delivered to the Irish Legal History Society on 22 Feb. 2014 at the Ulster Museum, Belfast. Editorial note: In this chapter the term 'Treaty' (with capital 'T') refers to the 'Articles of Agreement for a Treaty between Great Britain and Ireland' signed on 6 Dec. 1921 and the term 'Dominion' (with a capital 'D') is used to avoid confusion with the wider term 'his majesty's dominions', which refers to the British empire as a whole; there were five Dominions in 1917: Canada, Australia, New Zealand, South Africa and Newfoundland.

1 On the negotiations that preceded the signing of the Treaty see F. Pakenham, *Peace by ordeal* (London, 1935); F. Gallagher, *The Anglo-Irish Treaty* (London, 1965) and J.M. Curran, *The birth of the Irish Free State, 1921–1923* (Alabama, 1980). For more recent accounts that were published during the centenary, see C. Kenny, *Midnight in London: the Anglo-Irish Treaty crisis* (Dublin, 2021); G. Friemann, *The Treaty* (Newbridge, 2021) and M. Ó Fathartaigh and L. Weeks, *Birth of a state: the Anglo-Irish Treaty* (Newbridge, 2021).

2 E.g., Garvin has argued that the use of the term 'oath of allegiance' represents 'a marvellous lie of silence that has become institutionalized in Irish popular culture'. T. Garvin, *1922: the birth of Irish democracy* (Dublin, 1996), p. 51. See also M. Laffan, *Judging W.T. Cosgrave: the foundation of the Irish state* (Dublin, 2014), pp 103, 313.

This chapter also examines another important provision of the 1922 constitution of the Irish Free State that never captured public attention on the same level as the controversial oath but, nevertheless, was of far greater legal significance. This was the provision known as the 'repugnancy clause' that placed all sources of Irish law in a subordinate position to the provisions of the Treaty.[3] The abolition of the oath and the repugnancy clause were intertwined, because the former could not have been achieved without eliminating the latter. The oath and the repugnancy clause were, in fact, abolished by the same legal instrument; the Constitution (Removal of Oath) Act 1933. The removal of these two features of the 1922 constitution paved the way for a wider programme of constitutional reform that would gradually dismantle the settlement imposed by the Treaty and culminate in the creation of the 1937 constitution of Ireland.

This chapter also considers the changed legal environment created by the Statute of Westminster Act 1931 that made these important reforms possible. In addition, it examines why the abolition of the oath overshadowed the abolition of the repugnancy clause in the 1930s and afterwards even though, in legal terms, the latter was far more significant. The conclusion assesses the importance of the removal of the repugnancy clause in facilitating the dismantling of the settlement imposed by the Treaty and the emergence of a new constitutional order in 1937.

THE REPUGNANCY CLAUSE

The origins of the repugnancy clause were founded on British distrust of Irish intentions to abide by the provisions of the Treaty. Soon after the signature of that agreement, the British government sought a guarantee that the Irish Free State would continue to adhere to its provisions in the years that followed. This guarantee was finally secured in the summer of 1922 during British-Irish negotiations on the provisions of the draft Irish constitution. The final wording of this guarantee, which would later become known as the 'repugnancy clause', was enacted alongside the substantive articles of the constitution of the Irish Free State.[4] It provided:

> The said Constitution shall be construed with reference to the Articles of Agreement for a Treaty between Great Britain and Ireland set forth in the Second Schedule hereto annexed (hereinafter referred to as "the scheduled Treaty") which are hereby given the force of law, and if any

3 Constitution of the Irish Free State (Saorstát Éireann) Act 1922 [Irl.], s. 2, and Irish Free State Constitution Act 1922 (Session 2) [UK], preamble.

4 The use of the term 'repugnancy clause' for these provisions was created by Kohn: L. Kohn, *The constitution of the Irish Free State* (Dublin, 1932), p. 98.

> provision of the said Constitution or of any amendment thereof or of any law made thereunder is in any respect repugnant to any of the provisions of the scheduled Treaty, it shall to the extent only of such repugnancy, be absolutely void and inoperative and the Parliament and the Executive Council of the Irish Free State (Saorstát Éireann) shall respectively pass such further legislation and do all such other things as may be necessary to implement the Scheduled Treaty.[5]

The repugnancy clause made clear that the substantive articles of the 1922 Irish constitution and all future constitutional amendments would be subservient to the provisions of the Treaty. These considerations proved important in overcoming opposition to the draft Irish constitution at Westminster and in facilitating its enactment by that parliament in late 1922 without amendment of any of the substantive articles.[6] The repugnancy clause appeared as a legal padlock that would bind the Irish state to the Treaty in perpetuity, and prevent evolution towards greater sovereignty. The Irish anti-Treaty newspaper *Poblacht na h-Éireann* made dire predictions that the Treaty would bind Ireland to the empire 'for good and all' and prophesized that the Free State parliament of 1990 would still be unable to escape its grasp.[7]

THE PARLIAMENTARY OATH

The origins of the controversial parliamentary oath lay in the negotiations that preceded the signing of the Treaty. The British government proposed granting Dominion status to the island of Ireland with the exception of six north-eastern counties. All of the constitutions of the existing Dominions contained an 'oath of allegiance' that was sworn by their members of parliament. For example, in Canada the oath was 'I A.B. do swear, That I will be faithful and bear true Allegiance to Her Majesty Queen Victoria'.[8] This wording, with its unambiguous reference to allegiance to the British monarch, was unacceptable to the Irish delegation sent to negotiate with the British

5 See fn. 3 above.

6 E.g., the *Morning Post* noted that the repugnancy clause seemed to satisfy the 'average easy going politician' notwithstanding the remaining contents of the draft constitution. *Morning Post*, 17 June 1922.

7 *Poblacht na h-Éireann*, 10 Jan. 1922. The name 'Republic of Ireland' appeared in much larger print than the Irish equivalent of 'Poblacht na h-Éireann' on the banner of this newspaper. Nevertheless, this chapter will use the Irish equivalent because it predominated in other editions using this name. These include *Poblacht na h-Éireann (Scottish Edition)*, *Poblacht na h-Éireann (Southern Edition)* and *Poblacht na h-Éireann (War News)*.

8 British North America Act 1867 (30 & 31 Vic., c. 46), sch. 5. Kohn argues that the institution of oaths of allegiance 'has scarcely any parallel in monarchical constitutions on the continent'. Kohn, *Constitution of the Irish Free State*, p. 55.

government in late 1921. Lengthy negotiations produced a compromise wording that finally appeared in Article 4 of the Treaty:

> I .... do solemnly swear true faith and allegiance to the Constitution of the Irish Free State as by law established and that I will be faithful to H.M. King George V, his heirs and successors by law, in virtue of the common citizenship of Ireland with Great Britain and her adherence to and membership of the group of nations forming the British Commonwealth of Nations.

This wording allowed Irish supporters of the Treaty to argue that Irish parliamentarians would not swear allegiance to the King but to the Irish constitution. It could also be argued that this wording only promised faithfulness to the King as head of the commonwealth.[9] This interpretation was not accepted by opponents of the Treaty who insisted on using the term 'oath of allegiance'. The Dáil debates on the Treaty in late 1921 and early 1922 saw Irish opponents of that settlement make accurate predictions that the king would appear throughout the provisions of the anticipated Irish constitution.[10] This permitted them to argue that an oath to the Irish constitution would be 'an indirect oath to the King'.[11] The term 'oath of allegiance' would become entrenched in popular use although many commentators have questioned its accuracy.[12]

The dispute over the oath featured prominently in the divisive Dáil debates on acceptance or rejection of the Treaty. Although the Treaty was finally accepted by the Dáil in January 1922 by 64 votes to 57, the oath remained one of the most controversial aspects of the settlement. It became the symbol of divisions that would eventually lead to the outbreak of the Irish Civil War on 28 June 1922.[13] This ensured that controversies concerning the oath tended to overshadow matters of far greater practical significance in 1922 and in the years that followed. These included partition, the defence provisions of the

9 E.g., see *Dáil Éireann deb.*, vol. T, no. 6, cols 22–3 and 46–7 (19 Dec. 1921) and no. 8, col. 98 (21 Dec. 1921). See also *Dáil Éireann deb.*, vol. 1, col. 1039 (3 Oct. 1922). See also A.B. Keith, 'Notes on imperial constitutional Law', *Journal of Comparative Legislation and International Law* 4 (1922), 104 at 105.

10 E.g., see Articles 12, 17, 51 and 83 of the 1922 constitution of the Irish Free State. See also Anon., *What the Treaty means* (Dublin, 1922), pp 6–8. It should be noted that predictions of the king being recognized as commander-in-chief of the Irish armed forces proved inaccurate.

11 *Dáil Éireann deb.*, vol. T, no. 6, cols 24 and 27–8 (19 Dec. 1921); no. 7, col. 60 (20 Dec. 1921) and no. 15. col. 330 (7 Jan. 1922). See also *What the Treaty means*, p. 9 and *Poblacht na h-Éireann*, 22 June 1922.

12 See fn. 2 above.

13 E.g., de Valera declared on the enactment of the legislation abolishing the oath 'We are ending this Civil War and the causes of this Civil War'. *Dáil Éireann deb.*, vol. 47, col. 433 (3 May 1933).

Treaty, British retention of the 'Treaty ports', economic considerations and the repugnancy clause.[14]

The overshadowing of the repugnancy clause by the oath became apparent during the latter half of 1922. George Gavan Duffy, a signatory of the Treaty and a future judge of the Irish high court, opposed the repugnancy clause in 1922 and described it as 'thoroughly rotten'.[15] Nevertheless, he prioritized the oath over the repugnancy clause in terms of importance in private correspondence concerning the draft constitution.[16] This priority may also have influenced his stance in the Irish constituent assembly that considered the final text of the draft constitution in late 1922. Here, Gavan Duffy made an unsuccessful attempt to amend the provisions relating to the oath but made no corresponding effort with respect to the repugnancy clause.[17] This prioritization of the oath can be contrasted with the perspective of an international observer unfamiliar with Irish politics. In 1922 Henri Bourassa, a French Canadian politician and newspaper editor with strong nationalist views, concluded that the repugnancy clause was by far the most significant aspect of the draft constitution and attempted to convince the Irish provisional government that it might have serious implications for Irish sovereignty in the future.[18] Yet, the conclusion of the *Irish Times* that 'the oath is the Treaty's key stone' was more typical of Irish popular perceptions in the 1920s.[19] This prioritization of the oath is also evident in scholarship produced many decades after the removal of both the oath and the repugnancy clause.[20]

14 E.g., in 1922 Countess Markievicz argued that provisions such as the surrender of the 'Treaty ports' could not be compared to the oath which was dishonest 'before God and my own soul'. *Dáil Éireann deb.*, vol. T, no. 4, col. 204 (16 Dec. 1921). The British government also appear to have prioritized the oath over the financial disputes that underpinned the 'economic war' in the early 1930s. D. McMahon, *Republicans and imperialists – Anglo-Irish relations in the 1930s* (New Haven and London, 1984), p. 50.

15 Gavan Duffy to Collins, 14 June 1922; Gavan Duffy papers UCDA, P152/209.

16 Ibid.

17 *Dáil Éireann deb.*, vol. 1, cols 1041–5 (3 Oct. 1922). The debates on the repugnancy clause came near the end of the debates of the constituent assembly and Gavan Duffy may have become bruised by the failure of most of his previous efforts to secure amendment. See T. Mohr, 'George Gavan Duffy and the legal consequences of the Anglo-Irish Treaty, 1921–1923', *NILQ*, 72:4 (2021).

18 Memorandum of conversation between James Douglas and Henri Bourassa, 8 July 1922; Kennedy papers, UCDA P4/348.

19 *Irish Times*, 12 Aug. 1927, p. 6.

20 E.g., Coffey criticizes Paul M. Canning's analysis of the 'economic war' of the 1930s for overstating the importance of the oath at the expense of the issue of the land annuities. D.K. Coffey, 'The commonwealth and the oath of allegiance crisis: a study in inter-war commonwealth relations', *Journal of Imperial and Commonwealth History*, 44:3 (2016), 492 at 508 and 509. Canning also concludes that the removal of the oath 'would place in jeopardy the whole Treaty of 1921' while ignoring the removal of the repugnancy clause. P.M. Canning, 'The impact of Eamon de Valera: domestic causes of the Anglo-Irish economic war', *Albion,* 15:3 (1983), 179 at 186.

The conclusion of the Civil War in the summer of 1923 did not result in any resolution of divisions over the oath as a symbol of the Treaty settlement. The 1923 election saw a decisive victory for political parties that supported the Treaty and were prepared to accept the oath. These included Cumann na nGaedheal, the Labour Party and the Farmers' Party. Remnants of the old Sinn Féin party that continued to oppose the Treaty won 44 seats out of 153. This party, led by Eamon de Valera, refused to take its seats in Leinster House. There were many reasons behind this refusal. These included rejection of the 1922 constitution and its institutions and a belief that only anti-Treaty members of the second Dáil Éireann, which it was argued had not been validly dissolved, were entitled to constitute a legitimate Irish parliament. Nevertheless, the issue of the oath soon overshadowed all other objections to the point that they largely dropped out of public consciousness. For many observers the cause of abstention was less important than its effects. The absence of the largest opposition party appeared to augur badly for the future of the Irish state as a successful parliamentary democracy.

THE OATH AND THE IRISH FREE STATE, 1922–32

The Cumann na nGaedheal government led by W.T. Cosgrave, which held power between 1922 and 1932, refused to commit itself to abolishing the oath throughout its decade in office. It is worth noting that this government had little enthusiasm for the oath. The drafters of the 1922 constitution had hoped to exclude the oath from the main text and confine it to statute or even to parliamentary standing orders. George Gavan Duffy warned the Irish provisional government that the British government would make 'desperate efforts' to insert provisions derived from the Treaty including the parliamentary oath into the draft constitution but recommended that Irish negotiators maintain an 'unyielding attitude' in the face of 'idiotic British sentiment'.[21]

The British government refused to accept this position and, after difficult negotiations in London in the summer of 1922, an agreed text of the draft constitution recognized the oath in Articles 17 and 55 and in a schedule that contained the text of the Treaty. Although the Irish provisional government accepted the oath, it made little effort to hide its distaste. Kevin O'Higgins introduced the parliamentary oath to the Irish constituent assembly that would approve the final text of the constitution by admitting 'it is not a pleasing task to stand over it, and it is not a pleasant task to submit it here to an Irish assembly'.[22] William Peters, the British trade commissioner in Dublin

21 Gavan Duffy to Collins, 26 May 1922; Gavan Duffy papers, UCDA P152/202.

22 *Dáil Éireann deb.*, vol. 1, col. 1041 (3 Oct. 1922). O'Higgins had made his own opinion on the oath clear. See *Dáil Éireann deb.*, vol. T, no. 3, cols 173–4 (15 Dec. 1921).

in the early 1930s wrote 'no one in the Irish Free State outside a politically insignificant minority will ever dare to defend the oath as in itself a good thing. The oath is simply a lesser evil than the evil of being exposed to the consequences of its abolition.'[23] For Irish supporters of the Treaty, the oath was a bitter pill that had to be swallowed in order to secure more desirable aspects of the settlement. In these circumstances, the best that the provisional government and its immediate successors could do was to encourage their political opponents to swallow it too.

In March 1926 Éamon de Valera attempted to deflect Sinn Féin from its position of opposition to the Irish Free State as a whole to a position of opposition to the specific issue of the oath. He proposed, at the 1926 Sinn Féin ard fheis, that if the obstacle of the oath were removed the party should perceive entry into the Dáil as a matter of tactics rather than principle. When this proposal was defeated he and his followers withdrew from Sinn Féin and formed Fianna Fáil.[24]

The assassination of Kevin O'Higgins in 1927 was followed by the enactment of the Electoral (Amendment) (No. 2) Act 1927. This required all candidates for Dáil and Seanad elections to swear an affidavit of their intention, if elected, to take their seats and to take the oath required by Article 17 of the constitution. Failure to do so would result in a person losing their seat and being disqualified from further elections for a period of five years.[25] This legislation gave de Valera the stark choice of taking the oath or surrendering all hope of reforming the Irish Free State by following a parliamentary route. If the former option was unpalatable, the latter was unthinkable. This fateful choice persuaded de Valera and his colleagues to declare that the 'required declaration was not an oath' and was merely an 'empty political formula' that had 'no binding significance in conscience or in law'.[26] Concerns over legal commitments were repeated in their declaration that signing the oath 'implies no contractual obligation'.[27] Nevertheless, this bravado and obsession with law hid a great deal of personal unease. De Valera admitted that the decision was 'a step painful and humiliating to us' and admitted that 'it is never easy to pass under the yoke'.[28] Seán MacEntee also admitted that he and his colleagues had 'humiliated themselves' but declared

23 McMahon, *Republicans and imperialists*, p. 44.

24 D. O'Sullivan, *The Irish Free State and its Senate: a study in contemporary politics* (London, 1940), pp 186–7.

25 Electoral (Amendment) (No.2) Act 1927, s. 4.

26 *Irish Times*, 11 Aug. 1927, p. 7. Keogh credits senior figures in the Catholic church, in particular Monsignor John Hagan and Daniel Mannix, archbishop of Melbourne, in persuading de Valera to take this step. D. Keogh, *The Vatican, the bishops and Irish politics, 1919–39* (Cambridge, 1986), pp 131–3, 159, 226. See also P. Murray, *Oracles of God: the Roman Catholic church and Irish politics, 1922–1937* (Dublin, 2000), pp 206–10.

27 *Irish Times*, 11 Aug. 1927.

28 Ibid., 22 Aug. 1927.

that they 'were not going to allow a punctilio of personal pride to prevent them from taking the oath'.[29]

The change in stance on the oath resulted in hostile heckling at political events and predictable ridicule.[30] The *Irish Times* mocked 'Mr de Valera's casuistry' and noted that while it might convince members of his own party, '[i]t certainly will convince nobody else'.[31] Nevertheless, taking the oath did little to dent Fianna Fáil's electoral support. At a stroke a new opposition party had entered the Oireachtas. Parliamentary debate became more antagonistic but the status of the Irish Free State as a parliamentary democracy was placed on a more secure footing. W.T. Cosgrave recognized this reality when he declared that he was pleased to see Fianna Fáil TDs enter the Dáil and concluded 'I think that it is the best thing that has happened during the last five years.[32]

As seen earlier, the Cumann na nGaedheal government led by W.T. Cosgrave came under intense pressure throughout its decade in power over the issue of the parliamentary oath. This pressure came from Sinn Féin, Fianna Fáil and other opposition parties. Cumann na nGaedheal never won a majority of seats in the Dáil but the absence of anti-Treaty TDs ensured that it had little difficulty in forming a government before 1927. This changed when Fianna Fáil TDs took their seats in Leinster House. The Labour Party and the National League, a party founded in 1926 with links to the former Irish Parliamentary Party, proposed the formation of a government with the support of Fianna Fáil that would be pledged to negotiate with the British government over the compulsory nature of the oath.[33] This plan fell apart in the aftermath of the second election of 1927, which allowed Cumann na nGaedheal to stay in power for another five years.

The next initiative concerning the oath had serious implications for the 1922 constitution. Article 48 provided a means whereby the electorate could play a direct role in the legislative process. This provision reflected the importance of the principle of popular sovereignty to the drafters of the constitution. Exposure to the realities of government did not endear this provision to the Cosgrave administration, which declined to pass the legislation that was required to bring the relevant provision into force. Nevertheless, Article 48 provided a mechanism whereby the government could be obliged to introduce such legislation following the presentation of a petition signed by 75,000 registered voters. In 1928 Fianna Fáil circulated a petition of this nature that was signed by 96,000 voters. The response of the

29 Ibid., 15 Aug. 1927.
30 E.g., see *Irish Times*, 15 Aug. 1927 and Cumann na nGaedheal election posters such as that reproduced in Laffan, *Judging W.T. Cosgrave*, p. 281.
31 *Irish Times*, 12 Aug. 1927.
32 Ibid.
33 *Irish Times*, 12 Aug. 1927.

Cosgrave administration was the immediate removal of Article 48 by the Constitution (Amendment No. 10) Act 1928, which also abolished certain powers to hold referenda on ordinary bills contained in Article 47.[34] The government had long considered these provisions as unworkable[35] and it had also become obvious that this provision could also lead to a clash with the Treaty and the activation of the repugnancy clause.[36] The removal of Articles 47 and 48 had been recommended by a special committee in 1926 and a final cabinet decision to remove these provisions was made soon after the assassination of Kevin O'Higgins in 1927.[37] Nevertheless, the context in which the removal of these provisions was introduced created an indelible connection with the oath and, in the eyes of some observers, represented the first step in dismantling the 1922 constitution.[38]

WHY DID THE IRISH FREE STATE DECLINE TO ABOLISH THE OATH AND THE REPUGNANCY CLAUSE BETWEEN 1922 AND 1932?

Why did the Cumann na nGaedheal administration, which had no real enthusiasm for the oath, endure intense political pressure and decline to actively pursue its abolition during its decade in power? This government also resisted pressure to revise other constitutional provisions related to the Treaty that might have required a removal of the repugnancy clause. Why did it decline to follow a path that might have enhanced its popularity and lengthened its period in power?

One reason is the Cumann na nGaedheal government defined itself as the party that had created the settlement contained in the Treaty and insisted that

34 N. Mansergh, *The Irish Free State: its government and politics* (London, 1934), pp 137–46 and Kohn, *Constitution of the Irish Free State,* pp 238–46.

35 Memorandum on Article 48 of the constitution, undated, and draft speech by Michael McDunphy on 'bill no. 10', undated, NAI TSCH, S4469/10.

36 Constitution (amendment no. 10) bill, 2nd reading brief, 15 June 1928, NAI TSCH, S4469/10. See also *Dáil Éireann deb.*, vol. 23, cols 1737–8 and 1752 (18 May 1928) and vol. 23, cols 1903–4 (23 May 1928) and *Seanad Éireann deb.*, vol. 10, cols 1045 (12 July 1928).

37 Amendments to constitution committee report, 1926, NAI TSCH, S4650, and memorandum on Article 48 of the constitution, undated and decision of the cabinet, 15 July 1927, NAI TSCH S4469/10. A proposed constitutional amendment entitled the Constitution (Amendment No. 6) Bill 1927 was introduced to the Dáil in 1927 which would have limited Article 47 and removed Article 48. This measure reached a second reading before the dissolution of the Oireachtas and a general election intervened and terminated its progress. *Dáil Éireann deb.*, vol. 20, cols 810–11 (20 July 1927) and vol. 20, cols 982–1026 (27 July 1927).

38 E.g., see Laffan, *Judging W.T. Cosgrave*, pp 253–4. Hogan begins his account of the 'Irish Free State constitution undermined 1928–34' with an account of the Constitution (Amendment No. 10) Act 1929. G. Hogan, *The origins of the Irish constitution, 1928–1941* (Dublin, 2012), pp 26–8.

this settlement could only be amended by means of bilateral British-Irish agreement. This approach was designed to buttress the status of the Treaty as the perceived title deed of Irish statehood and protect it from encroachment. It was a strategy that found expression in the attempt to register the agreement in the League of Nations' Treaty series in 1924.[39] This position hampered any attempt to secure unilateral removal of the repugnancy clause or the oath. It is worth noting that this perspective was maintained in the earliest legal analyses commissioned by the new de Valera administration in 1932 concerning possible means of abolishing the oath. John Hearne, legal adviser at the Department of External Affairs who would later become close to de Valera and assist in the drafting of the 1937 constitution, concluded that 'the only wise course open to the government is that of diplomatic discussion with Great Britain'.[40] This advice could not have been welcome reading for de Valera who had made clear that he would not seek to abolish the oath by means of bilateral negotiation.[41]

The second reason behind the Cosgrave administration's failure to abolish the repugnancy clause and the oath was because it had other priorities. It focused on wider issues of autonomy within the commonwealth at the imperial conferences held between 1923 and 1930. This strategy paid off when the parliament at Westminster passed an imperial statute in 1931 that offered enhanced autonomy to all Dominions, including the Irish Free State. The Statute of Westminster Act 1931, which will be described in greater detail at a later stage, offered unfettered powers of constitutional amendment. These powers might have been used to override the repugnancy clause and might also have led to a unilateral effort to abolish the oath. However, once again, the Cosgrave administration had other priorities.

The provisions of the 1922 constitution that first came within the crosshairs of the Cosgrave government were those concerning the appeal from the Irish courts to the judicial committee of the privy council.[42] The potential powers of the judicial committee of the privy council, in overruling Irish courts and in acting as the final arbiter of the Treaty, were perceived as being far more significant in practical terms than the largely symbolic parliamentary oath. The unhappy history of the cases that were granted leave to appeal to the privy council in the 1920s and 1930s provided greater impetus to prioritizing the abolition of this institution over the oath.[43] It was also easier to target the privy council appeal as it was not mentioned directly in

39 League of Nations, Treaty series, XXVI, 10.

40 John Hearne, memorandum on the oath, 21 Mar. 1932, NAI TSCH, S2264. By contrast, Joseph Walshe, sec. dept. External Affairs, was prepared to contemplate unilateral abolition: Walshe to de Valera, 12 Mar. 1932, NAI TSCH, S2264.

41 E.g., see *Irish Press*, 17 Mar. 1932.

42 Constitution of the Irish Free State, art. 66.

43 T. Mohr, *Guardian of the Treaty: the privy council appeal and Irish sovereignty* (Dublin, 2016).

the provisions of the Treaty. This made it possible for the Cosgrave administration to argue that the privy council appeal was not actually a legal requirement under that settlement.[44] In 1931 the Cumann na nGaedheal government did consider the possibility of removing the repugnancy clause to facilitate the abolition of the privy council appeal but, as will be described at a later stage, it concluded that this would undermine their argument that this institution was not a legal requirement under the Treaty.[45]

In 1925 Winston Churchill raised the possibility of making the oath optional during the negotiations that followed the collapse of the boundary commission that had attempted to redraw the border with Northern Ireland. Laffan concludes that 'The idea was probably no more than a gambit' and the Irish negotiators chose not to pursue it.[46] The Cosgrave government also made efforts during its final months in power to remove the oath by means of bilateral agreement. Seán Murphy, a high-ranking civil servant in the Department of External Affairs, was sent to London in 1931 to persuade the British government that an agreed removal of the oath would lessen the possibility of de Valera coming to power at the next election.[47] These efforts proved unsuccessful and the oath became an election issue when the Dáil dissolved in early 1932.

The Statute of Westminster, which enhanced the powers of the Dominions to amend their own constitutions, came into force in December 1931. The dissolution of the Dáil in January 1932 ensured that the Cosgrave administration did not have the time to fulfil its own plans for constitutional reform. It now faced an election against opponents who openly advertised their own plans for constitutional reform and prioritized abolition of the oath. How could the Statute of Westminster facilitate constitutional reforms that might include the removal of the repugnancy clause or the parliamentary oath?

THE STATUTE OF WESTMINSTER

The Statute of Westminster Act 1931 was an important milestone in the evolution of the Dominions, which included the Irish Free State, in their progress towards full unfettered sovereignty. It was the product of several imperial conferences in the 1920s and early 1930s that saw the Irish Free State join with Canada and South Africa to push for greater autonomy from the United Kingdom. The final provisions were enacted by the parliament at Westminster as an 'imperial statute' in December 1931. The most important

44 Ibid., p. 105.
45 Ibid. p. 115.
46 Laffan, *Judging W.T. Cosgrave*, pp 206, 208.
47 D.W. Harkness, *The restless Dominion* (London, 1969), pp 239–40.

provision, from an Irish perspective, was contained in section 2 of the Statute of Westminster which removed the supremacy of British imperial statutes over Dominion laws. This opened the possibility of removing the repugnancy clause from the imperial statute that purported to create the 1922 constitution of the Irish Free State.[48] However, the situation was complicated because there was another statute that also claimed to have created this constitution.

The Irish constitution of 1922 was enacted in two parallel statutes, one passed by an Irish constituent assembly in Dublin and the other by the imperial parliament at Westminster. The repugnancy clause was included in both statutes.[49] The dual origin of the Irish Free State and its constitution was problematic as the British and Irish governments only recognized the statute enacted by their own parliament as legally valid. Yet, no Irish government could completely ignore the British claim. Removing the repugnancy clause was not possible in the 1920s under the British theory of the origin of the 1922 constitution because British imperial statutes outranked Dominion laws in terms of legal hierarchy. This position was maintained by means of a rule of common law and also by means of the Colonial Laws Validity Act 1865.

In 1931 the Statute of Westminster provided the Irish Free State with a means of removing the repugnancy clause that was compatible with British legal theory. The removal of the supremacy of British imperial statutes over Dominion laws meant that the Irish Free State was now free to remove the repugnancy clause even though it was enshrined in the imperial statute enacting the Irish constitution. It was less certain in the early 1930s whether the repugnancy clause could be removed in a manner compatible with Irish legal theory, which recognized the statute passed by the Irish constituent assembly as the legal source of the Irish constitution. These doubts were confirmed in 1934 when the Irish supreme court decided the historic case of *State (Ryan) v. Lennon*,[50] which will be examined at a later stage, and raised serious obstacles to its removal. This complicated situation ensured that although the Irish Free State could unilaterally remove the repugnancy clause it could only do so by accepting British theories as to the origins of the constitution and the state.

One of the first acts undertaken by the new Fianna Fáil government in 1932 was to order a series of legal analyses of the position of the Irish Free State under the Statute of Westminster. De Valera examined the possibility of breaking with the position taken by his predecessors and recognizing the position that the Irish Free State had been created by British statute. This *volte face* would have allowed the Irish government to make unfettered use of the Statute of Westminster in pursuing its programme of constitutional reform. De Valera was soon dissuaded from this approach by the legal advisers

48 Irish Free State Constitution Act 1922 (Session 2) [UK].
49 See fn. 3 above.
50 [1935] IR 170.

that he had inherited from his predecessors. John Hearne feared that an admission that the Irish Free State had been created by British statute would downgrade British-Irish disputes from the domain of international affairs to a less advantageous realm of intra-commonwealth affairs. He warned that '[i]f the status of this country is derived from a British statute there is no doubt that it can as a matter of law be destroyed by a British statute'.[51] Irish legal advisers remained uneasy even though this theoretical threat was minimized by political realities. Hearne concluded that

> [t]here is no legal competence within or without this state to destroy this state but if we derive its legal origin from the British parliament, that is from a source which has the inherent legal power to revoke its own acts, we are likely to put ourselves in the position of jeopardizing the internal and external sovereignty of this country.[52]

It is difficult to know how seriously de Valera considered the possibility of accepting the British legal theory in facilitating the reforms to the Irish 1922 constitution by means of the Statute of Westminster.[53] Notwithstanding arguments in the legal sphere, it would have been very difficult to justify such a *volte face* in political terms. These difficulties would have been enhanced by the position that de Valera and his followers had adopted while in opposition. In 1931 members of Fianna Fáil had condemned the Cosgrave government for participation in the conferences that led to the enactment of the Statute of Westminster and of having recognized British hegemony and of having 'used its power to fasten for ever upon us, in so far as they can do so, this Dominion status'.[54] In any case, acceptance of a position that the Irish Free State owed its origins to British statutes was incompatible with deeply-held sentiments as to the nature and origins of the Irish Free State that persist to this day.[55]

De Valera finally decided to follow the counsel of his legal advisers and played down the significance of the Statute of Westminster in relation to the Irish Free State. Instead, he tended to base his arguments, at least when speaking before a domestic audience, on the principle of co-equality and a general enhancement in the status of the Dominions. On occasion, de Valera and his attorney general, Conor Maguire, slipped up in the heat of parliamentary debates and made use of the Statute of Westminster to justify

51 John Hearne, 'The legal basis of the establishment of the Irish Free State', 31 Mar. 1932, NAI TSCH, S12046.

52 Ibid.

53 Alfred O'Rahilly recommended that de Valera make open use of the Statute of Westminster in abolishing the oath. A. O'Rahilly, 'The truth about the oath', undated, NAI TSCH, S2264.

54 *Dáil Éireann deb.*, vol. 39, col. 2309 (16 July 1931).

55 E.g., see *Re Article 26 and the Criminal Law (Jurisdiction) Bill, 1975* [1977] IR 129.

constitutional reforms.[56] However, in general, the Irish government was reluctant to place too much emphasis on the Statute of Westminster apart from signifying British recognition of the changed situation within the commonwealth.[57] De Valera made this position clear in a speech delivered in Ennis in April 1932 when he declared:

> Ireland is not a British colony. It is one of the oldest nations in the world, with all the rights of nationhood. Unlike the British Dominions, we cannot admit, and we have never freely admitted, that our right to sovereign independence is derived from a British statute. It is older than any British statute, older than the British parliament, older than the British nation itself.[58]

THE CONSTITUTION (REMOVAL OF OATH) BILL

The 1932 election saw Fianna Fáil win 72 seats out of 153 and form a minority government with the support of the Labour Party. De Valera's election manifesto had promised the removal of the oath in Article 17 of the constitution. Yet, de Valera insisted that this would not constitute a violation of the Treaty, a position that he would maintain with dogged determination when he introduced his Constitution (Removal of Oath) Bill.[59]

The symbolic importance attached to the oath by Fianna Fáil ensured that its removal was the first proposal for legislation introduced after that party assumed office. Its exceptional nature can be seen in its short title of 'Constitution (Removal of Oath) Bill', which broke from the existing convention of simply giving a number to a constitutional amendment.[60] Yet, this symbolism obscured the position that the bill went further than the simple removal of Article 17 of the constitution. The bill also purported to remove the repugnancy clause contained in section 2 of the constitution of the Irish Free State (Saorstát Éireann) Act 1922 and related provisions in Article 50 of the constitution.[61] Although the drafting of the bill implied that

56 E.g., see *Dáil Éireann deb.*, vol. 41, cols 1015, 1090 (29 Apr. 1932).

57 E.g., de Valera had considered making extensive use of the Statute of Westminster in the early drafts of his speech on the introduction of legislation for the abolition of the privy council appeal. De Valera seems to have thought better of this and all references to the Statute of Westminster were removed from the speech that was finally delivered. Draft speech for Constitution (Amendment No. 22) Act 1933, NAI DFA, 3/1, and *Dáil Éireann deb.*, vol. 49, cols 2115–16 (4 Oct. 1933).

58 *Irish Press*, 11 Apr. 1932.

59 *Irish Independent*, 11 Feb. 1932.

60 The original title of this amendment, as evident from government files, was 'constitution (amendment no. 18) bill 1932'. E.g., see NAI TSCH S4469/18. The name of this file was later changed when the reference to 'Amendment No. 18' was crossed out and replaced by 'Removal of Oath'.

61 Constitution (Removal of Oath) Act 1933, s. 2.

the amendment of these provisions were secondary matters, their importance, in the legal sphere, outweighed that of the oath. The removal of these provisions was an important preliminary to the unravelling of the entire Treaty settlement.

Section 1 of the bill deleted Article 17 of the constitution that set out the wording of the oath and made clear that it had to be taken by every member of the Oireachtas before taking their seats. The opening provision of the bill also amended Article 55 to remove the obligation to take the oath from ministers who might not be members of the Oireachtas.[62] Section 2 removed the repugnancy clause from the text of the Constitution of the Irish Free State (Saorstát Éireann) Act 1922. The removal of the repugnancy clause also necessitated a corresponding amendment to Article 50 of the constitution. Section 3 of the bill deleted the restrictive words in Article 50 that ensured that all constitutional amendments had to be 'within the terms of the Scheduled Treaty'.

The bill did not propose to delete Article 4 of the Treaty that appeared in the schedule to the constitution. John Hearne suggested, during the brief period in which de Valera considered adopting the 'British approach' to the origins of the Irish Free State, a section in the bill that would have provided that 'Article 4 of the Schedule to the Irish Free State Agreement Act, 1922 shall be and is hereby repealed'.[63] This would have been a controversial move and in the end de Valera wisely refrained from interfering with the actual text of the Treaty. Consequently, the provision of the Treaty that set out the wording of the oath to be taken in the Irish Free State remained intact in the schedule of the Irish constitution after the enactment of the Constitution (Removal of Oath) Bill. However, the removal of the repugnancy clause meant that its presence would be devoid of all legal effect.

On 22 March 1932 de Valera communicated his intention to remove the oath to the British government. The result was a series of acrimonious exchanges between de Valera and the Dominions secretary, James Thomas, that was published in the press.[64] More than a month passed before it was revealed that de Valera's proposed constitutional amendment also proposed to abolish the repugnancy clause and related provisions in Article 50. The British government made clear that it considered all of these measures as

62 The Constitution (Removal of Oath) Act 1933, s. 1, deleted the words 'and shall comply with the provisions of Article 17 of this Constitution'.

63 John Hearne, 'The legal basis of the establishment of the Irish Free State', 31 Mar. 1932, NAI TSCH, S12046. The quote refers to the Irish Free State (Agreement) Act 1922 that was enacted by Westminster on 31 Mar. 1922. This statute gave force of law to the Treaty and included the text of the Treaty in a schedule.

64 See *Text of notes exchanged between the Irish Free State government and the British government relating to the oath and land purchase annuities* (Dublin, 1932). A copy of this pamphlet can be found in NAI TSCH, S2264.

repudiations of the Treaty.[65] Nevertheless, it soon became clear that the British government had no desire to drive the Irish Free State out of the commonwealth. Even if British ministers had been inclined to seek expulsion, it seems likely that they would have been prevented from doing so by the other Dominions.

REMOVING THE OATH – LEGAL ARGUMENTS

Before examining the legal arguments that surrounded the removal of the oath it is necessary, for the sake of completeness, to briefly mention some of the political arguments that were raised in parliamentary debates. The repugnancy clause was largely overshadowed in these debates.

The parliamentary debates on the Constitution (Removal of Oath) Bill included the question of whether or not the Fianna Fáil government that took power in 1932 had received an electoral mandate to undertake this important constitutional reform.[66] These debates also raised wider questions as to the future of the Irish Free State in the commonwealth.[67] The question of whether the Irish Free State could and should act unilaterally in removing the oath also featured prominently in the parliamentary debates on this topic.[68] De Valera remained unimpressed with demands that his government should initiate negotiations with London concerning the oath. While he was publicly prepared to negotiate with the British government over a parallel dispute that had arisen over land annuities, which concerned repayment of loans made by the British government to Irish tenant farmers from the late nineteenth century onwards, he was not prepared to make a similar public commitment with respect to the oath. De Valera insisted that the oath was a purely domestic matter.[69] As events transpired, the oath was raised in British-Irish negotiations in 1932 and 1933 that included discussions as to possible amendment of the wording of the oath. In all cases, the negotiations failed to break the impasse between the two governments.[70]

65 *Hansard's Parl. deb., 5th series* (commons), vol. 265, cols 183–4 (26 Apr. 1932).

66 E.g., see *Seanad Éireann deb.*, vol. 15, cols 579, 592, 609–11 (22 Mar. 1932).

67 The communications from all three Dominion prime ministers and the responses were published in the *Irish Press*, 9 Apr. 1932. This aspect of the dispute was also the main source of interest to the state department in the United States of America. McMahon, *Republicans and imperialists*, p. 42.

68 E.g., see *Dáil Éireann deb.*, vol. 41, cols 576–667 (27 Apr. 1932) and vol. 46, cols 70–3 (1 Mar. 1933).

69 E.g., see *Irish Press*, 17 Mar. 1932.

70 TNA DO 35/398/1, note of conversation between Edward Harding and Joseph Walshe, 28 Oct. 1932. The possibility of international arbitration was also raised in these talks. In addition, McMahon outlines a number of low level negotiations in London involving P.J. Fleming, a personal friend of de Valera and an apparent intermediary, that proposed a wholescale revision of the Treaty, including the oath. These negotiations proved unsuccessful. McMahon, *Republicans and imperialists*, pp 43, 45–6, 56, 116–18.

The Fianna Fáil government argued that removal of the oath was necessary in order to guarantee the internal peace and stability of the Irish Free State. It argued that the oath prevented some Irish people from recognizing and giving their allegiance to the Irish Free State. The new government argued that much of the emergency legislation passed by the state had been necessitated by the alienation of these people and added that the removal of this obstacle might alter the entire political life of the Irish Free State.[71] The opposition rejected this argument and accused the government of acquiescing to the violent tactics of opponents of the State.[72]

One of the main legal justifications for the removal of the Article 17 was the contention that the Treaty did not actually require a mandatory oath. This position had been the subject of debate throughout the lifetime of the Irish Free State.[73] This contention had been championed in the 1920s by influential figures such as George Gavan Duffy, one of the signatories of the Treaty, who may have been the creator of this line of argument. Gavan Duffy's contentions were directly refuted by Eamonn Duggan, another signatory of the Treaty, and failed to persuade the Irish constituent assembly in 1922. Nevertheless, Gavan Duffy stubbornly continued to champion this argument which would be resurrected in the remainder of the decade by opponents of the Treaty.[74]

The contention that the oath had not been intended to be mandatory was popularly known as the 'whiskey argument'. According to this explanation the provision of the form of oath to be taken by members of the Oireachtas in Article 4 of the Treaty was akin to a rule saying that if the members of a certain club wished to take whiskey it had to be 'John Jameson's Three Star'. However, the rules of the club did not forbid teetotalism and no rule could be found requiring members to drink whiskey. In the same way, it was argued, no clause of the Treaty could be found that required all members of the Oireachtas to take the oath. Article 4 of the Treaty provided that 'The oath to be taken by Members of the Parliament of the Irish Free State shall be in the following form'. It was argued that these words merely provided that if members of the Oireachtas chose to take an oath it had to be in the form set out in Article 4.[75] This line of reasoning was dependent on the inference that the words 'to be' implied an optional, as opposed to a compulsory, nature. The proponents of this argument concluded that Article 17 of the constitution, which provided that the oath was mandatory for all members of the

71 *Dáil Éireann deb.*, vol. 41, cols 568 and 574–5 (27 Apr. 1932) and vol. 47, col. 438 (3 May 1933).
72 Ibid., col. 641–2 (27 Apr. 1932).
73 E.g., see D. Ó Crudhlaoich, *The oath of allegiance* (Dublin, 1925), pp 67–93.
74 Ibid., and *Dáil Éireann deb.*, vol. 3, col. 798 (10 May 1923).
75 'Does the draft constitution surrender more than the Treaty?', undated 1922; Gavan Duffy papers, UCDA P152/213, and *Irish Independent*, 25 Sept. 1922.

Oireachtas and external ministers, went beyond the strict demands of the Treaty.

The rejection of the 'whiskey argument' by the constituent assembly in 1922 and by the British government in the 1930s did little to dent its popularity.[76] In 1927 de Valera used this argument to attack the Cosgrave government by arguing that a non-obligatory oath was being retained for 'political party purposes, and for no other reason'.[77] It was resurrected again in the 1930s by members of Fianna Fáil, including de Valera, the minister for finance Seán MacEntee and the attorney general Conor Maguire.[78]

The 'whiskey argument' was not the only revival from 1922 that accompanied the introduction of the constitution (removal of oath) bill. The Fianna Fáil government made use of its access to the files of its predecessor to confirm the long-held suspicions that the draft constitution that had been taken to London in 1922 by Michael Collins and Arthur Griffith had not contained any provision concerning the oath. Seán MacEntee raised this point in the Dáil in 1932 to show that the drafters of the Free State constitution had not considered that the Treaty demanded a mandatory oath.[79] Members of Cumann na nGaedheal responded by insisting that the drafters had not doubted the mandatory nature of the oath. They argued that the drafters had merely considered that it would be sufficient to give effect to Article 4 of the Treaty in subsequent legislation or in parliamentary standing orders.[80] This position was emphasized by Senator James Douglas who had been directly involved in drafting the 1922 constitution.[81]

De Valera made it clear that the justification for the removal of Article 17 of the constitution was not based exclusively on the 'whiskey argument'.[82] This was a prudent step as there was always a vocal body of opinion within Irish nationalism that rejected it.[83] As the dispute over the abolition of the

76 E.g., see Thomas to de Valera, 23 Mar. 1932, NAI TSCH, S2264, and *Hansard's Parl. deb., 5th series*, vol. 263, col. 1044 (23 Mar. 1932).

77 *Irish Times*, 22 Aug. 1927, p. 5. For another example of de Valera's use of the 'whiskey argument' see *Dáil Éireann deb.*, vol. 23, col. 2531 (1 June 1928).

78 *Irish Press*, 17 Mar. 1932. See also *Dáil Éireann deb.*, vol. 41, cols 591–6 (27 Apr. 1932) and col. 1010 (29 Apr. 1932).

79 *Dáil Éireann deb.*, vol. 41, cols 740–2 (28 Apr. 1932) and cols 2021–2 (19 May 1932).

80 Ibid., cols 753–4 (28 Apr. 1932).

81 *Seanad Éireann deb.*, vol. 15, cols 686–7 (25 May 1932).

82 *Dáil Éireann deb.*, vol. 41, col. 927 (29 Apr. 1932).

83 The 'whiskey argument' had been rejected by the constituent assembly in 1922. In addition, John Hearne's legal analyses in the 1930s also rejected it. J. Hearne, 'Memorandum on the oath', 21 Mar. 1932, NAI TSCH, S2264. Alfred O'Rahilly, a professor of mathematical physics who assisted in the drafting of the 1922 constitution, sent voluminous correspondence to the Irish government on the subject of the oath in which he concluded that the whiskey argument 'is a very weak basis on which to base our case'. A. O'Rahilly, 'The truth about the oath', undated, NAI TSCH, S2264. Arthur Berriedale Keith, a professor at the University of Edinburgh and author of numerous texts on British imperial law, admitted that the contention that the oath was not mandatory 'is not wholly impossible of defence as

oath wore on, de Valera placed less and less emphasis on it.[84] De Valera's main legal argument was based on the principle of co-equality of members of the commonwealth and on developments in the status of the Irish Free State. This was a consequence of the constitutional advances made at successive imperial conferences and recognized by the Statute of Westminster in 1931. Government supporters often asked whether Canada or the United Kingdom were free to abolish their parliamentary oaths if they were so inclined. If so, the co-equal position of the Irish Free State ensured that it was also entitled to remove its parliamentary oath contained in Article 17 of the Irish constitution.[85]

De Valera's reliance on the progress of the Irish Free State within the commonwealth, culminating in the Statute of Westminster, must have been a bitter pill for Cumann na nGaedheal to swallow. While in opposition, Fianna Fáil had maintained that the labours of their opponents at the imperial conferences had actually retarded rather than advanced the status of the Irish Free State.[86] Even the long dead spectre of imperial federation, the objective of uniting the United Kingdom and the Dominions as a federal state, had been resurrected by Fianna Fáil in 1930 and 1931 in order to illustrate how the status and autonomy of the Irish Free State had been diminished at the imperial conferences.[87] In 1931 Sean T. O'Kelly, a future Fianna Fáil minister and president of Ireland, condemned the Statute of Westminster by arguing that its object was 'to nail us, to copper-fasten us, for ever to the British Empire and its king'.[88] He also accused the Cosgrave administration of having 'worked with all their might to bind us more closely to the British empire, politically, economically and financially'.[89] By 1932 de Valera accepted that

a mere matter of Treaty interpretation' but concluded that the wider context ensured that there was 'not the slightest possibility' of its acceptance. A.B. Keith, *The sovereignty of the British Dominions* (London, 1929), p. 190. It should be noted that Keith had already concluded on the subject of the Irish parliamentary oath that 'it appears impossible in the long run to insist on imposing on the Free State an obligation of the most dubious moral value'. A.B. Keith, *Responsible government in the Dominions*, 2 vols (Oxford, 1928), ii, p. 1255.

84 This argument was used by John W. Dulanty, Irish high commissioner in London, in the earliest communications with the British government on the abolition of the oath. However, one month later, de Valera wrote to J.H. Thomas that 'Whether the oath was or was not "an integral part of the Treaty made ten years ago" is not now the issue'. Dulanty to Thomas, 22 Mar. 1932 and de Valera to Thomas, 5 Apr. 1932, NAI TSCH, S2264.

85 *Dáil Éireann deb.*, vol. 41, col. 570 (27 Apr. 1932).

86 E.g., ibid., vol. 39, col. 2296 (16 July 1931) and *Seanad Éireann deb.*, vol. 14, cols 1621–2 and 1627 (23 July 1931). Thomas Johnson did, however, propose a resolution in the Seanad that would have commended the minister for external affairs for his efforts in 'procuring the full establishment and international recognition of the independence and sovereign status of Saorstát Éireann'. *Seanad Éireann deb.*, vol. 14, col. 1607 (23 July 1931).

87 *Dáil Éireann deb.*, vol. 39, col. 2296 (16 July 1931) and *Seanad Éireann deb.*, vol. 14, cols 1621–2 and 1627 (23 July 1931).

88 *Dáil Éireann deb.*, vol. 39, col. 2310 (16 July 1931).

89 Ibid., cols 2309–10 (16 July 1931).

Irish participation in the imperial conferences had actually enhanced Irish autonomy but declined to offer his political opponents credit for this achievement.

Members of the opposition in the Oireachtas concluded their attacks on the Constitution (Removal of Oath) Bill by returning to basics. They argued that the oath was a clear provision of the Treaty and that it was nonsensical to argue that it was not intended to be mandatory. The 'whiskey argument' was completely at odds with the historical background to the oath. Members of the opposition concluded that no international tribunal could possibly uphold the argument put forward by the government.[90]

The opposition also noted that the provisions of the Constitution (Removal of Oath) Bill refuted the argument that the oath was not mandatory under the Treaty. If this were the case, why had the government felt the need to break the overriding force of the Treaty contained in the provisions of the repugnancy clause? The opposition concluded that the removal of the oath and the removal of the repugnancy clause were clearly interlinked.[91] The legal arguments that were raised to justify the removal of the repugnancy clause, a provision that linked the Treaty and the 1922 constitution, must now be examined.

REMOVING THE REPUGNANCY CLAUSE – LEGAL ARGUMENTS

Once again, it is necessary for the sake of completeness to briefly outline political arguments raised during parliamentary debates before moving on to legal analysis. These debates witnessed relatively few arguments that specifically related to the repugnancy clause but often raised wider issues concerning the Treaty. It was often argued within Ireland and beyond that breaking the Treaty might mean that other countries would be reluctant to make new treaties with the Irish Free State.[92] Breaking the Treaty was also presented as a betrayal of guarantees provided to southern Protestants, many of whom had identified with unionist traditions, as a minority within the Irish Free State. It was also argued that northern unionists would be reluctant to accept legal guarantees from future Irish governments when the administration in power in the early 1930s had so blithely violated the Treaty.[93]

The contention that the new government had not received an electoral mandate to alter the repugnancy clause or its corresponding provision in

90 E.g., ibid., vol. 41, cols 600–1 (27 Apr. 1932).

91 Ibid., col. 616 (27 Apr. 1932).

92 E.g., see *Irish Independent*, 21 May 1932 and *Hansard's Parl. deb., 5th series* (commons), vol. 266, col. 1319 (2 June 1932).

93 *Dáil Éireann deb.*, vol. 41, cols 922–33 (29 Apr. 1932).

Article 50 was raised in the Oireachtas.[94] It was also argued that the title of the Constitution (Removal of Oath) Bill had been chosen to mask the removal of force of law from the Treaty as represented by the repugnancy clause.[95] These political arguments did not enjoy equivalent attention to those relating to the oath. However, legal analysis as to the possibility of abolishing the repugnancy clause pre-dated the initiative to abolish the oath.

The preparatory work in removing the repugnancy clause had already been carried out during the tenure of the Cumann na nGaedheal government that remained in power until 1932. This had been completed during the drafting of the measures that were intended to abolish the privy council appeal in 1931. John Hearne had advocated the removal of the repugnancy clause and the limiting provisions of Article 50 in 1931 in conjunction with the proposed abolition of the privy council appeal. Hearne tended to overlook the repugnancy clause as he was convinced that Article 50, which provided that '[a]mendments of this constitution within the terms of the Scheduled Treaty may be made by the Oireachtas', was the main limiting provision of the Irish constitution. However, Hearne believed that the Article 50 had never been intended to limit the legislative competence of the Oireachtas. He concluded that Article 50 was a voluntary declaration that did no more than recognize the obligations of the Irish Free State under the Treaty.[96] Consequently, Hearne saw no legal barrier to an amendment to Article 50 that removed this voluntary declaration.

Hearne openly admitted that he did not know the history behind the drafting of the repugnancy clause in 1922, a reality that hindered his understanding of its legal provisions.[97] The only significance that Hearne was prepared to attribute to the repugnancy clause was that it gave the force of law to the Treaty.[98] Consequently, draft legislation produced by Hearne in 1931 would have repealed all of the provisions of the repugnancy clause save those giving force of law to the Treaty.[99] De Valera had no sentimental ties to the Treaty and, when he took power in 1932, was not even prepared to give it a legal status that was bereft of all powers of enforcement. Section 2 of the Constitution (Removal of Oath) Bill purported to repeal the repugnancy clause in its entirety.

94 Ibid., col. 633 (27 Apr. 1932) and col. 816 (28 Apr. 1932).

95 Ibid., cols 745–6 (28 Apr. 1932).

96 This line of argument was also raised in the Oireachtas: *Dáil Éireann deb.*, vol. 41, col. 839 (28 Apr. 1932). See also the conclusions of Alfred O'Rahilly who dismissed the repugnancy clause by concluding that '[t]his can have no legal validity, it is merely a pious exhortation'. A. O'Rahilly, 'For the president', undated, NAI TSCH, S2264.

97 Hearne to S. Murphy, 27 May 1931, NAI DFA, 3/1.

98 Ibid. Hearne maintained this dismissive attitude towards the repugnancy clause in legal analyses for de Valera but, nevertheless, recommended its ultimate abolition. Hearne, 'Memorandum on the oath', 21 Mar. 1932.

99 Constitution (Amendment No. 18) Bill, 1931, NAI DFA, 3/1.

In 1931 the Cosgrave government, after some consideration, had decided to reject Hearne's proposal to remove constitutional links to the Treaty in the context of the proposed abolition of the privy council appeal. One of the considerations behind this rejection had been that any such move would have given the impression that the Cosgrave government did not believe its own argument that the abolition of the privy council appeal would not violate the terms of the Treaty.[100] By contrast, de Valera was prepared to put this abandoned plan into action in 1932. He was also prepared to brazen out the obvious accusation that this course of action undermined his claim that the removal of the oath did not violate the terms of the Treaty.

The Fianna Fáil administration dusted down and publicized legal arguments put forward by civil servants who had formerly advised their predecessors. These included the contention that it was not normal for a Treaty to form part of the constitutional law of a state or to have overriding effect over municipal law. The normal position under Irish law was that municipal law prevailed over the provisions of international treaties. Why, it was contended, should the Treaty be placed in such an exceptional position? The Irish government argued that it was doing nothing more than placing the purported Treaty signed in London on 6 December 1921 in the same legal position of every other Treaty involving the Irish Free State.[101]

All this was to assume that the 'Articles of Agreement for a Treaty' signed in 1921 did constitute an international Treaty, a position that the British government had never been prepared to recognize.[102] Although de Valera seemed to be embracing the position of his predecessors that the instrument signed in 1921 was an international Treaty, he remained tight-lipped as to his own views on the legal position and validity of the 1921 settlement. On one occasion he remarked that '[w]e are simply putting the Treaty in its place. What that place is and what its effect may be is another question altogether'.[103]

Members of the previous administration, now in opposition, responded by contending that the removal of the repugnancy clause showed that the de Valera government was aware that what it was doing was a violation of the Treaty and was afraid to have this tested in the courts. They added that this admission showed that Fianna Fáil did not believe the claims it had made to the electorate that the removal of the oath could be achieved without any violation of the Treaty.[104] Some members of the opposition raised the possibility of arbitration by another member of the commonwealth and even

100 *Dáil Éireann deb.*, vol. 41, cols 2115–16 (19 May 1932).
101 Ibid., cols 572–3 (27 Apr. 1932).
102 E.g., see T. Mohr, 'The Anglo-Irish Treaty: legal interpretation, 1921–1925', *Irish Jurist*, 66 (2021), 1 at 11–15. For an example of an Irish assertion that the 1921 settlement was not an international Treaty see O'Rahilly, 'The truth about the oath'.
103 *Dáil Éireann deb.*, vol. 41, col. 1132 (3 May 1932).
104 Ibid., col. 615 (27 Apr. 1932).

referral of the dispute to the permanent court of international justice.[105] The debates in the Oireachtas even raised the possibility of holding a referendum on the measures contained in the Constitution (Removal of Oath) Bill.[106] The previous government came in for some criticism in this context for removing this possibility by passing the Constitution (Amendment No. 10) Act 1928.[107]

The Cosgrave and de Valera governments shared an aversion to having any court, even an Irish court, act as arbiter of the Treaty and its impact on the legislative competence of the Oireachtas.[108] Nevertheless, there were voices in the Oireachtas that called for the referral of the Constitution (Removal of Oath) Bill to the supreme court.[109] De Valera responded that it would be wrong for domestic courts to decide an international matter.[110] He also raised hard-headed practical objections to submitting the matter to the Irish courts. As he explained to the Dáil:

> The courts, if they gave a verdict in our favour, would not help our position a whit, because it would be said: 'Oh, it is your own courts did it.' If, on the other hand, they decided against us, if they made a mistake and decided against us – as I said before, mistakes can be made by judges just as well as they can be made by other people – then in that case the mistake would be irretrievable. We would be told that 'even your own courts would not find in your favour'.[111]

This line of reasoning allowed the government to justify the removal of the repugnancy clause in the same statute as the provisions relating to the oath on the basis that it was a 'precautionary measure'.[112] This precaution was based on de Valera's assumption that any decision of the courts on this matter that did not correspond with his views would be 'wrong-minded' or, quite simply, a 'mistake'.[113] Conor Maguire, the attorney general, suggested that it would be 'monstrously unfair' to the Irish courts to oblige them to thrash out such matters.[114] Thomas Derrig, the minister for education, added that the government could not be sure that elements within the opposition might not challenge the decision of the Irish supreme court before the judicial

105 *Seanad Éireann deb.*, vol. 15, cols 958–9 (8 June 1932) and vol. 16, col. 692 (15 Mar. 1933).
106 *Dáil Éireann deb.*, vol. 41, col. 174 (20 Apr. 1932).
107 E.g., see *Dáil Éireann deb.*, vol. 41, col. 664 (27 Apr. 1932) and col. 739 (28 Apr. 1932).
108 E.g., see meeting of 25 Apr. in report on London discussions, 1 May 1931; McGilligan papers, UCDA P35/197, and J. Hearne to S. Murphy, 27 May 1931, NAI DFA, 3/1.
109 *Dáil Éireann deb.*, vol. 41, col. 630 (27 Apr. 1932) and cols 719, 838–9 (28 Apr. 1932).
110 Ibid., col. 1183 (3 May 1932) and *Seanad Éireann deb.*, vol. 15, col. 682 (25 May 1932).
111 *Dáil Éireann deb.*, vol. 41, col. 1176 (3 May 1932). See also *Seanad Éireann deb.*, vol. 15, cols 682–3 (25 May 1932).
112 *Dáil Éireann deb.*, vol. 41, cols 2032, 2137 (19 May 1932).
113 Ibid., col. 1176 (3 May 1932) and cols 2022–3 (19 May 1932).
114 Ibid., col. 2055 (19 May 1932).

committee of the privy council. Derrig singled out the small portion of the opposition led by Professor Thrift, who was seen as representing southern Protestant interests. However, he also claimed that the government could not be sure that the portion of the opposition led by W.T. Cosgrave would also refrain from taking the matter to the privy council.[115] This was a calculated insult to Cumann na nGaedheal whose opposition to the privy council appeal and repeated attempts to secure its abolition were now evident to the present government.

The Fianna Fáil government firmly refused to submit the contents of the Constitution (Removal of Oath) Bill to any tribunal, foreign or domestic. Members of the opposition could do little more than grumble that a single political party was, in effect, assuming the role of the judiciary. However, Fianna Fáil now had access to government files and argued that the possibility of removing the repugnancy clause had been submitted to the Cumann na nGaedheal government by their legal advisers.[116] The de Valera government was attempting to blunt the criticism of the opposition by suggesting that there was far more continuity than divergence between the policies of the two administrations.

DIVERGENCE AND CONTINUITY IN IRISH GOVERNMENTAL POLICY

In 1932 Fianna Fáil ministers argued that the Constitution (Removal of Oath) Bill mirrored the plans of the previous government with respect to the appeal to the judicial committee of the privy council.[117] They argued that the British government had regarded the abolition of the privy council appeal as being just as much a breach of the Treaty as the removal of the oath.[118] Leading figures in the former government denied the comparison on repeated occasions by emphasizing that the privy council appeal had never been mentioned in the Treaty whereas an entire article of that instrument was devoted to the oath.[119] They noted that the proposed removal of the repugnancy clause had merely appeared in one of several draft measures and had been firmly rejected by them.[120] De Valera responded that the decision made by Cumann na nGaedheal not to abolish the repugnancy clause in 1931

115 Ibid., col. 1203 (3 May 1932). See also de Valera's remarks at ibid., col. 2024 (19 May 1932).
116 Ibid., cols 573–4 (27 Apr. 1932) and col. 1018 (29 Apr. 1932).
117 Ibid., cols 1150–4 (3 May 1932); col. 2055 (19 May 1932); vol. 43, cols 651–2 (12 July 1932) and *Seanad Éireann deb.*, vol. 15, col. 982 (8 June 1932).
118 *Dáil Éireann deb.*, vol. 43, col. 701 (12 July 1932).
119 Ibid., vol. 41, col. 604 (27 Apr. 1932); col. 998 (29 Apr. 1932); col. 1152 (3 May 1932); col. 2114 (19 May 1932) and vol. 43, col. 713 (12 July 1932).
120 Ibid., vol. 41, col. 2055 (19 May 1932).

had been based on matters of policy rather than on legal considerations.[121] He continued to vex his predecessors by insisting that the difference between the position of the privy council and the position of the oath was the difference between 'tweedledum and tweedledee'.[122]

Although there were certain undeniable continuities between the Cumann na nGaedheal and the Fianna Fáil governments in their approach to constitutional reform, there were also important differences. The proposal put forward by the Cumann na nGaedheal government in 1931 was limited to the removal of the privy council in its roles as arbiter and sentinel of the Treaty. There is no evidence that it was intended as a prelude to the dismembering of the entire Treaty settlement. The policy of the Cosgrave administration was always to seek changes in the Treaty settlement by bilateral means.[123] Second, there is a wide gulf between merely considering a course of action and actually putting it into practice. Patrick McGilligan, minister for external affairs from 1927 to 1932, claimed that the proposal was nothing more than 'research work, done at my request, as to what might happen if certain steps were taken'.[124] Third, the proposal put forward by McGilligan and John Hearne was rejected by the Cumann na nGaedheal government as a whole. McGilligan himself seems to have changed his mind as to the wisdom of removing the repugnancy clause. He later claimed that the removal of the repugnancy clause had been rejected by the previous government on the grounds that it was felt to constitute a breach of the Treaty.[125]

THE DEBATES ON THE CONSTITUTION (REMOVAL OF OATH) BILL

The debates in the Dáil on the Constitution (Removal of Oath) Bill were lengthy and strayed over the entire span of recent and not so recent Irish history. A large number of amendments were moved by the opposition during these lengthy discussions. One attempted to change the wording of Article 17 to make clear that taking the oath would not be mandatory.[126] This would have meant that the words of the oath itself could be retained in the constitution. Another amendment sought to replace the permanent removal of the repugnancy clause with a temporary removal that would only apply to the removal of the oath.[127] There was also an amendment that sought to maintain the legal force of Article 10 of the Treaty which provided for the

121 Ibid., col. 2055 (19 May 1932).
122 Ibid., cols 1174–5 (3 May 1932).
123 Cosgrave to MacDonald, 21 Nov. 1931, NAI TSCH, S5340/19.
124 *Dáil Éireann deb.*, vol. 43, cols 656–7 (12 July 1932).
125 Ibid., cols 655–6, 707 (12 July 1932).
126 Ibid., vol. 41, col. 1128 (3 May 1932).
127 Ibid., col. 2012 (19 May 1932).

compensation of transferred civil servants.[128] All these amendments were defeated in the Dáil and the bill passed in the same form as was introduced by the government.

The Seanad proved to be a tougher proposition. Fianna Fáil only had thirteen seats out of sixty in the upper house. Their allies in the Labour Party could only muster six senators.[129] The nature of Seanad elections ensured that it would take some years for the formation of a government majority. The Seanad made a number of key amendments that altered the entire nature of the bill. First, the Seanad took out sections 2 and 3 of the bill that removed the repugnancy clause and the words 'within the terms of the Scheduled Treaty' from Article 50 of the constitution. Although the removal of Article 17 of the constitution by section 1 of the bill was left intact, the Seanad added a new section 4 that would delay it from coming into force pending the conclusion of a new British-Irish agreement on the removal of the oath.[130] It also altered the long title of the bill to reflect these changes.[131] When the Seanad refused to retract these amendments, the bill was suspended under Article 38A of the constitution.[132] In ordinary circumstances this meant a delay of twenty months. However, Article 38A also provided that a bill could be deemed to be passed sixty days after the reassembly of the Dáil following a general election. A general election intervened in January 1933 and this allowed for the enactment of the Constitution (Removal of Oath) Act 1933 on 3 May 1933.

Members of the Seanad, who had infuriated an already hostile government over the Constitution (Removal of Oath) Act 1933, appear to have concluded that they now had little to lose by imposing delays on subsequent legislation. For example, the Seanad delayed legislation removing university representation in the Dáil and rejected legislation intended to prohibit the wearing of political uniforms.[133] De Valera's response was entirely predictable.

128 This had been the subject of litigation in *Wigg and Cochrane v. Att Gen of the Irish Free State* [1927] IR 293 (high court), [1925] 1 IR 149 (supreme court) and [1927] IR 285 (privy council) and *In re Compensation to Civil Servants under Article X of the Treaty* [1929] IR 44.

129 O'Sullivan, *The Irish Free State and its Senate*, p. 302.

130 The proposed section 4 read as follows: 'This Act shall not come into force until an agreement has been entered into between the government of the Irish Free State and the British government providing that Article 4 of the Treaty of 1921 shall cease to have effect and such agreement has been ratified and approved by resolution of Dáil Éireann'. *Seanad Éireann deb.*, vol. 15, col. 1430 (20 July 1932).

131 The long title of the bill was as follows: 'An Act to remove the obligation now imposed by law on members of the Oireachtas and ministers who are not members of the executive council to take an oath, and for that purpose to amend the constitution and also the Constitution of the Irish Free State (Saorstát Éireann) Act 1922'. A Seanad amendment proposed the removal of the words 'and also the constitution of the Irish Free State (Saorstát Éireann) Act 1922'. *Seanad Éireann deb.*, vol. 15, col. 1429 (20 July 1932).

132 Article 38A was inserted by the Constitution (Amendment No. 13) Act 1928.

133 Constitution (Amendment No. 23) Act 1936 and the Wearing of Uniform (Restriction) Bill 1934, never enacted.

In 1933 he oversaw a constitutional amendment that reduced the period of delay that could be imposed by the Seanad to three months.[134] When this bill was itself delayed, it was replaced by a measure that provided for the complete abolition of Seanad Éireann. Although this measure was also delayed, it finally came into force on 29 May 1936.[135]

REACTION TO THE REMOVAL OF THE REPUGNANCY CLAUSE IN THE COURTS

The removal of the oath attracted by far the most attention in London, in the Dominions and in the press. For example, in early April de Valera received telegrams from the prime ministers of New Zealand, South Africa and Australia and the resulting correspondence on the oath would later be published in the newspapers.[136] The removal of the repugnancy clause rarely attracted attention in the press comparable to that of the oath in the 1920s and 1930s. Yet, this position was reversed in the courts. The facts of the historic case of *State (Ryan) v. Lennon*,[137] which was decided by the Irish supreme court in 1934, did not directly concern the repugnancy clause. The case focussed on Constitution (Amendment No. 16) Act 1929, which extended the period in which the constitution could be amended by means of ordinary legislation, and the Constitution (Amendment No. 17) Act 1931, which imposed severe emergency laws. Both amendments were upheld by the majority of the court despite a spirited dissent by Kennedy CJ. Nevertheless, the repugnancy clause was raised in *obiter dicta* by all three judges. The three judges of the supreme court had been divided on the issue of the two contested constitutional amendments but all three cast serious doubt on the legality of the removal of the repugnancy clause by the Constitution (Removal of Oath) Act 1933.

Kennedy CJ distinguished the status of the third Dáil Éireann, sitting as a constituent assembly, from subsequent Irish legislatures.[138] This suggested that the Oireachtas had no power to amend the provisions of the Constitution of the Irish Free State (Saorstát Éireann) Act 1922, including section 2 which contained the repugnancy clause, which had been enacted by the constituent

134 Constitution (Amendment No. 19) Bill 1933, never enacted.

135 Constitution (Amendment No. 24) Act 1936.

136 See NAI TSCH, S2264. The original telegrams were the result of a coordinated action that had been arranged by Dominions secretary, J.H. Thomas. None of the original telegrams referred directly to the dispute over the oath but simply expressed diplomatic concern at the emergence of a dispute with the United Kingdom. De Valera responded by referring to the oath as a 'conscience test' that his government had received a mandate from the Irish people to remove. *Irish Press*, 9 Apr. 1932, p. 1. The background to these telegrams is outlined in McMahon, *Republicans and imperialists*, pp 48–9.

137 [1935] IR 170.

138 Ibid., at 203.

assembly. Fitzgibbon J added that 'an amendment of Article 50 by the deletion of the words "within the terms of the Scheduled Treaty" would be totally ineffective, as effect is given to those words by the Constituent Act itself, which the Oireachtas has no power to amend'.[139] All three judges – Kennedy CJ, Fitzgibbon J and Murnaghan J – made reference to the repugnancy clause and treated it as if it still had legal effect.[140] If the validity of the Constitution (Removal of Oath) Act 1933 had ever been successfully challenged in the Irish courts the results would have been catastrophic. All of the subsequent constitutional reforms dismantling the settlement imposed by the Treaty would have fallen like dominos since they were all reliant on the removal of the repugnancy clause.

Ironically, the enactment of the Statute of Westminster ensured that the contention that the 1922 constitution had been created by British legislation and not the Irish constituent assembly offered greater autonomy to the Irish Free State. A challenge to de Valera's constitutional amendments, including the removal of the repugnancy clause, would be rejected in 1935 by the judicial committee of the privy council in *Moore v. Attorney General*.[141] The petitioners tried to use the decision in *State (Ryan) v. Lennon* to challenge the removal of the repugnancy clause but the court in London could not accept the argument that the constitution of the Irish Free State had been created by an Irish constituent assembly. It insisted that the constitution had been created by an imperial statute which could now be amended by a Dominion legislature as a result of the reforms ushered in by the Statute of Westminster. The argument that the Oireachtas had only purported to act under Irish law and not under the Statute of Westminster was also rejected. The privy council held that the actions of the Oireachtas must 'be deemed to have been done in the way in which alone it could legally be done, that is by virtue of the powers given by the Statute [of Westminster]'.[142] The privy council summarized its judgment by concluding:

> The simplest way of stating the situation is to say that the Statute of Westminster gave to the Irish Free State a power under which they could abrogate the Treaty, and that, as a matter of law, they have availed themselves of that power.[143]

It was now confirmed that a British theory of origin for the 1922 constitution offered more autonomy than an Irish one. However, de Valera proved reluctant to make use of this precedent. It is worth repeating de Valera's

139 Ibid., at 227.
140 Ibid., at 205, 226, 241.
141 [1935] IR 472 and [1935] AC 484.
142 [1935] IR 472 at 486 and [1935] AC 484 at 498.
143 [1935] IR 472 at 486–7 and [1935] AC 484 at 499.

declaration made in 1932 that 'we cannot admit, and we have never freely admitted, that our right to sovereign independence is derived from a British statute'.[144]

Reliance on an Irish origin for the 1922 constitution, as interpreted by the Irish supreme court in *State (Ryan) v. Lennon*, created serious challenges for the Irish government. The need to protect the removal of the repugnancy clause and all subsequent constitutional reforms from legal challenge gave de Valera a powerful incentive to usher in a new constitutional order in 1937. Some commentators even argue that the resurrection of the spectre of the repugnancy clause was the primary reason behind the creation of the Irish constitution of 1937.[145]

WHY DID THE OATH OVERSHADOW THE REPUGNANCY CLAUSE IN THE 1930S?

The oath proved to be one of the most controversial provisions of the Treaty and was widely blamed as a major cause of the Irish Civil War. In the years that followed it was one of the most important reasons behind the refusal of opponents of the Treaty to enter the Oireachtas. The abolition of the oath remained at the top of Fianna Fáil's political agenda after its abandonment of abstentionism. When that party formed a government in March 1932, its very first legislative initiative focused on abolishing the oath. The reaction in London to the proposed constitutional amendment was almost completely dominated by the oath. McMahon concludes 'In abolishing the oath, de Valera had chosen a symbol calculated to excite maximum alarm in Britain'.[146] It was not until April 1932, with the publication of the Constitution (Removal of Oath) Bill that the British government learned that Dublin was also aiming at the abolition of the repugnancy clause and the related provisions of Article 50 of the constitution. By this time, the debate in Ireland and beyond had long since crystallized as one focused on the parliamentary oath.

As contemporaries pointed out, the very title of the legislation containing relevant amendments, 'Constitution (Removal of Oath) Act 1933', obscured the removal of the repugnancy clause.[147] John Hearne's 1931 analysis as to the possibility of removing the constitutional provisions giving legal supremacy

144 *Irish Press*, 11 Apr. 1932.

145 E.g., see G. Quinn, 'Dangerous constitutional moments: the "tactic of legality" in Nazi Germany and the Irish Free State compared' in J. Morison, K. McEvoy and G. Anthony (eds), *Judges, transition and human rights* (Oxford, 2007), p. 224; Hogan, *The origins of the Irish constitution*, pp 101–13; and D.K. Coffey, 'The need for a new constitution: Irish constitutional change 1932–1935', *Irish Jurist*, 48 (2012), 275.

146 McMahon, *Republicans and imperialists*, p. 289.

147 *Dáil Éireann deb.*, vol. 41, cols 745–6 (28 Apr. 1932). See also *Seanad Éireann deb.*, vol. 15, col. 982 (8 June 1932).

to the Treaty had stressed that such important reforms would have to appear in a separate statute to other constitutional amendments.[148] This advice was ignored during the drafting of the constitution (removal of oath) bill. It is worth noting that such tactics would be forbidden under Article 46.4 of de Valera's 1937 constitution, which provides that 'A Bill containing a proposal or proposals for the amendment of this constitution shall not contain any other proposal'.

The repugnancy clause, a long and technical legal provision, could never hope to compete with the more accessible and highly emotive debate on the oath. It was also hampered by the reality that it lacked a single accessible name used in popular discourse. The term 'repugnancy clause' was created by Leo Kohn, a German scholar who wrote a major work on the Free State constitution in 1932. Its official name in Ireland was section 2 of the Constitution of the Irish Free State (Saorstát Éireann) Act 1922 while in the United Kingdom it was the preamble to the Irish Free State Constitution Act 1922 (Session 2). These lengthy and technical names were hardly accessible and the situation was made worse by the position that alternative short names were occasionally used such as the 'overhead clause'[149] and the 'preliminary clause'.[150] If this provision had been known by a single accessible name its removal could not have been so easily dismissed as a mere appendage to the provisions relating to the oath

CONCLUSION

The removal of the oath dominated Irish political debate in the early 1930s. Yet, it was the removal of the repugnancy clause that facilitated the programme of constitutional change over the course of that decade. The settlement imposed by the Treaty was dismantled piece by piece. Constitutional amendments reducing the powers of the governor general and abolishing the Irish appeal to the judicial committee of the privy council were passed in 1933.[151] The abdication of King Edward VIII provided de Valera with the opportunity to enact Constitution (Amendment No. 27) Act 1936 which sought to remove the king from any role in the internal affairs of the Irish Free State. This amendment also abolished the office of governor-general and removed the power of reservation, a delaying measure that could

148 J. Hearne to S. Murphy, 27 May 1931, and Constitution (Amendment No. 19) Bill, 1931, NAI DFA 3/1.

149 This was the term that was often used by British governments. See *Hansard's Parl. deb., 5th series* (commons), vol. 60, col. 109 (30 Nov. 1922).

150 It was usually called the 'preliminary clause' in the constituent assembly. See *Dáil Éireann deb.*, vol. 1, cols 1174–5 (4 Oct. 1922).

151 Constitution (Amendment No. 20) Act 1933, Constitution (Amendment No. 21) Act 1933 and Constitution (Amendment No. 22) Act 1933.

ultimately prevent a bill passed by the Oireachtas from coming into force. The abolition of the Seanad effected by Constitution (Amendment No. 24) Act 1936 was not strictly concerned with the provisions of the Treaty. Nevertheless, it removed a concession to the southern Protestant community promised by Arthur Griffith one day after the Treaty was signed. The most radical step was the replacement of the 1922 constitution with the current Irish constitution of 1937. This came into force on 29 December 1937 in the aftermath of a plebiscite. The defence provisions imposed by the Treaty settlement were removed by British-Irish agreements completed in 1938.[152] These agreements included the handover of the 'Treaty ports' of Berehaven, Cobh and Lough Swilly. The Irish state would formally become a republic on Easter Sunday 1949.[153]

The importance of the parliamentary oath, enshrined in the Treaty and the 1922 constitution, in the early history of the Irish state cannot be contested. It provided a rallying cry for opponents of the Treaty before and after the outbreak of Civil War. Leo Kohn concludes that 'No provision of the constitution has more deeply influenced the course of the parliamentary history of the Free State'.[154] It proved to be an important obstacle in preventing the largest opposition party from taking its seats in the Oireachtas during the first precarious years in the life of the Irish state. The removal of the oath in the 1930s attracted media attention on a global level.

Yet, important as the oath was, it should not be allowed to overshadow the significance of the repugnancy clause in Irish history. The existence and removal of the repugnancy clause never received a level of public attention comparable to the oath. This position was only reversed in the courts where the importance of the repugnancy clause could not be denied. The repugnancy clause was the lynchpin of the Treaty settlement and profoundly influenced the early years of the self-governing Irish state. Its removal facilitated the dismantling of the settlement imposed by the Treaty. This paved the way for the emergence of a new constitutional order which remains in force to this day.

152 The removal of the defence provisions of the Treaty were reflected in a British statute. This was the Éire (Confirmation of Agreements) Act 1938. In 1942 the British courts denied that this legislation constituted British recognition of the secession of 'Éire' from the commonwealth. *Murray v. Parkes* [1942] 2 KB 123. No equivalent provision was ever enacted in Irish legislation. While the trade and financial agreements were given statutory force in Ireland by the Finance (Agreement with the United Kingdom) Act 1938 and Agreement with United Kingdom (Capital Sum) Act 1938, the defence agreement only received recognition by a motion of approval passed by the Dáil. *Dáil Éireann deb.*, vol. 71, col. 456 (29 Apr. 1938).

153 Republic of Ireland Act 1948 and Republic of Ireland Act 1948 (Commencement) Order 1949, S.I. No. 27/1949.

154 Kohn, *Constitution of the Irish Free State*, p. 218.

The asinine law: Irish legal cartoons

FELIX M. LARKIN*

There is a rich history of cartooning in Ireland, and cartoons fit comfortably into what Vivian Mercier called the 'Irish comic tradition'. Mercier argued that this tradition is the central one of Irish and Anglo-Irish literature, and can be traced back to oral Gaelic roots in the ninth century. He identified the elements of this tradition as 'a bent for wild humour, a delight in witty word play, and a tendency to regard satire as one of the indispensable functions of the literary man'.[1]

Satire, whether in literary form or in cartoons, is generally associated with anti-establishment sentiment. It usually 'punches up', a weapon of the powerless against dominant groups and people.[2] Accordingly, lawyers and the law are obvious targets – and they have featured prominently in cartoons everywhere. The arcane and archaic rituals of the law invite ridicule, and so too does the showy – sometimes bombastic – style of many of its successful practitioners. Moreover, the fact that the law often has what seems – at least to an outsider – perverse outcomes makes it fair game for satire, laughter being a way of bridging the gap between common sense and the peculiar logic of the law. In this regard, the British humorist, J.B. Morton – better known as 'Beachcomber' – wrote that 'justice must not only be seen to be done; it must be seen to be believed'.[3]

It is the perverse outcomes of the law that give rise to the expression 'the law is an ass', famously associated with Charles Dickens. When, in *Oliver Twist*, a particular aspect of law is explained to Mr Bumble, he responds as

* The revised text of the thirty-first 'Hugh M. Fitzpatrick lecture in legal bibliography' delivered in the library of the Royal Dublin Society on 11 Nov. 2015. Shorter versions of this discourse were given at the Daniel O'Connell Summer School in Derrynane House, Cahirdaniel, Co. Kerry, on 28 Oct. 2022 and at the national meeting of the American Conference for Irish Studies in San José State University, California, on 8 June 2023. Many people have helped me gather the cartoons that I consider in this chapter, but I would like to acknowledge in particular the assistance of Mary Broderick in the National Library of Ireland. A special word of thanks goes to Martyn Turner for agreeing to let me reproduce so many of his cartoons.

1 V. Mercier, *The Irish comic tradition* (Oxford, 1962), p. ix.

2 See F.M. Larkin, 'Satirical journalism' in M. Conboy and A. Bingham (eds), *The Edinburgh history of the British and Irish press*, vol. iii: *competition and disruption, 1900–2017* (Edinburgh, 2020), pp 556–7.

3 R. Irving, *'The law is a ass': an illustrated anthology of legal quotations* (London, 2010), p. 17.

16.1 Ernest Kavanagh, 'The assinine law', *Irish Worker*, 14 Sept. 1912

follows: 'If the law supposes that … the law is a ass – a idiot [*sic*].'[4] A cartoon published in 1912 in the *Irish Worker*, the organ of the Irish Transport and General Workers' Union (ITGWU), illustrates the point (Figure 16.1). It shows a donkey dressed as a judge, administering 'law by the classes for the masses'. It is by Ernest Kavanagh, an insurance clerk employed by the ITGWU who moonlighted as a cartoonist. Tragically, he was shot dead on the front steps of Liberty Hall by a military sniper on Easter Tuesday 1916. What he was doing there is unclear, but he was definitely not a combatant in the Rising and may simply have been attempting – naïvely – to go to work.[5] The title of his cartoon is 'The assinine law' – with two Ss, just to ram home the

4 C. Dickens, *Oliver Twist* (1838), ch. 51. The remark, 'I am ashamed the law is such an ass', had earlier appeared in George Chapman's play *Revenge for honour* (1654), act 3, sc. 2.

5 J. Curry, *Artist of the revolution: the cartoons of Ernest Kavanagh, 1884–1916* (Cork, 2012). 'The assinine law' cartoon was published in the *Irish Worker*, 14 Sept. 1912.

16.1 Henry Brocas (?), 'The master of the scrolls', caricature of John Philpot Curran, 1809

16.2 Henry Brocas (?), 'A view of the Four Courts', with the four separate courts represented by the appropriate judicial figures in caricature (n.d. but likely between 1809 and 1822)

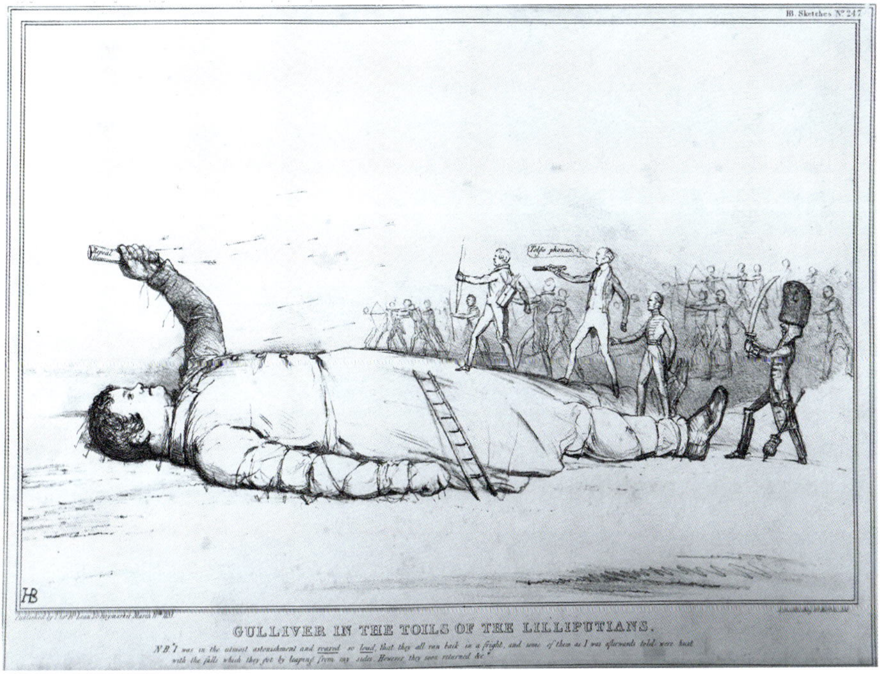

16.3 John Doyle ('HB'), 'Gulliver in the toils of the Lilliputians', caricature of Daniel O'Connell and others, 1833

16.4 William Sadler, 'Court in session at Ballyragget, Co. Kilkenny', *c.*1867 (NLI PD 3176 TX 29)

16.5 John Fergus O'Hea, 'What villains have done this?', *Weekly Freeman*, 13 May 1882

16.6 'Portraits of the counsel for the traversers in the State prosecutions of the Land League', *Weekly Freeman*, 1 Jan. 1881

16.7 'Justice unal(l)oyd', *Weekly Freeman*, 16 July 1881

16.8 'Direland in 1982: a peep into the future', *Pat*, 28 Jan. 1882

16.9 'The monkey and the cheese', *Pat*, 30 Apr. 1881

16.10 John Fergus O'Hea ('Spex'), 'Law-less state of the country', *Weekly Freeman*, 22 Mar. 1884

16.11 John Fergus O'Hea, 'The most noble', caricature of the marquess of Clanricarde, *Weekly Freeman*, 17 Dec. 1887

16.12 John D. Reigh, 'The consecration of Kilmainham jail: the two archbishops bless Father Keller and his prison', *United Ireland*, 26 Mar. 1887

16.13 John D. Reigh, 'The bumptious pigmy and the contemptuous giant', ridiculing the cross-examination of Parnell at the Special Commission, *United Ireland*, 11 May 1889

16.14 'Verdict and sentence', the cartoonist's 'verdict and sentence' on the London *Times* in the aftermath of the Report of the Special Commission, *Weekly Freeman*, 22 Feb. 1890

16.15 Leslie Ward ('Spy'), 'Richard Pigott', *Vanity Fair*, 9 Mar. 1889

16.16 John Page Mellor ('Quiz'), 'Cross examination', caricature of Charles Russell, *Vanity Fair*, 29 Mar. 1890

16.17 Leslie Ward ('Spy'), 'South Donegal', caricature of J.G. Swift MacNeill, *Vanity Fair*, 13 Mar. 1902

16.18 Leslie Ward ('Spy'), 'The Rt. Hon. James', caricature of James Campbell (later Lord Glenavy), *Vanity Fair*, 25 Aug. 1909

16.19 Liborio Prosperi ('Lib'), 'Dublin University', caricature of Edward Carson, *Vanity Fair*, 9 Nov. 1893

16.20 Alick P.F. Ritchie, 'Rt Hon. Lord Carson', cigarette card, 1926, NPG D2660

16.21 Ernest Forbes ('Shemus'), 'The Carson kids', caricature of Edward Carson with Lloyd George and Sir Hamar Greenwood, *Freeman's Journal*, 18 Nov. 1920

16.22 C.E. Kelly, 'So perhaps if you'd call back later …', caricature of Éamon de Valera with the ghost of Robert Emmet, *Dublin Opinion*, Apr. 1937

"When my country takes her place amongst the nations of the Six, then, and not till then, let her epitaph be written."

16.23 C.E. Kelly, caricature of Taoiseach Jack Lynch with the ghost of Robert Emmet, *Dublin Opinion*, July 1967

16.24 C.E. Kelly, 'A dream of fair women', with Queen Maeve and Granuaile attacking de Valera about the 1937 constitution, *Dublin Opinion*, June 1937

16.25 Martyn Turner, 'The law is a Pass machine', *Irish Times*, 13 Nov. 2013

16.26 Martyn Turner, 'A sad history of Ireland in four phrases', *Irish Times*, 23 Nov. 2012

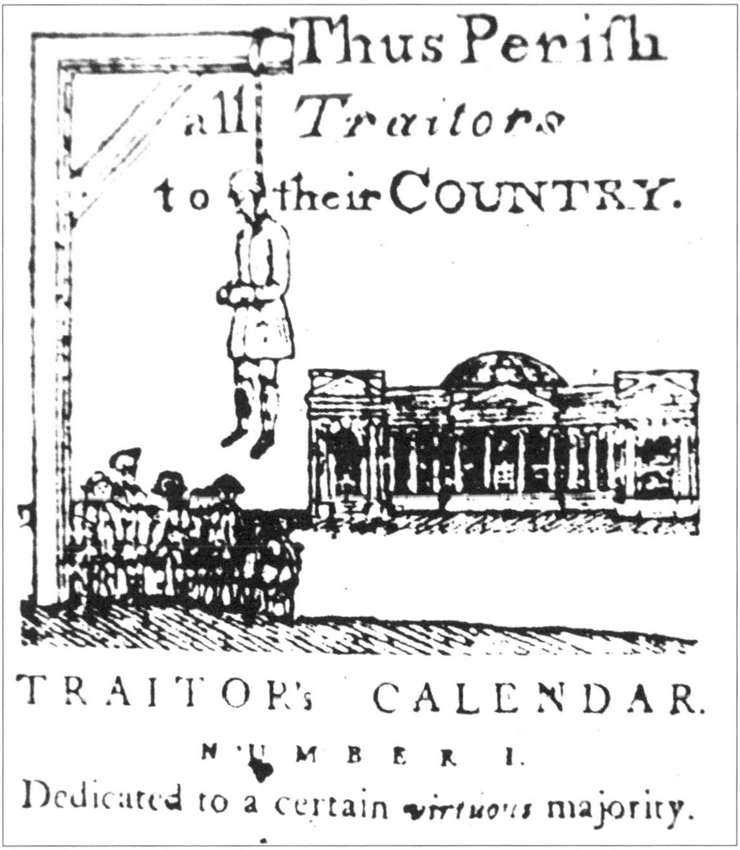

16.2 'Thus perish all traitors to their country', *Volunteer's Journal*, 5 Apr. 1784

message. I have appropriated that title for this chapter, but – pedant that I am – I have dropped the superfluous second S.

My purpose in this chapter is to examine how the law and lawyers have been depicted in a representative selection of Irish cartoons over more than two centuries. I am not concerned with the legal constraints within which Irish cartoonists have pursued their quirky craft, other than to note that there are such constraints – most obviously, the law of libel. Thus, for example, a cartoon by Martyn Turner – the resident cartoonist in the *Irish Times* since 1976 – on the occasion of Charles Haughey's resignation as taoiseach in 1992 was not published at that time because it was considered libellous by the newspaper's lawyers; its theme was Haughey's accumulation of wealth during his years in public office.[6]

6 M. Turner, *Turner's taoisigh: my brush with Kildare Street* (Dublin, 2014), p. 21. Later in 1992 the *Irish Times* also rejected a cartoon by Turner about Bishop Eamonn Casey after it was

One of the very first satirical cartoons published in Ireland likewise fell afoul of the law and the result was the imprisonment of the editor of the newspaper in which it appeared, the *Volunteer's Journal*. The editor was Mathew Carey, and he published the offending cartoon (Figure 16.2) on 5 April 1784 – and again in the next two issues of the newspaper. Entitled 'Thus perish all traitors to their country', the target of the cartoon was John Foster, then acting chancellor of the exchequer – but soon to be appointed chancellor – in the Irish parliament at College Green, which is seen in the background. Foster was variously referred to in these issues of the *Journal* as 'Jacky Finance' and 'Jack the Bloodsucker'.[7] He was later the last speaker of the Irish parliament before the Union of 1801.[8] Carey was arraigned before the Irish House of Commons on account of this cartoon and held for a time in Newgate prison in Dublin. On his release, but with a libel case still pending against him, he fled to America and had a highly successful career as a publisher in Philadelphia.[9]

Among the most prominent lawyers in Ireland in the 1780s and for some time afterwards was John Philpot Curran, whose daughter Sarah was the inamorata of Robert Emmet. He served as Irish master of the rolls from 1806 to 1814. In that capacity – though re-imagined as 'The master of the scrolls' – he was caricatured in the cartoon at Plate 16.1. Note that the scrolls in his pouch include petitions, affidavits, briefs, etc. The cartoon is thought to date from 1809.

A roughly contemporaneous cartoon is 'A view of the Four Courts' (Plate 13.2), with the Four Courts represented by appropriate judicial figures of the period in caricature: William Downes, first Baron Downes and chief justice of the king's bench, 1803–21; Thomas Manners-Sutton, first Baron Manners and lord chancellor, 1807–27; John Toler, first earl of Norbury and chief justice of the court of common pleas, 1800–27; and Standish O'Grady, first Viscount Guillamore and chief baron of the exchequer, 1805–31. There is an image of Gandon's Four Courts building in the background, and also a copy of the cartoon of Curran as 'The master of the scrolls'. A cartoon within a cartoon is indeed a rarity.

revealed that the bishop had fathered a child; but, to quote Turner, 'it was kept out of the paper on the question of taste' – not on legal considerations. *Irish Times*, 11 June 2011; see also M. O'Brien, *The* Irish Times*: a history* (Dublin, 2008), p. 246.

7 *Volunteer's Journal*, 5, 7, 9 Apr. 1784.

8 The Union had effect from 1 Jan. 1801 under parallel acts of the British and Irish parliaments, both entitled An Act for the Union of Great Britain and Ireland (39 & 40 Geo. III, c. 67 and 40 Geo. III, c. 38).

9 J. Archbold and S. Kleinman, 'Mathew Carey' in *DIB*. For Carey's career in America, see also D. Reddin van Tuyll, 'Seditionists and revolutionaries: planting the radical roots of the Irish American press during the "reign of witches"' in D. Reddin van Tuyll, M. O'Brien and M. Broersma (eds), *Politics, culture and the Irish American press, 1784–1963* (Syracuse, New York, 2021), pp 7–11.

These two cartoons – 'The master of the scrolls' and 'A view of the Four Courts' – are attributed to 'a member [not specified] of the Brocas family' in the catalogue of the National Library of Ireland.[10] They were published and sold as single sheets – artefacts in their own right, as distinct from a feature in or a supplement to newspapers. As Kelly has observed, such single-sheet cartoons were produced in small editions in Ireland in the late eighteenth and early nineteenth centuries: 'engraved from original drawings, then etched, printed and hand-coloured'. Since they were hand-coloured, each one was unique in its own way. They ranged in price from 5*d*. to as much as 6*s*. They are, in Kelly's words, an 'overlooked dimension of Irish visual culture'.[11]

Daniel O'Connell is acknowledged as the greatest Irish lawyer of the early nineteenth century, and perhaps the greatest in Irish history.[12] He was the focus of innumerable cartoons produced in Dublin and in London, most of them hostile and savagely anti-Catholic. Many were by John Doyle, the most notable caricaturist of the early nineteenth century. He was a Catholic Irishman, but plied his trade exclusively in London. His medium was the single-sheet cartoon, for which there was still a vibrant market in London until the advent of the comic periodical in the 1840s.[13] Gray has written that Doyle was 'preoccupied with Daniel O'Connell' and that O'Connell's career 'appeared to Doyle to embody a demagogic combination of radicalism, nationalism and Catholic grievance politics'.[14] One of Doyle's cleverest cartoons about O'Connell, published in London in March 1833, shows him as Gulliver brandishing a scroll bearing the word REPEAL – shorthand for his demand for repeal of the Union – and being restrained and attacked ineffectively by his political opponents, who are dismissed as Lilliputians (Plate 16.3). The inspiration for this cartoon was Swift's *Gulliver's travels*. In *Gulliver's travels*, one of the Lilliputians shouts out the phrase 'Tolgo Phonac' – whatever that means in the Lilliputian language – after which all the Lilliputians start firing arrows at Gulliver.[15] In the cartoon, the phrase is

10 If the attribution is correct, the artist is probably Henry Brocas *père* (1762/5–1837).

11 J. Kelly, 'Satirical fun: Irish single-sheet caricature in the late 18th and early 19th centuries', lecture given at the John J. Burns Library, Boston College, 17 Mar. 2022.

12 See P.M. Geoghegan, 'Daniel O'Connell and the law' in F.M. Larkin and N.M. Dawson (eds), *Lawyers, the law and history* (Dublin, 2013), p. 83. Geoghegan quotes the opinion of former Irish supreme court judge Hugh O'Flaherty that O'Connell was the greatest lawyer in Irish history.

13 Regarding single-sheet cartoons published in London from the 1780s to *c.*1820, see A. Loxton, *Uproar: satire, scandal and printmakers in Georgian London* (London, 2023). See also N.K. Robinson, *Caricature and the Irish: satirical prints from the Library of Trinity College Dublin,* c.*1780–1830* (Dublin, 2024).

14 P. Gray, 'HB's Famine cartoons: satirical art in a time of catastrophe' in M. Corporaal, O. Frawley and E. Mark-Fitzgerald (eds), *The Great Irish Famine: visual and material culture* (Liverpool, 2018), p. 37. See also F. Cullen, 'Visual parody and political commentary: John Doyle and Daniel O'Connell' in Ciaran O'Neill (ed.), *Irish elites in the nineteenth century* (Dublin, 2013).

15 J. Swift, *Gulliver's travels* (1726), part 1, ch. 1.

16.3 John Leech, 'The O'Connell rent', *Punch*, vol. 18 (1845)

attributed to Earl Grey, the British prime minister – and the arrows are directed towards the REPEAL scroll held by O'Connell. Other identifiable Lilliputians include the chief secretary for Ireland, Edward Stanley, later the earl of Derby, and the lord lieutenant, the marquess of Anglesey.

Punch, the 'quintessential Victorian comic periodical' launched in 1841, carried many cartoons about O'Connell in its early years.[16] The best of them – because of the detailed illustrations in its border – is 'The O'Connell rent', the derogatory term for the subscriptions raised from the public for O'Connell's Repeal Association (Figure 16.3). It is by John Leech and was published in *Punch* in 1845. The main image shows abject and deferential peasants paying the so-called rent to the great man. This is a pretty crude caricature – unlike the wonderfully whimsical drawings of incidents in O'Connell's life that appear in the border. The upper border shows the military presence at Clontarf to prevent the 'monster meeting' there that O'Connell cancelled at the last moment in 1843, and this is juxtaposed against a police 'assault on gingerbread stands' – presumably, hawkers plying for business on the margins of the 'monster meeting'. Thus is the abandoned 'monster meeting' trivialized. The lower border focuses on the trial of O'Connell and others in 1844 for conspiracy against the state: O'Connell is

16 M. de Nie, 'Satirical journalism' in D. Finkelstein (ed.), *The Edinburgh history of the British and Irish press*, vol. ii*: expansion and evolution, 1800–1900* (Edinburgh, 2020), p. 421.

16.4 John Tenniel, 'The Irish Frankenstein', *Punch*, 20 May 1882

in the dock, the presiding judges are opposite him, and in between there is an incident involving duelling pistols – a not-too-subtle allusion to the duel in 1815 between O'Connell and John D'Esterre, in which D'Esterre was killed. At either end of the lower border, the prime minister, Robert Peel, and the duke of Wellington, a leading member of Peel's government, keep an eye on what is going on. Similar items appear in the side borders: for example, 'King Dan' being crowned at the 'monster meeting' held at Tara and an impish O'Connell in a carriage going to his trial.

The respect for O'Connell in the memory of his fellow-countrymen is revealed in a delightful cartoon print of a petty sessions court in Ballyragget, Co. Kilkenny, dated *c.*1867 (Plate 16.4).[17] Note O'Connell's bust high up on the wall, apparently overseeing the proceedings. Petty sessions were relatively informal affairs, presided over by a justice of the peace who often had no legal training. This is a case of assault, probably a trivial matter: the plaintiff's head is bandaged, and he is pointing out his assailant.

John Leech – the artist of 'The O'Connell rent' – and other *Punch* cartoonists, notably Henry Furniss and John Tenniel, are notorious today for their 'siminianization' of the Irish. Curtis wrote about 'the steady stream of derogatory or denigrating stereotypes emanating from London [in the late

17 NLI PD 3176 TX 29, attributed to William Sadler.

16.5 'Persons and places associated with the Phoenix Park assassination trial', *Weekly Freeman*, 2 June 1883

nineteenth century] – mostly vividly expressed by the cartoonists' transformation of militant Irish nationalists, especially Fenian or republican rebels, into apelike or bestial creatures'.[18] Curiously, both Leech and Furniss had strong Irish connections: Leech was of Irish extraction, and Furniss was born in Wexford – albeit of English parents – and had begun his career with the Irish satirical magazine, *Zozimus*. One of the worst, but also best known, of *Punch*'s offensive cartoons is John Tenniel's 'Irish Frankenstein' (Figure 16.4), which appeared shortly after the Phoenix Park murders in 1882 – the killing of Lord Frederick Cavendish, the chief secretary for Ireland, and his principal civil servant, Thomas Burke, by the Invincibles, an extremist Fenian society. This loathsome crime shocked British public opinion and must have seemed to confirm the image of the Irish as lawless monsters as depicted in the cartoons of Leech, Furniss and Tenniel.[19]

18 L.P. Curtis Jr, *Images of Erin in the age of Parnell* (Dublin, 2000), p. 8.

19 See L.P. Curtis Jr, *Apes and angels: the Irishman in Victorian caricatures* (Newton Abbot, 1971), pp 38, 43. This was a truly pioneering study: nobody before Curtis had made use of cartoons as a source for Irish history.

A cartoon published by the *Weekly Freeman* in June 1883 provides an extraordinary panorama of the chief actors in the Phoenix Park murders (Figure 16.5).[20] Centre stage is the murder scene in the Phoenix Park, with the instruments the Invincibles used to kill Cavendish and Burke – long surgical knives – on display. Among the *dramatis personae* are the six Invincibles who were condemned to death for the murders. One, Patrick Delaney, had his sentence commuted to penal servitude for life, but the other five were hanged. They are shown at the bottom of the cartoon. Within the archway is the executioner, William Marwood, carrying the bag containing the rope that he would use for his grim task. Until 1888, the hangman supplied the rope himself; subsequently, it was the prison service that supplied it.[21]

John Fergus O'Hea's cartoon 'What villains have done this?' (Plate 16.5), published by the *Weekly Freeman* in response to the Phoenix Park murders, is in stark contrast to Tenniel's 'Irish Frankenstein'.[22] It features the female figure of Erin decrying the murders, and this clearly reflected majority Irish nationalist opinion. The *Freeman's Journal* was the principal nationalist daily newspaper published in Dublin in the second half of the nineteenth century. Its weekly compendium edition – the *Weekly Freeman* – began publishing cartoons such as this in 1880, thus introducing a satirical note into the newspaper press in Ireland for the first time. Printed as chromolithographs using up to four or five colours, they were given away with the newspaper as supplements. These cartoons addressed political themes with great immediacy, and the fact that they were in colour added greatly to their impact. They were duly copied by other Irish newspapers – notably, *United Ireland*. The aforementioned John Fergus O'Hea was the principal artist of the *Weekly Freeman* cartoons until 1891. He was then succeeded by his protégé, Thomas Fitzpatrick. The principal cartoonist of *United Ireland* was John D. Reigh.[23]

The cartoons in the *Weekly Freeman* and *United Ireland* document the land war of the 1880s, and are still often reproduced today in studies of that period.[24] A good example is one published by the *Weekly Freeman* on 1 January 1881 in tribute to the lawyers who defended the leaders of the Land League being prosecuted at that time for seditious conspiracy (Plate 16.6). It is unusual for a cartoon about lawyers to adopt a positive, or even neutral, tone; this cartoon is worthy of note for that reason. The lawyers depicted in

20 *Weekly Freeman*, 2 June 1883.

21 This change was introduced following the report of the Aberdare committee on the arrangements for executions by hanging.

22 *Weekly Freeman*, 13 May 1882. It pre-dated Tenniel's 'Irish Frankenstein', published in *Punch*, 20 May 1882.

23 For an overview of the work of these artists, see Curtis, *Images of Erin*. See also F.M. Larkin, 'Icons of freedom: the work of John Fergus O'Hea', *Irish Arts Review*, 39:2 (Summer 2022), 106.

24 Curtis makes good use of one such cartoon in his chapter in this volume, 'Exploring the dynamic of the Irish land war, 1879–90' (see p. 130 and Plate 6.3).

the cartoon include A.M. Sullivan, Richard Adams and Peter O'Brien. O'Brien was, in fact, defending A.M. Sullivan's brother, T.D. Sullivan – but his political sympathies were not with the Land League or with Home Rule. He went on to become a notorious crown prosecutor, known as 'Peter the Packer' because of his skill in securing 'packed' juries to guarantee convictions. He was later attorney general for Ireland and lord chief justice. The Sullivan brothers were successively owners of the *Nation* newspaper between 1858 and 1890. Richard Adams had been a leader-writer on the *Freeman's Journal* before his career at the bar flourished. He is mentioned in the 'Aeolus' episode of *Ulysses*, which is set in the *Freeman*'s offices – lauded as 'the besthearted bloody Corkman the Lord ever put the breath of life in'.[25] He later became a county court judge.

The Ladies Land League is an important part of the story of the land war, and they too were prosecuted – as evidenced by a cartoon in the *Weekly Freeman* in July 1881 (Plate 16.7). It is a scene from Kilmallock petty sessions, and the presiding resident magistrate was a Major Clifford Lloyd, hence the title of the cartoon 'Justice unal(l)oyed'.[26]

Gladstone's second land act – the Land Law (Ireland) Act 1881[27] – was an attempt to address some of the concerns of the Land League. It gave power to civil bill courts to fix rents (termed 'judicial rents'), with provision for referral to a Land Commission to appeal the judicial rents.[28] The act was seen as creating endless possibilities for legal wrangling – a 'cash cow' for lawyers. Accordingly, the Irish satirical magazine *Pat* in January 1882 looked into the future with a cartoon of Ireland a hundred years later, with the lawyers so rich that they have displaced the old landlords as proprietors of the land and are sitting comfortably on their rents (Plate 16.8). The Atlantic Ocean has become the AT-LAW-NTIC, and St George's Channel the GORGE-ON-US Channel – and Ireland is DIRELAND. The same idea is suggested in another *Pat* cartoon, published in 1881 before the land act became law, about a dispute between two cats, representing a landlord and his tenant (Plate 16.9). It is the legal monkey who devours the spoils.

It seems, however, that remarkably little crime came before the courts in Ireland in the 1880s – as noted in a *Pat* cartoon dated 29 July 1880 (Figure 16.6). The judges are putting on white gloves – the convention being that, when there were no cases to be tried by jury, the judge was presented

25 J. Joyce, *Ulysses*, ed. H.W. Gabler (London, 2008), ch. 7, lines 679–80.

26 Regarding the Ladies Land League, see M. Ward, '"Short skirts and strong boots": the pioneering feminism of Anna Parnell' in A. Parnell, *The tale of a great sham*, ed. D. Hearne (Dublin, 2020), pp xi–xxx. See also D. Urquhart, '"We have found a better way, boys": Anna and Fanny Parnell' in S. Fitzpatrick and M. O'Dowd (eds), *Sisters: nine families of sisters who made a difference* (Dublin, 2022).

27 44 & 45 Vict. c., 46.

28 See P. Bull, *Land, politics and nationalism: a study of the Irish land question* (Dublin, 1996), pp 88–91, 196.

16.6 Unsigned, 'Crime in Ireland', *Pat*, 29 July 1880

with a pair of white gloves. The lawyers are crying because of the loss of business. The caption includes the words: 'English papers please copy'. Likewise, in 1884 a *Weekly Freeman* cartoon mocked the plight of lawyers without work: one of them – a skeletal figure – claims that he 'was once as round as a tub' (Plate 16.10).[29]

The land war entered its second phase – the so-called Plan of Campaign – in late 1886. The first two estates to join the Plan were the Ponsonby estate, near Youghal, in Co. Cork, and the Clanricarde estate in Woodford, Co. Galway.[30] Both were very bitter struggles, and a hard-hitting cartoon in the *Weekly Freeman* depicted the marquess of Clanricarde in shades of black and with devil's horns, undergoing a mock trial for his actions to defeat the Plan on his estate (Plate 16.11). His lawyer asks: 'Is my client as black as he is painted?' – and the jurors reply: 'Yes, blacker!' The caption to the cartoon

29 This cartoon is signed 'Spex', a pseudonym sometimes used by John Fergus O'Hea. O'Hea had drawn a number of caricatures of eminent legal personages for *Ireland's Eye*, a satirical magazine briefly published in Dublin in the 1870s. I am grateful to the late Professor Chris Williams for bringing O'Hea's *Ireland's Eye* caricatures to my attention, though I have not included any of them here.

30 The outworking of the Plan on another estate, the Headfort estate, is discussed in Marshall's chapter in this collection, 'Lisnafana: a townland in crisis on the Headfort Cavan estate, 1879–95'.

16.7 Thomas Fitzpatrick, 'Rival washer women', *The Lepracaun*, Mar. 1909

refers to Clanricarde as the 'Marquis of Clanrackrent'. The Plan of Campaign on the Ponsonby estate gave rise to a real court drama when the parish priest of Youghal, Fr Keller, was summoned to appear as a witness in a Dublin court seeking to locate the money paid into a fund by the tenants in lieu of the rent payable to their landlord. The fund was intended to support any tenant evicted for non-payment of rent. Fr Keller was thought to be the trustee of the fund, but in court he refused to answer any questions and was jailed for contempt. A cartoon in the *United Ireland* newspaper in March 1887 shows him in priestly garb about to enter Kilmainham jail (Plate 16.12) and accompanied to the prison door by Archbishops Walsh of Dublin and Croke of Cashel – symbolizing that he had the full support of his ecclesiastical superiors in Ireland. The distinctive tympanum of entwined serpents above the door of Kilmainham jail is faithfully reproduced. Fr Keller's fate became a great *cause célèbre*, and he was unconditionally released after three months.[31]

31 See F.M. Larkin, 'Canon Keller of Youghal' in B. Casey, *Defying the law of the land: agrarian radicals in Irish history* (Dublin, 2013), pp 154–63. See also D. Hogan and P. Maume (eds), *The reminiscences of Ignatius O'Brien, lord chancellor of Ireland, 1913–18* (Dublin, 2021), pp 167–71.

Plate 16.13 is how the *United Ireland* newspaper represented Parnell's cross-examination at the Special Commission established by statute in 1888 to inquire into the charges made by the London *Times* newspaper against him in a series of articles entitled 'Parnellism and crime'.[32] Parnell is a 'contemptuous giant', while his interrogator – wielding a sword marked 'cross-examination' – is a 'bumptious pigmy'. Ultimately, when the Special Commission issued its report, which largely exonerated Parnell and his followers, it was the *Times* that found itself, metaphorically, in the dock – as in a cartoon in the *Weekly Freeman* on 22 February 1890 (Plate 16.14). The sentence being handed down by the judges is that 'you shall be held in odium and contempt for the rest of your natural life'.[33]

The star witness against Parnell at the Commission, Richard Pigott, was the subject of a wonderful *Vanity Fair* cartoon in March 1889 (Plate 16.15). It is by Sir Leslie Ward, the greatest and most prolific of the *Vanity Fair* cartoonists, who used the pseudonym 'Spy'. Sir Charles Russell, the leading counsel for Parnell – under whose cross examination Pigott was exposed as the forger of the letters presented as evidence to support the accusations made by the *Times* – also featured in *Vanity Fair*, and on two separate occasions. Plate 16.16 is the better of the two images, entitled 'Cross examination' and drawn by 'Quiz', the pen-name of John Page Mellor who was himself a lawyer. Russell was born in Newry, Co. Down, and – as Lord Russell of Killowen – was lord chief justice of England from 1894 to 1900.

Not many Irish lawyers made it into the pages of *Vanity Fair*, and those that did tended to achieve that distinction because of their political activities rather than as lawyers. One example is J.G. Swift MacNeill, a Protestant Home Rule MP for nearly thirty years, who was also a professor of law at the King's Inns and later at University College Dublin (Plate 16.17). At the King's Inns, MacNeill taught a number of Irish political leaders when they were studying for the bar, including John Redmond and Tim Healy – both of whom were, in their turn, caricatured in *Vanity Fair*, Redmond twice (in 1892 and 1904). The MacNeill cartoon is by 'Spy'.

'Spy' also did a *Vanity Fair* portrait of Sir James Campbell, later Lord Glenavy (Plate 16.18) – considered by many the finest Irish barrister of his time. He portrays him as a rather louche figure. A staunch unionist, Campbell was appointed lord chief justice of Ireland in 1916 and he served as lord chancellor from 1917 until June 1921. He later became the first chairman of the Senate of the Irish Free State.[34] In the cartoon at Figure 16.7, dating from 1909, Campbell and Tim Healy are shown together speculating about what

32 The Special Commission Act 1888 (51 & 52 Vict., c. 35).

33 For a lively account of the proceedings of the Special Commission, see M. Dungan, *Conspiracy: Irish political trials* (Dublin, 2009), pp 219–63.

34 Campbell is the subject of Hogan's chapter in this volume, 'James Henry Mussen Campbell QC, MP: a life in law and unionist politics'.

16.8 *(left)* Thomas Fitzpatrick, 'Justice is satisfied', *The Lepracaun*, Jan. 1906
16.9 Thomas Fitzpatrick, 'The goose with the golden eggs', *The Lepracaun*, Apr. 1906

they would do for a living if work in the courts dried up – and Healy says, quite presciently: 'Shure, you'll be pitchforked to be the lord chancellor, and maybe it's meself will be riz to some other place'. Healy became the first governor-general of the Irish Free State. This cartoon appeared in the *Lepracaun*, a humorous monthly magazine published between 1905 and 1915. Its proprietor and principal cartoonist was the same Thomas Fitzpatrick who had succeeded John Fergus O'Hea as principal cartoonist of the *Weekly Freeman* in 1891.[35]

The *Lepracaun* had a particularly negative view of the law and lawyers, as exemplified by two cartoons from 1906. The first, titled 'Justice is satisfied' and depicting legal practitioners as vultures (Figure 16.8), echoes the earlier cartoon in which the legal monkey devours everything that is in dispute. The other one makes the same point – targeting solicitors specifically (Figure 16.9). Note the name of the firm 'Chiselem, Bilkem & Bunkem'.

35 See J. Curry and C. Wallace, *Thomas Fitzpatrick and the* Lepracaun Cartoon Monthly, *1905–1915* (Dublin, 2015).

16.10 Grace Gifford, 'Edward Carson about to rebel' (from M. O'Neill, *Grace Gifford Plunkett and Irish freedom*)

Sir Edward Carson was also the subject of a *Vanity Fair* cartoon (Plate 16.19). It is by Liborio Prosperi, one of a number of Italian artists who worked for *Vanity Fair*. Carson's elongated figure and doleful countenance made him an ideal subject for a caricaturist. McDowell wrote of him: 'Thin, tall, angular, with a straight nose, curving, mobile mouth, long jaw and jutting chin, he provided for his opponents a cartoonist's conception of the upholder of autocratic and alien law.'[36] Cartoon images of him abound, including one on a Player's cigarette card (Plate 16.20).[37] Another particularly good image is by Ernest Forbes, an English artist who, using the pseudonym 'Shemus', was the resident cartoonist in Dublin's *Freeman's Journal* newspaper from 1920 to 1924 (Plate 16.21). The *Freeman* was a moderate nationalist newspaper – it had been the organ of the Irish Parliamentary Party up to the party's defeat in the general election of 1918. Carson, the leader of the northern unionists, was a regular butt of its cartoons. Entitled 'The Carson kids', this cartoon portrays the prime minister, Lloyd George, and Sir Hamar Greenwood, chief secretary for Ireland, as children clutching Carson's apron strings. The implication is that, with Lloyd George dependent on the support of the

36 R.B. McDowell, 'Edward Carson' in C.C. O'Brien (ed.), *The shaping of modern Ireland* (London, 1970 [1960]), p. 87.
37 National Portrait Gallery (NPG), London, D2660.

16.11 Grace Gifford, 'Vote for de Valera, a felon of our land', NLI, EPH C465

Conservative Party to continue in office, Carson is dictating government policy on Ireland. The cartoon dates from November 1920, a particularly vicious time in the War of Independence in Ireland.[38]

Grace Gifford, who married Joseph Mary Plunkett in Kilmainham jail a few hours before he was executed in 1916, was a talented and prolific cartoonist. She caricatured Carson as readying himself for rebellion in Ulster as if he were dressing for dinner (Figure 16.10).[39] Gifford was politically active in the years after the 1916 Rising up to the end of the Civil War in 1923, and her principal service to the republican cause was the production of election cartoons and other pictorial propaganda. A good example of her work is an election leaflet she produced for the East Clare by-election in 1917 (Figure 16.11). It places the Sinn Féin candidate, Éamon de Valera, dressed in his Irish Volunteers uniform, in a courtroom scene with the Irish Party's candidate, Patrick Lynch, an eminent king's counsel who had been appointed senior crown prosecutor for Co. Kerry in 1908. The voter is asked to choose between 'a felon of our land' and the former crown prosecutor. The

38 *Freeman's Journal*, 18 Nov. 1920. See F.M. Larkin, *Terror and discord: the Shemus cartoons in the* Freeman's Journal, *1920–1924* (Dublin, 2009).

39 M. O'Neill, *Grace Gifford Plunkett and Irish freedom: tragic bride of 1916* (Dublin, 2000). The Carson cartoon is at p. 58.

16.12 David Low, 'The joy-jig-jazz', *Evening Star*, 8 Dec. 1921, © Solo Syndication, supplied by British Cartoon Archive, University of Kent magistrate, wrapped in the Union Jack, records the death sentence passed on de Valera in 1916 – later, of course, commuted to life imprisonment. Ironically, Lynch would serve as attorney general under de Valera from 1936 to 1940.[40] She signs these cartoons as Grace Plunkett.

The Anglo-Irish Treaty of December 1921 was the subject of a multifaceted cartoon by David Low, published in the London *Evening Star* newspaper on 8 December 1921, two days after the Treaty was signed (Figure 16.12). Entitled 'The joy-jig-jazz', it celebrates what Low assumed – or maybe just hoped – was the end of the long conflict between Britain and Ireland. The key image is of Michael Collins dancing with Lloyd George in front of a gravestone that reads: 'Here lies the Irish trouble, aged about 800 years'. The cartoon also records Ulster unionists' satisfaction with the fact that the Treaty confirmed their exclusion from what would become the Irish Free State: at the top of the cartoon, there is a disembodied person – identified as possibly Sir James Craig, the premier of Northern Ireland, or alternatively the editor of the unionist Belfast newspaper, the *Northern Whig*. Whoever he is, he is playing 'God save our gracious king' on a concertina. Is this the tune that Lloyd George and Michael Collins are dancing to – and, if so, what is the significance of that? It appears to be a not-too-subtle allusion to the acceptance of the crown as part of the new constitutional framework for Ireland. Not everyone is happy, however: in the bottom left-hand corner of the cartoon are two 'disgusted diehards' – southern Irish Protestants – and they are said to be 'about to flee the country' because 'their occupation [is] gone'. This presumably refers to their 'occupation' of the south of Ireland, rather than to their jobs or professions. Finally, Low inserts a self-portrait into the cartoon, at the bottom right-hand side, and he is shown as 'very busy today burning all the excellent cartoons he would have published if they hadn't made peace'. Note that his discarded cartoons – those that he is burning – include ones entitled 'Black and Tan' and 'Jackboot', thereby suggesting disapproval of British policy in Ireland in the period leading up to the Treaty.[41]

In 1921, when this cartoon was published, David Low – then aged 30 and newly arrived in London from Australia – was embarking on a career that would establish his reputation as the greatest cartoonist of the interwar years in Britain.[42] His cartoon about the 1921 Treaty presents a sympathetic view of the Irish, unusual in the British press and in sharp contrast to that of Leech, Furniss and Tenniel in *Punch* forty or so years earlier. As a fellow colonial, he did not demonize the Irish – not even Collins, the mastermind behind the IRA's campaign of terror during the War of Independence.

40 NLI, EPH C465.

41 See A. Martin, 'Michael Collins and the British press', *History Ireland*, 28:4 (July/August 2020).

42 See Larkin, 'Satirical journalism', p. 562.

16.13 Grace Gifford, 'The empire circus', *Irish Fun*, May 1922

Grace Gifford was among those in Ireland who would oppose the Treaty. An anti-Treaty cartoon that she produced in May 1922 shows Collins as a circus ringmaster inducing a dog to perform some tricks (Figure 16.13). The dog is identified as 'Ireland, a province', and it is carrying a Union Jack flag and balancing an oath of allegiance on its nose. At the ringside is a dissolute King George V, accompanied by representatives of a supposedly happy empire – crudely caricatured as primitive tribesmen. The subliminal message is that the Treaty implies equivalence between such tribesmen – lesser mortals – and the Irish people.[43]

A piece of 'emergency' legislation in the immediate aftermath of the Civil War – a public safety bill to permit *inter alia* the continued detention of anti-Treaty prisoners without trial[44] – occasioned a particularly interesting Shemus cartoon in the *Freeman's Journal* in July 1923 (Figure 16.14). The debate on the legislation had extended over an all night sitting of Dáil Éireann. In adjacent news columns, the *Freeman* reported that the Dáil had adjourned at 8 a.m. the previous day after a seventeen-hour debate and that 'at five o'clock

43 *Irish Fun*, May 1922. Gifford regularly contributed anti-Treaty cartoons to this humorous monthly periodical. See T. Ellis, 'Women, gender and masculinity in Irish political cartoons, *c.*1922–1939' (MA, QUB, 2016), pp 23–4, 43–4.

44 This bill became the Public Safety (Emergency Powers) Act 1923.

16.14 Ernest Forbes ('Shemus'), 'Internment', *Freeman's Journal*, 14 July 1923

yesterday morning a small number of deputies were sound asleep on the benches, but the debate went on with no sign of slackening'. The cartoon presents a view of the chamber during the debate – with W.T. Cosgrave, president of the executive council, and two other ministers seated on the government front bench, on the left-hand side.[45] Opposition to the measure was led by George Gavan Duffy, the bearded figure shown addressing the Dáil. The entry on Gavan Duffy in the *Oxford DNB* describes him as 'an unswerving advocate of human rights and the rule of law', and he had resigned from the government in 1922 in protest against the abolition of the republican courts and the increasingly arbitrary nature of the government's treatment of anti-Treaty prisoners. In 1936 he was appointed a high court judge, and was promoted to president of the high court ten years later. He is regarded by many authorities as the father of judicial review in Ireland.[46] A

45 *Freeman's Journal*, 14 July 1923. See Larkin, *Terror and discord*, p. 74.
46 M. Kotsonouris, 'George Gavan Duffy' in *Oxford DNB*. See also L. McRedmond (ed.), *Modern Irish lives: dictionary of 20th century biography* (Dublin, 1996), p. 89.

16.15 Ernest Forbes ('Shemus'), 'Charles Gavan Duffy', *Freeman's Journal*, 12 Mar. 1923

stand-alone portrait of him appeared in the *Freeman* on 12 March 1923, one of a series of caricatures of prominent figures in the new Irish Free State, entitled 'Snapped by Shemus' (Figure 16.15).[47]

Shemus wasn't the only cartoonist who 'snapped' the luminaries of the new Free State. Isa Macnie ('Mac') was another, and she published a selection of her work as *The celebrity zoo* in 1925. Her portrait of Hugh Kennedy, attorney general from 1922 to 1924 and later the first chief justice of Ireland, is at Figure 16.16. A heavy man, she drew him as a hippopotamus. A verse, presumably by Macnie, which accompanies this caricature reads: 'Look, for the graceful hippo comes in view. / His feet are huge, but not so huge as Hugh, / Who, as a foremost figure of the state / Finds he, and his opinion, carry weight.'[48] Kennedy was not universally popular – hence the anonymous drawing at Figure 16.17. It echoes the cartoon attacking John Foster published in the *Volunteer's Journal* in 1784. It is drawn on the back of Dáil Éireann official notepaper, which suggests that it may have been the work of

47 See Larkin, *Terror and discord*, p. 56.

48 Mac [I.M. Macnie], *The celebrity zoo: some desultory rhymes and caricatures* (Dublin, 1925). It is the fourth of twenty portraits of prominent persons in 'rhymes and caricatures' in this book. The others include Patrick McGilligan, later also an attorney general (1954–7) but in 1925 minister for industry and commerce.

16.16 Isa Macnie ('Mac'), 'Hugh Kennedy' (from Mac, *The celebrity zoo*)

one of his parliamentary colleagues or of an official of the Dáil; as well as being attorney general, Kennedy was TD for Dublin South from 1923 to 1924.[49]

In 1926, Kennedy – as chief justice – publicly took issue with the government about the Court Officers Bill then going through the Dáil.[50] He argued that the bill would deprive the judiciary of control of the officers of the courts by making them civil servants, subject to normal civil service recruitment and discipline. The bill, however, reflected the recommendations of the judiciary committee that sat in 1923 under the chairmanship of Lord Glenavy, and Kennedy had been a member of that committee. Kevin O'Higgins, minister for justice, pointed that out in the Dáil – hence the cartoon at Figure 16.18 by Gordon Brewster in the *Evening Herald*, entitled 'Chief Justice Kennedy disowns his grandchild'.[51] Kennedy and his wife were, in fact, childless – so this cartoon was less than tactful.

49 NLI, PD A96.
50 It became the Court Officers Act 1926.
51 *Evening Herald*, 27 Mar. 1926.

16.17 'Hugh Kennedy', NLI, PD A96

Brewster, a long-time cartoonist with the *Evening Herald*, addressed the controversy about the Hugh Lane pictures in another cartoon in that newspaper – published in August 1932 (Figure 16.19). The message here is that the Irish claim is being blocked by legal technicalities and quibbles, notwithstanding the justice of the claim.[52] The title of the cartoon is 'The law is a hass' (*sic*), which is clearly a play on Mr Bumble's *bon mot* in *Oliver Twist*. But why 'hass'? It is a German word meaning 'hatred' or 'spite', and presumably Brewster considered the denial of the Irish claim to the pictures to be a matter of spite.

The very concept of justice came under scrutiny in a cartoon published by *Dublin Opinion* magazine in March 1938 (Figure 16.20).[53] The concern conveyed by this image is whether justice is well served when lawyers huddle together and work out some deal, and the implication is that it is not. This was a daring cartoon for *Dublin Opinion*, arguably Ireland's most celebrated satirical magazine – published between 1922 and 1968. Generally speaking, it

52 Ibid., 27 Aug. 1932. For background information on Brewster, see P. Ó Duibhir, *Gordon Brewster and his cartoons* (Cork, 2024).

53 *Dublin Opinion*, Mar. 1938. The artist was W.H. Conn, a regular contributor to *Dublin Opinion*. For an account of the history of *Dublin Opinion*, see F.M. Larkin, '"Humour is the safety valve of a nation": *Dublin Opinion*, 1922–68' in M. O'Brien & F.M. Larkin (eds), *Periodicals and journalism in twentieth-century Ireland* (Dublin, 2014).

16.18 Gordon Brewster, 'Chief Justice Kennedy disowns his grandchild', *Evening Herald*, 27 Mar. 1926

confined itself to politics and social life. Some areas, such as the law and religion, were out-of-bounds – not fair game for satire.

This reticence about lampooning the law – evident in other publications at this time, as well as in *Dublin Opinion* – was largely because of the danger of being held in contempt of court. As Kotsonouris has written, contempt of court issues were particularly sensitive in the early days of the newly-independent Irish state. Given the distrust of the legal system under the old regime, it was all the more important that the administration of justice in the new dispensation should be accorded obedience and respect. The courts insisted on that, and this influenced press coverage. Kotsonouris adds: 'History was to show that the difficulties encountered in this area are common in post-colonial societies, where [in the past] it may have been one's patriotic duty to disobey the law.'[54]

54 M. Kotsonouris, 'Criticizing judges in Ireland', *Irish Judicial Studies Journal*, 2:1 (2002), 79–97 at 85. As regards the impossibility of lampooning religion, see C.E. Kelly, 'May we laugh, please?', *The Furrow*, 4:12 (Dec. 1953), 697.

16.19 Gordon Brewster, 'The law is a hass', *Evening Herald*, 27 Aug. 1932

While *Dublin Opinion* may have refrained from mocking judges and the law, it did publish from time to time some brilliant cartoons on constitutional questions drawn by C.E. Kelly, its principal cartoonist and joint-editor – who signed his work 'C.E.K.'. Thus, in its very first issue – in March 1922, just after the Anglo-Irish Treaty had been ratified by the Dáil – there is a cartoon in which a reporter asks the ghost of Robert Emmet whether his epitaph might now be written. The reply is an emphatic 'not yet'. Then, in 1937, when de Valera's new constitution was imminent, Emmet's ghost appears again but is told by de Valera to 'call back later' (Plate 16.22). The matter comes up for a third time when Ireland was formally declared a republic in 1949. A cartoon in the December 1948 issue shows Emmet's ghost anticipating the declaration and saying to the taoiseach, John A. Costello: 'One more step … and then let my epitaph be written.' This theme was given a further twist in *Dublin Opinion* in July 1967: the taoiseach, Jack Lynch, planning Ireland's second application to join the Common Market (now the European Union), is confronted by Emmet's ghost which tells him: 'When my country takes her

16.20 W.H. Conn, 'Legal interlude', *Dublin Opinion*, Mar. 1938

place amongst the nations of the six, then, and not till then, let *her* epitaph be written [my emphasis]' (Plate 16.23) – not exactly a ringing endorsement of our application. Before Ireland, Britain and Denmark joined in 1972, the Common Market comprised the six founder member states.[55]

Moreover, when de Valera unveiled his draft new constitution in 1937, *Dublin Opinion* reflected the widespread criticism of the position of women

55 *Dublin Opinion*, Mar. 1922, Apr. 1937, Dec. 1948 and July 1967. The first of these cartoons is unsigned, but from its style it is almost certainly by C.E. Kelly. See F.M. Larkin, 'Emmet's unwritten epitaph: a recurring theme in *Dublin Opinion* cartoons', *History Ireland*, 32:6 (Nov./Dec. 2024).

16.21 C.E. Kelly, 'Oh, goody, goody! I'm glad I'm not repugnant', *Dublin Opinion*, Aug. 1961

that it posited – the emphasis on a woman's 'life within the home'. A cover cartoon depicted de Valera asleep in bed and dreaming of being attacked by the iconic figures of Queen Maeve and Granuaile, carrying a spear and a sword respectively. The caption reads: 'Say, big boy, about those articles in the new constitution' (Plate 16.24).[56]

De Valera, as president of Ireland, referred the Electoral Amendment Bill of 1961 to the supreme court under Article 26 of the constitution for a decision on whether it was repugnant to the constitution. It passed muster, giving rise to a wonderful *Dublin Opinion* cartoon in which the court is shown waving the bill on its way. The bill itself rejoices that it is 'not repugnant' (Figure 16.21).[57]

The 'wind of change' was blowing in Ireland, as elsewhere, in the early 1960s.[58] One manifestation of this was that Charles Haughey, recently appointed minister for justice, initiated a wide-ranging programme of reform of the legal system. *Dublin Opinion* clearly approved, as indicated in its cover cartoon of February 1962 (Figure 16.22) – which also references obliquely the

56 Ibid., June 1937.
57 Ibid., Aug. 1961.
58 The phrase 'wind of change' was used by the Harold Macmillan, the British prime minister, in a speech to the parliament of South Africa, 3 Feb. 1960.

16.22 C.E.Kelly, 'Mr. Haughey: "Here's one façade nobody'll mind being pulled down"', *Dublin Opinion*, Feb. 1962

contemporary controversy about the demolition of Georgian houses in Dublin.[59] Those were the days when even the *Irish Times* could regard Haughey – without irony – as 'the golden boy' of Irish politics.[60] There is great distance, all of it downhill, from that cartoon to the one by Martyn Turner which the *Irish Times* rejected when Haughey retired as taoiseach in 1992.

Another Turner cartoon featuring Haughey celebrates the bonanza for lawyers represented by the tribunal of inquiry – the Moriarty tribunal – that investigated his and other politicians' financial affairs (Figure 16.23). The lawyer in the cartoon echoes Haughey's alleged words of thanks to Ben Dunne for the money he gave him; whereas Haughey was reported as saying to Dunne 'Thanks a million, big fella', the lawyer addresses Haughey as 'little fella'.[61] This is but one of a number of cartoons by Turner on the various tribunals of inquiry established in Ireland in the 1990s, all headed by senior figures in the judiciary. The cartoon at Figure 16.24 refers to the Flood tribunal – the tribunal of inquiry into certain planning matters, initially under Mr Justice Flood. Turner adopts a biblical motif suggested by that judge's

59 *Dublin Opinion*, Feb. 1962.
60 O'Brien, *The* Irish Times, pp 175–6.
61 Turner, *Turner's taoisigh*, p. 27. See S. Smyth, *Thanks a million, big fella* (Dublin, 1997).

16.23 Martyn Turner, 'Thanks, little fella!', *Irish Times*, 2006

16.24 Martyn Turner, 'Flood warning', *Irish Times*, 1999

name. His cartoon evokes Noah's flood in the Book of Genesis, with a multiplicity of lawyers entering the ark two by two; and he opines that, with all these lawyers on board, 'this thing isn't going to go anywhere'.[62] The cost to the state – in other words, to the taxpayer – of legal fees in relation to tribunals and otherwise prompted Turner to suggest that 'the law is a Pass machine' – in other words, an ATM (Plate 16.25). That is his apt variation on the idea that 'the law is an ass'.[63]

Turner's doubts about tribunals – more specifically, his disgust at the fees earned by lawyers at the tribunals – are reflected in a cartoon entitled 'A sad history of Ireland in four phrases', which addressed the collapse of confidence

62 M. Turner, *Up every tree: the bumper book of Bertie* (Dublin, 2006), p. 23.
63 *Irish Times*, 13 Nov. 2013.

16.25 Martyn Turner, 'No surrender', *Irish Times*, 1986

in so many pillars of Irish society in recent years (Plate 16.26). The four figures in the cartoon – politician, priest, banker and doctor – ask the Irish people to 'trust me' despite the fact that each one represents a discredited part of the Irish establishment. Redemption is offered tongue-in-cheek in an aside, as follows: 'A few more tribunals would sort the country out … Trust me, I'm a lawyer.'[64]

Brown, in his history of the *Irish Times*, has written that Turner's 'politically acute cartoons … add to the newspaper's reputation for sharply expressed and hard-hitting commentary'.[65] This is particularly true of his contributions on what might be called the 'liberal agenda'. A fine example of his work in this vein is the cartoon published after the defeat of a proposal to lift the constitutional ban on divorce in Ireland in 1986 (Figure 16.25).[66] Those who had resisted the change are compared to the obdurate Orange Order in Northern Ireland, with their propensity to say 'no' to every reform. The banner incorporates a portrait of de Valera clutching his constitution, in place of King Billy – William of Orange – on his white horse. The exhortation

64 Ibid., 23 Nov. 2012.

65 T. Brown, *The* Irish Times*: 150 years of influence* (London, 2015), pp 294–5. For a more detailed assessment of Turner's career as a cartoonist, see D. Ferriter, 'Sustained excellence of a satirical cartoonist that is unmatched', *Irish Times*, 1 Dec. 2018.

66 M. Turner, *Greatest hits* (Dublin, 2003), p. 27.

16.26 Martyn Turner, 'The introduction of internment in Ireland for 14 year old girls, *Irish Times*, 17 Feb. 1992

is to remember 1937 (the year of the adoption of de Valera's constitution) instead of 1690 (the year of the battle of the Boyne).

Without question, Turner's greatest cartoon to date is that published on the front page of the *Irish Times* on 17 February 1992, in response to the state's efforts to prevent a pregnant 14-year-old girl, Miss 'X', travelling to England for an abortion (Figure 16.26). Until 2018 there was a constitutional ban on abortion in Ireland. This cartoon linked the young girl's predicament with the outrage of internment without trial in Northern Ireland in the 1970s. The depiction of the girl, her hair in a pigtail and carrying a teddy bear, standing on a map of Ireland surrounded by a fence topped with razor wire helped define the subsequent debate in Ireland on the abortion issue.[67] It is a more impactful piece of satire, and more obviously influential, than any other cartoon considered in this chapter.

This chapter has taken a somewhat jaundiced view of the law and lawyers. I make no apology for that. As the eminent jurist Lord Bingham

67 Ibid., p. 34. See O'Brien, *The* Irish Times, p. 247; Brown, *The* Irish Times, p. 363; Larkin, 'Satirical journalism', p. 570.

of Cornhill wrote, respect for the rule of law does not require us 'to swoon in adulation of the law, let alone lawyers'. He elaborates as follows:

> belief in the rule of law does not import unqualified admiration of the law, or the legal profession, or the courts, or the judges. We can hang on to most of our prejudices [about the law and lawyers]. It does, however, call on us to accept that we would very much rather live in a country which complies, or at least seeks to comply, with [the rule of law] … than in one that does not. The hallmarks of a regime which flouts the rule of law are, alas, all too familiar: the midnight knock on the door, the sudden disappearance, the show trial, the subjection of prisoners to genetic experiment, the confession extracted by torture, the gulag and the concentration camp, the gas chamber, the practice of genocide or ethnic cleansing, the waging of aggressive war. The list is endless. Better to put up with some choleric judges and greedy lawyers.[68]

I agree, but it is great fun to lampoon such judges and lawyers – and also the multifarious, and sometimes nefarious, practices of the legal world. Let us rejoice that we are free to do so. The prevalence of cartoons such as those considered in this chapter is a measure of the freedom we enjoy under the rule of law, and that freedom is something to rejoice in – even if the price we pay for it is an asinine law.

68 T. Bingham, *The rule of law* (London, 2010), pp 8–9.

Bibliography

PUBLISHED WORKS

Abbot, C., *The freaks of cupid* (London, 1845)

Adams, R.J.Q., *Bonar Law* (London, 1999)

Ainsworth, John, 'Some abstracts of Chancery suits relating to Ireland', *Journal of the Royal Society of Antiquaries of Ireland* 9:1 (1939), 39

Anderson, Robert, 'Our absurd system of punishing crime', *The Nineteenth Century and After*, 49 (Feb. 1901), 268

Anderson, Robert, *Sidelights on the Home Rule movement* (London, 1907)

Anderson, Robert, *The lighter side of my official life* (London, 1910)

Annesley, Francis and Patrick Little, 'Select document. Providence and posterity: a letter from Lord Mountnorris to his daughter, 1642', *Irish Historical Studies*, 32:128 (2001), 556

Anon., 'A seventeenth century will', *The Irish Builder*, 33:763 (1891), 218

Anon., 'Bankruptcy legislation', *Irish Law Times and Solicitors' Journal*, *3* (1869), 193

Anon., 'Imprisonment for debt', *Irish Law Times & Solicitors' Journal*, 2 (1868) 1

Anon., 'Deutsche Frauen über die Suffragetten', *Berliner Lokal-Anzeiger*, 372 (1912)

Anon., 'Die VII. Generalversammlung des Allgemeinen, deutschen Frauenvereins (VIII. Frauentag) in Gotha vom 2. Bis 5. October 1875', *Neue Bahnen*, 22, 23 (1875)

Anon., 'Eine deutsche Verteidigung der englischen Stimmrechtsweiber', *Berliner Neueste Nachrichten*, Nr. 637 (1912)

Anon., *Report of the International Council of Women. Assembled by the National Woman Suffrage Association, Washington, DC, March 25 to April 1, 1888* (Washington, DC, 1888)

Anon., *Motive zu dem Entwurfe eines Bürgerlichen Gesetzbuchs für das Deutsche Reich*, vol. iv (Berlin, 1896)

Anon., *Report of the Second and Third Conferences of the IWSA, Berlin, Germany, 3–4 June, 1904; Copenhagen, Denmark, 7–11 Aug. 1906* (Copenhagen, 1906)

Anon., *Report of the Proceedings on the Irish Convention* (Dublin, 1918)

Anon., 'Testamentary records', *Irish Genealogist*, 2:6 (1948), 180

Anon., 'The second round', *Woman's Leader* (12 Mar. 1920), 1125

Anon., *An answer to Mr. Molyneux his case of Ireland's being bound by acts of parliament in England, stated … By reasoning from his own arguments and authorities* (London, 1698)

Anon., *Rhetorica ad Herennium* (ed. and trans. Harry Caplan) (Massachusetts, 1977)

Anon., *The present state of Ireland* (Dublin, 1673)

Anon., *What the Treaty means* (Dublin, 1922)

Anson, William Reynell, *The law and custom of the constitution*, 2 vols (3rd edn, Oxford, 1907 and 4th edn, 1935)

Aristotle, *The art of rhetoric* (ed. and trans. J.H. Freese) (Massachusetts, 1926)

Atwood, William, *The history, and reasons, of the dependency of Ireland upon the imperial crown of the kingdom of England* (London, 1698)

Bader-Zaar, Birgitta, 'Frauenwahlrechtsbewegungen und Verfassungsstaat: Deutschland, Großbritannien und Österreich im Vergleich, 1866–1918' in M. Kirsch et al. (eds), *Der Verfassungsstaat vor der Herausforderung der Massengesellschaft. Konstitutionalismus um 1900 im europäischen Vergleich* (Berlin, 2002)

Bader-Zaar, Birgitta, 'Politische partizipation als grundrecht in Europa und Nordamerika. Entwicklungsprozesse zum allgemeinen, gleichen, geheimen und direkten wahlrecht für Männer und Frauen vom späten 18. bis zum frühen 20. Jahrhundert' in M. Grandner et al. (eds), *Grund- und menschenrechte: historische Perspektiven – aktuelle Problematiken* (Vienna, 2002)

Bader-Zaar, Birgitta, 'Zur Geschichte des Frauenwahlrechts im langen 19. Jahrhundert. Eine international vergleichende Perspektive', *Ariadne*, 40 (2001), 6

Ball, Francis Elrington, *The judges in Ireland, 1221–1921* (England, 1926)

Ball, Stephen, *Policing the Irish land war: official responses to political protest and agrarian crime, 1879–91* (London, 2000)

Bardon, Jonathan, *A history of Ulster* (Belfast, 1992)

Barnard, T.C., 'Lawyers and the law in later seventeenth-century Ireland', *Irish Historical Studies*, 28:111 (1993), 256

Barnard, T.C., 'Local courts in seventeenth- and eighteenth-century Ireland' in Michael Brown and Seán Patrick Donlan (eds), *The laws and other legalities of Ireland* (Farnham, 2001)

Barnard, Toby and Jane Fenlon (eds), *The dukes of Ormonde, 1610–1745* (Woodbridge, 2000)

Bassett, George Henry, *The book of County Armagh: a manual and directory* (Dublin, 1888)

Bäumer, Gertrud, 'Zur Kampfesweise der Suffragettes. Erklärung des Gesamtvorstands des Bundes Deutscher Frauenvereine', *Die Frauenfrage*, 15:3 (1913/14), 17–18

Beaumont, Catríona, *Housewives and citizens: domesticity and the women's movement in England, 1928–64* (Manchester, 2013)

Beaumont, Catríona, 'Women, citizenship and Catholicism in the Irish Free State, 1922–1948', *Women's History Review*, 6:4 (1997), 563

Becker, Bernard H., *Disturbed Ireland: being the letters written during the winter of 1880–81* (London, 1881)

Beckett, James Camlin, 'Literature in English, 1691–1800' in T.W. Moody (ed.), *A new history of Ireland*, vol. iv (Oxford, 1986)

Beckett, Matthew, *Sir George Rawdon, a sketch of his life and times* (Belfast, 1935)

Begg, Paul and Jack Bennett, *Jack the Ripper: the forgotten victims* (London, 2014)

Begg, Paul, *Jack the Ripper: the definite history* (London, 2003)

Bence Jones, William, *The life's work in Ireland of a landlord who tried to do his duty* (London, 1880)

Bergin, John and Andrew Lyall (eds), *The acts of James II's Irish parliament of 1689* (Dublin, 2016)

Berridale Keith, Arthur, *The constitution, administration and laws of the empire* (London, 1924)

Berriedale Keith, Arthur, *Responsible government in the dominions* (Oxford, 1928)

Berriedale Keith, Arthur, *The sovereignty of the British dominions* (London, 1929)

Berriedale Keith, Arthur, 'Notes on imperial constitutional law', *Journal of Comparative Legislation and International Law,* 4 (1922), 104

Bew, Paul, *Land and the national question in Ireland, 1858–82* (Dublin, 1978)

Bingham, Tom, *The rule of law* (London, 2010)

Blackstone, William, *Commentaries on the laws of England,* 4 vols (London, 1765–9)

Blake, Robert, *The unknown prime minister: the life and times of Andrew Bonar Law, 1858–1923* (London, 1955)

Blount, Thomas, *Nomo-Λεξικον. A law dictionary* (rev. edn, London, 1691)

Bock, Gisela, 'Frauenwahlrecht. Deutschland um 1900 in vergleichender perspektive' in M. Grütter et al. (eds), *Geschichte und emanzipation. Festschrift für Reinhard Rürup* (Frankfurt am Main, 1999)

Bock, Gisela, '100 Jahre Frauenwahlrecht: Deutschland in transnationaler perspektive', *Zeitschrift fur geschichtswissenschaft,* 66:5 (2018), 395

Bock, Gisela and Patricia Thane (eds), *Maternity and gender politics* (London, 1994)

Bock, Gisela, *Women in European history* (Oxford, 2002)

Bolton, Richard (ed.), *The statutes of Ireland, beginning the 3rd yeare of k. Edward III until the … 13th yeare of k. James I* (Dublin, 1621)

Bolton, Richard, *A justice of peace for Ireland, consisting of two bookes; whereunto are added many presidents of indictments of treasons, felonies…* (Dublin, 1638 and London, 1683)

Boyce, David George, *Nineteenth-century Ireland* (2nd edn, Dublin, 2005)

Bradshaw, Brendan, *The Irish constitutional revolution of the sixteenth century* (Cambridge, 1979)

Breen, Oonagh and Noel McGrath (eds), *Palles: the legal legacy of the last Lord Chief Baron* (Dublin, 2022)

Brown, Terence, *The* Irish Times*: 150 years of influence* (London, 2015)

Buckley, David N., *James Fintan Lalor: radical* (Cork, 1990)

Bull, Philip, *Land, politics, and nationalism: a study of the Irish land question* (Dublin, 1996)

Cahillane, Laura, *Drafting the Irish Free State constitution* (Manchester, 2016)

Cahillane, Laura, 'An insight into the Irish Free State constitution', *American Journal of Legal History* 54:1 (2014), 1

Cahillane, Laura and Donal Coffey, *The centenary of the Irish Free State constitution, constituting a polity?* (London, 2023)

Caine, Barbara, *English feminism, 1780–1980* (Oxford, 1997)

Campbell, Patrick, *My life and easy times* (London, 1968)

Canning, Paul M., 'The impact of Eamon de Valera: domestic causes of the Anglo-Irish economic war', *Albion: A Quarterly Journal Concerned with British Studies,* 15:3 (1983), 179

Cary, John, *A vindication of the parliament of England, in answer to a book, written by William Molyneux of Dublin …* (London, 1698)

Casey, Brian (ed.), *Defying the law of the land: agrarian radicals in Irish history* (Dublin, 2013)

Casey, Brian, 'Constructing political consciousness in the West of Ireland, 1876–79: the case of the Ballinasloe Tenant Defence Association', *New Hibernia Review* (Spring 2016), 58

Casey, Brian, 'Matt Harris and the Irish land question, 1876–1882', *Rural History*, 25:2 (Oct. 2014), 183

Cauer, Minna, 'Gedanken über den Internationalen Frauenkongress in London', *Die Frauenbewegung* 14 (1899), 122

Chartres Molony, J., *The riddle of the Irish* (London, 1927)

Cherry, Richard R., *The Irish land law and Land Purchase Acts, 1860–1891* (2nd edn, Dublin, 1893)

Cicero, Marcus Tullius, *De inventione* and *Topica* (ed. and transl. H.M. Hubbell) (Massachusetts, 1936)

Cicero, Marcus Tullius, *De oratore* (ed. and trans. E.W. Sutton) (Massachusetts, 1942)

Clark, Samuel, *Social origins of the Irish land war* (Princeton, 1979)

Clarke, Aidan and Bríd McGrath (eds), *Letterbook of George, 16th earl of Kildare* (Dublin, 2013)

Coen, Mark and Niamh Howlin, 'The jury speaks: jury riders in the nineteenth and twentieth centuries', *American Journal of Legal History*, 58:4 (2018), 505

Coen, Mark, '"The work of some irresponsible women": jurors, ghosts, and embracery in the Irish Free State', *Law and History Review*, 38:4 (2020), 777

Coen, Mark, *The Offences Against the State Act at 80: a model counter-terrorism Act?* (Oxford, 2021)

Coffey, Donal K., 'The need for a new constitution: Irish constitutional change 1932–1935', *Irish Jurist*, 48 (2012), 275

Coffey, Donal K., 'The commonwealth and the oath of allegiance crisis: a study in inter-war commonwealth relations', *Journal of Imperial and Commonwealth History*, 44:3 (2016), 492

Coffey, Donal K., *Drafting the Irish constitution, 1935–1937: transnational influences in interwar Europe* (London, 2018)

Coffey, Donal K. *Constitutionalism in Ireland, 1932–1938: national, commonwealth, and international perspectives* (London, 2018)

Conan Doyle, Arthur, *The adventures of Sherlock Holmes* (London, 1892)

Conlon, Michael V., 'Debtors in Cork gaols, 1705–1872', *Journal of the Cork Historical & Archaeological Society*, 47 (1942), 9

Costello, Kevin, *The court of admiralty of Ireland, 1575–1893* (Dublin, 2011)

Costello, Kevin and Niamh Howlin (eds), *Law and religion in Ireland, 1700–1970* (Cham, 2021)

Côté, Jane Mc L., *Fanny and Anna Parnell: Ireland's patriot sisters* (Dublin, 1991)

Crawford, Elizabeth, *The women's suffrage movement: a reference guide* (London, 1999)

Crawford, Elizabeth, *The women's suffrage movement in Britain and Ireland: a regional study* (London, 2006)

Crawford, Jon G., *A star chamber court in Ireland: the court of castle chamber, 1571–1641* (Dublin, 2005)

Crawford, Jon G., *Anglicizing the government of Ireland* (Dublin, 1993)

Cregan, Donal F., 'Irish Catholic admissions to the English inns of court, 1558–1625', *Irish Jurist*, 5:1 (1970), 95

Crooks, Peter and Thomas Mohr (eds), *Law and the idea of liberty in Ireland from Magna Carta to the present* (Dublin, 2023)
Crosby, Travis L., *The unknown Lloyd George* (London, 2014)
Cruise O'Brien, Conor and Máire Cruise O'Brien, *A concise history of Ireland* (London, 1972)
Cullen, Fintan, 'Visual parody and political commentary: John Doyle and Daniel O'Connell' in Ciaran O'Neill (ed.), *Irish elites in the nineteenth century* (Dublin, 2013)
Cunningham, Bernadette (ed.), 'Clanricard letters: letters and papers, 1605–1673, preserved in the National Library of Ireland manuscript 3111', *Journal of the Galway Archaeological and Historical Society*, 48 (1996), 162
Curry, James and Ciarán Wallace, *Thomas Fitzpatrick and the* Lepracaun Cartoon *Monthly, 1905–1915* (Dublin, 2015)
Curry, James, *Artist of the revolution: the cartoons of Ernest Kavanagh, 1884–1916* (Cork, 2012)
Curtis Clayton, Margaret (ed.), *The council book for the province of Munster*, c.*1599–1649* (Dublin, 2008)
Curtis Jr, L. Perry, *Apes and angels: the Irishman in Victorian caricatures* (Newton Abbot, 1971)
Curtis Jr, L. Perry, 'Landlord responses to the Irish land war, 1879–1887', *Éire/Ireland*, 38:3&4 (Fall/Winter 2003), 169
Curtis Jr, L. Perry, *Coercion and conciliation in Ireland, 1880–92* (Princeton, 1963)
Curtis Jr, L. Perry, *The depiction of eviction in Ireland, 1845–1910* (Dublin, 2011)
Curtis Jr, L. Perry, *Images of Erin in the age of Parnell* (Dublin, 2000)
Curtis, Edmund and R.B. McDowell (eds), *Irish historical documents, 1172–1922* (London, 1943)
Daley Caroline, and Melanie Nolan, *Suffrage and beyond: international feminist perspectives* (Auckland, 1994)
Davenant, Charles, *An essay upon the probable methods of making the people gainers in the balance of trade* (London, 1699)
Davidoff, L. and C. Hall, *Family fortunes: men and women of the English middle class, 1780–1850* (Chicago, 1987)
Davitt, Michael, *Fall of feudalism in Ireland* (London, 1904)
Dawson, N.M. (ed.), *Reflections on law and history: Irish Legal History Society discourses and other papers, 2000–2005* (Dublin, 2006)
Dennehy, Coleman, 'Crime, criminal policy, and law reform in seventeenth-century Irish parliaments', *The Journal of Legal History*, 44.1 (2023), 2
Dennehy, Coleman (ed.), *Law and revolution in seventeenth-century Ireland* (Dublin, 2020)
de Nie, Michael, 'Satirical journalism' in Finkelstein, David (ed.), *The Edinburgh history of the British and Irish press, vol. 2: expansion and evolution, 1800–1900* (Edinburgh, 2020),
Delany, Vincent Thomas Hyginus, *Christopher Palles, Lord Chief Baron* (Dublin, 1960)
Deutsch, Regine, *The International Woman Suffrage Alliance: its history from 1904–1929* (London, 1929)
Diarmuid Mac Iomhair, 'The house of Louth in the seventeenth and eighteenth centuries', *Journal of the County Louth Archaeological Society*, 16:2 (1966), 67

Dodridge, John, *The English lawyer: describing a method for managing the lawes of this land* (London, 1631)

Donnelly Jr, James S., 'The journals of Sir John Benn-Walsh relating to the management of his Irish estates, 1823–64', *Journal of the Cork Historical and Archaeological Society*, 79 (1974), 86 and 80 (1975), 15

Donnelly Jr, James S., *The land and the people of nineteenth-century Cork* (London, 1975)

Dooley, Terence, *The decline and fall of the dukes of Leinster 1872–1948* (Dublin, 2015)

Douglas, Roy, Liam Harte and Jim O'Hara, *Drawing conclusions: a cartoon history of Anglo-Irish relations, 1798–1998* (Belfast, 1998)

Dublin Chamber of Commerce: *Report of the Council of the Chamber of Commerce 1841* (Dublin 1841)

Dun, Finlay, *Landlords and tenants in Ireland* (London, 1881)

Dungan, Myles, *Conspiracy: Irish political trials* (Dublin, 2009 and 2013)

Edgeworth, Maria, *Castle Rackrent* (New York, 1976)

Edgeworth, Maria, *The absentee* (New York, 1976)

Edgeworth, Maria, *Patronage* (London, 1814)

Edwards, David, 'Collaboration without anglicization: the MacGiollapadraig lordship and tudor reform' in Patrick Duffy, David Edwards and Elizabeth FitzPatrick (eds), *Gaelic Ireland: land, lordship and settlement,* c.*1250*–c.*1650* (Dublin, 2001),

Edwards, David, *The Ormond lordship in County Kilkenny, 1515–1642: the rise and fall of Butler feudal power* (Dublin, 2000)

Ellis, T., 'Women, gender and masculinity in Irish political cartoons, *c.*1922–1939' (MA, QUB, 2016)

Eustance, E. et al. (eds), *A suffrage reader: charting directions in British suffrage history* (London, 2000)

Evans, Stewart and Donald Rumbelow, *Jack the Ripper: Scotland Yard investigates* (London, 2010)

Evans, Stewart P. and Keith Skinner, *Jack the Ripper: letters from hell* (London, 2001)

Fallon, Aengus, 'The foundational legislation of the Garda Siochana (1922–1926)', *Irish Jurist,* 62 (2019) 119

Fawcett, M.G., *Woman's suffrage: a short history of a great movement* (London, 1912)

Fell, Alison S. and Ingrid Sharp (eds), *The women's movement in wartime: international perspectives, 1914–19* (London, 2007)

Ferguson, W.D., *A treatise on the practice of the queen's bench, common pleas, and exchequer of pleas in Ireland* (Dublin, 1841)

Fletcher, I. et al., *Women's suffrage in the British empire: citizenship, nation and race* (Abingdon, 2000)

Fletcher, Reginald J. (ed.), *The pension book of Gray's Inn, 1569–1669* (2 vols, London, 1901)

Fogarty, L., *James Fintan Lalor: patriot and political essayist* (Dublin, 1919)

Foley, Timothy P., 'Thomas Maguire and the Parnell forgeries', *Journal of the Galway Archaeological and Historical Society*, 46 (1994), 173

Foster, Joseph (ed.), *The register of admissions to Gray's Inn, 1521–1889* (London, 1889)

Foucault, Michel, *Discipline and punish: the birth of the prison*, trans. Alan Sheridan (New York, 1977)

Foucault, Michel, *Les mots et les choses* (Paris, 1966)
Foucault, Michel, *Power/knowledge: selected interviews and other writings* (New York, 1980)
Foucault, Michel, *Surveiller et Punir* (Paris, 1975)
Foucault, Michel, *The archaeology of knowledge* (Paris, 1969)
Frevert, Ute (ed.), *Bürgerinnen und Bürger. Geschlechterverhältnisse im 19. Jahrhundert* (Göttingen, 1988)
Friemann, Gretchen, *The Treaty* (Newbridge, 2021)
Gallagher, Frank, *The Anglo-Irish Treaty* (London, 1965)
Gamble, John, *Northern Irish tales* (Dublin, 1818)
Ganly, J., 'The new Irish Bankruptcy Amendment Act', *Freeman's Journal,* 15 May 1871
Gardner, Helen, *In defence of the imagination* (Cambridge MA, 1982)
Garvin, Tom, *1922: the birth of Irish democracy* (Dublin, 1996)
Geary, Laurence, *The Plan of Campaign* (Cork, 1986)
Geoghegan, Patrick, *Oratory and debate: the College Historical Society, 1770–2020* (Dublin, 2020)
Gerhard, Ute (ed.), *Frauen in der Geschichte des Rechts. Von der Frühen Neuzeit bis zur Gegenwart* (München, 1997)
Gibson, Dirk C., *Jack the writer: a verbal and visual analysis of the Ripper correspondence* (London, 2013)
Gillespie, Raymond, 'The trials of Bishop Spottiswood 1620–40', *Clogher Record,* 12:3 (1987), 323
Gillespie, Raymond, 'A manor court in seventeenth-century Ireland', *Irish Economic and Social History,* 25 (1998), 81
Gordon, R. Michael, *Alias Jack the Ripper: beyond the usual Whitechapel suspects* (London, 2001)
Gottlieb, Julie V. (ed.), *Feminism and feminists after suffrage* (New York, 2016)
Gray, Peter, 'HB's Famine cartoons: satirical art in a time of catastrophe' in M. Corporaal, O. Frawley and E. Mark-Fitzgerald (eds), *The Great Irish Famine: visual and material culture* (Liverpool, 2018)
Greer, Desmond S. and Norma M. Dawson (eds), *Mysteries and solutions in Irish legal history: Irish Legal History Society discourses and other papers, 1996–1999* (Dublin, 2001)
Grosart, Alexander B., *The Lismore papers, first [and second] series* (4 vols, London, 1886–8)
Grotius, Hugo, *De iure belli ac pacis, libri tres* (3 vols, London, 1625)
Gwynn, Denis, *The life of John Redmond* (London, 1932)
Habermas, R., *Frauen und Männer des Bürgertums: eine Familiengeschichte (1750–1850)* (Göttingen, 2000).
Hale, Matthew, *Prerogatives of the king* [ed. D.C. Hale] (London, 1976)
Hale, Matthew, *The history of the pleas of the crown,* 2 vols (London, 1716)
Hamilton, George, *A history of the house of Hamilton* (Edinburgh, 1933)
Hanly, John (ed.), *The letters of Saint Oliver Plunkett 1625–1681, archbishop of Armagh and primate of All Ireland* (Dublin, 1979)
Hanna, Adam, *Poetry, politics and the law in modern Ireland* (Syracuse, NY, 2022)

Hanna, Adam and Eugene McNulty (eds), *Law and literature: the Irish case* (Liverpool, 2022)

Hannam, J., *International encyclopedia of women's suffrage* (Santa Barbara, 2000)

Harkness, D.W., *The restless dominion* (London, 1969)

Harris, Ruth-Ann, 'Negotiating patriarchy: Irish women and the landlord' in Marilyn Cohen and Nancy J. Curtis (eds), *Reclaiming gender: transgressive identities in modern Ireland* (New York, 1999)

Hart, Anthony, *A history of the bar and inn of court of Northern Ireland* (Belfast, 2013)

Healy, Maurice, *The old Munster circuit* (Dublin, 1939)

Heinsohn, K., 'Ambivalente Entwicklungen. 150 Jahre Frauenbewegung, Politik und Parteien', *Ariadne*, 67:68 (2015), 40

Heron, J.C., 'Bankruptcy and insolvency statistics in 1861', *Journal of the Statistical and Social Inquiry Society of Ireland* 3 (1862), 198

Herrup, Cynthia, 'The patriarch at home: the trial of the 2nd earl of Castlehaven for rape and sodomy', *History Workshop Journal*, 41 (1996), 1

Herrup, Cynthia, '"To pluck bright honour from the pale-faced moon": gender and honour in the Castlehaven story', *Transactions of the Royal Historical Society*, 6 (1996), 137

Herrup, Cynthia, *A house in gross disorder: sex, law and the second earl of Castlehaven* (Oxford, 1999)

Heuston, R.F.V., *Lives of the Lord Chancellors, 1885–1940* (Oxford, 1964)

Heuston, R.V.F., 'Legal history and the author: some practical problems of authorship' in W.N. Osborough (ed.), *The Irish Legal History Society: inaugural addresses* (Dublin, 1989)

Heymann, Linda Gustiva and Anita Augspurg, *Erlebtes, Erschautes: deutsche Frauen kämpfen für Freiheit, Recht und Frieden, 1850–1949* (Frankfurt, 1992)

Hickey, Éanna, *Irish law and lawyers in modern folk tradition* (Dublin, 1999)

Hill, George (ed.), *The Montgomery manuscripts (1603–1706). Compiled from the family papers by William Montgomery of Rosemount* … (Belfast, 1869)

Hill, Jacqueline R., 'Ireland without union: Molyneux and his legacy' in John Robertson (ed.), *A union for empire: political thought and the union of 1707* (Cambridge, 1995)

Hindenburg, Barbara von, *Die Abgeordneten des Preußischen Landtags, 1919–1933: Biographie – Herkunft- Geschlecht* (Frankfurt am Main, 2017)

Historical Manuscripts Commission, *Ninth report. Part II, app.* (London, 1884)

Historical Manuscripts Commission, *Tenth report, app. 5* (London, 1885)

Historical Manuscripts Commission, *Twelfth report, app 1 and 2* (London, 1888)

Historical Manuscripts Commission, *Fifteenth report, app. 1, part ii* (London, 1897)

Historical Manuscripts Commission, *Report on manuscripts in various collections*, vol. iii (London, 1904)

Hogan, Daire and Patrick Maume (eds), *The reminiscences of Ignatius O'Brien, lord chancellor of Ireland, 1913–18: a life in Cork, Dublin and Westminster* (Dublin, 2021)

Hogan, Gerard, *The origins of the Irish constitution, 1928–1941* (Dublin, 2012)

Hogan, Gerard, 'The Count Plunkett *habeas corpus* application and the end of the Dáil supreme court', *Irish Jurist*, 68 (2022), 25

Hon. Society of Lincoln's Inns, *The records of the Honourable Society of Lincoln's Inn: admissions from AD 1420 to AD 1799*, 4 vols (London, 1896)

Howlin, Niamh, *Juries in Ireland: laypersons and law in the long nineteenth century* (Dublin, 2017)

Howlin, Niamh and Kevin Costello (eds), *Law and the family in Ireland, 1800–1950* (London, 2017)

Howlin, Niamh, *Report on the trial of Myles Joyce, 1882* (June 2017)

Howlin, Niamh, *Report on the trial of John Twiss, January 1895* (Apr. 2021)

Howlin, Niamh, *Convictions for homosexual acts in the Irish courts, 1922–1993* (May 2022)

Hubler, Katherine E., 'Man's duty to woman: men and the first wave of German feminism, 1865–1919' (PhD, Boston College, 2012)

Hume, L.P., *The National Union of Women's Suffrage Societies, 1897–1914* (New York, 1982)

Inner Temple Library, 'Admissions to the Inner Temple to 1659' (typescript by L. Rees Lloyd, [1954])

Irish, Tomás, *Trinity in war and revolution 1912–1923* (Dublin, 2015)

Irish Land Committee, *The land question, Ireland, II: the anarchy in Ireland* (Dublin, 1880)

Irving, R., *'The law is a ass': an illustrated anthology of legal quotations* (London, 2010)

Jackson, Alvin, 'The failure of unionism in Dublin, 1900', *Irish Historical Studies*, 36:104 (1989), 377

Jackson, Alvin, *Home Rule: an Irish history 1800–2000* (Oxford, 2003)

Jackson, C., 'Irish political opposition to the passage of reform, 1893–98: the Criminal Evidence Act 1898' in John McEldowney and Paul O'Higgins (eds), *The common law tradition: essays in Irish legal history* (Dublin, 1990)

James, Dermot, *The Gore-Booths of Lissadell* (Dublin, 2004)

Jefferies, Henry A., 'The Armagh registers and the re-interpretation of Irish church history on the eve of the reformations', *Seanchas Ardmhacha: Journal of the Armagh Diocesan Historical Society*, 18:1 (1999/2000), 81

Jones, David S., 'The cleavage between graziers and peasants in the land struggle, 1890–1900' in Samuel Clark and J.S. Donnelly (eds), *Irish peasants: violence and political unrest, 1780–1914* (Manchester, 1983)

Jones, David S., *Graziers, land reform, and political conflict in Ireland* (Washington, DC, 1995)

Jones, Emrys, 'Late Victorian Belfast, 1850–1900' in J.C. Beckett and R.E. Glasscock (eds) *Belfast: the origin and growth of an industrial city* (London, 1967)

Jones, T., *Whitehall diary, vol. III, Ireland, 1918–1925*, ed. K. Middlemas (London, 1971)

Jordan, Donald E., *Land and popular politics in Ireland: County Mayo from the plantation to the land war* (Cambridge, 1994)

Jordan, Donald, 'The Irish National League and the "unwritten law": rural protest and nation building in Ireland, 1882–1890', *Past and Present*, 158 (Feb. 1998), 146

Joyce, James, *Ulysses* (London, 2008)

Kelly, Charles E., 'May we laugh, please?', *The Furrow*, 4:12 (Dec. 1953)

Kelly, P., 'Nationalism and the historians of the Jacobite war in Ireland' in Michael O'Dea and Kevin Whelan (eds), *Nations and nationalism: France, Britain and Ireland in the eighteenth-century context* (Oxford, 1995)

Kelly, Patrick, 'Conquest versus consent in Molyneux's *Case of Ireland*' in Ciaran Brady and Jane Ohlmeyer (eds), *British interventions in early modern Ireland* (Cambridge, 2005)

Kelly, Patrick, 'The one that got away, or almost: the Molyneux family library and Trinity College, Dublin' in W.E. Vaughan (ed.), *The Old Library Trinity College, Dublin, 1712–2012* (Dublin, 2013)

Kelly, Patrick, 'The printer's copy of the MS of Molyneux's *The case of Ireland …*', *Long Room,* 18–19 (1979), 13

Kenny, Colum, '"Badge of servitude"? The Irish at England's inns of court', *Proceedings of the Royal Irish Academy,* 119C (Dublin, 2019)

Kenny, Colum, '"It is notorious that a lawyer cannot draft his own will clearly": framing the boundary commission in the Anglo-Irish Treaty 1921', *Irish Jurist,* 68 (2022), 1

Kenny, Colum, *Midnight in London – the Anglo-Irish Treaty crisis* (Dublin, 2021)

Keogh, Dermot, *The Vatican, the bishops and Irish politics, 1919–39* (Cambridge, 1986)

Kidd, Colin, *British identities before nationalism* (Cambridge, 1999)

Kingston, John, 'Catholic families of the Pale', *Reportum Novum: Dublin Diocesan Historical Record,* 2:1 (1957–8), 88

Kingston, John, 'Lord Dunboyne', *Reportum Novum Dublin Diocesan Historical Record,* 3:1 (1961–2), 62

Kohn, Leo, *The constitution of the Irish Free State* (London, 1932)

Kolbert, Colin Francis and Timothy O'Brien, *Land reform in Ireland* (Cambridge, 1975)

Kotsonouris, Mary, 'Criticizing judges in Ireland', *Irish Judicial Studies Journal*, 2:1 (2002), 79

Lacey, Candida Ann S., *Barbara Leigh Smith Bodichon and the Langham Place Group* (New York, 1987)

Laffan, Michael, *Judging W.T. Cosgrave – the foundation of the Irish state* (Dublin, 2014)

Laffan, Michael, *The resurrection of Ireland: the Sinn Féin party, 1916–1923* (Cambridge, 1999)

Laird, Helen, *Subversive law in Ireland, 1879–1920: from 'unwritten law' to Dáil courts* (Dublin, 2005)

Lange, Helene (ed.), *Kampfzeiten. Aufsätze und Reden aus vier Jahrzehnten*, vol. 1 (Berlin, 1928)

Lange, Helene, 'Über das Frauenwahlrecht', *Neue Bahnen,* 33:7 (1898), 68

Lange, Helene and G. Bäumer (eds), *Handbuch der Frauenbewegung I. Teil: die Geschichte der Frauenbewegung in den Kulturländern* (Weinheim, 1980)

Larkin, Felix M., 'Satirical journalism' in M. Conboy and A. Bingham (eds), *The Edinburgh history of the British and Irish press, vol. 3: competition and disruption, 1900–2017* (Edinburgh, 2020)

Larkin, Felix M., '"Humour is the safety valve of a nation": *Dublin Opinion*, 1922–68' in Mark O'Brien and Felix M Larkin (eds), *Periodicals and journalism in twentieth-century Ireland* (Dublin, 2014)

Larkin, Felix M. and N.M. Dawson (eds), *Lawyers, the law and history: Irish Legal History Society discourses and other papers, 2005–2011* (Dublin, 2013)

Larkin, Felix M., 'Icons of freedom: the work of John Fergus O'Hea', *Irish Arts Review*, 39:2 (Summer 2022), 106

Larkin, Felix M., *Terror and discord: the Shemus cartoons in the* Freeman's Journal, *1920–1924* (Dublin, 2009)

Lauterer, Heide-Marie, *Parlamentarierinnen in Deutschland* (Königstein, 2002)

Law, Vivien Cheryl, 'The women's cause: feminist campaigns 1918–1928' (PhD, University of London, 1993)

Leahy, Walter T., *The Catholic church of the diocese of Trenton* (Princeton, 1906).

Lee, Joseph J., *The modernization of Irish society, 1848–1918* (Dublin, 1973)

Leigh Smith Bodichon, B., *Brief summary in plain language of the most important laws of England concerning women* (London, 1854)

Liddington, Jill, 'Was the suffrage campaign truly international? Votes for women in Edwardian England, 1903–1914' in E. Schöck-Quinteros et al. (eds), *Politische Netzwerkerinnen. Internationale Zusammenarbeit von Frauen, 1830–1960* (Bremen, 2007)

Little, George A., 'Hungry Hamilton, Fellow of Trinity', *Dublin Historical Record,* 11 (1930–40), 7

Little, George A., *The Spottiswoode miscellany: a collection of original papers and tracts, illustrative of the civil and ecclesiastical history of Scotland* (2 vols, Spottiswoode Society, Edinburgh, 1844)

Little, Patrick, 'Select document. Providence and posterity: a letter from Lord Mountnorris to his daughter, 1642', *Irish Historical Studies,* 32:128 (Nov. 2001), 556

Locke, John, *Second treatise of government* (London, 1690)

Lodge, John (rev. Mervyn Archdall), *The peerage of Ireland or a genealogical history of the present nobility of that kingdom* (7 vols, Dublin, 1789)

Longley York, Niall, *Neither kingdom nor nation: the Irish quest for constitutional rights, 1698–1800* (Washington DC, 1994)

Loughlin, James, *The British monarchy and Ireland: 1800 to the present* (Cambridge, 2007)

Lowe, John (ed.), *Letter-book of the earl of Clanricarde, 1643–1647* (Dublin, 1983)

Loxton, Alice, *Uproar: satire, scandal and printmakers in Georgian London* (London, 2023)

Lynch-Robinson, Christopher, *The last of the Irish RMs* (London, 1951)

Lyons, Francis Stewart Leland, 'Parnellism and crime, 1887–90' *Transactions of the Royal Historical Society*, 24 (1974), 137.

Lyons, Francis Stewart Leland, *Charles Stewart Parnell* (London, 1977)

Lyons, Francis Stewart Leland, *Ireland since the Famine* (London, 1971 and 2nd ed., 1985)

Lyons, Francis Stewart Leland, *John Dillon: a biography* (London, 1968)

Mac [I.M. Mcnie], *The celebrity zoo: some desultory rhymes and caricatures* (Dublin, 1925)

Mac Philib, Séamas, 'Profile of a landlord in folk tradition and in contemporary accounts: the third earl of Leitrim', *Ulster Folklore,* 34 (1988), 26

Mac Suibhne, Breandán, 'Soggarth aroon and gombeen-priest: Canon James MacFadden (1842–1917)' in Gerard Moran (ed.), *Radical Irish priests, 1660–1970* (Dublin, 1998)

Macaulay, Ambrose, *The Holy See and the Plan of Campaign in Ireland, 1885–93* (Dublin, 2002)

MacDonnell, Antony Patrick, *Some suggestions concerning the future welfare of Ireland* (Dublin, 1911)

MacIlwaine, William, 'Notice of hitherto unpublished portion of the "Montgomery manuscripts"', *Ulster Journal of Archaeology*, 9 (1861–2), 154

Mack, Peter, *Elizabethan rhetoric: theory and practice* (Cambridge, 2002)

MacLysaght, Edward (ed.), *Calendar of the Orrery papers* (Dublin, 1941)

MacLysaght, Edward (ed.), *Kenmare manuscripts* (Dublin, 1942)

MacMillan, Ken, *Sovereignty and possession in the English new world. The legal foundations of empire, 1576–1640* (Cambridge, 2006)

Mahaffy, Robert Pentland (ed.), *Calendar of state papers Ireland 1647–1660* (London, 1903)

Mahaffy, Robert Pentland (ed.), *Calendar of state papers Ireland 1625–1632* (London, 1900)

Mahaffy, Robert Pentland (ed.), *Calendar of state papers Ireland 1633–1647* (London, 1901)

Mahaffy, Robert Pentland (ed.), *Calendar of state papers Ireland 1669–1670* (London, 1910)

Mahony, Robert, *Jonathan Swift: the Irish identity* (New Haven and London, 1995)

Malchow, Howard L., *Gothic images of race in nineteenth-century Britain* (Stanford, 1996)

Malcolmson, Anthony Peter William, *Virtues of a wicked earl: the life and legend of William Sydney Clements, 3rd earl of Leitrim (1806–78)* (Dublin, 2009)

Mansergh, Nicholas, *The Irish Free State: its government and politics* (London, 1934)

[Marsh, Narcissus], *Institutiones logicae: in usum juventutis academiae Dublinensis* (Dublin, 1679)

Martial, *Epigrams* (ed. and trans. D.P. Shackleton Bailey) (2 vols, Massachusetts, 1963)

Maume, Patrick, 'Parnell and the I.R.B. oath', *Irish Historical Studies*, 29:115 (May 1995), 363

Maynard, Hazel, 'Irish membership of the English inns of court, 1660–1699: lawyers, litigation and the legal profession' (PhD, University College Dublin, 2006)

McAsey, Carmel, 'Booterstown', *Dublin Historical Record*, 21:3 (1969), 81

McAtasney, Gerard and Christine Kinealy, *The Famine in Lurgan and Portadown* (Belfast, 1997)

McBride, Ian, '*The case of Ireland* (1698) in context: William Molyneux and his critics', *Proceedings of the Royal Irish Academy*, 118 (2018), 203

McCartney, Donal, *W.E.H. Lecky: historian and politician, 1838–1903* (Dublin, 1994)

McCavitt, John, '"Good planets in their several spheares" – the establishment of the assize circuits in early seventeenth-century Ireland', *Irish Jurist*, 24:2 (1989), 248

McDowell, Robert Brendan, 'Edward Carson' in Conor Cruise O'Brien (ed.), *The shaping of modern Ireland* (London, 1970 [1960])

McDowell, Robert Brendan, 'Trinity College Dublin and politics' in R.B. McDowell (ed.), *Historical essays, 1938–2001* (Dublin, 2003)
McDowell, Robert Brendan and David Allardice Webb, *Trinity College, Dublin: an academic history, 1592–1952* (Cambridge, 1972)
McDowell, Robert Brendan, *Crisis and decline: the fate of the southern unionists* (Dublin, 1997)
McDowell, Robert Brendan, *The Irish Convention 1917–18* (London, 1970)
McGough McCann, Michelle, *The Irish coroner: death, murder and politics in Co. Monaghan 1846–78* (Dublin, 2023)
McGowan-Doyle, Valerie, *The book of Howth: Elizabethan conquest and the Old English* (Cork, 2011)
McGrath, Bríd, 'Ireland and the third university: attendance at the inns of court, 1603–1649' in David Edwards (ed.), *Regions and rulers in Ireland, 1100–1650: essays for Kenneth Nicholls* (Dublin, 2004)
McGrath, Bríd, *The operations of the Irish House of Commons, 1613–48* (Dublin, 2023)
McMahon, Deirdre, *Republicans and imperialists: Anglo-Irish relations in the 1930s* (New Haven and London, 1984)
McRedmond, Louis (ed.), *Modern Irish lives: dictionary of 20th-century biography* (Dublin, 1996)
Mercier, Vivian, *The Irish comic tradition* (Oxford, 1962)
Meyler, Walter, *St Catherine's bells: an autobiography* (London, 1870)
Mohr, Thomas, 'The Anglo-Irish Treaty – legal interpretation, 1921–1925', *Irish Jurist,* 66 (2021), 1
Mohr, Thomas, 'George Gavan Duffy and the legal consequences of the Anglo-Irish Treaty, 1921–1923' *Northern Ireland Legal Quarterly,* 72:4 (2021)
Mohr, Thomas, *Guardian of the Treaty: the privy council appeal and Irish sovereignty* (Dublin, 2016)
Mohr, Thomas, 'The rights of women under the constitution of the Irish Free State', *Irish Jurist,* 41 (2006), 20
Mohr, Thomas, 'Natural law in early twentieth-century Ireland: *State (Ryan) v. Lennon* and its aftermath', *Journal of Legal History,* 42:1 (2021), 1
Mohr, Thomas, 'Religious minorities under the constitution of the Irish Free State, 1922–1937', *American Journal of Legal History,* 61:2 (2021), 1
Mohr, Thomas, 'Law journals and Irish history, 1922–1939', *Comparative Legal History,* 7:2 (2019), 1
Molesworth, Robert, *Account of Denmark* (London, 1694)
Molyneux, William, *The case of Ireland's being bound by acts of parliament in England, stated* [Dublin, 1698], ed. P.H. Kelly (Dublin, 2018)
Montaño, John Patrick, '"Dycheyng and hegeying": the material culture of the Tudor plantations in Ireland' in Fiona Bateman and Lionel Pilkington (eds), *Studies in settler colonialism: politics, identity and culture* (Basingstoke, 2011)
Montaño, John Patrick, *The roots of English colonialism in Ireland* (Cambridge, 2011)
Moody, Theodore William, *Davitt and Irish revolution, 1846–82* (Oxford, 1981)
Mooney, Joe, *The changing fortunes of the Headfort estate, 1870–1928* (Dublin, 2012)
Moran, Gerard, 'Laying the seeds for agrarian agitation: the Ballinasloe Tenant Defence Association, 1876–80' in Carla King and Conor McNamara (eds), *The West of Ireland* (Dublin, 2011)

Morrissey, Thomas J., *William J. Walsh, archbishop of Dublin* (Dublin, 2000)
Moss, Jean Dietz, 'Discordant consensus: old and new rhetoric at Trinity College, Dublin', *Rhetorica: a Journal of the History of Rhetoric*, 14 (1996), 383
Muldrew, Craig, 'Credit and the courts: debt litigation in a seventeenth-century urban community', *Economic History Review*, 46:1 (1993), 23
Muldrew, Craig, 'The culture of reconciliation: community and the settlement of disputes in early modern England', *The Historical Journal*, 39:4 (1996), 915.
Mulvey, Helen F., *Thomas Davis and Ireland* (Washington, DC, 2003)
Murray, Patrick, *Oracles of God: the Roman Catholic church and Irish politics, 1922–1937* (Dublin, 2000)
Nicholls, Kenneth W., 'A calendar of salved chancery pleadings concerning County Louth', *Journal of the County Louth Archaeological and Historical Society*, 17:4 (1972), 250
Nicholls, Kenneth W., 'A calendar of salved chancery pleadings concerning County Louth, continued', *Journal of the County Louth Archaeological and Historical Society*, 18:2 (1974), 112
Nicholls, Kenneth W., 'Irishwomen and property in the sixteenth century' in Margaret MacCurtain and Mary O'Dowd (eds), *Women in early modern Ireland* (Dublin, 1991)
Nicholls, Kenneth W., 'Some documents on Irish law and custom in the sixteenth century', *Analecta Hibernica*, 26 (1970), 105
Nicholls, Kenneth W., *Land, law and society in sixteenth-century Ireland* (O'Donnell Lecture, Dublin, 1976)
Nicholls, Kenneth W., 'The Lynch Blosse papers', *Analecta Hibernica*, 29 (1980), 115
Ó Broin, Leon, *The prime informer: a suppressed scandal* (London, 1971)
Ó Crudhlaoich, Diarmuid, *The oath of allegiance* (Dublin, 1925)
Ó Duibhir, Pól, *Gordon Brewster and his cartoons* (Cork, 2024)
Ó Fathartaigh, Micheál and Liam Weeks, *Birth of a state: the Anglo-Irish Treaty* (Newbridge, 2021)
Ó Hiorlaithe, Aogán, 'Changes in scholarly approaches to early Irish law in the period since the publication of D.A. Binchy's *Corpus Iuris Hibernici*', *Irish Jurist*, 67 (2022), 170
Ó Tuathaigh, Gearóid, *I mBeal an Bhais: the Great Famine and the language shift in nineteenth-century Ireland* (Hamden, 2015)
O'Brien, Mark, *The* Irish Times*: a history* (Dublin, 2008)
O'Brien, William, *Recollections* (London, 1905)
O'Brien, William, *The Parnell of real life* (London, 1926)
O'Dowd, Mary, 'Women and the Irish chancery court in the late sixteenth and early seventeenth centuries', *Irish Historical Studies*, 31:124 (1999), 470
O'Malley, Liam, 'Patrick Darcy, Galway lawyer and politician, 1598–1668' in Diarmuid Ó Cearbhaill (ed.), *Galway: town and crown, 1484–1984* (Dublin, 1984)
O'Neill, Marie, *Grace Gifford Plunkett and Irish freedom: tragic bride of 1916* (Dublin, 2000)
O'Riordan, Colum, Paul Burns and Ciaran O'Connor (eds), *Ireland's court houses* (Dublin, 2019)
Osborough, W.N., *The Irish stage: a legal history* (Dublin, 2015)

Osborough, W.N., 'The lawyers of the Irish novels of Anthony Trollope' in Daire Hogan and W.N. Osborough (eds), *Brehons, serjeants and attorneys: studies in the history of the Irish legal profession* (Dublin, 1990)

Osborough, W.N. (ed.), *Explorations in law and history: Irish Legal History Society discourses, 1988–1994* (Dublin, 1995)

Osborough, W.N., *An island's law: a bibliographical guide to Ireland's legal past* (Dublin, 2013)

O'Sullivan, Donal, *The Irish Free State and its Senate: a study in contemporary politics* (London, 1940)

O'Sullivan, Niamh, *Aloysius O'Kelly: art, nation, empire* (Dublin, 2010)

Ohlmeyer, Jane and Éamonn Ó Ciardha (eds), *The Irish statute staple, 1596–1687* (Dublin, 1998)

Ohlmeyer, Jane, 'A laboratory for empire? Early modern Ireland and English imperialism' in Kevin Kenny (ed.), *Ireland and the British empire* (Oxford, 2004)

Ohlmeyer, Jane, '"Civilizinge of those rude partes": the colonization of Ireland and Scotland, 1580s–1640s' in Nicholas Canny (ed.), *The Oxford history of the British empire* (5 vols, Oxford, 1998)

Ohlmeyer, Jane, 'Conquest, civilization, colonization: Ireland, 1540–1660' in Richard Bourke and Ian MacBride (eds), *The Princeton guide to modern Irish history* (Princeton, 2016)

Ohlmeyer, Jane, 'Eastward enterprises: colonial Ireland, colonial India', *Past & Present*, 240:1 (2018), 83

Ohlmeyer, Jane, 'Irish recusant lawyers during the reign of Charles I' in Micheál Ó Siochrú (ed.), *A kingdom in crisis: the confederates and the Irish civil wars* (Dublin, 2000)

Ohlmeyer, Jane, *Making Ireland English: the Irish aristocracy in the seventeenth century* (London, 2012)

Orridge, A.W., 'Who supported the land war? An aggregate-data analysis of Irish agrarian discontent, 1879–1882', *Irish Economic and Social Review*, 12:3 (Apr. 1981), 203

Pakenham, Frank, *Peace by ordeal* (London, 1935)

Pape, Charlotte, 'Briefe' *Neue Bahnen* 11:15 (1876), 119

Pape, Charlotte, 'Rechte der Mutter über ihre Kinder', *Neue Bahnen* (1876), 12

Passarella, Claudia, 'The juries' wisdom in the administration of criminal justice: Irish jurisdiction and the Italian justice system in the late nineteenth and early twentieth centuries', *Comparative Legal History*, 7:2 (2019), 157

Phillips, William, *Studii legalis ratio, or, directions for the study of the law [1660]* (London, 1675)

Philpin, Charles H.E. (ed.), *Nationalism and popular protest in Ireland* (Cambridge, 1987)

Plunkett, Horace, *The Irish Convention. Confidential report to His Majesty The King* (Dublin, 1918)

Pocock, John Greville Agard, *The ancient constitution and the feudal law: … a re-issue with a retrospect* (Cambridge, 1987)

Pomfret, John E., *The struggle for land in Ireland, 1800–1923* (Princeton, 1930)

Prest, Wilfrid R. (ed.), *Lawyers in early modern Europe and America* (London, 1981)

Prest, Wilfrid R., 'Legal education of the gentry at the inns of court, 1560–1640', *Past and Present,* 38 (1967), 20

Prest, Wilfrid R., *The inns of court under Elizabeth and the early Stuarts (1590–1640)* (London, 1972)

Quintilianus, Marcus Fabius, *Institutio oratoria* (ed. and trans. H.E. Butler) (4 vols, Massachusetts, 1920–2)

Rabinow, Paul, *The Foucault reader* (New York, 1984)

Ranieri, Filippo, 'From status to profession: the professionalization of lawyers as a research field in modern European legal history', *Journal of Legal History*, 10:1 (1989), 184

Rayner Belloc, Bessie, *Remarks on the education of girls* (3rd edn, London, 1856)

Remme, I, *Die internationalen Beziehungen der deutschen Frauenbewegung vom Ausgang des 19. Jahrhunderts bis 1933* (Berlin, 1955)

Richter, H., and K. Wolff (eds), *Demokratisierung der Demokratie in Deutschland und Europa* (Hamburg, 2018)

Ridges, E.W., *Constitutional law of England* (London, 1905)

Riedel, T.C., *Gleiches Recht für Frau und Mann. Die bürgerliche Frauenbewegung und die Entstehung des BGB* (Cologne, 2008)

Ronner, A.D., *Law, literature and therapeutic jurisprudence* (Durham, NC, 2010)

Rosenbusch, U., *Der Weg zum Frauenwahlrecht in Deutschland* (Baden-Baden, 1998)

Rubenhold, Hallie, *The five: the untold lives of the women killed by Jack the Ripper* (London, 2019)

Rubinstein, D., *A different world for women: the life of Millicent Garrett Fawcett* (Ohio, 1991)

Rumbelow, Donald, *The complete Jack the Ripper* (London, 1975)

Rupp, Leila, *Worlds of women: the making of an international women's movement* (Princeton, 1997)

Russell, Charles William and John Patrick Prendergast (eds), *Calendar of state papers Ireland 1615–1625* (London, 1880)

Russell, Charles William and John Patrick Prendergast (eds) *Calendar of state papers Ireland 1611–1614* (London, 1877)

Russell, Charles William and John Patrick Prendergast (eds), *Calendar of state papers Ireland 1606–1608* (London, 1874)

Ryan, Louise and Margaret Ward (eds), *Irish women and the vote: becoming citizens* (Newbridge, 2018)

Ryan, Louise, *Winning the vote for women: the* Irish Citizenship *newspaper and the suffrage movement in Ireland* (Dublin, 2018)

Schaser, Angelika, 'Zur Einführung des Frauenwahlrechts vor 90 Jahren am 12. November 1918', *Feministische Studien*, 27:1 (2009), 97

Schirmacher, K., *Die Suffragettes* (Weimar, 1912)

Schraut, Sylvia, 'Internationale Konferenzen, Publikationen und die Stiftung von Erinnerung: Mediale Strategien in den Richtungskämpfen der bürgerlichen Frauenbewegung im Kaiserreich', *Feministische Studien,* 35:1 (2017), 61

Schröder, Hannelore, *Widerspenstige, Rebellinnen, Suffragetten. Feministischer Aufbruch in England und Deutschland* (Aachen, 2001)

Shanley, Mary Lyndon, *Feminism, marriage, and the law in Victorian England* (Princeton, 1989)
Sheehy, Jeanne, *The rediscovery of Ireland's past: the Celtic revival, 1830–1930* (London, 1980)
Sheehy Skeffington, Hanna, 'Women in the Irish Free State', *Equal Rights*, 23:12 (1937), 96
Sheehy Skeffington, Andrée, and Rosemary Owens, *Votes for women: Irish women's struggle for the vote* (Dublin, 1975)
Simms, John Gerald, *Colonial nationalism, 1698–1776* (Cork, 1976)
Simms, John Gerald, *Jacobite Ireland* (Dublin, 2000)
Simms, John Gerald, *William Molyneux* (Dublin, 1982)
Skinner, Keith and Stewart Evans, *The ultimate Jack the Ripper sourcebook* (London, 2013)
Skinner, Quentin, *Reason and rhetoric in the philosophy of Thomas Hobbes* (Cambridge, 1996)
Smith, F.E., *International law* (2nd ed., London, 1903; repr. London, 2015)
Smith, George Hill, *The North-East bar: a sketch, historical and reminiscent* (Belfast, 1910)
Smith, Harold L., *The British women's suffrage campaign, 1866–1928* (London, 1998)
Smyth, John, *The memoirs and letters of Ulick, marquess of Clanricarde, and earl of Saint Albans* (London, 1758)
Smyth, S., *Thanks a million, big fella* (Dublin, 1997)
Sneeringer, J., *Winning women's votes: propaganda and politics in Weimar Germany* (Chapel Hill, 2002)
Spelman, Henry, *Glossarium archaiologicum ...* (London, 1687)
Spender, John Alfred and Cyril Asquith, *The life of H.H. Asquith, Lord Oxford and Asquith* (London, 1932)
Spring-Rice, Thomas, *An inquiry into the effects of the Irish grand jury laws: as affecting the industry, the improvement, and the moral character of the people of Ireland* (London, 1815)
Steele, Edward David, *Irish land and British politics: tenant right and nationality, 1864–70* (Cambridge, 1974)
Steer, Francis W. and Noel H. Osborne (eds), *The Petworth House archives: a catalogue* (4 vols, Chichester, 1968)
Stevenson, John, *Two centuries of life in Down, 1600–1800* (Belfast, 1920)
Students admitted to the Inner Temple, 1547–1660 [ed. W.H. Cooke] (London, 1877)
Sturgess, H.A.C. (ed.), *Register of admissions to the honourable society of the Middle Temple from the fifteenth century to the year 1944*, 3 vols (London, 1949)
Stritt, M., 'Der Internationale Frauenkongress in London', *Die Frau*, 6 (1899), 644
Stritt, M., 'Germany. Victory for woman suffrage', *International Women's News*, 13:4 (1919), 44
Stuart Mill, J., *The subjection of women* (London, 1869)
Stubley, Peter, *1888: London murders in the year of the Ripper* (London, 2012)
Sturgess, Herbert Arthur Charlie (ed.), *Register of admissions to the Honourable Society of the Middle Temple from the fifteenth century to the year 1944* (3 vols, London, 1949)

Sugden, Philip, *The complete history of Jack the Ripper* (London, 1995)
Sulkunen, Irma, S.L. Nevala-Nurmi and P. Markkola (eds), *Suffrage, gender and citizenship: international perspectives on parliamentary reform* (Cambridge, 2009)
Sweeney, Joseph C., *The life and times of Arthur Browne in Ireland and America, 1756–1805: civil law and civil liberties* (Dublin, 2017)
Swift, Jonathan, *Gulliver's travels* (1726)
Tallon, Geraldine (ed.), *Court of claims: submissions and evidence, 1663* (Dublin, 2006)
Teele, Dawn L., *Forging the franchise: the political origins of the women's vote* (Princeton, 2018)
Teeling, George (ed.), *Selected speeches and arguments of the right hon. Thomas, Baron O'Hagan* (London, 1885)
Thomson, David, *Woodbrook* (London, 1974)
Thurgood, Peter, *Abberline: The man who hunted Jack the Ripper* (London, 2013)
Thurston Hopkins, R., *Life and death at the Old Bailey* (London, 1935)
Treadwell, Victor, *Buckingham and Ireland, 1616–1628: a study in Anglo-Irish politics* (Dublin, 1998)
Turner, Martyn, *Greatest hits* (Dublin, 2003)
Turner, Martyn, *Turner's taoisigh: my brush with Kildare Street* (Dublin, 2014)
Turner, Martyn, *Up every tree: the bumper book of Bertie* (Dublin, 2006)
Valentine, Barry J.A.C., *Criminal procedure in Northern Ireland* (2nd edn, Belfast, 2010)
Vaughan, William E., *Landlords and tenants in mid-Victorian Ireland* (Oxford, 1994)
Vaughan, William E., *Murder trials in Ireland 1836–1914* (Dublin, 2009)
Valiulis, Maryann Gialanella, *The making of inequality in the Irish Free State, 1922–37: women, power and gender ideology* (Dublin, 2019)
Vickers, Brian, *In defence of rhetoric* (Oxford, 1988)
Ward, Margaret, 'Suffrage first – above all else: an account of the Irish suffrage movement', *Feminist Review*, 19 (1982), 21
Watkins, S.B., *Ireland's suffragettes: the women who fought for the vote* (Dublin, 2014)
Weber, Marianne, *Ehefrau und Mutter in der Rechtsentwicklung. Eine Einführung* (Aalen, 1971, np 1907)
Weldon, S. Laurel, *When protest makes policy* (Ann Arbor, 2011)
White, Hayden V., *Metahistory: the historical imagination in nineteenth-century Europe* (Baltimore, 1973)
White, Hayden V., *Tropics of discourse: essays in cultural criticism* (Baltimore, 1978)
White, Jerry, *Mansions of misery: a biography of the Marshalsea debtors' prison* (London, 2016)
Wickert, C. (ed.), *Heraus mit dem Frauenwahlrecht: die Kämpfe der Frauen in Deutschland und England um die politische Gleichberechtigung* (Pfaffenweiler, 1990)
Wischermann, U., *Frauenbewegung und Öffentlichkeiten um 1900. Netzwerke, Gegenöffentlichkeiten, Protestinszenierungen* (Königstein, 2003)
Wood, Herbert, *A guide to the records deposited in the public record office of Ireland* (Dublin, 1919)
Wood, Herbert, 'The public records of Ireland before and after 1922', *Transactions of the Royal Historical Society*, 13, 4th ser. (1930), 17
Wright, George Newenham, *An historical guide to the city of Dublin* (London, 1825)

Wroath, John, *Until they are seven: the origin of women's legal rights* (Winchester, 1998)
Wylie, John C.W., *Irish land law* (3rd edn, Dublin, 1997)
Zimmern, Alice, *Women's suffrage in many lands* (London, 1909)

ARCHIVES

Bodleian Library, Oxford
British Cartoon Archive, University of Kent
British Library, London
Bundesarchiv, Koblenz, Germany
Dublin Corporation Archives, Dublin
Landesarchiv Berlin
National Archives of Ireland
National Library of Ireland, Dublin
Oireachtas Library, Dublin
Parliamentary Archives, London
Public Record Office of Northern Ireland, Belfast
Registry of Deeds, Dublin
Royal Irish Academy Library, Dublin
The National Archives, Kew
Trinity College Dublin manuscripts, Dublin
University College Dublin Archives, Dublin
Women's Library Archives, London

NEWSPAPERS AND PERIODICALS

An Phoblacht
Anglo Celt
Armagh Guardian
Armagh Standard
Belfast News Letter
Belfast Telegraph
Blackwood's Magazine
Church of Ireland Gazette
Connaught Telegraph
Down Recorder
Drogheda Argus
Drogheda Independent
Dublin Daily Express
Dublin Evening Telegraph
Dublin Gazette
Dublin Opinion
Evening Herald
Fermanagh Times
Freeman's Journal
Irish Fun
Irish Law Times and Solicitors' Journal
Irish Press
Irish Times
Irish Worker
Jewish Chronicle
Law Times
London Gazette
Londonderry Sentinel
Meath Herald and Cavan Advertiser
Morning Post
Nation
Newry Reporter
North Down Herald
Punch
Republic of Ireland
Saunders Newsletter
The Referee
Weekly Freeman
Wexford People
Ulster Gazette
United Ireland
Volunteer's Journal

LEGAL SOURCES

Cases

Bannatyne v. Gorman, FJ, 7 Nov. 1851
Browne v. Sir Nicholas Brady, FJ, 2 Dec. 1841
Chapman v. Marlborough Park Co. Ltd, Belfast News Letter, 19 July 1898
Codd v. Hyde (1833) 1 Law Rec (ns) 90
Coughlan v. Monks [1918] 2 IR 306.
Deering v. Palmer, FJ, 3 June 1842
Dowd v. Cunningham, FJ, 26 Sept. 1842
Gage and Roper v. Pigott and de Jenner [1919] 1 IR 23
Headfort v. Cochrane (1892) 26 ILTR 112
In re Article 26 and the Criminal Law (Jurisdiction) Bill, 1975 [1977] IR 129
In re Boyd [1918] 2 IR 98
In re Compensation to Civil Servants under Article X of the Treaty [1929] IR 44
In re Connor [1919] 1 IR 361
Maguire v. Browne [1921] 1 IR 148
Moore and Others v. Attorney General [1935] IR 472 and [1935] AC 484
Murray v. Parkes [1942] 2 KB 123
O'Brien v. Moore, FJ, 20 Feb. 1847
O'Connell & others v. Regina (1844) 11 Cl & Fin 155
O'Doherty v. Fox (1833) 1 Law Rec (ns) 36
Pharmaceutical Society of Ireland v. Boyd & Co. [1896] 2 IR 394
R (Cleland) v. Pharmaceutical Society of Ireland [1896] 2 IR 368
R (Futter) v. Justices of Co. Cork [1917] 2 IR 430
R (McMorrow) v. Fitzpatrick [1918] 2 IR 103
R v. McNicholl [1917] 2 IR 557
Ramsey v. Crawe (1673) Case, p. 117
Re Joseph Dawson and Others (1696) 13 How St. Tr. 451
Re Reade [1927] IR 31
Re the Earl of Shaftsbury (1681) 8 How. St. Tr. 770
Scott v. Doyle (1833) 2 Law Rec 65
Seyman v. Gresham (1601) Cro Eliz 908; 78 ER 1131
Shelburne v. Burke (1833) 1 Law Rec (ns) 15
State (Ryan and others) v. Lennon (and others) [1935] IR 170
The Queen v. Sullivan (1887) 20 LR Ir 550
Tighe v. Abraham (1833) 2 Law Rec 35
Town and County Advance Company v. Provincial Bank [1917] 2 IR 421
Tyrell v. Sullivan, FJ, 17 June 1851
White v. Burrow (nd) Rowe's Reports 431
Wigg and Cochrane v. The Attorney General of the Irish Free State [1927] IR 293 (HC), [1925] 1 IR 149 (SC) and [1927] IR 285 (PC)
Woods v. Finnis (1852) 7 Exch R 363

Legislation

Poynings Law 1495 (10 Hen. VII, c. 4)
Crown of Ireland Act 1542 (33 Hen. VIII, c. 1)
An Act for turning of Countries that be not yet Shire Grounds into Shire Grounds 1569 (11 Eliz. sess. 3, c. 9).
Crown and Parliament Recognition Act 1689 (2 Will. and Mary, c. 1)
An Act for the Abrogating the Oath of Supremacy in Ireland and Appointing other Oaths 1691 (3 & 4 Will. and Mary, c. 2)
Sunday Observance Act 1695 (Ir) (7 Will. III, c. 17)
An Act for the Confirmation of Articles made at the Surrender of the City of Limerick, 1697 (9 Will. III, c. 2)
An Act for the more easy and speedy securing and recovery of small debts 1697 (9 Will. III, c. 15 [Ir])
Union with Ireland Act 1800 (39 & 40 Geo. III, c. 67 [G.B.])
Act for the Union of Great Britain and Ireland 1800 (40 Geo. III, c. 38 [Ir.])
Process (Ireland) Act 1803 (43 Geo. III, c. 53)
Insolvent Debtors Relief (Ireland) Act 1809 (49 Geo. III, c. 54)
Insolvent Debtors (Ireland) Act 1810 (50 Geo. III, c. 47)
Insolvent Debtors Relief (Ireland) Act 1811 (51 Geo. III, c. 123)
Insolvent Debtors Relief (Ireland) Act 1812 (52 Geo. III, c. 163)
Insolvent Debtors Act 1813 (53 Geo III, c. 102)
Insolvent Debtors (Ireland) Act 1814 (54 Geo. III, c. 114)
Grand Jury (Ireland) Act 1816 (56 Geo. III c. 87)
Prisons Act 1821 (1 & 2 Geo. IV, c. 57)
Prisons (Ireland) Act 1822 (3 Geo. IV, c. 64)
Arrest on Mesne Process (Ireland) Act 1829 (10 Geo. IV, c. 35)
Roman Catholic Relief Act 1829 (10 Geo. IV, c. 7)
Civil Bill Courts Act 1836 (6 & 7 Will. IV, c. 75)
Grand Jury (Ireland) Act 1838 (1 & 2 Vict., c. 37)
Small Tenements Recovery Act 1838 (1 & 2 Vict., c. 74)
Custody of Infants Act 1839 (2 & 3 Vict., c. 54)
Debtors (Ireland) Act 1840 (3 & 4 Vict., c. 105)
Insolvent Debtors Act 1840 (3 & 4 Vict., c. 107)
Insolvent Debtors (Ireland) Act 1840 (3 & 4 Vict., c. 108)
Four Courts Marshalsea Act 1842 (5 & 6 Vict., c. 95)
Coroners (Ireland) Act 1846 (9 & 10 Vict., c. 37)
Execution Act 1848 (11 & 12 Vict., c. 28)
Encumbered Estates (Ireland) Act 1849 (12 & 13 Vict., c. 77)
Civil Bill Courts (Ireland) Act 1851 (14 & 15 Vict., c. 57)
Common Law Procedure Act 1853 (16 & 17 Vict., c 113)
Probate and Letters of Administration Act 1857 (20 & 21 Vict., c. 79)
Bankrupt and Insolvent Act 1857 (20 & 21 Vict., c. 60)
Landlord and Tenant Amendment (Ireland) Act 1860 (23 & 24 Vict., c. 154)
Civil Bill Courts Procedure Amendment Act (Ireland) 1864 (27 & 28 Vict., c. 99)
Colonial Laws Validity Act 1865 (28 & 29 Vict., c. 63)
British North America Act 1867 (30 & 31 Vict., c. 3)

Landlord and Tenant (Ireland) Act 1870 (33 & 34 Vict., c. 46)
Married Women's Property Act 1870 (33 & 34 Vict., c. 93)
Debtors Ireland Act 1872 (35 & 36 Vict., c. 57)
Winter Assizes Act, 1876 (39 & 40 Vict., c. 57)
Appellate Jurisdiction Act 1876 (39 & 40 Vict., c. 59)
Supreme Court of Judicature (Ireland) Act, 1877 (40 & 41 Vict., c. 57)
Prisons Act 1877 (40 & 41 Vict., c. 21)
Coroners (Ireland) Act 1881 (48 & 49 Vict., c. 35)
Land Law (Ireland) Act 1881 (44 & 45 Vict., c. 49)
Protection of Persons and Property (Ireland) Act 1881 (44 & 45 Vict., c. 4).
Arrears of Rent (Ireland) Act 1882 (45 & 46 Vict., c. 47)
Purchase of Land (Ireland) Act 1885 (48 & 49 Vict., c. 73)
Criminal Law and Procedure (Ireland) Act 1887 (50 & 51 Vict., c. 20)
Land Law (Ireland) Act 1887 (50 & 51 Vict., c. 33)
Married Women's Property Act 1882 (45 & 46 Vict., c. 75)
Representation of the People Act 1884 (48 & 49 Vict., c. 3)
Criminal Law and Procedure (Ireland) Act 1887 (50 & 51 Vict., c. 20)
Special Commission Act 1888 (51 & 52 Vict., c. 35)
Criminal Evidence Act 1898 (61 & 62 Vict., c. 36)
Commonwealth of Australia Constitution Act 1900 (63 & 64 Vict., c. 12 [Aus])
Land Purchase (Ireland) Act 1903 (3 Ed. VII, c. 37)
Irish Universities Act 1908 (7 Ed. VII, c. 38)
Irish Land Act, 1909 (9 Ed. VII, c. 42)
Official Secrets Act 1911 (1 & 2 Geo. V, c. 28)
Termination of the Present War (Definition) Act 1918 (8 & 9 Geo. V, c. 59)
Government of Ireland Act 1914 (4 & 5 Geo. V, c. 90)
Government of Ireland Act 1920 (10 & 11 Geo. V, c. 67)
Constitution of the Irish Free State (Saorstát Éireann) Act 1922 [Irl.]
Irish Free State (Agreement) Act 1922 (12 & 13 Geo. V, c. 4)
Irish Free State Constitution Act 1922 (12 & 13 Geo. V, c. 1)
Criminal Evidence (NI) Act 1923
Electoral (Amendment) (No. 2) Act 1927
Constitution (Amendment No. 16) Act 1929
Constitution (Amendment No. 17) Act 1931
Constitution (Amendment No. 10) Act 1928
Statute of Westminster Act 1931
Constitution (Removal of Oath) Bill 1932
Constitution (Amendment No. 19) Bill 1933
Constitution (Amendment No. 20) Act 1933
Constitution (Amendment No. 21) Act 1933
Constitution (Amendment No. 22) Act 1933
Constitution (Removal of Oath) Act 1933
Wearing of Uniform (Restriction) Bill 1934
Constitution (Amendment No. 24) Act 1936
Constitution (Amendment No. 23) Act 1936
Constitution (Amendment No. 27) Act 1936
Éire (Confirmation of Agreements) Act 1938

Finance (Agreement with the United Kingdom) Act 1938
Agreement with United Kingdom (Capital Sum) Act 1938
Republic of Ireland Act 1948
Grand Jury (Abolition) Act (Northern Ireland), 1969

PARLIAMENTARY SOURCES

Dáil Debates
Seanad Debates
Hansard's Parliamentary Debates, series 2–5
Commons Journals

The inspector general's report on the state of the prisons in Ireland for the year 1818, HC 1819 xii.453 (534)

Sixth report of the commissioners appointed to enquire into the duties, salaries and emoluments of the officers, clerks and ministers of justice in all temporal and ecclesiastical courts in Ireland. The court of king's bench, HC 1819 xii.287 (6)

State of Ireland. Minutes of evidence taken before the select committee appointed to inquire into the disturbances in Ireland in the last session of parliament, 13 May–18 June 1824, HC 1828 vii.1 (20)

(Ireland.) The fifteenth report of the commissioners appointed to inquire into the duties, salaries and emoluments, of the officers, clerks, and ministers of justice, in all temporal and ecclesiastical courts in Ireland. Office of sheriff, HC 1825 xvii.29 (310)

Return of the number of prisoners imprisoned for debt [on the 19th April 1826] in the king's bench, Fleet, Marshalsea … also a similar return for Ireland, HC 1826–27 xix.201 (108)

Return of the number of prisoners in committed for debt in Ireland, in the years 1827 and 1828, HC 1829 xxii.379 (93)

Return of the number of prisoners committed for debt to the custody of the keepers of the four courts Marshalsea, city Marshalsea, and other prisons in Dublin, and to each of the other prisons in Ireland, in the year 1829, HC 1830–31 xxiii.209 (118)

Returns of the number of summonses issued, and decrees made, by the court of conscience, in Dublin, in each of the last three years, HC 1830 viii.57 (170)

Eighth report of the inspectors general on the state of the prisons in Ireland, HC 1830 xxiv.719 (48)

Courts of request: (power of committing.) An abstract return of the number of courts of law in England, Wales, and Ireland, whether under the name of courts of request, or any other name, which have the power of committing to prison for debts of £. 5. and under, HC 1830 xxiii.217 (15)

Court of conscience, Dublin. Returns of the number of summonses issued, and decrees made, by the court of conscience, in Dublin, in each of the last three years; with the annual amount of fees received by the judge and register of the court; and, the number of warrants or executions issued during the same period, HC 1830–31 vii.57 (170)

Copy of the fourth report made to His Majesty by the commissioners appointed to inquire into the practice and proceedings of the superior courts of common law, HC 1831–32 (239)

Eleventh report of the inspectors general on the general state of the prisons of Ireland, HC 1833 xvii.307 (67)

Imprisonment for debt. Ireland. A return of all persons imprisoned for the three years last past, HC 1833 xxix.361 (356)

Civil bill commitments (Ireland) A return of the number of persons committed to each prison in Ireland during the last five years under civil bill decrees, and the amount for which every such decree was obtained, HC 1836 xlii.459 (184)

Fourteenth report of the inspectors general on the general state of prisons, HC 1836 xxxv.431 (118)

Report of the commissioners appointed to inquire and report with a view to the revision of the offices of the superior courts of common law in Ireland, HC 1842 xxiii.1 (378)

Imprisonment for debt. Abstract of a return of the number of persons confined for debt in the prisons of London, Middlesex and Surrey … and for Ireland HC 1844 xxxviii.613 (292)

Twenty-fourth report of the inspectors general on the general state of prions in Ireland 1845, HC 1846 xx.257 (697)

Return of the number of prisoners confined for debt in the different gaols of Ireland on the first day of January in each of the years 1837 etc, HC 1847 lvi.175 (354)

Debtors (Ireland). Abstract of returns of the persons confined for debt in each gaol in Ireland, in each of the years ending the 1st day of May 1843, 1844, 1845, 1846 and 1847, under orders from the quarter sessions, and from the superior courts of law, &c, HC 1847 lvi.177 (565)

Twenty-sixth report of the inspectors general of the prisons of Ireland, HC 1847–48 xxxiv.253 (952)

Court of queen's bench, &c. (Ireland). Returns of the total amount of law fund duty received in or yielded by the courts of queen'sbBench, common pleas and exchequer in Ireland, in the years 1842, 1843, 1844, 1845, 1846, 1847 and 1848; &c, HC 1850 li.323 (316)

Thirty-sixth report of the inspectors-general on the general state of the prisons of Ireland, 1857; with appendices, HC 1857–58 lvi.177 (2394)

English and Irish Law and chancery commission. First report of Her Majesty's commissioners appointed to inquire into the superior courts of common law and courts of chancery of England and Ireland, HC 1863 xv.463 Cmnd. 3238

Forty-fourth report of the inspectors general on the general state of the prisons of Ireland 1865, HC 1866 xxxiv.235 Cmnd. 3690

Forty-fifth report of the inspectors-general on the general state of the prisons of Ireland, 1866, HC 1867 xxxv.1 Cmnd. 3915

Report from the select committee on Irish Land Act, 1870; together with the proceedings of the committee, minutes of evidence, and appendix, HC 1878 xv.1 (249)

Report of her majesty's commissioners of enquiry into the working of the Landlord and Tenant (Ireland) Act of 1870 and the acts amending the same, HC 1881 xviii.1, 73, xix.1, 825, Cmnd. 2779, 2779-I, 2779-II and 2779-III

Special commission to inquire into charges and allegations against certain members of parliament and others, 19 vols (London, 1899)

The fifty-fifth report of the deputy keeper of the public records and keeper of the state papers in Ireland (Dublin, 1928)

The fifty-sixth report of the deputy keeper of the public records and keeper of the state papers in Ireland (Dublin, 1931)

Index

Compiled by Julitta Clancy

Note: page references in *italics* denote illustrations; '*Pl.*' indicates Plate number

IRISH LEGAL HISTORY SOCIETY SERIES*

1 Daire Hogan and W.N. Osborough (eds), *Brehons, serjeants and attorneys: studies in the history of the Irish legal profession* (1990)
2 Colum Kenny, *King's Inns and the kingdom of Ireland: the Irish 'inn of court', 1541–1800* (1992)
3 Jon G. Crawford, *Anglicizing the government of Ireland: the Irish Privy Council and the expansion of Tudor rule, 1556–1578* (1993)
4 W.N. Osborough (ed.), *Explorations in law and history: Irish Legal History Society discourses, 1988–1994* (1995)
5 W.N. Osborough, *Law and the emergence of modern Dublin: a litigation topography for a capital city* (1996)
6 Colum Kenny, *Tristram Kennedy and the revival of Irish legal training, 1835–1885* (1996)
7 Brian Griffin, *The Bulkies: police and crime in Belfast, 1800–1865* (1997)
8 Éanna Hickey, *Irish law and lawyers in modern folk tradition* (1999)
9 A.R. Hart, *A history of the king's serjeants at law in Ireland: honour rather than advantage?* (2000)
10 D.S. Greer and N.M. Dawson (eds), *Mysteries and solutions in Irish legal history: Irish Legal History Society discourses and other papers, 1996–1999* (2000)
11 Colum Kenny, *King's Inns and the battle of the books, 1972: cultural controversy at a Dublin library* (2002)
12 Desmond Greer and James W. Nicolson, *The factory acts in Ireland, 1802–1914* (2003)
13 Mary Kotsonouris, *The winding-up of the Dáil courts, 1922–1925: an obvious duty* (2004)
14 Paul Brand, Kevin Costello and W.N. Osborough (eds), *Adventures of the law: proceedings of the 16th British Legal History Conference, Dublin 2003* (2005)
15 Jon G. Crawford, *A Star Chamber court in Ireland: the Court of Castle Chamber, 1571–1641* (2005)
16 A.P. Quinn, *Wigs and guns: Irish barristers and the Great War* (2006)
17 N.M. Dawson (ed.), *Reflections on law and history: Irish Legal History Society discourses and other papers, 2000–2005* (2006)
18 James Kelly, *Poynings' Law and the making of law in Ireland, 1660–1800* (2007)
19 W.E. Vaughan, *Murder trials in Ireland, 1836–1914* (2009)
20 Kevin Costello, *The Court of Admiralty of Ireland, 1575–1893* (2011)
21 W.N. Osborough, *An island's law: a bibliographical guide to Ireland's legal past* (2013)
22 Felix M. Larkin and N.M. Dawson (eds), *Lawyers, the law and history: Irish Legal History Society discourses and other papers, 2005–2011* (2013)
23 Daire Hogan and Colum Kenny (eds), *Changes in practice and law: a selection of essays by members of the legal profession to mark twenty-five years of the Irish Legal History Society* (2013)
24 W.N. Osborough, *The Irish stage: a legal history* (2015)
25 Thomas Mohr, *Guardian of the Treaty: the Privy Council appeal and Irish sovereignty* (2016)
26 Joseph C. Sweeney, *The life and times of Arthur Browne in Ireland and America, 1756–1805* (2017)
27 Niamh Howlin, *Juries in Ireland: laypersons and law in the long nineteenth century* (2017)
28 Patrick Hyde Kelly (ed.), *The case of Ireland's being bound by acts of parliament in England, stated, Dublin 1698* (2018)
29 Mary Phelan, *Irish speakers, interpreters and the courts, 1754–1921* (2019)
30 Coleman A. Dennehy (ed.), *Law and revolution in seventeenth-century Ireland* (2020)
31 Daire Hogan and Patrick Maume (eds), *The reminiscences of Ignatius O'Brien, lord chancellor of Ireland 1913–18: a life in Cork, Dublin and Westminster* (2021)
32 Peter Crooks and Thomas Mohr (eds), *Law and the idea of liberty in Ireland: from Magna Carta to the present* (2023)
33 Bríd McGrath, *The operations of the Irish House of Commons, 1613–48* (2023)
34 Niamh Howlin (ed.), *A century of courts: the Courts of Justice Act 1924* (2024)
35 Niamh Howlin and Felix M. Larkin (eds), *Confluences of law and history: Irish Legal History Society discourses and other papers, 2011–21* (2025)

ALSO AVAILABLE

The Irish Legal History Society (1989)

*Volumes 1–7 are published by Irish Academic Press

Irish Legal History Society

Established in 1988 to encourage the study and advance the knowledge of the history of Irish law, especially by the publication of original documents and of works relating to the history of Irish law, including its institutions, doctrines and personalities, and reprinting or editing of works of sufficient rarity or importance.

www.irishlegalhistorysociety.org